The Poetry of Slavery

THE POETRY
OF SLAVERY

An Anglo-American Anthology
1764–1865

MARCUS WOOD

OXFORD
UNIVERSITY PRESS

OXFORD

UNIVERSITY PRESS

Great Clarendon Street, Oxford OX2 6DP

Oxford University Press is a department of the University of Oxford.
It furthers the University's objective of excellence in research, scholarship,
and education by publishing worldwide in

Oxford New York

Auckland Bangkok Buenos Aires Cape Town Chennai
Dar es Salaam Delhi Hong Kong Istanbul Karachi Kolkata
Kuala Lumpur Madrid Melbourne Mexico City Mumbai Nairobi
São Paulo Shanghai Taipei Tokyo Toronto

Oxford is a registered trade mark of Oxford University Press
in the UK and in certain other countries

Published in the United States
by Oxford University Press Inc., New York

British Library Cataloguing in Publication Data

Data available

Library of Congress Cataloging in Publication Data

Data available

ISBN 0–19–818708–4
ISBN 0–19–818709–2 (pbk.)

1 3 5 7 9 10 8 6 4 2

Typeset in Bulmer MT by
Jayvee, Trivandrum, India
Printed in Great Britain
on acid-free paper by
T. J. International Ltd.,
Padstow, Cornwall

For Rufus, Athanase, Emily, and Alice

Acknowledgements

The Poetry of Slavery was compiled in fits and starts over a period of some twenty years during which time I was lucky enough to be helped by the staff at a number of British and American institutions. Many fellowships and awards enabled me to work at specific libraries where the 'dirty hands' research for this book happened. I first became interested in American abolition poetry as a Henry Fellow at Harvard in 1984–5, where Ken Carpenter, of the Harvard Library Bulletin, suggested that I look for abolition poems not just in books, but within popular and print culture. The American Antiquarian Society, where I spent several months as a Peterson Fellow in 1992, allowed me to gain my first overview for the American sections of this book, and I must thank Georgia Barnhill, Joanne Chaison, John Hench, and Caroline Sloat, long-term supporters of my work. In 1993 the Newberry Library awarded me a fellowship and while there I amassed much rare American poetry on slavery which made it into the final selection for this book. In 1997 as a Barra Fellow at the Library Company of Philadelphia, I was lucky enough to benefit from the advice of Jim Green and Phil Lapsansky. Jim was wonderful on Anglo-American literary perspectives, while Phil has remained committed to this project right up to the eleventh hour when he made some crucial transcriptions for me. In October 2001 I was invited to contribute to the 'England and the Deep South' conference at the University of Mississippi, an event of unique value for this project because of the Anglo-American perspectives it generated. I thank Joe Ward for inviting me. In October 2002 I had a brief research stint at the Huntington Library where, thanks to Robert C. Ritchie, I was able to make some late discoveries. I also had immensely valuable last minute discussions about this project with Gillian Brown, Thadious Davis, Judith Jackson Fossett, Stephen Railton, Karen Sanchez-Eppler, and Richard Yarborough, at the Huntington's 'Topsy Turvy: Uncle Tom's Cabin Turns 150' conference.

While a visiting fellow at the Humanities Research Centre of the Australian National University in 2002 I was able to work on the anthology in a stimulating environment. The Director of the HRC, Iain McCalman, is an inspirational person whose long-term interest in my work has directly influenced the form and balance of this anthology.

Many British institutions offered me their expertise in putting together the selections in this book. I am indebted to the British Library, to Oxford's research Libraries, and to the staff of Rhodes House, and the Upper Reading Room of the

Bodleian in particular. At different times and in different ways several major institutions committed to thinking about Britain's slavery inheritance have contributed to the project. I will single out Anthony Tibbles of the Transatlantic Slavery Gallery, National Museums and Galleries Merseyside, Liverpool, and the staff of Wilberforce House Museum, Hull. I am also grateful to the National Maritime Museum, and Robert J. Blyth in particular, who invited me to talk to the staff about the problematic nature of remembering slavery. My interactions with Anti-Slavery International have as ever inflected the current work.

This book would certainly not have seen the light of day without Worcester College Oxford, the British Academy, and the Arts and Humanities Research Board of Great Britain. As a Michael Bromberg Fellow and then as a British Academy Postdoctoral Fellow, at Worcester College, I first put the project together. Joseph and Ruth Bromberg have maintained a deep interest in my work, and I will always be in their debt. The British Academy has continued to offer support in the form of further travel grants and awards. I am deeply grateful to the Arts and Humanities Research Board, for their prolonged commitment to the project. In 2001–2 the AHRB awarded me a research fellowship which allowed me the time to begin putting the anthology into its final shape. During that time, as a Leverhulme Fellow I was able to finish writing the introduction and notes for *The Poetry of Slavery*.

I thank the University of Sussex, which has been very understanding in allowing me to go off for long periods of leave in order to complete my research. I am particularly grateful to my colleagues Peter Boxall, Andrew Crozier, Denise DeCaires Narain, Stephen Fender, Richard Follet, Debbie Foy-Everett, Siobhan Kilfeather, Maria Lauret, Laura Marcus, Vincent Quinn, Nicholas Royle, Minoli Salgado, Alan Sinfield, Lindsay Smith, Jenny Taylor, Norman Vance (Latinist extraordinary), Richard Whatmore, and Brian Young. My graduate students Chris Abuk, Cathy Bergin, Iman Hamam, Philip Kaisary, Juliette Myers, Carole Realf, and Anita Rupprecht also contributed in different ways.

Finally I name the following people in gratitude for what they have done for this book: Adam Ashforth, Robin Blackburn, Richard Blackett, Richard Brown, Luisa Calé, David Dabydeen, Michael Dash, Madge Dresser, Kai Easton, Cecille Fabre, Stephen Farthing, Moira Ferguson, Sandra Gunning, Sherry Jeffries, Steve Jones, Grevel Lindop, Jon Mee, Dwight Middleton, Catherine Molineux, Phil Morgan, Abbey Machado Newport, Benita Parry, Geoff Quilley, James Raven, Laura Roman, Michael Schmidt, Dillwyn Smith, Michael Suarez, Helen Thomas, John Walsh, Jim Walvin, Helen Weston, and Stephen Zagala.

Contents

List of Plates

Abolition Poetry: A Literary Introduction

This anthology is made up of poems produced in Britain and North America 1764–1865. All of this work concerns the subjects of the slave trade and plantation slavery. The anthology deliberately mixes up canonical distinctions. Much of the verse included is by a range of now almost forgotten, sometimes anonymous, abolition bards, a good number of them women. The more obscure work appears alongside verse by Cowper, Blake, Wordsworth, Shelley, Keats, Tennyson, and the Brownings in Britain, and Whitman, Longfellow, Whittier, Lowell, Melville, and Dickinson in the United States. Most of this work is now not read. In the case of the canonic figures if it is read, then it is read out of context, and most often through the filters which have been applied via the industry of literary biography. Literary biography is a soft-centred but voracious creature. Biographies construct the 'life' of the famous author, yet the myth of the artist's life is a curious structure, an amorphous bag, and just about anything may be stuffed into it. One effect of constructing the anthology has been to cut work by long famous, or currently fêted, and fashionable authors out of the biographical fat which surrounds and often protects them, and to place them back within the cultural environments in which they felt impelled to address slavery. The overall strategies for selection, and the reasons for inclusion of authors, are laid out in the relevant individual prefaces. This Introduction has a more general purpose and serves to set out some literary contexts for thinking about the vast range of poetry that was generated by the slavery debates in two continents during a century. The introduction also indicates some of the formal and performative forces which generated the poetry of slavery.

'The Abolition Blunderbuss': where are the pro-slavery bards?

The period 1807–65 saw the official abolition of the Atlantic slave trade and of plantation slavery in the British sugar colonies and in North America, after a series of propaganda drives which were without precedent. One thing which jumps out in this context is the small amount of pro-slavery verse which is included in the anthology. This does not result from a policy of exclusion, but reflects the simple fact that, as far as I can see, very little of the writing produced to defend the slave systems on either side of the Atlantic was produced in the form of poetry. The pro-slavery verse that was written differed significantly from abolition verse, in that it was often not written as propaganda, but occasionally or incidentally. It is very rare to find poems which *were* explicitly composed as defences of slavery: Boswell's *No Abolition of Slavery* or the anonymous American *The Ballad of the Abolition Blunderbuss* (pp. 184–94, 652–9) are unusual exceptions. Even here, however, it is misleading to talk of slavery being 'defended'. In these poems the best form of defence is deemed to be attack, and both authors launch into extended *ad hominem* assaults on individual abolition leaders. Poems which tolerate or celebrate the slavery systems, good examples being Grainger's *The Sugar Cane*, which defends plantation slavery at great length, and Teale's *The Voyage of the Sable Venus* (pp. 7–29, 30–5), which celebrates the middle passage, do so as a matter of course. Both were written before abolition had become a mainstream transatlantic movement and consequently the authors feel a cultural confidence about accepting slavery which cannot be matched in British or American poetry written after the late 1780s.

When one turns to consider the American South during the 1830–65 period, the years of the greatest production of Northern abolition publicity, the poetic silence is deafening. It is no coincidence that *The Abolition Blunderbuss*, written in 1861, was composed and published in Boston, and is a Northerner's attack on what is seen as the extremism and sentimentality of the leaders of East Coast abolition. It is a significant fact that the comprehensive bibliography to Larry E. Tise's magisterial *Proslavery: A History of the Defence of Slavery in America, 1701–1740* does not contain one volume of Southern poetry. There are novels, treatises, catechisms, orations, addresses, discourses, speeches, discussions, collections of essays, diaries, debates, testimonies, prophecies, speeches, a multitude of sermons, a 'forensic dispute', and even one satiric drama, but there are no poems. The only possible exception to this statement is highly ironic— the specially composed 'hymns' which are to be found at the back of Benjamin Morgan Parker's 1828 manual designed to help police slave exposure to religion, *A Plain and Easy Catechism, Designed Chiefly for the Benefit of Coloured Persons. To Which are Annexed Suitable Prayers and Hymns*. It is indeed fascinating that the only poet who is analysed in any detail in Tise's book is Timothy Dwight. He is seen by Tise as a central intellectual presence in the formation of an American counter-revolutionary conservatism from the mid-1790s until his death in 1817.[1]

Dwight's 1794 epic-pastoral *Greenfield Hill* (pp. 418–23) takes a highly ambivalent stance on slavery. Dwight invents a comparative slavery table where he feels confident to attack West Indian slavery as practised by the French and British. He

---

[1] For Parker and Dwight see Larry B. Tise, *Proslavery: A History of the Defence of Slavery in America, 1701–1840* (University of Georgia Press, 1987), 141–2, 205–24, 365, 409. For a more sympathetic analysis of Dwight and *Greenfield Hill* see Vernon Louis Parrington, *The Connecticut Wits* (Archon, 1963), pp. xxxv–xl, 200–47.

is, however, prepared to accept slavery in the Southern states and on the East Coast as benevolent, indeed almost utopian. Black slaves in Africa are presented according to a series of animalized stereotypes. So here is another strange fact; the first and only major poem to defend, or at least to excuse in comparative terms, plantation slavery in the newly independent United States is generated out of the North and penned by the president of Yale University. From its earliest days it seems that the poetic discussion of slavery was destined to be a Northern art form. The very first pro-slavery tract published in America appeared almost a century before, and was by a Northerner and slave holder from Massachusetts, John Saffin. His 1701 *A Brief and Candid Answer to a Late Printed Sheet, Entituled, The Selling of Joseph* was a general defence of slavery. Saffin rounded his arguments off with a nasty little poem of his own composition that stands as the first pro-slavery verse generated in America. The piece was called 'The Negro's Character' and ran:

> Cowardly and cruel are those *Blacks* Innate,
> Prone to Revenge, Imp of inveterate hate.
> He that exasperates them, soon espies
> Mischief and Murder in their very eyes.
> Libidinous, Deceitful, False and Rude,
> The Spume Issue of Ingratitude.[2]

This takes the shortest line to justifying slavery, the assassination of an entire ethnic minority through the creation of an inventory of false character traits—or, in a word, racism. Yet the picture of the corrupt, and corrupted, African slave which Saffin presents is still very much intact when Dwight is writing nearly one hundred years later.

The slavery canon: high art, low art, and publishing's new technologies

The period covered in this book saw the transformation of British and much of North American society into industrial centres with astonishing new media technologies. Abolition publicity in general, and poetry in particular, drew on the new publishing modes which became available. Abolition publicists grew alongside, and cleverly adapted to, new developments and the anthology is designed to bring out some of the intricate ways in which British and American anti-slavery activists bounced off each other. If American abolitionist authors in the 1820s and 1830s began their efforts under the shadow of a British formal and technological inheritance the traffic soon flowed back the other way.

[2] Quoted Tise, *Proslavery*, 18; for Saffin see 17–19, 30, 33, 36.

Consequently the work included in this book is from a very wide formal publishing base which takes in handbills, broadsides, print satire, song sheet, and chapbook songsters, illustrated adult and children's books, children's toys, novels, slave testimony and narrative, and private manuscripts as well as the expected published volumes of verse. In a sense what was happening with publishing technology and popular politics dictated the range of the selection.

In the 1940s Wylie Sypher, author of what is still the only volume with a claim to address the literatures of abolition generated in Britain in anything like their formal variety, considered the contribution of poetry to the English abolition movement and reached the following harsh conclusions:

The slave and his lot were a poetical *pons asinorum*: the worse the poet the more he felt obliged to elevate his subject by the cumbrous splendor of epithet, periphrasis and apostrophe, even at the cost of dealing with facts only by footnotes and appendices. The result was poetry false in the worst sense of the word—not alone in its inane phraseology, but in its heedlessness of the truth with which it purported to deal. There was a violent clash between historical and pseudo-poetic truth.[3]

Literary historians, cultural studies theorists, and post-colonialists no longer use Sypher's kind of language to describe literary texts. Maybe slavery aestheticians quite simply do not think in his terms any more, and this might be a healthy development, yet Sypher's way of reading things raises questions which still lack answers.[4] For Sypher anti-slavery poetry is bad art because it does not tell the truth about slavery. Sypher requires an art of slavery which will confront the historical facts, the records of events and atrocities, head on. He wants poems which deal with the horrors encased in the slavery archive in the main text not in a scholarly apparatus. In that strange metaphor of the 'bridge of donkeys', the *pons asinorum*, he sees the traumatic experience of the slaves as a conduit for any and every victim of the excesses of the age of sentiment. Sypher goes so far as to see in abolition verse not only the distortion of historical truth, but the abuse of humanist ethics, summing up that 'many a versifier . . . addressed not the humanity of the reader but his sentiment. Thus anti-slavery poetry was often ethically as well as aesthetically hollow.' Using the value judgements of his day Sypher is undoubtedly

---

[3] Wylie Sypher, *Guinea's Captive Kings: British Anti-Slavery Literature of the XVIII'th Century* (University of North Carolina Press, 1942), 157.

[4] Despite the relative neglect of slavery verse there has been some exceptional recent work on the British 18th-century abolition literatures: see Srinivas Aravamudan (ed.), *Slavery, Abolition and Emancipation* (Pickering & Chatto, 1999); Tim Fulford and Peter J. Kitson (eds.), *Romanticism and Colonialism: Writing and Empire, 1780–1830* (Cambridge University Press, 1998); Helen Thomas, *Romanticism and Slave Narratives* (Oxford University Press, 2000); and Marcus Wood, *Slavery, Empathy, and Pornography* (Oxford University Press, 2002). For recent publication of a great number of facsimile 18th- and early 19th-century texts on slavery see Peter J. Kitson and Debbie Lee (eds.), *Slavery, Abolition and Emancipation Writings in the British Romantic Period*, 8 vols. (Pickering & Chatto, 1999). For Anglo-American poetry on slavery to 1810 see James G. Basker's wonderful *Amazing Grace: An Anthology of Poems about Slavery, 1660–1810* (Yale University Press, 2002).

right; the majority of abolition verse does not constitute literary art as Harold
Bloom still understands it. Indeed Sypher is really accusing the abolition poets of
being victims of their version of political correctness; they are blinded by their
own self-righteousness. Grubbing around in archives across Britain and North
America, not to mention Brazil, I have now read a few hundred pages of the best,
and thousands of pages of the very worst, poetry generated by the explosion of
abolition as an Anglo-American propaganda phenomenon. Why make an anthology out of an archive which has remained more or less happily dead and buried to
all but a few *dry-as-dusts* for the best part of a century and a half?

There are many answers to this question, but I want to start with the most
important. The way in which English and American societies are prepared to
look at their very different slavery inheritances has changed. Over the last fifty
years, American scholars and literary theorists have opened up the unendingly
complicated inheritance of Atlantic slavery in an unprecedented manner. Recent
developments in trauma theory and the aesthetics of trauma coming out of Nazi
Holocaust studies have also provided useful theoretical developments which
have implications for the art generated around the Slavery Holocaust. The pioneering efforts of American scholars have enforced the necessary resurrection of
the African-American literary canon, for it must not be forgotten that most of the
authors who have been 'rediscovered', from Phyllis Wheatley to Frederick
Douglass and Ellen Watkins Harper (see pp. 404–10, 548–51, 602–7), were literary
celebrities in their day. There has also been a shift to thinking about the texts generated by white authors. Following Toni Morrison's brilliant lead in *Playing in
the Dark* there is now increased interest in trying to understand why abolitionists
and pro-slavery authors thought and created what they did, the way they did.
There is interest in thinking about why the counter-truths and bizarre narrative
fictions of the slavery archive were generated.[5] Obviously Britain lags behind
North America and has not produced anything like the same volume of informed
and confrontational analysis of the texts generated by the British slavery debates.
Much of the most valuable work even on the literatures of British slavery is the
work of American scholars. Despite these advances, however, it remains the case
that British and American slavery constitute largely discrete fields of study; works
in these areas are restricted to 'black studies', 'slavery studies', and occasionally
the 'post-colonial studies' shelves of the book supermarkets. This fact is probably the single most important justificatory impetus for this anthology. There
have been some brilliant comparative studies of Atlantic slavery by historians and
cultural theorists; the work of David Brion Davis, Robin Blackburn, Henri Louis
Gates, and Paul Gilroy stands out. Yet this work is a testament to the fact that it
takes a lifetime of reading and rethinking to get to a stage where it is possible to

---

[5] For crucial recent publications see Bibliography, and the works by Andrews, Dash, Gates, Gilroy,
Morrison, Wood (2000), and Basker, in particular.

work in comparative theoretical and cultural terms on the Atlantic slave systems. Within literary studies equivalent comparative work has really not happened, and this tends to create a highly distorted picture of the slavery debates. In this context the publication of James G. Basker's *Amazing Grace: An Anthology of Poems about Slavery, 1660–1810* is hugely important. This ground-breaking anthology has opened up the transatlantic poetry of slavery during the early phase of abolition to a general readership. Basker's exemplary, and scholarly, work has initiated the processes of thinking about the complicated cultural interactions between British and North American slavery verse.

From the very first abolition was an amazingly integrated Anglo-American enterprise, and it remained so, through various ups and downs, during the first half of the nineteenth century. A few months after Britain carried through slave trade abolition in 1807 Thomas Clarkson, who had emerged as the national icon of selfless anti-slavery philanthropic industry, published a monumental history of the movement. His *History of the Rise, Progress, and Accomplishment of the Abolition of the African Slave-Trade by the British Parliament* opens with the famous abolition map (Pl. 1). In this image he attempts quite literally to rise above abolition as a cultural phenomenon and to look down upon it as a mythic terrain which can be mapped. Although the book's title states that it is about the abolition of the British slave trade the map shows Britain and America as equal, and intellectually symbiotic, partners in the enterprise. For Clarkson this equality grows out of the remarkable transatlantic effects of the Quaker anti-slavery alliance, which inaugurated a fluid exchange of people and ideas from the south of England and the East Coast of America during the second half of the eighteenth century. The effects of the early abolition collaborations went very deep, and sustained a creative dialogue which ran, and outran, its initially narrow religious camaraderies. When American abolition began to hot up in the early 1830s, on until the outbreak of the Civil War, the activists rapidly shifted their sights from British abolition (British slavery officially ended with the introduction of the apprentice systems from 1834) to North American. In reality British domination of the Atlantic slave trade in the second half of the eighteenth century, and the British organization of plantations in the Caribbean, were very different from the development of slave systems in North America.

The manner in which North Americans, including abolitionists, experienced, and related to, the shifting political pressures exerted by and on the slave power, and the slaves themselves, was a world away from the manner in which eighteenth-century British abolitionists came at slavery. While most British abolitionists, unless they lived in one of the three great slaving ports, were unlikely to have first-hand contact with slaves, for Americans slavery was very much a domestic phenomenon. Developments in the 1840s and 1850s around the Mexican War, the Missouri Compromise, the free-soil debates around the

Kansas Nebraska Act, the Dred Scott case, and the Fugitive Slave Law saw the North increasingly forced to think about slavery, and the physical presence of black slaves, as its problem as well as the South's. It is an oversimplification, but in some ways a useful one, to say that for the South the only problem was not the slave systems but the attitude of the North to the slave systems.

Yet one rather amazing thing that emerges from the poetry in this volume is the fact that for both British and American poets these economic and historical differences (which are treated in more detail in the 'Key Notes' which directly follow the Introduction to this volume) are virtually invisible. Slavery was manifested as a set of fictive literary constructs in the late eighteenth century in Britain, and this inheritance still seems to provide the central paradigms for North American abolition verse in the nineteenth century. In other words abolition poets, along with other writers on slavery, were imaginatively, as well as politically, generally rather timid. Slaves, slavery, and their inheritance had to be rigorously controlled as artistic entities. The slave was still sentimentally constructed according to a series of precepts demanding passivity and victimhood (the middle passage, domestic and plantation tortures, rape, slave auction), abstraction, animalization, and Christianization (the latter reaches its apogee in literature celebrating the 'emancipation moment'). The slave power was still demonized according to a series of negative stereotypes relating to the plantation household (the patriarch's slave harem, the idle and/or sadistic slave mistress) or the gambling den (duels, whiskey drinking, and spitting). British slavery literatures of the late eighteenth century often concentrate on the horrors of the middle passage. This was a result of the fact that the British campaign was, until 1807, directed primarily against the slave trade and not the entire institution of Atlantic slavery. Consequently it is not surprising, for reasons of polemical precision, to see American abolition literature, including poetry, inclining away from this focus. Yet British abolition had also constructed plantation slavery according to a series of fictions which proved remarkably resilient in nineteenth-century America. The figures of the brutal overseer, the languid plantation mistress, the beautiful and preferably quadroon or mulatto slave girl as auction, and then rape, victim, and the good slave who accepts a pacifying version of Christianity as the reward for being given freedom, were all developed within British abolition verse and prose from 1780 to 1830 (pp. 36–48, 81–142, 241–99). American abolition fiction absorbed and, to a large degree, reconstituted this inheritance.

It is also important to remember that many popular literary contexts existed for the representation of blacks and slavery before the slavery debates proper were inaugurated in the late eighteenth century. These contexts reacted with abolition verse in complicated ways. For example the black female form as a focus for amatory and erotic fiction had existed within British poetry for centuries as both highly charged and ultimately comic. In this sense poets as different as Isaac Teale and William Wordsworth (pp. 30–5, 231–7) write about black slave women by looking back to, and in many ways perverting, a well-established Renaissance tradition. From the late fifteenth century, through to the late seventeenth, commonplace books regularly contained playful and punning experiments set on the premiss of white men wooing black women, and less regularly black women wooing black men, or sometimes boys. Black men wooing white women is a romantic premiss that did not seem to hold any attraction. Many of these poems circling interracial sexuality appear to be exercises in rhetorical sophistication and in the art of playing with oppositions and inversions. Some have an overtly satiric edge, many others do not, and some appear to have as their overriding motivation the aesthetic celebration of black over white.[6] With the exception of Dunbar's 'Ane Blacke Moire', which is much earlier than the other poems, and far more cynical, none of them is built upon the satiric exploitation of black–white power relations. None of this work deals explicitly with the social power relations growing out of slavery. It was in the context of verse-drama that this theme was to be explored first.

It is a fact that most of the English public from the late 1600s until the late nineteenth century would have gained their cultural ideas about Africans, Afro-Caribbeans, plantation life, and the slave trade not from reading poetry but from seeing 'nigger minstrels', pantomimes, melodramas, and plays. From the appearance of Thomas Southerne's phenomenally successful 1696 *Oroonoko: A Tragedy* (an extravagant theatrical adaptation of Aphra Behn's sentimental slave novella *Oroonoko*), until the incredible popularity of dramatic versions of Stowe's *Uncle Tom's Cabin* from 1852 onwards, slavery was never really off the English theatrical menu. Abolition gave a big fillip to slave dramas: not only was Southerne endlessly revived but new slave dramas appeared in the late eighteenth and early nineteenth centuries. The dates of the major plays focused on plantation slavery—George Coleman the Younger, *Inkle and Yarico* (1787; a musical four-act reworking of Mrs Weddell's *Incle and Yarico* which first appeared in 1742); Thomas Bellamy, *The Benevolent Planters* (1789); Mariana Starke, *The Sword of Peace* (1789); John Fawcett, *Obi; or, Three Fingered Jack* (1800); George Coleman the Younger, *The Africans* (1808); the anonymous *Furibond; or, Harlequin Negro;* Jacques-Henri Bernardin de Saint-Pierre, *Paul and Virginie* (1808); and Thomas Morton's *The Slave* (1816)—indicate how the plays followed the pattern of the rise of abolition publicity, which hits a high in 1787–90, and then undergoes an enormous popular regeneration 1807–8, in the wake of the passage of the 1807 bill for abolishing the slave trade.

---

[6]   The most detailed analysis of this body of love poetry is Gordon McMullan, *Renaissance Configurations: Voices/Bodies/Spaces, 1580–1960* (Macmillan Press, 1998). A representative body of amatory poetry focused on black–white conjunction and desire is reprinted chronologically arranged as an appendix titled 'Poems of Blackness', pp. 269–90. There is also a fine selection of poems about slavery extracted from British and American drama 1660–1810 in Basker, *Amazing Grace*.

For the purposes of this anthology *Obi* (pp. 227–30), in one of its later melo-dramatic reworkings, is the most relevant because of the strength and range of the song lyrics. While several of the dramas carried many songs, they are most commonly generalized love lyrics, or celebratory songs focused on dancing and singing. *Obi* is particularly important in showing the grip which slave-evolved religious ritual and magic had gained on the theatre-going imagination. This anthology could have been hugely expanded with selections from the blank verse and lyrics from the relevant plays, but the drama of slavery is, finally, a rather different project.[7]

Little white lies: Britain's abolition literature as a whited sepulchre

This anthology is necessary for two further reasons. First the fact that among the major slaving nations of Europe and the Americas Britain remains curiously uninterested in attempting the exhumation and re-examination of the cultural remains of its massive investment in slavery, an investment which was made over the best part of 300 years. Secondly there exists a general lack of interest in Ameri-can slavery poetry unless it is written by leading canonic figures, or by African Americans. Certainly among the African-American poets Wheatley, and to some extent Hammon, Horton, and Harper (pp. 404–15, 461–6, 602–7), are now regu-larly taught and studied, although one cannot help feeling that they are still to some extent corralled off within the sanctioned literary ghettos of slavery and African-American studies. With the exception of the work of Whitman, Lowell, and to a lesser extent Whittier, Longfellow, and Dickinson, virtually all the verse reproduced in the American section of this anthology by whites has been con-signed to oblivion.

There remains an attitude among literary scholars and theorists that there is no point studying slavery verse because its sentimentality and flat occasionality ren-der it aesthetically worthless. There is also, quite understandably, a lingering dis-taste for studying slave experience through the fantasies of white abolition versifiers. For historians, and even cultural historians, this material is given the body swerve on the grounds that it bears no relation to a 'real' history, that it is not the 'truth', that it does not pretend to objectivity. It is, however, the very fanciful-ness, the fictionality, the distortion, the superimposition, of an imagined narra-tive and an imagined ethical scenario, which make the fictions of slavery so very important. It is not enough to say that slavery poetry, some of which was hugely successful in its day in terms of sales *and* critical reception, is no longer to our

---

[7] There is a current reprinting of all the relevant texts combined with a fine scholarly discussion of the place of slavery in British theatre in Jeffrey N. Cox (ed.), *Slavery, Abolition and Emancipation: Writings in the British Romantic Period*, v: *Drama* (Pickering & Chatto, 1999).

taste because it does not fit current conceptions of historical truth, real testimony, or artistic quality. History is never what happened, but what a given society decides it wants to believe has happened. Art has no intrinsic value outside that value which a given culture decides to give or take away at a given time, and this give and take is not a stable or rational phenomenon. The poetry in this book is terribly important: what it provides is nothing less than a map of how a surprisingly wide cross section of educated British and American people wanted to project Africa, the Caribbean, Britain, sailors, slaves, and slavery. It shows the intellectual and aesthetic mechanisms that were already in place for the transformation of slavery from event to national myth. The extensive literary translation of slavery was both an immediate and a lasting phenomenon. What the poetry reproduced below shows is that British and American poets extensively erased, re-inscribed, denied, familiarized, falsified, narrativized, and generally metamorphosed slavery even while it was happening, even while it *was* 'real'. If we desire to understand not only why slavery happened, but what its legacies might mean for Britain and America now, then it is to the primary creative materials of the slavery archive that we must turn.

The agendas for the memorialization of abolition and the slavery debates in general were firmly in place from a very early date, and poetry held a vital place. The extent to which abolition verse was invented in canonic terms comes out plainly if we return to Clarkson's abolition map (Pl. 1) and look at another aspect of it. Not only does it set out a 'special relationship' *vis-à-vis* Britain and American anti-slavery, but authors and particularly poets dominate the British half of the map. Alexander Pope (1688–1744), William Warburton (1698–1779), William Shenstone (1714–63), William Cowper (1731–1800), James Beattie (1735–1803), Thomas Day (1748–89), and William Roscoe (1753–1831) are all named as formative abolitionists, and in the accompanying text Clarkson even claims Milton (1608–74) as the first abolition poet:

Several of our old English writers, though they have not mentioned the African Slave-trade, or the slavery consequent upon it, in their respective works, have yet given their testimony of condemnation against both. Thus our great Milton:

> O execrable, so to aspire
> Above his brethren, to himself assuming
> Authority usurp't, from god not given;
> He gave us only over beast, fish, fowl,
> Dominion absolute; that right we hold
> By his donation;—but man over men
> He made not lord, such title to himself
> Reserving, human left from human free.[8]

---

[8] Thomas Clarkson, *The History of the Rise, Progress, and Accomplishment of the Abolition of the African Slave-Trade by the British Parliament*, 2 vols. (Longman, Hurst, Rees & Orme, 1808), i. 44–5.

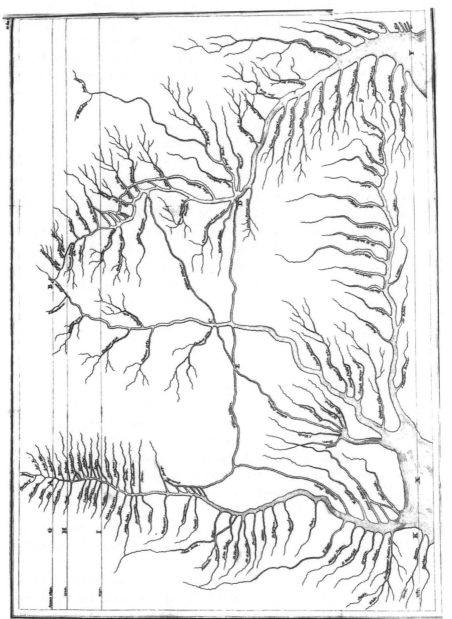

1. Thomas Clarkson, *Abolition Map* (copper-plate engraving, 1808).

Milton was to continue to be quoted by British and American abolitionists in the anti-slavery press; he represented, as did the Declaration of Independence, a primal site for the articulation of the basic right to liberty of all humans. Milton's centrality to abolition thought and writing is a terrain waiting to be mapped. In alluding to Clarkson's seizure of Milton for the cause here, it is only necessary to indicate that the abolitionists cast their net very wide, and that readers today will have to learn to do the same if they wish to understand the creative origins of abolition writing. But this observation brings in the subject of necessary limits: what has and has not been included.

Samson Agonistes can lay claim to being the first, and perhaps the greatest, major poem in English to articulate the agonies of enslavement on a free consciousness. Samson is not only 'Eyeless in Gaza, at the mill, with slaves', but a slave himself, subject, mutilated, abused, and worked as a beast. He ends as a figure of divine vengeance who destroys his enslavers. The poem has one typically momentous Miltonic insight: it establishes the chief suffering of the slave to lie in the consciousness that his present state exists in perfect opposition to a former or alternative state of liberty. And yet the appropriation of the terrible beauty of this poem by Clarkson is not innocent. Slavery is universalized, it is elevated to the realm of abstract discussion. Atlantic slavery is seen to exist in opposition to Liberty within a levelling humanistic agenda whereby all slavery is bad and all liberty is good, and where the two poles of slavery and liberty are transcultural, transhistorical, and transparent. Within such a vast definitional space there are no limits to what the poetry of slavery might be, or might talk about. Clarkson's idealizing but sloppy canonic method may however have a hidden agenda. The danger with Clarkson's 'happy-clappy' poetic theory of universal poetic brotherhood is that it constitutes a move which effectively writes Atlantic slavery out of the European consciousness as a unique phenomenon, a unique European crime. And indeed this is the assumption behind much Evangelical abolition verse. Yet it is not only within the ruthless comparative dynamic of an Evangelical conception of sin that Atlantic slavery can be in danger of slipping out of sight.

If Clarkson's treatment of Milton raises the unanswerable question, what are the limits of the poetry of slavery?, then we also need to address the concomitant problem that what passed for abolition poetry in the minds of some poets can completely pass by the minds of readers today. Take for example Walter Savage Landor's early poem *Crysaor*, a poem about the abuse of absolute political power. The dictator Crysaor blasphemes against the gods, and is struck down for his arrogance. The climax of his defiance as he raves at Jove is framed within a typically Landorean incoherence:

> Tell, and quickly, why should I adore,
> Adored myself by millions? Why invoke,

Invoked with all thy attributes? Men wrong
By their protestations, prayers, and sacrifice,
Either the gods, their rulers, or themselves:
But flame and thunder fright them from the *Gods*,
Themselves they cannot, dare not—they are ours,
Us—dare they, and they, *us*? But triumph, Jove!
Man for one moment hath engaged his lord,
Henceforth let merchants value him, not kings.[9]

For Landor this speech constituted a furious assault on the slave trade, and on George III's complicity in the nefarious traffic. An accompanying footnote to the final line explained:

This poem describes a period when the insolence of tyranny and the sufferings of mankind were at the utmost. They could not be so without slavery; and slavery could not generally exist without some sort of barter. Merchants then were necessary. It appears that Crysaor, wicked as he is represented, had no personal share in its propagation. He encouraged it. But, a Sovereign who is powerful enough, either by the fears or affection of his people, to abolish from amongst them this unhuman traffic, and who makes not one effort, uses not one persuasion, for the purpose, deserves the execration which followed, and the punishment which overtook Crysaor. Every man, instead of waiting with awe for some preternatural blow, should think *himself* a particle of those elements which Providence has decreed to crush so abominable a monster.[10]

The opacity of expression and of the historical allegory make it difficult to read this work now as a contribution to the abolition crusade. Atlantic slavery is discussed so abstrusely that it is off the map. It may be interesting to reread this verse now as a typical demonstration of the manner in which British complicity in a world crime can be culturally disguised to the point of disappearance. Yet I have tended to keep the anthology as a whole fairly tightly focused on verse which is much more directly concerned with addressing Atlantic slavery. There are, however, several major poets who tread a line between abstraction and engagement with the specifics of the slave trade and it was impossible to decide in some cases what to include and what to leave out. It has been argued, for example, that *The Rime of the Ancient Mariner* is, among other things, a poem quite explicitly addressing the guilt of British domination of the transatlantic slave trade in the eighteenth century.[11] Yet on reflection I cannot see this argument as really

---

[9] Walter Savage Landor, *The Complete Works of Walter Savage Landor*, 17 vols. (Chapman & Hall, 1933), xiii. 57.

[10] Ibid. 366.

[11] See J. R. Ebbatson, 'Coleridge's Mariner and the Rights of Man', *Studies in Romanticism*, 11 (1972), 171–206; James Twitchell, '"The Rime of the Ancient Mariner" as Vampire Poem', *College Literature*, 4 (1977), 21–39; Jerome J. McGann, 'The Meaning of "The Ancient Mariner"', *Critical Enquiry*, 8 (1981), 63–86.

holding up. To read the murder of the albatross as a symbolic allusion to the guilt of the slave trade, and the events that follow as an examination of the repercussions of that guilt, and of divine retribution, upon the English maritime interest, is to close Coleridge's poem down in quite drastic ways (pp. 204–5 for further discussion of the poem). Then again it is quite possible to argue that Act I of Shelley's *Prometheus Unbound* constitutes perhaps the most terrifying poetic articulation of the psychological effects of slave torture on both oppressor and victim. I finally included this wonderful writing as an ultimate creative antidote to Hegel's master–slave dialectic (pp. 305–10). Then again when I came to reread the dance around the winepresses of Luvah, the triumphalist ninth book of Blake's *Vala*, I felt that Blake had given enough clues to make it certain that this poetry, although not abolitionist in any simple sense, certainly does constitute a treatment of slave insurrection. I would even go so far as to see it as a visionary celebration of the San Domingue slave revolution (pp. 142–4, 147–50).

The wider exploration of slavery as a metaphorical presence in English literature is a task awaiting a labourer. Toni Morrison has already put out a moral marker encouraging this work to begin when she tells us that 'the scholarship that looks into the mind, imagination and behaviour of slaves is valuable. But equally valuable is a serious intellectual effort to see what racial ideology does to the mind, imagination and behaviour of masters.'[12] But anthologies require parameters and in this anthology the poetry by canonical authors which *has* been included is (with the exception of Shelley, Blake, and John Newton's *Olney Hymns* (pp. 77–80)) explicitly on the subject of enslavement, either of indigenous peoples in the Americas, or of Africans, taken to the New World and incorporated in the systems of plantation slavery.

American poetry of slavery: how different is it?

The creation of poetry concerning slavery in North America constitutes, as in England, a literary history of negotiation. In both Britain and America the bulk of publications appeared over a period of two decades: in Britain it was 1788–1808 and in America the early 1830s until the mid-1850s. Yet one major difference between American and British abolition verse relates both to the number of canonic poets who wrote major poetry about slavery, and to the extensive period over which these poets maintained an interest in the subject. After slave trade emancipation in the British colonies British slavery ceased to be a major issue for British poets. When they did become involved in writing anti-slavery verse it was primarily in connection with the American abolition movement, and in the context of accusing

---

[12]   Toni Morrison, *Playing in the Dark* (Picador, 1992), pp. 11–12.

America of hypocrisy. The evidence suggests there was no market for British poetry which set about examining the dark and traumatic aspects of the domestic inheritance of Atlantic slavery. There are odd flickers of poetic interest in the ugly origins and development of the British slave industries, and they come from unlikely quarters. For example the now almost forgotten Richard Harris Barham in the third volume of the once sensationally popular historical satire *The Ingoldsby Legends* (1840) manages to slip in a bitter reference to John Hawkins. Hawkins's inauguration of the slave trade is seen as the work of the Devil:

> . . . Nick [the Devil],—who, because
> He'd the gout in his claws,
> And his hoofs—(he's by no means as young as he was
> And is subject of late to a sort of rheumatic a-
> ttack that partakes both of gout and sciatica,)—
> All the night long had twisted and grinn'd,
> His pains much increased by an easterly wind,
> Which always compels him to hobble and limp,
> Was strongly advised by his Medical Imp
> To lie by a little, and give over work,
> For he'd lately been slaving away like a Turk,
> On the Guinea-coast, helping to open a brave trade
> In Niggers, with Hawkins who founded the slave trade.[13]

This is however a quite eccentric aside in Victorian mainstream poetry, which is no longer much interested in slavery except as a cultural blunt instrument with which to beat America over the head. American poets could not have been more different. American slavery was a central concern in the work of several of the major poets of the mid-century. Longfellow, although he worked on slavery mainly in one relatively short burst, wrote some of the most spectacular and widely disseminated slavery poetry of all time (pp. 528–31). Approximately one third of Whittier's massive poetic output is directly on slavery and abolition themes; it is without doubt the single most important issue in his life's work (pp. 496–514). Lowell scored his biggest national and international hit as a poet with *The Biglow Papers*, which make slavery and the free-soil debates during the Mexican War a central concern. The rest of his œuvre is scattered with slavery poems, some of which caught the public imagination (pp. 558–70). Whitman thought and wrote about slavery in a variety of contexts from his early journalism until the end of the Civil War, and continued obsessively to revise the discussions of race and slavery

---

[13] Richard Harris Barham, *The Ingoldsby Legends or Mirth and Marvels*, 2 vols. (Richard Bentley, 1840), ii. 294. Barham added the following footnote: 'Sir John Hawkins for "his worthye attempts and services" and because "in the same he had dyvers conflights with the Moryans and slew and toke dyvers of the same Moryans" received from Elizabeth an *honourable* augmentation to his coat armour including for his crest "*A demi-Moor sable, with two manacles on each arm or.*" '

in *Leaves of Grass* for the rest of his life. Whatever the final nature of his political take on slavery, and there is ultimately nothing logical in Whitman's thought, the one thing that cannot be disputed is the centrality of the subject to his art (pp. 626–37). With the exception of Cowper there is simply no equivalent for this commitment to writing poetry about slavery in the major British poets, be they proto-Romantics, Romantics, or Victorian post-Romantics.

Another difference between British and American slavery verse relates to the sheer volume, scale, and variety of work that came out of America. One of the most useful things about this anthology is the way in which it sets the work of the famous poets of American and British slavery alongside a mass of work by men and women who have been unjustly sentenced to cultural oblivion. Few of the figures who wrote about British slavery have remained obscure. Certainly there are some exceptions and Hugh Mulligan, Samuel Pratt, Samuel Whitchurch, and Richard Mant are not household names, even among British literary scholars. Yet in the case of American abolition it is quite remarkable how many of their generations of ambitious slavery poets have sunk without a trace despite the quality and cultural impact of their work. This includes the peculiar epics of such figures as Thomas Branagan, William Hebbard, and S. R. Philips. Perhaps one of the most necessary literary exhumations of this part of the anthology is the resurrection of Henry Pierpont, who, although not the intellectual equal of Cowper, has definite claims to be considered the most technically experimental of the mid-century American abolition poets. Pierpont, in his formal experiments, and striving to find the proper vessel to contain his thought, in many ways pinpoints an extreme 'anxiety of influence' in American verse.

The manner in which abolition poets culturally defined themselves was certainly not helped by British arrogance and intransigence over American slavery during the two decades leading up to the war. The British poetic achievement hangs over the American slavery propagandists, and it is worth considering some of the American attempts to create literary solutions to the problem of their British inheritance. I want to think about the texts of some of the more obscure American poets in this Introduction because the special problems and the literary context for this work are far less familiar to British and American readers than those surrounding the British poets, or the 'canonical' American poets.

Abolition verse and martyrological obsession

North Americans have been, and some would say still are, very good at mythologizing themselves as noble victims. The process begins with the fictionalization of the Pilgrim Fathers and saturates the poetry of slavery from an early stage. The first description of a slave in an American poem is of a white Englishwoman, not a black

African. The description was made by the Maryland tobacco merchant and plantation owner Ebenezor Cook in his Hudibrastic *The Sot-Weed Factor; or, A Voyage to Maryland*. Cook is a good place to start thinking about what distinguishes American slavery poetry from British. Cook was an early transatlantic commuter, spending much of his time in Britain, and his poem, although highly critical of British elitism, was first published in London in 1708. The fictional narrator, a supercilious young Englishman, arrives in Maryland and asks a young cattle-drover where he might find lodging. Because he is unknown in the place he is immediately mistaken for a white fugitive slave. Having corrected the mistake the narrator is directed to a nearby planter's house, and is led to his bedroom by a tattered chambermaid. He asks her where she comes from and she tells her story:

> In better Times, e'er to this Land,
> I was unappily Trapann'd;
> Perchance as well I did appear;
> As any Lord or Lady here,
> Not then a Slave for twice a Year . . .
> . . . I daily work and Bare-foot go
> In weeding Corn or feeding Swine,
> I spend my melancholy Time.
> Kidnap'd and Fool'd, I hither fled,
> To shun a hated Nuptial Bed,
> And to my cost already find
> Worse Plagues than those I left behind . . .
> . . . Quick as my thoughts the Slave was fled.[14]

She is then an indentured slave labourer working out a four-year contract, who claims to have fled an arranged marriage in England. And yet, nearly a century before the first African slaves were imported to Jamestown, Virginia, twenty abducted Africans arrived in the colony in 1619 as indentured labourers on seven-year contracts and effectively inaugurated African enslavement in North America. The invisibility in Cook's poem of what was by 1708 a substantial black slave population in Virginia is instructive. Equally instructive is the fact that the first slave to appear in an American poem is a suffering white European woman.

White martyrology takes a far more central role in American abolition verse than in British, and in this mirrors a general difference between the Anglo-American anti-slavery movements. When considering the abolition obsession with suffering for the ultimately just cause it is important to recognize that abolitionists in America had some sort of case. They did operate, in the North, in a very different and far more hostile environment than their British counterparts.

---

[14] Ebenezor Cook, *The Sot-Weed Factor; or, A Voyage to Maryland, &c* (William Park, 1708), repr. *The Heath Anthology of American Literature*, vol. i (3rd edn., Houghton Mifflin, 1998), 644–5, ll. 155–9, 163–9, 174.

Very few British abolitionists went out to do first-hand research in the colonies before the 1833 emancipation bill. After that there was a certain amount of Evangelical research carried out into the real fallout from the newly implemented 'apprentice' system. Yet it was very rare for British abolitionists to encounter any sort of personal danger, or even a sense that they were ruthless fanatics. It was only in late eighteenth-century Liverpool and, to a lesser extent, Bristol that there was a pro-slavery population that was concentrated and socially varied enough to lead to the violent reception of abolitionists. Thomas Clarkson did meet with violent opposition once or twice in Liverpool and Bristol, and William Roscoe (pp. 53–67) was manhandled by an enraged pro-slavery mob on entering Liverpool in the wake of the 1807 abolition bill, but this seems an extraordinary event. In reality the potential for abolition martyrdom was very limited compared to that experienced by Northern abolitionists in America. Those British abolition poets and writers who developed a cult of martyrdom around themselves, John Newton or William Cowper (pp. 77–93), did so in eccentric ways, which were tied into the peculiarities of their own masochistic Evangelicalism. They might take slavery and their tortured relationship with a personally vindictive God into a dark world of solipsistic persecution, but in reality nobody was going to destroy their property, shoot them, hang them, tar and feather them, or stone them to death. Even at its height in the London of the late 1780s abolition was not something that anyone white was going to have to die for.

American abolition really began to take off in the North in the 1820–40 period. During this time there was genuine antipathy and fury among large sections of the working population of most Northern cities directed against organized abolition. Meetings were broken up, printing presses and print works destroyed, and individuals assaulted. Abolition orators and authors, including some visiting British, were in danger of being attacked, beaten, and occasionally even killed by the mobs. Several abolitionists did die during this period, to become fully fledged martyrs. Elijah Lovejoy was the first, and the reaction to his death emphasizes how efficient the abolitionists were in drawing on the full machinery of the British literature of the Protestant martyrs, and on its American limb, the mythology of the *Mayflower*. Lovejoy, Jonathan Walker, William Lloyd Garrison, and most spectacularly John Brown were all elaborately constructed as martyrs using the Foxean models. Not only did the publicity material generate poetry directly around the trials and sufferings of these figures (see pp. 511–13, 536–40, 649–52, 663) but this general atmosphere of persecutory euphoria saturated a large variety of the poetry produced (see pp. 483–7, 584–601, 626–37, 641–52).[15] This

---

[15] The best overview of the neglected subject of abolition and martyrological obsession is still Hazel Catherine Wolf, *On Freedom's Altar: The Martyr Complex in the Abolition Movement* (University of Wisconsin Press, 1952); see also James Brewer Stewart, *Holy Warriors: The Abolitionists and American Slavery* (Farrar Straus & Giroux, 1993).

desire to out-vie the slave in terms of one's personal victimhood sometimes reaches comic proportions of exaggeration, and is perhaps humorously parodied in Whitman's famous lines on becoming a political martyr (p. 632). Yet Whitman stands apart from the body of New England literary abolitionists in his refusal to embrace simplistically, at any point, the tenets of extreme, one might say Bostonian, abolition. In this context it is crucial to understand that there were big regional differences in the profile of abolition in the North. New York, for example, Whitman's base for much of his life, and the environment he matured in as an artist, had a powerful Southern Democrat presence and a powerful anti-abolition lobby. It needs to be stressed that the mobs who attacked abolitionists in many of the East Coast ports and cities were not simply composed of homogeneous and rabid pro-slavery bigots. Often the primary motivation for those taking to the streets related to a series of anxieties. Many Northerners in the 1820–40 period were concerned about the practical ramifications of abolition theory in the North, not the South. Many who were definitely not in favour of the plantation slavery of the South were deeply worried about what the influx of a substantial free black population would mean for them and their jobs. These anxieties frequently unleashed deep and immovable prejudices based in race and colour theory. The compromised political vision which could result from such a variety of socio-political shifts and their resulting pressures is evident in the life and writings of figures as different as Bryant, Emerson, and Whitman (pp. 459–61, 554–8, 626–37). Abolitionists (certainly before the Kansas Nebraska Act, and most significantly the watershed of the 1850 Fugitive Slave Law) were widely constructed as fanatical political extremists, set on breaking up the Union. Even more terrifying was another widely held conviction, namely that abolition's ultimate aim was to enforce the mass migration of a black, ignorant, lustful, morally corrupted, and potentially violent slave, or ex-slave, population into the white, industrialized Northern urban centres. Riots directed against abolitionists were consequently primarily not pro-slavery, but a manifestation of terror. Fear grew out of a desire to protect the labour market and out of the horror of miscegenation. In this the reactions and actions of Northern anti-abolition mobs had no equivalent within the history of British abolition.

British radicalism strangely pervasive in American slavery verse

To take an early and influential American abolition anthology, *Songs of the Free and Hymns of Christian Freedom*, the location of culture is, not surprisingly, essentially Eurocentric. The primary influences are British Nonconformist hymnology (Watts and Wesley pre-eminent) and the tradition of British seventeenth-century radical dissent. It is not to the literary culture of nineteenth-century radicalism, to Paine and Cobbett, or even to Godwin and Hazlitt, that the poets turn, but to seventeenth-century religious disputation, particularly in terms of the way the conventions of martyrology are employed. Forgotten scaffold oratory in the form of the last speeches of Protestant martyrs, even martyrs as obscure as Henry Vane and Marion Harvey, is quoted as a commentary upon abolition verse.

Songs of the Free was an early abolition anthology of poetry published in 1836 and compiled by the 20-year-old Maria Weston Chapman (pp. 483–7). The literary inheritance Chapman draws on comes out of her initial definition of abolition as a religious mission. Abolition is justified as a moral duty, but more specifically in terms of a Bunyanesque 'Holy War' which grows out of heroic spiritual commitment and which will lead to spiritual revelation. The central impetus is the radical equation between slave and abolitionist as Christian martyrs. What any scholar of American abolition would consider to be the central issues of abolition polemic in the 1840s and 1850s do not feature at all. Political debate in the areas of recolonization, the constitutional imperative for slavery in new states, the status of fugitives in Northern free states, even the sanctity of the Union as an ideal beyond the slave question, are not present in the poetry and anthologies of the 1830s.

The poetry in *Songs of the Free* is stylistically and formally dominated by British Nonconformist hymns. The tendencies to masochistic physicality in Wesleyan poetics dwelling on the Passion, and the martial triumphalism of Watts, dominate. The devolved Victorian continuation of these themes within the English tradition has been transferred to America and is also heavily represented by Chapman in her copious selection of poems by the fabulously popular Felicia Hemans. She is represented by among others *The Graves of the Martyrs*, *The Heart of the Martyr*, *The Landing of the Pilgrim Fathers*, and *The Prisoner's Evening Prayer*.

In the context of both British abolition poetry from the period 1780–1830, and the poetry that was to be written by American abolitionists 1840–65, several things stand out about Chapman's compilation. With the exception of Whittier's anti-slavery poetry there is an absence of work which either confronts the political background to the continuation of slavery in America or, more intriguingly, in view of the powerful models provided by earlier English abolition, details the suffering or violence endured by the slaves. The vast majority of pieces deal tangentially with slavery either through association with extreme cases of English political martyrdom, or by appealing to notions of universal freedom and the equality of the races (as in the quotation of several of Isaac Watts's renditions of the Psalms).

The definitional parameters which anti-slavery had established for itself as a discourse of martyrdom and Holy War are forcefully set out in the preface to the anonymous 1837 abolition epic *Slavery Rhymes, Addressed to the Friends of*

Liberty (pp. 487–96). Abolition is described through a diction that incorporates not only the tradition of Foxean Protestant martyrology but also the rhetorically threadbare chivalric paraphernalia of Holy War and the apostolic parallels typical of conversion narratives.

[C]lothed in the 'armour of righteousness', and wielding the 'sword of the spirit', [abolitionists] throw themselves into the breach, wherein they mean to conquer or die. When they bring the subject to the test of Scripture, they feel a 'necessity laid upon them' 'to adopt the faith of abolitionism—and, like the apostle Paul, usually become the most strenuous defenders of the faith they once sought to destroy. Thus the cause is progressing, gathering increasing impetus from every triumph, until even now, in its early infancy, amidst bitter reproaches and persecutions, exposed to demoniac violence and wrong, it is overleaping the strong entrenchments raised by a nation's prejudices and consolidated by a nation's power.[16]

The spiritual battle of abolition is here aligned with the struggles of the first Christians. As the preface progresses this is linked with a further historical inheritance, that of British abolition and that of British reform agitation; both involve a journey through suffering, persecution, and darkness into the light of apotheosis:

having before them the example of the European reformers who though few and despised, triumphed gloriously over the spiritual slaveholders of a former age—and of the puritans of their father land, who (amidst a storm of contumely and persecution unequalled in modern history except by that which assails the abolitionists in the present day) rescued the ark of liberty from the grasp of a tyrant race, and through their sufferings and writings transmitted the precious seeds of civil and religious freedom to all succeeding generations; and above all fixing their eyes on the long protracted struggles of the British abolitionists they will doubtless persevere; and as certainly as they persevere they will ultimately triumph. The clouds of obloquy and prejudice under which they now labour will pass away, and their perfect cause emerge in perfect unity and splendour.[17]

The spirit of the European Reformation is preserved and passed on in its purest form in the example of the Pilgrim Fathers. This inheritance is seen as progressing through an uninterrupted lineage via British Puritanism into American abolition, while it also branches off in the late eighteenth century into British abolition. But where is the slave? Reform is both a sacred trust and an inherited tradition which finds its roots in the anti-papist Reformation in Europe. Abolition is seen as the last link in this European chain of religious dissent. The fight against slavery is the latest example of the fight against the corruption of the established Church. Hence the task of abolition is to scale 'the barriers of ecclesiastical

---

[16] A Looker On (pseud.), *Slavery Rhymes Addressed to the Friends of Liberty Throughout the United States* (John S. Taylor, 1837), p. iv.

[17] Ibid., p. vi.

domination treachery and pride' (p. x). But where is the slave? I am summarizing this increasingly prolix justificatory rhetoric because it is typical. This writing constructs a very clean model of the perverse manner in which abolition propagandas could exist within their own fiction of radical dissent without the presence of the slave registering at all. In such a moral scheme the slave is incidental, and indeed in this preface is not mentioned. The apotheosis outlined above is explicitly reserved for 'the cause', not the black body of the freed slave. The suffering of the slave, if it is important, is only important as a manifestation of the evil of the slave system. In this reform utopia the religious and moral corruption of the slave owner, and above all the suffering of the abolitionist, provide anti-slavery with its focus and its justification.

Slave and ex-slave contributions to the poetry of slavery: an Anglo-American divide

But I do not want to end this Introduction on such a negative note. Much of the poetry of slavery in both Britain and America may seem to get on very nicely without paying too much attention to the slaves. Yet one thing which comes out strongly is the extent to which slaves did have a vital and transformative creative input into the verse which responded to the operations of the slave systems. Again however the differences between America and Britain are enormous.

There is a general absence of black slave poets coming out of Britain during the period 1780–1865. Those black authors who did publish and reach a large audience generally chose to write in other forms than verse. Of the four most influential black ex-slave authors only Equiano and Wedderburn (pp. 150–4, 310–15) wrote substantial poems of their own. Even here these short pieces appeared incidentally within very different publications; in Equiano's case within a slave narrative, in Wedderburn's as filler in his ephemeral but wonderfully militant newspaper *The Axe Laid to the Root*. When it comes to the preservation of slave poetry produced in the English colonies there is an archival hole. It is astonishing, but sadly a fact, that there appear to be no slave poets from the eighteenth- or early nineteenth-century British slave colonies who published, or should one say were allowed to publish, any poetry at all. Unlike America there also seems to have been no interest in recording and printing the slave songs, anthems, or spirituals which the slaves of the British Antilles must have produced. Conversely North American spirituals and work songs were carefully recorded from an early date and have come to constitute the bedrock of black poetic and musical response to slavery. These works combine revolutionary politics with a beautiful solution to trauma survival (see pp. 399–404). Yet even within more conventional white Eurocentric verse forms the American inheritance could hardly be more differently weighted from the British. Phyllis Wheatley and Jupiter Hammon were writing accomplished poetry which addressed the issues of slavery and discrimination in the 1770s (pp. 404–15). The African-American slave and ex-slave traditions of poetry continue unbroken from then until the Civil War. Black poets frequently took up abolition themes with an intensity and ingenuity which their white abolition counterparts lacked. They were also, on occasion, not afraid of launching a critique into the hypocritical and self-serving mechanisms which can be seen to operate in white abolition thought. The poetry of Whitfield and Holly (pp. 584–94) did not merely reiterate white Northern abolitionist attacks on Southern corruption, the slave's passive suffering, and the heroic active suffering of white abolition martyrs. Northern prejudice and hypocrisy were forcefully interrogated, and even ridiculed as well. Several ex-slave and free black poets gained wide readerships, and even, as in the case of Ellen Watkins Harper, became mainstream literary figures. One thing this anthology has tried to bring out is the extent to which black figures not now remembered as poets (including such leading lights as Frederick Douglass, William Wells Brown, and Henry 'Box' Brown) incorporated original poetry into their works in unexpected ways (pp. 548–51, 570–6, 580–4).

What might the poetry of slavery mean now?

The central questions raised by this anthology are first, what sort of poetry did the Atlantic slavery systems generate? and secondly, what is the point of reading it now? This volume will have been successful if it puts readers in a position to form their own answers to these questions. One thing that comes out of this anthology is the remarkable homogeneity of almost all the verse. Despite the fact that a large number of individuals from vastly different cultural and geographical backgrounds are writing poetry about slavery for nearly a century the religious, race, and cultural agendas emerge as stable, even monolithic. The mythographers of slavery first invented, and then needed to believe in, the fictions of their own stability. The alternative, a radical literature which addressed the economic and cultural forces which enabled the Atlantic slave systems, was, and to a large extent remains, beyond the capacity of British and North American art. Among poets Blake and Whitman finally emerge as the only figures with the strength of vision to break the abolition mould, and to confront new, dark, unanswerable, and sometimes even humorous questions about the psychopathology of Atlantic slavery.

  This anthology makes available a body of work that will contribute to the accelerating processes of thinking through the Anglo-American cultural inheritance of slavery. It also puts readers in a position to judge why some of the poems are more helpful in accelerating these processes than other poems. For my money Whitman shares with Blake the ability to bring a weird energy to the task of making art about Atlantic slavery. In this sense these two poets break out of the mawkish, sentimental, self-righteous, or martyrological approaches which saturate much of the abolition poetry in the rest of this volume. Blake is prepared to say that an extreme form of cleansing violence is the inevitable, and necessary, response to the inheritance of slavery. He celebrates what bell hooks has termed 'killing rage', as the terrible price that must be paid for what was perpetrated. Whitman's ironic take on the bizarre power which money, exchange mechanisms, and commodity fetishism exert on our so-called civilization might have a particular resonance now, in a world where more human beings than ever before are bought and sold in the global market place, using the US dollar (pp. 626–37). What would the Whitman who sang the 'body electric' in the persona of a slave auctioneer have done with the sale of thousands of Thai children into the European and American sex industries? What would his art have done with those who auction teenaged Filipina girls off to European and American men, via the World Wide Web? If these acts of enslavement are subjects for art we do not seem to have the poets capable of dealing with them any more.

The poetry of slavery did not stop in the Diaspora in 1865. Maybe the final point of this volume lies in the manner in which it helps us reread what has been written since 1865. In the twentieth century a radical poetics of slavery emerged, produced by poets who were the descendants of slaves and who grew up in, and out of, the slave Diaspora. From the publication of Aimé Césaire's still shocking *Notebook of a Return to my Native Land*, through the work of the Caribbean Surrealist and Négritude poets, and on into the poetry of Derek Walcott, the reggae lyrics of Peter Tosh, Bob Marley, Burning Spear, and Jimmy Lindsay, and the extraordinary contributions of the dub poets, with Mikey Smith at their head, the inheritance of Atlantic slavery has generated beautiful and terrifying poetry in the Caribbean. In North America there have also been vital interventions into attempting to make poetic language do new things with the impossible task of remembering slavery. Langston Hughes and Robert Hayden wrote in conventional poetic form of slave experience, but it is perhaps in the prose experiments of Ralph Ellison and Toni Morrison that American writing has taken the memory of slavery to a new level of condensation. Ellison's poem/sermon 'The Blackness of Blackness' in *Invisible Man*, and Morrison's 'I am beloved and she is mine' monologue in *Beloved*, have shown that there are unprecedented ways of using poetic diction to explore the memory of slavery. All of these dense and beautiful twentieth-century poetic achievements are finally strangely enriched if they are read through, and against the grain of, the slave poetry that has preceded them. This is a body of work created by women and men, blacks and whites.

English and North American Slavery: Key Notes on Cultural and Historical Difference[1]

The following notes expand on some key concepts relevant both to the abolition poetry in this anthology, and to the international slavery abolition movements of Britain and North America, which gave rise to the majority of this work. It is particularly important to describe the basic differences between the British-Caribbean and North American slave systems. Despite many similarities, the abolition and pro-slavery movements these two regions generated were inflected by stark dissimilarities. It is also vital to outline some areas of the historiographies of slavery that were developed in Britain and America in order to acculturate and explain the slave systems. The historical fictions generated around slavery both inflected and were influenced by abolition. The abolition literatures which Britain and America produced consequently share a lot, but also have many quite distinct areas.

Origins and volume of Atlantic slavery

Africans made up the principal slave force in the American and Caribbean colonies, and former colonies, from the sixteenth to the late nineteenth centuries. Black Africans started to appear in Mediterranean slave markets as early as the fourteenth century. By the mid-fifteenth century the Portuguese had made contact with the sub-Saharan ports, and the European slave trade with Africa began, with Lisbon as the first significant European slave port. When Europeans arrived on the coast of tropical West Africa, looking for slaves, they found a network of trade routes organized around powerful African city states; these networks were inherited by the slave traders. Links were established with influential inland Arab and African traders, and with African coastal chiefs and leaders. The 'triangular trade', or 'Guinea trade', which increasingly gained its slaves from the interior of Africa, developed, and rapidly took on a vast scale. The total number of slaves taken from Africa as a result of this trade will never be accurately known. Estimates range between ten and sixty million human beings.

[1] The information contained in these notes has been synthesized from the texts listed in the first section of the Select Bibliography; see pp. 694–5 below.

Portugal had introduced significant sugar production in northern Brazil by the mid-1540s, and had established one pattern for subsequent New World plantation slavery. With the indigenous populations of the Caribbean and South America largely destroyed in any areas of Luso-Hispanic colonial contact, the industrial development of these areas was to depend on imported African slave labour. By 1600 the slave plantation labour system was fully developed around the production of refined sugar. It was a uniquely efficient system which, in the larger plantations, combined a social structure close to feudal hierarchy and a labour system which closely anticipated that of the capitalist industrial factory. The African slave populations on South American and Caribbean plantations were not regenerative (North America was a special case in this respect, as it was in the demographics and populations of its plantations). The sugar and mining industries were expanding markets in the Caribbean and Americas. Consequently the plantations and mines required ever-fresh supplies of African slave labour. In order to meet this fluctuating yet unending demand transportation of slave cargoes from the African coast to the Americas continued from 1600 until the late nineteenth century. Despite abolition decrees, laws, and treaties, slaves were still being smuggled to Brazil right up until 1888 when Brazilian slavery was finally abolished via the *lei d'ouro* or golden law. Plantation owners outside the United States, certainly up to the late eighteenth century, frequently did business in an economic climate where European monopoly capitalism produced a market in which the price of supporting a slave child until it could labour was more than that of buying a new slave out of Africa.

Development of British slavery and the slave trade

The British began settling the Caribbean colonies by the early 1620s, Barbados being the first successfully cultivated British island. The Luso-Brazilian plantation model was adopted across the entire Caribbean. Black slaves became the inevitable source of labour, once it was found that a certain percentage of them survived in the tropics, and sub-tropics, far longer and in greater numbers than white Europeans. This fact gave rise to the myth, still believed by many Europeans today, that Africans were not affected by heat and worked without distress in hot climates. The truth was that many slaves, depending on which part of the African continent they came from, had acquired and sometimes inherited immunity to diseases fatal for Europeans, the most destructive being yellow fever, and two of the worst strains of malaria.

The development of Barbados by the British is a convenient microcosm for viewing the expansion of sugar production in the Caribbean as a whole. In 1637 the island produced no sugar, by the 1670s it generated 65 per cent of the sugar consumed by the British, and by 1767 80 per cent of the island was covered with plantations. The British (Jamaica, Trinidad, Barbados, Demerara, St Kitts, and certain of the North American colonies), the Spanish (Cuba, Santo Domingo), and the French (San Domingue, later renamed Hayti) all developed mass slave plantation industries on their colonies. There was a craving for new slave labour to enable plantation development. James Walvin makes the remarkable statement that 'the influence of slave labour was so great that it was not until the 1840s that more Europeans than Africans crossed the Atlantic to populate the New World'.[2]

Slaves were transported from Africa to the Americas and the Caribbean primarily on European ships. This journey was called the 'middle passage' because it, typically but not invariably, constituted the central section of the three-part journey which a European slave ship would make. The boat would load up with trading stuffs for the African slave coast (guns, alcohol, textiles, metal household goods), barter these for slaves and often anything else they could get their hands on (ivory, gold, dyes, hardwoods, and 'cultural curiosities'). The slaves were then shipped, almost invariably under appalling conditions, to the New World plantations. Large numbers of slaves, and of the slaving crews, died on the middle passage. In the New World the slaves were sold and slave produce (at different times in different places sugar, tobacco, cotton, coffee, rice, and alcohol) was shipped and brought back to Europe. The British, French, Spanish, Portuguese, Dutch, and Danes all, at various times and to different degrees, took part in the 'Guinea trade', which generated substantial profits. Between 1670 and 1770, in the British West Indies alone, over two million African slaves who had survived the middle passage were bought.

American slavery structurally and socially different from that of the Caribbean

From the first North American slavery was atypical when compared with Brazil and the European colonies of the Caribbean. There was, proportionally, a much smaller percentage of blacks to whites, and the slaves existed on smaller and more varied plantations. Typical Caribbean plantations had between 50 and 200 slaves, some more than 300; when American plantation slavery was at its height in 1850 less than half the plantations had more than 30 slaves.

Only a very small number of mainland American colonies bought slaves in the seventeenth century. It was only by the mid-eighteenth century that plantation society became typical in some of the Southern states, and even then it was vastly different from the Caribbean slave societies. Where in Jamaica or Barbados the

---

[2] James Walvin, *Questioning Slavery* (Routledge, 1996), 13–14.

population was finally between 75 and 95 per cent black, in North America, even in the Southern states, white European-based populations always substantially outnumbered slaves. Another big difference was that in North America both white and slave populations actually grew; amazingly slave populations grew faster in the nineteenth century than European populations. Consequently there was a diminishing dependence on the African and Atlantic slave trade to provide labour. When plantation slavery developed substantially certain states, most notoriously Virginia, became increasingly breeding and marketing states, selling the slaves down south, or in the now proverbial phrase 'down the river'.

Consequently American abolition writing focuses far more on what is a home-grown institution. This fact underlies a fundamental shift between American and English abolition writing. In England the abolitionists were fighting a phenom-enon that had no significant manifestation on the British mainland, and slavery, despite the vagaries of the Mansfield decision, was popularly deemed, and by the early nineteenth century to all practical purposes was, illegal within Britain. Con-sequently both the horrors of the middle passage, and those of plantation slavery, could be set out as foreign evils which tainted, but in fact were no part of, British law, thought, or society. The West India planter, as Austen's *Mansfield Park* demonstrates with such precision, was not quite an Englishman. The planter lobby, although powerful in Parliament because of its economic clout, could finally be cut off as an unnecessary and alien attachment. The white Creoles, male and female, adults and children, were culturally even more eccentric than the British-born absentee planters, and were constructed in Britain as a strange set of creatures, difficult to define.

The popular perception of slavery in the United States, at least until the later 1830s, was entirely different. Immediately after the War of Independence slavery had been represented, even in many parts of the South, as contrary to the basic tenets of the Declaration of Independence, and as a minor and doomed element in the national economy. In the decade following the War of Independence the number of free blacks, many of whom had fought alongside the colonists against the British, increased dramatically.

Everything changed in the opening decades of the nineteenth century. In 1793 Eli Whitney invented the cotton gin, which separated the seed from the cotton mechanically. This made the cultivation of the short staple cotton crop possible across almost all of the South. In 1790 America produced 4,000 bales of cotton, in 1860 4,000,000. The slave population grew from 1.5 million in 1820 to over 4 million in 1860. The South's prosperity depended on slave labour, and the whole balance and approach of abolition shifted. The point can be made suc-cinctly with the following figures. In 1827 there were 130 anti-slavery societies in the United States of which 106 were in slave-holding states. By 1857 there were 1,057 anti-slavery societies, but not one of these was in the Southern slave-holding states. Abolition as a publishing and literary phenomenon went through a massive alteration. From being, in the period 1780–1830, as much a part of the South as the North, it became exclusively a Northern phenomenon in the period 1830–65, the period from which the majority of the abolition verse in this anthology is taken.

British abolition's 'great awakening': the anti-slave trade movement

The basic difference between British abolition in its first great phase from 1780 until the abolition of the slave trade in 1807 and North American abolition is that British abolition focused, for reasons of political strategy, almost exclusively on the conditions and operation of the Atlantic slave trade. It is not surprising that Britain should have produced the first effective national propaganda movement to call attention to the basic inhumanity and amorality of the slave trade, because by the 1740s England dominated the international slave trade with Africa. By the 1750s, primarily owing to its ruthless and notorious competitiveness, Liverpool had supplanted London to become the biggest slaving port in the world; Bristol was another substantial centre. By this stage only the great French slaving ports of Nantes and Bordeaux came anywhere near rivalling the leading British slave ports.

Why the abolition movement suddenly gained momentum in Britain in the early 1780s is not easily answered. In the context of this anthology it is certainly worth emphasizing that in terms of an intellectual and literary inheritance there was already a substantial European and American tradition to draw on, although this related to the development of theories of slavery generally, and only tangentially to the slave trade. Montesquieu had written against slavery as early as the *Persian Letters* (1721), but it was his *Spirit of the Laws* (1748) which annihilated defences of slavery drawn from the classics, ultimately Aristotle's *Politics*. Montesquieu had vast influence in England and determined the basis of legal theory, becoming a central influence in those parts of Blackstone's *Commentaries on the Laws of England* (1765) which treated slave rights in the courts.

Eighteenth-century Quakers in England and America also established a body of anti-slavery writing. The Americans John Woolman and Anthony Benezet wrote anti-slavery texts that were widely read on both sides of the Atlantic. Benezet's long pamphlet *Some Historical Account of Guinea* (1771) profoundly influenced Thomas Clarkson and Granville Sharp in their early abolition writing, and established the basic paradigms for the presentation of the slave trade which reappear in many of the texts in this anthology including Olaudah Equiano's *Interesting Narrative*, William Roscoe's *Mount Pleasant*, William

Cowper's second book of *The Task*, Thomas Day's *The Dying Negro*, Samuel Whitchurch's *Hispaniola*, and James Montgomery's *The West Indies* (pp. 150–4, 53–7, 86–8, 36–48, 168–80, 279–96). English Methodism also fed into the early stages of English abolition: in 1774 John Wesley published his *Thoughts on Slavery*, another text strongly influenced by Benezet.

One crucial fact to bear in mind when looking at abolition poetry is that slavery itself was popularly deemed to be, and finally did become, legally outlawed in mainland Britain. Consequently, unless they travelled to the colonies, the only direct contact which British people had with slavery was to be found through the impact and operations of the slave trade in British ports. The history of the first great phase of British abolition propaganda begins in the early 1780s with the publications and activities of the abolitionist Quakers, and with the legal battles of Granville Sharp. It ends with the passage of a parliamentary bill making slave trading in Britain and the British colonies illegal in 1807. Consequently the history of abolition initially bears a heavy anti-slave trade bias. It was not until after 1807 that attention in Britain shifted from the 'middle passage' almost exclusively to the question of abolishing chattel slavery on the colonial plantations. North American abolition had conversely a long-established tradition of tract literature directed to slave holding not only in the American South, but during much of the eighteenth century on the north-east coast as well.

Consequently the abolition writing in England which appears after 1807 carries very different emphases from that before 1807. There is an increasing English triumphalism which celebrates the national philanthropy leading to the first abolition bill, and which explodes into self-congratulation in 1833–4 with the abolition of slavery in the British sugar colonies. The period 1808–40, in English abolition publication, shifts to considering the condition of the slave on the plantation, and to the creation of what is virtually a bestiary of white plantation society. Prose and verse deal increasingly with plantation stereotypes such as the overseer, the absentee planter, the cruel plantation mistress jealous of her attractive young female slaves, and the lethargic Creole mistress, too idle almost to move. Stereotypes for the slave, however, had already been developed and always emphasized loyalty, obedience, docility, and Christianity. Thomas Day's *The Dying Negro* ultimately comes out of the same desire to soothe white fear of the black slave as Harriet Beecher Stowe's *Uncle Tom's Cabin*. The only exception to this rule is the development of the figure of the runaway, who however may also appear as pathetic victim, rather than victorious escapee. It is only in the writings of blacks themselves that these stereotypes are subverted or even annihilated. This literary process begins with the superb autobiography of the ex-slave Olaudah Equiano published in the momentous year of 1789 as Europe experienced the birth of the French Revolution. Mid-nineteenth-century America saw black ex-slaves (Moses Roper, Frederick Douglass, Harriet Jacobs, William

Wells Brown, Henry 'Box' Brown, William and Ellen Craft, to name a sample of the most prominent) expand on the inheritance of the black autobiography. They produced a body of work which redefined the imaginative construction of slavery, and which permanently altered the white literary stereotypes of the black. As this tradition was not poetic it is not followed up in detail in the present context.

Slave rebellion and literary taboo

In terms of this anthology it is necessary to underline that throughout white abolition literature there is a constant desire to sheer away from the notion that the slave can attain his or her freedom through violent rebellion. There is also a reluctance to admit that the slave can sustain a fulfilled life after a successful revolt. There are no British poems celebrating slave rebellion in the British colonies. There are no epics detailing the history of the Jamaican maroons, who remained independent in their isolated communities in the inaccessible cockpit country, and successfully fought off the British army for 200 years. Similarly there are no ballads or Spenserian cantos celebrating Nat Turner's bloody revolt in Virginia in 1831. Abolition poetry such as Samuel Whitchurch's 1804 *Hispaniola*, which docs treat the outrages of the San Domingue slave revolution directly, and which does contain descriptions of black military violence, does so in the context of the battle of the slaves against revolutionary and then Napoleonic France. Whitchurch presents the slaves as the latest victims in a series of terrible colonial actions carried out by non-British Europeans (pp. 168–81). The black rebellion is presented as the inevitable outcome of the violent amorality not only of the French colonists, but of the Spanish before them. The disastrous British attempt to take French San Domingue in the 1790s is passed over by all British poets.

San Domingue and slavery propagandas

In terms of its cultural fallout in Britain and America the San Domingue slave revolution, which began in 1790 and did not end until the final declaration of Hayti as an independent black republic in 1804, was a huge boon for pro-slavery propaganda. It is not surprising to see abolition poets in Britain and America largely giving the event a body swerve. Cultural commentators from Edmund Burke in the 1790s to George Fitzhugh in mid-nineteenth-century America had made San Domingue synonymous with black barbarity, sexual outrage, bloodlust, and anarchy. The imagery of black slave passivity and victimhood which had typified abolition literatures was suddenly decimated in wave after wave of atrocity literature fixated on the (largely imagined) depredations of the 'Black Jacobins'. It was only when Napoleonic France took on, and was defeated by, the rebel-slave armies that the tide of propaganda to some extent turned. Britain at war with France delighted in setting up Toussaint L'Ouverture as an inspirational and ideal black counter to Napoleon. Consequently Toussaint features in the work of several English and American poets, including Whitchurch, Wordsworth, and Whittier (pp. 176–80, 231–3, 503–10).

Impact of the British 1834 slave emancipation Act

The impact of emancipation in the British sugar colonies on British abolition writing is enormous. British emancipation generated a flood of celebratory publication, including a lot of verse (see pp. 297–9, 320–2). Thereafter the memory of slavery in British abolition verse and literature became primarily a cause for celebration, frequently at the expense of American claims to the constitutional enjoyment of 'life, liberty and the pursuit of happiness'. A European league table of colonial atrocity was set up from which the British were strangely absent. The Spanish and French were set up as bestial and hypocritical colonizers, slaughtering indigenous populations, and introducing Popery and African slavery on top of the wreckage. Tennyson's *Anacaona* and *Columbus* both play ingenious Victorian variations on this inheritance. (For poetry of the Spanish 'Black Legend' see pp. 85–8, 106–8, 133–8, 168–80, 280–8, 313–16, 445–7.)

After the early 1830s British abolitionists turned their attention to America, which from 1831 to 1835 became the literary and intellectual hub of world abolition. While there were magnificent poetical, and prose, contributions to American abolition by British poets, these frequently excoriated the continuation of the 'Peculiar Institution' in the context of American claims to enlightened democracy, and the achievement of slave emancipation in the British colonies. Elizabeth Barrett Browning's *The Runaway Slave at Pilgrim's Point* is a case in point (pp. 356–63). The poem opens by showing the American runaway symbolically collapsing at 'Pilgrim's Point', the site of the British establishment of a free settlement in North America.

Women and abolition in Britain and America

Abolition allowed women in Britain and North America to become involved in grass-roots political activism. The members of female abolition societies broke with social convention to hold their own political meetings and to canvass from door to door in the major cities of Britain and the Northern states of America.

Women also contributed to abolition propaganda in gender-specific ways. They produced and distributed hand-painted albums and work bags which were put up for auction at anti-slavery bazaars, and they also made poetry anthologies and pamphlets. This work was produced on a massive scale and was of central importance to the abolition movement.

As this anthology brings out forcefully, women were absolutely central to the production of abolition publication from its beginnings. Recent work, and that of Rosamund and Louis Billington in particular, has begun to reveal the extent of the transatlantic dialogue between British and American abolitionists. Perhaps more significantly this work also attempts to isolate differences between British and American female abolitionists in the nineteenth century. The American societies emerge as possessing far more radical agendas than their British counterparts, yet from the evidence of this anthology it would appear that their radicalism did not translate readily into their poetry.

What also emerges is the fact that from the appearance of Anne Yearsley's impassioned *Poem on the Inhumanity of the Slave-Trade* (pp. 120–30) to the moment when Julia Ward Howe composed the magnificent 'Battle Hymn of the Republic' to the tune of 'John Brown's Body' (p. 663), British and American women exploited a unique opportunity to put their slavery poetry out there, with a delighted promiscuity, for whoever would listen. One of the elements which comes out of this anthology most clearly is the range and polemical efficacy of women's abolition verse. The Christian, sentimental, and philanthropic justifications of abolition made it a movement to which women were invited to contribute at both an organizational and artistic level. Presented with the opportunity to write political propaganda for a huge audience both American and British women poets were capable of harnessing abolition to a series of issues relating to female oppression. The very different solutions that they adopted in order to subvert and re-interrogate abolition dogma again come out strongly in this anthology. The contribution of women to the British abolition movement throughout its different phases was constant. The poetry More, Yearsley, and Barbauld (pp. 99–132, 180–4) produced during the first phase of abolition publicity was as effective as anything their male counterparts produced. Yet as abolition became a less central concern in the period 1834–50 in Britain so American abolition came to hold an increasingly central place.

Janet Gray's 1997 anthology *She Wields a Pen: American Women Poets of the Nineteenth Century* has begun the task of uncovering the mass of poetry written by American women. Abolition in America existed as the key-site in which women could combine the creation of published literature, political rhetoric, and high-profile public performance. They did this at a level, over a period, and with a vigour and ingenuity that finds no real equivalent in nineteenth-century Britain. Lydia Maria Child, Maria Weston Chapman, and Eliza Lee Follen (pp. 472–87, 522–6) are just three of the more prominent women, authors, editors, activists, and intellectuals of real ability, who devoted some of their vast energies to abolition, while working during long careers in many areas of reform.

American abolition's 'great awakening'

The early 1830s were a watershed for American abolition. When on 1 January 1831 William Lloyd Garrison published the first issue of the *Liberator* he announced a fierce and totally uncompromising immediatist approach to abolition. He demanded that it should be instantaneous and nationwide. He castigated himself for his earlier support of gradualist approaches to abolition and in particular his sympathy with 're-Colonisation', in other words the immediate forced resettlement of free blacks in Africa, to be followed by the slaves, under compensatory schemes for the owners. Garrison stated that he 'undertook to look at the slave question the way the Negro looked at it'. Much of the financial support for the *Liberator*, at least in the first years, came from free blacks. A new radical 'Garrisonian' abolition suddenly swept the North, a movement which shunned compromise, excoriated the South, and focused upon the inherent pathos and nobility of the slave. Garrisonian abolition was also instrumental in developing the Northern abolitionist as ultimate martyrological victim.

Garrisonian immediatism conveniently marks the opening of the floodgates of abolition propaganda. The New England Anti-Slavery Society was formed in 1832; societies sprang up throughout the North. Elizur Wright masterminded the New York ASS's 'Great Postal Campaign' in 1855–6 and pamphlets, newspapers, journals, children's books, handbills, and broadsides carrying prose, poetry, and vivid woodcuts were sent out across the North. Garrison returned from a trip to co-ordinate with English abolition societies in October 1833 and together with Beriah Green, Lewis Tappan, and the poet J. G. Whittier established a National Convention. By 1838 there were 1,350 societies within the national organization with a membership in the region of a quarter of a million. Much of the American abolition poetry in this anthology dates from this period of remarkable abolition ferment and formal experimentation.

The major American themes 1830–1865

Unlike British abolition verse, which is in comparison ideologically static, American abolition propaganda focused on, and constantly responded to, issues arising out of the geographical and economic shifts of the 1830–60 period. Nineteenth-century America, as it pushed out south into Mexico, fighting a brutal colonial war which ended with the annexation of the southwestern states, and out across the new territories of Kansas and Nebraska, was not a stable entity, but it was a single mainland which supposedly constituted a single economic and political 'union'. Whether the newly settled areas would be slave states or not was perceived as a matter of crucial importance for the future balance of political power between North and South. Abolition responded to the threat of the expansion of the slave power with fury. A sub-Miltonic epic such as *Nebraska*, rewriting *Paradise Lost* in the shadow of Daniel Webster's political chicanery over the Kansas Nebraska Act, is an ambitious, gloriously clumsy, and typically American poem (pp. 594–602).

In the years directly preceding the outbreak of war it is difficult to overstate the propagandistic centrality of the Fugitive Slave Law. This was a crucial turning point in terms of the Northern consciousness, marking for many an absolute split from the South on slavery. Congress had passed a law that made the Northern states directly answerable to the South in terms of their treatment of fugitive blacks. Northerners were now legally obliged to turn fugitives over to Southern owners, or their agents. The North was forced to admit that the Union demanded that the legal rights of the slave power over its human 'property' could practically extend into the North. One immediate result of the passage of the Act was the creation of Harriet Beecher Stowe's *Uncle Tom's Cabin* of 1852. This was merely the spearhead for a vast production of art and literature which now concentrated on the figure of the fugitive slave, and which reflected the newly felt outrage. Slavery had moved from the North's backyard into its front garden.

Observations on Anglo-American abolition in the ante-bellum decades

American abolition inherited some literary tropes from British slave trade propaganda of 1780–1807 (the Negro mother's lament at being parted from her children, the basic humanitarian equation of slave and master typified in the British abolition aphorism 'am I not a man and a brother') but its primary emphasis is on the treatment of slaves in its own Southern states, and the Northerner's complacent acceptance of these horrors. American slavery's literary masterpiece *Uncle Tom's Cabin* (1852) does not treat the international slave trade at all but concerns two major geographical themes: first the selling of Tom down the river from Kentucky deeper and deeper into the cotton country, and secondly the movement from Kentucky to the free states of the mulatto 'runaways' George Harris and his wife Eliza.

American abolition poetry and literature generally developed its own domestic subject areas and tropes for the discussion of the abolition question. These worked in different areas, some of them directed primarily at the Southern slave holders, others aimed at pricking the conscience of the complicitous Northerner. As is amply demonstrated in the poems reproduced in this anthology there are two prominent themes. The first is the emphatic assertion that slavery as an institution is not compatible with the ideals of the new nation. These ideals are seen as set out formally in the Declaration of Independence, but are also essentialized in a series of key myths beginning with the story of the Pilgrim Fathers, and moving through the narratives of the War of Independence (pp. 483–95, 584–9, 618–23, 641–59). The second theme was the demonization of the South, as a land of atrocity, darkness, and bondage, and the celebration of the North as a place of enlightenment, sanctuary, and freedom. It is only really after the 1830s that a concerted propaganda campaign directed at the demonization of the South, in moral and institutional terms, takes off. Before this abolition tended to concentrate on foregrounding the suffering of the slave, and to some extent the moral damage which slave holding exerted on the slave owner. This increasingly explicit denigration of the South comes out clearly in the overall balance of the American section of this anthology. Abolition poets and authors increasingly turned to satire during the 1840–60 period. If the expansion of the slave states into the new territories was to be quelled then part of the job of anti-slavery propaganda was to prove that the Southern states were rotten at the core. A number of poetical satires in this anthology including *Slavery Vindicated; or, The Beauty and Glory of the 'Patriarchal System' Illustrated*, Daniel Mann's *The Virginia Philosopher; or, A Few Lucky Slave Catchers: A Poem*, John Pierpont's 'Slave Holder's Address to the North Star', and *Southern Chivalry*, by 'a citizen of the Cotton Country', are part of this tendency (pp. 515–22, 532–5, 544–6, 664–9).

British abolition's peculiar line on America's dilemmas

If British abolition seemed initially to lay down the basic paradigms for abolition verse, the transatlantic dialogue became a complicated two-way process. Leading abolition celebrities from Britain were very much in demand in the 1830–50 period: Harriet Martineau and George Thompson are sensational, but typical, examples. They both toured the United States, were celebrated in abolition strongholds, and deliberately sought martyrological abuse in the mid-west, and the South. Their lectures and experiences were then publicized in newspapers on both sides of the Atlantic. Martineau in particular was a brilliant journalist and self-promoter. The foremost anti-slavery journals frequently looked to Britain for their stylistic models and even for their contributors. Cowper, Wordsworth, and (strangely, given that he did not write about Atlantic slavery directly) Byron were the most frequently reprinted of a huge variety of British poets who appeared in

American anti-slavery journals. Elizabeth Barrett Browning wrote her most important slavery poems not for the British market but for *The Liberty Bell*, a volume published annually by the Boston Women's Anti-Slavery Society as a Christmas stocking filler (pp. 356–63, 365–8). Blake was first widely printed in North America as an abolition poet in the poetry column of the *National Anti-Slavery Standard* (see pp. 142–3). This paper, along with Garrison's *Liberator*, was far and away America's biggest anti-slavery newspaper. A very brief perusal of the fat poetry column of the *National Anti-Slavery Standard*, when under the inspirational editorship of Lydia Maria Child (p. 472), could serve as a sort of shorthand for the manner in which British poetry impacted on American abolition publicity. British Romantic poetry was seen as a central abolition reservoir and saturates the work. The poetry column in volume 1 number 1 opened with two Coleridge quotations and followed this up with Wordsworth's 'Truth for a Free State': 'The discipline of slavery is unknown | Among us,—hence the more we do require | The discipline of virtue: order else | Cannot subsist, nor confidence nor peace.'[3] The succeeding issues quoted vast amounts of British poetry beginning with Milton's sonnets, but focusing on the late eighteenth and nineteenth centuries. Wordsworth and Coleridge remain favourites, but Burns, Leigh Hunt, Byron, Eliza Cook, Harriet Martineau, and even Ebenezer Elliott are all well represented.

Yet in the 1840s and 1850s the major stars of American abolition were also touring and lecturing in Britain. Ex-slaves and fugitive slaves were popular with British audiences north and south and travelled a well-established lecture circuit. The abolitionists strictly policed who was allowed in and what they were allowed to say, but as long as the rules were obeyed ex-slaves found a ready audience in Britain. Virtually every major black polemicist visited Britain at least once during this period, many had their works republished in British editions, and several emulated William Wells Brown and even toured the rest of Europe. The brilliant scholarship that has resulted in the publication of the massive *Black Abolitionist Papers* has revealed for the first time something of the extent of involvement of black polemicists in the construction of a cultural network connecting Britain, Canada, and the United States.[4] Contemporary accounts reveal the ecstatic responses which the extemporized verse performances of Henry 'Box' Brown received from British audiences from London to Leeds, and the disquiet which his extemporized psalms and hilarious ballads caused to the abolition establishment (pp. 580–4). Brown's success reveals, however, the extent to which abolition was big business, and the manner in which it could easily drift into publishing and performative contexts which were genuinely popular and

[3] *National Anti-Slavery Standard*, 1/1 (11 June 1840), 4.
[4] Peter Ripley (ed.), *The Black Abolitionist Papers*, 5 vols. (University of North Carolina Press, 1985–92).

beyond the control of British or American abolition societies. It is difficult now to comprehend how big abolition was as a publishing and marketing phenomenon. American abolition generated some of the biggest-selling popular works in the British market. The popularity of major abolition texts from the United States in Britain can hardly be exaggerated. Harriet Beecher Stowe was an author super-star, and *Uncle Tom's Cabin* had a global impact, yet its biggest market by far in the 1850s was in Britain (pp. 382–92). Stowe, and abolition generally, once they reached a certain level of popularity, fed into extant popular forms developed for the representation of black language and culture. This is manifested most clearly in this volume in the treatment of slave and race themes in the 'songsters' gener-ated by black-face minstrelsy (pp. 685–93).

Stowe was not a unique phenomenon, simply the centrepiece in a flourishing publicity trade. Slave narratives became popular with an English reading public: the works of Frederick Douglass, William Wells Brown, William and Ellen Craft, and Henry 'Box' Brown were all popular in Britain and the majority appeared in English editions, some even in Welsh editions. The early Gothic slavery novel *Archie More; or, The White Slave* was marketed in a number of cheap 'railway edi-tions', the equivalent of today's airport best-sellers. Abolition poetry by leading American authors could have a huge market: Lowell and Whittier both had big British followings, yet perhaps the most unexpected success was the sly slavery satire of James Russell Lowell. The first pirated English edition of Lowell's *Biglow Papers* shared with the pirated editions of *Uncle Tom's Cabin* the privilege of attracting the talents of George Cruikshank, the greatest graphic satirist living. The work raced through editions in London, and its success was partly the result of the manner in which it enforced British cultural stereotypes about Americans.

And yet, from the 1840s to the outbreak of the Civil War, American slavery reg-isters sporadically in the British poetic, and indeed literary, consciousness. As the war appeared inevitable British journalism and media generally were primar-ily concerned not with slavery, but with the economic and diplomatic implica-tions of the war for Britain. Douglas Lorimer's *Colour, Class and the Victorians* sums up the caricatured and fundamentally confused British response, stating that for British writers and politicians 'the American Civil War takes on the appearance of a great morality play. Lincoln the knight in shining armour, and his Federal Forces of Good fight for abolition, while a Satanic South vainly struggles for slavery, and justly falls because of its hellish institution. As interested specta-tors in this great moral drama, many mid-Victorians became confused, and ended up cheering for the South in flagrant violation of England's honoured anti-slavery traditions.'[5] For the purposes of this anthology the compromised and

---

[5] Douglas Lorimer, *Colour, Class and the Victorians: English Attitudes to the Negro in the Mid-Nineteenth Century* (Leicester University Press, 1978), 162–3.

morally suspended British reaction comes out in the satiric poem 'King Cotton Bound; or, The Modern Prometheus', which appeared in *Punch* at the end of 1861 (pp. 368–72). Indeed *Punch* provides a wonderful and economic overview of the Victorian middle class's reaction to the war, and fully illustrates every aspect of Victorian Negrophobia. Maybe one print satire above all sums up British response, 'JOHN BULL'S NEUTRALITY'.[6] This shows John Bull standing in his shop door, while two shamefaced urchins, the American North and South, furtively drop the stones they are carrying. Bull announces sternly, 'Look here boys, I don't care twopence for your noise, but if you throw stones at my window, I must *thrash you both*.' British culture invariably brought some pretty blunt ideological tools to bear on the construction of the American Civil War. In many ways it seems that the British popular psyche, when it responded to the Civil War, operated almost neurotically out of two main areas. The first, incredible though it seems, was a continuing inability to deal with the *fact* of American independence even though it had happened nearly a century before. There is a determined British refusal to get creatively involved in thinking about the remarkably complex socio-economic developments occurring across a vast land mass. Consequently America was boiled down to a set of lowest common denominators, a greedy North and a barbaric South, both presented in graphic terms most commonly as angry men, or spoilt children. The second area was a bitter-sweet self-righteousness over the issue of slavery which could only lead British writers to abstract the issue. From the perspective of mid-nineteenth-century London, American slavery was a vicious evil which placed Britain on the moral high ground. It was easy to empathize with the sentimental extremes of Stowe's *Uncle Tom's Cabin* or the humorous outrage of Lowell, yet throughout the 1850s and into the 1860s the slaves themselves tend to be abstracted, when they are not ignored, or even worse positively denigrated. A survey of *Punch* from 1850 to 1865 provides an unstinting exhibition of blacks in the slave Diaspora, and America in particular, as debased and risible. African Americans are represented purely according to the stereotypes not of so-called scientific racism, but of a brute racism which was rapidly gaining the ascendancy when English Negrophobes, from Carlyle to Dickens and Thackeray, represented blacks of any type on any issue. The groundwork for this brutally reductionist construction of the black slave and ex-slave had been formed in a variety of publishing areas within Britain for over fifty years. We now live with the effects of this horrific inheritance.[7]

Yet for the most part when British poets decided to treat the early phases of colonization and slavery they turned to narratives from the Spanish Black Legend.

---

[6]   *Punch*, 45 (1864), 136.

[7]   For the new brutalist racisms see Marcus Wood, *Slavery, Empathy, and Pornography* (Oxford University Press, 2002), 346–97.

So Tennyson focuses on Columbus and the obscure Haytian princess Anacoana (pp. 313–16). Within the British mythography of slavery a self-serving account of the 'heroes' of abolition had taken centre stage. Abolition emerges very much in the terms that G. M. Trevelyan essentializes in his immensely popular *British History in the Nineteenth Century*. He summarizes his minute discussion of slavery with a paragraph that in many ways encapsulates the Victorian cultural orthodoxy on Wilberforce and British abolition:

It is good to think that a movement of such immense and beneficent import to the whole world should have been begun and mainly carried through by the humanity and enlightenment of the British people as a whole, under the guidance of an entirely unselfish agitation . . . The systematic propaganda begun by Sharp and Wilberforce . . . became the model for the conduct of hundreds, even thousands of other movements—political, humanitarian, social, educational—which have been and still are the arteries and life-blood of modern Britain, where every man and woman with a little belief and a little public spirit is constantly joining Leagues, Unions or Committees . . . The life of William Wilberforce is therefore a fact of importance in the general history of the world.[8]

Here abolition is set out as the paradigm for the evolving middle class's ability to keep itself busy through the setting up of philanthropic societies. For the majority of British people this was how slavery was remembered for the next century.

Competitive slavery paradigms: white factory slave versus black plantation slave

When considering pro-slavery literatures in Britain and the Northern United States it should also be remembered that abolition publicity was produced against a background in which the first experiments with factory modes of production according to a capitalist model were the big sugar, tobacco, and rice plantations of the Americas. By 1865 Atlantic slavery was, on paper, no longer a part of the labour systems of Britain or North America, yet factory systems constituted the productive norm for white labour within industrial Europe and North America. The new labour masses of the white proletariat increasingly inflected how North Americans and English people thought about slavery and slaves. The 'white factory slavery/black plantation slavery' antithesis came out in pro-slavery literature in both Britain and America. The polemical origins for these writings lay in positions that had been developed by radical proto-socialists in the late eighteenth and early nineteenth centuries. The most influential figure in this con-

---

[8] G. M. Trevelyan, *British History in the Nineteenth Century* (Longman, 1922), 51–2.

text was William Cobbett. Yet among the Victorian social prophets Thomas Carlyle was Cobbett's biggest fan and primary stylistic disciple. He developed Cobbett's Negrophobe defence of white labour into a discourse. Then John Ruskin in Britain, and George Fitzhugh in the United States, took up Carlyle's legacy and provided the brilliant spearhead for a body of popular work which elaborated arguments concerning the extent of industrial enslavement of white labouring populations and the benevolent nature of plantation slavery. The effects of these developments have direct and indirect bearing on the contents of this book. The Chartist poems on 'white slavery' (pp. 322–8) grow directly out of the Carlyle/Cobbett inheritance, and Elizabeth Barrett Browning is engaged with it in the prologue to *Curse for a Nation* (pp. 365–6). Ebenezer Elliott (Carlyle was a huge fan), Thomas Hood, and Tennyson wrote brilliant poetry on the sufferings of the new industrialized labouring poor in Britain. These poets wrote nothing about the plight of the blacks or new immigrant workforces in the Caribbean, and nothing about American plantation slavery. This fact reflects both the literary fashions relating to labour exploitation, and the political pressures that produced them.

Chronology

A list of important literary, artistic, and historical events relating to colonial slavery and abolition in Britain, France, and America 1764–1865. A = America; GB = Great Britain; F = France.

1764 [GB and A] Sugar Act passed by British Parliament on American colonies, imposing heavy duty on molasses not imported from the British West Indies. This attempt to protect produce of the slave colonies causes massive resentment in America.
[GB] James Grainger, *The Sugar Cane: A Poem. In Four Books*

1765 [GB and A] Stamp Act imposed by Britain on American colonies, requiring that official documentation be printed on 'stamped' (very expensive) paper. Brings American rebellion closer.
[GB] Isaac Teale, *The Voyage of the Sable Venus*

1766 [GB and A] Stamp Act repealed by Britain.

1767–8 [GB and A] Further trade restrictions imposed on America, including restriction of right to trade with non-British West Indies.

1770 [F and GB] Abbé Raynal publishes *Histoire de deux Indes* (immediately translated into English as *Philosophical and Political History of the East and West Indies*; eighteen English editions printed in 1770s). Gives detailed accounts of the emotional sufferings of Africans in slavery and the middle passage. Furiously refutes the argument that there is any moral justification for slavery.
[A] Crispus Attucks, a free black, is murdered by British troops as one of the martyrs of the Boston Massacre.
[A] James Albert Gronniosaw, *A Narrative of the Most Remarkable Particulars in the Life of James Albert Ukawsaw Gronniosaw, an African Prince, as Related by Himself.*

1771 [A] Anthony Benezet publishes *Some Historical Account of Guinea*. The first comprehensive account of the economic and emotional devastation inflicted on Africa and Africans by the slave trade. The horrors of the middle passage described by an eminent white American for the first time.

1772 [GB] Court ruling on the case of James Somerset, popularly known as the 'Mansfield decision', generally interpreted as declaring illegality of slavery in Britain. Granville Sharp in London initiates correspondence with the

American Quaker Anthony Benezet, beginning organized Anglo-American abolition co-operation.

1773   [GB and A] Boston Tea Party: three shiploads of tea dumped in Boston harbour as demonstration against British tax on American tea.
[A] 6 January. The Massachusetts legislature is petitioned by slaves for their freedom.
[A] Phyllis Wheatley, *Poems on Various Subjects*. The first book of poetry written in America by a black ex-slave. Wheatley sails for England in May, and her poems are published in London in September.

1774   [GB] Edward Long, *The History of Jamaica; or, General Survey of the Antient and Modern State of that Island*.
John Wesley, *Thoughts on Slavery*. States 'Liberty is the right of every human creature, as soon as he breathes the vital air; no human law can deprive him of that right which he derives from the law of nature.'
[A] Massachusetts sets up Revolutionary Government, First Continental Congress, in Philadelphia where twelve colonies send delegates in support of Massachusetts. American War of Independence inevitable.

1775   [GB and A] Lord Dunmore the British Governor of Virginia offers to grant freedom to any slave who has run away from his master and agreed to fight for the British army. Later in the year the Dunmore Proclamation is intended to get indentured servants and freed blacks to enlist in the British army.
Freed slaves fight with the British against the colonies, at the Battle of Great Bridge, Virginia.
During the war approximately 5,000 slaves, mainly from the North, fight with the continental army.
The first abolition society is founded; the Pennsylvania Abolition Society aims to protect free blacks, and any blacks held unlawfully in bondage.
August. George III makes a proclamation stating that the colonies are in a state of rebellion and must be dealt with.

1776   [GB] David Hartley puts the first motion to outlaw slavery before the House of Commons: the motion is a massive failure.
[A] Second Continental Congress resolves that 'no slaves be imported into any of the Thirteen United Colonies'.
4 July. Continental Congress endorses the 'Declaration of Independence' which is adopted *without* the anti-slavery statement drawn up by Thomas Jefferson.

1777   [GB] William Roscoe, *Mount Pleasant*. The first poem to attack Liverpool for its involvement with the Guinea trade.
[A] Vermont abolishes slavery, the first American territory to do so.

1778   [GB] House of Commons appoints a committee to look into the British slave trade.

[A] Maryland Quakers outlaw slavery among members. An autonomous black regiment fights heroically against the British at the Battle of Portsmouth, Rhode Island.

1780 [A] Pennsylvania Gradual Abolition Act passed, the first emancipation Act in America. Pennsylvania also becomes the first state to sanction interracial marriage.

1781 [A] A group of pioneers predominantly of black African descent settles the Los Angeles area.

1782 [A and GB] Peace treaty signed between Britain and America; Britain loses American War of Independence.
[GB] Ignatius Sancho's *Letters* posthumously published. Sancho, a black ex-slave and friend of Lawrence Sterne, is embraced as a master of sentimental prose. His message is, in fact, rather more subversive.
[A] George Washington is recorded as the major slave holder in Fairfax County, Virginia, with 188 slaves.

1783 [GB] British Quakers form Committee for Sufferings committed to the production of abolition propaganda. Ten thousand copies of *The Case of our Fellow Creatures, the Oppressed Africans* printed.
Granville Sharp records the court hearing concerning the drowning at sea, for insurance purposes, of 133 slaves carried on the slave ship *Zong*. The case becomes a national scandal.
[A] Maryland forbids further importation of slaves.

1786 **[GB] Thomas Clarkson publishes *An Essay on the Slavery and Commerce of the Human Species*.**

1787 [GB] Society for Effecting the Abolition of the Slave Trade formed. Thomas Clarkson visits the great slave ports of Liverpool and Bristol to collect evidence.
[GB] Thomas Day, *The Dying Negro*.
Adam Smith, *An Essay on Complexion*.
Ottobah Cugoano, *Thoughts and Sentiments on the Evil and Wicked Traffic of the Slavery and Commerce of the Human Species, Humbly Submitted to the Inhabitants of Great Britain, by Ottobah Cugoano, a Native of Africa*.
[A] The Constitution is approved, and slavery is officially extended for twenty years. Freedman Richard Allen founds the Free African Society in Philadelphia.

1788 [F] Société des Amis des Noirs formed.
[GB] June. A bill to establish space allocations for the transportation of slaves on British ships is passed, known as Dolben's Bill.
[GB] John Newton, *Thoughts upon the African Slave Trade*.
William Roscoe, *The Wrongs of Africa*.
Hannah More, *The Black Slave Trade: A Poem*.

1789   [F] Thomas Clarkson visits Amis des Noirs in Paris, and distributes the plan
        of slave ship *Brookes* to sensational effect.
        [GB] Following mass petitioning Wilberforce first introduces twelve
        resolutions against the slave trade. House of Commons demands more
        evidence. John Newton testifies before the Commons Committee on Slavery.
        **[GB] Olaudah Equiano, *The Interesting Narrative of the Life of Olaudah
        Equiano, or Gustavas Vassa, the African. Written by Himself.* The book
        runs into several editions and is a literary event. The ex-slave narrative is
        established as a central form of abolition propaganda.**
        William Blake, *Songs of Innocence and of Experience.*
        **Robert Norris, *Memoirs of the Reign of Bossa Ahadee, King of Dahomey . . .
        To Which are Added the Author's Journey to Abomey, the Capital; and a
        Short Account of the African Slave Trade.***
        [A] Society for Abolishing the Slave Trade formed Providence, Rhode Island.

1790   [F] Vincent Ogé leads a mulatto rebellion in San Domingue. He is captured
        and publicly tortured to death.
        [GB] A select committee of the House of Commons undertakes extensive
        interviewing of witnesses involved in the slave trade.
        **[GB] John Gabriel Stedman, *Narrative of a Five Years Expedition against
        the Revolted Negroes of Surinam.***

1791   [F] National Assembly extends suffrage to all freeborn colonists with no
        restriction on colour. Mass slave uprising across the North Plain of
        San Domingue. Assembly renounces the suffrage extension.
        [GB] Wilberforce's motion to introduce slave bill rejected.
        **[GB] *Account by the Planter Deputies of San Domingo before the French
        National Assembly at the Beginning of November 1791.***
        Anna Laetitia Barbauld, *Epistle to Wilberforce.*
        [A] Benjamin Banneker publishes his *Almanac.*

1792   [F] Legislative Assembly declares equal rights for all free blacks and mulattos.
        [GB] House of Commons votes to end British slave trade in 1796, the motion
        blocked in the House of Lords. Anti-saccharitism (boycott on slave-produced
        sugar) becomes fashionable.
        **[GB] Samuel Taylor Coleridge wins Browne Medal at Cambridge University
        for his 'Ode on the Slave Trade'.**
        [A] Kentucky admitted to Union as first new slave state.

1793   [F] San Domingue is invaded by Britain and Spain, both of which are now at
        war with France. French commission in San Domingue: Santhonax proclaims
        all slaves free in the North Province; a general emancipation decree follows.
        [GB] Parliament rejects yet another motion by Wilberforce to introduce a slave
        trade abolition bill.
        **[GB] Bryan Edwards, *History, Civil and Commercial of the British Colonies
        in the West Indies.***

[A] Congress passes the first Fugitive Slave Law. Eli Whitney invents the cotton gin: this will revolutionize cotton production across the South and lead to mass expansion of slave labour.

1794   [F] Convention abolishes slavery in all French colonies, and makes citizenship a universal right of all Frenchmen of any colour.
[GB] Robert Southey, *Slave Trade Sonnets*.
[A] Congress makes it illegal for Americans to trade in slaves abroad.

1795   [GB] Wilberforce's abolition bill is defeated by a big margin.

1796   [GB] Wilberforce's abolition bill is defeated by four votes.

1797   [F] Black revolutionary leader Toussaint L'Ouverture joins with the mulatto leader Rigaud; they brilliantly resist all invasion attempts.
[GB] Twenty thousand British troops committed to San Domingue to fight rebel slaves, and take the 'Jewel of the Antilles' for England.

1798   [F] A power struggle between the black forces of San Domingue (led by Toussaint) and mulattos (represented by Rigaud and Hédouville).
[GB] British forces decimated by yellow fever are withdrawn from San Domingue.

1799   [A] New York adopts a gradual emancipation law.

1800   [F] Toussaint gains total control of San Domingue, Dessalines put in charge of South Province.
[A] Gabriel Prosser and Jack Bowler plan for a slave insurrection in Richmond, Virginia; they are discovered and executed along with several of their followers.
American citizens officially banned from all further slave exportation.

1801   [F] Toussaint gains control of Spanish Santo Domingo, and has control of whole island of Hayti. Napoleon sends big invasion force under Leclerc to attempt reinvasion of San Domingue.

1802   [F] Napoleon reinstates slavery in former French colonies. Toussaint's armies resist the French. Toussaint is captured through diplomatic treachery and shipped to a secret prison in the Alps.

1803   [F] Franco-British war isolates Napoleon's troops in San Domingue. Decimated by yellow fever, and the brilliant guerrilla tactics of the black revolutionaries, they withdraw, and surrender to the British.
[A] United States purchases Louisiana Territory from France. South Carolina reopens slave trade with Africa.

1804   [F] Hayti (formerly French San Domingue) is declared an independent country; Dessalines proclaimed Emperor Jacques I.
[GB] Bill for slave trade abolition passed by Commons, blocked in Lords.
[GB] Samuel Whitchurch, *Hispaniola*.

1805 [GB] Robert Bisset, *The History of the Negro Slave Trade, in its Connection with the Commerce and Prosperity of the West Indies and the Wealth and Power of the British Empire.*
Marcus Rainsford, *An Historical Account of the Black Empire of Hayti.*

1806 [GB] Thomas Moore, *Poems Relating to America.*
[A] The African Meeting House, the oldest black church building in America, is constructed by free blacks.

1807 [GB] Bill abolishing British slave trade is passed in Commons and Lords. African Institution formed to work towards international enforcement.
[GB] William Wordsworth composes sonnet 'To Toussaint L'Ouverture'.
[A] Congress bans American participation in the African slave trade from 1 January. Ban is widely ignored.

1808 [GB] Thomas Clarkson, *History of the Rise, Progress and Accomplishment of the Abolition of the African Slave-Trade by the British Parliament.*

1809 [GB] James Montgomery, *The West Indies: A Poem in Four Parts.*

1815 [A] Black troops fight with Andrew Jackson at the Battle of New Orleans.

1816 [A] American Colonization Society formed to initiate 'repatriation' of American free blacks to Africa.
[A] George Bourne, *The Book and Slavery Irreconcilable.*

1819 **[A] Robert Walsh, *An Appeal from the Judgements of Great Britain.***

1820 [A] Congress passes 'Missouri Compromise' whereby Missouri will be admitted to the Union under the conditions that although slavery will be legal in the state, it will be illegal in the unsettled Louisiana territory north of latitude 36° 30'.

1821 [A] Benjamin Lundy, first issue of the *Genius of Universal Emancipation.*

1822 [A] The slave and free black uprising purportedly planned by Denmark Vesey in Charleston, South Carolina, leads to hideous reprisals and persecution of the black community. Liberia is officially founded by African-American colonizers.

1823 [GB] Zacharay Macaulay, *East and West India Sugar.*
William Wilberforce, *An Appeal in Behalf of the Negro Slaves in the West Indies.*

1824 [GB] James Stephen, *The Slavery of the British West India Colonies Delineated*, vol. i.

1829 [A] William Lloyd Garrison and Benjamin Lundy unite and begin publishing *Genius of Universal Emancipation* in Baltimore.
David Walker, *David Walker's Appeal.*
George Moses Horton, *The Hope of Liberty.*

1831   [GB] Mary Prince, *The History of Mary Prince, a West Indian Slave, Related by Herself.*
Simon Strickland, *Negro Slavery Described by a Negro.*
[A] Nat Turner's Rebellion. Turner leads a band of blacks in a violent revolt, in which they execute every white who falls in their way, a total of sixty men, women, and children. The revolt is suppressed and Turner executed. The whites take terrible reprisals on the blacks of Virginia. Repressive legislation against blacks follows the rebellion in the majority of Southern states.
[A] Nat Turner dictates *The Confessions of Nat Turner.*
1 January. William Lloyd Garrison publishes the first issue of the *Liberator.* Overnight Garrison abandons gradualist approaches to emancipation and demands immediate and total abolition of slavery across America.

1832   [GB] Harriet Martineau, *Demerara.*
[A] New England Anti-Slavery Society adopts and publishes its constitution.
[A] William Lloyd Garrison, *Thoughts on African Colonisation.*

1833   [A] James Greenleaf Whittier publishes radical abolition pamphlet *Justice and Expediency.*
Lydia Maria Child, *An Appeal in Favour of That Class of Americans Called Africans.*

1834   [GB] Emancipation Act liberating all slaves in British sugar colonies. Ex-slaves to serve four- to six-year apprenticeship, under conditions which amount to continued slavery. Children under 6 freed immediately. Slave owners are paid a total of £20,000,000 in compensation.

1835   [A] Pro-slavery 'Snow Riot' sweeps Washington for two days sparked by discovery of Reuben Crendall's possession of abolition literature, and a free black, Beverly Snow's, verbal attacks on the rioters.

1837   [A] Murder of abolitionist Elijah P. Lovejoy by mob in Illinois.
[A] John Greenleaf Whittier, *Poems Written During the Progress of the Abolition Question.*

1838   [A] 'Underground railroad' steps up transportation of escaped slaves to freedom in Canada. Pennsylvania Hall in Philadelphia burned in May by an anti-abolition mob.
3 September. Frederick Douglass escapes from slavery.
[A] Horace Kimball and James Thome, *Emancipation in the West Indies.*
Angelina Grimké, *Letters to Catherine E. Beecher in Reply to an Essay on Slavery and Abolitionism.*

1839   [A] Slaves rebel aboard the Spanish slaver *Amistad*, seize the boat, and are taken by coastguard to New York. In ensuing legal battles over their status they become international celebrities.
[A] Theodore Dwight Weld and Angelina Grimké publish their monumental collection of slavery advertisements and personal testimony, *American Slavery As It Is: Testimony of a Thousand Witnesses.*

1840   [GB] World's Anti-Slavery Convention in London; Garrison refuses to attend
in protest at exclusion of women.
[A] Josiah Henson, escaped slave and model for Stowe's 'Uncle Tom', sets up
British-American Institute, Dresden, Ontario.

1841   [GB] Harriet Martineau, *The Hour and the Man*.
[A] A court in Washington, DC, finally rules on the *Amistad* case. Cinque and
his fellow revolutionaries are released. Thirty-two ex-slaves are returned to
their homeland Sierra Leone. Many had already died at sea or waiting for their
trial. Slave rebellion on board the *Creole* sailing from Hampton, Virginia, to
New Orleans. The revolutionaries successfully sail the boat to freedom and
asylum in the Bahamas.

1842   [GB] J. M. W. Turner, *Slavers Throwing Overboard the Dead and Dying:
Typhoon Coming On*, and Auguste-François Biard, *Scene on the African
Coast*, both exhibited at the Royal Academy in London. Aesthetically these
works articulate the polarization between the official memory of the British
slave trade (Biard) and its genuine and uncontrollable horror (Turner).

1843   [A] John Pierpont, *The Anti-Slavery Poems of John Pierpont*.

1845   [A] Annexation of Texas by United States.
[A] Frederick Douglass, *Narrative of the Life of Frederick Douglass, an
American Slave*.
William Wells Brown, *The Travels of William Wells Brown*.

1846   [A] May. America acknowledges that it is at war with Mexico following
annexation of Texas. President Polk states deployment of military forces is
necessary to prevent Mexican invasion.

1847   [A] Steam-powered cotton mills first operate in United States. First Dred
Scott trial begins defining legal status of fugitive slaves in the free North.
Free-soil party formed to prevent expansion of slavery into the territories
newly gained from Mexico.
[A] Frederick Douglass publishes the *North Star*.

1848   [A] March. Mexican War ends.
[GB and A] Elizabeth Barrett Browning, *The Runaway Slave at Pilgrim's
Point*, written for the American abolition anthology *The Liberty Bell*.
[F] France abolishes slavery in all of its colonies.

1849   [GB] Thomas Carlyle, *Occasional Discourse on the Negro Question*
(republished 1853 as 'the Nigger Question').
[A] Harriet Tubman escapes slavery in Maryland and becomes a moving force
in the underground railroad. Tubman subsequently makes nineteen trips to
the South to free over 300 slaves including her own parents in 1857.
[A] Henry 'Box' Brown, *Narrative of Henry Box Brown, Who Escaped
from Slavery in a Box Three Feet Long, Two Wide, and Two and a
Half High*.

1850 [A] Compromise of 1850 attempts a legislative cocktail to finally placate North and South over slavery. This involves passage of the new Fugitive Slave Law. This supersedes the law of 1793: it allows slave holders to enter the Northern states and the free territories and to retrieve slaves. The law also demands the participation of the North in helping Southerners recapture escaped slaves.
[A] Sojourner Truth, *Narrative of Sojourner Truth, a Northern Slave.*

1851 [A] Constant agitation in North and South over status of fugitive slaves in North. Myrtilla Miner opens a 'Normal School for Coloured Girls' in DC. Despite intimidation and attack the school flourishes. By 1858 six former pupils have opened their own schools for blacks.
Sojourner Truth performs *Aren't I a Woman* at Women's Conference in Akron, Ohio.

1852 [A and GB] Harriet Beecher Stowe, *Uncle Tom's Cabin.* The book becomes an instantaneous and massive hit all over the Northern free states and Europe. Its success in Britain is even greater than America, and it is adapted into a variety of art forms.

1853 [A] Wendell Phillips makes speech, 'Philosophy of the Abolition Movement'.
William Wells Brown, *Clotel; or, The President's Daughter: A Narrative of Slave Life in the United States.*
[A and GB] Harriet Beecher Stowe, *Key to Uncle Tom's Cabin*; Stowe also publishes *Dred: A Tale of the Great Dismal Swamp*, the remarkable follow-up to *Uncle Tom's Cabin.*

1854 [A] Kansas Nebraska Act passed, fudging issue of whether slavery will exist in new states and leading to guerrilla skirmishes over slavery question in the new territories.
[A] George Boyer Vashon, *Vincent Ogé.*
Ellen Watkins Harper, *Poems on Miscellaneous Subjects.*

1855 [A] Frederick Douglass, *My Bondage my Freedom.*
Walt Whitman, *Leaves of Grass.*

1856 [A] Kansas 'free-soil war'. John Brown 'executes' five colonists who he claims are slave holders. Charles Sumner caned by irate Southerner in Congress.
[A] George Fitzhugh, *Cannibals All! or, Slaves without Masters.*

1857 [A] Dred Scott decision, widely held to give slave states legal rights over escaped slaves in North.

1858 [A] The celebrated campaign debates between Abraham Lincoln and Senator Stephen Douglas. Slavery is the central bone of contention.
[A] Charles Ball, *Fifty Years in Chains; or, The Life of an American Slave.*
Sally Williams, *Aunt Sally; or, The Cross the Way to Freedom. Narrative of and Battle of New Orleans.*

1859   [GB] Frederick Douglass makes second tour of Britain.
        [A] Last publicly acknowledged slave ship is scuttled in Mobile, Alabama.
        October. John Brown and twenty-one followers take the United States
        armoury at Harper's Ferry and hope to spark a slave insurrection across the
        South. The event is a military debacle, but a publicity triumph. Brown and the
        abolitionists brilliantly choreograph his death, which becomes a central
        martyrological icon during the Civil War.
        [A] Harriet Wilson, *Our Nig; or, Sketches from the Life of a Free Black.*

1860   [A] South Carolina first state to secede from Union.
        [A] Jane Brown, *A Narrative of the Life of Jane Brown and her Two
        Children.*

1861   [A] Secession of the Southern states and formation of the Confederacy. The
        Civil War begins.
        [A] J. W. C. Pennington, *A Narrative of Events of the Life of J. H. Banks, an
        Escaped Slave.*

1862   [A] April. Congress abolishes slavery in the District of Columbia.

1863   [A] 1 January. Emancipation Proclamation takes effect.
        Frederick Douglass meets with Lincoln to discuss treatment of black soldiers
        in Civil War.

1864   [A] Frederick Douglass meets with Lincoln to plan exodus of blacks from
        South in event of a Union defeat.
        Maryland slaves emancipated.

1865   [GB and Jamaica] The Governor Eyre affair in Jamaica. 11 October. A black
        mob burns the courthouse in Morant Bay, Jamaica, and commit several
        murders. Governor Eyre declares marshal law and 439 blacks are murdered,
        600 flogged, 1,000 black homes destroyed. Thomas Carlyle, then John
        Ruskin, head the Eyre Defence and Aid Committee in London, celebrating
        Eyre as a national hero. The event splits the British intellectual elite down the
        middle. Eyre is subsequently vindicated by the British government.
        [A] 9 April. Confederates surrender; Robert E. Lee surrenders with his troops
        to Grant at Appotomax.
        Good Friday, 14 April. President Lincoln is assassinated.
        6 December. Congress finally ratifies Amendment XIII. 'Neither slavery nor
        involuntary servitude, except as a punishment for crime whereof the party
        shall have been duly convicted, shall exist within the United States, or any
        place subject to their jurisdiction.'
        The 'Black Codes' are issued in former Confederate states taking civil rights
        from freed blacks. Ku Klux Klan founded in Tennessee.

PART I

British Poems

Contents of Part I

James Grainger (1721?-1766), *The Sugar Cane: A Poem. In Four Books*, Book IV (1764)

Grainger was born in Berwickshire and was trained as a physician in Edinburgh. He was active as an English army surgeon in the Scottish rebellion of 1745 and also in the wars against the Dutch over the next three years. He returned to his medical studies after leaving the army and gained his MD in 1753. Yet Grainger had always maintained a taste for literature and when he moved to London in the early 1750s he came to know most of the leading lights of Johnsonian literary London. Bishop Percy and Oliver Goldsmith became particular friends. Once close to Tobias Smollett, he had a massive falling out, following Smollett's savaging of Grainger's woeful efforts at classical translation.

In 1759 with his literary career in London going nowhere, and having become something of a figure of fun, the destitute Grainger agreed to accompany a young planter heir, Pierre Brumoy, to the island of St Christopher in the British Caribbean. It was during the next four years, while working on the island as a physician tending slaves on various estates, that Grainger wrote the long, and extensively annotated, *The Sugar Cane*. The poem was sent to London, and supported by no less a figure than Samuel Johnson. Johnson wrote supportive notices in the *London Chronicle* and in the *Critical Review*. Johnson was, however, an inveterate enemy both of the slave trade and of plantation slavery, and criticized the poem for not positively attacking plantation slavery. Grainger is in fact a firm supporter of the benevolist position and argues throughout that a well-run plantation constitutes a social ideal for slave and slave owner. In this sense *The Sugar Cane* is strangely utopian. Grainger published a second edition of the poem in 1764, with even longer notes, and worked the notes up into a separate publication which was basically a medical field guide to keeping slaves healthy, *Essay on the More Common West India Diseases; and the Remedies which That Country Itself Produces. To which are added some Hints on the Management &c. of Negroes*. It is worth noting that both the essay and the poem were reprinted in 1802 in Jamaica alongside one Colonel Martin's *Essay on Plantership* under the blanket title *Three Tracts on West Indian Agriculture*. It would appear that in Jamaica the poem functioned as a blank verse guide to running a plantation, rather than as the epic of the Caribbean sugar industry Grainger had hoped to write. Yet Grainger never saw his Jamaican publication; by the end of 1766 he was dead of the West Indian fever.

The Sugar Cane was, until recently, neglected; when it was noticed it was as a benchmark for late Augustan poetic absurdity, and it has often been cited as the worst long poem in English. Even the well-disposed Dr Johnson is reputed to have snapped at one point. Grainger was reciting the poem to him, and got to a long section concerning vermin infestation of the sugar fields. At the line 'Shall I sing of rats' Johnson shouted out 'No!' Yet the recent rise in interest in the literature of Empire has seen a reassessment of Grainger, and even the production of a new scholarly edition of his masterpiece. In aesthetic terms conventionalists might find a grotesque mismatch in form and content, as Grainger discusses in sub-Miltonic pentameters various problems of plantation

2. Anon., 'Sugar Cane' (copper-plate engraving, 1764), frontispiece to
James Grainger, *The Sugar Cane.*

management including not only the notorious rats but worm infestation. It is, however, precisely the oblivious literary luxuriance with which Grainger festoons his practical and brutal assessment of slave life which now makes the poem such a compelling part of the British slave archive.

Grainger, a shabby and poor travelling physician, who was trying to eke out extra cash by doing a sideline in slave trading as he travelled the plantations, aspired to become a planter. *The Sugar Cane* is consequently a strange fantasy which attempts to set out the planter's calling in epic terms, and to aggrandize the role of medicine within the plantation society. Grainger's poem is also valuable as a sort of catch-all for consequent pro-slavery arguments. The arguments on the relative well-being of the Caribbean slave populations when compared with the lot of the European labouring classes were to prove particularly fertile ground for future slavery apologists. His arguments were repeated not only by the plantocracy, but subsequently by English radicals from Cobbett to the Chartists.

The Sugar Cane

ARGUMENT

Invocation to the Genius of Africa.[1] Address. Negroes when bought should be young, and strong. The Congo-negroes[2] are fitter for the house and trades, than for the field. The Gold-Coast,[3] but especially the Papaw-negroes, make the best field-negroes: but even these, if advanced in years, should not be purchased. The marks of a sound negroe at a negroe sale. Where the men do nothing but hunt, fish or fight, and all field drudgery is left to the women; these are to be preferred to their husbands. The Minnahs[4] make good tradesmen, but addicted to suicide. The Mandingos,[5] in particular, subject to worms; and the Congas, to dropsical disorders. How salt-water, or new negroes should be seasoned. Some negroes eat dirt. Negroes should be habituated by gentle degrees to field labour. This labour, when compared to that in lead-mines, or of those who work in the gold and silver mines of South America, is not only less toilsome, but far more healthy. Negroes should always be treated with humanity. Praise of freedom. Of the dracunculus, or dragon-worm. Of chigres.[6] Of the yaws. Might not this disease be imparted by inoculation? Of worms, and their multiform appearance. Praise of commerce. Of the imaginary disorders of negroes, especially those caused by their conjurers or Obia-men.[7] The composition and supposed virtues of a magic-phiol. Field-negroes should not begin to work before six in the morning, and should leave off between eleven and

---

[1] Genius here is being used strictly in the Latin sense of *genius loci*, the spirit of the place.

[2] Slaves taken from that part of Africa near the Congo river, approximately modern Zaire.

[3] That part of coastal Africa around the gulf of Guinea, approximately the modern Ghanaian coast.

[4] Slaves taken from Minnah, in central Nigeria.

[5] Slaves taken from Mande, a West African province. Mandingos were notorious among slave captains for their rebelliousness; the majority were devout Muslims.

[6] Chigres, also known as chigoes or chiggers, a West Indian and South American form of flea: the larvae burrow into the skin, particularly beneath the toenails, causing excruciating pain.

[7] Obeah is a general term covering the entire range of slave-evolved polytheistic religions which grew out of the fusion of African forms of belief and Christianity. In this sense Obeah relates closely to Santeria in Cuba, Umbanda, Macumba, and Condomblé in Brazil, and to Voodoo in Hayti.

twelve; and beginning again at two, should finish before sun-set. Of the weekly allowance of negroes. The young, the old, the sickly, and even the lazy, must have their victuals prepared for them. Of negroe-ground, and its various productions. To be fenced in, and watched. Of an American garden. Of the situation of the negroe-huts. How best defended from fire. The great negroe-dance described. Drumming, and intoxicating spirits not to be allowed. Negroes should be made to marry in their masters plantation. Inconveniences arising from the contrary practice. Negroes to be cloathed once a year, and before Christmas. Praise of Lewis XIV for the Code Noir.[8] A body of laws of this kind recommended to the English sugar colonies. Praise of the river Thames. A moon-light landscape and vision.

BOOK IV

Genius of Africk! whether thou bestrid'st
The castled elephant; or at the source,
(While howls the desart fearfully around,)
Of thine own Niger, sadly thou reclin'st
Thy temples shaded by the tremulous palm,
Or quick papaw, whose top is necklac'd round
With numerous rows of party-colour'd fruit:
Or hear'st thou rather from the rocky banks
Of Rio Grandê,[9] or black Sanaga?[10]
Where dauntless thou the headlong torrent brav'st
In search of gold, to brede thy wooly locks,
Or with bright ringlets ornament thine ears,
Thine arms, and ankles: O attend my song.
A muse that pities thy distressful state;
Who sees, with grief, thy sons in fetters bound;
Who wishes freedom to the race of man;
Thy nod assenting craves: dread Genius, come!

Yet vain thy presence, vain thy favouring nod;
Unless once more the muses, that erewhile
Upheld me fainting in my past career,
Through Caribbe's cane-isles; kind condescend
To guide my footsteps, through parch'd Libya's wilds;
And bind my sun-burnt brow with other bays,
Than ever deck'd the Sylvan bard before.

[8] The Code Noir was instigated in 1685 by Louis XIV, and attempted to introduce some legal limits to the abuses carried out on slaves in the French colonies.

[9] Now the Corubal river in Guinea-Bissau, West Africa.

[10] A West African river in present-day Cameroon.

Say, will my Melvil,[11] from the public care,
Withdraw one moment, to the muses shrine?
Who smit with thy fair fame, industrious cull
An Indian wreath to mingle with thy bays,
And deck the hero, and the scholar's brow!
Wilt thou, whose mildness smooths the face of war,
Who round the victor-blade the myrtle twin'st,
And mak'st subjection loyal and sincere;
O wilt thou gracious hear the unartful strain,
Whose mild instructions teach, no trivial theme,
What care the jetty African requires?
Yes, thou wilt deign to hear; a man thou art
Who deem'st nought foreign that belongs to man.

In mind, and aptitude for useful toil,
The negroes differ: muse that difference sing.

Whether to wield the hoe, or guide the plane;
Or for domestic uses thou intend'st
The sunny Libyan: from what clime they spring,
It not imports; if strength and youth be theirs.

Yet those from Congo's wide-extended plains,
Through which the long Zaire winds with chrystal stream,
Where lavish Nature sends indulgent forth
Fruits of high flavour, and spontaneous seeds
Of bland nutritious quality, ill bear
The toilsome field; but boast a docile mind,
And happiness of features. These, with care,
Be taught each nice mechanic art: or train'd
To houshold offices: their ductile souls
Will all thy care, and all thy gold repay.

But, if the labours of the field demand
Thy chief attention; and the ambrosial cane
Thou long'st to see, with spiry frequence, shade
Many an acre: planter, chuse the slave,
Who sails from barren climes; where art alone,
Offspring of rude necessity, compells
The sturdy native, or to plant the soil,
Or stem vast rivers for his daily food.

---

[11] Count de Melvil is one of the benevolent characters in Smollet's *Adventures of Ferdinand Count Fathom.*

Such are the children of the Golden Coast;
Such the Papaws, of negroes far the best:
And such the numerous tribes, that skirt the shore,
From rapid Volta to the distant Rey.[12]

But, planter, from what coast soe'er they sail,
Buy not the old: they ever sullen prove;
With heart-felt anguish, they lament their home;
They will not, cannot work; they never learn
Thy native language; they are prone to ails;
And oft by suicide their being end.—

Must thou from Africk reinforce thy gang?—
Let health and youth their every sinew firm;
Clear roll their ample eye; their tongue be red;
Broad swell their chest; their shoulders wide expand;
Not prominent their belly; clean and strong
Their thighs and legs, in just proportion rise.
Such soon will brave the fervours of the clime;
And free from ails, that kill thy negroe-train,
A useful servitude will long support.

Yet, if thine own, thy children's life, be dear;
Buy not a Cormantee,[13] tho' healthy, young.
Of breed too generous for the servile field;
They, born to freedom in their native land,
Chuse death before dishonourable bonds:
Or, fir'd with vengeance, at the midnight hour,
Sudden they seize thine unsuspecting watch,
And thine own poinard bury in thy breast.

At home, the men, in many a sylvan realm,
Their rank tobacco, charm of sauntering minds,
From clayey tubes inhale; or, vacant, beat
For prey the forest; or, in war's dread ranks,
Their country's foes affront: while, in the field,
Their wives plant rice, or yams, or lofty maize,
Fell hunger to repel. Be these thy choice:
They, hardy, with the labours of the Cane
Soon grow familiar; while unusual toil,
And new severities their husbands kill.

---

[12] A river in what is now Ghana, West Africa.
[13] Slaves who came from Cormantyne, a Dutch-dominated slaving region in what is now Ghana.

The slaves from Minnah are of stubborn breed:
But, when the bill, or hammer, they affect;
They soon perfection reach. But fly, with care,
The Moco-nation;[14] they themselves destroy.

Worms lurk in all: yet, pronest they to worms,
Who from Mundingo[15] sail. When therefore such
Thou buy'st, for sturdy and laborious they,
Straight let some learned leach[16] strong medicines give,
Till food and climate both familiar grow.
Thus, tho' from rise to set, in Phoebus' eye,[17]
They toil, unceasing; yet, at night, they'll sleep,
Lap'd in Elysium; and, each day, at dawn,
Spring from their couch, as blythsome as the sun.

One precept more, it much imports to know.—
The Blacks, who drink the Quanza's[18] lucid stream,
Fed by ten thousand springs, are prone to bloat,
Whether at home or in these ocean-isles:
And tho' nice art the water may subdue,
Yet many die; and few, for many a year,
Just strength attain to labour for their lord.

Would'st thou secure thine Ethiop from those ails,
Which change of climate, change of waters breed,
And food unusual? let Machaon[19] draw
From each some blood, as age and sex require;
And well with vervain,[20] well with sempre-vive,[21]
Unload their bowels.—These, in every hedge,
Spontaneous grow.—Nor will it not conduce
To give what chemists, in mysterious phrase,
Term the white eagle; deadly foe to worms.
But chief do thou, my friend, with hearty food,
Yet easy of digestion, likest that
Which they at home regal'd on; renovate
Their sea-worn appetites. Let gentle work,
Or rather playful exercise, amuse
The novel gang: and far be angry words;

[14] Slaves who had originated from the Arab, Red Sea, port of Mocha.   [15] See n. 5.
[16] A medical doctor. Doctors commonly applied leeches in order to let blood.
[17] Phoebus Apollo, the sun god.   [18] The Kwanza river in present-day Angola.
[19] Physician to the Greek army during the Trojan War.
[20] A wild form of *Verbena* supposed to have both magic and medicinal powers.
[21] The house leek, a European succulent plant.

Far ponderous chains; and far disheartning blows.—
From fruits restrain their eagerness; yet if
The acajou, haply, in thy garden bloom,
With cherries,[22] or of white or purple hue,
Thrice wholesome fruit in this relaxing clime!
Safely thou may'st their appetite indulge.
Their arid skins will plump, their features shine:
No rheums,[23] no dysenteric ails torment:
The thirsty hydrops[24] flies.—'Tis even averr'd,
(Ah, did experience sanctify the fact;
How many Lybians now would dig the soil,
Who pine in hourly agonies away!)
This pleasing fruit, if turtle join its aid,
Removes that worst of ails, disgrace of art,
The loathsome leprosy's infectious bane.

There are, the muse hath oft abhorrent seen,
Who swallow dirt;[25] (so the chlorotic fair
Oft chalk prefer to the most poignant cates:[26])
Such, dropsy bloats, and to sure death consigns;
Unless restrain'd from this unwholesome food,
By soothing words, by menaces, by blows:
Nor yet will threats, or blows, or soothing words,
Perfect their cure; unless thou, Paean,[27] deign'st
By medicine's power their cravings to subdue.

To easy labour first inure thy slaves;
Extremes are dangerous. With industrous search,
Let them fit grassy provender collect
For thy keen stomach'd herds.—But when the earth
Hath made her annual progress round the sun,
What time the conch[28] or bell resounds, they may
All to the Cane-ground, with thy gang, repair.

---

[22] 'The tree which produces this wholesome fruit is tall shady and of quick growth. Its Indian name is *Acajou*.' [Grainger]

[23] Either rheumatic pains, or mucous discharges.

[24] Now called oedema: a disease involving fluid build-up in the body.

[25] Slaves were known to eat dirt as a form of suicide; consequently a steel mask with perforated mouth-piece was placed on the offenders, known as a 'dirt-eating mask'. See p. 289 n. 9.

[26] Luxurious food.

[27] In Homer the physician of the gods; the word was subsequently applied to Apollo.

[28] The conch shell, used as a musical instrument in Africa, was subsequently used to call slaves to work on many Caribbean plantations.

Nor, Negroe, at thy destiny repine,
Tho' doom'd to toil from dawn to setting sun.
How far more pleasant is thy rural task,
Than theirs who sweat, sequester'd from the day,
In dark tartarean caves, sunk far beneath
The earth's dark surface; where sulphureous flames,
Oft from their vapoury prisons bursting wild,
To dire explosion give the cavern'd deep,
And in dread ruin all its inmates whelm?—
Nor fateful only is the bursting flame;
The exhalations of the deep-dug mine,
Tho' slow, shake from their wings as sure a death.
With what intense severity of pain
Hath the afflicted muse, in Seotia seen
The miners rack'd, who toil for fatal lead?
What cramps, what palsies shake their feeble limbs,
Who, on the margin of the rocky Drave,[29]
Trace silver's fluent ore? Yet white men these!

How far more happy ye, than those poor slaves,
Who, whilom, under native, gracious chiefs,
Incas and emperors, long time enjoy'd
Mild government, with every sweet of life,
In blissful climates? See them dragg'd in chains,
By proud insulting tyrants, to the mines
Which once they call'd their own, and then despis'd!
See, in the mineral bosom of their land,
How hard they toil! how soon their youthful limbs
Feel the decrepitude of age! how soon
Their teeth desert their sockets! and how soon
Shaking paralysis unstrings their frame!
Yet scarce, even then, are they allow'd to view
The glorious God of day, of whom they beg,
With earnest hourly supplications, death;
Yet death slow comes, to torture them the more!

With these compar'd, ye sons of Afric, say,
How far more happy is your lot? Bland health,
Of ardent eye, and limb robust, attends
Your custom'd labour; and, should sickness seize,

---

[29] 'A river in Hungary, on whose banks are found mines of quicksilver.' [Grainger]

With what solicitude are ye not nurs'd!—
Ye Negroes, then, your pleasing task pursue;
And, by your toil, deserve your master's care.

   When first your Blacks are novel to the hoe;
Study their humours: Some, soft-soothing words;
Some, presents; and some, menaces subdue;
And some I've known, so stubborn is their kind,
Whom blows, alas! could win alone to toil.

   Yet, planter, let humanity prevail.—
Perhaps thy Negroe, in his native land,
Possest large fertile plains, and slaves, and herds:
Perhaps, whene'er he deign'd to walk abroad,
The richest silks, from where the Indus rolls,
His limbs invested in their gorgeous pleats:
Perhaps he wails his wife, his children, left
To struggle with adversity: Perhaps
Fortune, in battle for his country fought,
Gave him a captive to his deadliest foe:
Perhaps, incautious, in his native fields,
(On pleasurable scenes his mind intent)
All as he wandered; from the neighbouring grove,
Fell ambush dragg'd him to the hated main.—
Were they even sold for crimes; ye polish'd, say!
Ye, to whom Learning opes her amplest page!
Ye, whom the knowledge of a living God
Should lead to virtue! Are ye free from crimes?
Ah pity, then, these uninstructed swains;
And still let mercy soften the decrees
Of rigid justice, with her lenient hand.

   Oh, did the tender muse possess the power,
Which monarchs have, and monarchs oft abuse:
'T would be the fond ambition of her soul,
To quell tyrannic sway; knock off the chains
Of heart-debasing slavery; give to man,
Of every colour and of every clime,
Freedom, which stamps him image of his God.
Then laws, Oppression's scourge, fair Virtue's prop,
Offspring of Wisdom! should impartial reign,
To knit the whole in well-accorded strife:

Servants, not slaves; of choice, and not compell'd;
The Blacks should cultivate the Cane-land isles.

Say, shall the muse the various ills recount,
Which Negroe-nations feel? Shall she describe
The worm that subtly winds into their flesh,
All as they bathe them in their native streams?
There, with fell increment, it soon attains
A direful length of harm. Yet, if due skill,
And proper circumspection are employed,
It may be won its volumes to wind round
A leaden cylinder: But, O, beware,
No rashness practise; else 'twill surely snap,
And suddenly, retreating, dire produce
An annual lameness to the tortured Moor.

Nor only is the dragon worm to dread:
Fell, winged insects, which the visual ray
Scarcely discerns, their sable feet and hands
Oft penetrate; and, in the fleshy nest,
Myriads of young produce; which soon destroy
The parts they breed in; if assiduous care,
With art, extract not the prolific foe.

Or, shall she sing, and not debase her lay,
The pest peculiar to the Aethiop-kind,
The yaw's[30] infestious bane?—The infected far
In huts, to leeward, lodge; or near the main.
With heartning food, with turtle, and with conchs;
The flowers of sulphur, and hard niccars[31] burnt,
The lurking evil from the blood expel,
And throw it on the surface: There in spots
Which cause no pain, and scanty ichor[32] yield,
It chiefly breaks about the arms and hips,
A virulent contagion!—When no more
Round knobby spots deform, but the disease
Seems at a pause: then let the learned leach
Give, in due dose, live-silver[33] from the mine;

---

[30] The yaws is an infectious skin disease of the tropics, also known as framboesia and button scurvy.
[31] 'The botanical name of this shrub is Guilandina.' [Grainger]
[32] Here 'ichor' is being used medically to mean the watery fluid discharged from an ulcer. There is also the ironic weight of the more common meaning, ichor being the blood of the Greek deities.
[33] 'Live-silver', or 'quick-silver', were words for the metallic element mercury.

Till copious spitting the whole taint exhaust.—
Nor thou repine, tho' half-way round the sun,
This globe, her annual progress shall absolve;
Ere, clear'd, thy slave from all infection shine.
Nor then be confident; successive crops
Of defoedations[34] oft will spot the skin:
These thou, with turpentine and guaiac[35] pods,
Reduc'd by coction to a wholesome draught,
Total remove, and give the blood its balm.

　　Say, as this malady but once infests
The sons of Guinea, might not skill ingraft
(Thus, the small-pox are happily convey'd;)
This ailment early to thy Negroe-train?

　　Yet, of the ills which torture Libya's sons,
Worms tyrannize the worst. They, Proteus-like,[36]
Each symptom of each malady assume;
And, under every mask, the assassins kill.
Now, in the guise of horrid spasms, they writhe
The tortured body, and all sense o'er-power.
Sometimes, like Mania,[37] with her head downcast,
They cause the wretch in solitude to pine;
Or frantic, bursting from the strongest chains,
To frown with look terrific, not his own.
Sometimes like Ague,[38] with a shivering mien,
The teeth gnash fearful, and the blood runs chill:
Anon the ferment maddens in the veins,
And a false vigour animates the frame.
Again, the dropsy's bloated mask they steal;
Or, "melt with minings of the hectic fire."

　　Say, to such various mimic forms of death;
What remedies shall puzzled art oppose?—
Thanks to the Almighty, in each path-way hedge,
Rank cow-itch[39] grows, whose sharp unnumber'd stings,

---

[34] Exudations, pollutions.

[35] *Guaiacum*, a family of tropical bean caper trees; their green resin has medicinal properties.

[36] An ancient Greek sea god, who could assume different forms, which he did in order to avoid having to foretell the future.

[37] 'Mania' here is the personification of madness, or insanity.

[38] 'Ague' is an acute form of fever, and personified it assumes a dramatic character.

[39] 'This extraordinary vine should not be allowed to grow in a Cane-piece; for Negroes have been

Sheath'd in Melasses,[40] from their dens expell,
Fell dens of death, the reptile lurking foe.—
A powerful vermifuge,[41] in skilful hands,
The worm-grass proves; yet, even in hands of skill,
Sudden, I've known it dim the visual ray
For a whole day and night. There are who use
(And sage Experience justifies the use)
The mineral product of the Cornish mine;
Which in old times, ere Britain laws enjoyed,
The polish'd Tyrians,[42] monarchs of the main,
In their swift ships convey'd to foreign realms:
The sun by day, by night the northern star,
Their course conducted.—Mighty commerce, hail!
By thee the sons of Attic's sterile land,
A scanty number, laws impos'd on Greece:
Nor aw'd they Greece alone; vast Asia's King,
Tho' girt by rich arm'd myriads, at their frown
Felt his heart wither on his farthest throne.
Perennial source of population thou!
While scanty peasants plough the flowery plains
Of purple Enna;[43] from the Belgian fens,
What swarms of useful citizens spring up,
Hatch'd by thy fostering wing. Ah where is flown
That dauntless free-born spirit, which of old,
Taught them to shake off the tyrannic yoke
Of Spains insulting King;[44] on whose wide realms,
The sun still shone with undiminished beam?
Parent of wealth! in vain, coy nature hoards
Her gold and diamonds; toil, thy firm compeer,
And industry of unremitting nerve,
Scale the cleft mountain, the loud torrent brave,
Plunge to the center, and thro' Nature's wiles,
(Led on by skill of penetrative soul)
Her following close, her secret treasures find,

known to fire the Canes, to save themselves from the torture which attends working the grounds where it has abounded.' [Grainger]

[40] *Mélasse* is the French form of 'molasses', the black treacle extracted during the process of refining sugar.
[41] A drug that expels worms, from *vermes*, the Latin for worms.
[42] Inhabitants of ancient Tyre, the Phoenicians.
[43] Province of ancient Sicily, in ancient times devoted to the cult of Ceres.
[44] Belgium and the Netherlands finally achieved independence from Spain in 1581.

To pour them plenteous on the laughing world.
On thee Sylvanus,[45] thee each rural god,
On thee chief Ceres,[46] with unfailing love
And fond distinction, emulously gaze.
In vain hath nature pour'd vast seas between
Far-distant kingdoms; endless storms in vain
With double night brood o'er them; thou dost throw,
O'er far-divided nature's realms, a chain
To bind in sweet society mankind.
By thee white Albion,[47] once a barbarous clime,
Grew fam'd for arms, for wisdom, and for laws;
By thee she holds the balance of the world,
Acknowledg'd now sole empress of the main.
Coy though thou art, and mutable of love,
There may'st thou ever fix thy wandering steps;
While Eurus[48] rules the wide atlantic foam!
By thee, thy favourite, great Columbus found
That world, where now thy praises I rehearse
To the resounding main and palmy shore;
And Lusitania's[49] chiefs those realms explor'd,
Whence negroes spring, the subject of my song.

 Nor pine the Blacks, alone, with real ills,
That baffle oft the wisest rules of art:
They likewise feel imaginary woes;
Woes no less deadly. Luckless he who owns
The slave, who thinks himself bewitch'd; and whom,
In wrath, a conjurer's snake-mark'd staff[50] hath struck!
They mope, love silence, every friend avoid;
They inly pine; all aliment reject;
Or insufficient for nutrition take:
Their features droop; a sickly yellowish hue
Their skin deforms; their strength and beauty fly.
Then comes the feverish fiend, with firy eyes,

---

[45] Minor Roman deity of the woods and forest.
[46] Roman version of the Greek Demeter, goddess of the harvest, and symbol of fertility.
[47] The ancient name for England.
[48] Latin name for the east wind, and in this context the Eastern trade winds.
[49] The ancient name for Portugal.
[50] 'The negro-conjurors, or Obia-men, as they are called, carry about them a staff which is marked with frogs, snakes, &c. The blacks imagine that its blow if not mortal, will at least occasion long and troublesome disorders . . . as the negroe magician can do mischief, so they can also do good on a plantation, provided they are kept by the white people in proper subordination.' [Grainger]

Whom drowth, convulsions, and whom death surround,
Fatal attendants! if some subtle slave
(Such, Obia-men are stil'd) do not engage,
To save the wretch by antidote or spell.

    In magic spells, in Obia, all the sons
Of sable Africk trust:—Ye, sacred nine![51]
(For ye each hidden preparation know)
Transpierce the gloom, which ignorance and fraud
Have render'd awful; tell the laughing world
Of what these wonder-working charms are made.

    Fern root cut small, and tied with many a knot;
Old teeth extracted from a white man's skull;
A lizard's skeleton; a serpent's head:
These mix'd with salt, and water from the spring,
Are in a phial pour'd; o'er these the leach
Mutters strange jargon, and wild circles forms.

    Of this possest, each negroe deems himself
Secure from poison; for to poison they
Are infamously prone: and arm'd with this,
Their sable country daemons[52] they defy,
Who fearful haunt them at the midnight hour,
To work them mischief. This, diseases fly;
Diseases follow: such its wonderous power!
This o'er the threshold of their cottage hung,
No thieves break in; or, if they dare to steal,
Their feet in blotches, which admit no cure,
Burst loathsome out: but should its owner filch,
As slaves were ever of the pilfering kind,
This from detection screens;—so conjurers swear.

    'Till morning dawn, and Lucifer withdraw
His beamy chariot; let not the loud bell
Call forth thy negroes from their rushy couch:
And ere the sun with mid-day fervour glow,
When every broom-bush opes her yellow flower;
Let thy black labourers from their toil desist:
Nor till the broom her every petal lock,
Let the loud bell recall them to the hoe.

[51] The nine muses.
[52] Daemons are supernatural beings, halfway between humans and gods.

But when the jalap[53] her bright tint displays,
When the solanum[54] fills her cup with dew,
And crickets, snakes, and lizards 'gin their coil;
Let them find shelter in their cane-thatch'd huts:
Or, if constrain'd unusual hours to toil,
(For even the best must sometimes urge their gang)
With double nutriment reward their pains.

Howe'er insensate some may deem their slaves,
Nor 'bove the bestial rank, far other thoughts
The muse, soft daughter of humanity!
Will ever entertain.—The Ethiop knows,
The Ethiop feels, when treated like a man;
Nor grudges, should necessity compell,
By day, by night, to labour for his lord.

Not less inhuman, than unthrifty those;
Who, half the year's rotation round the sun,
Deny subsistence to their labouring slaves.
But would'st thou see thy negroe-train encrease,
Free from disorders; and thine acres clad
With groves of sugar: every week dispense
Or English beans, or Carolinian rice;
Iërne's[55] beef, or Pensilvanian flour;
Newfoundland cod, or herrings from the main
That howls tempestuous round the Scotian isles!

Yet some there are so lazily inclin'd,
And so neglectful of their food, that thou,
Would'st thou preserve them from the jaws of death;
Daily, their wholesome viands must prepare:
With these let all the young, and childless old,
And all the morbid share;—so heaven will bless,
With manifold encrease, thy costly care.

Suffice not this; to every slave assign
Some mountain-ground: or, if waste broken land
To thee belong, that broken land divide.
This let them cultivate, one day, each week;
And there raise yams, and there cassada's[56] root:

---

[53] The root of *Ipomopea* which is a powerful purgative.
[54] The potato, and nightshade genus of plants.   [55] Iërne: ancient name for Ireland.
[56] 'To an ancient Caribbean, bemoaning the savage uncomfortable life of his countrymen, a Deity clad

From a good daemon's staff cassada sprang,
Tradition says, and Caribbees[57] believe;
Which into three the white-rob'd genius broke,
And bade them plant, their hunger to repel.
There let angola's bloomy bush[58] supply,
For many a year, with wholesome pulse their board.
There let the bonavist,[59] his fringed pods
Throw liberal o'er the prop; while ochra bears
Aloft his slimy pulp, and help disdains.
There let potatos[60] mantle o'er the ground;
Sweet as the cane-juice is the root they bear.
There too let eddas[61] spring in order meet,
With Indian cale,[62] and foodful calaloo:[63]
While mint, thyme, balm, and Europe's coyer herbs,
Shoot gladsome forth, nor reprobate the clime.

   This tract secure, with hedges or of limes,
Or bushy citrons, or the shapely tree
That glows at once with aromatic blooms,
And golden fruit mature. To these be join'd,
In comely neighbourhood, the cotton shrub;
In this delicious clime the cotton bursts
On rocky soils.—The coffee also plant;
White as the skin of Albion's lovely fair,
Are the thick snowy fragrant blooms it boasts:
Nor wilt thou, cocô, thy rich pods refuse;
Tho' years, and heat, and moisture they require,
Ere the stone grind them to the food of health.
Of thee, perhaps, and of thy various sorts,
And that kind sheltering tree, thy mother nam'd,[64]
With crimson flowerets prodigally grac'd;

in white apparel appeared, and told him, he would have come sooner to have taught him the ways of civilised life had he been addressed before. He then showed him sharp-cutting stones to fell trees and build houses; and bade them cover themselves with the palm leaves. Then he broke his staff in three which being planted soon after produced cassada . . .' [Grainger]

[57] The indigenous inhabitants of the Caribbean.
[58] 'This is called *pidgeon pea.*' [Grainger]
[59] 'This is the Spanish name of a plant that produces an excellent bean.' [Grainger]
[60] 'They are sweet. There are four kinds, the red the white the long and the round. The juice of each may be made into a pleasant cool drink.' [Grainger]
[61] 'This wholesome root . . . called Edda.' [Grainger]
[62] 'This green, which is a native of the New World, equals any of the greens in the Old.' [Grainger]
[63] 'Species of Indian pot herb.' [Grainger]
[64] 'It is also called *Cacao.*' [Grainger] The tree from the seeds of which chocolate is extracted.

In future times, the enraptur'd muse may sing:
If public favour crown her present lay.

  But let some antient, faithful slave erect
His sheltered mansion near; and with his dog,
His loaded gun, and cutlass, guard the whole:
Else negro-fugitives, who skulk 'mid rocks
And shrubby wilds, in bands will soon destroy
Thy labourer's honest wealth; their loss and yours.

  Perhaps, of Indian gardens I could sing,
Beyond what bloom'd on blest Phaeacia's isle,[65]
Or eastern climes admir'd in days of yore:
How Europe's foodful, culinary plants;
How gay Pomona's[66] ruby-tinctured births;
And gawdy Flora's[67] various-vested train;
Might be instructed to unlearn their clime,
And by due discipline adopt the sun.
The muse might tell what culture will entice
The ripened melon, to perfume each month;
And with the anana[68] load the fragrant board.
The muse might tell, what trees will best exclude
("Insuperable height of airiest shade"[69])
With their vast umbrage the noon's fervent ray.
Thee, verdant mammey,[70] first, her song should praise:
Thee, the first natives of these Ocean-isles,
Fell anthropophagi,[71] still sacred held;
And from thy large high-flavour'd fruit abstain'd,
With pious awe; for thine high-flavoured fruit,
The airy phantoms of their friends deceas'd
Joy'd to regale on.—Such their simple creed.
The tamarind[72] likewise should adorn her theme,
With whose tart fruit the sweltering fever loves
To quench his thirst, whose breezy umbrage soon
Shades the pleas'd planter, shades his children long.

---

[65] Phaeacians, ancient Greek people notorious for their luxuriousness.
[66] Roman goddess of fruit.   [67] Roman goddess of flowers.   [68] Pineapple.
[69] Milton, *Paradise Lost*, IV. 138. The lines describe Satan's first entrance into Eden, and his perception of a vast but beautiful forest lying before the wall around the garden of Paradise itself.
[70] 'A lofty shady and beautiful tree.' [Grainger]
[71] Man-eaters, cannibals.
[72] 'This large, shady and beautiful tree grows fast even in the driest soils, and lasts long.' [Grainger]

Nor, lofty cassia,[73] should she not recount
Thy woodland honours! See, what yellow flowers
Dance in the gale, and scent the ambient air;
While thy long pods, full-fraught with nectared sweets,
Relieve the bowels from their lagging load.
Nor chirimoia,[74] though these torrid isles
Boast not thy fruit, to which the anana yields
In taste and flavour, wilt thou coy refuse
Thy fragrant shade to beautify the scene.
But, chief of palms, and pride of Indian-groves,
Thee, fair palmetto,[75] should her song resound:
What swelling columns, form'd by Jones or Wren,[76]
Or great Palladio,[77] may with thee compare?
Not nice-proportion'd, but of size immense,
Swells the wild fig-tree, and should claim her lay:
For, from its numerous bearded twigs proceed
A filial train, stupendous as their fire,
In quick succession; and, o'er many a rood,
Extend their uncouth limbs; which not the bolt
Of heaven can scathe; nor yet the all-wasting rage
Of Typhon, or of hurricane, destroy.
Nor should, tho' small, the anata[78] not be sung:
Thy purple dye, the silk and cotton fleece
Delighted drink; thy purple dye the tribes
Of Northern-Ind,[79] a fierce and wily race,
Carouse, assembled; and with it they paint
Their manly make in many a horrid form,
To add new terrors to the face of war.
The muse might teach to twine the verdant arch.
And the cool alcove's lofty roof adorn,
With ponderous granadillas,[80] and the fruit
Call'd water-lemon; grateful to the taste:
Nor should she not pursue the mountain-streams,

---

[73] A coarse form of cinnamon.   [74] Peruvian fruit, very like the custard apple.
[75] 'This being the most beautiful of palms, nay, perhaps superior to any tree in the world, has with propriety obtained the name of *Royal*.' [Grainger]
[76] Inigo Jones and Christopher Wren, the two greatest English Renaissance architects.
[77] Andrea Palladio, creator of the 'Palladian' style of neoclassical architecture, which was hugely influential on the style not only of English country houses, but of the planters' mansions throughout the eighteenth-century slave Diaspora of the Caribbean and Americas.
[78] '*Anotto* or *Arnotta*; thence corruptly called Indian Otter by the English.' [Grainger]
[79] Indigenous peoples of North America, formerly known as 'Red Indians'.
[80] A type of passionflower.

But pleas'd decoy them from their shady haunts,
In rills, to visit every tree and herb;
Or fall o'er fern-clad cliffs, with foaming rage;
Or in huge basons float, a fair expanse;
Or, bound in chains of artificial force,
Arise thro' sculptured stone, or breathing brass.—
But I'm in haste to furl my wind-worn sails,
And anchor my tir'd vessel on the shore.

It much imports to build thy Negroe-huts,
Or on the sounding margin of the main,
Or on some dry hill's gently-sloping sides,
In streets, at distance due.—When near the beach,
Let frequent coco cast its wavy shade;
'Tis Neptune's tree; and, nourish'd by the spray,
Soon round the bending stem's aerial height,
Clusters of mighty nuts, with milk and fruit
Delicious fraught, hang clattering in the sky.
There let the bay-grape,[81] too, its crooked limbs
Project enormous; of impurpled hue
Its frequent clusters glow. And there, if thou
Would'st make the sand yield salutary food,
Let Indian millet[82] rear its corny reed,
Like arm'd battalions in array of war.
But, round the upland huts, bananas plant;
A wholesome nutriment bananas yield,
And sun-burnt Labour loves its breezy shade.
Their graceful screen let kindred plantanes join,
And with their broad vans shiver in the breeze;
So flames design'd, or by imprudence caught,
Shall spread no ruin to the neighbouring roof.

Yet nor the sounding margin of the main,
Nor gently sloping side of breezy hill,
Nor streets, at distance due, imbower'd in trees;
Will half the health, or half the pleasure yield,
Unless some pitying naiad[83] deign to lave,
With an unceasing stream, thy thirsty bounds.

---

[81] 'Or sea side grape as it is more commonly called.' [Grainger]
[82] 'Or maise. This is commonly called Guinea corn . . . Negroes and poor white people make many (not unsavoury) dishes with them.' [Grainger]
[83] A nymph inhabiting springs or rivers.

On festal days; or when their work is done;
Permit thy slaves to lead the choral dance,
To the wild banshaw's[84] melancholy sound.
Responsive to the sound, head feet and frame
Move aukwardly harmonious: hand in hand
Now lock'd, the gay troop circularly wheels,
And frisks and capers with intemperate joy.
Halts the vast circle, all clap hands and sing;
While those distinguish'd for their heels and air,
Bound in the center, and fantastic twine.
Meanwhile some stripling, from the choral ring,
Trips forth; and, not ungallantly, bestows
On her who nimblest hath the greensward beat,
And whose flush'd beauties have inthrall'd his soul,
A silver token of his fond applause.
Anon they form in ranks; nor inexpert
A thousand tuneful intricacies weave,
Shaking their sable limbs; and oft a kiss
Steal from their partners; who, with neck reclin'd,
And semblant scorn, resent the ravish'd bliss.
But let not thou the drum their mirth inspire;
Nor vinous spirits: else, to madness fir'd,
(What will not bacchanalian frenzy dare?)
Fell acts of blood, and vengeance they pursue.

Compel by threats, or win by soothing arts,
Thy slaves to wed their fellow slaves at home;
So shall they not their vigorous prime destroy,
By distant journeys, at untimely hours,
When muffled midnight decks her raven-hair
With the white plumage of the prickly vine.[85]

Would'st thou from countless ails preserve thy gang;
To every Negroe, as the candle-weed[86]
Expands his blossoms to the cloudy sky,
And moist Aquarius melts in daily showers;
A woolly vestment give, (this Wiltshire weaves)
Warm to repel chill Night's unwholesome dews:

---

[84] 'A sort of rude guitar invented by the Negroes.' [Grainger]
[85] 'This lovely white rosaceous flower is as large as the crown of ones hat.' [Grainger]
[86] 'This shrub . . . produces a yellow flower somewhat resembling a narcissus.' [Grainger]

While strong coarse linen, from the Scotian loom,
Wards off the fervours of the burning day.

The truly great, tho' from a hostile clime,
The sacred Nine embalm; then, Muses, chant,
In grateful numbers, Gallic Lewis[87] praise:
For private murder quell'd; for laurel'd arts,
Invented, cherish'd in his native realm;
For rapine punish'd; for grim famine fed;
For sly chicane expell'd the wrangling bar;
And rightful Themis[88] seated on her throne:
But, chief, for those mild laws his wisdom fram'd,
To guard the Aethiop from tyrannic sway!

Did such, in these green isles which Albion claims,
Did such obtain; the muse, at midnight-hour,
This last brain-racking study had not ply'd:
But, sunk in slumbers of immortal bliss,
To bards had listned on a fancied Thames!

All hail, old father Thames! tho' not from far
Thy springing waters roll; nor countless streams,
Of name conspicuous, swell thy watery store;
Tho' thou, no Plata,[89] to the sea devolve
Vast humid offerings, thou art king of streams:
Delighted Commerce broods upon thy wave;
And every quarter of this sea-girt globe
To thee due tribute pays; but chief the world
By great Columbus found, where now the muse
Beholds, transported, slow vast fleecy clouds,
Alps pil'd on Alps romantically high,
Which charm the sight with many a pleasing form.
The moon, in virgin-glory, gilds the pole,
And tips yon tamarinds, tips yon Cane-crown'd vale,
With fluent silver; while unnumbered stars
Gild the vast concave with their lively beams.
The main, a moving burnish'd mirror, shines;
No noise is heard, save when the distant surge
With drouzy murmurings breaks upon the shore!—

---

[87] Louis XIV, the 'Sun King'.   [88] Ancient Greek goddess, personification of Justice.
[89] Great South American river.

Ah me, what thunders roll! the sky's on fire!
Now sudden darkness muffles up the pole!
Heavens! What wild scenes, before the affrighted sense,
Imperfect swim!—See! in that flaming scroll,
Which Time unfolds, the future germs bud forth,
Of mighty empires! independent realms!—
And must Britannia, Neptune's favourite queen,
Protect'ress of true science, freedom, arts;
Must she, ah! must she, to her offspring crouch?
Ah, must my Thames, old Ocean's favourite son,
Resign his trident to barbaric streams;
His banks neglected, and his waves unsought,
No bards to sing them, and no fleets to grace?—
Again the fleecy clouds amuse the eye,
And sparkling stars the vast horizon gild—
She shall not crouch; if Wisdom guide the helm,
Wisdom that bade loud Fame, with justest praise,
Record her triumphs! bade the lacquaying winds
Transport, to every quarter of the globe,
Her winged navies! bade the scepter'd sons
Of earth acknowledge her pre-eminence!—
She shall not crouch; if these Cane ocean-isles,
Isles which on Britain for their all depend,
And must for ever, still indulgent share
Her fostering smile: and other isles be given,
From vanquish'd foes—And, see, another race!
A golden aera dazzles my fond sight!
That other race, that long'd-for aera, hail!
THE BRITISH GEORGE[90] NOW REIGNS, THE PATRIOT KING!
BRITAIN SHALL EVER TRIUMPH O'ER THE MAIN.

[90] King George III of England, who had massive interests in the slave trade, and in the East India
Company.

Isaac Teale, *The Voyage of the Sable Venus from Angola to the West Indies* (1765, first printed in Bryan Edwards, *The History, Civil and Commercial of the British Colonies in the West Indies* (1793))

This is a nasty piece of work. The Jamaican planter and pro-slavery apologist Bryan Edwards (see pp. 67–72) had, in 1793, printed a long parodic love poem entitled *The Voyage of the Sable Venus, from Angola to the West Indies* to garnish his defence of plantation slavery within his pro-slavery masterpiece *The History, Civil and Commercial of the British Colonies in the West Indies.* The title given to Teale's poem consequently constitutes a poetic locution for what was to become notorious as 'the middle passage'. *The Voyage of the Sable Venus* was written at Edwards's own suggestion nearly thirty years before. The poem ironically celebrates the delights of interracial sex between sailors and black women on the middle passage (slave rape) and then of slave owners and black women within the Caribbean (slave rape, and slave prostitution). The poem was published at the precise historical moment when the ground swell within Quaker, Evangelical, and some radical circles was just beginning to build up against the immorality, inefficiency, and moral inexcusability of the slave trade. Yet it was also written at a point when the trade was still seen by many as legitimate business, and when the great fact-finding missions of the abolition movement in the 1780s had not yet exposed the full enormity and scale of the trade to a wide readership.

At the heart of the satire is the mechanism whereby disempowerment is presented as its opposite. The 'Sable Venus' is shown to be the sexual magnet that draws the crowds of men, including 'some great ones'. Yet there is a real and often repeated scene related to the realities of slave trading and the middle passage which lies behind this image of the arrival of the frenzied crowds to greet the slave ship. It was not uncommon, on the arrival of a slave ship, for the captain to prepare the slaves for sale, and then allow potential purchasers to rush on board and fight for possession of the most likely bargains. The experience by all accounts caused the slaves, and the women and children in particular, an indescribable terror (see p. 250). Yet in this poem, as the sexually obsessed men swarm around her, the Sable Venus is again shown to be patronizingly in control of the situation: 'Gay Goddess of the sable smile! | Propitious still, this grateful isle | With thy protection bless!' The poem ends with the author, Teale, claiming that he will pursue sexual encounters with slave women throughout the Caribbean plantation systems. Pro-slavery satire can take some pretty bizarre turns. What is to be done with this work now? The poem was no doubt seen as good healthy fun, but it climaxes with a claim that because of the beauty of the 'Sable Venus' it is the author's duty to sexually abuse any black woman in the slave Diaspora he can get his hands on. Not only this but the women are assumed to desire the process. This fantasy is of course the oldest rape defence in the world. Mimba 'pouts' and is 'wanton'; in Isaac Teale's world of rape fantasy, of course she wants it. One of the most terrifying aspects of the satire lies in the collision between diction and thought. Teale fantasizes at the poem's conclusion about the types of female beauty over which, as a planter, he has a total right of abuse. Yet the potential victims are introduced in a sort of plantation pastoral which substitutes Bennebas, Quashebas, and Mimbas for the Phyllises and Cynthias of Ben Jonson or the Cavalier poets.

The Voyage of the Sable Venus, from Angola to the West Indies

I long had my gay lyre forsook,
But strung it t'other day, and took
    T'wards Helicon[1] my way;
The muses all, th'assembly graced,
The president himself was placed,
    By chance 'twas concert-day.

Erato[2] smil'd to see me come;
Ask'd why I staid so much at home;
    I own'd my conduct wrong;
But now, the sable queen of love,
Resolv'd my gratitude to prove,
    Had sent me for a song.

The ladies look'd extremely shy,
Apollo's smile was arch and sly,
    But not one word they said.—
I gaz'd,—sure silence is content,—
I made my bow, away I went;
    Was not my duty paid?

Come to my bosom, genial fire,
Soft sounds, and lively thoughts inspire;
    Unusual is my theme:
Not such dissolving *Ovid*[3] sung,
Nor melting *Sappho*'s[4] glowing tongue,—
    More dainty mine I deem.

---

[1] The mountain in Boeotia supposed to be the favourite home of the muses.
[2] The muse of amatory and erotic lyric poetry.
[3] The great Latin poet (43 BC–AD 17), author of the *Metamorphoses*.
[4] The great Greek lyric and amatory poetess who lived *c.*600 BC, and who has remained notorious as a supposed lesbian.

Sweet is the beam of morning bright,
Yet sweet the sober shade of night;
   On rich *Angola*'s shores,
While beauty clad in sable dye,
Enchanting fires the wondering eye,
   Farewel! ye *Paphian*[5] bow'rs.

O sable queen! thy mild domain
I seek, and court thy gentle reign,
   So soothing soft and sweet;
Where meeting love, sincere delight,
Fond pleasure, ready joys invite,
   And all true raptures meet.

The prating *Frank*, the *Spaniard* proud,
The double *Scot*, *Hibernian* loud,
   And sullen *English* own,
The pleasing softness of thy sway,
And here, transferr'd allegiance pay,
   For gracious is thy throne.

From East to West, o'er either Ind"[6]
Thy sceptre sways; thy pow'r we find
   By both the tropics felt;
The blazing sun that gilds the zone,
Waits but the triumph of thy throne,
   Quite round the burning belt.

When thou, this large domain to view,
Jamaica's isle, thy conquest new,
   First left thy native shore,
Bright was the morn, and soft the breeze,
With wanton joy the curling seas
   The beauteous burden bore.

Of iv'ry was the car, inlaid
With ev'ry shell of lively shade;
   The throne was burnish'd gold;
The footstool gay with coral beam'd,
The wheels with brightest amber gleam'd,
   And glist'ring round they rowl'd.

---

[5] Pertaining to Paphos, in Cyprus, a place sacred to Aphrodite, goddess of love; hence the word carries associations of lasciviousness, and can even imply that a person is a whore.
[6] An abbreviation for West or East Indies.

The peacock and the ostrich spread
Their beauteous plumes, a trembling shade,
   From noon-day's sultry flame:
Sent by their fire, the careful East,
The wanton breezes fann'd her breast,
   And fluttered round the dame.

The winged fish, in purple trace
The chariot drew; with easy grace
   Their azure rein she guides:
And now they fly, and now they swim;
Now o'er the wave they lightly skim,
   Or dart beneath the tides.

Each bird that haunts the rock and bay,
Each scaly native of the sea,
   Came crowding o'er the main:
The dolphin shows his thousand dyes,
The grampus his enormous size,
   And gambol in her train.

Her skin excell'd the raven plume,
Her breath the fragrant orange bloom,
   Her eye the tropic beam:
Soft was her lip as silken down,
And mild her look as evening sun
   That gilds the *Cobre*[7] stream.

The loveliest limbs her form compose,
Such as her sister *Venus* chose,
   In *Florence*, where she's seen;[8]
But just alike, except the white,
No difference, no—none at night,
   The beauteous dames between.

With native ease, serene she sat,
In elegance of charms compleat,
   And ev'ry heart she won:
False dress deformity may shade,
True beauty courts no foreign aid:
   Can tapers light the sun?—

---

[7] A river in St Catherine's Parish, in central and south Jamaica; it flows into Kingston harbour.
[8] An allusion to the painting *The Birth of Venus* by Sandro Botticelli in the Uffizi Gallery in Florence.

The pow'r that rules old ocean wide,[9]
'Twas he, they say, had calm'd the tide,
   Beheld the chariot rowl:
Assum'd the figure of a tar,
The Captain of a man of war,
   And told her all his soul.

She smil'd with kind consenting eyes;—
Beauty was ever valour's prize;
   He raised a murky cloud:
The tritons sound, the sirens sing,
The dolphins dance, the billows ring,
   And joy fills all the croud.

Blest offspring of the warm embrace!
Fond ruler of the saffron race!
   Tho' strong thy bow, dear boy,[10]
Thy mingled shafts of black and white,
Are wing'd with feathers of delight,
   Their points are tipped with joy.

But, when her step had touch'd the strand,
Wild rapture seiz'd the ravish'd land,
   From ev'ry part they came:
Each mountain, valley, plain, and grove
Haste eagerly to show their love;—
   Right welcome was the dame.

Port-Royal shouts were heard aloud,
Gay *St. Iago* sent a croud,
   Grave *Kingston*[11] not a few:
No rabble rout,—I heard it said,
Some great ones joined the cavalcade—
   The muse will not say who.

Gay Goddess of the sable smile!
Propitious still, this grateful isle
   With thy protection bless!
Here fix, secure, thy constant throne;
Where all, adoring thee, do ONE
   ONE Deity confess.

[9] The power that rules the ocean is Neptune.   [10] Cupid is the 'dear boy'.
[11] Port-Royal, St Iago, Kingston were the major slave trading centres in Jamaica.

For me, if I no longer own
Allegiance to the Cyprian[12] throne,
   I play no fickle part;
It were ingratitude to slight
Superior kindness; I delight
   To feel a grateful heart.

Then, playful goddess! cease to change,
 Nor in new beauties vainly range;
   Tho' whatso'er thy view,
Try every form thou canst put on,
I'll follow thee thro' every one;
   So staunch am I, so true.

Do thou in gentle *Phibba* smile,
In artful *Benneba* beguile,
   In wanton *Mimba* pout;
In sprightly *Cuba*'s eyes look gay,
Or grave in sober *Quasheba*,
   I still shall find thee out.[13]

Thus have I sung; perhaps too gay
Such subject for such time of day,
   And fitter far for youth:
Should then the song too wanton seem,
You know who chose t' unlucky theme,
   Dear Bryan,[14] tell the truth.

---

[12] Relating to Cyprus, a place where there was a cult of Aphrodite; consequently the word has many lewd and erotic associations.

[13] Phibba, Benneba, Mimba, Quasheba are all fanciful and derogatory diminutives for imagined young black women. Quasheba is a feminized version of Quashee, which was originally an Ashanti name given to one born on a Sunday, but was generally adopted as a slave name in the West Indies; the name then entered racist discourse, most notoriously in Thomas Carlyle's *Discourse on the Nigger Question* (1849).

[14] Bryan Edwards, ingenious slavery apologist and author of *The History, Civil and Commercial of the British Colonies in the West Indies*, in which Teale's poem was first published.

Thomas Day (1748–89) and John Bicknell, *The Dying Negro: A Poetical Epistle* (1773)

Day, whose father died when he was young, left him in comfortable circumstances. He ended up at Corpus Christi College, Oxford, where he came under the spell of Rousseau's major writings, which were suddenly making their impact felt in the early 1760s. He remained throughout his life obsessed with the alleviation of human suffering, and with the necessity of living a good life. His most famous work *Sandford and Merton* was an Enlightenment polemic setting out his ideal of generous manliness, and remained a children's educational classic well into the nineteenth century. Day was not merely a theorist and by the end of his life had given almost his entire fortune away, mostly to help the local labouring poor in Ottershaw in Surrey. A philanthropist with a philosophical bent, Day was interested in the plight of the poor, but he was also interested in finding a wife. This combination of interests led to his most notorious experiment, the attempt to rear a wife 'on philosophical principles'. He and his friend Bicknell accordingly selected a beautiful blonde girl from an orphanage, and a brunette from a foundling hospital, whom he renamed Sabrina and Lucretia respectively. He undertook to educate them, and then select one for a wife, and support the other. The experiment generated a series of strange anecdotes, including stories of his torture of one of the girls in order to investigate her capacity for stoicism. It was, however, Bicknell who ended up marrying Lucretia, while Sabrina was apprenticed to a milliner. Bicknell's inveterate sentimental humanism, and his capacity to become romantically infatuated with young women whom he hopelessly idealized, are both fully played out within *The Dying Negro*.

The poem, Day's first publication, was popular from its appearance and remained a firm favourite with Anglo-American abolition readerships. It is the first significant piece of verse propaganda directed explicitly against the English slave systems. The verses were published in the main newspapers and periodicals (the version given here appeared in the *Gentleman's Magazine* in 1814, over forty years after its first printing). The poem, written in crude form by Bicknell shortly before his early death, and then expanded by his friend Day into the version reprinted here, was created before there were any established models for abolition literatures attempting to give the slave victim a voice. The poem consequently looks back to the tragic sentimentalism of Southerne's *Oroonoko*. The poem in taking as its central character the figure of the lovelorn and suicidal black male, separated from his beloved, follows a familiar pattern. What is particularly unusual about this poem, and what separates it from subsequent abolition poetry, is the manner in which it argues for the right of the slave to love and marry a white woman in England. The language in which the slave expresses his emotional infatuation is, however, grafted on from populist sentimental love poetry. One reason for the poem's enduring appeal lies in the manner in which it emphatically follows a series of moves which present the black as completely passive, and as effectively paralysed, in terms of any effective political action, by an excess of sensibility.

The Dying Negro

ADVERTISEMENT.

The following Poem was occasioned by a fact which had recently happened at the time of its first publication, in 1773. A negro, belonging to the Captain of a West Indiaman, having agreed to marry a white woman, his fellow-servant, in order to effect his purpose, had left his master's house, and procured himself to be baptized; but being detected and taken, he was sent on board the Captain's vessel, then lying in the river; where, finding no chance of escaping, and preferring death to another voyage to America, he took an opportunity of stabbing himself. As soon as his determination is fixed, he is supposed to write this epistle to his intended wife.

> Arm'd with thy sad last gift—the power to die;
> Thy shafts, stern Fortune, now I can defy;
> Thy dreadful mercy points at length the shore,
> Where all is peace, and men enslave no more;
> This weapon, even in chains, the brave can wield,
> And vanquish'd quit triumphantly the field:
> Beneath such wrongs let pallid Christians live,
> Such they can perpetrate, and may forgive.
> Yet while I tread that gulph's tremendous brink,
> Where nature shudders, and where beings sink,
> Ere yet this hand a life of sorrow close,
> And end by one determin'd stroke my woes,
> Is there a fond regret, which moves my mind
> To pause, and cast a lingering look behind?
> —O my lov'd bride!—for I have call'd thee mine,
> Dearer than life, whom I with life resign,
> For thee even here this faithful heart shall glow,
> A pang shall rend me, and a tear shall flow.—
> How shall I soothe thy grief, since fate denies
> Thy pious duties to my closing eyes?
> I cannot clasp thee in a last embrace,
> Nor gaze in silent anguish on thy face;
> I cannot raise these fetter'd arms for thee,
> To ask that mercy heaven denies to me;
> Yet let thy tender breast my sorrows share,
> Bleed for my wounds, and feel my deep despair.
> Yet let thy tears bedew a wretch's grave,
> Whom Fate forbade thy tenderness to save.

Receive these sighs, to thee my soul I breathe,
Fond love in dying groans is all I can bequeathe.
   Why did I, slave, beyond my lot aspire?
Why didst thou fan the inauspicious fire?
For thee I bade my drooping soul revive;
For thee alone I could have borne to live;
And love, I said, shall make me large amends,
For persecuting foes, and faithless friends:
Fool that I was! enur'd so long to pain,
To trust to hope, or dream of joy again.
Joy, stranger guest, my easy faith betray'd,
And Love now points to death's eternal shade;
There, while I rest from misery's galling load,
Be thou the care of every pitying god;
Nor many that demon's unpropitious power,
Who shed his influence on my natal hour,
Pursue thee too with unrelenting hate,
And blend with mine the colour of thy fate.
For thee may those soft hours return again,
When pleasure led thee smiling o'er the plain:
Ere, like some hell-born spectre of dismay,
I cross'd thy path, and darken'd all the way.
Ye waving groves, which from this cell I view!
Ye meads, now glittering with the morning dew!
Ye flowers, which blush on yonder hated shore,
That at my baneful step shall fade no more,
A long farewell!—I ask no vernal bloom—
No pageant wreaths to wither on my tomb.
—Let serpents hiss, and night-shade blacken there,
To mark the friendless victim of despair!
   And better in th' untimely grave to rot,
The world and all its cruelties forgot,
Than, dragg'd once more beyond the western main,
To groan beneath some dastard planter's chain,
Where my poor countrymen in bondage wait
The slow enfranchisement of lingering fate.
Oh! my heart sinks, my dying eyes o'erflow,
When Memory paints the picture of their woe!
For I have seen them, ere the dawn of day,
Rous'd by the lash, begin their cheerless way;
Greeting with groans unwelcome morn's return,

While rage and shame their gloomy bosoms burn;
And, chiding every hour the slow-pac'd sun,
Endure their toils till all his race was run;
No eye to mark their sufferings with a tear,
No friend to comfort, and no hope to cheer;
Then like the dull unpitied brutes repair
To stalls as wretched, and as coarse a fare;
Thank heaven, one day of misery was o'er,
And sink to sleep, and wish to wake no more.—
Sleep on! ye lost companions of my woes,
For whom in death this tear of pity flows;
Sleep, and enjoy the only boon of heaven,
To you in common with your tyrants given!
O while soft slumber from their couches flies,
Still may the balmy blessing steep your eyes;
In sweet oblivion lull awhile your woes,
And brightest visions gladden the repose!
Let fancy, then, unconscious of the change,
Thro' our own fields and native forests range;
Waft ye to each once-haunted stream and grove,
And visit every long-lost scene ye love!
—I sleep no more—nor in the midnight shade
Invoke ideal phantoms to my aid;
Nor wake again abandon'd and forlorn,
To find each dear delusion fled at morn;
A slow consuming death let others wait,
I snatch destruction from unwilling fate:—
Yon ruddy streaks the rising sun proclaim,
That never more shall beam upon my shame;
Bright orb! for others let thy glory shine,
Mature the golden grain and purple vine,
While fetter'd Afric still for Europe toils,
And Nature's plunderers riot on her spoils;
Be theirs the gifts thy partial rays supply,
Be mine the gloomy privilege to die.

    And thou, whose impious avarice and pride
The holy cross to my sad brows denied,
Forbade me Nature's common rights to claim,
Or share with thee a Christian's sacred name;
Thou too, farewell! for not beyond the grave
Extends thy power, nor is my dust thy slave.

In vain heaven spread so wide the swelling sea,
Vast watery barrier, 'twixt thy world and me;
Swift round the globe, by earth nor heaven controll'd,
Fly stern oppression, and dire lust of gold.
Where'er the hell-hounds mark their bloody way,
Still Nature groans, and man becomes their prey.
In the wild wastes of Afric's sandy plain,
Where roars the lion thro' his drear domain,
To curb the savage monarch of the chace,
There too heaven planted man's majestic race;
Bade reason's sons with nobler titles rise,
Lift high their brow sublime, and scan the skies.
What tho' the sun in his meridian blaze,
Dart on their naked limbs his scorching rays;
What tho' no rosy tints adorn their face,
No silken tresses shine with flowing grace;
Yet of ethereal temper are their souls,
And in their veins the tide of honour rolls;
And valour kindles there the hero's flame,
Contempt of death, and thirst of martial fame;
And pity melts the sympathizing breast,
Ah! fatal virtue! for the brave distrest.
My tortur'd bosom, sad remembrance spare!
Why dost thou plant thy keenest daggers there?
And shew me what I was, and aggravate despair?
Ye streams of Gambia, and thou sacred shade!
Where in my youth's first dawn I joyful stray'd,
Oft have I rous'd, amid your caverns dim,
The howling tyger, and the lion grim;
In vain they gloried in their headlong force,
My javelin pierc'd them in their raging course.
But little did my boding mind bewray,
The victor and his hopes were doom'd a prey
To human brutes more fell, more cruel far than they.
Ah! what avails the conqueror's bloody meed,
The generous purpose, or the dauntless deed!
This hapless breast expos'd on every plain,
And liberty preferr'd to life in vain?
Fallen are my trophies, blasted is my fame,
Myself become a thing without a name,
The sport of haughty lords, and even of slaves the shame.

Curst be the winds, and curst the tides which bore
These European robbers to our shore!
O be that hour involv'd in endless night,
When first their streamers met my wondering sight!
I call'd the warriors from the mountain's steep,
To meet these unknown terrors of the deep;
Rous'd by my voice, their generous bosoms glow,
They rush indignant, and demand the foe,
And poise the darts of death, and twang the bended bow:
When lo! advancing o'er the sea-beat plain,
I mark'd the leader of a warlike train:
Unlike his features to our swarthy race;
And golden hair play'd round his ruddy face.
While with insidious smile, and lifted hand,
He thus accosts our unsuspecting band:
'Ye valiant chiefs, whom love of glory leads
To martial combats, and heroic deeds;
No fierce invader your retreat explores,
No hostile banner waves along your shores.
From the dread tempests of the deep we fly,
They lay, ye chiefs, these pointed terrors by:
And O, your hospitable cares extend,
So may ye never need the aid ye lend!
So may ye still repeat to every grove
The songs of freedom, and the strains of love!'
Soft as the accents of the traitor flow,
We melt with pity, and unbend the bow;
With liberal hand our choicest gifts we bring,
And point the wanderers to the freshest spring.
Nine days we feasted on the Gambian strand,
And songs of friendship echoed o'er the land.[1]
When the tenth morn her rising lustre gave,
The chief approach'd me by the sounding wave.
'O, youth,' he said, 'what gifts can we bestow,
Or how requite the mighty debt we owe?
For lo! propitious to our vows, the gale

---

[1] '"Which way soever I turned my eyes on this spot, I beheld a perfect image of pure nature, an agreeable solitude, bounded on every side by charming landscapes; the rural situation of cottages in the midst of trees; the ease and indolence of the negroes, reclined under the shade of their spreading foliage; the simplicity of their dress and manners; the whole revived in my mind the idea of our first parents, and I seemed to contemplate the world in its primitive state. They are, generally speaking, very good-natured, sociable, and obliging."—M. Adanson's Voyage to Senegal, &c.' [Day]

With milder omens fills the swelling sail.
To-morrow's sun shall see our ships explore
These deeps, and quit your hospitable shore.
Yet while we linger, let us still employ
The number'd hours in friendship and in joy;
Ascend our ships, their treasures are your own,
And taste the produce of a world unknown.'
He spoke; with fatal eagerness we burn,—
And quit the shores, undestin'd to return!
The smiling traitors with insidious care
The goblet proffer, and the feast prepare,
Till dark oblivion shades our closing eyes,
And all disarm'd each fainting warrior lies.
O wretches! to your future evils blind!
O morn for ever present to my mind!
When bursting from the treacherous bands of sleep,
Rous'd by the murmurs of the dashing deep,
I woke to bondage and ignoble pains,
And all the horrors of a life in chains.[2]
Ye gods of Afric! in that dreadful hour
Where were your thunders and avenging power!
Did not my prayers, my groans, my tears invoke
Your slumbering justice to direct the stroke?
No power descended to assist the brave,
No lightnings flash'd, and I became a slave.
From lord to lord my wretched carcase sold,
In Christian traffic, for their sordid gold:
Fate's blackest clouds were gather'd o'er my head;
And, bursting now, they mix me with the dead.
Yet when my fortune cast my lot with thine,
And bade beneath one roof our labours join,
Surpris'd I felt the tumults of my breast
Lull'd by thy beauties to unwonted rest.
Delusive hopes my changing soul inflame,
And gentler transports agitate my frame.

---

[2] '"As we passed along the coast, we very often lay before a town, and fired a gun for the natives to come off, but no soul came near us. At length we learned by some ships that were trading down the coast, that the natives seldom came on board an English ship, for fear of being detained or carried off; yet at last some ventured on board; but if these chanced to spy any arms, they would all immediately take to their canoes, and make the best of their way home."—*Smith's Voyage to Guinea*.' [Day]

What tho' obscure thy birth, superior grace
Shone in the glowing features of thy face.
Ne'er had my youth such winning softness seen,
Where Afric's sable beauties dance the green,
When some sweet maid receives her lover's vow,
And binds the offer'd chaplet to her brow.
While on thy languid eyes I fondly gaze,
And trembling meet the lustre of their rays,
Thou, gentle virgin, thou didst not despise
The humble homage of a captive's sighs.
By heaven abandon'd, and by man betray'd,
Each hope resign'd of comfort or of aid,
Thy generous love could every sorrow end,
In thee I found a mistress and a friend;
Still as I told the story of my woes,
With heaving sighs thy lovely bosom rose;
The trickling drops of liquid crystal stole
Down thy fair cheek, and mark'd thy pitying soul:
Dear drops! upon my bleeding heart, like balm
They fell, and soon my tortur'd mind grew calm;
Then my lov'd country, parents, friends forgot,
Heaven I absolved, nor murmur'd at my lot;
Thy sacred smiles could every pang remove,
And liberty became less dear than love.
    —And I have lov'd thee with as pure a fire,
As man e'er felt, or woman could inspire:
No pangs like these my pallid tyrants know,
Not such their transports, and not such their woe.
Their softer frames a feeble soul conceal,
A soul unus'd to pity or to feel;
Damp'd by base lucre, and repell'd by fear,
Each nobler passion faintly blazes here.
Not such the mortals burning Afric breeds,
Mother of virtues and heroic deeds!
Descended from yon radiant orb, they claim
Sublimer courage, and a fiercer flame.
Nature has there, unchill'd by art, imprest
Her awful majesty on every breast.
Where'er she leads, impatient of controul,
The dauntless Negro rushes to the goal;
Firm in his love, resistless in his hate,

His arm is conquest, and his frown is fate.
 What fond affection in my bosom reigns!
What soft emotions mingle with my pains!
Still as thy form before my mind appears,
My haggard eyes are bathed in gushing tears;
Thy lov'd idea rushes to my heart,
And stern Despair suspends the lifted dart.—
O could I burst these fetters, which restrain
My struggling limbs, and waft thee o'er the main
To some far distant land, where Ocean roars
In horrid tempests round the gloomy shores;
To some wild mountain's solitary shade,
Where never European faith betray'd;
How joyful could I, of thy love secure,
Meet every danger, every toil endure.
For thee I'd climb the rock, explore the flood,
And tame the famish'd savage of the wood.
When scorching summer drinks the shrinking streams,
My care should screen thee from his sultry beams;
At noon I'd crown thee with the fairest flowers,
At eve I'd lead thee to the safest bowers;
And when bleak winter howl'd around the cave,
For thee his horrors and his storms I'd brave;
Nor snows nor raging winds should damp my soul,
Nor such a night as shrouds the dusky pole:
O'er the dark waves my bounding skiff I'd guide,
To pierce each mightier monster of the tide;
Thro' frozen forests force my dreary way,
In their own dens to rouse the beasts of prey;
Nor other blessing ask, if this might prove
How fix'd my passion, and how fond my love.
—Then should vain fortune to my sight display
All that her anger now has snatch'd away;
Treasures more vast than Avarice e'er design'd
In midnight visions to a Christian's mind;
The Monarch's diadem, the Conqueror's meed,
That empty prize for which the valiant bleed;
All that Ambition strives to snatch from fate,
All that the Gods e'er lavish'd in their hate;
Not these should win thy lover from thy arms,
Or tempt a moment's absence from thy charms;

Indignant would I fly these guilty climes,
And scorn their glories as I hate their crimes!
But whither does my wandering fancy rove?
Hence ye wild wishes of desponding love!
Ah! where is now that voice which lull'd my woes;
That Angel face, which sooth'd me to repose?
By Nature tempted, and with passion blind,
Are these the joys Hope whisper'd to my mind?
Is this the end of constancy like thine?
Are these the transports of a love like mine?
My hopes, my joys, are vanish'd into air,
And now of all that once engag'd my care,
These chains alone remain, this weapon and despair.   }
  —So be thy life's gay prospects all o'ercast,
All thy fond hopes dire disappointment blast!
Thus end thy golden visions, son of pride!
Whose ruthless ruffians tore me from my bride;
That beauteous prize Heaven had reserv'd at last,
Sweet recompence for all my sorrows past.
O may thy harden'd bosom never prove
The tender joys of friendship or of love!
Yet may'st thou, doom'd to hopeless flames a prey,
In unrequited passion pine away!
May every transport violate thy rest,
Which tears the jealous lover's gloomy breast!
May secret anguish gnaw thy cruel heart,
Till death in all his terrors wing the dart;
Then, to complete the horror of thy doom,
A favour'd rival smile upon thy tomb!
  Why does my lingering soul her flight delay?
Come, lovely maid, and gild the dreary way!
Come, wildly rushing with disorder'd charms,
And clasp thy bleeding lover in thy arms;
Close his sad eyes, receive his parting breath,
And soothe him sinking to the shades of death!
O come—thy presence can my pangs beguile,
And bid th' inexorable tyrant smile;
Transported will I languish on thy breast,
And sink enraptur'd to eternal rest:
The hate of men, the wrongs of fate forgive,
Forget my woes, and almost wish to live.

Ah! rather fly, lest aught of doubt controul
The dreadful purpose labouring in my soul;
Tears must not bend me, nor thy beauties move,
This hour I triumph over fate and love.
    Again with tenfold rage my bosom burns,
And all the tempest of my soul returns;
Again the furies fire my madding brain,
And death extends his sheltering arms in vain;
For unreveng'd I fall, unpitied die,
And with my blood glut Pride's insatiate eye.
    Thou Christian God! to whom so late I bow'd,
To whom my soul its new allegiance vow'd,
When crimes like these thy injur'd power prophane,
O God of Nature! art thou call'd in vain?
Didst thou for this sustain a mortal wound,
While Heaven, and Earth, and Hell, hung trembling round?
That these vile fetters might my body bind,
And agony like this distract my mind?
On thee I call'd with reverential awe,
Ador'd thy wisdom, and embrac'd thy law;
Yet mark thy destin'd convert as he lies,
His groans of anguish, and his livid eyes,
These galling chains, polluted with his blood,
Then bid his tongue proclaim thee just and good!
But if too weak thy vaunted power to spare,
Or sufferings move thee not, O hear despair!
Thy hopes and blessings I alike resign,
But let revenge, let swift revenge be mine!
Be this proud bark, which now triumphant rides,
Toss'd by the winds, and shatter'd by the tides!
And may these fiends, who now exulting view
The horrors of my fortune, feel them too!
Be theirs the torment of a lingering fate,
Slow as thy justice, dreadful as my hate;
Condemn'd to grasp the riven plank in vain,
And chac'd by all the monsters of the main;
And while they spread their sinking arms to thee,
Then let their fainting souls remember me!
    —Thanks, righteous God!—Revenge shall yet be mine;
Yon flashing lightning gave the dreadful sign,
I see the flames of heavenly anger hurl'd,

I hear your thunders shake a guilty world.
The time shall come, the fated hour is nigh,
When guiltless blood shall penetrate the sky.
Amid these horrors, and involving night,
Prophetic visions flash before my sight;
Eternal justice wakes, and in their turn
The vanquish'd triumph, and the victors mourn;—.
Lo! Discord, fiercest of the infernal band,
Fires all her snakes, and waves her flaming brand;
No more proud Commerce courts the western gales,
But marks the lurid skies, and furls her sails;
War mounts his iron car, and at his wheels
In vain soft Pity weeps, and Mercy kneels;
He breathes a savage rage thro' all the host,
And stains with kindred blood the impious coast;
Then, while with horror sickening Nature groans,
And earth and heaven the monstrous race disowns,
Then the stern genius of my native land,
With delegated vengeance in his hand,
Shall raging cross the troubled seas, and pour
The plagues of Hell on yon devoted shore.
What tides of ruin mark his ruthless way!
How shriek the fiends exulting o'er their prey!
I see their warriors gasping on the ground,—
I hear their flaming cities crash around.—
In vain with trembling heart the coward turns,
In vain with generous rage the valiant burns.—
One common ruin, one promiscuous grave,
O'erwhelms the dastard, and receives the brave—
For Afric triumphs!—his avenging rage
No tears can soften, and no blood assuage.
He smites the trembling waves, and at the shock
Their fleets are dash'd upon the pointed rock.
He waves his flaming dart, and o'er their plains,
In mournful silence, Desolation reigns—
Fly swift, ye years!—Arise, thou glorious morn!
Thou great avenger of thy race be born!
The conqueror's palm, and deathless fame be thine!
One generous stroke, and liberty be mine!
—And now, ye Powers, to whom the brave are dear,
Receive me falling, and your suppliant hear.

> To you this unpolluted blood I pour,
> To you that spirit which ye gave restore!
> I ask no lazy pleasures to possess,
> No long eternity of happiness;—
> But if, unstain'd by voluntary guilt,
> At your great call this being I have spilt,
> For all the wrongs which innocent I share,
> For all I've suffer'd, and for all I dare;
> O lead me to that spot, that sacred shore,
> Where souls are free, and men oppress no more!

Mary Robinson (1758–1800), 'The Linnet's Petition', in *Poems* (1775); 'The Negro Girl', in *Poetical Works of the Late Mary Robinson* (1806)

Mary Robinson's life was an extraordinary one, and she lived the excesses of the English Regency in every aspect of her thought and writing. From 1776 to 1783 she was, periodically, the most celebrated actress in England, and one of the most celebrated beauties in Europe. Her performance as Perdita in the *Winter's Tale* led to the Prince of Wales's infatuation with her and a subsequent massively publicized liaison which had burned itself out in a year. Her subsequent career as stage writer, novelist, woman of fashion, mistress, and finally recluse has often been rehearsed. The ups and downs of Robinson's stage career and amatory experience have, however, tended to drown out the extent to which she was a serious literary player for nearly twenty years during a period when London was uniquely saturated with literary genius. That Robinson was no intellectual lightweight is testified to by the fact that she was admired and befriended by some of the great thinkers and poets of the age. That the socialite and pseudo-radical satirist John Wolcot (Peter Pindar) should have been an admirer is not that surprising but her deep friendship with William Godwin and Mary Wollstonecraft certainly is. Coleridge was also a fan, although his praise of her indicates both her strengths and weaknesses. When he observed of her 'I never knew a human being with so *full* a mind—bad, good and indifferent, I grant you, but full and overflowing,' he suggests that the distinguishing feature is energy of mind, not necessarily quality of mind. Certainly her vast output of poems, plays, and novels is primarily distinguished by the apparent indefatigability which produced it. Yet Robinson's saturation in the spirit of the age, and her lively interest in contemporary politics, led to some extraordinary poems, many focused on the suffering of the poor. She held passionate beliefs on individual liberty. Albeit sentimental, 'The Linnet's Petition' indicates a conventional ability to extend libertarian argument to the whole of creation. This approach anticipates what was to become a commonplace of abolition polemic, the paralleling of the rights of animals and the rights of slaves. Given her championing of the socially and politically disenfranchised Robinson inevitably became influenced by abolition propaganda and felt the need to write about the slave's suffering. Her most central treatment of the theme 'The Negro Girl' displays the elements of emotional excess, and the Gothic trappings that hang about most of her poetry. Yet in focusing so exclusively upon the sufferings of the female slave deprived of her male lover this poem opened the way for a brand of abolition verse written almost exclusively by white women and exploring the suffering of black women. The climax of this development within Anglo-American abolition was Elizabeth Barrett Browning's *The Runaway Slave* (see pp. 356–64).

The Linnet's Petition

I

As Stella sat the other day,
    Beneath a myrtle shade,
A tender bird in plaintive notes,
    Address'd the pensive maid.

II

Upon a bough in gaudy cage,
    The feather'd warbler hung,
And in melodious accents thus,
    His fond petition sung.

III

"Ah! pity my unhappy fate,
    And set a captive free,
So may you never feel the loss,
    Of peace, or liberty."

The Negro Girl

Dark was the dawn, and o'er the deep
    The boist'rous whirlwinds blew;
The Sea-bird wheel'd its circling sweep,
    And all was drear to view—
When on the beach that binds the western shore
The love-lorn ZELMA stood, list'ning the tempest's roar.

Her eager Eyes beheld the main,
   While on Her DRACO dear
She madly call'd, but call'd in vain,
   No sound could DRACO hear,
Save the shrill yelling of the fateful blast,
While ev'ry Seaman's heart quick shudder'd as it past.

White were the billows, wide display'd
   The clouds were black and low;
The Bittern shriek'd, a gliding shade
   Seem'd o'er the waves to go!
The livid flash illum'd the clam'rous main,
While ZELMA pour'd, unmark'd her melancholy strain.

"Be still!" she cries, "loud tempest cease!
   O! spare the gallant souls!"
The thunder rolls—the winds increase—
   The Sea like mountains rolls.
While from the deck the storm-worn victims leap,
And o'er their struggling limbs the furious billows sweep.

"O! barb'rous Pow'r! relentless Fate!
   Does Heaven's high will decree
That some should sleep on beds of state—
   Some in the roaring Sea?
Some nurs'd in splendour deal Oppression's blow,
While worth and DRACO pine—in Slavery and woe!

"Yon vessel oft has plough'd the main
   With human traffic fraught;
Its cargo—our dark Sons of pain—
   For worldly treasure bought!
What had they done? O Nature tell me why
Is taunting scorn the lot of thy dark progeny?

"Thou gav'st, in thy caprice, the Soul
   Peculiarly enshrin'd;
Nor from the ebon Casket stole
   The Jewel of the mind!
Then wherefore let the suff'ring Negro's breast
Bow to his fellow MAN, in brighter colours drest.

"Is it the dim and glossy hue
   That marks him for despair?

While men with blood their hands embrue,
　　And mock the wretch's pray'r,
Shall guiltless Slaves the scourge of tyrants feel,
And, e'en before their GOD! unheard, unpitied kneel.

"Could the proud rulers of the land
　　Our Sable race behold;
Some bow'd by Torture's giant hand,
　　And others basely sold!
Then would they pity Slaves, and cry, with shame,
What'er their TINTS may be, their SOULS are still the same!

"Why seek to mock the Ethiop's face?
　　Why goad our hapless kind?
Can features alienate the race—
　　Is there no kindred mind?
Does not the cheek which vaunts the roseate hue
Oft blush for crimes that Ethiops never knew?

"Behold! the angry waves conspire
　　To check the barb'rous toil!
While wounded Nature's vengeful ire
　　Roars round this trembling Isle!
And hark! her voice re-echoes in the wind—
Man was not form'd by Heav'n to trample on his kind!

"Torn from my mother's aching breast,
　　My Tyrant sought my love—
But in the grave shall ZELMA rest,
　　Ere she will faithless prove;
No, DRACO!—Thy companion I will be
To that celestial realm where Negros shall be free!

"The Tyrant WHITE MAN taught my mind
　　The letter'd page to trace;
He taught me in the Soul to find
　　No tint, as in the face:
He bade my reason blossom like the tree—
But fond affection gave the ripen'd fruits to thee.

"With jealous rage he mark'd my love;
　　He sent thee far away;
And prison'd in the plantain grove
　　Poor ZELMA pass'd the day;

But ere the moon rose high above the main
ZELMA and Love contriv'd to break the Tyrant's chain.

"Swift, o'er the plain of burning Sand
   My course I bent to thee;
And soon I reach'd the billowy strand
   Which bounds the stormy Sea.
DRACO! my Love! Oh yet thy ZELMA's soul
Springs ardently to thee, impatient of controul.

"Again the lightning flashes white
   The rattling cords among!
Now, by the transient vivid light,
   I mark the frantic throng!
Now up the tatter'd shrouds my DRACO flies.
While o'er the plunging prow the curling billows rise.

"The topmast falls—three shackled slaves
   Cling to the Vessel's side!
Now lost amid the madd'ning waves—
   Now on the mast they ride—
See! on the forecastle my DRACO stands,
And now he waves his chain, now clasps his bleeding hands.

"Why, cruel WHITE-MAN! when away
   My sable Love was torn,
Why did you let poor ZELMA stay,
   On Afric's sands to mourn?
No! ZELMA is not left, for she will prove
In the deep troubled main her fond—her faithful Love."

The lab'ring Ship was now a wreck,
   The shrouds were flutt'ring wide;
The rudder gone, the lofty deck
   Was rock'd from side to side—
Poor ZELMA's eyes now dropp'd their last big tear,
While from her tawny cheek the blood recoil'd with fear.

Now frantic, on the sands she roam'd,
   Now shrieking stopp'd to view
Where high the liquid mountains foam'd
   Around the exhausted crew—
'Till, from the deck, her DRACO's well-known form
Sprung 'mid the yawning waves, and buffetted the storm.

Long, on the swelling surge sustain'd,
  Brave DRACO sought the shore,
Watch'd the dark Maid, but ne'er complain'd,
  Then sunk, to gaze no more!
Poor ZELMA saw him buried by the wave,
And, with her heart's true Love, plung'd in a wat'ry grave.

William Roscoe (1753–1831), from *Mount Pleasant* (1777); from *The Wrongs of Africa* (1787)

Roscoe was born in Liverpool in exactly the year that John Newton (pp. 77–80) sailed into Liverpool on his final voyage as captain of a slave ship. Roscoe remained in Liverpool his whole life and became a successful attorney at the court of King's Bench, then a banker and, briefly, an MP. Yet throughout his varied careers he also remained a central figure in the cultural establishment of the vastly expanding slave port. Roscoe's artistic and literary tastes were remarkably varied. He tried to establish a variety of societies and projects around printing and design in Liverpool. He also developed a serious interest in botany. Throughout his adult life Roscoe wrote, in many different forms and disciplines. He wrote occasional political pamphlets including the excoriating *Strictures on Mr Burke's Two Letters* which coolly laid bare the barmy assumptions driving Burke's *Letters on the Regicide Peace*. Roscoe also produced important botanical studies, and works of Renaissance history. His profound humanism and philanthropic disposition made it inevitable that he should see a terrible contradiction at the heart of Liverpool's newly found prosperity.

Mount Pleasant is an ambitious work that meditates upon the workings of commerce. The poem famously considers the moral implications of Liverpool's massively expanding wealth, given that this wealth was founded upon the slave trade, a trade which Liverpool had come to dominate internationally in the period 1750–80. Roscoe wrote several subsequent poems attacking the trade during the late 1780s, when abolition publication was at its height. His *Wrongs of Africa* is distinguished by the breadth of the moral and sociological perspectives with which the Atlantic slave trade is treated although the narrative shifts are handled with great crudity. Roscoe's slavery poetry may finally appear stiff and over-declamatory, but it reflects the profound liberationist philosophy of a brave anti-slavery activist. Of all the centres of the slave trade Liverpool was, as Thomas Clarkson found, the most ruthless, intransigent, hard bitten, and violent. Throughout a long career as writer and activist Roscoe attacked Liverpool's slaving economy with energy and common sense. When he was elected MP at the end of 1806 he went in on what was a highly controversial anti-slave trade ticket. He openly supported the finally successful abolition bill through Parliament in 1807, and returned to Liverpool in a public triumph. This infuriated local seamen and a violent riot ensued in which a magistrate was stabbed, and many anti-slavery supporters were bludgeoned, although Roscoe himself escaped injury. Roscoe's open support of abolition effectively terminated his political career; he was never re-elected. He maintained his anti-slavery position but died in 1831, three years before slavery was officially ended in the British sugar colonies.

from *Mount Pleasant*

When WINDSOR-FOREST's loveliest scenes decay,
Still shall they live in POPE's unrivall'd lay.[1]
Led on by Hope an equal theme I choose:
—O might the subject boast an equal Muse!
Then should her name the force of time defy,
When sunk in ruin LIVERPOOL shall lie.

   How numerous now her thronging buildings rise!
What varied objects strike the wandering eyes!
Where rise yon masts her crowded navies ride,
And the broad rampire checks the beating tide;
Along the beach her spacious streets extend,
Her areas open, and her spires ascend;

      .   .   .   .   .

   Far as the eye can trace the prospect round,
The splendid tracks of opulence are found:
Yet scarce an hundred annual rounds have run,
Since first the fabric of this power begun

      .   .   .   .   .

   Now o'er the wondering world her name resounds,
From Northern climes, to INDIA's distant bounds.
—Where-e'er his shores the broad ATLANTIC laves;
Where-e'er the BALTIC rolls his wintry waves;
Where-e'er the honour'd flood extends his tide,
That clasps SICILIA like a favour'd bride;
Whose waves in ages past so oft have bore
The storm of battle on the Punic[2] shore;

---

[1] Alexander Pope published his 'Windsor-Forrest' in 1713, and the poem was soon accepted as the most perfect Augustan pastoral.
[2] Carthaginian, from ancient Carthage. Because the Romans constructed the Carthaginians as deceitful and treacherous 'Punic' also carries these associations.

Have wash'd the banks of GREECE's learned bow'rs,
And view'd at distance ROME's imperial tow'rs;
In every clime her prosperous fleets are known,
She makes the wealth of every clime her own:
GREENLAND for her its bulky whale resigns,
And temperate GALLIA[3] rears her generous vines;
'Midst warm IBERIA[4] citron-orchards blow,
And the ripe fruitage bends the laboring bough:
The OCCIDENT[5] a richer tribute yields,
Far diffcrent produce swells their cultured fields;
Hence the strong cordial that inflames the brain,
The honey'd sweetness of the juicy cane,
The vegetative fleece,[6] the azure dye,
And every product of a warmer sky.

There AFRIC's swarthy sons their toils repeat,
Beneath the fervors of the noon-tide heat;
Torn from each joy that crown'd their native soil,
No sweet reflections mitigate their toil;
From morn, to eve, by rigorous hands opprest,
Dull fly their hours, of every hope unblest.
Till, broke with labour, helpless, and forlorn,
From their weak grasp the lingering morsel torn;
The reed-built hovel's friendly shade deny'd;
The jest of folly, and the scorn of pride;
Drooping beneath meridian suns they lie,
Lift the faint head, and bend th' imploring eye;
Till Death, in kindness, from the tortur'd breast
Calls the free spirit to the realms of rest.

Shame to Mankind! But shame to BRITONS most,
Who all the sweets of Liberty can boast;
Yet, deaf to every human claim, deny
That bliss to others, which themselves enjoy:
Life's bitter draught with harsher bitter fill;
Blast every joy, and add to every ill;
The trembling limbs with galling iron bind,
Nor loose the heavier bondage of the mind.

---

[3] Derived from the Latin name for France.   [4] Latin name for Spain.
  [5] The quarter of the sky in which the heavenly bodies set. The West, as opposed to the Orient, or East.
   [6] A locution for the cotton plant, raw cotton when it bursts from the pod resembling a sheep's fleece.

Yet whence these horrors? this inhuman rage,
That brands with blackest infamy the age?
Is it, our varied interests disagree,
And BRITAIN sinks if AFRIC's sons be free?
—No—Hence a few superfluous stores we claim,
That tempt our avarice, but increase our shame;
The sickly palate touch with more delight,
Or swell the senseless riot of the night.—
—Blest were the days ere Foreign Climes were known,
Our wants contracted, and our wealth our own;
When Health could crown, and Innocence endear,
The temperate meal, that cost no eye a tear:
Our drink, the beverage of the chrystal flood,
—Not madly purchas'd by a brother's blood—
Ere the wide spreading ills of Trade began,
Or Luxury trampled on the rights of Man.

When COMMERCE, yet an infant, rais'd her head,
'T was mutual want her growing empire spread:
Those mutual wants a distant realm supply'd,
And like advantage every clime enjoy'd.
Distrustless then of every treacherous view,
An open welcome met the stranger crew;
And whilst the whitening fleet approach'd to land,
The wondering natives hail'd them from the strand;
Fearless to meet, amidst the flow of soul,
The lurking dagger, or the poison'd bowl.

Now, more destructive than a blighting storm,
A bloated monster, Commerce rears her form;
Throws the meek olive from her daring hand,
Grasps the red sword, and whirls the flaming brand:
True to no faith; by no restraints controul'd;
By guilt made cautious, and by avarice bold.
Each feature reddens with the tinge of shame,
Whilst PATNA's[7] plain, and BUXAR's[8] fields I name;
How droops BENGAL beneath Oppression's reign!
How groans ORISSA[9] with the weight of slain!

[7] A town in what is now north-eastern India, Bihar state, mainly on the Ganga.
[8] Area of India in Bihar. British victory in a war here enabled British imperial control of the whole of Bengal.
[9] Orissa in east central India, Bay of Bengal. When Roscoe was writing the area was notorious for

To glut her rage, what thousands there have bled,
What thrones are vacant, and what princes dead!
In vain may War's relenting fury spare,
Attendant Famine follows in the rear;
And the poor natives but survive, to know
The lingering horrors of severer woe.
—Can this be she, who promis'd once to bind
In leagues of strictest amity, mankind?
This fiend, whose breath inflames the spark of strife,
And pays with trivial toys the price of life?

from *The Wrongs of Africa*

PART I

Offspring of love divine, Humanity!
To whom, his eldest born, th' Eternal gave
Dominion o'er the heart; and taught to touch
Its varied stops in sweetest unison;
And strike the string that from a kindred breast
Responsive vibrates! from the noisy haunts
Of mercantile confusion, where thy voice
Is heard not; from the meretricious glare
Of crowded theatres, where in thy place
Sits Sensibility, with wat'ry eye,
Dropping o'er fancied woes her useless tear;
Come thou, and weep with me substantial ills;
And execrate the wrongs, that Afric's sons,
Torn from their natal shore, and doom'd to bear
The yoke of servitude in western climes,
Sustain. Nor vainly let our sorrows flow,
Nor let the strong emotion rise in vain,
But may the kind contagion widely spread,
Till in its flame the unrelenting heart
Of Avarice, melt in softest sympathy;—
And one bright blaze of universal love,
In grateful incense, rises up to heaven.

bloody interventions by the British, and Orissa was finally 'conquered' by the British in 1803, a few years after this poem was written.

Form'd with the same capacity of pain,
The same desire of pleasure and of ease,
Why feels not man for man? When nature shrinks
From the slight puncture of an insect's sting,
Faints if not screen'd from sultry suns, and pines
Beneath the hardship of an hour's delay
Of needful nutriment; when liberty

.   .   .   .   .   .

Is priz'd so dearly, that the slightest breath
That ruffles but her mantle, can awake
To arms, unwarlike nations, and can rouse
Confederate states to vindicate her claims;
How shall the sufferer man, his fellow doom
To ills he mourns, or spurns at? tear with stripes
His quivering flesh; with hunger and with thirst
Waste his emaciate frame? in ceaseless toils
Exhaust his vital powers; and bind his limbs
In galling chains? Shall he whose fragile form
Demands continual blessings, to support
Its complicated texture; air, and food,
Raiment, alternate rest, and kindly skies,
And healthful seasons, dare with impious voice
To ask those mercies, whilst his selfish aim
Arrests the general freedom of their course?
And gratified beyond his utmost wish,
Debars another from the bounteous store?
But thou, the master of the sable crew!
Lord of their lives and ruler of their fate,
For whom they toil and bleed! what powers unknown
Of keen enjoyment can thy nature boast,
That thus thy single bliss can grasp the sum
Of hapless numbers, sacrificed to thee?
—Say, can their tears delight thee? Can their groans
Add poignance to thy pleasures? Or when death
Alarms thee with his summons, canst thou add
The total of their ravish'd lives to thine?
Or spring not rather thy detested joys,
From some perversion of each nobler sense
Indulgent nature gave thee? For the glow
Of melting charity, that looks on all
With eyes impartial; and receives delight

Most exquisite, whene'er her ready aid
Diffuses gladness, or represses pain,
Thro' the minutest particle of life;
Feels not thine harden'd breast a horrid bliss
In the wild shriek of anguish? in the groan
Of speechless misery? Hence with tyrant voice
Thou bidst the trembling victim to thy wrath
Devoted, writhe beneath the torturing whip,
Or for some trivial fault, (to which compar'd
The daily crime, which thou without remorse
Committ'st against him, is as oceans depth,
To the shoal current of the scantiest rill)
To mutilation doom'st him, and to death.
—Dear to the heart is freedom's generous flame,
And dear th' exulting glow, that warms the soul,
When struggling virtue from the tyrant's grasp
Indignant rushes, and asserts her rights;
But for this nameless transport, thou hast found
A gloomy substitute, and from the depths
Of loathsome dungeons, manacles, and chains,
Canst draw strange pleasure, and preposterous joy.
And thou th' inferior minister of ill!
Inferior in degree, but in thy scorn
Of every milder virtue, in the love
Of rapine, and the quenchless thirst of gold
His more than equal! O'er th' Atlantic deep,
That rolls in vain to screen its eastern shores
From thy fierce purpose, on thou plough'st thy way;
And firm, and fearless, as thy voyage were meant
On messages of mercy, seest unmov'd
The lightnings glare, and hear'st the thunders roll,
Regardless of their threats; when o'er the main,
Rides in dread state the equinoctial blast,
And swells th' insulted ocean, when thy bark
(The thin partition 'twixt thy fate and thee)
Labours thro' all her frame, and loudly threats
Thine instantaneous doom; thou still preserv'st
Thine execrable aim; nor storms, nor fire,
Nor fell diseases, nor impending death,
Arrest thy purpose; till the distant shores
Of hapless Afric open on thy sight.

From northern Gambia, to the southern climes
Of sad ANGOLA, lie the fated lands,
Whose genius mourns thy coming: wak'd by him,
In vain the elemental fury rag'd,
For thou hast triumph'd: joyful on the strand,
His sable sons receive thy wearied crew;
And bid them share their vegetable store,
Pow'rful to purify the tainted blood
And grateful to the palate, long inur'd
To nutriment half putrid: in return,
Thou to their dazzled sight disclosest wide
Thy magazine of wonders, cull'd with care,
From all the splendid trifles, that adorn
Thine own luxurious region; mimic gems
That emulate the true; fictitious gold
To various uses fashion'd, pointing out
Wants which before they knew not; mirrors bright,
Reflecting to their quick and curious eye
Their sable features; shells, and beads, and rings,
And all fantastic folly's gingling bells,
That catch'd th' unpractis'd ear, and thence convey
Their unsuspected poison to the mind.
Yet not delightless pass'd their cloudless days.
The cheerful natives, ere the wasteful rage
Of European avarice chang'd the scene;
—Strangers alike to luxury and toil,
They, with assiduous labour, never woo'd
A coy and stubborn soil, that gave its fruits
Reluctant; but on some devoted day,
Perform'd the task, that for their future lives
Suffic'd, and to the moist and vigorous earth
The youthful shoots committed: fervid suns,
And plenteous showers, the rising juices sent
Thro' all the turgid branches; and ere long,
Screen'd from the scorching beam, beneath the shade
Himself had rais'd, the careless planter sat;
And from the bending branches cropt the fruit;
More grateful to his unperverted taste,
Than all that glads the glutton's pamper'd meal.
Nor was amusement wanting; oft at morn,
Lord of his time, the healthful native rose,

And seiz'd his faithful bow, and took his way
Midst tangled woods, or over distant plains,
To pierce the murd'rous Pard; when glowing noon
Pour'd its meridian fervors, in cool shades
He slept away th' uncounted hours, till eve
Recall'd him home; then midst the village train
He join'd the mazy dance; then all his pow'rs
Were wak'd to action; vigorous and alert,
He bounded o'er the plain; or in due time
Plied his unwearied feet, and beat his hands;
Whilst bursts of laughter, and loud shouts of joy,
Spoke the keen pleasures of th' admiring throng.

But when the active labours of the chace
No more delighted, in the shady bower
Idly industrious, sat reclin'd at ease
The sable artist; to the jav'lin's shaft,
The ebon staff, or maple goblet, gave
Fantastic decorations; simply carv'd,
Yet not inelegant: beneath his hands,
Oft too a cloth of firmer texture grew,
That steep'd in azure, mocks the brittle threads,
And fleeting tincture, of our boasted arts.
The task, perform'd beneath no master's eye,
Of trivial worth esteem'd, successive months
Unfinish'd saw, whilst objects interven'd,
Deem'd more important: that by grateful change,
Cheer'd the slow progress of his guiltless life.

Nor yet unknown to more refin'd delights,
Nor to the soft and social feelings lost,
Was the swart African: wherever man
Erects his dwelling, whether on the bleak
And frozen cliffs of Zembla's northern coast,
Or in meridian regions; Love attends
And shares his habitation: in his train
Come fond affections, come endearing joys,
And confidence, and tenderness, and truth;
For not to polish'd life alone confin'd,
Are these primaeval blessings; rather there
Destroyed, or injured; mercenary ties
There bind ill suited tempers; avarice there,

And pride, and low'ring superstition, cross
The tender union; but where nature reigns,
And universal freedom, love exults
As in his native clime; there aims secure
His brightest arrow, steep'd in keen delights,
To cultur'd minds, and colder skies, unknown.

Dark, and portentous, as the sable cloud,
That bears unseen contagion on its wings,
And drops destruction on the race of man,
Came the foul plague, that, brought from Europe, spread
O'er Afric's peaceful shores, with sudden change
Perverting good, to evil: at the sight
Nature recoil'd, and tore with frantic hands
Her own immortal features: broke at once,
Were all the bonds of social life, and rage,
And deadly hatred, and uncheck'd revenge,
In every bosom burn'd. The dance, the song
Were now no more, for treachery's secret snare
Impended o'er their revels, and distrust
Had alienated man from man: no more,
At early dawn, o'er hills and plains unknown,
The hunter took his solitary range,
Lest, fiercer than the tyger or the pard,
He there shou'd meet his fellows, and become
Himself the prey. Then mutual wars arose,
And neighbouring states, that never knew before
A motive of contention, took the field;
Not with the glorious hope of conquest fir'd,
But with detested avarice, to purloin
Their foes, and sell to Europe's shameless race,
Their unoffending neighbours; soon themselves
To share their lot, and mourn the self-same chains.

PART II

.   .   .   .   .   .

—Yes, thanks to man; whose follies, and whose crimes,
Change the fair face of nature, and pervert
Her dearest gifts to evil:—breathes the air
Its healthful fragrance, his misguided rage
With foul contagion loads its dropping wings,

Swept from the carnage of the reeking field.
O'er the broad ocean, whose encircling arms
Were meant to join the far dissever'd land
In friendly intercourse, and wide diffuse
The blessings of each different state to all,
His mad ambition, sends in dread array,
His messengers of terror; prompt to pour
Their fiery vengeance, on each distant shore,
Whose natives, to his absolute command,
Their soil, their produce, liberties, and lives,
Resign not. He, amidst the spicy climes
Of Asia, where prolific nature pours
Her unappropriate, and superfluous wealth,
Within his hoarded magazine confines
A nation's produce; and around its doors,
With lifted hands, and unaccusing voice,
Hears the meek native supplicate for food,
And bids him perish; and, as tho' he fear'd
Some happier spot of earth should yet remain,
That bore not bleeding witness of his guilt,
He, from their parent-shore, relentless tears
The sons of Afric; to the madding wave,
To strange diseases, to the piercing taunts
Of wanton insolence, and all the wrongs
That man from man can suffer, dooms their days!

Deep freighted now with human merchandize,
The vessel quits the shore; prepar'd to meet
The storms, and dangers, of th' Atlantick main;
Her motion scarce observ'd, save when the flood
In frequent murmurs beats against her prow,
And the tall cocoas slowly seem to change
Their former station. Lessening on the sight,
The distant mountains bow'd their cloud capt heads;
And all the bright and variegated scene,
Of hills, and groves, and lawns, and reed-built sheds,
That oft had caught the prisoner's ardent eye,
Not hopeless of escape, now gradual sunk
To one dim hue. Amongst the sable tribes
Soon spread th' alarm; when sudden from the depths
Of crouded holds, and loathsome caverns, rose

One universal yell, of dread despair,
And anguish inexpressible; for now
Hope's slender thread was broke; extinguished now
The spark of expectation, that had lurk'd
Beneath the ashes of their former joys,
And o'er despondency's surrounding gloom,
Had shed its languid lustre. Bold, and fierce,
Of high indignant spirit, some their chains
Shook menacing, and from their low'ring eyes,
Flash'd earnest of the flame that burnt within:
Whilst groans, and loud laments, and scalding tears,
Mark'd the keen pangs of others.—Female shrieks,
At intervals, in dreadful concert heard,
To wild distraction manly sorrow turn'd;
And ineffectual, o'er their heedless limbs,
Was wav'd the wiry whip, that dropp'd with blood.

Now sunk the mournful day; but mournful still
The night that followed: and the rising morn,
That spread before the hopeless captives view,
Nought, but the wide expanse of air, and sea,
Heard all their cries with double rage renew'd.
Nor did the storm of headstrong passions rest,
Till the third evening clos'd; nor by degrees
Was hush'd; but sudden as th' autumnal blast,
Its rage exhausted sinks at once to rest;
Whilst the wide wood, that bow'd beneath its course,
Declines its wearied branches, thus the strife
Ceas'd—not a groan, and not a voice was heard;
But, as one soul had influenc'd every breast,
A sullen stillness reign'd. Resign'd and mild,
As if forgot their former sense of wrong,
They took the scanty fare they lately spurn'd;
And if a tear should mingle with their food,
No prying eye perceiv'd it: day by day
Saw the same scene renew'd; whilst prosperous gales
Full towards her destin'd port the vessel bore;
And gently breathing o'er the seaman's mind,
Came the remembrance of his native land;
The thoughts of former pleasures, former friends,
Of rest and independance; heedless he,

That on the miseries of others, rose
The fabrick of his joys; and gratified
His selfish views, whilst multitudes bewail'd
Th' eternal loss of nature's dearest gifts;
To them irreparable wrong, to him
A slight accession to his stores of bliss.

'Twas night; and now the ship, with steady course,
Pursued her midway voyage; subsided now
The tyrant's dread, a more indulgent lot
The slaves experienc'd; and their chains relax'd
Their biting cincture. Fearless trod the deck
The unsuspicious guard; whilst, from below,
Amidst the croud of captives, not a sound
Of louder note ascended. Yet, even then,
Each eye was wake, and ev'ry heaving breast
Was panting for revenge. For now approach'd
The awful hour, long hop'd for, long forefix'd,
Sacred to vengeance, to the thirst of blood,
And bitter retribution. Slowly roll'd
The moments, whilst with anxious minds, the slaves
Waited the voice that loos'd them from restraint,
And turn'd them on their tyrants: not more prompt
The nitrous grain, that, at the touch of fire,
Bursts in resistless flame. Nor yet the voice
Is heard; but thro' each deep and dark recess
A hollow murmur rises, that upbraids
The long delay—nor yet the voice is heard!
Whilst in each agitated breast, by turns,
Dismay, and doubt, and desperation reign;
And fancy, now triumphant, now depress'd,
Luxuriant wantons thro' the scene of blood,
Or feels the fiery torture.—"Rise, revenge,
Revenge your wrongs," th' expected voice exclaims,
And meets a ready answer, from the tongues
Of countless numbers, from each gloomy cell,
In dreadful cries return'd. But who shall tell
The wild commotion; who the frantic rage
Of savage fury, when, with joint accord,
They burst th' opposing gratings, and pour'd forth,
Impetuous as the flood that breaks its mound?

—What tho' unarm'd!—upon th' unsparing steel
They rush'd regardless; and th' expected wound
Deep, but not always deadly, rous'd their minds
To fiercer desperation: thronging close,
Fearless, and firm, they join'd th' unequal war;
And when the fatal weapon pierc'd their side,
They struggled to retain it, and in death
Disarm'd the hand that conquer'd.—Thick they fell,
But oft not unreveng'd, for fastening close
Upon the foe some gain'd the vessel's side,
And rush'd together to a wat'ry death;
Whilst from the yawning hold, emerging throngs
Replac'd the vanquish'd, and, with hideous cries,
Struck terror thro' the tyrants chilling veins,
And bad oppression tremble. Nerveless stood
The harden'd seamen: but recovering soon,
They gain'd the barrier, that across the deck
Its firm defence projected; then began
The scene of blood; then pour'd amongst the slaves,
Frantic, and fierce, and madding with their wrongs,
The volley'd vengeance; whilst without a foe,
Misguided courage urg'd the strife in vain;
And check'd by hands unseen, relax'd its powers
In sudden weakness.—Terror, and surprise,
Like deadly blood-hounds, seiz'd the vanquish'd crew,
That stood defenceless, and expos'd, the mark
Of uncontroll'd revenge; and as they fell,
Without reluctance saw the purple stream,
Slow welling from the fount of life, and join'd
In kindred currents pour along the deck,
Tinging with guiltless blood the western wave.

But hark! the sound of conquest and of joy
Bursts from th' exulting victors.—Hark again!
The thrice repeated triumph, tells the heavens,
That innocence once more has felt the fangs,
Th' insatiate fangs of guilt, and weeps in blood
Her just resistance, and her rightful aims!

Peace to your shades, ye favour'd train, who fell
Amidst the generous struggle! o'er whose limbs
The friendly hand of Death has interpos'd

His fated curtain; that, nor human force,
Nor human malice, nor the deep regret
Of disappointed avarice, nor the pang
Of keen remorse, that gnaws the murderer's peace,
And blasts his future joys, can e'er remove.
—Secure beneath its guardian gloom, ye sleep,
In undisturb'd repose: no more ye start
At misery's kindred shriek; no more ye weep
O'er fond domestic ties, untimely torn;
No longer from th' oppressor's hand, ye ask
The slender pittance, that prolongs your lives
To lengthen'd anguish; nor for you prepares,
Th' unfeeling planter, 'midst his cultur'd isles,
(Isles moist with tears, and fertiliz'd with blood)
His whips, his racks, his gibbets, and his chains.
—Yours is the palm of conquest;—you have found
A shelter from the hovering storm, that waits
Your less successful fellows; who lament,
And vainly wish to share your happier lot.

Bryan Edwards (1743–1800), 'Stanzas, Occasioned by the Death of ALICO, an African Slave, Condemned for Rebellion, in Jamaica, 1760' (1777); 'Ode on Seeing a Negro Funeral' (1777); 'Inscription at the Entrance of a Burial Ground for Negro Slaves' (c.1776)

Edwards was famously described by Wilberforce as a 'powerful opponent of the slave trade abolition'. Edwards emerged as one of the most effective of the pro-slavery advocates within the West India lobby because of the combination of a number of factors. He had been relatively well educated first in a French boarding school in Bristol and then by a private tutor in Jamaica, and was an unusually erudite opponent of abolition. He also had an unusual knowledge of the politics surrounding slavery both in the West Indies and in Europe. Finally as a polemicist for the slave interest he is exceptional in the common sense of his arguments and the linguistic restraint in which they were framed. Edwards's two-volume *History, Civil and Commercial of the British Colonies in the West Indies* was marked out by all of these qualities. It was indeed only with the occurrence of the slave revolution in San Domingue in the early 1790s that Edwards moved into a more openly propagandistic rhetoric. Edwards's *Historical Survey of the French Colony in the Island of San Domingue* of 1797 was one of the most hard-hitting pieces of atrocity literature to come out of British reaction to the Haytian revolution. Blacks, when contaminated by popular Jacobinism, are painted as inhuman monsters. Yet the main body of Edwards's work, including the poetry reproduced below, takes a far more benevolent approach to the depiction of the Caribbean slave. Edwards's early works show him to have believed that blacks were capable of intellectual and moral development, and he consequently believed in a very slow and gradual reform of Caribbean society, so that finally blacks would be prepared to 'look after themselves'. The combination of sentimentality and patronizing paternalism which mark Edwards's mythologization of slave life come out clearly in the three poems here.

The 'Inscription at the Entrance of a Burial Ground for Negro Slaves' which was taken up and printed in anti-slavery anthologies (see pp. 316–28) indicates that the literary codes used to describe white power and propriety can be shared by both the abolitionists and the slave power. The printing of the poem in the 1827 *Anti-Slavery Scrapbook* carried the following introduction by the editor:

> On a plantation in Jamaica, belonging to Bryan Edwards, his Negroes had chosen for their burial ground, a retired spot in a grove of pimento. It was a place extremely solemn and singularly beautiful; and B. Edwards directed, that in case of his death in Jamaica he should be buried in the midst of them. As the ground was exposed to the intrusion of cattle, he caused a fence to be raised round it, and inscribed these lines on the little wicket at the entrance.

The decorousness of Edwards's verse, and his gesture of desiring to be placed in the simple and beautiful burial ground of his slaves, are read by the abolition editor as attractive. His erection of a fence around the burial ground is seen as noble. But it is significant that the fence only goes up after we have been told that Edwards has decided that this will be his own burial ground should he die on his plantation. Why didn't he put the fence up before if he cared about the slaves' graves being disturbed by cattle? Then again what does this gesture of having his own tomb among his slaves mean? Is it a gesture testifying to a belief that beyond the grave there is no distinction between slave and master or is it a final proprietorial gesture?

The gestures of ownership extend into the poetry. The codes and burial rituals of the slaves, quiet, self-contained, private, are written over by the 'Inscription' Edwards now places over the graveyard, *his* graveyard. The inscription is in fact directed at a white readership, at the slave-owning class, and is a pompous justification by Edwards of his own decision to be buried in so unassuming and even 'unconsecrated' a spot. He also makes it clear that this is now not simply a slave burial ground but the precise equivalent of an English country churchyard. When he states that the sight is as sacred as an English church, although 'not here are found | The solemn aisle and consecrated ground', Edwards is in fact saying the opposite, that his presence has a transforming impact on the place. The final line is couched in terrible irony. The statement that 'o'er the turf-built shrine, | Where virtue sleeps, presides the Power Divine' is a conflation; we are not merely reminded of Edwards's God, there is a suggestion that Edwards is

God. It is Edwards who 'presides' over this burial ground, and as the embodiment of the power of life and death over the slaves when alive, he maintains authority as the Power Divine even in death. For his slaves even death offers no escape.

Stanzas, Occasioned by the Death of ALICO, an African Slave, Condemned for Rebellion, in Jamaica, 1760

I

'Tis past:—Ah! calm thy cares and rest!
  Firm and unmoved am I:
In freedom's cause I bar'd my breast—
  In freedom's cause I die.

II

Ah stop! thou dost me fatal wrong—
  Nature will yet rebel;
For I have loved thee very long,
  And loved thee very well.

III

To native skies and peaceful bow'rs,
  I soon shall wing my way;
Where joy shall lead the circling hours,
  Unless too long they stay.

IV

O speed, fair sun! thy course divine;
  My Abala remove—
There thy bright beams shall ever shine,
  And I forever love!

V

On those blest shores a slave no more!
  In peaceful ease I'll stray;
Or rouse to chase the mountain boar,
  As unconfined as day!

VI

No Christian tyrant there is known
  To mark his steps with blood,

Nor sable mis'ry's piercing moan
　　Resounds thro' ev'ry wood!

VII

Yet have I heard the melting tongue,
　　Have seen the falling tear;
Known the good heart by pity wrung,
　　Ah! that such hearts are rare!

VIII

Now, Christian, glut thy ravish't eyes—
　　I reach the joyful hour;
Now bid the scorching flames arise,
　　And these poor limbs devour.

IX

But know pale tyrant, 'tis not thine
　　Eternal war to wage;
The death thou giv'st shall but combine
　　To mock thy baffled rage.

X

O death, how welcome to th'opprest!
　　Thy kind embrace I crave;
Thou bring'st to mis'ry's bosom rest,
　　And *freedom to the slave!*

Ode on Seeing a Negro Funeral

Omalco dies! o'er yonder plain
　　His bier is borne; the sable train
By youthful virgins led:
　　Daughters of injur'd Africk, say
Why raise ye thus th' heroic lay,
　　Why triumph o'er the dead?

No tear bedews their fixed eye!—
'Tis now the hero lives they cry,
　　Releas'd from slav'ry's chain:
Far o'er the billowy surge he flies,
And joyful views his native skies,
　　And long-lost bow'rs again.

On Koromantin's[1] palmy soil,
Heroic deeds and martial toil
   Shall fill each glorious day:
Love, fond and faithful, crown thy nights,
And artless joys, unbought delights,
    Past cruel wrongs repay.

Nor lordly pride's stern av'rice there,
Alone shall nature's bounties share;
   To all her children free:
For thee, the dulcet reed shall spring,
Her milky bowl the coco bring,
    Th'anana[2] bloom for thee.

The thunder, hark!—'Tis Africk's god!
He wakes; he lifts th'avenging rod,
   And speeds th' impatient hours:
From Niger's golden stream he calls;
Fair Freedom comes; oppression falls,
    And vengeance yet is ours!

Soon, Christian, thou, in wild dismay,
Of Africk's ruthless rage the prey,
   Shalt roam th'affrighted wood:
Transformed to tygers, fierce and fell,
Thy race shall prowl with savage yell,
    And glut their rage for blood!

But soft—beneath yon tam'rind shade,
Now let the hero's limbs be laid;
   Sweet slumbers bless the brave:
There shall the breeze spread perfume,
Nor livid light'nings blast the bloom
    That decks Omalco's grave.

---

[1] Koromantin, or Coromantee: black slaves from the coastal Ghanaian region Koromantin, where the British had built a slave fort. These slaves were renowned for their violent spirit, and in Jamaica for their adherence to Obeah.

[2] Pineapple.

Inscription at the Entrance of a Burial Ground for Negro Slaves

Stranger! whoe'er thou art, with reverence tread,
Lo! these, the silent mansions of the dead!
His life of labour o'er the wearied slave
Here finds at length, soft quiet in the grave.
View not with proud disdain the unsculptur'd heap,
Where injur'd innocence forgets to weep;
Nor idly deem, although not here are found
The solemn aisle and consecrated ground,
The spot less sacred;—o'er the turf-built shrine,
Where virtue sleeps, presides the Power Divine.

Thomas Chatterton (1752–70), *Heccar and Gaira: An African Eclogue* (written 1770, published 1778)

Chatterton's brief and largely obscure life is primarily remembered for his authorship of supposed antique poetry (mainly romances and ballads), and for his spectacularly miserable suicide in a garret. His death was rapidly constructed into an ideal of wasted genius by leading Romantics including Coleridge, Wordsworth, Shelley, and Keats. One thing typifies Chatterton's verse: its uncompromising otherworldliness. Virtually everything he wrote is separated, by apparently absolute barriers of fictive time, place, and diction, from the reality of a Britain saturated with signs of imperial expansion and the nascent Industrial Revolution. Chatterton spent the majority of his short life in Bristol, Britain's third largest slaving port after Liverpool and London, during the period when England dominated the Guinea trade. *Heccar and Gaira* is the one poem where Chatterton's peculiar sensibility was turned to consider the effects of slave trading on Africa.

Chatterton, very near the end of his life, composed three 'African Eclogues'. All of them use Africa as an exotic setting in order to pursue themes of doomed love and martial achievement. Africa provides a dramatic backdrop to these neo-Gothic narratives, in much the way in which Chatterton's immediate literary model, Collins's *Oriental Eclogues*, had reinvented the 'Orient'. Exotic nomenclature and essentialized, not to say mythologized, 'desart' and jungle settings are taken up with the same confident oblivion towards African culture which Collins showed toward his imagined 'Orient'. While in most essentials *Heccar and Gaira* conforms to late eighteenth-century stereotypes of African cultural misrepresentation it is unusual in its construction of the Atlantic slave trade. *Heccar and Gaira* is the only one of Chatterton's works to deal with the theme of African retribution. Significantly it was one of the few poems produced in English which full-bloodedly celebrates the abused African's right to perpetual 'Vengeance' as a result of the enormities of the slave trade. Chatterton is not, however, aware of the complexities of the African trade and of the extent to which a variety of Africans were complicit, a pro-slavery theme long used to justify the trade.

The poem is a loose dialogue between two African warriors. The poem opens with the warrior Gaira addressing 'the Companion of his soul' Heccar and the two of them talking of a terrible and insatiable desire for 'Vengeance'. The enemy they desire to annihilate is white, in fact the white slave traders who are responsible for kidnapping Cawna (Gaira's wife) and her children into slavery. When vengeance is discussed in later abolition poetry (see Cowper, pp. 87–8, 92; More, p. 108; Pratt, pp. 139–40; Edward Rushton's *West India Eclogues*) it is seen as God's prerogative. If the slave power is to be destroyed through violence it will be the violence of natural cataclysm, storm, earthquake, and resultant fire. The black, Caribbean slave or free African, only needs to sit back and wait for God to act. Chatterton's blacks do not require such divine intervention but are quite capable of bringing about their own violent justice. Chatterton is also unusual in this poem in working through a subtle negativizing of whites and whiteness. One hundred and fifty years before Aimé Césaire in the *Notebook of a Return to my Native Land* was to construct an ironic set of tropes for negative whiteness Chatterton suggests what can be done. It is only halfway through the poem that Chatterton makes it explicit that the 'reeking slain . . . pil'd in Mountains on the sanguine sand' are white bodies. These white bodies are first introduced not as beautiful flesh, but the stark white of bleached skeletons: 'The scatter'd bones mantled in silver White.' Both silver and white become increasingly associated with death, disease, and terror, the terror of the whites making them appear ghastly: 'Fear with a sick'ned Silver ting'd their hue.' White people emerge as spectral, unreal, a 'palid race' with 'languid face' who dare not look on the sun. Nature emerges strong and beautiful in single colour adjectives: 'the brown desart and the glossy green . . . the azure wave' among which the 'pallid shadows' of the 'Children of the Wave' vanish. White bodies only seem to gain form and beauty in this poem when dyed in blood. The final image of the dead white slave crew shows them to 'strew the Beaches' while their blood is seen to 'tinge the Lilly of their Features red'.

There were other poets who attempted to articulate extreme black revolutionary violence. The Jacobin sympathizer Percival Stockdale wrote occasional poems celebrating black insurrectionaries, and in this anthology Whitchurch's *Hispaniola* celebrates black vengeance on the planters through a spectral vision (pp. 178–80). What makes Chatterton's work exceptional, and finally disturbing, is the manner in which he uses the delicate peculiarities of his deliberately aestheticized and antiquated diction to describe the subject of the massacre of contemporary slave crews who were at that moment sailing to and from Bristol.

Heccar and Gaira: An African Eclogue[1]

Where the rough Caigra[2] rolls the surgy Wave,
Urging his Thunders thro' the echoing Cave
Where the sharp Rocks in distant Horror seen
Drive the white Currents thro' the spreading green
Where the loud Tiger pawing in his rage
Bids the black Archers of the wilds engage
Stretch'd on the Sand two panting Warriors lay
In all the burning Torments of the day
Their bloody Javlins reek'd a living Steem
Their bows were broken at the roaring stream
Heccar the Chief of Jarra's fruitful Hill
Where the dark Vapors nightly dews distil
Saw Gaira the Companion of his Soul
Extended where loud Caigra's Billows roll
Gaira the King of warring Archers found
Where daily Lightnings plow the sandy ground
Where brooding Tempests howl along the Sky
Where rising Desarts whirl'd in Circles fly

Heccar
Gaira 'tis useless to attempt the Chace
Swifter than hunted Wolves they urge the race
Their less'ning forms elude the straining Eye
Upon the Plumage of Macaws they fly
Let us return and Strip the reeking Slain
Leaving the Bodys on the burning Plain

Gaira
Heccar, my Vengeance still exclaims for blood
Twould drink a wider Stream than Caigra's flood
This Jav'lin oft in nobler Quarrels try'd
Put the loud thunder of their Arms aside
Fast as the streaming Rain I pour'd the dart
Hurling a Whirlwind thro' the trembling heart

---

[1]   A short pastoral poem, a classic example being Virgil's *Bucolics*.
[2]   Chatterton was using contemporary maps and atlases to glean the place names he uses throughout the *African Eclogues*. Some place names he seems to have adapted or even made up. Caigra probably refers to a river in the Congo.

But now my ling'ring Feet Revenge denies
O could I thro' my Javlin from my Eyes

Heccar
When Gaira the united Armys broke
Death wing'd the Arrow. Death impell'd the stroke.
See pil'd in Mountains on the sanguine sand
The blasted of the Lightnings of thy hand
Search the brown desart and the glossy green
There are the Trophys of thy Valor seen
The scatter'd bones mantled in silver White
Once animated dared thy force in fight
The Children of the Wave whose palid race
Views the faint Sun display a languid face
From the red fury of thy Justice fled
Swifter than Torrents from their rocky bed.
Fear with a sick'ned Silver ting'd their hue:
The guilty fear when Vengeance is their due

Gaira
Rouze not Remembrance from her shadwy Cell
Nor of those bloody Sons of Mischief tell
Cawna, O Cawna: deck'd in sable Charms
What distant region holds thee from my arms
Cawna the Pride of Afric's sultry Vales
Soft, as the cooling Murmur of the Gales
Majestic as the many color'd Snake
Trailing his Glorys thro' the blossom'd brake
Black as the glossy Rocks where Eascal roars
Foaming thro' sandy Wastes to Jagirs[3] Shores
Swift as the Arrow hasting to the breast
Was Cawna the Companion of my rest
The Sun sat lowring in the Western Sky
The Swelling Tempests spread around the Eye
Upon my Cawna's Bosom I reclin'd
Catching the breathing Whispers of the Wind
Swift from the Wood a prowling Tiger came
Dreadful his Voice his Eyes a glowing flame
I bent the Bow, the never erring dart
Pierc'd his rough Armor but escap'd his heart

---

[3] Eascal and Jagir are fictional African district names invented by Chatterton.

He fled tho' wounded to a distant Waste
I urg'd the furious flight with fatal haste
He fell he dy'd, spent in the fiery toil
I stripp'd his Carcase of the furry Spoil
And as the varied Spangles met my Eye
On this I cry'd shall my lov'd Cawna lie
The dusky Midnight hung the Skies in grey
Impelled by Love I wing'd the airy way
In the deep Valley and the mossy Plain
I sought my Cawna but I sought in vain
The palid shadows of the Azure Waves
Had made my Cawna and my Children slaves
Reflection maddens to recall the hour
The Gods had giv'n me to the Daemons[4] Power
The Dusk slow vanish'd from the hated Lawn
I gain'd a Mountain glaring with the Dawn
There the full Sails expanded to the Wind
Struck Horror and Distraction in my Mind
There Cawna mingled with a worthless train
In common slav'ry drags the hated Chain
Now judge my Heccar have I cause for Rage?
Should aught the thunder of my Arm asswage?
In ever reeking blood this Javlin dy'd
With Vengeance shall be never satisfied
I'll strew the Beaches with the mighty dead
And tinge the Lilly of their Features red

Heccar
When the loud shriekings of the hostile Cry
Roughly salute my Ear enrag'd I'll fly
Send the sharp Arrow quivering thro: the heart
Chill the hot Vitals with the venom'd dart
Nor heed the shining Steel or noisy smoke
Gaira and Vengeance shall inspire the stroke.

---

[4] See p. 21 n. 52.

John Newton (1725–1807), 'Amazing Grace', 'Alas! by Nature how Deprav'd', in *Olney Hymns* (1779); from *The Journal of a Slave Trader* ([1751–2] 1962); from *Thoughts upon the African Slave Trade* (1788)

Why include the hymn 'Amazing Grace' or any of *Olney Hymns* in an anthology about the poetry of slavery? Newton's beautiful hymns are locked into a spiritual dynamic of violent suffering, sin, guilt, pain, enslavement to sin, and ultimate redemption. His writings on slavery as both a slave captain and an abolitionist exist in peculiar and frequently agonized relation to these lovely lyrics. Read together they take us as close as written words can to understanding why the slave industry could be such an enormous and respectable operation for such a long time.

The bare facts of Newton's life are as follows. Born in 1725, his mother died when he was 7, and his father started taking him on voyages with him. At the age of 18 he was impressed onto a British warship, and although promoted to midshipman, deserted, was captured, flogged, and reduced to the ranks, and at his own request exchanged to a slaving boat in 1745. He ended up on the coast of Sierra Leone and effectively became the slave of a white slave factor in the Plantane islands, whose black African wife persecuted and brutalized Newton over a period of months. This became a central element in the fascination of his legend, and he became known as 'the white slave'. Newton was finally rescued by a friend of his father's in 1748. Up to this point Newton remembers himself as a godless and totally debauched character, but sailing home on 10 March 1748 he underwent an ecstatic Christian conversion.

He returned to England, married his childhood sweetheart Mary Catlett, and at this point entered the slave trade. From 1750 to 1753 he made three voyages as captain of slave vessels. During this period Newton kept a journal of his voyages for the ship's owners, a document in which he set down the day-to-day business events on his ship. At the same time that he was keeping the journal Newton was also composing emotionally highly complex love letters to Mary Catlett. In 1754 a convulsive fit convinced him to retire from the hazards of slaving; Newton decided on a career change, and tried to enter the Church. He was quickly taken up by Lord Dartmouth, a young, fervent, wealthy, and very influential Evangelical nobleman. Newton acquired the curacy of Olney in 1764 and in the same year he published the first of his autobiographical works describing his early life, the *Authentic Narrative*, which immediately became an Evangelical classic. While at Olney Newton consolidated his position within the Church and developed an international literary career. He came to exert a charismatic power over his parishioners who included the mentally unstable but brilliant proto-Romantic poet William Cowper. Cowper and Newton became creatively inseparable, and worked together on the *Olney Hymns*.

Newton moved to London in 1780 and became a preaching celebrity. The glamour of trauma which was attached to him was a marketable commodity, of which the capital demanded a share. At this point Newton moved in the establishment mainstream, and became one of the most influential preachers and spiritual guides in London until his death in 1807, the year the slave trade was abolished. Newton's importance for this anthology lies in the fact that his writings constitute a very special resource for considering the traumatic inheritance of transatlantic slavery now. His writings provide a set of blueprints for thinking through how eighteenth-century Evangelical Christianity (and hymnology) provided Britain and America with a set of structures for dealing with sin, guilt, shame, and evil within the context of imperial and industrial expansion. While working in the slave trade Newton did terrible things. He tortured little children, and personally ordered and supervised the thumbscrewing of four small boys. He then spent the rest of his life examining and re-examining his sin within the context of an enthusiastic redemptive theology which was an applied form of Calvinism. The body of writing that resulted is not easy to understand, but might be seen as a set of tools with which to lay bare the disguises that surround the damage which slavery inflicted upon the ethical consciousness of Britain and the Americas.

Amazing Grace

Faith's Review and Expectation, 1 Chronicles 17: 16, 17

> Amazing grace! (how sweet the sound)
>   That sav'd a wretch like me!
> I once was lost, but now am found,
>   Was blind, but now I see.
>
> 'Twas grace that taught my heart to fear,
>   And grace my fears reliev'd;
> How precious did that grace appear
>   The hour I first believ'd!
>
> Through many dangers, toils, and snares,
>   I have already come;
> 'Tis grace that brought me safe thus far,
>   And grace will lead me home.
>
> The Lord has promis'd good to me,
>   His word my hope secures:
> He will my shield and portion be,
>   As long as life endures.
>
> Yes, when this flesh and heart shall fail,
>   And mortal life shall cease,

I shall possess, within the veil,
  A life of joy and peace.

The earth shall soon dissolve like snow,
  The sun forbear to shine;
But God, who call'd me here below,
  Will be for ever mine.

from *Thoughts upon the African Slave Trade* (19)

With our ships, the great object is, to be full. When the ship is there, it is thought desirable, she should take as many as possible. The cargo of a vessel of a hundred tons, or little more, is calculated to purchase from two hundred and twenty to two hundred and fifty slaves. Their lodging-rooms below the deck, which are three (for the men, the boys, and the women) besides a place for the sick, are sometimes more than five feet high, and sometimes less; and this height is divided towards the middle, for the Slaves lie in two rows, one above the other, on each side of the ship, close to each other, like books upon a shelf. I have known them so close, that the shelf would not, easily, contain one more.

Alas! by Nature how Deprav'd

XXIX. *How shall I put thee among the Children?* Jeremiah 3: 19

    Alas! by nature how deprav'd,
      How prone to ev'ry ill!
    Our lives to Satan how enslav'd,
      How obstinate our will!

    And can such sinners be restor'd,
      Such rebels reconcil'd!
    Can grace itself the means afford
      To make a foe a child?

    Yes, grace has found the wondrous means
      Which shall effectual prove,
    To cleanse us from the countless sins,
      And teach our hearts to love.

Jesus for sinners undertakes,
 And dy'd that they may live;
His blood a full atonement makes,
 And cries aloud, "Forgive."

Yet one thing more must grace provide,
 To bring us home to God,
Or we shall slight the Lord who dy'd,
 And trample on his blood.

The Holy Spirit must reveal
 The Saviour's work and worth;
Then the hard heart begins to feel
 A new and heavenly birth.

Thus bought with blood, and born again,
 Redeem'd, and sav'd by grace,
Rebels in God's own house obtain
 A son's and daughter's place.

from *The Journal of a Slave Trader*

Monday 11th December . . . By the favour of Divine Providence made a timely discovery to day that the slaves were forming a plot for an insurrection. Surprised 2 of them attempting to get off their irons, and upon farther search in their rooms, upon the information of 3 of the boys, found some knives, stones, shot etc., and a cold chissel. Upon enquiry there appeared 8 principally concerned to move in projecting the business and 4 boys with supplying them with the above instruments. Put the boys in irons and slightly in the thumbscrews to urge them to a full confession.

This entry provides a challenging answer to Newton's later question, in the form of biblical quotation, *How shall I put thee among the Children?*

William Cowper (1731–1800), from *Charity* (written 1781, published 1782); from *The Task*, Book II, 'The Time Piece' (1785); 'Sweet Meat Has Sour Sauce' (written 1788, published 1836); 'The Morning Dream' (1788); 'The Negro's Complaint' (written 1788, published 1793); 'Epigram (Printed in the *Northampton Mercury*)' (1815)

Cowper, with the possible exception of Christopher Smart, has come to be seen as the most significant and experimental inheritor of the 'high' Augustan tradition, and simultaneously as a leading formal and thematic precursor of various aspects of Romanticism, and as a model for Wordsworth in particular. His writings also show him to have thought about slavery with unique ambition.

Cowper had an almost pathological desire to sympathize with victims. He consequently appealed to the age of sentiment in a number of ways. He wrote elegies on almost anything including the death of his mother, the caging and shooting of birds, and even a comic yet strangely haunting lament on a halibut he had eaten. He could express intense sorrow for the sickness of animals, especially his pet hares. He produced moving laments on the destruction of trees, and articulated the terror with which he confronted his own periodic bouts of insanity. Cowper was also a poet abreast of contemporary developments, whether recent exploration in the South Seas, the expansion of the press and leisure industries in the eighteenth century, or the economic and moral implications of plantation slavery. Cowper consequently comes at slavery from a variety of perspectives—moral, theological, historical, and emotional.

Cowper's letters and autobiographical writings show him to have felt a keen sympathy for enslaved Africans which was based in a comparison between their suffering and his own sense of spiritual desolation. He was enslaved to despair as the slave was in thrall to the slave power. At times this could lead Cowper into a nihilistic vision with the slave at its centre. He also continually agonized over whether he could make poetry out of slavery at all:

> The more I have consider'd it [the slave trade] the more I have convinced myself that it is not a promising theme for verse. General censure on the iniquity of the practise will avail nothing, the world has been overwhelm'd with such remarks already, and to particularise all the horrors of it were an employment for the mind both of the poet and his readers of which they would necessarily soon grow weary. For my own part I cannot contemplate the subject very nearly without a degree of abhorrence that affects my spirits and sinks them below the pitch requisite for success in verse. (*The Letters and Prose Writings of William Cowper*, ed. James King (Oxford University Press, 1988), iii. 172)

Cowper refers to the theme again and again; another passage from the letters is worth quoting because it shows that many of the problems relating to art and trauma which we now consider distinctly 'modern' hit Cowper full in the face a long time ago:

> Slavery and especially Negro Slavery, because the cruellest, is an odious and disgusting subject. Twice or thrice I have been assailed with entreaties to write a poem on that theme; but . . . I felt myself so much hurt in my spirits the moment I enter'd on the contemplation of it, that I have at last determined absolutely to have nothing more to do with it. There are some scenes of horror on which my imagination can dwell not without some complaisance, but then they are such scenes as God not man produces. In earthquakes, high winds, tempestuous seas, there is the grand as well as the terrible. But when man is active to disturb there is such meanness in the design and cruelty in the execution that I both hate and despise the whole operation, and feel it a degradation of poetry to employ her in the description of it. (*Letters*, iii. 177–8)

Cowper is articulating the argument, so often rehearsed since the Holocaust, that the mass destruction of humankind by humankind on the grounds of economic competition and race hatred does not furnish a suitable subject for art. In suggesting that natural calamities possess 'grandeur', while human ones do not, he poses a central problem for the art of slavery. It was not until Turner painted *Slavers Throwing Overboard the Dead and Dying* that a great Romantic artist was to evolve a solution as to how the monumentally mean realities of the slave trade and the grandeur of natural calamity could be fused into a single tragic vision.

Cowper finally did take up the challenge of writing about slavery and then produced a brilliantly unstable body of work. He could condense the ethical essence of abolition argument into the majestic blank verse of *The Task*, or conduct debates over entire paragraphs of heroic couplets in *Charity*, with an intellectual authority which tempts comparison with Dryden. When he came to write for the Society for Effecting the Abolition of Slavery he had a different agenda. He was asked to turn out ballads with genuine popular appeal. Thomas Clarkson noted:

> circumstances occurred to keep up a hatred of the trade among the people in this interval, which trivial as they were ought not to be forgotten. The amiable poet Cowper had frequently made the Slave-trade the subject of his contemplation . . . now he had written three little fugitive pieces on it. Of these the most impressive was that, which he called *The Negro's Complaint* . . . This little piece Cowper presented in manuscript to some of his friends in London . . . having ordered it on the finest hot-pressed paper, and folded it up in a small and neat form, they gave it the printed title of 'A Subject for Conversation at the Tea Table'. After this, they sent many thousand copies of it in franks into the country. From one it spread to another till it travelled almost over the whole island. Falling at length into the hands of a musician, it was set to music; and it then found its way into the streets both of the metropolis and of the country where it was sung as a ballad; and where it gave a plain account of the subject, with an appropriate feeling to those who heard it. (Thomas Clarkson, *The History of the Rise, Progress, and*

Accomplishment of the Abolition of the African Slave-Trade (Longman, Hurst, Rees & Orme, 1808), i. 188)

The impact of Cowper's abolition writing was lasting here and in America: Cowper was more frequently reprinted by American abolitionists than any other poet with the exception of Wordsworth.

Cowper's impact as a propagandist for the abolition cause lay in his range. He tries several approaches to the description of slave suffering. Formally the boldest and certainly the most dramatic is 'Sweet Meat Has Sour Sauce' where Cowper takes the step of speaking out ironically in the assumed voice of a slave captain. The poem as a description of white depravity contrives to possess an ironic freedom that not only enables, but in fact demands, the most brutalized and objectified descriptions of the black slave. What we are given is the way the abolitionist liked to see the slave trader seeing his slaves. In its extremity, vulgarity, cruelty, and stupidity, this version of the slave trader's views represents an abolition ideal, or anti-ideal. Yet it might be asked what perception of black slave or black African societies this poem projects. The same question might be asked of Cowper's other anti-slavery satire the little 'Epigram (Printed in the *Northampton Mercury*)'. It is certainly a tight little joke at the fictional planter's expense, but the slave is again excluded, and animalized. It is a central and virtually unbroken tenet of abolition thought that blacks must be portrayed as harmless and passive victims if they are to merit pity.

Charity (ll. 123–243)

.   .   .   .   .   .

Heav'n speed the canvass gallantly unfurl'd
To furnish and accommodate a world;
To give the pole the produce of the sun,
And knit th'unsocial climates into one.
Soft airs and gentle heavings of the wave
Impel the fleet whose errand is to save,
To succour wasted regions and replace
The smile of opulence in sorrow's face.
Let nothing adverse, nothing unforeseen,
Impede the bark that ploughs the deep serene,
Charg'd with a freight transcending in its worth
The gems of India, nature's rarest birth,
That flies like Gabriel[1] on his Lord's commands,
An herald of God's love to pagan lands.

---

[1] The name means 'God is my strength': one of the two greatest angels in the Judaeo-Christian and Muslim lore. The angel of annunciation, resurrection, mercy, vengeance, death, and revelation.

But ah! what wish can prosper, or what pray'r,
For merchants rich in cargoes of despair,
Who drive a loathsome traffic, gage and span,
And buy the muscles and the bones of man?
The tender ties of father, husband, friend,
All bonds of nature in that moment end;
And each endures while yet he draws his breath,
A stroke as fatal as the scythe of death.
The sable warrior, frantic with regret
Of her he loves, and never can forget,
Loses in tears the far receding shore,
But not the thought that they must meet no more;
Depriv'd of her and freedom at a blow,
What has he left that he can yet forego?
Yes, to deep sadness sullenly resign'd,
He feels his body's bondage in his mind,
Puts off his gen'rous nature, and to suit
His manners with his fate, puts on the brute.
    Oh most degrading of all ills that wait
On man, a mourner in his best estate!
All other sorrows virtue may endure,
And find submission more than half a cure;
Grief is itself a med'cine, and bestow'd
T'improve the fortitude that bears the load,
To teach the wand'rer, as his woes increase,
The path of wisdom, all whose paths are peace;
But slav'ry!—virtue dreads it as her grave:
Patience itself is meanness in a slave:
Or if the will and sovereignty of God
Bid suffer it awhile and kiss the rod,
Wait for the dawning of a brighter day,
And snap't the chain the moment when you may.
Nature impress'd upon what'er we see
That has a heart and life in it—Be free!
The beasts are chartered—neither age nor force
Can quell the love of freedom in a horse:
He breaks the cord that held him at the rack;
And, conscious of an unencumber'd back,
Snuffs up the morning air, forgets the rein,
Loose fly his forelock and his ample mane;
Responsive to the distant neigh he neighs,

Nor stops, till overleaping all delays,
He finds the pasture where his fellows graze.
  Canst thou, and honour'd with a Christian name,
Buy what is woman-born, and feel no shame?
Trade in the blood of innocence and plead
Expedience as a warrant for the deed?
So may the wolf whom famine has made bold
To quit the forest and invade the fold;
So may the ruffian who with ghostly glide,
Dagger in hand, steals close to your bed side;
Not he, but his emergence forc'd the door,
He found it inconvenient to be poor.
Has God then giv'n its sweetness to the cane—
Unless his laws be trampled on—in vain?
Built a brave world, which cannot yet subsist,
Unless his right to rule it be dismiss'd?
Impudent blasphemy! So folly pleads,
And av'rice, being judge, with ease succeeds.
  But grant the plea, and let it stand for just,
That man make man his prey, because he *must*,
Still there is room for pity to abate,
And soothe the sorrows of so sad a state.
A Briton knows,—or if he knows it not,
The Scripture plac'd within his reach, he ought,—
That souls have no discriminating hue,
Alike important in their Maker's view,
That none are free from blemish since the fall,
And love divine has paid one price for all.
The wretch that works and weeps without relief,
Has one that notices his silent grief,
He from whose hands alone all pow'r proceeds,
Ranks its abuse among the foulest deeds,
Considers *all* injustice with a frown,
But *marks* the man that treads his fellow down.
Begone! the whip and bell in that hard hand
Are hateful ensigns of usurp'd command.
Not Mexico could purchase kings a claim
To scourge him, weariness his only blame.
Remember, heav'n has an avenging rod—
To smite the poor is treason against God!
  Trouble is grudgingly and hardly brook'd,

While life's sublimest joys are overlook'd,
We wander o'er a sun-burnt thirsty soil,
Murm'ring and weary of our daily toil,
Forget t'enjoy the palm-tree's offer'd shade,
Or taste the fountain in the neighb'ring glade:
Else who would lose that had the pow'r t'improve
Th'occasion of transmuting fear to love?
Oh 'tis a godlike privilege to save,
And he that scorns it is himself a slave!
Inform his mind; one flash of heav'nly day
Would heal his heart and melt his chains away.
"Beauty for ashes" is a gift indeed!
And slaves, by truth enlarg'd, are doubly freed:
Then would he say, submissive at thy feet,
While gratitude and love made service sweet,
My dear deliv'rer out of hopeless night,
Whose bounty bought me but to give me light,
I was a bondsman on my native plain,
Sin forg'd and ignorance made fast the chain;
Thy lips have shed instruction as the dew,
Taught me what path to shun, and what pursue;
Farewell my former joys! I sigh no more
For Africa's once lov'd, benighted shore,
Serving a benefactor I am free,
At my best home if not exiled from thee.

The Task, Book II, 'The Time Piece' (ll. 1–65)

Oh for a lodge in some vast wilderness,
Some boundless contiguity of shade,
Where rumour of oppression and deceit,
Of unsuccessful or successful war,
Might never reach me more. My ear is pain'd,
My soul is sick with ev'ry day's report
Of wrong and outrage with which earth is fill'd.
There is no flesh in man's obdurate heart,
It does not feel for man. The natural bond
Of brotherhood is sever'd as the flax[1]

---

[1] The fibres of the plant *Linum* which are woven into linen.

That falls asunder at the touch of fire.
He finds his fellow guilty of a skin
Not colour'd like his own, and, having pow'r
T''inforce the wrong, for such a worthy cause
Dooms and devotes him as his lawful prey.
Lands intersected by a narrow frith
Abhor each other. Mountains interpos'd,
Make enemies of nations who had else
Like kindred drops, been mingled into one.
Thus man devotes his brother, and destroys;
And worse than all, and most to be deplor'd
As human nature's broadest, foulest blot,
Chains him, and tasks him, and exacts his sweat
With stripes, that mercy with a bleeding heart
Weeps when she sees inflicted on a beast.
Then what is man? And what man seeing this,
And having human feelings, does not blush
And hang his head to think himself a man?
I would not have a slave to till my ground,
To carry me, to fan me while I sleep,
And tremble while I wake, for all the wealth
That sinews bought and sold have ever earn'd.
No: dear as freedom is, and in my heart's
Just estimation priz'd above all price,
I had much rather be myself the slave
And wear the bonds, than fasten them on him.
We have no slaves at home.—Then why abroad?
And they themselves once ferried o'er the wave
That parts us, are emancipate and loos'd.
Slaves cannot breathe in England; if their lungs
Receive our air, that moment they are free;
They touch our country and their shackles fall.
That's noble, and bespeaks a nation proud
And jealous of the blessing. Spread it then,
And let it circulate through every vein
Of all your empire; that where Britain's power
Is felt, mankind may feel her mercy too.
   Sure there is need of social intercourse,
Benevolence, and peace, and mutual aid,
Between the nations, in a world that seems
To toll the death-bell of its own decease,

And by the voice of all its elements
To preach the gen'ral doom.[2] When were the winds
Let slip with such a warrant to destroy?
When did the waves so haughtily o'erleap
Their ancient barriers, deluging the dry?
Fires from beneath, and meteors from above,
Portentous, unexampled, unexplained,
Have kindled beacons in the skies, and th'old
And crazy earth has had her shaking fits
More frequent, and foregone her usual rest.
Is it a time to wrangle, when the props
And pillars of our planet seem to fail,
And Nature[3] with a dim and sickly eye
To wait the close of all?

Sweet Meat has Sour Sauce; or, The Slave Trader in the Dumps

A trader I am to the African shore,
But since that my trading is like to be o'er,
I'll sing you a song that you ne'er heard before,
    Which nobody can deny, deny,
    Which nobody can deny.

When I first heard the news it gave me a shock,
Much like what they call an electrical knock,
And now I am going to sell off my stock,
    Which nobody, &c.

'Tis a curious assortment of dainty regales,
To tickle the Negroes when the ship sails,
Fine chains for the neck, and a cat with nine tails,
    Which nobody, &c.

Here's a supple-jack plenty, and store of rat-tan,[1]
That will wind itself round the sides of a man,

---

[2] 'Alluding the late calamities in Jamaica.' [Cowper]
[3] 'Alluding to the fog that covered both Europe and Asia during the whole summer of 1783.' [Cowper]

[1] A very supple form of cane, made from the stems of certain types of climbing palm.

As close as a hoop round a bucket or can,
    Which nobody, &c.

Here's padlocks and bolts, and screws for the thumbs,
That squeeze them so lovingly till the blood comes,
They sweeten the temper like comfits or plumbs,
    Which nobody, &c.

When a Negro his head from his victuals withdraws,
And clenches his teeth and thrusts out his paws,
Here's a notable engine to open his jaws,[2]
    Which nobody, &c.

Thus going to market we kindly prepare
A pretty black cargo of African ware,
For what they must meet with when they get there,
    Which nobody, &c.

'Twould do your heart good to see 'em below,
Lie flat on their backs all the way as we go,
Like sprats on a gridiron, scores in a row,
    Which nobody, &c.

But ah! if in vain I have studied an art
So gainful to me, all boasting apart,
I think it will break my compassionate heart,
    Which nobody, &c.

For oh! how it enters my soul like an awl!
This pity, which some people self-pity call,
Is sure the most heart-piercing pity of all,
    Which nobody, &c.

So this is my song, as I told you before;
Come, buy off my stock, for I must no more
Carry Caesars and Pompeys[3] to Sugar-cane shore,
    Which nobody can deny, deny,
    Which nobody can deny.

---

[2] The *speculum oris*, an adjustable clamp, originally invented as a medical tool to open the mouths of lockjaw patients, it was then taken up and used for force-feeding slaves on the middle passage.
[3] Slaves were frequently named after Roman emperors and nobles.

The Morning Dream

'Twas in the glad season of Spring,
　Asleep at the dawn of the day
I dream'd what I cannot but sing,
　So pleasant it seem'd as I lay.
I dream'd that on Ocean afloat,
　Far hence to the westward I sail'd,
While billows high-lifted the boat,
　And the fresh-blowing breeze never fail'd.

In the steerage[1] a woman[2] I saw,
　(Such at least was the form that she wore)
Whose beauty impress'd me with awe,
　Ne'er taught me by woman before.
She sat, and a shield at her side
　Shed light like a sun on the waves,
And smiling divinely, she cried,
　I go to make Freemen of Slaves—

Then raising her voice to a strain
　The sweetest that ear ever heard,
She sung of the Slave's broken chain,
　Wherever her glory appear'd.
Some clouds which had over us hung
　Fled chased by her melody clear,
And methought while she Liberty sung,
　'Twas liberty only to hear.

Thus swiftly dividing the flood
　To a slave-cultur'd island we came,
Where a daemon,[3] her enemy, stood,
　Oppression his terrible name.
In his hand, as the sign of his sway,
　A scourge hung with lashes he bore,
And stood looking out for his prey
　From Africa's sorrowful shore.

But soon as approaching the land
　That goddess-like Woman he view'd,

[1] That part of a sailing ship, in front of the captain's cabin, from which it was steered.
[2] The woman is the allegorical figure of Britannia.　　[3] See p. 21 n. 52.

The scourge he let fall from his hand
    With blood of his subjects imbrued.
I saw him both sicken and die,
    And the moment the monster expired
Heard shouts that extended the sky
    From thousands with rapture inspired.

Awaking, how could I but muse
    At what such a Dream should betide?
But soon my ear caught the glad news
    Which serv'd my weak thought for a guide—
That Britannia, renown'd o'er the waves
    For the hatred she ever had shown
To the black-sceptred rulers of slaves,
    Resolves to have *none of her own*.

The Negro's Complaint

Forced from home and all its pleasures
    Afric's coast I left forlorn,
To increase a stranger's treasures
    O'er the raging billows borne;
Men from England bought and sold me,
    Pay'd my price in paltry gold;
But, though slave they have enroll'd me
    Minds are never to be sold.

Still in thought as free as ever,
    What are England's rights, I ask,
Me from my delight to sever,
    Me to torture, me to task?
Fleecy locks, and black complexion
    Cannot forfeit Nature's claim;
Sins may differ, but affection
    Dwells in White and Black the same.

Why did all-creating Nature
    Make the plant for which we toil?
Sighs must fan it, tears must water,
    Sweat of ours must dress the soil.

Think, ye Masters iron-hearted
   Lolling at your jovial boards;
Think how many backs have smarted
   For the sweets your Cane affords.

Is there, as ye sometimes tell us,
   Is there one who reigns on high?
Has he bid you buy and sell us,
   Speaking from his throne the sky?
Ask him if your knotted scourges,
   Matches, blood-extorting screws
Are the means that Duty urges
   Agents of his Will to use?

Hark!—He answers—Wild tornadoes
   Strewing yonder flood with wrecks,
Wasting Towns, Plantations, Meadows,
   Are the voice with which he speaks.
He, foreseeing what vexations
   Afric's sons should undergo,
Fix'd their Tyrants' habitations
   Where his whirlwinds answer—No.

By our blood in Afric wasted
   Ere our necks receiv'd the chain;
By the mis'ries that we tasted,
   Crossing in your barks the main;
By our suff'rings since ye brought us
   To the man-degrading mart;
All sustain'd with patience taught us
   Only by a broken heart—

Deem our nation Brutes no longer
   'Till some reason ye shall find
Worthier of regard and stronger
   Than the Colour of our Kind.
Slaves of gold, whose sordid dealings
   Tarnish all your boasted pow'rs,
Prove that *You* have human feelings
   Ere ye proudly question *Ours*!

Epigram (Printed in the Northampton Mercury)

To purify their wine some people bleed
A *Lamb* into the barrel, and succeed;
No Nostrum, Planters say, is half so good
To make fine sugar, as a *Negro's* blood.
Now lambs and negroes both are harmless things,
And thence, perhaps, this wondr'ous Virtue springs,
'Tis in the blood of Innocence alone—
Good cause why Planters never try their own.

Hugh Mulligan (d. 1798/9), from 'The Slave: An American Eclogue'; from 'The Lovers: An African Eclogue' (1784), in *Poems Chiefly on Slavery and Oppression* (1788)

Mulligan's desire to be considered part of the Clapham sect mainstream of abolition comes out in the oleaginous dedication of his *Poems* to William Wilberforce. Mulligan sets the little Tory's recent bout of ill health up as a matter of international concern for humanity. He states that 'the interests of humanity, truth, and justice' are 'intimately connected with the welfare of an individual' so that 'private danger or calamity is converted into a public concern'. He concludes: 'May this humble compliment, flowing from a free and independent mind, prove to you the harbinger of returning health.' Yet Mulligan's poems are not nearly as compromised as their grovelling introduction would suggest. The *Poems* are unusual in coming at slavery from a relatively well-researched comparative perspective which considers English colonial depredations in India, Ireland, and Africa, and which opens with a discussion of American slavery. Mulligan is unique among abolition poets in seeing Atlantic slavery as one aspect of a ruthless and global imperial policy inaugurated by England and then bequeathed to the new American nation. Other abolition poets writing of slavery in the late 1780s are careful to set the English slave trade out as a single and unique blemish upon an otherwise benign system of English global mercantilism (see More, pp. 101–10; and Cowper, pp. 83–6). Mulligan completely breaks ranks with this fictional orthodoxy. His account of the slave trade and American slavery, in the form of a sentimental lament spoken by Adala, occurs in the context of two other eclogues of oppression. The first, 'The Virgins: An Asiatic Eclogue', set in 'Indostan', although framed in the form of a sentimental dialogue between two Indian virgins is a hard-hitting attack on corrupt English policy in India. The subject was very topical, following the interminable corruption proceedings against Warren Hastings, the first Governor General of India, who was finally impeached in 1788. Although he was ultimately cleared, the case, and Edmund Burke's brilliant muck-raking exercises in his attacks on Hastings, had left a filthy taste in the English imperial mouth. Mulligan brings his treatment of English imperial abuse even closer to home in 'The Herdsmen, An European Eclogue'. This is set upon 'A promontory in the West of Ireland' and attacks the suffering and ruin brought on the island by absentee landlordism, and by the 'churlish squire' and his 'ruddy boys'. Mulligan was himself Irish and the subject is clearly a particularly charged one.

Mulligan is unusual among slavery poets in casting his net so wide. His discussions of African and American slavery are constrained in terms of form and diction by the conventions of the African eclogues of Chatterton (see pp. 72–6). Yet while the sentimentalized and idealized portraits of African existence are tame, the excoriation of the white slave traders, and the planters, and the extended prayers for vengeance on the part of the blacks, are more radical.

The Slave: An American Eclogue[1] (ll. 1–80, 139–60)

Time—Morning. Scene—A plantation in Virginia.

> Safe from the wild banditti's fierce alarms,
> From civil strife and foreign despot's arms,
> Tho' mild Virginia boast her peaceful plain,
> Yet there in blood her petty tyrants reign.
> With pines wide waving tho' the woods be crown'd,
> Tho' the green vales with living wealth abound,
> Bright on her fields tho' ripening rays descend,
> And rich with blushing fruit the branches bend;
> To those who ne'er must freedom's blessings taste,
> 'Tis barren all, 'tis all a cheerless waste.
>
>> Whilst hoarse the cat'ract murmurs on the gale,
> And the chill night-dew sweeps along the vale;
> Whilst the loud storm amidst the mountains howls,
> And lightning gleams, and deep the thunder rolls,
> Beneath a leafless tree, ere morn arose,
> The slave ADALA thus laments his woes:
>> 'Ye grisly spectres, gather round my seat,
> From caves unblest, that wretches groans repeat!
> Terrific forms from misty lakes arise!
> And bloody meteors threaten thro' the skies!
> Oh! curs'd destroyers of our hapless race,

[1] See p. 74 n. 1.

Of human-kind the terror and disgrace!
Lo! hosts of dusky captives, to my view,
Demand a deep revenge! Demand their due!
And frowning chiefs now dart athwart the gloom,
And o'er the salt-sea wave pronounce your doom—
But Gods are just, and oft the stroke forbear,
To plunge the guilty deeper in despair.
Lift high the scourge, my soul the rack disdains,
I pant for freedom and my native plains!
　　With limbs benumb'd my poor companions lie;
Oppress'd by pain and want the aged sigh:
Thro' reedy huts the driving tempest pours;
Their festr'ing wounds receive the sickly show'rs.
In madd'ning draughts our Lords their senses steep,
And doom their slaves to stripes and death in sleep;
Now, while the bitter blast surrounds my head,
To times long past my restless soul is led,
Far, far beyond the azure hills to groves
Of ruddy fruit, where beauty fearless roves—
O blissful feats! O self-approving joys!
Nature's plain dictates! ignorance of vice!
O guiltless hours! Our cares and wants were few,
No arts of luxury, or deceit, we knew:
Our labour sport—to tend our cottage care,
Or from the palm the luscious juice prepare;
To sit, indulging love's delusive dream,
And snare the silver tenants of the stream;
Or (nobler toil) to aim the deadly blow,
With dext'rous art, against the spotted foe.
O days, with youthful daring mark'd!—'twas then
I dragg'd the shaggy monster from his den;
And boldly down the rocky mountain's side
Hurl'd the fierce panther in the foaming tide:
Our healthful sports a daily feast afford,
And ev'ning found us at the social board.
　　Can I forget? Ah me! the fatal day;
When half the vale of peace was swept away!
Affrighted maids in vain the gods implore,
And weeping view from far the happy shore;
The frantic dames impatient ruffians seize,
And infants shriek and seize their mothers' knees;

With galling fetters soon their limbs are bound,
And groans throughout the noisome bark resound.
   Why was I bound? Why did not WHIDAH see
ADALA gain or death or victory?
No storms arise, no waves revengeful roar,
To dash the monsters on our injured shore.
   Long o'er the foaming deep to worlds unknown
By *envious winds* the *bulky ship* was blown.
While by disease and chains the weak expire,
Or parch'd, endure the slow consuming fire.
Who in this land of many griefs would live?
Where Death's the only comfort tyrants give!
Tyrants unblest! each proud of strict command,
Nor age nor sickness stays the driver's hand;
Whose hearts in adamant involv'd, despise
The drooping female's tears, the infant's cries;
From whose stern brows no grateful look e'er beams,
Whose *blushless* front nor death nor murder shames
.   .   .   .

Thou God, who gild'st with light the rising day!
Who life dispensest by thy genial ray!
Will thy slow vengeance never never fall,
But undistinguish'd favour shine on all?
Oh hear a suppliant wretch's last sad prayer!
Dart fiercest rage! infect the ambient air!
This pallid race, whose hearts are bound in steel,
By dint of suff'ring teach them how to feel.
   Or to some Despot's lawless will betray'd,
Give them to know, what wretches they have made!
Beneath the lash let them resign their breath,
Or curse, in chains the clay-cold hand of death,
Or, worst of ills! within each callous breast
Cherish, uncurb'd, the dark internal pest,
Bid AV'RICE swell the undiminsh'd rage,
While no new worlds th'accursed thirst assuage;
Then bid the monsters on each other turn,
The fury passions in disorder burn;
Bid Discord flourish, civil crimes increase,
Nor one fond wish arise that pleads for Peace—
'Til with their crimes, in wild confusion hurl'd,
They wake the anguish in a future world.

The Lovers: An African Eclogue (ll. 1–16, 96–129, 163–81)

'Time.—Midnight Scene—Guinea.'

When Afric's Genius mourn'd an injur'd land,
And wrapt in clouds, her foe's destruction plann'd;
Tremendous, oft she shews her mangled form,
Derides the suff'rers, and enjoys the storm.
She sees the wild, the dread tornado driven
By all th'avenging ministers of Heav'n;
Bids the plague rage, disease in rivers flow,
And on her spoilers pours the cup of woe.
   Beneath her ken the British bark was moor'd;
The traders vainly thought their prey secur'd:
What time the watch proclaim'd the midnight sound,
Their sickly mates in horrid slumbers bound;
High o'er the poop[1] two sable Lovers glide,
And toil for freedom on the swelling tide.
The beach now gain'd, they joyful, hand in hand,
With ardent souls salute their native strand,

.   .   .   .   .   .

ZELMA

Unheard-of crimes and tortures met my eyes,
That call'd for vengeance from th'impartial skies;
My gloomy thoughts oft sunk me in despair—
Blown by the winds thro' seas, we knew not where;
And, worse than all, to be their passion's slave!
T'avoid his suit, I brav'd the dashing wave.
That morn, thou know'st, when Sestro bold and strong,
(Who to the moon could chaunt the mystic song)
Sprung o'er the prow—breasting the briny waves—
In frantic mood the curst commander raves.
Now the rude engine sent forth sulph'rous flame,
The mortal thunder miss'd its deadly aim,
And happy Sestro gain'd his native shore—

BURA

Yet what ensu'd must pity's self deplore:

---

[1] The after part of the ship, the raised part of the stern.

I saw the White, the trembling guard secur'd,
On his chief's unpitying vengeance pour'd;
The furies rag'd within the tyrant's breast,
While cringing minions act the damn'd behest;
His arms extended to the shrouds were ty'd,
While clotted gore the pale beholders dy'd.
That pow'r which hears the dying victim's pray'rs,
Beneath the knotted whip closed all his cares—
What the reward? Oh what the mighty meed!
In foreign lands ye make each other bleed:
Or are ye exiles, doom'd to drag your lives
On hellish schemes—from country and from wives?
No lenient herbs your ulcer'd bodies heal,
The wrathful vengeance you severely feel,
And draw-in pest'lence with your latest breath,
With putrid meals devour the seeds of death.—

ZELMA

Drowning and pale, I view'd the sickly race;
Alas they're men! Tho' crimes their souls debase,
In fev'rous fits they talk of wives and friends;
The hand of death alone their torture ends

.   .   .   .   .   .

ZELMA

Why shook the earth?—Behold the darken'd air!

BURA

Thus rapt in clouds the lofty mountain shakes,
When from the skies the vivid light'ning breaks;
Tremendous thus, rebounds the thunder's roar,
When rueful swains their fields and flocks deplore.
The Whites no more at suff'ring wretches smile,
No more majestic floats their lofty pile.
See o'er the deep its shatter'd fragments roll,
Our injur'd Gods their dark designs controul.

ZELMA

Now all their fears, and tears, and suff'rings cease;
The gods are good, and take their souls to peace:
Guilty and guiltless now are seen no more.
Alas! my love, fly, fly this fatal shore.

BURA

The barren beach, ye sons of rapine, prize;
Yes fertile fields and groves shall meet our eyes.
Say what are all your treasures brought from far,
But vice, intemp'rance, and a rage for war?
Then, Zelma, haste! to distant wilds we bend;
Content and peace shall on our steps attend.

Hannah More (1745-1833), *The Black Slave Trade: A Poem* (originally published as *Slavery: A Poem*, 1788); *The Sorrows of Yamba; or, The Negro Woman's Lamentation* (1795); *The Feast of Freedom; or, The Abolition of Domestic Slavery in Ceylon* (1816)

More, like Chatterton, grew up in and around Bristol when it was one of the world's biggest slaving ports. She did not become interested in producing slavery literature, however, until well on in her career. In the early 1770s through an introduction to the great actor and theatrical entrepreneur David Garrick she went to London where she was introduced to Sir Joshua Reynolds and became a favourite of Dr Johnson. During the late 1770s More began literary production in earnest, writing ballads and plays. Her tragedy *Percy* was hugely successful both on the stage and as a text. When Garrick died in 1779 it was something of a watershed for her, and More backed off from the fashionable London literary scene. She rejected the theatre on moral grounds and began to produce polemical and didactic writings aimed at teaching Tory politics and Evangelical morals to children and the British labouring poor. Her exposure to John Newton's writings (pp. 77–80) and then in the late 1780s to his sermons was the single force most responsible for making More seriously interested in the slave trade. In 1787 she was introduced to Wilberforce just as he was throwing himself into the orchestration of the political activities of the abolitionists and they became fast friends and abolition collaborators. It was at this point that More wrote *Slavery: A Poem*.

Abolition for More was, as it was for Wilberforce, merely one area of social reform within a far bigger project. During the 1790s More threw herself into producing loyalist propaganda directed against French Jacobinism. She wrote and published more than fifty titles between 1794 and 1797. These 'Cheap Repository Tracts' were supported and printed by the Loyalist Associations and distributed in several million copies across the country. More's 'Tracts' set out to defend the established Church and the aristocracy against the claims of the English radicals, and particularly Tom Paine's arguments in *The Rights of Man* ridiculing privilege and its institutions. The 'Tracts' attempted to persuade the poor that they should show obedience, respect, and above all gratitude to the local clergy and the squirearchy. More took a very similar line on the attitudes which black Afro-Caribbean, and later Indian, slaves should show to their white 'liberators'. More's slaves may be lavishly pitied in the abstract, but they must remain passive, and above all good Christians. Both *The Sorrows of Yamba* and *The Feast of Freedom* are powerful demonstrations that for More it was axiomatic that a free slave become a subservient Christian slave.

More maintained close links with Wilberforce, and continued to support slavery abolition as a cause after the trade was abolished in 1807. As late as 1816 she penned *The Feast of Freedom* which was translated into a variety of south Indian languages, as well as being translated by Buddhist monks and circulated in Ceylon. This ecstatic celebration of British imperial patriarchy is also an uncompromising elaboration of the policing role of Christianity within Empire. In becoming simultaneously emancipated and Christianized the slave swaps one master for another, or as More succinctly summarizes: 'We'll show that we indeed are free, | Because we serve the Lord.' In this poem More goes so far as to argue that the Sinhalese will now willingly give all their trade goods to Britain as a literal trade-off for having been given access to Christianity. The sinister links between Evangelical missionary fervour and British imperial ambition could hardly be more straightforwardly set out.

More's work continues to be sidelined. The recently reconstructed Anglo-American-female-Romantic poetic canon has not easily found a place for More. Her unwavering patriarchalism, and her belief first in the subservient role of women, and secondly in the innate inferiority of all non-white non-British peoples, have not made her immediately attractive to late twentieth-century editors in search of proto-feminist icons. Yet More is a typical case of a once highly influential author who *must* now be read precisely because her assumptions regarding race, slavery, religion, and the economics of Empire are so far removed from the catechisms of contemporary Western liberalism. More's abolition verse was massively popular, and is the most fluent and intellectually the most hidebound verse to come out of mainstream state-backed Evangelical abolition. Both *The Sorrows of Yamba* (first published as one of the Cheap Repository Tracts) and *Slavery: A Poem* encapsulate the assumptions upon which Clapham sect abolition was founded.

Textual note: The publishing history and authorship of *The Sorrows of Yamba* are complicated. More did not sign the poem Z, her normal way of indicating her authorship within the multi-authored Cheap Repository Tracts. It has recently been convincingly argued that the first part of the narrative was composed by a little-known poet called Eaglesfield Smith, who submitted the poem to More for publication in the Tracts. More then emended the poem, the most important change being the inclusion of the long missionary conversion narrative. For a detailed account see Srinivas Aravamudan (ed.), *Slavery, Abolition and Emancipation: Writings in the British Romantic Period* (Pickering & Chatto, 1999), 224.

The Black Slave Trade: A Poem

> —O great design!
> Ye Sons of Mercy! O complete your work;
> Wrench from Oppression's hand the iron rod,
> And bid the cruel feel the pains they give.
> —Thompson's "Liberty"[1]

If Heaven has into being deign'd to call
Thy light, O LIBERTY! to shine on all;
Bright intellectual Sun! why does thy ray
To earth distribute only partial day?
Since no resisting cause from *spirit* flows
Thy universal presence to oppose;
No obstacles by Nature's hand impress'd,
Thy subtle and ethereal beams arrest;
Not sway'd by *matter* is thy course benign,
Or more direct or more oblique to shine;
Nor motion's laws can speed thy active course;
Nor strong repulsion's pow'rs obstruct thy force:
Since there is no convexity in MIND,
Why are thy genial rays to parts confin'd?
While the chill North with thy bright beam is blest,
Why should fell darkness half the South invest?
Was it decreed, fair Freedom! at thy birth,
That thou should'st ne'er irradiate *all* the earth?
While Britain basks in thy full blaze of light,
Why lies sad Afric quench'd in total night?

   Thee only, *sober* Goddess! I attest,
In smiles chastis'd, and decent graces dress'd;
To thee alone, pure daughter of the skies,
The hallow'd incense of the Bard should rise:
Not that mad Liberty,[2] in whose wild praise
Too oft he trims his prostituted bays;
Not that unlicens'd monster of the crowd,
Whose roar terrific bursts in peals so loud,
Deaf'ning the ear of Peace; fierce Faction's tool,
Of rash Sedition born, and mad Misrule;

---

[1] The epigraph is by James Thompson (1700–48), whose most renowned poem *The Seasons* contained a famous attack on the slave trade.

[2] '"Mad Liberty", alluding to the riots in London in the year 1800.' [More]

Whose stubborn mouth, rejecting Reason's rein,
No strength can govern, and no skill restrain;
Whose magic cries the frantic vulgar draw
To spurn at Order, and to outrage Law;
To tread on grave Authority and Pow'r,
And shake the work of ages in an hour:
Convuls'd her voice, and pestilent her breath,
She raves of mercy, while she deals out death:
Each blast is fate; she darts from either hand
Red conflagration o'er th' astonish'd land;
Clamouring for peace, she rends the air with noise,
And, to reform a part, the whole destroys.
Reviles oppression only to oppress,
And, in the act of murder, breathes redress.
Such have we seen on Freedom's genuine coast,
Bellowing for blessings which were never lost.
'Tis past, and Reason rules the lucid hour,
And beauteous ORDER reassumes his power:
Lord of the bright ascendant may he reign,
Till perfect Peace eternal sway maintain!

    O, plaintive Southerne![3] whose impassion'd page
Can melt the soul to grief, or rouse to rage;
Now, when congenial themes engage the Muse,
She burns to emulate thy generous views;
Her failing efforts mock her fond desires,
She shares thy feelings, not partakes thy fires.
Strange pow'r of song! the strain that warms the heart
Seems the same inspiration to impart;
Touch'd by th' extrinsic energy alone,
We think the flame which melts us is our own;
Deceiv'd, for genius we mistake delight,
Charm'd as we read, we fancy we can write.

    Though not to me, sweet Bard, thy pow'rs belong,
The cause I plead shall sanctify my song.
The Muse awakes no artificial fire,
For Truth rejects what Fancy would inspire:
Here Art would weave her gayest flow'rs in vain,
The bright invention Nature would disdain.

---

[3] 'Author of Oroonoko.' [More] Thomas Southerne (1660–1746) based his 1696 dramatic tragedy on a novella by Aphra Behn, *Oroonoko*, a romance focused on slave revolt in Surinam.

For no fictitious ills these numbers flow,
But living anguish, and substantial woe;
No individual griefs my bosom melt,
For millions feel what Oronoko felt:
Fir'd by no single wrongs, the countless host
I mourn, by rapine dragg'd from Afric's coast.
    Perish th' illiberal thought which would debase
The native genius of the sable race!
Perish the proud philosophy, which sought
To rob them of the pow'rs of equal thought!
What! does th' immortal principle within
Change with the casual colour of a skin?
Does matter govern spirit? or is MIND
Degraded by the form to which 'tis join'd?
    No: they have heads to think, and hearts to feel.
And souls to act, with firm, though erring zeal;
For they have keen affections, soft desires,
Love strong as death, and active patriot fires:
All the rude energy, the fervid flame
Of high-soul'd passion, and ingenuous shame:
Strong, but luxuriant virtues, boldly shoot
From the wild vigour of a savage root.
    Nor weak their sense of honour's proud control,
For pride is virtue in a Pagan soul;
A sense of worth, a conscience of desert,
A high, unbroken haughtiness of heart;
That self-same stuff which erst proud empires sway'd,
Of which the conquerors of the world were made.
Capricious fate of men! that very pride
In Afric scourg'd, in Rome was deified.
    No Muse, O Qua-shi![4] shall thy deeds relate,
No statue snatch thee from oblivious fate!

---

[4] '"It is a point of honour among Negroes of a high spirit to die rather than to suffer their glossy skin to bear the mark of the whip. Qua-shi had somehow offended his master, a young planter, with whom he had been bred up in the endearing intimacy of a play-fellow. His services had been faithful; his attachment affectionate. The master resolved to punish him and pursued him for that purpose. In trying to escape, Qua-shi stumbled and fell; the master fell upon him, they wrestled long and with doubtful victory, at length Qua-shi got uppermost, and, being fairly seated on his master's breast, he secured his legs with one hand, and with the other drew a sharp knife: then said, 'Master, I have been bred up with you from a child; I have loved you as myself; in return, you have condemned me to a punishment of which I must ever have borne the marks—thus only I can avoid them;' so saying, he drew the knife with all his strength across his own throat and fell down dead, without a groan, on his master's body." Ramsay's, *Essay on the Treatment of African slaves.*' [More]

For thou wast born where never gentle Muse
On Valour's grave the flow'rs of Genius strews;
And thou wast born where no recording page
Plucks the fair deed from Time's devouring rage.
Had Fortune plac'd thee on some happier coast,
Where *polish'd* Pagans souls heroic boast,
To thee, who sought'st a voluntary grave,
Th' uninjur'd honours of thy name to save,
Whose generous arm thy barbarous Master spar'd,
Altars had smok'd, and temples had been rear'd.

    Whene'er to Afric's shores I turn my eyes,
Horrors of deepest, deadliest guilt arise;
I see, by more than Fancy's mirror shown,
The burning village, and the blazing town:
See the dire victim torn from social life,
See the scar'd infant, hear the shrieking wife!
She, wretch forlorn! is dragg'd by hostile hands,
To distant tyrants sold, in distant lands:
Transmitted miseries, and successive chains,
The sole sad heritage her child obtains.
E'en this last wretched boon their foes deny,
To weep together, or together die.
By felon hands, by one relentless stroke,
See the fond vital links of Nature broke!
The fibres twisting round a parent's heart,
Torn from their grasp, and bleeding as they part.

    Hold, murderers! hold! nor aggravate distress;
Respect the passions you yourselves possess:
Ev'n you, of ruffian heart, and ruthless hand,
Love your own offspring, love your native land;
Ev'n you, with fond impatient feelings burn,
Though free as air, though certain of return.
Then, if to you, who voluntary roam,
So dear the memory of your distant home,
O think how absence the lov'd scene endears
To him, whose food is groans, whose drink is tears;
Think on the wretch whose aggravated pains
To exile misery adds, to misery chains.
If warm *your* heart, to British feelings true,
As dear his land to him as yours to you;
And Liberty, in you a hallow'd flame,

Burns, unextinguish'd, in his breast the same.
Then leave him holy Freedom's cheering smile,
The heav'n-taught fondness for the parent soil;
Revere affections mingled with our frame,
In every nature, every clime the same;
In all, these feelings equal sway maintain;
In all, the love of HOME and FREEDOM reign:
And Tempe's[5] vale, and parch'd Angola's sand,
One equal fondness of their sons command.
Th' unconquer'd Savage laughs at pain and toil,
Basking in Freedom's beams which gild his native soil.

    Does thirst of empire, does desire of fame,
(For these are specious crimes,) our rage inflame?
No: sordid lust of gold their fate controls,
The basest appetite of basest souls;
Gold, better gain'd by what their ripening sky,
Their fertile fields, their arts,[6] and mines supply.

    What wrongs, what injuries does Oppression plead,
To smooth the crime and sanctify the deed?
What strange offence, what aggravated sin?
They stand convicted—of a darker skin!
Barbarians, hold! th' opprobrious commerce spare,
Respect HIS sacred image which they bear.
Though dark and savage, ignorant and blind,
They claim the common privilege of *kind*;
Let Malice strip them of each other plea,
They still are men, and men should still be free.
Insulted Reason loathes th' inverted trade—
Loathes, as she views the human purchase made;
The outrag'd Goddess, with abhorrent eyes,
Sees MAN the traffic, SOULS the merchandize!
Man, whom fair Commerce taught with judging eye,
And liberal hand, to barter or to buy,
Indignant Nature blushes to behold,
Degraded Man himself, truck'd, barter'd, sold;
Of ev'ry native privilege bereft,
Yet curs'd with ev'ry wounded feeling left.

---

  [5] A sacred valley between the mountains of Olympus and Ossa in Thessaly, praised by poets as of absolute beauty; Tempe is consequently associated with consummate loveliness.

  [6] 'Besides many valuable productions of the soil, cloths and carpets of exquisite manufacture are brought from the coast of Guinea.' [More]

Hard lot! each brutal suff 'ring to sustain,
Yet keep the sense acute of human pain.
Plead not, in reason's palpable abuse,
Their sense of feeling callous and obtuse:[7]
From heads to hearts lies Nature's plain appeal,
Though few can reason, all mankind can feel.
Though wit may boast a livelier dread of shame,
A loftier sense of wrong refinement claim;
Though polish'd manners may fresh wants invent,
And nice distinctions nicer souls torment;
Though these on finer spirits heavier fall,
Yet natural evils are the same to all.
Though wounds there are which reason's force may heal,
There needs no logic sure to make us feel.
The nerve, howe'er untutor'd, can sustain
A sharp, unutterable sense of pain;
As exquisitely fashion'd in a slave,
As where unequal fate a sceptre gave.
Sense is as keen where Gambia's waters glide,
As where proud Tiber rolls his classic tide.
Though verse or rhetoric point the feeling line,
They do not whet sensation, but define.
Did ever wretch less feel the galling chain,
When Zeno[8] prov'd there was no ill in pain?
In vain the sage to smooth its horror tries;
Spartans and Helots see with different eyes;
Their miseries philosophic quirks deride,
Slaves groan in pangs disown'd by Stoic pride.
    When the fierce Sun darts vertical his beams,
And thirst and hunger mix their wild extremes;
When the sharp iron[9] wounds his inmost soul,
And his strain'd eyes in burning anguish roll;
Will the parch'd Negro own, ere he expire,
No pain in hunger, and no heat in fire?

---

[7] 'Nothing is more frequent than this cruel stupid argument, that they do not *feel* the miseries inflicted on them as Europeans would do.' [More]

[8] Greek philosopher who founded the Stoic school of philosophy.

[9] 'This is not said figuratively. The writer of these lines has seen a complete set of chains fitted to every separate limb of these unhappy, innocent, men; together with instruments for wrenching open the jaws, contrived with such ingenious cruelty as would gratify the tender mercies of an inquisitor.' [More] With the ironic reference to the Inquisition More is typically buying into the Spanish 'Black Legend'.

For him, when agony his frame destroys.
What hope of present fame or future joys?
For *that* have Heroes shorten'd Nature's date;
For *this* have Martyrs gladly met their fate;
But him, forlorn, no Hero's pride sustains,
No Martyr's blissful visions soothe his pains;
Sullen, he mingles with his kindred dust,
For he has learn'd to dread the Christian's trust;
To him what mercy can that GOD display,
Whose servants murder, and whose sons betray?
Savage! thy venial error I deplore,
They are *not* Christians who invest thy shore.

    O thou sad spirit, whose preposterous yoke
The great deliverer Death, at length, has broke!
Releas'd from misery, and escap'd from care,
Go, meet that mercy man denied thee here.
In thy dark home, sure refuge of th' oppress'd,
The wicked vex not, and the weary rest.
And, if some notions, vague and undefin'd,
Of future terrors have assail'd thy mind;
If such thy masters have presum'd to teach,
As terrors only they are prone to preach;
(For should they paint eternal Mercy's reign,
Where were th' oppressor's rod, the captive's chain?)
If, then, thy troubled soul has learn'd to dread
The dark unknown thy trembling footsteps tread;
On HIM, who made thee what thou art, depend;
HE, who withholds the means, accepts the end.
Thy mental night thy Saviour will not blame,
He died for those who never heard his name.
Not *thine* the reckoning dire of LIGHT abus'd,
KNOWLEDGE disgrac'd, and LIBERTY misus'd;
On *thee* no awful judge incens'd shall sit
For parts perverted, and dishonour'd wit.
Where ignorance will be found the safest plea,
How many learn'd and wise shall envy *thee!*

    And thou, WHITE SAVAGE! whether lust of gold
Or lust of conquest rule thee uncontroll'd!
Hero, or robber!—by whatever name
Thou plead thy impious claim to wealth or fame;

Whether inferior mischief be thy boast,
A tyrant trader rifling *Congo's* coast:
Or bolder carnage track thy crimson way,
Kings dispossess'd, and provinces thy prey;
Whether thou pant to tame earth's distant bound;
All Cortez[10] murder'd, all Columbus found;
O'er plunder'd realms to reign, detested Lord,
Make millions wretched, and thyself abhorr'd:—
Whether Cartouche[11] in forests break the law,
Or bolder Caesar keep the world in awe;
In Reason's eye, in Wisdom's fair account,
Your sum of glory boasts a like amount:
The means may differ, but the end's the same;
Conquest is pillage with a nobler name.
Who makes the sum of human blessings less,
Or sinks the stock of general happiness,
Though erring fame may grace, though false renown
His life may blazon or his memory crown,
Yet the last audit shall reverse the cause,
And God shall vindicate his broken laws.
    Had those advent'rous spirits who explore
Through ocean's trackless wastes, the far-sought shore;
Whether of wealth insatiate, or of pow'r,
Conquerors who waste, or ruffians who devour;
Had these possess'd, O COOK![12] thy gentle mind,
Thy love of arts, thy love of human kind;
Had these pursued thy mild and liberal plan,
DISCOVERERS had not been a curse to man.
Then, bless'd Philanthropy! thy social hands
Had link'd dissever'd worlds in brothers' bands;
Careless, if colour, or if clime divide;
Then, lov'd and loving, man had liv'd, and died.
Then with pernicious skill we had not known
To bring their vices back and leave our own.

---

[10] Hernán Cortez, the legendary conquistador who invaded the Mexican empire and enslaved its people. Cortez's actions in Mexico led to incalculable deaths among Mexican people.
[11] Louis Dominique Cartouche was a legendary criminal in early 18th-century France; he was eventually publicly executed in 1721.
[12] James Cook (1728–79), the celebrated naval explorer, most commonly remembered for his voyages round Australia and New Zealand.

The purest wreaths which hang on glory's shrine
For empires founded, peaceful PENN![13] are thine;
No blood-stain'd laurels crown'd thy virtuous toil,
No slaughter'd natives drench'd thy fair-earn'd soil.

Still thy meek spirit in thy flock survives,
Consistent still, *their* doctrines rule their lives;
Thy followers only have effac'd the shame
Inscrib'd by SLAVERY on the Christian name.

Shall Britain, where the soul of Freedom reigns,
Forge chains for others she herself disdains?
Forbid it, Heaven! O let the nations know
The liberty she tastes she will bestow;
Not to herself the glorious gift confin'd,
She spreads the blessing wide as human kind;
And scorning narrow views of time and place,
Bids all be free in earth's extended space.

What page of human annals can record
A deed so bright as human rights restor'd?
O may that god-like deed, that shining page
Redeem OUR fame, and consecrate OUR age,
And let this glory mark our favour'd shore,
To curb FALSE FREEDOM and the TRUE restore!

And see the cherub MERCY from above,
Descending softly, quits the sphere of love!
On Britain's Isle she sheds her heavenly dew,
And breathes her spirit o'er th' enlighten'd few;
From soul to soul the generous influence steals,
Till every breast the soft contagion feels.
She speeds, exulting, to the burning shore,
With the best message Angel ever bore;
Hark! 'tis the note which spoke a Saviour's birth,
Glory to God on high, and peace on Earth!
She vindicates the Pow'r in Heaven ador'd,
She stills the clank of chains, and sheathes the sword;
She cheers the mourner, and with soothing hands
From bursting hearts unbinds th' Oppressor's bands;
Restores the lustre of the Christian name,
And clears the foulest blot that dimm'd its fame.

---

[13]   William Penn (1644–1718), early North American colonist who founded the modestly named Pennsylvania.

As the mild Spirit hovers o'er the coast,
A fresher hue the wither'd landscapes boast;
Her healing smiles the ruin'd scenes repair,
And blasted Nature wears a joyous air;
While she proclaims through all their spicy groves,
"Henceforth your fruits, your labours, and your loves,
All that your Sires possess'd, or you have sown,
Sacred from plunder—all is now YOUR OWN."
　　And now, her high commission from above,
Stamp'd with the holy characters of love,
The meek-ey'd spirit waving in her hand,
Breathes manumission o'er the rescu'd land:
She tears the banner stain'd with blood and tears,
And, LIBERTY! thy shining standard rears!
As the bright ensign's glory she displays,
See pale OPPRESSION faints beneath the blaze!
The giant dies! no more his frown appals,
The chain, untouch'd, drops off, the fetter falls.
Astonish'd echo tells the vocal shore,
Oppression's fall'n, and Slavery is no more!
The dusky myriads crowd the sultry plain,
And hail that MERCY long invok'd in vain.
Victorious pow'r! she bursts their two-fold bands,
And FAITH and FREEDOM spring from Britain's hands.
　　And THOU! great source of Nature and of Grace,
Who of one blood didst form the human race,
Look down in mercy in thy chosen time,
With equal eye on Afric's suff'ring clime:
Disperse her shades of intellectual night,
Repeat thy high behest—LET THERE BE LIGHT!
Bring each benighted soul, great GOD, to Thee,
And with thy wide Salvation make them free!

The Sorrows of Yamba; or, The Negro Woman's Lamentation

'In St. Lucie's[1] distant isle,
　　Still with Afric's love I burn;
Parted many a thousand mile,
　　Never, never to return.

[1] A variant name for the small Caribbean island of St Lucia.

Come kind death! and give me rest,
    Yamba has no friend but thee;
Thou canst ease my throbbing breast,
    Thou canst set the Prisoner free.

Down my cheeks the tears are dripping,
    Broken is my heart with grief;
Mangled my poor flesh with whipping,
    Come kind death! and bring relief.

Born on Afric's Golden Coast,
    Once I was as blessed as you;
Parents tender I could boast,
    Husband dear, and children too.

Whity man he came from far,
    Sailing o'er the briny flood,
Who, with help of British Tar,[2]
    Buys up human flesh and blood.

With the Baby at my breast
    (Other two were sleeping by)
In my Hut I sat at rest,
    With no thought of danger nigh.

From the Bush at even tide
    Rushed the fierce man-stealing Crew;
Seized the Children by my side,
    Seized the wretched Yamba too.

Then for love of filthy Gold
    Straight they bore me to the Sea;
Crammed me down a Slave Ship's hold,
    Where were Hundreds stowed like me.

Naked on the Platform lying,
    Now we cross the tumbling wave;
Shrieking, sickening, fainting, dying.
    Deed of shame for Britons brave.

At the savage Captain's beck
    Now like Brutes they make us prance.
Smack the Cat about the Deck,
    And in scorn they bid us dance.

---

[2] A British sailor, so named because they smelt of Amsterdam tar, from continually painting the rigging and rope-work with it.

Nauseous horse-beans they bring nigh,
　　Sick and sad we cannot eat;
Cat must cure the Sulks they cry,
　　Down their throats we'll force the meat.

I in groaning passed the night,
　　And did roll my aching head;
At the break of morning light,
　　My poor Child was cold and dead.

Happy, happy, there she lies,
　　Thou shalt feel the lash no more.
Thus full many a Negro dies
　　Ere we reach the destined shore.

Thee, sweet infant, none shall sell,
　　Thou hast gained a watery Grave;
Clean escaped the Tyrants fell,
　　While thy mother lives a Slave.

Driven like Cattle to a fair,
　　See they sell us young and old;
Child from Mother too they tear,
　　All for love of filthy Gold.

I was sold to Massa hard,
　　Some have Massas kind and good;
And again my back was scarred,
　　Bad and stinted was my food.

Poor and wounded, faint and sick,
　　All exposed to burning sky,
Massa bids me grass to pick,
　　And I now am near to die.

What and if to death he send me,
　　Savage murder though it be,
British Law shall ne'er befriend me,
　　They protect not Slaves like me.'

Mourning thus my wretched state,
　　(Ne'er may I forget the day)
Once in dusk of evening late
　　Far from home I dared to stray;

Dared, alas! with impious haste
   Towards the roaring Sea to fly,
Death itself I longed to taste,
   Longed to cast me in and Die.

There I met upon the Strand
   English Missionary Good,
He had Bible book in hand,
   Which poor me no understood.

Led by pity from afar
   He had left his native ground;
Thus if some inflict a scar,
   Others fly to cure the wound.

Straight he pulled me from the shore,
   Bid me no self-murder do;
Talked of state when life is o'er,
   All from Bible good and true.

Then he led me to his Cot,
   Soothed and pitied all my woe;
Told me 'twas the Christian's lot
   Much to suffer here below.

Told me then of God's dear Son,
   (Strange and wondrous is the story;)
What sad wrong to him was done,
   Though he was the Lord of Glory.

Told me too, like one who knew him,
   (Can such love as this be true?)
How he died for them that slew him,
   Died for wretched Yamba too.

Freely he his mercy proffered,
   And to Sinners he was sent:
E'en to Massa pardon's offered:
   O if Massa would repent!

Wicked deed full many a time
   Sinful Yamba too hath done;
But she wails to God her crime,
   But she trusts his only Son.

O ye slaves whom Massas beat,
   Ye are stained with guilt within;
As ye hope for mercy sweet,
   So forgive your Massas' sin.

And with grief when sinking low,
   Mark the Road that Yamba trod;
Think how all her pain and woe
   Brought the Captive home to God.

Now let Yamba too adore
   Gracious Heaven's mysterious Plan;
Now I'll count my mercies o'er,
   Flowing through the guilt of man.

Now I'll bless my cruel capture,
   (Hence I've known a Saviour's name)
Till my Grief is turned to Rapture,
   And I half forget the blame.

But though here a Convert rare
   Thanks her God for Grace divine,
Let not man the glory share,
   Sinner, still the guilt is thine.

Here an injured Slave forgives,
   There a Host for vengeance cry;
Here a single Yamba lives,
   There a thousand droop and die.

Duly now baptised am I
   By good Missionary Man:
Lord my nature purify
   As no outward water can!

All my former thoughts abhorred,
   Teach me now to pray and praise:
Joy and Glory in my Lord,
   Trust and serve him all my days.

Worn indeed with Grief and Pain,
   Death I now will welcome in:
O the Heavenly Prize to gain!
   O to escape the power of Sin!

True of heart, and meek and lowly,
   Pure and blameless let me grow!
Holy may I be, for Holy,
   Is the place to which I go.

But though death this hour may find me,
   Still with Afric's love I burn,
(There I've left a spouse behind me)
   Still to native land I turn.

And when Yamba sinks in death,
   This my latest prayer shall be,
While I yield my parting breath,
   O that Afric might be free.

Cease, ye British Sons of murder!
   Cease from forging Afric's chain;
Mock your Saviour's name no further,
   Cease your savage lust of gain.

Ye that boast '*Ye rule the waves*',
   Bid no Slave Ship soil the sea,
Ye that '*never will be slaves,*'
   Bid poor Afric's land be free.

Where ye gave to war its birth,
   Where your traders fixed their den,
There go publish '*Peace on Earth,*'
   Go proclaim '*good-will to men.*'

Where ye once have carried slaughter,
   Vice, and Slavery,—and Sin;
Seized on Husband, Wife, and Daughter,
   Let the Gospel enter in.

Thus where Yamba's native home,
   Humble Hut of Rushes stood,
Oh if there should chance to roam
   Some dear Missionary good;

Thou in Afric's distant land,
   Still shall see the man I love;
Join him to the Christian band,
   Guide his Soul to Realms above.

> There no Fiend again shall sever
>   Those whom God hath joined and blessed:
> There they dwell with Him for ever,
>   There '*the weary are at rest.*'

The Feast of Freedom; or, The Abolition of Domestic Slavery in Ceylon: Written to commemorate that event, which took place on his Majesty's birth-day, August 12, 1816

This little piece has already been rendered into many of the Indian languages: its first translation was made into the Cingalese by the Budhoo priests who were brought to this country by Sir Alexander Johnston.

The Feast of freedom, or the Twelfth of August

Scene, Ceylon.

Sabat, Dumal, Cingalese, &c.

[*The first three stanzas are sung*]

DUMAL
Let's be merry, sing and play,—
This is freedom's holiday!

SABAT
Bless the day that sets us free!
Hail the morn of liberty!
Our children's children still shall meet,
Fair freedom's birth to celebrate.

DUMAL
Spread the blessing far and wide,
Care and thought be laid aside;
Let us drink, rejoice, and sing,
Till with our mirth the valleys ring!

CHORUS

Let's be merry sing and play,—
this is Freedom's holiday!
    [song ends]

SABAT

But ere our joyful sports begin,
Aright of freedom think;
'Tis not a liberty to sing,
A liberty to drink.

DUMAL

Yes, let us hail the cocoa-tree,
With all the joys it gives;
To laugh and drink is to be free,—
The thought my heart revives.

SABAT

O let us not the gift abuse,
Nor thank the Powers amiss:
Our Freedom rightly let us use,—
Intemperance is not bliss.

Our groves of cinnamon we prize,
No islands such possess;
They send their fragrance to the skies,
Their sweets our labours bless.

Yet there's a balm of nobler end
Our spirits to recruit:
England, fair Freedom's choicest friend,
Conveys the sacred fruit.

One Tree of sov'reign virtue grows,
All other trees excelling:
This Tree all joy and peace bestows,
Wher'er it makes its dwelling.

Its root is deep, its branches wide,
A Tree to make one wise;
Beneath its shelter sinners hide—
Its head is in the skies.

There is a Book contains the leaves
Might heal a dying nation;
This Book, who faithfully receives,
Secures his own salvation.

DUMAL

O give us then this friendly Tree,
This healing Book produce:
So shall we give all praise to thee,
If thou wilt shew their use.

SABAT

Not that rich juice our cocoa lends
Such sober joys imparts:
That many a life untimely ends,—
This heals the broken hearts.

DUMAL

With riddles puzzle us no more,
But tell us what you mean:
What is that Tree, what is that Book
Which you, I trust, have seen?

SABAT

Your tree's sweet juice drunk to excess,
Produces hate and strife;
That Tree, which more than all can bless,
Is call'd the TREE OF LIFE.

The Cocoa juice distracts the brain,
You crave it o'er and o'er;
But who *this* Tree's fair fruit obtain,
Shall thirst, my friends, no more

[Sabat *holding out a bible*]
This is the boon which England sends,
It breaks the chains of sin;
O blest exchange for fragrant groves!
O barter most divine!

It yields a trade of noblest gain,
Which other trades may miss;
A few short years of care and pain,
For endless, perfect bliss.

This shows us freedom how to use,
To love our daily labour;
Forbids our time in sloth to lose,
Or riot with our neighbour.

Then let our masters gladly find,
A freeman works the faster;
Who serves his God with heart and mind,
Will better serve his master.

When soul and body both are free,
How swift will pass the days!
The sun our cheerful work shall see,
The night our prayer and praise.

CHORUS OF CINGALESE
O give us Sabat's precious tree,
We join with one accord;
We'll show that we indeed are free,
Because we serve the Lord.

O give us Sabat's holy Book,
With transport we will read;
There we shall see, when'er we look,
God's freedman's free indeed.

SABAT
The twelfth of August then shall be
By us forgotten never;
From this blest period we are free,
For ever, and for ever.

CHORUS
Bless the day that sets us free!
Hail the Morn of Liberty.

Ann Yearsley (1752–1806), *A Poem on the Inhumanity of the Slave-Trade Humbly Inscribed to the Right Honourable and Right Reverend Frederic Earl of Bristol Bishop of Derry* (1788)

Yearsley was initially the literary discovery of Hannah More, but rapidly threw off the constraints imposed by her mentor and produced a large body of verse on a variety of subjects. In 1784 More's cook showed her some poems written by a local woman who made her living delivering milk. More was impressed and immediately set about organizing the publication of a volume of Yearsley's poems by subscription. The resultant 1785 volume *Poems on Several Occasions* was a big success, with over 1,000 subscribers. As it ran into several editions and the profits mounted Yearsley became resentful that More had decided to act as her literary 'trustee' investing the profits for an annuity. Yearsley wanted all her money up front in a lump sum and after a brief and bitter fight she got what she wanted. She continued successfully writing and publishing occasional and romantic poems until 1796.

Yearsley wrote and published her abolition poem in 1788, the year when abolition propaganda first began to be produced on a national scale. Slavery had suddenly become a 'hot' publishing area, yet Yearsley would also have been aware that More was writing her own major verse treatment of the subject, *Slavery: A Poem*, which also appeared in 1788. Certainly Yearsley's poem is a slap in the face for the kind of pious platitudes in which More specializes. Yearsley's poem is eccentric to other abolition verse in its obsessive assault on the hypocrisy of state religion. The fact that the slave power, both in the colonies and as manifested in business interest within the British planter lobby, claimed Christian credentials is a trigger for Yearsley's fury throughout the poem. She operates an inverse colonial demonology in which she sets other European forms of imperialism, including Spanish, against the supreme evil of British moral hypocrisy. The poem is first and foremost an attack on the religious and political status quo within Bristol, and as such a veiled assault on the social values which More, despite her sentimental forays into abolition, sought to protect.

A Poem on the Inhumanity of the Slave-Trade

Bristol,[1] thine heart hath throbbed to glory.—Slaves,
E'en Christian slaves, have shook their chains, and gazed
With wonder and amazement on thee. Hence

---

[1] Bristol was not only Yearsley's home town but, at this date, England's third largest slave-trading port, after Liverpool and London.

Ye grovelling souls, who think the term I give,
Of Christian slave, a paradox! to *you*
I do not turn, but leave you to conception
Narrow; with that be blessed, nor dare to stretch
Your shackled souls along the course of *Freedom*.

   Yet, Bristol, list! nor deem Lactilla's[2] soul
Lessened by distance; snatch her rustic thought,
Her crude ideas, from their panting state,
And let them fly in wide expansion; lend
Thine energy, so little understood
By the rude million, and I'll dare the strain
Of Heaven-born Liberty till Nature moves
Obedient to her voice. Alas! my friend,
Strong rapture dies within the soul, while Power
Drags on his bleeding victims. Custom, Law,
Ye blessings, and ye curses of mankind,
What evils do ye cause? We feel enslaved,
Yet move in your direction. Custom, thou
Wilt preach up filial piety; thy sons
Will groan, and stare with impudence at Heaven,
As if they did abjure the act, where Sin
Sits full on Inhumanity; the church
They fill with mouthing, vaporous sighs and tears,
Which, like the guileful crocodile's, oft fall,
Nor fall, but at the cost of human bliss.

   Custom, thou hast undone us! led us far
From God-like probity,[3] from truth, and heaven.

   But come, ye souls who feel for human woe,
Though dressed in savage guise! Approach, thou son,
Whose heart would shudder at a father's chains,
And melt o'er thy loved brother as he lies
Gasping in torment undeserved. Oh, sight
Horrid and insupportable! far worse
Than an immediate, an heroic death;
Yet to this sight I summon thee. Approach,
Thou slave of avarice, that canst see the maid
Weep o'er her inky fire! Spare me, thou God

---

[2] Lactilla is a Latin name for a milkmaid, and consequently a poeticized reference to Yearsley's job.
[3] Moral integrity, upright character, from the Latin *probitas* meaning honest.

Of all-indulgent Mercy, if I scorn
This gloomy wretch, and turn my tearful eye
To more enlightened beings. Yes, my tear
Shall hang on the green furze, like pearly dew
Upon the blossom of the morn. My song
Shall teach sad Philomel[4] a louder note,
When Nature swells her woe. O'er suffering *man*
My soul with sorrow bends! Then come, ye few
Who feel a more than cold, material essence;
Here ye may vent your sighs, till the bleak North
Find its adherents aided.—Ah, no more!
The dingy youth comes on, sullen in chains;
He smiles on the rough sailor, who aloud
Strikes at the spacious heaven, the earth, the sea,
In breath too blasphemous; yet not to *him*
Blasphemous, for *he* dreads not either:—lost
In dear internal imagery, the soul
Of Indian Luco rises to his eyes,
Silent, not inexpressive: the strong beams
With eager wildness yet drink in the view
Of his too humble home, where he had left
His mourning father, and his Incilanda.

Curse on the toils spread by a Christian hand
To rob the Indian of his freedom! Curse
On him who from a bending parent steals
His dear support of age, his darling child;
Perhaps a son, or a *more tender* daughter,
Who might have closed his eyelids, as the spark
Of life gently retired. Oh, thou poor world!
Thou fleeting good to individuals! see
How much for thee they care, how wide they ope
Their helpless arms to clasp thee; vapour thou!
More swift than passing wind! thou leav'st them nought
Amid the unreal scene, but a *scant grave*.

I know the crafty merchant will oppose
The plea of nature to my strain, and urge
His toils are for his children: the lost plea

---

[4] A nightingale, from the Greek myth where Philomela, daughter of Pandeon, was turned into a songbird.

Dissolves my soul—*but when I sell a son,*
Thou God of nature, let it be my own!

    Behold that Christian! see what horrid joy
Lights up his moody features, while he grasps
The wished-for gold, purchase of human blood!
Away, thou seller of mankind! Bring on
Thy daughter to this market! bring thy wife!
Thine aged mother, though of little worth,
With all thy ruddy boys! Sell them, thou wretch,
And swell the price of Luco! Why that start?
Why gaze as thou wouldst fright me from my challenge
With look of anguish? Is it *Nature* strains
Thine heart-strings at the image? Yes, my charge
Is full against her, and she rends thy soul,
While I but strike upon thy pitiless ear,
Fearing her rights are violated.—Speak,
Astound the voice of *Justice*! bid thy tears
Melt the unpitying power, while thus she claims
The pledges of thy love. Oh, throw thine arm
Around thy little ones, and loudly plead
Thou *canst not* sell thy children.—Yet, beware
Lest Luco's groan be heard; should *that* prevail,
Justice will scorn thee in her turn, and hold
Thine *act* against thy *prayer*. Why clasp, she cries,
That blooming youth? Is it because thou lov'st him?
Why Luco was beloved: then wilt thou feel,
Thou selfish Christian, for thy private woe,
Yet cause such pangs to him that is a father?
Whence comes thy right to barter for thy fellows?
Where are thy statutes? Whose the iron pen
That gave thee precedent? Give me the seal
Of virtue, or religion, for thy trade,
And I will ne'er upbraid thee; but if force
Superior, hard brutality alone
Become thy boast, hence to some savage haunt,
Nor claim protection from my social laws.
Luco is gone; his little brothers weep,
While his fond mother climbs the hoary rock
Whose point o'er-hangs the main. No Luco there,
No sound, save the hoarse billows. On she roves,

With love, fear, hope, holding alternate rage
In her too anxious bosom. Dreary main!
Thy murmurs now are riot, while she stands
Listening to every breeze, waiting the step
Of gentle Luco. Ah. return! return!
Too hapless mother, thy indulgent arms
Shall never clasp thy fettered Luco more.
See Incilanda! artless maid, my soul
Keeps pace with thee, and mourns. Now o'er the hill
She creeps, with timid foot, while Sol[5] embrowns
The bosom of the isle, to where she left
Her faithful lover: here the well-known cave,
By Nature formed amid the rock, endears
The image of her Luco; here his pipe,
Formed of the polished cane, neglected lies,
No more to vibrate; here the useless dart,
The twanging bow, and the fierce panther's skin,
Salute the virgin's eye. But where is Luco?
He comes not down the steep, though he had vowed,
When the sun's beams at noon should sidelong gild
The cave's wide entrance, he would swift descend
To bless his Incilanda. Ten pale moons
Had glided by, since to his generous breast
He clasped the tender maid, and whispered love.

Oh, mutual sentiment! thou dangerous bliss!
So exquisite, that Heaven had been unjust
Had it bestowed less exquisite of ill;
When thou art held no more, thy pangs are deep,
Thy joys convulsive to the soul; yet all
Are meant to smooth the uneven road of life.

For Incilanda, Luco ranged the wild,
Holding her image to his panting heart;
For her he strained the bow, for her he stripped
The bird of beauteous plumage; happy hour,
When with these guiltless trophies he adorned
The brow of her he loved. Her gentle breast
With gratitude was filled, nor knew she aught
Of language strong enough to paint her soul,

---

[5] Latin name for the sun.

Or ease the great emotion; whilst her eye
Pursued the generous Luco to the field,
And glowed with rapture at his wished return.

    Ah, sweet suspense! betwixt the mingled cares
Of friendship, love, and gratitude, so mixed,
That ev'n the soul may cheat herself.—Down, down,
Intruding Memory! bid thy struggles cease,
At this soft scene of innate war. What sounds
Break on her ear? She, starting, whispers 'Luco.'
Be still, fond maid; lift to the tardy step
Of leaden-footed woe. A father comes,
But not to seek his son, who from the deck
Had breathed a last adieu: no, he shuts out
The soft, fallacious gleam of hope, and turns
Within upon the mind: horrid and dark
Are his wild, unenlightened powers: no ray
Of *forced* philosophy to calm his soul,
But all the anarchy of wounded nature.

    Now he arraigns his country's gods, who sit,
In his bright fancy, far beyond the hills,
Unriveting the chains of slaves: his heart
Beats quick with stubborn fury, while he doubts
Their justice to his child. Weeping old man,
Hate not a Christian God, whose record holds
Thine injured Luco's name. Frighted he starts,
Blasphemes the Deity, whose altars rise
Upon the Indian's helpless neck, and sinks,
Despising comfort, till by grief and age
His angry spirit is forced out. Oh, guide,
Ye angel-forms, this joyless shade to worlds
Where the poor *Indian*, with the *sage*, is proved
The work of a Creator. Pause not here,
Distracted maid! ah, leave the breathless form,
On whose cold cheek thy tears so swiftly fall,
Too unavailing! On this stone, she cries,
My Luco sat, and to the wandering stars
Pointed my eye, while from his gentle tongue
Fell old traditions of his country's woe.
Where now shall Incilanda seek him? Hence,
Defenceless mourner, ere the dreary night

Wrap thee in added horror. Oh, Despair,
How eagerly thou rend'st the heart! She pines
In anguish deep, and sullen: Luco's form
Pursues her, lives in restless thought, and chides
Soft consolation. Banished from his arms,
She seeks the cold embrace of death; her soul
Escapes in one sad sigh. Too hapless maid!
Yet happier far than he thou lov'dst; his tear,
His sigh, his groan avail not, for they plead
Most weakly with a Christian. Sink, thou wretch,
Whose act shall on the cheek of Albion's sons
Throw Shame's red blush: thou, who hast frighted far
Those simple wretches from thy God, and taught
Their erring minds to mourn his partial love,
Profusely poured on thee; while they are left
Neglected to *thy* mercy. Thus deceived,
How doubly dark must be *their* road to death!

Luco is borne around the neighbouring isles,
Losing the knowledge of his native shore
Amid the pathless wave; destined to plant
The sweet luxuriant cane. He strives to please,
Nor once complains, but greatly smothers grief.
His hands are blistered, and his feet are worn,
Till every stroke dealt by his mattock gives
Keen agony to life; while from his breast
The sigh arises, burthened with the name
Of Incilanda. Time inures the youth,
His limbs grow nervous, strained by willing toil;
And resignation, or a calm despair,
(Most useful either) lulls him to repose
A Christian renegade, that from his soul,
Abjures the tenets of our schools, nor dreads
A future punishment, nor hopes for mercy,
Had fled from England, to avoid those laws
Which must have made his life a retribution
To violated justice, and had gained,
By fawning guile, the confidence (ill placed)
Of Luco's master. O'er the slave he stands
With knotted whip, lest fainting nature shun
The task too arduous, while his cruel soul,

Unnatural, ever feeds, with gross delight,
Upon his sufferings. Many slaves there were,
But none who could suppress the sigh, and bend,
So quietly as Luco: long he bore
The stripes, that from his manly bosom drew
The sanguine stream (too little prized); at length
Hope fled his soul, giving her struggles o'er,
And he resolved to die. The sun had reached
His zenith—pausing faintly, Luco stood,
Leaning upon his hoe, while memory brought,
In piteous imagery, his aged father,
His poor fond mother, and his faithful maid:
The mental group in wildest motion set
Fruitless imagination; fury, grief,
Alternate shame, the sense of insult, all
Conspire to aid the inward storm; yet words
Were no relief, he stood in silent woe.

    Gorgon, remorseless Christian, saw the slave
Stand musing, 'mid the ranks, and, stealing soft
Behind the studious Luco, struck his cheek
With a too-heavy whip, that reached his eye,
Making it dark for ever. Luco turned,
In strongest agony, and with his hoe
Struck the rude Christian on the forehead. Pride,
With hateful malice, seize on the Gorgon's soul,
By nature fierce; while Luco sought the beach,
And plunged beneath the wave; but near him lay
A planter's barge, whose seamen grasped his hair,
Dragging to life a wretch who wished to die.

    Rumour now spreads the tale, while Gorgon's breath
Envenomed, aids her blast: imputed crimes
Oppose the plea of Luco, till he scorns
Even a just defence, and stands prepared.
The planters, conscious that to fear alone
They owe their cruel power, resolve to blend
New torment with the pangs of death, and hold
Their victims high in dreadful view, to fright
The wretched number left. Luco is chained
To a huge tree, his fellow-slaves are ranged
To share the horrid sight; fuel is placed

In an increasing train, some paces back,
To kindle slowly, and approach the youth,
With more than native terror. See, it burns!
He gazes on the growing flame, and calls
For 'water, water!' The small boon's denied.
E'en Christians throng each other, to behold
The different alterations of his face,
As the hot death approaches. (Oh, shame, shame
Upon the followers of Jesus! shame
On him that dares avow a God!) He writhes,
While down his breast glide the unpitied tears,
And in their sockets strain their scorched balls.
'Burn, burn me quick! I cannot die!' he cries:
'Bring fire more close!' The planters heed him not,
But still prolonging Luco's torture, threat
Their trembling slaves around. His lips are dry,
His senses seem to quiver, e'er they quit
His frame for ever, rallying strong, then driven
From the tremendous conflict. Sigh no more
Is Luco's, his parched tongue is ever mute;
Yet in his soul his Incilanda stays,
Till both escape together. Turn, my muse,
From this sad scene; lead Bristol's milder soul
To where the solitary spirit roves,
Wrapped in the robe of innocence, to shades
Why thus in mercy let thy whirlwinds sleep
O'er a vile race of Christians, who profane
Thy glorious attributes? Sweep them from earth,
Or check their cruel power: the savage tribes
Are angels when compared to brutes like these.

Advance, ye Christians, and oppose my strain:
Who dares condemn it? Prove from laws divine,
From deep philosophy, or social love,
That ye derive your privilege. I scorn
The cry of Avarice, or the trade that drains
A fellow-creature's blood: bid Commerce plead
Her public good, her nation's many wants,
Her sons thrown idly on the beach, forbade
To seize the image of their God and sell it:—
I'll hear her voice, and Virtue's hundred tongues

Shall sound against her. Hath our public good
Fell rapine for its basis? Must our wants
Find their supply in murder? Shall the sons
Of Commerce shivering stand, if not employed
Worse than the midnight robber? Curses fall
On the destructive system that shall need
Such base supports! Doth England need them? No;
Her laws, with prudence, hang the meagre thief
That from his neighbour steals a slender sum,
Though famine drove him on. O'er *him* the priest,
Beneath the fatal tree, laments the crime,
Approves the law, and bids him calmly die.
Say, doth this law, that dooms the thief, protect
The wretch who makes another's life his prey,
By hellish force to take it at his will?
Is this an English law, whose guidance fails
When crimes are swelled to magnitude so vast,
That *Justice* dare not scan them? Or does *Law*
Bid *Justice* an eternal distance keep
From England's great tribunal, when the slave
Calls loud on *Justice only*? Speak, ye few
Who fill Britannia's senate, and are deemed
The fathers of your country! Boast your laws,
Defend the *honour* of a land so fallen,
That Fame from every battlement is flown,
And Heathens start, even at a Christian's name.

    Hail, social love! true soul of *order*, hail!
Thy softest emanations, pity, grief,
Lively emotion, sudden joy, and pangs,
Too deep for language, are thy own: then rise,
Thou gentle angel! spread thy silken wings
O'er drowsy *man*, breathe in his *soul*, and give
Her God-like powers thy animating force,
To banish Inhumanity. Oh, loose
The fetters of his mind, enlarge his views,
Break down for him the bound of avarice, lift
His feeble faculties beyond a world
To which he soon must prove a stranger! Spread
Before his ravished eye the varied tints
Of future glory; bid them live to *Fame*,

Whose banners wave for ever. Thus inspired,
All that is great, and good, and sweetly mild,
Shall fill his noble bosom. He shall melt,
Yea, by thy sympathy unseen, shall feel
Another's pang: for the lamenting maid
His heart shall heave a sigh; with the old slave
(Whose head is bent with sorrow) he shall cast
His eye back on the joys of youth, and say,
'Thou *once* couldst feel, as I do, love's pure bliss;
Parental fondness, and the dear returns
Of filial tenderness were thine, till torn
From the dissolving scene.'—Oh, social love,
Thou universal good, thou that canst fill
The vacuum of immensity, and live
In endless void! thou that in motion first
Set'st the long lazy atoms, by thy force
Quickly assimilating, and restrained
By strong attraction; touch the soul of man;
Subdue him; make a fellow-creature's woe
His own by heart-felt sympathy, whilst wealth
Is made subservient to his soft disease.

And when thou hast to high perfection wrought
This mighty work, say, *'such is Bristol's soul.'*

Edward Jerningham (1737–1812), *The African Boy* (1788)

Jerningham was an aristocratic *littérateur* and philanthropist. The third son of a baronet he was educated in France, and moved in highly fashionable circles in London, numbering the Prince of Wales among his intimates. He had a varied social life, however, and helped in practical ways many less fortunate than himself, including Cowper. He wrote very much in the spirit of the age of sentiment, and frequently chose subjects relating to his philanthropic interests, including the suffering of animals, the establishment of a foundling hospital, and slavery. His sentimental approach was not, however, to the taste of all his contemporaries. William Gifford, the savage editor of the *Anti-Jacobin*, went so far as to lambaste him for 'snivelling' and 'weeping at the age of fifty o'er love-lorn oxen and deserted sheep'. *The African Boy* is a good example of the manner in which the benevolent fantasies of abolition could be superimposed upon real events which, for the blacks involved, were rather different. The poem is supposedly a monologue spoken by a '*little mournful* MOOR' on the dockside, about to sail from England to be reunited with his mother in Sierra Leone. In Jerningham's poem the boy presents a utopian vision whereby his mother, sexually and physically abused while in slavery, will start a new idyllic life with her infant in the new colony. In fact the reality bore no relation to this idealized vision of voluntary 'recolonization'.

During and after the American War several thousand blacks, the majority ex-slaves, travelled to England in the hope that they would be given paid work in return for having supported the British against the colonies. Not knowing what to do with this refugee population the founding of a free black state in Sierra Leone seemed a useful way of moving them on. The Committee for the Relief of the Black Poor, mainly composed of Clapham sect abolitionists, organized a boat to take a force of 700 blacks to the new settlement. The whole enterprise rapidly became a disaster. The black and white leaders fell into dispute; Equiano (pp. 150–4), who was initially put in charge of the venture, was dismissed after complaining about white corruption. Eventually a much-reduced company of over 300 blacks arrived without sufficient food and supplies in Sierra Leone in May 1787. Within a year a third of them were dead. The remainder found themselves starving and constantly at war with their African neighbours.

The African Boy

Ah, tell me, *little mournful* MOOR.
Why still you linger on the shore?
Haste to your play-mates, haste away,
Nor loiter here with fond delay:
When Morn unveil'd her radiant eye,
You hail'd me as I wander'd by;
Returning at th' approach of Eve,
Your meek salute I still receive.

"*Benign Enquirer*, thou shalt know
Why here my lonesome moments flow:
'Tis said thy Countrymen (no more
Like rav'ning sharks that haunt the shore)
Return to bless, to raise, to cheer,
And pay *Compassion's long arrear*.

"'Tis said the num'rous Captive Train,
Late bound by the degrading Chain,
Triumphant come, with swelling sails,
'Mid smiling skies, and western gales;
They come with festive heart and glee,
Their hands unshackled—minds as free;

They come at Mercy's great command,
To repossess their native land.

"The gales that o'er the Ocean stray,
And chase the waves in gentle play,
Methinks they whisper as they fly,
JUELLEN *soon will meet thine eye!*
'Tis this that sooths her little Son,
Blends all his wishes into one:
Ah! were I clasp'd in her embrace,
I wou'd forgive her past disgrace:
Forgive the memorable hour
She fell a prey to tyrant pow'r;
Forgive her lost, distracted air,
Her sorrowing voice, her kneeling pray'r;
The suppliant tears that gall'd her cheek,
And last, her agonizing shriek.
Lock'd in her hair, a ruthless hand
Trail'd her along the flinty strand;
A ruffian train, with clamours rude,
The impious spectacle pursu'd:
Still as she mov'd, in accents wild,
She cried aloud, *My child! my child!*
The lofty bark she now ascends;
With screams of woe, the air she rends:
The vessel less'ning from the shore,
Her piteous wails I heard no more;
Now as I stretch'd my last survey,
Her distant form dissolv'd away.

"That day is past: I cease to mourn—
Succeeding joy shall have its turn,
Beside the hoarse-resounding deep
A pleasing anxious watch I keep:
For when the morning clouds shall break,
And darts of day the darkness streak,
Perchance along the glitt'ring main,
(Oh, may this hope not throb in vain!)
To meet these long-desiring eyes,
JUELLEN and the Sun may rise."

Samuel Jackson Pratt (1749–1814), from *Humanity; or, The Rights of Nature: A Poem* (1788)

The aptly named Pratt is an exemplary abolition opportunist. Pratt was born to a relatively well-connected family in St Ives yet rejected a career in the Church for that of a theatrical and literary adventurer. He appeared in theatres in Ireland and London in 1773 and 1774 and even played Hamlet at Covent Garden Theatre. After trying his hand as an itinerant showman and even fortune teller, from about 1776 onwards Pratt supported himself as a freelance writer. He published a huge quantity of essays, plays, elegies, and other occasional verse, and always had an eye out for fashionable topics. In 1788 he decided, quite sensibly, to jump on the anti-slave trade bandwagon, publishing *Humanity*. In this prolix and pompous poem he pursued his stated aim 'to consider SLAVERY; but not only that species of it which consists in buying and selling our *Fellow-Creatures* in Africa—BUT EVERY OTHER KIND, in EVERY OTHER PLACE' (preface, p. i). The poem contains a continuous anti-papist and anti-Hispanic agenda. Much of the poem is given over to rehearsing in the most fulsome terms the anti-Spanish and Portuguese colonial 'Black Legend'. The first extract shows how Pratt takes great delight in linking Spanish depravity in the Americas with the operations of the Inquisition. The second extract deals with English colonization under the Romans and then subsequently under the barbarian invasions, ending with the Norman enslavement of the Saxons. Ingeniously Pratt suggests that it is the fact that the Normans are papists that leads them to enforce a slavery system on their Saxon victims. After this England is forced into a vicious history as 'Rome sent her *Monks*, and superstition reign'd, | Freedom in bonds, and even *Conscience* chain'd'. *Humanity* demonstrates how easily abolition could be locked into an already extant, indeed exhausted, colonial mythology which was primarily concerned to demonize Spain and Catholicism. This theme existed long before, and was to outlive, English abolition propaganda. Anti-papist paranoia and the myths of the Black Legend (pp. xlii, 85–8, 106–8, 168–80, 280–8, 313–16, 445–7) remained a mainstay of the rhetoric justifying British imperial expansion in the second half of the nineteenth century.

from *Humanity; or The Rights of Nature: A Poem*

· · · · · ·

Wouldst thou the map of slavery survey,
And the dire circuit of the trade display,
Dart thy astonish'd eye o'er distant lands;
From Senegal to Gambia's burning sands,
Pursue the blushing lines to Congo's shore,

Then traverse many a league, Benguela[1] o'er,
Career immense! o'er which the merchant reigns,
And drags reluctant MILLIONS in his chains!
　COMMERCE! thou sailest on a sanguine flood,
On a red sea of Man's devoted blood:
Thy pompous robe, tho' gemm'd as India's store,
Proud, tho' it flows, is dy'd in human gore.
The tears of millions bathe thy fatal cane,
And half thy treasure springs from human pain,
And not an idol on thy altars shine
But human victims stain the crimson shrine!

　　　·　　·　　·　　·　　·　　·

But ah! once more to stain the bloody shrine
And sell mankind, O PORTUGAL, was thine;
To thee ill-fated Afric owes her pain,
The scourge fresh pointed and the new forg'd chain;
Thine the base arts the sons of gold applaud,
The smile deceptive, and the snare of fraud,
Th' extended hand that chases fear away,
Th' embrace that wins affection to betray,
The league of peace in policy devis'd,
The compact broken and the oath despis'd,
To lure the heart all smooth seductions try'd,
And the heart gain'd, disguise's thrown aside:
The plot avow'd, the promise boldly broke,
By the harsh driver and the galling yoke.

Accurs'd GONZALES[2] taught thee first the art,
To fix this stigma on his country's heart;
The dire example spread with barbarous rage,
Thrift was the vice, and spar'd nor sex nor age;
At length the traffic into *system* came,
Th' infection flew, till Britain caught the flame;
Detested HAWKINS[3] arm'd his pirate host,
And wolfe-like prowl'd on Guinea's fated coast;

---

[1] Port developed by the Portuguese in Angola, which became a significant trading centre in the 18th century.

[2] Sebastián González (1592–1790), born in Coimbra, Portugal; he went to New Mexico where he operated as a particularly ruthless conquistador.

[3] John Hawkins, an Elizabethan explorer and sea-dog who was responsible for fitting out and successfully completing the first three slaving voyages to Africa; he then traded his slaves to the Spanish colonists in the Caribbean. See p. xxv.

Force, brib'ry, stratagem, were all employ'd,
O shame! till twice ten millions were destroy'd.
The work of Christians this, whose lawless rage
Taught milder savages foul wars to wage;
Christians taught savages new modes of strife,
And burst asunder all the ties of life;
Christians taught savages to worship gold,
Till, for their idol, sons and sires were sold:
Till sleeping tribes at midnight's hour were caught,
And seiz'd as prey, to *public market* brought;
Till from the breast the babe was stol'n away,
And children kidnapp'd in the face of day.
   Next tawny SPAIN the shameful trade pursu'd,
Theft grew familiar, tyranny ensued;
The tawny slave on his oppressor pour'd,
And mad with smart, his haughty lord devour'd:
Insidious SPAIN! still vanity thy guide,
Thou mixture loath'd of penury and pride,
Slothful in dignity, supine in state,
Active alone in cruelty and hate:
Commerce, like this, might well command thy zeal,
O! patron of the agonizing wheel!
From where wild Biscay throws its foam around,
And aids the deaf'ning tempests frantic sound;
Ev'n to the steeps where Pyrenees ascend,
And like a rocky chain their links extend,
The nations shuddered as it sprang to birth,
And throes unwonted shook the lab'ring earth!
Thou, TORQUEMADA,[4] thy assistance gave,
To fix this engine which the thoughts enslave;
Sedately savage, thou could'st calm behold,
Men scatter'd piece-meal, tho' thy rage was cold:
Quaff'd the warm blood, enforc'd the torturing power,
And view'd with horrid joy the flames devour.
School'd in thy climes demoniac arts, could bear
To see the cord inflict, the pincers tear;
Array'd thy victims in the rich attire,
And danc'd, like Satan, round thy feast of fire.

[4] Tomás de Torquemada, notoriously severe Dominican priest who became Spanish Grand Inquisitor in 1483, and in 1492 implemented the expulsion of all Jews who refused to convert to the Catholic Church, with its resultant atrocities.

Ah! well might SLAVERY thrive in such a hand,
For all are slaves in a despotic land;
Precarious life is pass'd in trembling awe,
And the proud tyrant owns the breath they draw.
POWER, like a miser, spreads the greedy hand,
Still stepping onward, never at a stand,
A subtle miner working still his way,
In av'rice of accumulating sway;
Tools would be statesmen, statesmen would be kings,
And *they* would mount upon the angels wings;
POWER first advances with a modest air,
But, born a tyrant, quickly learns to dare;
By due degrees he throws each barrier down,
Thinks *strength* is *right*, and calls the world his own;
At length grown absolute, assumes the God,
And proves at once a pestilence and rod,
Till, grown incautious, some rash point he tries,
And in the ruin of his project lies.

.   .   .   .   .   .

Behold where fated FLORIDA extends,
His blood-track'd course the fell VELASQUEZ⁵ bends,
Launches his guilty bark upon the waves,
To kidnap free-born men and make them slaves!
See, as he gains the chain-devoted land,
The sable natives hurry to the strand,
His sailing castle on the waves they view,
And gaz'd with wonder as it near them drew;
But on the deck when *human* forms appear'd,
And peaceful signals smil'd, no more they fear'd;
'Twas MAN they trusted, MAN who spoke them fair,
Cajol'd their faith, and lur'd them to the snare!
And now as guests they land, as guests are led,
Thro' palmy groves to every Indian shed;
The Spaniards there their glitt'ring stores unfold,
The shining mirrour, and the toy of gold;

---

⁵ Diego de Velásquez, Spanish conquistador and first Governor of Cuba. He sailed on Columbus' second voyage of 1493 and in 1511 Diego Columbus sent him on an expedition to conquer Cuba. By 1514 he had control of the island, split with Columbus, and named himself Governor. He then gathered together another military force and sent Hernán Cortez in command of it, to explore Mexico. Cortez, following his Mexican 'triumphs', then split with Velásquez.

Each gaudy bauble, cheats the Indian's eyes,
And tricks his passions into fond surprise,
Teaches new luxuries and wants unknown,
Till Europe's vice and folly is his own;
The useless ornaments his senses fire,
And each fresh gewgaw kindles fresh desire;
Fair in the glass another self he sees,
Till harmless wonder swells to vanities:
From lures like these the baneful passions grow,
And what began in pleasure ends in woe:
Frauds heap'd on frauds to purchase these were taught,
And every trinket was with blood-shed bought.

　　But soon as guests, in turn, the Indian bands
Condemn'd, alas! to quit their native lands
No fraud suspecting, mount the treacherous ship,
Where, as in ambush, lie the chains and whip;
Like nested snakes, whose poisons are enroll'd
Mid'st wreaths of flowers, in many a shining fold;
The faithless Spaniard leaves the plunder'd shore,
His fraud succeeds, and freedom is no more.
Then o'er th' affrighted waves is heard the yell
Of mingled thousands in their wat'ry Hell,
Shut from the light, unknowing yet their doom,
The vessel proves a prison and a tomb:
In the dark caverns of the bark they lie,
Live to fresh horrors or in bondage die;
While the base tyrant glorying in his snare,
Mocks at the loud rebuke and dumb despair.

　　Soon as the vessel bore the tribes away,
What horrors seiz'd upon the trembling prey!
Ah! hear the shrieks of kindred left behind,
Roll to the wave and gather in the wind!
Matrons with orphans, sons with sires appear,
But vain affection's shriek and nature's tear:
The Spanish pirate ploughs the watr'y plains,
And plants his cannon at the thin remains;
The flaming balls the wailing natives reach,
And added slaughter stains the crimson beach;
All, all is lost; but with a generous pride,
E'en slaves spurn life, when freedom is deny'd:

"Free, still be free, loud echoes to the sky,
Dare not to live in bondage, dare to die!"

But oh! ye Christian savages, declare
On what unknown prerogative ye dare?
Peaceful and blest, where rich Bananas grew,
And nature freshen'd as the sea-breeze blew,
Where harvests smil'd without the aid of toil,
And verdure gladden'd the exuberant soil,
Where summer held so bountiful a sway,
Scarce claim'd their year, the culture of a day,
The plants at twilight trusted to the earth,
The following morn sprang blooming into birth,
Grac'd with the bow, the Indians harmless ran,
And undisturb'd enjoy'd the rights of man:
The rights of man by nature still are due,
To men of ev'ry clime and every hue;

.   .   .   .   .   .

See FREEDOM smiling thro' the realms of frost,
And glow on Labradore's inclement coast,
Tho' darkness sheds deep night thro' half the year,
And snow invests the clime,—that clime is dear,
For there fair LIBERTY resides, and there
At large the native breasts the searching air,
Where blows the arctic tempests icy gale,
And famine seizes on the spermy whale,
The bearded Esquimaux half robb'd of sight,
Roves uncontroul'd content with FREEDOM's light,
His country loves, to all its ills conforms,
Endures its caverns and accepts its storms;
For the huge Sea-dog spreads the nimble oar,
Nor sighs for blessings of a softer shore,
No languid Suns unnerve his hardy race,
Which bless'd with Freedom range from place to place.

Such too, BRITANNIA, were THY savage Sons,
Thro' all thy tribes the dread of Slav'ry runs,
Th' mild heroic, honest without laws,
They brav'd each peril in fair Freedom's cause.
But ah! full many an age in Gothic night,
Was veil'd th' effulgence of their native right;

Tho' like the rocky Barrier of their coast,
That Freedom now is her sublimest boast,
Full many an age dissension shook her Fane,
From Rome's fierce Cæsar to the stormy Dane.
In whelming tides pour'd in the Saxon clan,
And Normans finish'd what their rage began;
The savage Briton to his Mountains fled,
Alternate triumph'd and alternate bled;
War upon wars, on conquest conquests throng,
Vandal drove Goth, and Goth urg'd Gaul along;
On human flesh the savage Victors eat,
And mistic Druids shar'd the sanguine treat;
These to their altars, e'en while truth they taught,
The trembling sacrifice rapacious brought;
Impostor-priests before their Idols stood,
And talk'd of Heav'n with hands embru'd in blood;
Before their eyes imagin'd spectres glare,
Spirits were heard, and fancy'd ghosts were there,
Religion, Law, and Government their own,
Bloody their Altars, bloody was their Throne;
Thro' the vex'd Isle the sanguine edict spread
That Heav'n demanded mountains of the dead;
In the dark grove which Superstition trod,
Priests hid their spoils, yet commun'd with their God,
And muttering rights within the fearful gloom,
Stab a fresh victim and the feast resume;
Unfelt as yet the soft'ning ties of life,
Deep in the prisoner's breast the ruthless knife
The Female plung'd—could savage man do more!
Then idly prophesied as flow'd the gore;
A rage of slaughter then *that* sex possess'd,
Now with each grace of melting Pity blest.

But soon the Tyrants sought themselves to save,
For soon Invaders pierc'd the Druid cave;
Forth from the Baltic pour'd the deathful host,
And train'd to havock, crimson'd all the coast,
The Northern Hive swarm'd terrible around,
And every Altar smoak'd upon the ground,
Fire, sword, and carnage, spotted every hand,
Swell'd the gorg'd tomb and delug'd all the land.

Different in mind, and manners, as in face,
The Normans came, an innovating race;
Their power, their passions, and their pride, they brought,
Fierce, bold, and bloody, and with conquest fraught,
From the forc'd mixture of a foreign breed,
Unnatural customs, laws, and wars succeed;
The *Saxon* superstition, weak as dire,
In two extremes of water and of fire,
The burning ploughshare and the cauldron hot,
To prove the Culprit innocent or not,
Were lenient mercies to the cruel strife,
That *then* with horror hung a cloud on life,
Then, by no ties of law or nature bound,
Assassination took its deathful round;
In every grove the lurking stabber lay,
And human bloodshed clotted all the way,
In every street the mangled corpse appear'd,
And mutual hate the sanguine standard rear'd;
In slavish homage to an haughty Lord,
All social joy was broken at the board,
From house to house the Tyrant's edict ran,
And the Feast ended ere the Mirth began,
At the eighth hour toll'd out by dread command,
The dreary knell that darken'd all the land;
Wisdom, her lessons could no more impart,
Nor Friendship gladden or improve the heart,
Ere to their bliss the genial hours invite,
Oppression shed impenetrable night,
The friendly faggot chear'd the heart no more,
And all the soft'ning blooms of life were o'er;
To ruin'd Juries the dire sword succeeds,
And at each pore insulted Justice bleeds,
Ev'n rural pastime in that iron age,
No more to jovial sports the youth engage,
The savage beasts, which Nature gave to all,
To glut th' infatiate pride of *one* must fall;
No more the chace, no more the woods were free,
All, all was Hate,—for all was SLAVERY.
The Lawyer, *Clergy* too, and *Baron* proud,
Aping their Prince, struck terror thro' the croud;
Next, bigot *Priests*, th' imposing mandate bring,

And yoke the Neck of each succeeding King;
Rome sent her *Monks*, and superstition reign'd,
Freedom in bonds, and even *Conscience* chain'd;
Impious as vain, the Pope his terrors laid,
Ignorance was awed and folly was afraid;
Fair Truth in fetters was like Reason bound,
And dread Anathema's[6] were peal'd around,
Pomp of procession, and parade of prayer,
Pardon, and curse, dealt mercy or despair:
The heart was tainted, and the head confus'd,
And all the attributes of God abus'd;
People and Prince were in one chaos hurl'd,
Law, Justice, Order, Virtue, left the World!

    Eventful BRITAIN! should the Muse display,
The various blood-tracks which then mark'd thy way,
Should she pursue the havoc of the sword,
That gash'd thee first, then crouching, call'd thee Lord,
Or trace the Deluges of Foreign Gore,
That ran in purple torrents thro' thy shore,
As conquest oft her crimson pinion spread,
And different victors different mischiefs bred;
Thy hardiest Sons would tremble but to view,
The fearful picture that her pencil drew:
Then let her pause ere she these deeds rehearse
A subject sacred to her future verse.

    Last, and what greater proofs can now remain,
Touch we the border of SURINAM'S[7] plain,
Lo, there the purchas'd NEGROES may'st thou see,
Bursting their bonds and daring to be free,
In daring bands from caves and rocks they come,
And wrought to blood like trooping Panthers roam;
The swart Mulattoes to the forests fly,
Resolv'd to live in freedom, or to die.

---

[6] A solemn ecclesiastical curse or pronouncement involving excommunication. Any execrated person or thing.

[7] The British colony of Surinam on the north-east coast of South America had been notorious since the mid-17th century for slave revolts. A slave revolution features in Aphra Behn's *Oroonoko* set in late 16th- century Surinam.

Blest be the man and worthy to be blest,
Friend of the Wretched, Guardian of th' oppress'd,
Blest be the Man—ye Negroes bow the knee,
And bless him, Thou, Oh! sweet HUMANITY—

William Blake (1757-1827), 'The Little Black Boy', in *Songs of Innocence and of Experience* (1789-90); from *America* (1793); from *Vala; or, The Four Zoas*, Book IX (1797-1803)

There are two publications in which Blake confronted Atlantic slavery in direct ways. The first is Captain John Stedman's *Narrative of a Five Years Expedition against the Revolted Negroes of Surinam* for which Blake produced several engravings, worked up from Stedman's sketches, which showed scenes of slave life, including slave torture and execution. The second is the illuminated book *The Visions of the Daughters of Albion.* Yet, as the selections that follow demonstrate, the critique of slavery which Blake generated is one that does not fall into any easy polemical category. Blake never preached a narrow political agenda, and he does not produce straightforward propaganda on slavery.

Blake's *Songs of Innocence and of Experience* are a fascinating proof that what mid-nineteenth-century Anglo-American audiences saw as abolition verse might not correspond with what we see now. Blake's general concern to confront abuses of power, and the suffering of the innocent, in a variety of contexts, influenced the concerns of the transatlantic abolition crusade in unexpected ways. It is a strange fact that Blake's first substantial printing in North America was as an abolition poet. The inspirational American abolition polemicist Lydia Maria Child (pp. 472–82) printed, over a period of seven months in 1842, a substantial selection of Blake's *Songs* in the mass circulated *National Anti-Slavery Standard.* At this point Blake was, even in Britain, virtually unknown as an author or artist. Child selected the poems from the first popularly available edition of the *Songs,* printed in London in 1839. Child chose to begin her mini-anthology of Blake with the poem in *Songs of Innocence* most directly, though ambivalently, engaged with the question of interracial conflict and colour, 'The Little Black Boy'. It was a good poem with which to confront a prejudiced Northern readership, because while it appears to be endorsing a conventional set of beliefs relating to the superiority of whites the poem has a sting in its tail. The poem is a forceful meditation on the dangers of Christian Evangelical indoctrination on the mind of the African, or African American. The black boy is presented in the first stanza as having internalized the stereotypical colour symbolism of European Christianity and has consequently accepted the resulting encoded readings of black and white in absolute moral and spiritual terms. Blackness is seen to indicate a soulless state of unenlightenment; the soul to which the black boy aspires is a white one. This approach to whiteness supports racist stereotypes; yet if the poem is ironic then Blake is not asserting but subverting the rhetoric of racism. Blake seems finally to be questioning the basis and adequacy of conventional British constructions of blackness. Child, in placing this work before a mass American readership, reinvented Blake as an effective propagandist for, yet critic of, abolition race agendas. In doing so she indicated how Blake's unorthodox and ironic approaches to the languages of race had a potency which more historically specific and stylistically conventional abolition literatures lacked.

Slavery, and the reactions of Europe and America to its existence during the revolutionary period, is a central theme in *Visions of the Daughters of Albion*. What is unique about the *Visions* is the way it sets up an abusive triangular relationship between a male slave owner and rapist, his female victim, and her former partner. In analysing the destructive effects of female slave rape on the powerless male Blake examines an area which is neglected by other eighteenth- and nineteenth-century slave literatures. The central theme of the *Visions* is a bold and horrific one. It concerns the seemingly irreparable effects of slave rape upon the consciousness of the victims, who, with a typical Blakean imaginative amplitude, are finally seen to include the slave owner as well as the slaves.

In his subsequent work Blake increasingly moves from the psychological despair at the end of the *Visions* to explore the possibility of violent liberation. The implications of slave insurrection and the process of emancipation through revolutionary violence are treated in *America*, which paves the way for the climactic ninth book of *Vala; or, The Four Zoas*. In both cases Blake suggests new ways of thinking about how spiritual renewal might, or might not, be possible within the damaged psychology of the ex-slave.

The ninth book of *Vala* constitutes Blake's central expression of the overthrow of colonial slavery. Blake's emancipation moment is articulated in stark counterpoint to the abolition establishment's preferred rendition of the theme, nicely encapsulated within the concluding stanza's of Cowper's 'The Morning Dream' (pp. 90–1). In *Vala* Blake is careful to make sure that the association of this moment of liberation for all enslaved people is located within Africa and the Atlantic slave trade. In that ecstatic instant when 'all the slaves from every earth in the wide universe | Sing a new song, drowning confusion in its happy notes' there is a crucial detail. Before launching into an extended and terrifying paean to the destruction of the slave power Blake slows down, to point out that: 'the song that they [the emancipated slaves] sung was this, | Composed by an African black, from the little earth of Sotha.' The aesthetic touch paper for the explosively violent process of emancipation which follows is created by a black African-American slave.

The poem may never have been published in Blake's lifetime, but what he achieved here nevertheless constitutes an extreme affirmation of the Atlantic slave's right to the violent act of self-liberation, even if it means the destruction of the slave power in a maelstrom of bloodlust. Blake was the only major British Romantic poet who dared to celebrate slave revolution. It is significant that he wrote this account before the abolition of the slave trade when the pro-slavery propaganda machine was deluging London with horror stories about San Domingue. Blake delightedly feeds off this anti-black atrocity literature in an act of inspirational parody. The horrific accounts of massacre, sexual abuse, and bloodlust which flooded Britain from the early 1790s onwards in the wake of the 1790 slave-led massacres in the great Northern Plain of San Domingue are here transmogrified into a universal hymn of triumph. Blake shifts attention away from the 'black beast' stereotypes of this counter-literature of emancipation, and places the cause of violence at the door of the slave power.

The Little Black Boy

My mother bore me in the southern wild,
And I am black, but oh! my soul is white;
White as an angel is the English child;
But I am black, as if bereaved of light.

My mother taught me underneath a tree;
And sitting down before the heat of day,
She took me on her lap and kissed me,
And pointing to the east began to say:—

'Look on the rising sun: there God does live,
And gives his light, and gives his heat away;
And flowers, and trees, and beasts, and men receive,
Comfort in morning, joy in the noon day.

'And we are put on earth a little space,
That we may learn to bear the beams of love;
And these black bodies, and this sun-burnt face,
Is but a cloud, and like a shady grove.

'For when our souls have learned the heat to bear,
The clouds shall vanish; we shall hear his voice,
Saying: "Come from the grove, my love and care,
And round my golden tent like lambs rejoice."'

Thus did my mother say, and kissed me;
And thus I say to little English boy:
When I from black and he from white cloud free
And round the tent of God like lambs we joy,

I'll shade him from the heat, 'till he can bear,
To lean in joy upon our Father's knee;
And then I'll stand, and stroke his silver hair,
And be like him, and he will then love me.

America

Preludium (ll. 11–16, 26–37)

.   .   .   .   .   .

'Dark virgin', said the hairy youth, 'thy father stern abhorred
Rivets my tenfold chains while still on high my spirit soars.
Sometimes an eagle screaming in the sky, sometimes a lion
Stalking upon the mountains, and sometimes a whale I lash
The raging fathomless abyss, anon a serpent folding
Around the pillars of Urthona,[1] and round thy dark, dark limbs

.   .   .   .   .   .

Soon as she saw the terrible boy, then burst the virgin cry:
'I know thee, I have found thee, and I will not let thee go.
Thou art the image of God who dwells in darkness of Africa,
And thou art fallen to give me life in regions of dark death.
On my American plains I feel the struggling afflictions
Endured by roots that writhe their arms into the nether deep;
I see a serpent in Canada, who courts me to his love;
In Mexico an Eagle, and a lion in Peru;
I see a Whale in the South-Sea, drinking my soul away.
Oh, what limb-rending pains I feel! Thy fire and my frost
Mingle in howling pains, in furrows by thy lightnings rent;
This is eternal death, and this the torment long foretold.'

A Prophecy (ll. 3–51)

.   .   .   .   .   .

Washington[2] spoke: 'Friends of America, look over the Atlantic sea;
A bended bow is lifted in heaven, and a heavy iron chain

---

[1]   Urthona within Blake's mythography is one of the 'Four Mighty Ones', the four elemental spirits
who make up the character of the Eternal Man. In *America* Urthona is a grim dictatorial presence who
imprisons the youthful and revolutionary Orc. Urthona's daughter is kind to Orc.

[2]   George Washington (1732–99), commander in chief of the Continental Army during the American
War of Independence. Blake's *America* is a complex meditation on the American War and his Washington

Descends link by link from Albion's cliffs across the sea to bind
Brothers and sons of America, till our faces pale and yellow,
Heads depressed, voices weak, eyes downcast, hands work-bruised,
Feet bleeding on the sultry sands, and the furrows of the whip
Descend to generations that in future times forget.'

The strong voice ceased; for a terrible blast swept over the heaving sea.
The eastern cloud rent; on his cliffs stood Albion's wrathful Prince,
A dragon form clashing his scales! At midnight he arose,
And flamed red meteors round the land of Albion beneath.
His voice, his locks, his awful shoulders, and his glowing eyes
Appear to the Americans upon the cloudy night.

Solemn heave the Atlantic waves between the gloomy nations,
Swelling, belching from its depths red clouds and raging fires.
Albion is sick; America faints. Enraged the zenith grew.
As human blood shooting its veins all round the orbed heaven
Red rose the clouds from the Atlantic in vast wheels of blood,
And in the red clouds rose a wonder o'er the Atlantic sea—
Intense, naked, a human fire, fierce glowing as the wedge
Of iron heated in the furnace. His terrible limbs were fire,
With myriads of cloudy terrors, banners dark and towers
Surrounded; heat but not light went through the murky atmosphere.
The king of England looking Westward trembles at the vision.
Albion's Angel stood beside the Stone of Night, and saw
The terror like a comet, or more like the planet red
That once enclosed the terrible wandering comets in its sphere.
Then, Mars, thou wast our centre, and the planets flew round
Thy crimson disc; so ere the sun was rent from thy red sphere.
The spectre glowed, his horrid length staining the temple long
With beams of blood, and thus a voice came froth and shook the temple:
'The morning comes, the night decays, the watchmen leave their stations;
The grave is burst, the spices shed, the linen wrapped up;
The bones of death, the covering clay, the sinews shrunk and dried
Reviving shake, inspiring move, breathing, awakening,
Spring like redeemed captives when their bonds and bars are burst.

---

is not that closely related to the historical figure. *America* opens with the 'Prophecy' in which Washington defies Britain. In this speech Washington develops his accusations against British imperialism with the metaphor of an enormous transatlantic chain, which stands for enslavement of both black and white colonists.

Let the slave grinding at the mill run out in to the field;
Let him look up into the heavens and laugh in the bright air;
Let the enchained soul shut up in dark ness and in sighing,
Whose face has never seen a smile in thirty weary years,
Rise and look out—his chains are loose, his dungeon doors are open.
And let his wife and children return from the oppressor's scourge—
They look behind at every step and believe it is a dream,
Singing, "The sun has left his blackness, and has found a fresher morning,
And the fair moon rejoices in the clear and cloudless night;
For empire is no more, and now the lion and wolf shall cease." '

Vala; or, The Four Zoas (from Book IX)

Go down, ye kings & councillors & giant warriors!
Go down into the depths, go down & hide yourselves beneath!
Go down, with horse & chariots & trumpets of hoarse war!

'Lo! how the pomp of Mystery[1] goes down into the caves!
Her great men howl & throw the dust & rend their hoary hair;
Her delicate women and children shriek upon the bitter wind,
Spoiled of their beauty, their hair rent and their skin shrivelled up.
Lo, darkness covers the long pomp of banners on the wind,
And black horses & armed men & miserable bound captives.
Where shall the graves receive them all, & where shall be their place,
And who shall mourn for Mystery, who never loosed her captives?

'Let[2] the slave grinding at the mill run out in to the field;
Let him look up into the heavens and laugh in the bright air;
Let the enchained soul, shut up in dark ness and in sighing,
Whose face has never seen a smile in thirty weary years,
Rise and look out—his chains are loose, his dungeon doors are open
And let his wife and children return from the oppressor's scourge—

---

[1] Blake is using the word Mystery here in its biblical sense as the whore of Babylon from Revelation: 'I saw a woman sit upon a scarlet coloured beast, full of names of blasphemy, having seven heads and ten horns . . . And upon her forehead was a name written, MYSTERY, BABYLON THE GREAT, THE MOTHER OF HARLOTS AND ABOMINATIONS OF THE EARTH' (Revelation 18: 3–5).

[2] The next fourteen lines are a slightly revised version of the famous passage on emancipation in *America*, top of this page.

They look behind at every step and believe it is a dream:
Are these the slaves that groaned along the streets of Mystery?
Where are your bonds & taskmasters? Are these the prisoners?
Where are your chains, where are your tears? Why do you look around?
If you are thirsty, there is the river: go bathe your parched limbs.
The good of all the land is before you; for Mystery is no more!'

Then all the slaves from every earth in the wide universe
Sing a new song, drowning confusion in its happy notes
(While the flail of Urizen[3] sounded loud, & the winnowing
    wind of Tharmas[4])
So loud, so clear in the wide heavens; & the song that they sung was this,
Composed by an African black, from the little earth of Sotha:[5]

'Aha! Aha! How came I here so soon in my sweet native land?
How came I here? Methinks I am as I was in my youth,
When in my father's house I sat & heard his cheering voice;
Methinks I see his flocks & herds & feel my limbs renewed;
And lo, my brethren in their tents & their little ones around them!'

The song arose to the golden feast, the Eternal Man rejoiced:
Then the Eternal man said: 'Luvah,[6] the vintage is ripe: arise!
   .   .   .   .   .   .

Then Luvah stood before the winepress; all his fiery sons
Brought up the loaded wagons with shoutings; ramping tigers play
In the jingling traces, furious lions sound the song of joy
To the golden wheels circling upon the pavement of heaven; & all
The villages of Luvah ring: the golden tiles of the villages
Reply to violins & tabors, to the pipe, flute, lyre & cymbal.

---

[3] Urizen is another of the 'Four Mighty Ones' who constitute Eternal Man. At the start of *Vala* he has been involved in a conspiracy with Luvah to seize total control of Eternal Man, one of the actions which causes the fall of the world and the Chaos in which the poem starts. He is not, as with most of Blake's emanations, a stable fictive entity, but generally represents powers of rationality; his name at one level constitutes a pun on 'Your reason'.

[4] Tharmas is another of the 'Four Mighty Ones'. He quarrels with his female counterpart Enion at the opening of *Vala*. He spends most of the poem in search of her, as she wanders 'on the verge of nonentity'. They are only reunited after the dance round the winepresses, in Eternity.

[5] This probably refers to Sotho, or what is now called Lesotho in Africa, although Blake may also be alluding to Egypt, and the Sothic year, a cyclic period of 1,460 years. In the latter case the African is singing in a new Egyptian millennium with the song that sets off the dance.

[6] Luvah is the last of the 'Four Mighty Ones'; he is vital to the action of the poem's opening because of his conspiracy to take over Eternal Man. As representative of the passions both of sexual love and love in its widest sense (his name puns on 'Lover', 'Luvah') he oversees the violent sado-masochism unleashed by the dance round his winepresses. His children are responsible for the 'cruel delights' with which the sons of Mystery are destroyed.

Then fell the legions of Mystery in maddening confusion
Down, down, through the immense, with outcry, fury & despair
Into the winepresses of Luvah. Howling fell the clusters
Of human families through the deep. The winepresses were filled,
The blood of life flowed plentiful, odours of life arose
All round the heavenly arches & the odours rose, singing this song:

'O terrible winepresses of Luvah! O caverns of the grave!
How lovely the delights of those risen again from death.
O trembling joy! Excess of joy is like excess of grief.'

So sang the human odours round the winepresses of Luvah.
But in the winepresses is wailing, terror & despair.
Forsaken of their elements they vanish & are no more;
No more but a desire of being, distracted ravening desire,
Desiring like the hungry earth and the gaping grave

. . . .

How red the sons and daughters of Luvah! How they tread the grapes
Laughing & shouting drunk with odours; many fall o'erwearied;
Drowned in the wine is many a youth & maiden. Those around them
Lay them on skins of tigers or the spotted leopard or wild ass
Till they revive, or bury them in the cool grots making lamentation.
But in the winepresses the human grapes sing not nor dance:
They howl & writhe in shoals of torment, in fierce flames consuming,
In chains & irons & in dungeons, circle with ceaseless fires
In pits & dens & shades of death, in shapes of torment & woe.
The plates, the screws and wracks & saws & cords & fires & floods,
The cruel joy of Luvah's daughters, lacerating with knives
And whips their victims, & the deadly sports of Luvah's sons.

Timbrels & violins sport around the winepresses. The little seed,
The sportive root, the earthworm, the small beetle, the wise emmet
Dance round the winepresses of Luvah. The centipede is there,
The ground spider with many eyes, the mole clothed in velvet,
The earwig armed, the tender maggot, emblem of immortality,
The slow slug, the grasshopper that sings & laughs & drinks—
The winter comes, he folds his slender bones without a murmur—
There is the nettle that stings with soft down, & there
The indignant thistle whose bitterness is bred in his milk
And who lives in the contempt of his neighbour; there all the idle weeds
That creep about the obscure places show their various limbs
Naked in all their beauty, dancing round the winepresses.

They dance around the dying & they drink the howl and groan;
They catch the shrieks in cups of gold, they hand them to one another.

Olaudah Equiano (1745–97), 'Miscellaneous Verses; or, Reflections on the State of my Mind during my First Convictions of the Necessity of Believing the Truth, and of experiencing the Inestimable Benefits of Christianity', from *The Interesting Narrative of the Life of Olaudah Equiano, or Gustavas Vassa, the African* (1789)

Equiano has emerged during the last twenty years, after almost 200 years of neglect, as one of the most remarkable writers and social activists to engage with eighteenth-century slavery. Equiano was kidnapped into African slavery when he was about 10. He was shipped first to the West Indies, then Virginia, and was bought as a slave by a British naval captain in 1756 who changed his name to Gustavas Vassa. In 1762 he was sold on to a merchant in the West Indies and finally bought his own freedom in 1766. During the remainder of his life Equiano travelled mainly between England and the Caribbean, although in 1773 he even enrolled in an Arctic expedition. While a free black Equiano was several times involved in trading slaves, or running slave plantations. In 1776 he finally resigned from his position as plantation overseer and from his return to London appears to have become increasingly involved in attempts to help poor blacks. Equiano also became linked with leading London radicals and is known to have stayed in the house of Thomas Hardy, leader of the London Corresponding Society, who was notoriously prosecuted in the Treason Trials of 1794. Equiano published his momentous *Narrative* in the equally momentous year of 1789, and the book went through many editions in England and Ireland and had been translated into Dutch, German, and Russian by 1794.

Equiano's *Narrative* is an immensely complicated text which inverts and problematizes abolition rhetoric and the eighteenth-century genre of the confessional spiritual narrative. Equiano's shifting takes on racial prejudice, his own complicity in the slave systems, and his personal quest to find a form of Christianity produced a text of multiple ironies. The debates over the extent to which Equiano was aware of the moral and political contradictions within his text continue. The 'Miscellaneous Verses' printed below are caught up in these multiple ironies. At one level this is a confessional religious poem justifying Equiano's conversion to a white readership. Yet there is a level at which Equiano plays his indescribable sufferings as a slave off against Christ's gesture of sacrifice.

Miscellaneous Verses; or, Reflections on the State of my Mind

Well may I say my life has been
One scene of sorrow and of pain;
From early days I griefs have known,
And as I grew my griefs have grown.

Dangers were always in my path,
And fear of wrath and sometimes death;
While pale dejection in me reign'd
I often wept, by grief constrain'd.

When taken from my native land,
By an unjust and cruel band,
How did uncommon dread prevail!
My sighs no more I could conceal.

To ease my mind I often strove,
And tried my trouble to remove:
I sung and utter'd sighs between—
Assay'd to stifle guilt with sin.

But, O! not all that I could do
Would stop the current of my woe;
Conviction still my vileness shew'd;
How great my guilt—how lost to good.

"Prevented that I could not die,
Nor could to one sure refuge fly;
An orphan state I had to mourn,—
Forsook by all, and left forlorn."

Those who beheld my downcast mien,
Could not guess at my woes unseen:

They by appearance could not know
The troubles that I waded through.

Lust, anger, blasphemy, and pride,
With legions of such ills beside,
"Troubled my thoughts," while doubts and fears
Clouded and darken'd most my years.

"Sighs now no more would be confin'd—
They breath'd the trouble of my mind:"
I wish'd for death, but check'd the word,
And often pray'd unto the Lord.

Unhappy, more than some on earth,
I thought the place that gave me birth—
Strange thoughts oppress'd—while I replied,
"Why not in Ethiopia died?"

And why thus spar'd, when nigh to hell!—
God only knew—I could not tell!—
"A tott'ring fence, a bowing wall,
I thought myself e'er since the fall."

Oft times I mus'd, and nigh despair,
While birds melodious fill'd the air.
"Thrice happy songsters, ever free,"
How blest were they compar'd to me!

Thus all things added to my pain;
While grief compel'd me to complain;
When sable clouds began to rise,
My mind grew darker than the skies.

The English nation forc'd to leave,
Now did my breast with sorrow heave!
I long'd for rest—cried "Help me, Lord!
Some mitigation, Lord, afford!"

Yet on, dejected, still I went—
Heart-throbbing woes within me pent;
Nor land, nor sea, could comfort give,
Nor aught my anxious mind relieve.

Weary with troubles yet unknown
To all but God and self alone,
Numerous months for peace I strove,
Numerous foes I had to prove.

Inur'd to dangers, grief, and woes,
Train'd up 'midst perils, death, and foes,
I said, "Must it thus ever be?
No quiet is permitted me."

Hard hap, and more than heavy lot!
I pray'd to God, "Forget me not—
What thou ordain'st help me to bear;
But, O! deliver from despair!"

Striving and wrestling seem'd in vain;
Nothing I did could ease my pain:
Then gave I up my work and will,
Confess'd and own'd my doom was hell!

Like some poor pris'ner at the bar,
Conscious of guilt, of sin, and fear,
Arraign'd, and self 'condem'd, I stood,
"Lost in the world and in my blood!"

Yet here, 'midst blackest clouds confin'd,
A beam from Christ, the day-star, shin'd;
Surely, thought I, if Jesus please,
He can at once sign my release.

I, ignorant of his righteousness,
Set up my labours in its place;
"Forgot for why his blood was shed,
And pray'd and fasted in his stead."

He dy'd for sinners—I am one;
Might not his blood for me atone?
Tho' I am nothing else but sin,
Yet surely he can make me clean!

Thus light came in and I believ'd;
Myself forgot, and help receiv'd!

My Saviour then I know I found,
For, eas'd from guilt, no more I groan'd.

O, happy hour, in which I ceas'd
To mourn, for then I found a rest!
My soul and Christ were now as one—
Thy light, O Jesus, in me shone!

Bless'd be thy name; for now I know
I and my works can nothing do;
"The Lord alone can ransom man—
For this the spotless Lamb was slain!"

When sacrifices, works, and pray'r,
Prov'd vain, and ineffectual were,
"Lo then I come!" the Saviour cry'd
And, bleeding, bow'd his head and dy'd.

He dy'd for all who ever saw
No help in them, or by the law:
I this have seen and gladly own
"Salvation is by Christ alone!"

Samuel Whitchurch, from *The Negro Convert: A Poem* (1791); from *Hispaniola* (1804)

Whitchurch appended a long self-explanatory title to his first slavery poem *The Negro Convert: A Poem; being the Substance of the Experience Of Mr John Marrant, Negro, As related by himself previous to his Ordination, at the Countess of Huntingdon's Chapel in Bath, On Sunday the 15th of May 1785, together With a concise Account of the most Remarkable Events in his very singular Life*. Whitchurch explains in his preface that he took down Marrant's narrative in shorthand while he was being examined for the ministry, and that he has worked his poem out of these raw materials.

The first part of the poem tells how Marrant, a free black in North Carolina, lived a life of sin and sensuality in Charleston before being struck with guilt on hearing George Whitefield preach. He subsequently underwent a violent conversion experience. The following extract takes the poem up at the point where Marrant was press-ganged into an English man of war, where he worked under the conditions of a slave for six years. After several suicide attempts, and action in the Battle of Dogger Bank against the Dutch in 1781, he finally returned to Britain and freedom. Although wounded in battle he was unable to gain a penny in compensation or pay. At this point he decided seriously to devote himself to the ministry and after being helped by a series of religious mentors achieved his goal.

Marrant's story in many ways closely mirrors that set out in Equiano's *Interesting Narrative*. It is presented as part travel and adventure story, part slave narrative, and part spiritual autobiography. Marrant's biography, however, is not his own to tell, and is being translated into the normalizing fictions of a white pietistic versifier. Whitchurch's take on the narrative presents Marrant's religious quest as glorious and finally unproblematic. The dark and subversive approach to white society and its religious factionalism which seeps out into Equiano's prose is absent.

Over a decade after writing *The Negro Servant* Whitchurch returned to the theme of blacks and slavery in the context of the San Domingue revolution. The subject allowed the nationalistic but radical Whitchurch more latitude. He composed his epic *Hispaniola* in order to absorb the San Domingue rebellion into the flood of publicity directed in Britain against Napoleon's imperial ambitions. The black revolution is used to set up a bloodthirsty assault not only on Bonaparte but upon the entire history of the French Revolution. Whitchurch's poem demonstrates that the cult of Toussaint, and especially the British myth of his moral and military superiority to Bonaparte, was firmly in place at the turn of the nineteenth century. The cultural fictions explaining the slave revolt had shifted, and it is no longer the British abolitionists and the Amis des Noirs who are given responsibility for the carnage in San Domingue. Bonaparte, as the incarnation of French Jacobin bloodlust, has gained the sole credit. For Whitchurch Toussaint is the spiritual embodiment of a terrible but implacably active spirit of vengefulness. In this sense he could not be further from Wordsworth's Toussaint (pp. 231–3). In the poem's conclusion the spectre of Toussaint appears and speaks in apocalyptic language of French responsibility for the violence and atrocity they have unleashed. The abused slaves are shown to have learned their trade from the excesses of the Revolution, and perform a hideous colonial mimicry of the September massacres upon the bodies of the planters. It is a bitter irony that when Dessalines, first leader of the black Haytian republic, finally did order the massacre of all French whites on the island in 1805, it was under the specific influence of British colonial advisers. Whitchurch maintains a typical British oblivion to this fact. In Whitchurch's fantasy it is not Dessalines, but the spirit of Toussaint that appears and calls down a terrible vengeance on Napoleon and his troops. The poetry is, in aesthetic terms, pretty bad, but Whitchurch has, nevertheless, produced verse that is powerful in its commitment to black violence as the inevitable response to the slave systems of the French Caribbean.

from *The Negro Convert*

I Sing, "no Indian whose untutor'd mind,
Sees God in clouds, or hears him in the wind,
Whose soul proud science never taught to stray
Far as the solar walk, or milky way."[1]
More grand my theme—for lo! my daring muse,
With the young Negro shall extend her views;
His notions of a God are not confin'd
To flying clouds, nor to the whistling wind!
His soul has Heav'nly wisdom taught to stray
Beyond the solar walk, and milky way;
His heart enlighten'd, warm devotion fires,
And pure religion all his soul inspires;
Cheer'd by the sunshine of a Saviour's love,
E'en Pisgah's[2] lofty top he soars above;
No middle skies can bound his future views,
His happier soul sublimer heights pursues,
For faith in Jesus to his hope has giv'n
Beyond uncertain life—a certain Heav'n.—

   Yet ere my muse pursues her destin'd way,
To great *Selina*[3] I would homage pay;
To you, blest ornament of Heav'nly grace!
Whose bounteous deeds are known in every place;
Proud your firm zeal, your actions to rehearse,
To you I'd sing—to you direct my verse!
But since too low the highest of my lays
To sound your worth—to celebrate your praise,
The noble task alas! I must decline,
And for *effects*, the honor'd *cause* resign;—
Yet wheresoe'er the Gospel banner flies,
Myriads your worth, your gen'rous zeal shall prize;
Yet wheresoe'er the Gospel trump shall sound,
Dear shall the name of *Huntingdon*[4] be found!—

---

[1]   A slightly rearranged quotation of Alexander Pope's 1733 *An Essay on Man*, ll. 99–102. In fact Pope's passage goes on to celebrate the harmony and contentment of his imagined 'Indian's' consciousness, existing outside European corruption.

[2]   There are three American mountains carrying this name, two in the Catskill Mountains, and one which is the highest peak in the Blue-Ridge Mountains of Virginia.

[3]   Selina, or Selene, the Greek moon goddess, Artemis.

[4]   The Countess of Huntingdon, abolitionist and philanthropist, to whom the poem is dedicated.

Lo! Christ its head—its nursing mother you,
On distant shores a rising Church I view,
Where with commission sent, the sable youth
Shall to Barbarians preach the Word of Truth,
Shall in those gloomy corners of the earth
Spread the glad tidings of a Saviour's birth!
His blameless life shall paint, and to them shew
His painful death, and resurrection too;
Shall warn the sinner from his evil way,
And preach the blessings of the Gospel day;
Shall paint a Christ triumphing o'er the grave,
To anger slow, and ready still to save;
He like a Paul of righteousness shall treat,
Of temp'rance, reason, and the judgment seat!—
Their bosoms smote with reverential fear,
The joyful news, shall happy Negroes hear.—
Thus, thus great Lady shall the truth be known,
In climes remote, and in a distant zone;
'Midst savage plants thus SHARON'S ROSE shall rise,
And Eden smile beneath inclement skies!
Thus shall the *Negro Convert* publish still
To fellow blacks, the great Jehovah's will;
And num'rous hearts can from experience tell
A task so great befits our hero well.—

And now fam'd Patroness of saints below,
In whose great Master's cause my numbers flow,
O! deign t'attend—while gladly I display
The solemn grandeur of that sacred day,
When in your Chapel, lo! each pious youth,
Receiv'd the charge in godliness, and truth,
By rev'rend hands ordain'd—when each declar'd
What grace, what favor, his experience shar'd.—
And now the eighth in conscious wisdom bold
His pious tale had eloquently told,
His honey'd tongue the congregation charm'd,
And in his cause each feeling bosom warm'd;
His melting accents so had pleas'd the ear,
That still they listen'd—still they seem'd to hear—
When on the throne, high rais'd above the rest,
His soul's experience thus the *Black* exprest—

Since here I'm brought by Providence to tell
What checquer'd scenes my christian life befell,
How wounded conscience flung with poignant smart
When saving grace had reach'd my stubborn heart;
Dear list'ning brethren! I beseech you pray
That God will own me on this solemn day!
O! beg of Christ, my pious friends, to grant
A kind supply for every present want,
To check the sallies of impetuous youth,
And teach my falt'ring tongue to speak the truth.—

First on Columbia's shores my breath I drew
Where pleasing fast my years of childhood flew;
Each art was try'd to please my vacant mind,
To pleasure prone—to vanity inclin'd;
But grown to riper years, I soon began
To change from infant toys—to toys of man;
On various instruments intent to play
To Charlestown now I eager bent my way,
There the French-horn I learnt with skill to blow
In lofty notes, or modulations flow;
There at the midnight dance I oft was seen
To rouse to motion by the violin.—
Thus pass'd my days, and thus my nights would pass,
Still charm'd by music, and the chearful glass.—
But O my friends, twas giv'n me soon to know
That pleasures ways would terminate in woe,
That down the fearful steep her foosteps led,
To the dark regions of the second dead!—
For lo! in proud rebellion now I rose
Against my God, and deem'd his saints my foes;
In his own house I strove my horn to sound,
To spread confusion thro' his flock around;
In vain I strove, for Heav'nly grace decreed,
That in the black attempt my heart should bleed;
For lo! the trumpet of the Gospel sounds,
My soul disarms—my every scheme confounds;
The champion *Whitefield*[5] like an angel spoke,
And from his lips this awful sentence broke,

---

[5] George Whitefield (1714–70), English Evangelical follower of John Wesley. He made seven trips to
America, and his charismatic preaching was a contributory factor in the 'Great Awakening' of religious

"Prepare O Israel to meet thy GOD!"
Fear seiz'd my soul—I felt the vengeful rod!
Like Saul of Tarsus[6] to the ground I fell,
While in my conscience blaz'd a fiery Hell!
Convictions barbed arrows pierc'd my heart,
And conscious guilt, and shame increas'd its smart;
Thus see the wretch who dar'd with impious rage
The great Ambassador of Heav'n t'engage,
Who dar'd presume the sounding horn to blow,
Now fearful sink beneath a load of woe!
Trembling, and prostrate now upon the ground,
I cry'd for mercy, but no mercy found;
My crimes I thought too black to be forgiv'n,
My sins against me shut the door of Heav'n!
Stung to the inmost soul I roar'd aloud,
And still around me press'd the list'ning croud;
At length the service o'er great Whitefield came,
At his approach I felt unusual shame;
His Heav'nly presence work'd my soul's disgrace,
I turn'd aside, nor dar'd to shew my face;
When spoke the holy man I late defy'd,
"And art thou caught at last?" he joyful cry'd,
"Thy trembling limbs, and downcast looks declare,
That Christ has caught thee in the Gospel snare."
Unfit to walk—almost depriv'd of sense,
He bade some standers by to take me thence,
Said he would see me ere from town he went,
If leisure time should favor his intent.—
Now to my home in misery convey'd,
I loath'd myself—was for myself afraid!
My sinful conduct star'd me in the face,
No hope of mercy—none of Heav'nly grace!
But black despair, and conscious guilt combin'd
To light an Aetna in my tortur'd mind!—
Ye chosen of the Lord!—tis ye have known
The spirit wounded, and the contrite groan;

consciousness on the East Coast. He finally broke with the Wesleyans and became an extreme Calvin-istic Methodist.

   [6] St Paul, who died in AD 67, a Jew, but son of a Roman citizen, was instrumental in persecuting the early Christians until he underwent a miraculous conversion experience on the road to Damascus, struck temporarily blind by a white light. After recovering he was instrumental in setting up the early Christian missions.

'Tis ye alone can tell a man may stand
When God afflicts him with a chast'ning hand,
When dire disease shall rack his feeble frame,
And dim the lustre of his vital flame;
That this he may sustain—nor shed one tear,
But O! a wounded conscience, who can bear?—
—Three days I sigh'd, and fed the growing flame,
When to my room a Baptist preacher came,
He came to my relief—when lo! he found
My room with various nostrums spread around;
There too he found—fresh med'cine to prescribe,
Two famous Doctors of the healing tribe;
For them, my friends, mistaking my disease,
Had sent to physic, bleed, and give me ease;
But vain their art—their skill united vain;
There was but *One* could heal my bosom's pain;
There was but one Physician could be found
To soothe my anguish, or to heal my wound;
He who for man resign'd his sacred breath,
Alone could save my guilty soul from death!
These said the Preacher—these may now depart,
They have no med'cine for a wounded heart;
Then strove the holy man with anxious care
To raise my hope—to brighten my despair;
On bended knees, with fervency of soul,
He begg'd of Christ my anguish to controul,
Some Heav'nly grace—some mercy to impart,
To check my grief, and ease my aching heart;
In vain he begg'd—invok'd a Saviour's name,
To my sad soul no ray of comfort came!
But all was dark, and doubt; and fell despair,
And every horror reign'd triumphant there!
As love his breast, and pity mov'd his tongue,
An hymn of tuneful WATTS's[7] now he sung;
But ah! nor bard divine, nor music's charms
Could quell my grief, could quiet my alarms!
I deem'd myself beneath th'Almighty's curse,
And told my pious friend—he made me worse—

---

[7] Isaac Watts (1674–1748), Nonconformist poet and hymn writer, best remembered for the children's classic *Divine Songs for Children* (1715).

But he undaunted—to his Master true
Resolv'd to try again what pray'r could do;—
He pray'd again, and O! what Heav'nly love,
What wondrous grace came smiling from above!
My soul enlighten'd felt the saving pow'r,
And mercy triumph'd in that happy hour!
Like Bunyan's joyful pilgrim now I found
My christian burden tumble to the ground!
Before my faith, lo! *Doubting-Castle* fell,
And grim *Despair* sunk to his native Hell![8]

    Thus my good friends—I have in truth confess'd
How Grace divine reclaim'd this stubborn breast;
And now as time permits me, I shall tell
What strange events my future life befell.—

    The sin subdu'd that caus'd my bosom's smart,
And all the venom rankling at my heart;
My former pleasures can no more delight,
The daily pastimes, nor the dance by night;
The violin that charm'd my soul before,
My lov'd French-horn, can charm my soul no more!
Pleasure that woo'd me in my wanton hours,
Whose thorns I seiz'd, and vainly deem'd them flow'rs;
The gay companions of my youth, I shun,
From all their snares, and from the town I run.—
Now to my home, my friends, I bend my way,
But they deride me, and deny my stay;
They know not *Christ*—their hearts with malice burn,
And me a wand'rer out of doors they turn;
Yet still supported by a Saviour's love,
Thro' dang'rous woods, and fearful wilds I rove;
Successive days and nights alternate shed
Sunshine, and dews, obnoxious on my head;
In search of food I roam the sultry day,
By night I'm chac'd by savage beasts of prey;
Now the tall tree presents its giddy height,
Haunted—pursu'd, I climb with wild affright!
I stride some trembling branch to shun the foe,
While death, and devastation lurks below,

[8] Both 'Doubting Castle' and the giant 'Despair' are allegorical obstacles which Christian must over-come in John Bunyan's Evangelical classic *The Pilgrim's Progress* (1678).

While hungry monsters vent their rage around,
Raise the loud yell, and vengeful tear the ground;
Yet still to me the Saviour's care was known,
I still rely'd upon his strength alone;
Yet still the Lord was pleas'd to be my guide,
He knew my wants, and every want supply'd;
Tho' hunger pinch'd—he staid my fleeting breath,
Nor gave to taste the bitter cup of death;
By his Almighty Arm sustain'd, I stood
Unhurt amidst the dangers of the wood;
In my distress, I cry'd unto the Lord,
Who did sweet comfort to my soul afford.—

    Freed from the wilderness, at length I came
To men who bore the injur'd christian name;
Christians by name—for savage beasts of prey
I found more kind, more merciful than they.—

    Twas at the time when thunders from afar
In lofty tone provok'd unnat'ral war;
When thro' our Colonies from man to man,
Revengeful strife, and fatal discord ran;
When friends, and brothers 'gainst each other rose,
And sons rebellious deem'd their sires their foes;
When the mad sire, by party rage misled,
Aim'd the fell weapon at his offspring's head;
'Twas then, as wand'ring near the sea-beat shore,
Where vessels ride, and waves incessant roar,
A British party me by force detain'd,
By which a tedious servitude I gain'd;
On board the warlike vessel now confin'd,
Lo! new distresses mortify my mind;
Here forc'd to bend beneath tyrannic sway,
To haughty chiefs, I servile homage pay;
Here mock'd, and scourg'd for JESU's sake—I find
The Boatswain cruel, and his mates unkind.—
All this I bore—but O! my faithless heart,
Oppress'd by ills, and griefs most pungent smart,
Forgot its Lord, and doubt, and fell despair,
And unbelief again found entrance there!
And now the fiend who erst with impious rage,
Dar'd the blest army of his God engage,

Began his art, his cunning to employ,
To cause this hand its master to destroy;
From the bow port I thrice essay'd to find
A wat'ry grave to ease my troubled mind,
But there as oft—so pleas'd the Power divine,
Some person stood, and check'd my rash design;
And still I liv'd, and still by fervent prayer,
I triumph'd o'er the tempter, and despair.—

    But O! my friends, 'twould tire you here to tell
What various incidents my life befell;
'Twould wound your tender hearts, 'twould make you weep
Did I recount the dangers of the deep;
How big with rage the furious tempest roar'd,
And threat'ned instant death to all on board!
How the huge wave high mounting to the skies,
Struck every soul with terror and surprise,
Lest on the ship its monstrous weight should fall,
And in one fearful ruin bury all!—
Hurl'd from the ship, and struggling with the wave,
I once was sinking in the boist'rous grave,
But then unto my Saviour God I cry'd,
Who sav'd me from the fury of the tide;
He gave command, and lo! the swelling main
Hove me secure on board my ship again!—
In perils oft—in num'rous battles try'd,
I pray'd to God, and God was on my side;
All this he did, and more a God can do,
He can afflict—but he can comfort too;
And with an heart-felt joy I can declare
That he will hear, that he will answer prayer;
And though awhile his glorious face he hides,
Though Satan buffets, and a Saviour chides,
Yet, yet at last the Christian shall prevail,
And find his God, whose mercies never fail!
Yet, shall at last like wrestling Jacob[9] prove
How vast his goodness, infinite his love!—

    And now six years of tedious service past,
I come to the decisive fray at last;

[9] Jacob and the angel is an episode in Genesis 32. Jacob returning from Laban to Canaan encountered, at Peniel, an angel with whom he wrestled. The angel gave him a new name, 'Israel'.

To me decisive—for from that I found
My hopes of liberty successful crown'd.—

To meet the foe, brave *Parker*[10] spreads his sail,
And soon the horrors of the fight prevail;
The stubborn Dutch, though in their motions slow,
Form the firm line, and wait their English foe;
Now swells the tumult—now each squadron fires,
And rage, and fury every breast inspires!
The battle's smoky clouds invade the sky,
And big with death the balls impetuous fly!
In this dread scene, my brethren, who could stand
Unless supported by th'Almighty's hand?—
To God alone, my life, my all I owe,
'Twas he alone could save me from the foe;
'Twas He, when war's tumultuous thunders rag'd,
When fleet with fleet, and ship with ship engag'd,
When all around me, death and horror spread,
'Twas He, as with an helmet, screen'd my head;
'Twas God alone, by His Almighty pow'r
Could me preserve in that tremendous hour!
'Twas He preserv'd my life, but yet I found
My body mark'd with many a gaping wound.—

And now had ceas'd the fury of the fight,
And now each squadron in disabled plight,
Their diff'rent havens anxious to regain,
Shape diff'rent courses o'er the northern main;
And O! how glad was every heart on board
When in the Downes our shatter'd Fleet we moor'd.—
And there arriv'd, and all our dangers o'er,
I with the wounded was convey'd on shore,
Where in a few months time I haply found
My prospects pleasing, and my wishes crown'd;
My wounds were heal'd—my hateful bondage o'er,
I saw no tempest—heard no cannons roar.—

Now safe on shore, and free from war's alarms,
Anticipation paints her thousand charms;

---

[10]   Sir Hyde Parker (1739–1807). In 1801 he was sent to command the British fleet in the Baltic. Nelson defied Parker's orders to fight the Battle of Copenhagen in which Parker took no part.

'Midst her luxuriant scenes, I fondly find
A thousand distant views, to please my mind!
My wages paid—re-cross'd the western main—
My native shores, my friends, I greet again!—
But all was fancy, in whose flatt'ring glass,
The scenes that please us, instantaneous pass!

    To claim my share of captures from the foe,
Elate with hope, to London now I go;
I urge my claim—but ah! I urge in vain;
I plead my cause—but scarce a hearing gain—
No wages there—no share of warlike spoils
Reward the sailor for his num'rous toils;
In lieu of these—lo! purse-proud Agents stand;
And Clerks in office, an imperious band,
Perplex the Sailor by contriv'd delay,
And with him share, the pittance of his pay.—
All this I found, still JESUS was my friend,
I look'd to Him—on Him I could depend;
His presence buoy'd my sinking spirits up!
His loving kindness sweeten'd sorrow's cup!

    But since too fast for what I have to say,
On rapid wing our moments fly away,
I shall relate by aid of Grace divine
My first acquaintance with this present line;
In humble diction, and in language weak
Shall of my ministerial calling speak.—
No pay receiv'd—by artful men detain'd,
In Town, to claim my right, I still remain'd.—
To learn what things our gracious Lord had done,
To hear his word, from place to place I run.—
Sometimes the great *Romaine* relieves my soul,
When o'er my head the waves of trouble roll!
Sometimes the Reverend *Willes*[11] salutes mine ear;
My heart delighted—I with pleasure hear!—
But still those friends I long since left behind,
My dear connexions hang upon my mind;

[11] George Wickers Willes (1785–1846), naval captain and hero, present (aged 12) at the Battle of St Vincent under Parker.

To preach a Christ—to shew them all their wants,
To teach their precious souls—my bosom pants!—
One night, my mind, with thoughts like these impress'd,
I laid me down to take my usual rest,
When soon, as starting from a trance, I woke,
For thus methought some Heav'nly Agent spoke—
"Go forth! go forth!"—I hail the grateful voice,
I hear—I tremble—yet I would rejoice;
But the dire foe to Eden's early bloom
Said—"'Twas some person in a neigh'bring room."—
Lull'd by his artful wiles, mine eyes I close,
And on my pillow sink to soft repose;
'Till rous'd again—"*go forth*" assails mine ears,
Creates new hopes—yet stimulates my fears!
Still with suggestions would the foe deceive,
Which still ungrateful I would fain believe!
Like our first parents thus we frequent find
The fiend invade with unbelief the mind;—
But faith my shield—I now victorious rise,
Each doubt cimmerian[12] instantaneous flies!
To my lov'd relatives abroad, I write
'Till morning's dawn succeeds the gloom of night.—
And now to God for counsel I apply,
To him I look—on him I now rely;
That he'd reveal his blessed Will I pray,
Mark out my steps, and put me in the way!
Then to my friends beyond the seas I send,
And still I pray—God's blessing may attend.—
My prayers were heard—the letter found its way—

An answer came—which you have heard to day.—
But ere the answer came—my restless mind,
As yet unsettled—anxious strove to find
Some sweet society, where praise, and pray'r,
And holy friendship rivall'd worldly care;
And now, as if some secret impulse prest
The happy thought which struck my panting breast,
To pious *Willes* my eager steps I bend,
Who strait admits me as a christian friend;

---

[12]   Related to the Cimmerii, a tribe reputed to have lived in perpetual darkness.

In this connnexion thus admission gain'd,
In this connexion I have still remain'd;
And still I hope, as God shall be my guide,
Firm in this faith to cross the raging tide.—
But yet I trembled—still some doubts, and fears
Deject my soul, and melt me into tears,
Lest, when I haply cross the foaming main,
Reach the far shore, and see my friends again,
Lest then I should, unknowing what to say,
Lead them bewilder'd from salvation's way!
And fearing God, would in his day of fire,
Of my foul hands their sinful blood require!
But to God's Word these fears and doubts give place,
For still—"sufficient for me is his Grace!"—
And still I know, that when my stamm'ring tongue,
Which oft God's holy praise had feebly sung,
That when on earth its feeble accents cease,
Angels shall waft me to eternal peace!
That, with his saints I shall triumphant sing
Perpetual praises to our Heav'nly King!
Shall join his saints who now his Throne surround,
And in his presence evermore be found!

    And now my friends, let me beseech you pray,
That God will guide me o'er the watry way!
O! pray, that I may in the lowly sphere
Of meek humility continual steer!
O! pray that distant Negroes soon may know,
How pure the fountains of salvation flow!
That they may for a Saviour's ransom sue.
Whose cleansing blood can make them white as you.

    O! may on us Holy Ghost descend,
And God's sweet presence all our lives attend!
O! may my ministerial brethren find,
A GOD their guide—a SAVIOUR ever kind!

from *Hispaniola*

. . . . .

Oh happy isle! ere bigot Spain
Pushed venturous o'er the western main,
And scared thy nations with the voice of war;
Ere from Savanna's ever green,
Or from thy sun-gilt hills was seen
The rash invader rising from afar:

Or ere his swelling sails all white
Crowded upon the astonished sight,
With rampant banners on the trade-wind borne
Or ere the foe with thundering guns
Destroyed thine inoffensive sons,
Or thou had'st wept—a childless queen forlorn!

Or ere was seen the stranger band
Marshalled upon thy burning strand,
With Romish priests in saint-like cowl and vest;
The holy crucifix they bore,
But falsehood's painted vizor wore,
And scandalized the doctrines they profess'd.

O justly praised by all mankind!
Gifted with comprehensive mind,
Who ventured first by ardent zeal inspir'd,
O'er unplough'd seas his course to bend[1]
To watch the car of day descend,
Or hail new worlds by vertic sun-beams fir'd!

Long ere they blessed the hero's eyes
His fancy painted brighter skies,
And pictured realms beyond the western star
O'er beds of gold where rivers glide,
And gem-decked shrines in splendid pride
Reflect the solar blaze, and shine afar.

He wanted not, humane as brave,
One child of nature to enslave,

[1] Christopher Columbus.

For deed so base he never sail unfurl'd;
Though bound for gold to unknown lands,
He fondly hoped with pious hands
To plant the cross, and bless a heathen world.

Intrepid veteran! though his name
Live, blazoned by immortal fame,
Whose pendant first o'er western billows flew;
Had he, green island, ne'er descried
Thy landscapes o'er th'encircling tide
Rise in majestic grandeur to his view:

If whelmed in perilous distress,
Outcast on ocean's wilderness,
Had all his hopes of enterprise been cross'd;
Or when by love of home inspir'd,
'Gainst him his rebel crew conspir'd,
Had he been friendless to the wild waves toss'd;

Then had no foreign barbarous pow'r,
In bold discovery's fatal hour,
Delightful island! desolated thee:
Where pined the sickly slave enchain'd,
Where proud Iberia's viceroys reign'd,
Unmurdered millions had been blessed and free.

In nature's peerless charms array'd,
Of no rude ravisher afraid
Then lovely innocents had dwelt secure;
Then still unstained by Indian blood
Thy fountains to the deep sea's flood
Their constant streams had poured for ever pure.

Still might the lover fearless rove
Where to the high-arched shady grove
Beauty retired unconscious of a crime;
Where fragrant flowers and fruits grew wild,
And where simplicity's meek child
Plucked new-born pleasures from the wing of time.

Too soon the cruel spoiler came,
And kindled war's destructive flame,

And ruin spread and devastation wide;
On thee he rush'd—his heart of stone
Felt not when sorrow made its moan,
Thy soil he deluged with life's crimson tide!

He doomed thy children to explore
The caverned earth for golden ore,
He wrung their limbs with slavery's galling chain;
Unheeded then the prisoner's cry
For pity passed a stranger by,
And misery poured the silent tear in vain!

As wave by wave incessant pressed
On ocean's ever heaving breast
Successive beats against the naked strand,
Thus woe, wronged isle, succeeded woe
Thus on thee fell each deathful blow,
Remorseless dealt by thy destroyer's hand.

Then blessed with mercy's smile no more
Injustice triumphed on thy shore,
And thou wert crushed beneath his iron sway;
Thy grief-fed eye beheld stern pow'r
The harmless sons of peace devour,
And sweep the remnant of the meek away!

Then, queen of isles! dismayed, forlorn,
Thy plains were on the whirlwind borne,
Sunk in the distant surge, or lost in air;
Death hailed thee in the blood-hounds yell,
Tornadoes rang thy funeral knell,
And terror haunted thee and wild despair!

Against thee, leagued with other foes,
The giant superstition rose;
Saint though he seemed, beneath his lowering brow
The ruffian lurked—his crafty eye
Shot lewdness, and fierce cruelty,
And foul misdeeds belied his holy vow.

He much delighted was to dwell
On dreadful punishments in hell

Prepared for heretics of every name;
And though he praised the gospel's lore,
A sword all stained with blood he wore,
And flung around mad persecution's flame.

He mounted fury's blood-stained car,
And poured on thee his thickest war,
He smote thy bare head with his tempest blast;
O'erwhelmed in sorrow's deepest flood,
Then thou didst weep big tears of blood—
Destruction's ploughshare o'er thy bosom pass'd!

Was it for this thy friendly hand
Saved the invader on the stand
When ocean dashed him shipwrecked on thy shore?
Was it for this with grief sincere
Thy eye ran o'er with pity's tear
When his heart failed to hear the tempest roar?

Was it for this thy virgin train
Welcomed in friendship's artless strain
The stern oppressor, and the foe ador'd?
Was it for this thy matrons bore
The green palm branch that waved before,
And offered homage to a foreign lord?

And was for this the feast prepar'd
At which th'ungrateful stranger shar'd
Each rare production of thy summer clime?
Most foul return—his honor sold,
He sacrificed alone to gold,
And mildewed fame's proud meed with every crime.

Alas! the Spaniard's hateful rage
Nor cries nor tears could aught assuage;
Nor beauty's charms, nor misery's plaints inspire
With pity's zeal one sordid breast
To feel for innocence oppress'd,
Or check the fury of inhuman ire.

Even *Anacoana* charm'd in vain,
She saw her friends around her slain;

Whils't ignominious bound, and doomed to die,
Herself unpitied and forlorn,
The mark of base *Ovando's* scorn,
A martyr fell to hospitality![2]

Then, queen of isles! no more for thee
Flew the wild notes of minstrelsy
From instruments by untaught artists made,
When danced the sportive youthful throng,
And sung love's soft inchanting song
In the cool freshness of the tamarind's shade.

Their race extinct—'twas then in vain
That flowers of every verdant plain
Mingled sweet fragrance with the mountain's breeze;
Or that the cocoa nut should swell
With food nutritious in its shell,
Or that perpetual verdure decked thy trees.

[2] 'Although I am unfriendly to such long notes and quotations, yet the unexampled barbarity and treachery which the merciless *Ovando* exercised towards the kind-hearted and inoffensive *Anacoana*, and her faithful and unsuspecting adherents, induce me to transcribe the following particular account of it:

"The province anciently named Xaragua, which extends from the fertile plain where Leogane is now situated, to the Eastern extremity of the island, was subject to a female cacique, named Anacoana, highly respected by the natives. She had always courted the friendship of the Spaniards, and loaded them with benefits; but some of the adherents of Roldan having settled in her country, were so much exasperated at her endeavoring to restrain their excesses, that they accused her of having formed a plan to throw off the yoke, and to exterminate the Spaniards. Ovando, though he knew well what little credit was due to such profligate men, marched, without further inquiry, towards Xaragua, with three hundred foot and seventy horsemen. To prevent the Indians from taking alarm at this hostile appearance, he gave out that his sole intention was to visit Anacoana, to whom his countrymen had been so much indebted, in the most respectful manner, and to regulate with her the mode of levying the tribute payable to the King of Spain. Anacoana, in order to receive this illustrious guest with due honor, assembled the principal men in her dominions, to the number of three hundred; and advancing at the head of these, accompanied by a great crowd of persons of inferior rank, she welcomed Ovando with songs and dances, according to the mode of the country, and conducted him to the place of her residence. There he was feasted for some days, with all the kindness of simple hospitality, and amused with the games and spectacles usual to the Americans upon such occasions of mirth and festivity. But amidst the security which this inspired, Ovando was meditating the destruction of his unsuspicious entertainer and her subjects; and the mean perfidy with which he executed his scheme equaled his barbarity in forming it. Under colour of exhibiting to the Indians the parade of an European tournament, he advanced with his troops, in battle array, towards the house in which Anacoana and the chiefs who attended her were assembled. The infantry took possession of all the avenues which led to the village. The horsemen encompassed the house. The movements were the object of admirations without any mixture of fear, until, upon a signal which had been concerted the Spaniards suddenly drew their swords and rushed upon the Indians, defenceless and astonished at an act of treachery which exceeded the conception of undesigning men. In a moment Anacoana was secured. All her attendants were seized and bound. Fire was set to the house; and without examination or conviction, all these unhappy persons, the most illustrious in their own country, were consumed in flames. Anacoana was reserved for a more ignominious fate. She was carried in chains to St Domingo (the capital of the island) and after the formality of a trial before Spanish judges, she was condemned, upon the evidence of those very men who had betrayed her, to be publicly hanged." Robertson's *History of America*.' [Whitchurch]

Or that gay birds with beauteous plumes
Walked in thy gardens of perfumes,
Or to thy bowers of love delighted flew;
Or that his voice of mimic song
Bade travellers oft their stay prolong
Where orchards lovelier than Hesperia's grew.

Never shall harmless Indian more
Thy boundless forest wilds explore;
Or thro' umbrageous arbours fearless stray,
Where *cedars* and *palmettos* rise,
Spread their green honours in the skies,
And yield cool refuge from the burning day.

Or where the mightier *ceiba*[3] grows,
And wide his friendly shadow throws,
No more shall nature's children peaceful rove,
Where mountain torrents pour their streams
Screen'd from the sun's all-powerful beams
Beneath the ancient giants of the grove.

Thy *fire-fly* wonders of the night
Then winged unseen their silent flight,
And vainly glowed and living lustre shed;
O'er observation's curious eye
That watched the meteor beauties fly,
Cheerless oblivion's thickest veil was spread.

Then triumphed war's devouring brood
Within their own made solitude;
Destruction's mighty angel o'er thee past,
He poured from his fate-guided hand
Wrath's plague-full vials on thy land
And loud he blew his tramp's heart-chilling blast!

Impartial muse of history!
Thy records stained with blood I see;
For led by memory to thy foulest page,
I turn far back when giant crimes
Damned the proud victories of the times,
And blasted all the laurels of the age.

[3] A giant tropical tree which grows on all the islands of the greater Antilles. In both Hayti and Cuba it is worshipped as the seat of gods and witches in the slave-evolved religious cults of Voodoo and Santeria.

Wafted across the billowy flood
I hear vehement cries for blood,
And murders voice on *Hayti's* ravaged coast
Outroar the torrent waves that sweep
Down the huge mountain's towering steep;
Whilst pass before me many an injured ghost!

The wing of fancy bears me nigh
Some world beneath a happier sky,
Whither the martyred of mankind have fled;
Where pleasure walks o'er verdant plains,
Where peace, perpetual empress reigns,
And where reside the spirits of the dead.

Hark! melody's soft sounds I hear
Steal on my rapture-ravished ear;
Some matchless beauty beams upon my eye,
Than evening's lustrous star more bright,
Or the refulgent queen of night
When walking forth in cloudless majesty.

'Tis murdered *Anacoana's* voice,
She bids thee sun-bright isle rejoice,
She bids the spirits of the murdered rest:
Ocean's proud waves forget to roar,
And silent break upon thy shore
While her kind accents soothe the listener's breast.

Behold her angel spirit rise—
Mark her bright mercy-beaming eyes
Weep o'er Xaragua's solitary fate;
Though thus she mourns forsaken vales
That echoed murder's dreadful tales,
She sees far off and hails thy happier state.

"Alas! what hearts by hardships broke,
Who bowed, who died beneath the yoke,
None of my faithful friends survive to tell;
Them bondage held 'till life's last breath,
Their toils ne'er ceased 'till sunk in death,
Their wounded spirits bade the world farewel.

But famine smote the blood-hound crew,
That from their bleeding vitals drew

The carnage banquet, and the feast of blood;
They rolled their eager eyes in vain
Around each desolated plain
Where murder prowled, and poured life's purple flood.

And thou, stern foe! more base than brave,
Bold traveller o'er yon wide sea wave,
Though thou hast conquered and thy millions slain,
Though Mexico's rich spoils be thine,
And Peru's far-famed golden mine,
Thou shalt be cursed with thy unrighteous gain.

Anon some rival will arise,
And share with thee this paradise—
When shineth here the star of liberty
Thou shalt in darkness still remain,
And hug thy own proud tyrant's chain,
Blind foe to truth, and slave of bigotry!

Then mourn not much-loved summer isle,
Again on thee shall freedom smile,
Though on thee prey the vultures of the north:
Brave sable nations shall arise,
And rout thy future enemies,
Though Europe send her hostile legions forth.

Yet ere the victor's flag be borne
Millions will from their friends be torn,
Kidnapped and bound on Afric's distant shore;
From the green banks that Niger laves,
Or realms o'erlooking ocean's caves,
Dragged forth to bondage—to return no more!

But they shall rise! the hour will come
Big with the proud oppressor's doom;
Though times and seasons pass away,
That sun which saw his ruffian hand
Spread desolation o'er the land,
Will smile at retribution's holy day!"

Thus said-the star-bright beauty flies
To *Coyaba's*[4] green paradise,

[4] Coyaba, or Coyah, pineapple-growing region.

Where kindred souls with kindred ardour burn,
And where from many an Eden grove
Thro' which departed spirits rove
Ten thousand thousand hail her glad return.

From shades where murdered myriads lie
Impatient souls for vengeance cry—
"How long, how long, great God of Holiness,
With slave-ship fleets shall men of blood
Ride every navigable flood
Thine unprotected children to oppress?"

Rise, mighty shade of *Toussaint*[5]—rise!
Thou though by freedom's enemies
Wert doomed in hopeless solitude to death;
O rise, and haunt thy murderer's bed,
And thus assail in accents dread
His ears oft soothed by flattry's poisoned breath:

"Though nerveless now I lift in vain
This arm that many a Gaul hath slain,
Yet tyrant list! my brethren shall be free,
For though thou send forth host on host,
Vanquished on *Hayti's* sea-girt coast,
They shall not strike the flag of liberty.

Though by their faithless chief's command
Thine armed brigands with ruthless hand
Spurning man's rights and honor's sacred ties,
Me seized at midnight, and in chains,
Dragged from war-wasted distant plains
To where pale tyrants frown, and wintry skies.

Bold trampler on all human laws!
Heaven will avenge my righteous cause;
Thou hast not sacrificed my life in vain;
E'en now the sable heroes rise;
Revenge! revenge! each warrior cries—
They charge the hosts, and strew their route with slain!

Rivers of blood now run around
Drenching the burnt up thirsty ground;

[5] Toussaint L'Ouverture, see pp. 231–3.

But thou art chief in perfidy and guilt;
The outraged children of the sun
But mimic what thy Gauls have done—
Thou must account for all the blood that's spilt!

What though imperial robes await
To deck thy limbs in regal state;
Though servile artist carve thy kingly bust;
Thou shalt not long usurp the throne
Of princely grandeur not thine own—
Time may soon tread thy honours in the dust!

Death's shadow pointeth to the hour,
The last of all thy pomp and power—
See! that hand-writing on thy palace wall![6]
Its blood red characters portray
Fortune's changed scenes, and tell the day
When Afric's sons will triumph at thy fall!

Vexed spirits, residents of hell—
Fallen tyrants who in darkness dwell,
Hail thy approach from thrones of misery:
Great conqueror art thou humbled thus?
Art thou become like unto us?
Enslaver of nations!—Is it thee?

Insulted African, arise!
Just Heaven regards the captive's cries.
Lo! vengeance rideth on this swift-wheeled car;
Though orient India loud demand
Redress from his uplifted hand,
Westward he drives for thee victorious war.

Not HE, famed warrior! who of late
Weighed in his balance *Egypt's*[7] fate,

---

[6] In Daniel 5 King Belshazzar has a great feast. When he orders the gold and silver vessels which his father Nebuchadnezzar had taken out of the temple in Jerusalem to be brought in, a supernatural hand appears and writes the words MENE TEKEL UPHARSIN on the wall. The text cannot be deciphered until Daniel is brought in. He tells Belshazzar that the text means 'thou art weighed in the balance and art found wanting'.

[7] Referring to Napoleon's Egyptian campaign.

And on his pale horse oft to victory rode;
Who broke on *Nilus* fertile banks
The warlike Mamaluke's[8] stubborn ranks,
And o'er the haughty neck of Ismael stood.

Not HE, who burning desarts past,
Swept by the Simoom's[9] sultry blast,
To plant his standard in the holy land;
Whom Zion's[10] watchmen heard from far,
And fear'd him, mighty man of war!
Soon backward driven by England's chosen band.

Not HE, though millions own his sway,
And vassal crowds his nod obey;
Though bannered squadrons from his ports may sail
To pour his fury on thy plains,
And rivet fast the captive's chains—
Not HE, pale tyrant! shall 'gainst thee prevail.

But O to hear the story told
'Twould make the warm heart's blood run cold;
The crimes revealed by truth's impartial tale
Might from the unfeeling stoic's eye
Force the strange tear of sympathy,
And make the ruddiest cheek of man turn pale.

O grave upon the lone sea shore,
Thou shalt thy tenant crowds restore:
O hidden caverns of the ocean deep,
Ye shall give up the death-doomed host
That bound on *Hayti's* blood-stained coast,
Sank whelmed by thousands down the watery steep.

Then martyred multitudes will rise,
And shame their fear struck enemies:
Yet ere the hour of final reckoning come
Stern justice will the crimes pursue
Of murder's unrelenting crew,
And them to death or lingering suffering doom.

---

[8] Or Mameluke, originally one of a military force of Circassian slaves, who later became the ruling class and the sultans of Egypt.

[9] A hot, stifling desert wind of Africa.

[10] Zion can signify Jerusalem, the Christian Church, or heaven.

Brought forth on slavery's iron bed,
Midst savage wilds of ignorance bred,
Where mercy's smiling angel seldom came;
Spurned—outcast of the human race—
Of untaught mind—in manners base—
The negro panteth not for virtuous fame.

Unmoved he hears the sufferer's moan;
Untouched by sorrow's mournful groan,
His callous heart no soft compunction knows;
But burning with revengeful rage,
He spareth not or sex or age;
The white skin only designates his foes.

Proud European, blame him not—
Would'st thou act better, if, hard lot!
Thou like the African wert bought and sold?
If unprotected by the laws
'Twere vain to plead thy desperate cause
Where justice asks but for the murderer's gold?

If thou wert thus to misery born,
Treated with insolence and scorn;
The book of knowledge never op'ed to thee;
When by the voice of freedom hail'd,
If by the tyrant's sword assail'd,
Would'st thou not march thro' blood to liberty?

Hark! the loud trumpet's hostile breath
Proclaims or liberty or death;
March the black squadrons, vengeance leads the van;
Oppression's cheerless day is past,
Th' insulted slave hath risen at last,
And claimed the rights and dignity of man.

Fierce burns the fire of marital strife,
Fast flow the crimson streams of life;
Grim horror strides across th'ensanguined plain;
Lift, son of Ham,[11] thy wrath-red eye,
Behold thy prostrate enemy
Where victory stalks o'er mountain heaps of slain.

---

[11]   The curse of Ham, by his father Noah in Genesis 9: 22–8, states that Ham shall be 'a servant of servants unto his brethren'. The text was used by pro-slavery advocates as a biblical sanction for the enslavement of Africans, whose blackness was the mark of Ham, and consequently signified them to be 'sons of Ham'.

> Gaul's vanquished myrmidons have felt
> The dreadful blow by justice dealt—
> Heart-smote by sickness, or by famine driven;
> Some few escaped the warriors hands;
> Some prisoners bound to distant lands,
> Routed like chaff before the winds of heaven.

Anna Laetitia Barbauld (1743–1825), *Epistle to William Wilberforce, Esq. On the Rejection of the Bill for Abolishing the Slave Trade* (1791)

Barbauld's writings cover a very large formal range, and have intellectual authority. Due to the enlightened attitudes of her parents (mainly her mother), Barbauld was well educated, learning Latin and Greek and exposed to the English classics. Her family moved to Warrington in 1758 where she came in contact with some of the leading Dissenting intellectuals of the day, including Joseph Priestley and the great prison reformer John Howard. By 1773 she had published her first book, *Poems*, which raced through four editions and was widely admired. The young Coleridge and Wordsworth were among the fans of her early verse. She married in 1774 and opened a school with her husband which she taught in until 1785. It was during this period that Barbauld wrote a series of highly influential children's books. She toured France just before the Revolution broke out, returning in 1786. Barbauld's passionate Dissenting nature increasingly began to come through in her writing. Her *Address to the Opposers of the Repeal of the Corporation and Test Acts* came out a year before the *Epistle to Wilberforce*, and showed her to be a forthright supporter of the ideals of the French Revolution, as well as of the rights of slaves.

The *Epistle* is a strongly argued and unusual intervention in the slavery debates. It was written at a point when the slavery bill, wittily described by C. L. R. James as a 'hardy annual', had again been defeated, and Barbauld's sense of anger and futility comes through. She also emerges as a hard-nosed pragmatist, as she argues that abolition idealizations are futile in a world ultimately ruled by greed and the slave power, where the 'seasoned tools of avarice prevail'. There are several surprising intellectual subtleties in the poem. Barbauld is not afraid to parody and attack abolition rhetoric which presents the suffering of slaves according to the absurd diction of sentimental pastoral verse. She also takes an almost sceptical line on the activities of the abolition leaders, concluding that despite their best efforts the only people they really help are themselves. Not many abolitionists would dare to stand up and say straight out to Wilberforce: 'But seek no more to save a Nation's fall | For ye have saved yourselves and that is all.'

Epistle to William Wilberforce, Esq. On the Rejection of the Bill for Abolishing the Slave Trade

Cease, Wilberforce, to urge thy generous aim—
Thy country knows the sin and stands the shame!
The preacher, poet, senator, in vain
Has rattled in her sight the Negro's chain,
With his deep groans assailed her startled ear
And rent the veil that hid his constant tear,
Forced her averted eyes his stripes to scan,
Beneath the bloody scourge laid bare the man,
Claimed pity's tear, urged conscience's strong control
And flashed conviction on her shrinking soul.
The muse, too soon awaked, with ready tongue
At mercy's shrine applausive paeans rung,
And freedom's eager sons in vain foretold
A new astrean reign, an age of gold!
She knows and she persists—still Afric bleeds;
Unchecked, the human traffic still proceeds;
She stamps her infamy to future time
And on her hardened forehead seals the crime.
    In vain, to thy white standard gathering round,
Wit, worth, and parts and eloquence are found;
In vain to push to birth thy great design
Contending chiefs and hostile virtues join;
All from conflicting ranks, of power possessed
To rouse, to melt, or to inform the breast.
Where seasoned tools of avarice prevail,
A nation's eloquence, combined, must fail.
Each flimsy sophistry by turns they try—
The plausive argument, the daring lie.
The artful gloss that moral sense confounds,
Th' acknowledged thirst of gain that honour wounds,
(Bane of ingenuous minds!) th' unfeeling sneer
Which sudden turns to stone the falling tear.
They search assiduous with inverted skill
For forms of wrong, and precedents of ill;
With impious mockery wrest the sacred page,
And glean up crimes from each remoter age;

Wrung nature's tortures, shuddering, while you tell,
From scoffing fiends bursts forth the laugh of hell;
In Britain's senate, misery's pangs give birth
To jests unseemly, and to horrid mirth—
Forbear! thy virtues but provoke our doom
And swell th' account of vengeance yet to come.
For (not unmarked in Heaven's impartial plan)
Shall man, proud worm, contemn his fellow man?
And injured Afric, by herself redressed,
Darts her own serpents at her tyrant's breast.
Each vice, to minds depraved by bondage known,
With sure contagion fastens on his own;
In sickly languors melts his nerveless frame,
And blows to rage impetuous passion's flame;
Fermenting swift, the fiery venom gains
The milky innocence of infant veins;
There swells the stubborn will, damps learning's fire,
The whirlwind wakes of uncontrolled desire,
Sears the young heart to images of woe
And blasts the buds of virtue as they blow.
　　Lo! where reclined, pale beauty courts the breeze,
Diffused on sofas of voluptuous ease;
With anxious awe, her menial train around
Catch her faint whispers of half-uttered sound.
See her, in monstrous fellowship, unite
At once the Scythian and the Sybarite;[1]
Blending repugnant vices, misallied,
Which frugal nature purposed to divide;
See her, with indolence to fierceness joined,
Of body delicate, infirm of mind,
With languid tones imperious mandates urge,
With arm recumbent wield the household scourge,
And with unruffled mien, and placid sounds,
Contriving torture and inflicting wounds.
　　Nor in their palmy walks and spicy groves
The form benign of rural pleasure roves;
No milkmaid's song or hum of village talk
Soothes the lone poet in his evening walk;

---

[1] Originally an inhabitant of Sybaris, an ancient Greek town notorious for luxury; hence one steeped in luxury of excess.

No willing arm the flail unwearied plies
Where the mixed sounds of cheerful labour rise;
No blooming maids and frolic swains are seen
To pay gay homage to their harvest queen;
No heart-expanding scenes their eyes must prove
Of thriving industry and faithful love:
But shrieks and yells disturb the balmy air,
Dumb sullen looks of woe announce despair
And angry eyes through dusky features glare.
Far from the sounding lash the muses fly
And sensual riot drowns each finer joy.

   Nor less from the gay east on essenced wings,
Breathing unnamed perfumes, contagion springs;
The soft luxurious plague alike pervades
The marble palaces and rural shades;
Hence thronged Augusta builds her rosy bowers
And decks in summer wreaths her smoky towers;
And hence in summer bow'rs art's costly hand
Pours courtly splendours o'er the dazzled land.
The manners melt, one undistinguished blaze
O'erwhelms the sober pomp of elder days;
Corruption follows with gigantic stride
And scarce vouchsafes his shameless front to hide;
The spreading leprosy taints ev'ry part,
Infects each limb, and sickens at the heart.
Simplicity! most dear of rural maids,
Weeping resigns her violated shades;
Stern independence from his glebe retires
And anxious freedom eyes her drooping fires;
By foreign wealth are British morals changed,
And Afric's sons, and India's, smile avenged.

   For you whose tempered ardour long has borne
Untired the labour, and unmoved the scorn.
In virtue's fasti be inscribed your fame,
And uttered yours with Howard's honoured name.
Friends of the friendless—hail, ye generous band
Whose efforts yet arrest Heaven's lifted hand,
Around whose steady brows in union bright
The civic wreath and Christian's palm unite!
Your merit stands, no greater and no less,
Without or with the varnish of success;

But seek no more to break a nation's fall,
For ye have saved yourselves, and that is all.
Succeeding times your struggles, and their fate,
With mingled shame and triumph shall relate,
While faithful history in her various page,
Marking the features of this motley age,
To shed a glory, and to fix a stain,
Tells how you strove, and that you strove in vain.

James Boswell (1740–95), *No Abolition of Slavery; or, The Universal Empire of Love: A Poem* (1791)

Boswell, Dr Johnson's great biographer, did not agree with Johnson on many political issues. Johnson was, of course, a renowned enemy of slavery and Boswell takes issue with him in the *Life*:

> [Johnson] had always been very zealous against slavery in every form, in which I with all deference thought that he discovered 'a zeal without knowledge'. Upon one occasion, when in company with some very grave men at Oxford, his toast was, 'Here's to the next insurrection of the negroes in the West Indies.'

Boswell remained a staunch slavery apologist. In this poem he bizarrely combines a love poem to a young lady he is pursuing with a series of increasingly obscene *ad hominem* satiric attacks on leading abolitionists. In order to understand how such an apparently crazy literary hybrid could be produced it is important to remember that slavery had long existed as a literary device to describe romantic love. Boswell was deeply steeped in this tradition before he wrote *No Abolition of Slavery*.

As a young man he wrote a good deal of conventional and aesthetically weak love poetry. The second section of Boswell's poetic juvenilia is entitled 'Amorous' and contains many verses constructed around the trope of the lover enslaved by his desire for the beloved. Sometimes the slavery is presented as the, almost, desirable fantasy of bondage through marriage, as in this platitudinous quatrain from the *Song to Mira*: 'O, were I with my Mira bound | In Hymen's silken chain, | In transports we should run life's round | And scarcely think of Pain.' Pain is killed by the gentle chains of marriage. Voluntary enslavement to the object of desire is presented in other contexts as a total sacrifice of will power, an effacement of personality by the lover: 'You say my charmer, that I swore, | When sighing at your feet, | That I should have a will no more . . .' Unremarkable as these little love games are as poetry they do indicate the extent to which a late eighteenth-century literary gentleman and libertine felt at his ease linking the metaphorics of enslavement with the love lyric. Enslavement through love is, of course, an old trope which is most fully and ironically searched in Shakespeare's *Tempest*. Shakespeare sets off Caliban's, and later Ferdinand's, enslavement by Prospero against Ferdinand's amorous fantasies of enslavement, through love, to Miranda. In devolved and far less challenging forms the 'slave to love' formula was repeated in innumerable seventeenth-century lyrics, climaxing in the love poems of the Cavalier poets.

Boswell's youthful appropriations of this tradition are at one level the fag end of a well-worn tradition. Yet in the early 1790s Boswell entered the slavery debates, and gave the love-as-slavery trope a cynical and clever new twist. Boswell was a staunch supporter of the planter lobby in Parliament. He decided to publish a satiric verse attack upon the leading abolitionists and further to defend the property rights of the West India planters. One of the dangers inherent in writing pro-slavery satire is that of taking the slave too seriously as a subject. Merely by deciding to write satire on the subject of the abolition of the slave trade the satirist runs the danger of placing African enslavement centre stage as a social and human rights issue. Boswell's cynical formula for avoiding this danger lay in the facetious coupling of his amorous bondage fantasy with the serious political issue of abolition of the slave trade. He manages to produce a poem which is saturated with strange sexual tensions which extend finally beyond the presentation of his own attempts at seduction and into his presentation of the leading abolitionists.

Perhaps the most disturbing part of the poem is when Boswell describes the process of falling in love and then getting married in terms of a slave's progress through the Atlantic slave trade. The process begins with kidnapping in Africa, Boswell identifying himself with a type of African slave who, as his footnotes set out, was seen as the most rebellious. He then relates his transportation below decks on the middle passage in a state of fear, his subsequent 'seasoning' on the plantation, and final labour and torture ('REGULATION') on the plantations under the conditions of the slave code. Boswell in placing himself in competition with the slave victim through this curiously precise parodic narrative is making a move which is unnervingly close to that of many of the abolitionists.

In this poem the attacks on individual Clapham sect abolitionists repeatedly turn to themes of licentiousness and repressed libidinousness. There are many examples but the attack on Sir William Dolben is particularly extreme in its perverted sexual metaphorics. Boswell uses Greek, and an elaborate scholarly apparatus, in order to introduce a particularly nasty little pun on the concept of 'planting'. Boswell, with a knowing disgracefulness, couples prostituted sex and plantation slavery as areas which allow the white male to prosper. 'Slavery and licentious joy' coexist as opportunities for the empowered white male. Dolben is set out, with a quite deliberately literal perversity, as a killjoy. Dolben's activities within the Evangelical Societies for the Suppression of Vice, attempting to keep a lid on street prostitution in urban centres in Britain, are set against his activities in support of abolition of the slave trade. 'Planting' sperm in a prostitute, a habit to which Boswell, by his own rather overstrained profession, was addicted throughout his adult life, and planting plantations in the colonies, are aligned as legitimate areas of activity/productivity for a British gentleman. In this strange British literary world of satire, slave trade abolition somehow becomes synonymous with prudery, and slavery exists in the same company as a good night in a bawdy house. Although, of course, the final crudity is wrapped up in Greek and put into the mouth of Diogenes the Cynic.

No Abolition of Slavery; or, The Universal Empire of Love: A Poem

—— Most pleasing of thy sex,
Born to delight and never vex;
Whose kindness gently can controul
My wayward turbulence of soul.

Pry'thee, my dearest, dost thou read,
The Morning *Prints,* and ever heed
Minutes, which tell how time's mispent,
In either House of Parliament?
See T——,[1] with the front of Jove!
    But not like Jove with thunder grac'd
In Westminster's superb alcove
    Like the unhappy Theseus[2] plac'd.
Day after day indignant swells
    His generous breast, while still he hears
Impeachment's fierce relentless yells,
    Which stir his bile and grate his ears.

And what a dull vain barren shew
    St. Stephen's luckless Chapel fills;
Our notions of respect how low,
    While fools bring in their idle Bills.
Noodles, who rave for abolition
Of *th' African's improv'd condition,*
At your own cost fine projects try;
Dont *rob*—from *pure humanity.*
Go, W——,[3] with narrow scull,
Go home, and preach away at Hull,

---

[1] Edward, Lord Thurlow, lawyer and judge, best remembered for his part as prosecutor during the 1794 Treason Trials.

[2] 'Sedet eternumque sedebit, Infelix Theseus Virg.' [Boswell] He sits and through eternity will sit, unhappy Theseus. In one of the many myths relating to Theseus he is said to have gone down to Hades with Pirithous the Lapith in an attempt to carry back Persephone.

[3] William Wilberforce, leader of the parliamentary push for abolition of the slave trade.

No longer to the Senate cackle,
In strains which suit the Tabernacle;
I hate your little wittling sneer,
Your pert and self-sufficient leer,
Mischief to Trade sits on thy lip,
Insects will gnaw the noblest ship;
Go, W——, be gone, for shame,
Thou dwarf, with a big-sounding name.

Poor inefficient B——,[4] we see
No *capability* in thee,
Th' immortal spirit of thy Sire
Has borne away th' aethereal fire,
And left thee but the earthy dregs,—
Let's never have thee on thy legs;
'Tis too provoking, sure, to feel,
A kick from such a puny heel.

Pedantick pupil of old Sherry,[5]
Whose shrugs and jerks would make us merry,
If not by tedious languor wrung—
Hold thy intolerable tongue.

Drawcansir DOLBEN[6] would destroy
Both slavery and licentious joy;
Foe to all sorts of *planters*,[7] he
Will suffer neither *bond* nor *free*.

Go we to the Committee room,
There gleams of light conflict with gloom,
While unread rheams in chaos lye,
Our water closets to supply.

What frenzies will a rabble seize
In lax luxurious days, like these;
THE PEOPLE'S MAJESTY, forsooth,
Must fix our rights, define our truth;

[4] Brown, punning on the name of the great landscape gardener 'Capability' Brown.
[5] Richard Brinsley Sheridan (1751–1816), dramatist, libertine, and Member of Parliament with liberal Whig leanings.
[6] Sir William Dolben, fierce supporter of abolition of the slave trade, and responsible for the drafting and passage of 'Dolben's Bill' which for the first time laid down minimum space allowances for slaves on the middle passage.
[7] 'Diogenes being discovered in the street in fond intercourse with one of those pretty misses whom Sir William Dolben dislikes, steadily said, "Θοτευο Ανρας—I plant men."' [Boswell]

Weavers become our Lords of Trade,
And every clown throw by his spade,
T' *instruct* our ministers of state,
And *foreign commerce* regulate:
Ev'n *bony* Scotland with her dirk,
Nay, her starv'd presbyterian *kirk*,
With ignorant effrontery prays
Britain to dim the western rays,
Which while they on our island fall
Give warmth and splendour to us all.

See in a stall three feet by four,
Where door is window, window door,
Saloop a hump-back'd cobler drink;
"With *him* the muse shall sit and think;"
He shall in *sentimental* strain,
That *negroes* are *oppress'd*, complain.
What mutters the decrepit creature?
THE DIGNITY OF HUMAN NATURE!

WINDHAM;[8] I won't suppress a gibe
Whilst THOU art with the whining tribe;
Thou who hast sail'd in a balloon,
And touch'd, intrepid, at the moon,
(Hence, as the Ladies say you wander,
By much too fickle a Philander:[9])
Shalt THOU, a Roman free and rough,
Descend to weak *blue stocking*[10] stuff,
And cherish feelings soft and kind,
Till you emasculate your mind.

Let COURTENAY[11] sneer, and gibe, and hack,
We know Ham's[12] sons are always black;
On sceptick themes he wildly raves,
Yet Africk's sons were always slaves;
I'd have the rogue beware of libel,
And spare a jest—when on the Bible.

---

[8] William Windham (1750–1810), English politician and statesman, follower of Pitt with liberal leanings.
[9] A lover, a flirt, a 'dangler after women'.
[10] An over-learned lady, especially a pedantic one.
[11] Sir William Courtenay (1796–1838), the name adopted by a popular prophet and madman who believed he was the Messiah. He and a band of armed followers were finally killed by English troops near Canterbury.
[12] See Whitchurch, *Hispaniola*, n. 10 above.

Burke,[13] art Thou here too? thou, whose pen,
Can blast the fancied *rights of men*:[14]
Pray, by what logick are those rights
Allow'd to *Blacks*—deny'd to *Whites?*

But Thou! bold Faction's chief *Antistes*,[15]
Thou, more than Samson Agonistes![16]
Who, Rumour tells us, would pull down
Our charter'd rights, our church, our crown;
Of talents vast, but with a mind
Unaw'd, ungovern'd, unconfin'd;
Best humour'd man, worst politician,
Most dangerous, desp'rate state physician;
Thy manly character why stain
By canting, when 'tis all in vain?
For thy tumultuous reign is o'er;
The People's Man thou art no more.

And Thou, in whom the mighty name
Of William Pitt[17] still gathers fame,
Who could at once exalted stand,
Spurning subordinate command;
Ev'n when a stripling sit with ease,
The mighty helm of state to seise;
Whom now (a thousand storms endur'd)
Years of experience have matur'd;
For whom, in glory's race untir'd,
Th' events of nations have conspir'd;
For whom, eer many suns revolv'd,
Holland has crouch'd, and France dissolv'd;
And Spain, in a Don Quixote fit,
Has bullied only to submit;

---

[13] Edmund Burke (1729–97), aesthetician, author, and politician.

[14] Burke's *Reflections on the Revolution in France* (1790) led Thomas Paine to write the scathing rejoinder *The Rights of Man* (1791–2); Burke is here seen as standing against Paine's egalitarianism.

[15] Antistes is probably Boswell's adaptation of Antistius, who was a tribune, in other words a magistrate elected by the Roman plebeians, or common people, to defend their rights. Antestia stamped on coins meant 'plebeian'.

[16] The title of Milton's famous poem recounting the tale of the biblical figure.

[17] William Pitt (1708–78), politician, and brilliant imperial diplomatist, instrumental in masterminding British imperial expansion in the mid-18th century. Known as the 'Great Commoner' because of his passionate defence of constitutional rights.

Why stoop to nonsense? why cajole
Blockheads who vent their *rigmarole?*[18]

And yet, where *influence* must rule,
'Tis sometimes wise to play the fool;
Thus, like a witch, you raise a storm,
Whether the *Parliament's Reform,*
A set of *Irish Propositions,*
Impeachment—on your *own conditions,*
Or RICHMOND's[19] wild *fortifications,*
Enough to ruin twenty nations,
Or any thing you know can't fail,
To be a tub to Party's whale.
Then whilst they nibble, growl, and worry,
All keen and busy, hurry-scurry;
Britannia's ship you onward guide,
Wrapt in security and pride.

Accept fair praise; but while I live
Your *Regency* I can't forgive;
My Tory soul with anger swell'd,
When I a parcel'd Crown beheld;
Prerogative put under hatches,
A Monarchy of shreds and patches;
And lo! a *Phantom!* to create,
A huge HERMAPHRODITE OF STATE!
A monster, more alarming still
Than FOX's raw-head India Bill![20]

THURLOW, forbear thy awful frown;
I beg you may not *look* me down;
My honest fervour do not scout,
I too like thee can be devout,
And in a solemn invocation,
Of loyalty make protestation.

---

[18]   A long, rambling discourse, prolix, incoherent.
[19]   Legh Richmond (1772–1827), English clergyman who wrote *The Negro Servant* and the great Evangelical tract *Annals of the Poor.*
[20]   Charles James Fox (1749–1806), the great Whig statesman, was a continual critic of British abuse of its colonies. He was a leading critic of Warren Hastings, and tried to have him impeached over his behaviour in India.

Courtiers, who chanc'd to guess aright,
And bask now in the Royal sight,
Gold sticks and silver, and white wands,
Ensigns of favour in your hands,
Glitt'ring with stars, and envied seen
Adorn'd with ribbands blue, red, green!
I charge you of deceit keep clear,
And poison not the Sovereign's ear:
O ne'er let Majesty suppose
The *Prince's* friends must be HIS foes.
There is not one amongst you all
Whose sword is readier at his call;
An ancient Baron of the land,
I by my King shall ever stand;
But when it pleases Heav'n to shroud
The Royal image in a cloud,
That image in the Heir I see,
The Prince is then as King to me.
Let's have, altho' the skies should lour,
No interval of Regal pow'r.

Where have I wander'd? do I dream?
Sure slaves of power are not my theme;
But honest slaves, the sons of toil,
Who cultivate the Planter's soil.

He who to thwart GOD's system tries,
Bids mountains sink, and vallies rise;
Slavery, subjection, what you will,
Has ever been, and will be still:
Trust me, that in this world of woe
Mankind must different burthens know;
Each bear his own, th' Apostle spoke;
And chiefly they who bear the yoke.

From wise subordination's plan
Springs the chief happiness of man;
Yet from that source to numbers flow
Varieties of pain and woe;
Look round this land of freedom, pray,
And all its lower ranks survey;
Bid the hard-working labourer speak,
What are his scanty gains a week?

All huddled in a smoaky shed,
How are his wife and children fed?
Are not the poor in constant fear
Of the relentless Overseer?

LONDON! Metropolis of bliss!
Ev'n there sad sights we cannot miss;
Beggars at every corner stand,
With doleful look and trembling hand;
Hear the shrill piteous cry of *sweep*,
See wretches riddling an ash heap;
The streets some for old iron scrape,
And scarce the crush of wheels escape;
Some share with dogs the half-eat bones,
From dunghills pick'd with weary groans.

Dear CUMBERLAND,[21] whose various powers
Preserve thy life from languid hours,
Thou scholar, statesman, traveller, wit,
Who prose and verse alike canst hit;
Whose gay *West-Indian* on our stage,
Alone might check this stupid rage;
Fastidious—yet O! condescend
To range with an advent'rous friend:
Together let us beat the rounds,
St. Giles's ample blackguard bounds:
Try what th' accurs'd *Short's Garden* yields,
His bludgeon where the *Flash-man*[22] wields;
Where female votaries of sin,
With fetid rags and breath of gin,
Like antique statues stand in rows,
Fine fragments sure, but ne'er a nose.
Let us with calmness ascertain
The liberty of *Lewkner's Lane*,
And *Cockpit-Alley—Stewart's Rents*,
Where the fleec'd drunkard oft repents.
With BENTLEY's critical *acumen*
Explore the haunts of evil's *Numen*;

[21] Richard Cumberland (1732–1811), Secretary to the Board of Trade (1776–82), also a prolific play-wright whose titles included *The West Indian.*
[22] A bully to a bawdy house, a whore's bully, a pimp.

And in the *hundreds* of *Old Drury*,
Descant *de legibus Naturae*.
Let's prowl the courts of *Newton-Street*,
Where infamy and murder meet;
Where CARPMEAL must with caution tread,
MACMANUS tremble for his head,
JEALOUS look sharp with all his eyes,
And TOWNSHEND apprehend surprise;
And having view'd the horrid maze,
Let's justify the Planter's ways.

   Lo then, in yonder fragrant isle
Where Nature ever seems to smile,
The cheerful *gang*!—the negroes see
Perform the task of industry:
Ev'n at their labour hear them sing,
While time flies quick on downy wing;
Finish'd the bus'ness of the day,
No human beings are more gay:
Of food, clothes, cleanly lodging sure,
Each has his property secure;
Their wives and children are protected,
In sickness they are not neglected;
And when old age brings a release,
Their grateful days they end in peace.

   But should our Wrongheads have their will,
Should Parliament approve their bill,
Pernicious as th' effect would be,
T' abolish negro slavery,
Such partial freedom would be vain,
Since Love's strong empire must remain.

   VENUS, Czarina of the skies,
Despotick by her killing eyes,
Millions of slaves who don't complain,
Confess her universal reign:
And *Cupid* too well-us'd to try
His bow-string lash, and darts to ply,
Her little *Driver* still we find,
A wicked rogue, although he's blind.

Bring me not maxims from the schools;
Experience now my conduct rules;
O ——! trust thy lover true,
I must and will be slave to you.

 Yet I must say—but pr'ythee smile,—
'Twas a hard trip to Paphos isle;
By your keen roving glances caught,
And to a beauteous tyrant brought;
My head with giddiness turn'd round,
With strongest fetters I was bound;
I fancy from my frame and face,
You thought me of th' Angola race:
You kept me long indeed, my dear,
Between the decks of hope and fear;
But this and all the *seasoning* o'er,
My blessings I enjoy the more.

 Contented with my situation,
I want but little REGULATION;
At intervals *Chanson à boire*[23]
And good old port in my *Code noire*;[24]
Nor care I when I've once begun,
How long I labour, in the sun
Of your bright eyes!—which beam with joy,
Warm, cheer, enchant, but don't destroy.

 My charming friend! it is full time
To close this argument in rhime;
The rhapsody: must now be ended,
My proposition, I've defended;
For, Slavery there must ever be,
While we have Mistresses like thee!

THE END.

___

[23] Drinking song.　　[24] See Grainger, *Sugar Cane*, n. 8.

Captain John Marjoribanks, *Slavery: An Essay in Verse . . . Humbly Inscribed to Planters, Merchants, and Others Concerned in the Management or Sale of Negro Slaves* (1792)

Marjoribanks states in his preface that the 'verses were written in Jamaica, in October 1786', and adds that he has not changed a word since the establishment of the abolition societies. He adds that he is publishing the poem because it bears such a close relation to the facts which are laid out in Clarkson's notorious 'Abstract', which collated a mass of eyewitness evidence against the slave trade. Marjoribanks also talks of how when living in the West Indies he recorded all his experiences and reactions to slavery in poems which he set down in a commonplace book. 'Slavery' was composed out of these. He concludes by emphasizing his special role as an eyewitness: 'This little production . . . is not the offspring of hypothesis, the dream of theory, but the simple recital of what fell under the cognisance of my own senses; and may be considered as an additional link in the chain of evidence.'

It is the precision of the testimony, and the ghastly nature of the details recorded, which give this poem a unique place within the poetry generated by abolition. Marjoribanks is particularly unusual in focusing criticism on the cruelty which women slave holders inflict upon their female slaves. It is, however, within the extensive footnotes that the horrific factual details of slave torture and abuse are fully developed. Marjoribanks seems to feel an aesthetic reluctance to introduce the worst factual details into his elegant couplets.

Slavery: An Essay in Verse

Britannia's heroes for fair Freedom fought,
And gained, at length, the prize they nobly sought.
On our brave ancestors did Freedom smile,
And fix'd her empire in their happy isle.
There still she flourishes in all her charms,
Each heart enlivens, and each bosom warms.
    Ungrateful men! to whom such boons she gave!
Who dare whole nations of mankind enslave!
From the rich ports, where she triumphant reigns,
Forth fly the fleets that carry freights of chains!
From peaceful counting houses edicts pour,
Afric's wide realms rapaciously to scour.

By Freedom's sons o'er distant oceans borne,
Are helpless wretches from their country torn!
In noisome cells, where fell Distemper glows,
A favour'd part *Death* frees from future woes!
Or happy they, who in the friendly deep
Fly from their tyrants to eternal sleep!
    What horrid fears must haunt the untutor'd mind
(Too *just*, alas!) of torments yet behind!
On shocking feasts must savage fancy brood,[1]
Where pale Europeans prey on human food!
His bloody limbs, yet quiv'ring on the board,
Glut the keen stomach of the ruthless lord!
Or on the shrine of vengeful gods he lies;
And, in atonement for a christian, dies!
Yes! every slave must yield a master food,
Who slowly fattens on his vital blood!
Blest, if at once his cruel tortures ceas'd,
And gave white cannibals a short liv'd feast!
Yes! Afric's sons must stain the bloody shrine!
But all those victims, Avarice, are *thine!*
On Mercy's God, those tyrants dare to call;
But Av'rice only is their lord of all!
To him their rites incessantly they pay;
And waste for him the Negro's life away!
    "But hear!" say you. Philosophy will hear;
Whoever argues, he will lend an ear.
"On their own shore those wretches *slaves* we found,[2]
And only mov'd them to a fairer ground.
Captives in war they met this wayward fate;
Or birth had doom'd them to a servile state.
Oft they are convicts sentenc'd for their crimes
To endless exile from their native climes.
With plants they knew not on those sterile lands,
Here are they nourish'd by our friendly hands;
Of our own properties we give them share,
And food or raiment never costs them care.

---

[1] 'The general idea of the new Negroes seems to be, that they are to be devoured.' [Marjoribanks]
[2] 'This and every other argument I have put into their mouths, I have frequently heard the planters use.' [Marjoribanks]

On them no debts, no difficulties prey,
Not Briton's peasants half so blest as they!"[3]
Hold, impious men! the odious theme forbear!
Nor with such treason wound a Briton's ear!
The British peasant! healthy, bold and *free!*
Nor wealth, nor grandeur, half so blest as he!
The state of life, for *happiness the first*,[4]
Dare you compare with this the *most accurs'd*.
You found them slaves—but who that title gave!
The God of Nature never form'd a slave!
Though Fraud, or Force acquire a master's name,
Nature and Justice must remain the same!
He who from theives their booty, conscious, buys,
May use an argument as sound and wise:
That he conceives no guilt attends his trade,
Because the booty is already made.
     For your own honour, name not Afric's wars!
Ye, whose curs'd commerce rais'd those civil jars!
Each petty chief whose tribe was drain'd for you,
For *your vile traffic* roams in quest of new;
For you in guiltless blood imbrues his hands,
And carries havoc o'er his neighbour's lands!
They whom the feebler rage of war may spare,
A harder fate from you and slavery share!
For you—*sole instigators to the wrong*,
The brutal victor hurries them along.
From Afric's far interior regions driven,
To you—and anguish are those wretches given!
     Nor yet are you, for any *righteous cause*,
The *executioners of Afric's laws;*
Th' *atrocious criminals* I oft have view'd,
European justice has so far pursu'd;
Emblems of Innocence they met my eyes,
In soft simplicity and young surprise!
     But I, alas! may spare my idle strains,
Which ne'er can wrest them from European chains!
For int'rest speaks in language far too strong,
Either to heed a sermon or a song!

---

[3] The preceding paragraph is a succinct summary of arguments commonly used by pro-slavery apologists.

[4] 'I would here be understood to allude to the peasantry of England.' [Marjoribanks]

Yet happy I, and not in vain I write,
If I could render but their chains more light;
Could I but wipe one tear from SLAVERY's eye,
Or save his heart one agonizing sigh!
　　Grant then your plea:—"Necessity demands
The toil of foreign slaves' unwilling hands."
Yet no necessity could e'er excuse,
The more than savage cruelty you use!⁵
　　"Those creatures are so obstinate," you say,
"That but for punishment they will obey;
No kindness soothes! no gratitude they know"—
Ah! little gratitude, indeed, they owe!
Ere you this virtue to their race denied,
Th' effects of kindness might have well been tried!
Come, now, reflect what *tender* modes you take
To make those beings labour—*for your sake!*
First, then, you are so generous and good
To give them time to rear a *little* food;
On the same selfish principle, of course,
You feed *(far better though)* your mule or horse.
Small is the portion, poor the granted soil,
Till'd by the Negro's restless Sabbath's toil!
What loud applause a master must deserve,
Not to permit his property⁶ to *starve!*
　　But worn by toils he can no more renew,
The helpless wretch is turn'd adrift by you!⁷
Ye, who destroyed, refusing to sustain
The few unhappy days that yet remain!
To render misery itself more hard,
You term it favour, freedom, and reward:
Can we your generosity deny;
Who grant your victims—*liberty to die!*
　　Soon as the trembling crew are landed *here*,
Their quiv'ring flesh the burning pincers sear;

---

⁵ 'While I speak of the cruelty practised by planters in general, I would not be understood to say, that there may not be many exceptions.' [Marjoribanks]
⁶ 'So they term them, but I deny that, in the sight of God, any human being can be the *property of another*.' [Marjoribanks]
⁷ 'I have seen several of these unfortunates expire, literally of hunger, who had been picked up on the road by soldiers; but too late for their preservation. I have known a good many others, who had been abandoned by their owners, supported for years by the humanity of those poor fellows.' [Marjoribanks]

Proudly imprinting your degrading brand
On men, created by your Maker's hand!
A dreadful specimen, we may suppose,
This *warm* reception gives of future woes!
　　Ere the poor savage yet can understand
The haughty language of a foreign land;
Ere he conceives your meaning, or your view,
The whip directs him what he is to do.
No sex, no age, you ever learn'd to spare,
But female limbs indecently lay bare;
See the poor mother lay her babe aside,[8]
And stoop to punishment she must abide!
Nor midst her pangs, her tears, her horrid cries,
Dare the sad husband turn his pitying eyes.
　　Amongst your numbers, do we never meet
Villains so most atrociously complete,
Who, with accurs'd accuracy, count the days,
The hours of labour pregnancy delays;
Who nature's wond'rous work attempt to spoil
By stripes, by terrors, and excess of toil.[9]
　　Agualta's stream by rains becomes a flood;
Once by its side a fearful female stood;
Th' attempt to cross it was a certain death—
To tarry, worse, perhaps—her tyrants wrath!
Some anxious hours, *unwilling*, did she stay,
Then through the less'ning torrent fought her way.
Prostrate she lay before her despot's feet,
Imploring mercy she was not to meet!
For ah! the ruffian's heart was hard as steel!
No pity *he* had e'er been known to feel!
While the lash tore her tir'd and tortur'd frame,
The pangs of labour prematurely came.
She clasp'd her murder'd infant to her breast!
Stretch'd her sore limbs, and sunk in endless rest![10]

---

[8] 'The Negro women who have young children carry them fastened on their backs, while they are at work in the field.' [Marjoribanks]

[9] 'To the villainous principle, that it is *cheaper* to purchase Guinea Negroes, than by better usage, and lighter labour, to encourage population among those of *this* country, may, in a great measure, be ascribed the necessity of so vast and annual importation from Africa.' [Marjoribanks]

[10] 'This happened during my residence here, within little more than a mile of the spot where I now sit: viz. On Norbrook mountain; the property of Long, compiler of the history of Jamaica. Stonyhill, 16th October, 1786.' [Marjoribanks]

Your ingenuity we must confess,
In finding various methods to distress:
See the wretch fastened on an emmet's nest,
Whose stings in myriads his whole frame molest!
Or smeared with cowhage all his body o'er,
His burning skin intolerably sore!
Chains, hooks, and horns, of every size and shape,
Mark those who've once attempted an escape.
A sister isle once us'd, but *this* improves,
That curs'd invention called Barbadoes Gloves.[11]
For your own sakes, your malice, and your whim
But *rarely* sacrifice a Negro's limb.
Unless a slave of sedentary trade,
(A luckless tailor well may be afraid);
Where there's no great occasion for a pair,
You may lop off the leg he has to spare.[12]
Were there a surgeon—and there may be such,[13]
Whose heart compassion had the power to touch;
Who dar'd the horrid office to decline,
Your laws condemn him in a heavy fine.[14]
If int'rest teaches you their limbs to spare,
Immediate[15] *murders* must be still more *rare*.
Though 'tis this selfish sentiment alone
That oft deters you to destroy *your own*.
But should your passions hurry you away
Another person's property to slay,
The guilt's consider'd in a venial light,
The proof is difficult; the sentence slight.[16]
Nay, malice, safe, may find a thousand times
When no *white evidence* can prove his crimes.

[11] 'Slips of wood are placed between every two fingers, and the whole screwed or wedged close together, so as to give most exquisite torture. I have known this infernal machine kept on house slaves for many days together.' [Marjoribanks]

[12] 'The reason assigned to a gentleman of my acquaintance, by his overseer, for cutting off the leg of one of his Negroes in his absence, was, that the fellow having run off, he thought this the most effectual method of preventing his trying it a second time; adding, that as *he was a tailor* the *property* was not a bit less valuable.' [Marjoribanks]

[13] 'I mean even in the West Indies.' [Marjoribanks]

[14] 'The penalty I think is 50 l currency.' [Marjoribanks]

[15] '*Immediate* as opposed to the slow murder of toil and torment.' [Marjoribanks]

[16] 'Generally payment of the price of the Negro to his owner. It is then, it may be, remarked, as expensive to kill another man's slave as your own.' [Marjoribanks]

Since, 'tis establish'd by your partial laws,
No slave bears witness in a *white* man's cause.[17]
'Tis said your equitable laws confine
The negro's punishment to *thirty-nine*.[18]
A specious sound!—which never gave redress,
Since who on earth can prove when you transgress.
Or curs'd pretences you can find with ease,
For nine and thirties num'rous as you please.
A jealous mistress finds a ready sham
To give a handsome maid the sugar dram;[19]
With her fair hands prepares the nauseous draught,
And pours the scalding mixture down her throat;
Closely confin'd for mad'ning nights and days,
Her burning thirst no liquid drop allays.
Nay, well I know a proud revengeful dame,
Who gave a dose too loathsome here to name.[20]
It must be own'd you *all* do wond'rous well,
Yet still in *torturing* the fair excel.
What strange inventions has their genius found,
(Impell'd by jealousy) to plague and wound!
And in *those modes* we should the least suppose
That *female delicacy* would have chose.
Self interested men have met your ear;
I, *without int'rest*, will be more sincere!
Wretches by want expell'd from foreign climes;[21]
Escap'd from debts, or justice due their crimes;
The base, the ignorant, the ruffian steer,
And find a desperate asylum *here*.
Abject and servile though themselves may be
To those above them but in one degree;
O'er the subordinate, sad, sable crew
They have as absolute control as you.

[17] 'Not only slaves but free Negroes, and people of colour are excluded. They are, however, admitted as evidences *against each other*.' [Marjoribanks]

[18] 'As there is seldom more than one white man in the field, the futility of the law is clear.' [Marjoribanks]

[19] 'An equal mixture of rum and salt.' [Marjoribanks]

[20] 'A lady of my acquaintance caused a slave, in presence of her family and strangers, to swallow a glass of rum mixed with human excrement.' [Marjoribanks]

[21] 'The life of a *book-keeper* is, in general, such a combination of drudgery and disease, pride and poverty, despotism and servility, that no man of birth, education, spirit and sensibility would, if previously acquainted with its nature, ever engage in it.' [Marjoribanks]

Men uninform'd, uncultivated, rude,
Whose boist'rous passions ne'er have been subdu'd;
Whose tempers, never naturally mild,
Care and misfortune render still more wild;
Their furious hearts a short relief procure,
To wreak on others more than they endure;
By such caprice, are negroes doom'd to bleed,
The Slaves of Slavery—They are low indeed!
    Bad is at best the slave's most easy state
Yet some are destin'd to a harder fate.
Villains there are, who, doubly bent on gain,
Most nicely calculate the toil and pain;
Who fix the time (Oh! Heav'n! why sleeps thy wrath?)
They may, *with profit*, work their gangs to death.
"Whether shall we," those precious scoundrels say,
"Grasp fortune quickly, or make long delay?
A hundred slaves we have no fund to buy;
The strength of *half that number* let us try,
With *mod'rate toil*, from practice it appears,
These slaves might live, perhaps, a dozen years;
To us, you know, the matter will be even,
If we can make as much of them in seven."[22]
The price of property they only weigh,
Regardless, else, what *lives they take away!*
    In mild Britannia many of you dwell,
Where tortur'd slavery ne'er is heard to yell.
You fly wherever luxury invites,
And dissipation crowns your days and nights;
The dire reflection never meets your view,
What pangs, what bloodshed, buy those joys for you!
Your injur'd slaves, perhaps, you *never saw;* [23]
And doubt the picture I *so truly* draw
Such would not willingly, I hope, impose
The last extremity of human woes.
But, if from freedom's land you never stray'd;
By false descriptions you may be betray'd.
    He who has made an independence *here*,
At home in splendour hurries to appear;

---

[22] 'This diabolical practice is called *driving* a gang.' [Marjoribanks]
[23] 'Many proprietors of estates in this country have never been in the island.' [Marjoribanks]

London, or Bath, with lying fame resounds,
"A fresh Creole!—worth Fifty Thousand Pounds!"
Though ten he knows the limit of his store,
He must keep up the figure first he wore.
Thoughtless he riots in the gay career;
And finds himself half ruin'd in the year.
Duns grow importunate—and friends but cool,
Back to Jamaica comes the bankrupt fool.
First goes the Pen;[24] the Polink;[25] worse and worse;
At last the sugar work is put to nurse.
He strives with Jews and Marshals long—in vain—
Once thus involv'd, he ne'er gets clear again.
Worse ev'ry year his situation grows,
'Till in a prison he concludes his woes;
Unless, perhaps, a seat at Council-board
A sure protection should for life afford;
Or in the lower house enacting laws—
The law eluding faster than he draws.
But while he parties off from year to year,
The Negro's sufferings are indeed severe!
For their vain lord the most supplies to raise,
Ill fed; hard work'd; they know no resting days![26]
Perhaps to greedy jobbers lent on hire,[27]
Who from excess of toil their gain acquire;
Who have no int'rest in them to preserve;
And if they labour, care not how they starve.
Or seiz'd by marshalls, and to market brought;
By various masters families are bought.
Amidst their unregarded sighs and tears,
The wife and husband fall to different shares;
Their clinging offspring from their arms are tore,
And hurried from them, ne'er to meet them more?
    I knew a fœtus, in mere wanton play,
Sold from the mother in whose womb it lay.

---

[24] 'The Villa.' [Marjoribanks]
[25] 'A mountain farm for raising provisions and stock.' [Marjoribanks]
[26] 'Indeed none of them do; but the Sunday, which they ought to be allowed to work for themselves, is generally styled a resting day.' [Marjoribanks]
[27] 'Bad as the situation of the slaves is in general it will easily be credited that those on bankrupt estates (of which God knows there is no scarcity) are more peculiarly wretched. But the most super-eminently miserable of the human race are, undoubtedly the Negroes belonging to *jobbing gangs*.' [Marjoribanks]

Unhappy mother! doom'd for months to bear
The luckless burden thou wert not to rear![28]
   What dreadful partings, for revenge's sake,
Do furious females in a moment make!
Their fav'rite maids, with whom from youth they grew,
As fine their shape, and scarce less fair their hue;[29]
For some slight error, some unlucky chance;
A tea-cup broken, or a lover's glance;
Feel all the fury of their quenchless flame;
And meet the punishment of pain and shame.
The parent's, sister's, ev'ry tender tie—
All are dissolv'd—and round the isle they fly!
   Accursed state! where nature, and where love,
Rude violations must for ever prove!
You, brutal ravishers! pretend in vain
That Afric's children feel no jealous pain.
Untaught Europeans, with illiberal pride,
Look with contempt on all the world beside;
And vainly think no virtue ever grew,
No passion glow'd beneath a sable hue.
Beings you deem them of inferior kind;[30]
Denied a human, or a thinking mind.
Happy for Negroes were this doctrine true!
Were *feelings lost to them—or giv'n to you!*

Samuel Taylor Coleridge (1772–1834), 'Greek Prize Ode on the Slave Trade' (1792) (translated from the Greek by Anthea Morrison); four stanzas from the 'Ode on the Slave Trade' in *Joan of Arc* (1796)

There have been many, indeed too many, efforts over the last thirty years to prove that Coleridge's masterpiece, and his major contribution to the *Lyrical Ballads, The Rime of the Ancient Mariner*, is a poem centrally concerned with the British slave trade. It is not a

---

[28] 'The bargain was struck in the hearing of the unfortunate mother.' [Marjoribanks]

[29] 'The ladies are generally attended by girls of colour, who, frequently, are their near relations; in the third or fourth generations, many of them are almost as fair as Europeans.' [Marjoribanks]

[30] 'I have often heard planters, talking of their Negroes, very gravely style them their *Cattle*.' [Marjoribanks]

good idea to try and read slavery too literally into the *Rime*, which seems to have been so constructed as to avoid any crude contextualizing readings which draw exclusively on contemporary politics. It is not, after all, as if Coleridge were not capable of addressing the question of slavery head on when he wanted to. He wrote about the subject throughout his career and his views changed radically over time. The 'Greek Prize Ode' on the slave trade reproduced here is an early effort but one of which Coleridge was proud. The 'Ode' bagged Coleridge the prestigious Browne gold medal for Greek composition in 1792 at Cambridge. Decades later when he wrote his effusive review of Thomas Clarkson's mammoth *History* of the slave trade Coleridge opened by stating how sorry he was that Clarkson had not included him as one of the names on the famous abolition map which opens the volume (p. xxi). He went on: 'your book and your little map were the only publication I wished to see my name in . . . my first public Effort was a Greek Ode against the Slave Trade . . . and I published a long Essay in the *Watchman* against the trade in general.' The lecture and essay against the slave trade which Coleridge produced in 1795 repeat many current abolition arguments relating to the inefficiency of the trade and the fact that it was devoted to producing unnecessary luxury goods. Yet this journalism also includes a subtle analysis of the emotionally exploitative dynamic which lies behind sentimental abolition literature. Coleridge's 'Greek Prize Ode' is intriguing in that it both exploits what Coleridge had termed the 'bastard sensibility' of sentimental slavery literature, and yet warns against the dangers of attempting to appropriate the suffering of the slave. The appearance of Wilberforce as a 'herald of pity' marks the nadir of Coleridge's lip service to abolition orthodoxy, yet the treatment of the slaves in the poem is unusual. Above all the poem shies away from a conventional pietism of the sort exemplified in Southey's 'Sailor who Had Served in the Slave Trade' (pp. 219–22). The religious longings expressed by the slaves are to return to be with their ancestors in Africa. Coleridge's high opinion of the 'Greek Prize Ode' comes out in the way he translated his favourite section into English and included it within the early radical verse-drama *Joan of Arc*.

The 'Greek Prize Ode' stands as a tribute to Coleridge's early and passionate hatred of slavery, and his desire for an immediate and universal emancipation. Unfortunately these beliefs were diluted and trimmed as his life progressed. Coleridge's thoughts on Caribbean slavery after the 1790s are marked by a regression into a certain politicized application of Christianity. Coleridge's views on slavery and Africans became increasingly ambivalent and pragmatic. He is recorded in his *Table Talk* as having grave doubts in the early 1830s over the feasibility of the emancipation bill.

Greek Prize Ode on the Slave Trade

On the wretched lot of the Slaves in the Isles of Western India.
In the highest Assembly Jul.3.1792.

O Death, leaving the gates of darkness, come
hastening to a race yoked to misery; thou

wilt not be received with tearings of cheeks
or with lamentation, but, on the contrary,
with circles beating out the dance and with the
joy of songs: thou art Fearful indeed, but still thou
dwellest with Liberty, hateful Tyrant. Raised
on thy murky wings, through the rough swell of
the vast Ocean, let them fly to the dear
resorts of pleasure, and to their fatherland.
There, verily, beside the springs
beneath the citron groves, lovers tell to their
beloved what terrible things, being men,
they suffered from men Alas! Islands
full of murderous excess, abounding in
evils ill to look upon, where Hunger is
sick, and a bloody blow roars,
woe for us; how often a mist has come over
the tearful eyes, and how often at the same time
the heart has groaned! For I grieve deeply
with the race of slaves suffering dire ills,
just as they groan with unspeakable grief,
so they circle round in eddies of loathsome
labours, children of Necessity.
Since burning Heat, and Plague, and insufferable
Weariness rage round them on loveless days, and
the relentless phantoms of baneful Memory.
Alas! the watchful Scourge drives them on
exhausted, before Dawn wakes the sun; and the
sweet-looking star of Day sets, but griefs
blossom for ever: for midnight terrors smite
the soul, breathing wrath; the eyes of the
wretched ones fall asleep, but Fear never sleeps.
And if they seek after any sweet delusion with the
shadows of hope that appear in dreams, as they
are roused they are promptly driven mad with
the torments of wanton violence.
O you who revel in the evils of Slavery, O you
who feed on the persecution of the wretched,
wanton children of Excess, snatching your
brother's blood, does not an inescapable Eye
behold? Does not Nemesis[1] brandish fire-breathing

---

[1] Greek goddess of retribution. Extreme retributive justice.

requital? Do you hear? Or do you not hear?
Because winds shake the earth from its foundations,
and the recesses of the earth moan, and the
depths bellow terribly, guaranteeing that those
below are angry with those who slav!
But what sweet-voiced echo, what throbbings
of the Dorian[2] lyre, hovers towards me?
What soft voice lets fall a sweet whispering?
O! I see a Herald of Pity, his head shaded
with branches of olive! O! the golden joy of
thy words, Wilberforce, I hear! 'Holy spring
of Tears, now [there is] enough of thy drops:
smitten with the stranger-helping lightning
of Justice, the misery having been quelled
shall die. And the abominable thankless Favour of
Gold shall no longer fall upon African shores,
as the breath of Pestilence rides with
parching winds. Far from fatherland
and kinsfolk, old age shall not wrestle with
lawless labours, breathing out wild cries, ah! ah!
when life is setting.
No longer with prophetic fear shall the Mother
take her grimy babe to her breast: no; because
the Day of Slavery has already been stretched
too far. You who, Slaves of puffed-up Masters,
have never, wretches, seen a tear moisten Pity's
cheek, [though] suffering things shattering to
hear, for you, your Children taste of [?] Justice,
gathering the roses of Tranquillity, and surely the holy
reverence for Liberty, mother of prizes.[']

Translation: Anthea Morrison

from *Ode on the Slave Trade*

But long time pass'd not, ere that brighter Cloud
Return'd more bright: along the Plain it swept;
And soon from forth its bursting sides emerg'd
A dazzling Form, broad-bosom'd, bold of Eye,

---

[2] Belonging to the Dorians, Greek.

And wild her hair save where by Laurels bound.
Not more majestic stood the healing God
When from his Bow the arrow sped, that slew
Huge Python.[1] Shriek'd AMBITION's ghastly throng,
And with them those, the locust Fiends that crawl'd
And glitter'd in CORRUPTION's slimy track.
Great was their wrath, for short they knew their reign.
And such Commotion made they and Uproar
As when the mad Tornado bellows thro'
The guilty Islands of the western main,
What time departing for their native shores,
Eboe, or Koromantyn's[2] plain of Palms,
The infuriate Spirits of the Murder'd make
Fierce merriment, and vengeance ask of Heaven.
Warm'd with new Influence the unwholsome Plain
Sent up its foulest fogs to meet the Morn:
The Sun, that rose on FREEDOM, rose in blood!

Anon., 'Ode: The Insurrection of the Slaves at St Domingo' ([1792] this text *The Spirit of the Public Journals for 1797*)

This is an unusual poem, in that San Domingue was a subject largely written out of abolition during the 1790s. The uprising of over 100,000 slaves on the great plain of north San Domingue in the winter of 1790–1, and the ensuing carnage in the French sugar colony over the next two years, unleashed a barrage of anti-Jacobin and anti-black propaganda of unparalleled ferocity. Leading critics of the Revolution, with Edmund Burke at their head, saw the San Domingue slave revolution as an ultimate sign of the revolutionary depravity of France and the inhuman barbarity of the black Caribbean slave populations. When this ode was originally published in the radical *Courier* in 1792 it constituted a spirited and marginal defence of some aspects of the 'insurrection'. When it was republished in 1797, the year in which British troops were committed en masse to an attempt to invade the colony and claim it for Britain, the climate was beginning to change. The blacks could be constructed as a revolutionary force willing to take on the French. The construction of the black forces as heroic

[1] Apollo, god of archery, who slew the Python.
[2] See Edwards, 'On Seeing a Negro Funeral', n. 2, above.

enemies of initially revolutionary, and then Napoleonic imperialist, France were to culminate in mythologization of Toussaint L'Ouverture. The central device of having the personified 'Genius of Africa' rise up and utter a curse against the French was also taken up by Whitchurch in extended form in his *Hispaniola* (for later poetic constructions of San Domingue see Whitchurch and Wordsworth, pp. 168–80, 231–3).

Ode: The Insurrection of the Slaves at St Domingo

Lowly sinks the ruddy sun,
Sheathe the blade, the war is done;
Cried Orrah, to his murderous band,
Who wearied stood on Cuba's strand.
But hark! what sound invades the ear?
Hark!—Sheathe the blade, no danger's near:
'T is the gasp of parting breath,
'T is the hollow voice of death,
'T is the sigh, the groan of those,
Once our tyrants, once our foes.
Loud, loud, ye fiends, shriek loud! your cries
Pour loud! a grateful sacrifice
To him, at whose behest ye bleed,
Who smil'd propitious on the deed!
And, ye hoar cliffs, that frown around,
The echos of our shouts resound,
While around the votive fire
We've sooth'd the spirit of our fire.
'T was night, when bound in servile chains,
We sail'd from Afric's golden plains;
The moon had reach'd its utmost height,
Its orb disclos'd but half its light;
Darkling clouds hung o'er the deep,
And the hush'd murmurs seem'd to sleep.
Sudden floating in the skies
A shadowy cloud appear'd to rise;
Sudden gliding o'er the flood
The dim-seen shade before me stood;
Through its form the moon's pale beam
Shed a faint, a sickly gleam;

Thrice its arm I saw it rear,
Thrice my mighty soul did fear.
The stillness dread a hollow murmur broke;—
It was the Genius groan'd; and, lo!—it spoke!
   "O, my troubled spirit sighs
   When I hear my people's cries!
   Now, the blood which swells their veins
   Flows debas'd by servile chains:
   Desert now my country lies;
   Moss grown now my altars rise:
   O, my troubled spirit sighs
   When I hear my people's cries!
   Hurry, Orrah, o'er the flood,
   Bathe thy sword in Christian blood!
   Whidah will thy side protect;
   Whidah will thy arm direct."
Low'ring frown'd the burden'd cloud,
Shrilly roar'd the whirlwind loud,
Livid lightnings gleam'd on high,
And big waves billow'd to the sky.
   Astonish'd I, in wild affright,
   Knew not 't was vanish'd from my sight;
   Whether on the storm it rode,
   Or sunk beneath the troubled flood.
Again! along the beam gilt tide,
Ah! see again the spirit glide!
It joins our triumph! on the sight
It bursts in majesty of light.
Mark! how it bows its wondrous head,
And hails our deed! Ah! see—'t is fled!
   Now, now, ye cliffs, that frown around,
   The echoes of our shouts resound,
   While around the votive fire
   We've sooth'd the spirit of our sire.

Anon., 'The African's Complaint on Board a Slave Ship' (*Gentleman's Magazine*, 1793)

This poem was published at the point when the impact of the slave revolution on San Domingue and the successive failures of the bill for slave trade abolition had put a serious damper on the abolition propaganda drive. The poem is an attempt to reimpose the image of the black on the middle passage as an entirely helpless and harmless victim. Here the trauma of the middle passage is translated into an ideological pap easily digestible for the respectable middle-brow readers of the *Gentleman's Magazine*. Black Caribbean dialect is brutally parodied, the linguistic mimesis of the richness and subtleties of the slave languages being reduced to the substitution of 'dis' for 'this' and 'dat' for 'that'.

In *The Signifying Monkey* (Oxford University Press, 1988) Henri Louis Gates warns that Western perceptions of the middle passage were deliberately constructed in ways which prevented an understanding of how African civilizations were transposed into the societies of the New World slave, and ex-slave, communities: 'The notion that the Middle Passage was so traumatic that it functioned to create in the African a tabula rasa of consciousness is as odd as it is a fiction, a fiction that has served many economic orders and their attendant ideologies. The full erasure of traces of cultures as splendid, as ancient, and as shared by the slave traveller as the classic cultures of traditional West Africa, would have been extraordinarily difficult' (p. 4). This poem is a fine illustration of how the processes of erasure Gates alludes to were put into effect. The voice in this poem has nothing to do with black suffering and everything to do with white sentimental fictions of black suffering. It is not simply that the black voice is silenced; it is drowned out in the din of an obscenely appropriative white 'sympathy'.

The African's Complaint on Board a Slave Ship

Trembling, naked, wounded, sighing,
On dis winged house I stand,
Dat with poor black-man is flying
Far away from their own land!

Fearful water all around me!
Strange de sight on every hand,
Hurry, noise, and shouts, confound me
When I look for Negro land.

Every thing I see affright me,
   Nothing I can understand,
With de scourges white man fight me,
   None of dis in Negro land.

Here de white man beat de black man,
   'Till he's sick and cannot stand,
Sure de black be eat by white man!
   Will not go to white man land!

Here in chains poor black man lying
   Put so tick dey on us stand,
Ah! with heat and smells we're dying!
   'Twas not dus in Negro land.

Dere we've room and air, and freedom,
   Dere our little dwellings stand;
Families, and rice to feed 'em!
   Oh I weep for Negro land!

Joyful dere before de doors
   Play our children hand in hand;
Fresh de fields, and sweet de flow'rs,
   Green de hills, in Negro land.

Dere I often go when sleeping,
   See my kindred round me stand;
Hear 'em take—den wak in weeping,
   Dat I've lost my Negro land.

Dere my black love arms were round me,
   De whole night! not like dis hand,
Close dey held, but did not wound me;
   Oh! I die for Negro land!

De bad traders stole and sold me,
   Den was put in iron hand—
When I'm dead dey cannot hold me
   Soon I'll be in black man land.

John Wolcot (1738–1819) ['Peter Pindar'], *Azid; or, The Song of the Captive Negro* (1795)

Wolcot began his professional life as a doctor and, having trained in Edinburgh, following family connections went out to work in Jamaica; he then returned to Britain, trained as a minister, and went back to Jamaica where he worked both as a rector and as an army surgeon. On returning to Britain in 1779 he rapidly made a name for himself as a social and political satirist. An irreverent critic both of the establishment and of pretension in the visual and literary arts, Wolcot had a slightly Juvenalian edge, never really committing himself in any steadfast way to the radical cause although he could be a devastating critic of the loyalists. He made no lasting or intelligent commitment to the anti-slavery cause. The poem reproduced below is an utterly conventional song lyric, which again attempts to mimic Afro-Caribbean language as a way of entering the psyche of the slave victim. Although a little more varied than the previous poem, the rendition of black, presumably Jamaican, dialect boils down to the predictable substitutions of 'wid', 'de', and 'den' for 'with', 'the', and 'then'. If this linguistic window dressing is removed then the poem emerges for what it is, a piece of torpid gesturalization. The, by now, overused abolition device of presenting the slave as piteously wishing for death in order to escape to the ancestral homeland has become redundant.

Azid; or, The Song of the Captive Negro

Poor Mora eye be wet wid tear,
    And heart like lead sink down wid woe;
She seem her mournful friends to hear,
    And see der eye like fountain flow.

No more she give me song so gay,
But sigh, 'Adieu, dear Domahay.'[1]

No more for deck her head and hair,
    Me look in stream, bright gold to find;
Nor seek de field for flow'r so fair,
    Wid garland Mora hair to bind.

'Far off de stream!' I weeping say,
' Far off de fields of Domahay.'

---

[1] Fanciful variant spelling of Dahomey, an area of West Africa within present-day Benin.

But why do Azid live a slave,
    And see a slave his Mora dear?
Come, let we seek at once de grave—
    No chain, to tyrant den we fear.

Ah, me! I hear a spirit say,
'Come, Azid, come to Domahay.'

Den gold I find for thee once more,
    For thee to fields for flow'r depart;
To please de idol I adore,
    And give wid gold and flow'r my heart.

Den let we die and haste away,
And live in groves of Domahay.

Robert Southey (1774–1843), 'Poems on the Slave Trade', in *Poems 1797* (1797); 'The Sailor Who Had Served in the Slave Trade', in *Poems 1799* (1799); 'Verses Spoken in the Theatre at Oxford, upon the Installation of Lord Grenville', in *Collected Poems of Robert Southey* (1810)

Southey wrote the majority of his slavery verse as a young political idealist, in the early to mid-1790s while he was still under Coleridge's intellectual influence, and while the two of them were actively engaged in the abolition cause in Bristol. These poems are not, in retrospect, either his best or his most important writing on the subject. Southey's most sustained and profound work on colonial plantation slavery came not in the context of the early abolition poetry but in his later prose works and particularly the *History of Brazil* and the closely related *History of Ursua and Crimes of Aguirre*. The *History of Brazil* contained a deeply sympathetic discussion of the Brazilian rebel slave community in Palmares, and constitutes the first serious study of slave marronage. In 1807, the very year that the British slave trade was finally abolished, Southey also published the laconic mock travel book *Letters from England: By Don Manuel Alvarez Espriella. Translated from the Spanish*. These epistles introduced the subjects of chattel slavery in the West Indies and wage slavery in Britain in radical and intriguing ways. It is however, the poetry which is the subject here.

'Poems on the Slave Trade' was Robert Southey's public reaction to the first phase of English abolition, and the volume outlines the limitations of his aesthetic response to slavery during the heady days of his early radicalism. Thematically the sonnets are, when compared to the establishment abolition verse of Hannah More, or even of Cowper (pp. 81–93, 99–116), frequently very bold. His sonnet sequence constructs a logical narrative, which begins on the African mainland, contemplating the interrelations of African and European slave traders. The narrative then moves through the middle passage and on to delineate the outrages of the plantation. Southey is intellectually ambitious in attempting to look beyond atrocity and provide an overview of the intercontinental economic forces which enable slavery. The basic problem lies in the diction and the histrionic narrative persona which Southey has constructed for himself. The poetry fails as political discourse because the diction, simultaneously emotionally effusive and aesthetically burned out, destroys the clarity of the social analysis. Southey's unquenchable desire to invent himself as suffering witness to the enormities of slavery threatens to crowd out the slave victim altogether.

Southey's 'The Sailor Who Had Served in the Slave Trade' provides an extreme example of the extent to which abolition poetry is capable of appropriating or rather misappropriating the suffering of the slave through empathetic projection. The poem is a parodic rewriting of Coleridge's *Rime of the Ancient Mariner* in which a Bristol clergyman hears the sound of human agony coming out of a cowhouse. The clergyman asks the sailor what the problem is, which prompts the sailor to retell the narrative of how he whipped a slave girl to death, under his captain's instructions, during the middle passage. Southey's sinner is a dull and familiar figure, who emerges simply as a victim of demonic possession. His sin has made him the property of the Devil, and his terror is a banal selfish fear of orthodox Evangelical damnation. When it comes to narrating the murder of a woman the sailor is forced to whip because she will not eat, the slave inevitably emerges not as a suffering human, but as a catalyst for the sailor's suffering. Indeed Southey goes to the bizarre extreme of placing his white torturing narrator in direct competition with the victim. By 1810 Southey, as poet laureate, was writing verses in which the black body had been written out completely. Within the grandiose self-satisfaction of the 'Verses Spoken in the Theatre at Oxford, upon the Installation of Lord Grenville' Southey takes what is to become the standard British line on the history of Atlantic slavery. This poem is a test case for how British involvement in slavery could be effectively mythologized as a cause not only for national celebration but for missionary expansion into Africa. The central premiss is one which is to become fundamental to Victorian imperialistic fiction. The evil of slavery is constructed as necessary because it enables the altruistic glories of the British abolition movement to flourish. By this stage Southey can also use Atlantic slavery as a handy rhetorical club with which to beat the myth of Napoleon over the head. Consequently abolition is set in a wider triumphalist context relating to the war with France, and what is seen as Britain's fight against Napoleonic slavery within Europe.

Sonnet I

Hold your mad hands! for ever on your plain
   Must the gorged vulture clog his beak with blood?
   For ever must your Nigers tainted flood
Roll to the ravenous shark his banquet slain?
Hold your mad hands! what daemon[1] prompts to rear
   The arm of Slaughter? on your savage shore
   Can hell-sprung Glory claim the feast of gore,
With laurels water'd by the widow's tear
Wreathing his helmet crown? lift high the spear!
   And like the desolating whirlwinds sweep,
   Plunge ye yon bark of anguish in the deep;
For the pale fiend, cold-hearted Commerce there
Breathes his gold-gender'd pestilence afar,
And calls to share the prey his kindred Daemon War.

Sonnet II

Why dost thou beat thy breast and rend thine hair,
   And to the deaf sea pour thy frantic cries?
   Before the gale the laden vessel flies;
The Heavens all-favoring smile, the breeze is fair;
Hark to the clamors of the exulting crew!
   Hark how their thunders mock the patient skies!
   Why dost thou shriek and strain thy red-swoln eyes
As the white sail dim lessens from thy view?
Go pine in want and anguish and despair,
   There is no mercy found in human-kind—
Go Widow to thy grave and rest thee there!
   But may the God of Justice bid the wind
Whelm that curst bark beneath the mountain wave,
And bless with Liberty and Death the Slave!

[1] See p. 21 n. 52.

Sonnet III

Oh he is worn with toil! the big drops run
    Down his dark cheek; hold—hold thy merciless hand,
    Pale tyrant! for beneath thy hard command
O'erwearied Nature sinks. The scorching Sun,
As pityless as proud Prosperity,
    Darts on him his full beams; gasping he lies
    Arraigning with his looks the patient skies,
While that inhuman trader lifts on high
    The mangling scourge. Oh ye who at your ease
    Sip the blood-sweeten'd beverage![2] thoughts like these
Haply ye scorn: I thank thee Gracious God!
    That I do feel upon my cheek the glow
Of indignation, when beneath the rod
    A sable brother writhes in silent woe.

Sonnet IV

'Tis night; the mercenary tyrants sleep
    As undisturb'd as Justice! but no more
    The wretched Slave, as on his native shore,
Rests on his reedy couch: he wakes to weep!
Tho' thro' the toil and anguish of the day
    No tear escap'd him, not one suffering groan
    Beneath the twisted thong, he weeps alone
In bitterness; thinking that far away
Tho' the gay negroes join the midnight song,
    Tho' merriment resounds on Niger's shore,
She whom he loves far from the chearful throng
    Stands sad, and gazes from her lowly door
With dim grown eye, silent and woe begone,
    And weeps for him who will return no more.

---

[2] Referring to the principal use of sugar as a sweetener in tea and coffee. When Southey was writing the English abolitionists had organized a boycott on slave sugar consumption. Those participating were called anti-saccharites.

Sonnet V

Did then the bold Slave rear at last the Sword
    Of Vengeance? drench'd he deep its thirsty blade
In the cold bosom of his tyrant lord?
    Oh! who shall blame him? thro' the midnight shade
Still o'er his tortur'd memory rush'd the thought
    Of every past delight; his native grove,
    Friendship's best joys, and Liberty and Love,
All lost for ever! then Remembrance wrought
His soul to madness; round his restless bed
    Freedom's pale spectre stalk'd, with a stern smile
    Pointing the wounds of slavery, the while
She shook her chains and hung her sullen head:
No more on Heaven he calls with fruitless breath,
But sweetens with revenge, the draught of death.

Sonnet VI

High in the air expos'd the Slave is hung
    To all the birds of Heaven, their living food![3]
He groans not, tho' awaked by that fierce Sun
    New torturers live to drink their parent blood!
He groans not, tho' the gorging Vulture tear
    The quivering fibre! hither gaze O ye
    Who tore this Man from Peace and Liberty!
Gaze hither ye who weigh with scrupulous care
The right and prudent; for beyond the grave
    There is another world! and call to mind,
    Ere your decrees proclaim to all mankind
Murder is legalized, that there the Slave
Before the Eternal, "thunder-tongued shall plead
Against the deep damnation of your deed."[4]

---

[3] A common form of slave punishment in the Caribbean, to be suspended alive in an iron cage usually in a public space. Thirst was the usual cause of death.
[4] Adapted from *Macbeth*, I. vii. 19–20.

The Sailor Who Had Served in the Slave Trade

In September, 1798, a Dissenting Minister of Bristol, discovered a Sailor in the neighbourhood of that City, groaning and praying in a hovel. The circumstance that occasioned his agony of mind is detailed in the annexed Ballad, without the slightest addition or alteration. By presenting it as a Poem the story is made more public, and such stories ought to be made as public as possible.

> He stopt,—it surely was a groan
>   That from the hovel came!
> He stopt and listened anxiously
>   Again it sounds the same.
>
> It surely from the hovel comes!
>   And now he hastens there,
> And thence he hears the name of Christ
>   Amidst a broken prayer.
>
> He entered in the hovel now,
>   A sailor there he sees,
> His hands were lifted up to Heaven
>   And he was on his knees.
>
> Nor did the Sailor so intent
>   His entering footsteps heed,
> But now the Lord's prayer said, and now
>   His half-forgotten creed.
>
> And often on his Saviour call'd
>   With many a bitter groan,
> In such heart-anguish as could spring
>   From deepest guilt alone.
>
> He ask'd the miserable man
>   Why he was kneeling there,
> And what the crime had been that caus'd
>   The anguish of his prayer.
>
> Oh I have done a wicked thing![1]
>   It haunts me night and day,
> And I have sought this lonely place
>   Here undisturb'd to pray.

[1]   Rearrangement of Coleridge's 'I had done a hellish thing' when the Mariner refers to the killing of the Albatross.

I have no place to pray on board
   So I came here alone,
That I might freely kneel and pray,
   And call on Christ and groan.

If to the main-mast head I go,
   The wicked one is there,
From place to place, from rope to rope,
   He follows every where.

I shut my eyes,—it matters not—
   Still still the same I see,—
And when I lie me down at night
   'Tis always day with me.

He follows follows every where,
   And every place is Hell!
O God—and I must go with him
   In endless fire to dwell.

He follows follows every where,
   He's still above—below,
Oh tell me where to fly from him!
   Oh tell me where to go!

But tell me, quoth the Stranger then,
   What this thy crime hath been,
So haply I may comfort give
   To one that grieves for sin.

O I have done a cursed deed[2]
   The wretched man replies,
And night and day and every where
   'Tis still before my eyes.

I sail'd on board a Guinea-man
   And to the slave-coast went;
Would that the sea had swallowed me
   When I was innocent!

And we took in our cargo there,
   Three hundred negroe slaves,
And we sail'd homeward merrily
   Over the ocean waves.

[2] Another rearrangement of the Coleridge line; see n. 1.

But some were sulky of the slaves
   And would not touch their meat,
So therefore we were forced by threats
   And blows to make them eat.

One woman sulkier than the rest
   Would still refuse her food,—
O Jesus God! I hear her cries—
   I see her in her blood!

The Captain made me tie her up
   And flog while he stood by,
And then he curs'd me if I staid
   My hand to hear her cry.

She groan'd, she shriek'd—I could not spare
   For the Captain he stood by—
Dear God! that I might rest one night
   From that poor woman's cry!

She twisted from the blows—her blood
   Her mangled flesh I see—
And still the Captain would not spare—
   Oh he was worse than me!

She could not be more glad than I
   When she was taken down,
A blessed minute—'twas the last
   That I have ever known!

I did not close my eyes all night,
   Thinking what I had done;
I heard her groans and they grew faint
   About the rising sun.

She groan'd and groan'd, but her groans grew
   Fainter at morning tide,
Fainter and fainter still they came
   Till at the noon she died.

They flung her overboard;—poor wretch
   She rested from her pain,—
But when—o Christ! o blessed God!
   Shall I have rest again!

I saw the sea close over her,
    Yet she was still in sight;
I see her twisting every where;
    I see her day and night.

Go where I will, do what I can
    The wicked one I see—
Dear Christ have mercy on my soul,
    O God deliver me!

To morrow I set sail again
    Not to the Negroe shore—
Wretch that I am I will at least
    Commit that sin no more.

O give me comfort if you can—
    Oh tell me where to fly—
And bid me hope, if there be hope,
    For one so lost as I.

Poor wretch, the stranger he replied,
    Put thou thy trust in heaven,
And call on him for whose dear sake
    All sins shall be forgiven.

This night at least is thine, go thou
    And seek the house of prayer,
There shalt thou hear the word of God
    And he will help thee there!

Spoken in the Theatre at Oxford, upon the Installation of Lord Grenville

GRENVILLE,[1] few years have had their course, since last
Exulting Oxford view'd a spectacle
Like this day's pomp; and yet to those who throng'd
These walls, which echo'd then with Portland's praise,

[1] William Wyndham Grenville, 1st Baron (1759–1834). English politician and statesman, in 1806 he formed the ministry of 'All the Talents' and it was this coalition which, before its dissolution in 1807, finally saw through the abolition of the slave trade.

What change hath intervened! The bloom of spring
Is fled from many a cheek, where roseate joy
And beauty bloom'd; the inexorable Grave
Hath claimed its portion; and the band of youths,
Who then, collected here as in a port
From whence to launch on life's adventurous sea,
Stood on the beach, ere this have found their lots
Of good or evil.   Thus the lapse of years,
Evolving all things in its quiet course,
Hath wrought for them; and though those years have seen
Fearful vicissitudes, of wilder change
Than history yet had learnt, or old romance
In wildest mood imagined, yet these too,
Portentous as they seem, not less have risen
Each of its natural cause the sure effect,
All righteously ordain'd. Lo! kingdoms wreck'd,
Thrones overturn'd, built up, then swept away
Like fabrics in the summer clouds, dispersed
By the same breath that heap'd them; rightful kings,
Who, from a line of long-drawn ancestry
Held the transmitted sceptre, to the axe
Bowing the anointed head; or dragg'd away
To eat the bread of bondage; or escaped
Beneath the shadow of Britannia's shield,
There only safe.   Such fate have vicious courts,
Statesmen corrupt, and fear-struck policy,
Upon themselves drawn down; till Europe, bound
In iron chains, lies bleeding in the dust,
Beneath the feet of upstart tyranny:
Only the heroic Spaniard, he alone
Yet unsubdued in these degenerate days,
With desperate virtue, such as in old time
Hallow'd Saguntum and Numantia's[2] name,
Stands up against the oppressor undismay'd.
So may the Almighty bless the noble race,
And crown with happy end their holiest cause!
     Deem not these dread events the monstrous birth

[2] Saguntum was a Spanish city besieged and then sacked by Hannibal in 219 BC. Numantia was a strategically important location in the Douro in Spain; after a year's blockade it surrendered to Scipio Aemilianus and was sacked.

Of chance! And thou, O England, who dost ride
Serene amid the waters of the flood,
Preserving, even like the Ark of old,
Amid the general wreck, thy purer faith,
Domestic loves, and ancient liberty,
Look to thyself, O England! for be sure,
Even to the measure of thine own desert,
The cup of retribution to thy lips
Shall soon or late be dealt! . . a thought that well
Might fill the stoutest heart of all thy sons
With aweful apprehension. Therefore, they
Who fear the Eternal's justice, bless thy name,
Grenville, because the wrongs of Africa
Cry out no more to draw a curse from Heaven
On England!—for if still the trooping sharks
Track by the scent of death the accursed ship
Freighted with human anguish, in her wake
Pursue the chace, crowd round her keel, and dart
Toward the sound contending, when they hear
The frequent carcass from her guilty deck
Dash in the opening deep, no longer now
The guilt shall rest on England; but if yet
There be among her children, hard of heart
And sear'd of conscience, men who set at nought
Her laws and God's own word, upon themselves
Their sin be visited! . . the red-cross flag,
Redeem'd from stain so foul, no longer now
Covereth the abomination.
                                    This thy praise,
O Grenville, and while ages roll away
This shall be thy remembrance.   Yea, when all
For which the tyrant of these abject times
Hath given his honourable name on earth,
His nights of innocent sleep, his hopes of heaven;
When all his triumphs and his deeds of blood,
The fretful changes of his feverish pride,
His midnight murders and perfidious plots,
Are but a tale of years so long gone by,
That they who read distrust the hideous truth,
Willing to let a charitable doubt
Abate their horror; Grenville, even then

Thy memory will be fresh among mankind;
Afric with all her tongues will speak of thee,
With Wilberforce and Clarkson, he whom Heaven,
To be the apostle of this holy work,
Raised up and strengthen'd, and upheld through all
His arduous toil.   To end the glorious task,
That blessed, that redeeming deed was thine:
Be it thy pride in life, thy thought in death,
Thy praise beyond the tomb. The statesman's fame
Will fade, the conqueror's laurel crown grow sere;
Fame's loudest trump upon the ear of Time
Leaves but a dying echo; they alone
Are held in everlasting memory,
Whose deeds partake of heaven.   Long ages hence,
Nations unborn, in cities that shall rise
Along the palmy coast, will bless thy name;
And Senegal and secret Niger's shore,
And Calabar, no longer startled then
With sounds of murder, will, like Isis now,
Ring with the songs that tell of Grenville's praise.

Revd Ford, 'I do Remember a Poor Negro' (1799) [parody of *Romeo and Juliet* V.i.37–52, 'I do remember an apothecary']

Literary, and particularly Shakespearian and Miltonic, parodies were massively popular in England in the late eighteenth and early nineteenth centuries. The radical antiquarian William Hone managed to conduct a three-day trial defence for a charge of blasphemous libel by simply reading out hundreds of literary parodies. His argument was that a parody does not ridicule the form of the original but the new subject. Consequently his parodies of the Bible were attacking not the Bible but corrupt politicians. If this theory of parody is accepted then where does that leave the slave in the present example? Romeo's monologue relates to his recollection of a poverty-stricken chemist he can buy poison from cheaply:

> I do remember an apothecary,
> And hereabouts a dwells, which late I noted,
> In tattered weeds with overwhelming brows,
> Culling of simples. Meagre were his looks.

Sharp misery had worn him to the bones,
And in his needy shop a tortoise hung,
An alligator stuffed and other skins
Of ill-shaped fishes; and about his shelves
A beggarly account of empty boxes,
Green earthen pots, bladders, and musty seeds,
Remnants of packthread, and old cakes of roses
Were thinly scattered to make up a show.
Noting this penury, to myself I said
'An if a man did need a poison now,
Whose sale is present death in Mantua,
Here lives a caitiff wretch would sell it him.'

Romeo's monologue describes how poverty can lead to the destruction of an individual's moral will even to the extent that they will deal in death. Yet the poor apothecary is in fact empowered by his capacity to do anything for money. His corruption draws Romeo to him like a magnet. In Ford's parody the emotional dynamic of the original is completely altered because it has to accord with the passive presentation of the abused black. The first half of the monologue follows the original logically: the abused slave fittingly takes the place of the suffering chemist. Yet description of the run-down shop makes way for an inventory of slave tortures which owes more to Gothic fancy than fact. The landscape of despair is complete with 'air-piercing shrieks . . . dismal groans; wire platted whips, fetters, and massy chains, Remnants of cords and old spikes of iron' and it appears to be more an attempt to describe one of Piranesi's *Carcery* prints than a description of plantation life. Yet despite the extremity of this vision, having set up this platform for the slave victim it would make sense to follow through the processes of the model and replace the apothecary's capacity for embittered wickedness with that of the abused slave. This of course is not an abolition option. Ford makes the standard move of calling upon God to avenge the sufferings of slavery, while the slave ends the poem by simply falling down dead. The problem of the suffering slave consciousness was probably never more economically written out of Western thought: 'the sufferer drops, | And enters into rest', as, presumably, does the reader.

I do remember a poor Negro,
Under the torrid sun by parching thirst
Oppress'd; with sweat-bestreamed brow he slaved,
Planting of sugar-canes; fierce were his looks,
Curs'd Tyranny had almost made him mad;
And on his goary back a blanket hung,
To hide his fester'd sores, and torn-up back
By deep-indented lashes; within the huts
Air-piercing shrieks are heard, and dismal groans;
Wire-platted whips, fetters, and massy chains,
Remnants of cords, and old spikes of iron,

Were scatter'd here and there to make up terror.
Noting these cruelties, I cried aloud,
If Heaven hath store of right-aim'd thunder-bolts,
Scourges for guilt, and pains for damned men,
Here are unfeeling traders, that grow rich,
And fatten on the blood of human victims.
Oh! this same thought doth harrow up the soul,
Knock at the heart, and bid soft Pity weep!
No holiday allow'd, the sufferer drops,
And enters into rest.

W. H. Murrey, 'Overseer's Song', 'Possum up a Gum Tree', 'Magic Fire Duly Placed', in *Obi; or, Three-Fingered Jack: the plot and principal incidents taken from the highly popular pantomime of the celebrated Mr. Fawcett first performed at the Theatre Royal, Haymarket, July 2nd. 1800* [c.1830]

This hugely popular drama presents a dumbed-down version of the racial tensions within British Jamaica. The original version by John Fawcett was published in 1800, and was based on the story of Jack Mansong in Benjamin Moseley's *Treatise on Sugar* (1799). This version differs markedly from the later reworking by Murrey used here. Murrey's play in some ways makes the black characters conform more crudely to race stereotypes. The songs in this version are however more confrontational than the conventional love songs and black dance anthems in the earlier play.

Obi, or Three-Fingered Jack, is an escaped slave rebel, or maroon, who has murdered a white woman in revenge for the murder of his wife and daughter at the hands of white slave takers in Africa. He is presented as an evil villain who gains his power over the black slaves through his close connection with his mother who is an 'Obi' (Obeah) woman, or Afro-Caribbean leader, who is in control of the magical powers of the Jamaican equivalent of Voodoo. The play basically shows the slaves as loyal to an enlightened white master, and it is the loyal black Quashee who finally kills Jack and frees the white hero. The slaves are all then freed.

The exact creative and publishing history of *Obi* remains something of a mystery. By 1800, as the title of the earliest text version of the play makes clear, 'the celebrated Mr. Fawcett' was famous for his pantomime rendition of the story. This was apparently a version with no dialogue, but purely mime and song. No transcription of this text has been located, if indeed it exists. Murrey's text was then a development in more conventional theatrical form of Fawcett's original. Several elements, however, suggest that Murrey's version is closely related to its pantomimic roots. Most of the crucial dramatic action occurs in long and isolated dumb-show, indicated via protracted stage direction, as for example Three-Fingered Jack's attempted murder of the white hero Orford at the end of Act I, Scene v. The tableau opens with the child slave Tuckey leaving his master alone:

> *Music.—Tuckey, somewhat reluctantly obeys, and exits, whilst the Captain, preparing to load his fowling-piece, crosses to R.H., Jack now rushes upon him, wrests his gun from his and severely wounds him with a dagger, ere he has time to call for aid. The* Captain *falls at* Jack's *feet.—Horns sound nearer.—Jack looks cautiously and keenly off in the direction of the sound, and all around, then raising the body of* ORFORD, *bears it to his cave, and the scene closes on picture.*

The low comedy and the frequent use of set-piece songs would also suggest that Murrey's version is heavily dependent on its primitive source. The play was genuinely popular in London and the provinces and underwent many subsequent formal transformations, appearing for example as a beautiful children's book brought out by the famous Dean and Munday company in 1821 under the title *Obi; or, Three-Fingered Jack. Embellished with handsome Engravings on Wood.*

The songs/poems reproduced here give a sense of the manner in which plantation life and race politics can be essentialized within primitive drama for a broad-based and not necessarily literate audience. Significantly Jack is not given a song himself. The three songs are each by a key character and define race stereotypes. The first is sung by the jovial overseer, who sings to the happy slaves a hymn celebrating the coming birthday of the plantation mistress. The slaves join in, in a crude imitation of Jamaican patois. The second song is by the comic black slave youth Tuckey, and involves a comparison between the playful mischievous opossum, and the equally simple mischievous slaves. The third, and most interesting of the songs, is a curse on all white people by the Obeah woman. She sings an incantation which owes more to the Witches in *Macbeth* than to any observed Afro-Caribbean religious slave ritual. These songs would have gained wider public exposure than any of the verse in this anthology, with the single exception of the songs from *Uncle Tom's Cabin*. They present a reassuring vision of Afro-Caribbeans who are easily forced into the black and white political morality of melodrama.

The text used here is from *Obi; or, Three-Fingered Jack: A Melodrama* (London, c.1830).

Overseer's Song

Negroes discovered at work; they come forward, and the Overseer sings,

> Black ladies and gentlemen, I pray you draw near,
> And attend to the words of your grand overseer.

Leave work till to-morrow, my hearts—in the morning
      Be jovial and gay,
      For this is the day,
Miss Rosa, the good planter's daughter was born in.
  ' Tis our lady's birth-day,
  Therefore we'll make holyday,
    And you shall all be merry,
    And you shall all be merry,
      Sing ting—a—ring, &c.
      CHORUS.
Good massa we find,
  Sing ting a ring, sing terry,
Where buckra man kind,
  Then Negro heart merry,
     Sing ting—a—ring, terry.
      Huzza! Huzza!

Possum up a Gum Tree

Air,—Native Melody.

Opossum up a gum tree,
  His tail his body follow,
Racoon quickly him see
  Looking out o' hollow—
Pull him by the long tail,
  Opossum squall—opossum squall,
Racoon stick his long nail,
  Him louder squall—him louder squeak,
    Opossum up, &c.

Opossum him look shy now,
  Racoon grin, Racoon grin,
Opossum wink his eye now,
  Move him chin, move him chin,
Opossum down him tumble
  From the tree, from the tree,
And make him 'gin to tremble,

Racoon he, he, Racoon he, he,
   Opossum up, &c.

Black boy him love Jill Jenkins,
   Tink he'll wed—tink he'll wed,
His massa chide him thinking,
   Beat him head—beat him head,
Black boy him love rum, too,
   Make him groggy—make him groggy,
But massa make him come to
   When him floggy—when him floggy.
     Opossum up, &c.

Magic Fire Duly Placed

*OBI WOMAN discovered, sitting near fire, forming an Obi.
After performing several incantations, she speaks.*

Magic fire duly placed
In square within a circle traced,
   Boil the mystic herbs I've brought,
   Till the Obi charm be wrought;
Bones I've raked from the burial ground,
When night and the storm were black around;
Give strength to my work, till I've fixed my dart,
Like a cankerous thorn in the white man's heart—
Till I pierce him and wring him in nerve and spleen
By the arrows felt, but never seen.
   Then by flame unbodied burn him,
   Then on racking windlass turn him,
Till his sinews quiver and ache anew,
And the cold sweat falls like drops of dew,
Toil him and moil him again and again,
Sicken his heart and madden his brain;
Till strength, and sense, and life depart,
As I tear the last pulse from the white man's heart.

William Wordsworth (1770–1850), 'To Toussaint L'Ouverture', 'September 1, 1802' (both written 1802, published in *Poems in Two Volumes, 1800–1807*); from *The Prelude*, Book X (1805); from *The Prelude*, Book X (1850); 'To Thomas Clarkson' (1807); 'Queen and Negress Chaste and Fair!' (1821)

Even in the 1790s Wordsworth felt detached from the slave trade as a general political issue, and this comes out clearly in the curious discussion of the subject in the 1805 *Prelude*. In the quotation reproduced here from Book X Wordsworth describes his return from France after a year's absence. He gauges the moral health of the nation initially via the success of the abolition movement, yet rapidly moves on to see this as symptomatic of a general desire to support libertarian causes. Wordsworth reads the agitation for slave trade abolition as a preparatory move for a more general reform. Wordsworth, finally, does not appear to be summarizing the political situation so much as justifying his own take on abolition as part of a general moral groundswell. He places the slave trade in a wider picture, arguing that as long as the ideals of the French Revolution triumph then slavery will naturally fade away, as simply one particularly rotten branch on the tree of 'human shame'. Slavery and its traumatic effect on thousands of African individuals is not seen as a unique challenge to the consciences of England and France. While figures as diverse as Cowper, Coleridge, and Hazlitt saw the middle passage as a site of horror which reaches beyond the resources of the creative imagination, Wordsworth simply is not that interested in thinking about the subject as raw material for his art.

When Wordsworth came to deal with slavery directly in his poetry it was by concentrating on individual black victims of the corrupted French revolutionary process. His two greatest poems on slavery are also about the processes of imperial chaos which were part of the fallout of the French revolutionary wars.

Wordsworth's most famous poem about a slave is the sonnet 'To Toussaint L'Ouverture'. The crucial point with regard to the timing of Wordsworth's sonnet to Toussaint is that it was written after the withdrawal of British troops from San Domingue. The disastrous six-year attempt by Pitt to establish control in the colony had put a new slant on how the British looked at the black revolutionaries. With the rise of Bonaparte and the real threat of French invasion, the cynical entrapment and fatal imprisonment of Toussaint L'Ouverture by the French had provided the British with the chance to create the myth of a noble black who had been fighting, and winning, against the common enemy. Wordsworth certainly had his weather eye open when he wrote the sonnet to Toussaint; it would have been a lot more remarkable had he composed an equivalent paean to the martyred and forgotten Boukman in the early 1790s.

Wordsworth's other great sonnet devoted to a black subject, 'September 1, 1802', shares with 'To Toussaint L'Ouverture' a passive construction of the black. This terrifying poem defines new limits for the creative disempowerment of the colonial subject. The poem ends as an attack on the 'Ordinances' of Napoleonic France, which, in the wake of the disastrous San Domingue campaign, banned all colonial blacks from the French mainland. Yet even here the objection to racist French policy is reserved for the poet, and his way of expressing that objection is implicit. The fact that the black victim is incapable of articulating resentment at her treatment allows the poet to suggest his own. Yet this conclusion also suggests a lack of political consciousness in the victim. The black woman can state the facts of what has happened to her, but cannot even 'murmur' her anger, or despair. Wordsworth's final poetic treatment of the subject of the black colonial refugee seeking asylum in England, 'Queen and Negress Chaste and Fair', is stupidly unpleasant. This poem constitutes Wordsworth's final word in verse on the subject of the slave rebellion in San Domingue. The disastrous dictatorship of Henri Christophe, self-appointed Emperor of Hayti, ended in rebellion and his suicide in 1820. His wife and daughters were allowed passage to Britain where they stayed with the Clarksons. Thomas Clarkson had in fact conducted a voluminous correspondence with Christophe over many years. The arrival of the Christophe household was an event which caused much hilarity in the papers of the day, and also obviously to Mary and William Wordsworth. One evening, amidst outbursts of mirth, Wordsworth composed 'Queen and Negress Chaste and Fair'. The poem is an ingenious parody of Ben Jonson's beautiful lyric celebrating Queen Elizabeth in *Cynthia's Revels*:

> Queen and huntress, chaste and fair,
> Now the sun is laid to sleep,
> Seated in thy silver chair,
> State in wonted manner keep:
> Hesperus entreats thy light,
>   Goddess excellently bright.
>
> Earth, let not thy envious shade
> Dare itself to interpose;
> Cynthia's shining orb was made
> Heaven to clear, when day did close:
> Bless us then with wished sight,
>   Goddess excellently bright.
>
> Lay thy bow of pearl apart,
> And thy crystal-shining quiver;
> Give unto the flying hart
> Space to breathe, how short soever:
> Thou that mak'st a day of night,
>   Goddess, excellently bright.

Wordsworth's view of the Haytian revolution, which began with such elevated patronization in the sonnet to Toussaint, ends in sniggering bathos. Beyond this Wordsworth's poem is embedded in a series of moves which relate to the Negrophobe humour of the popular prints of the day. The idea that abolition leaders would be seduced by hugely endowed black women had long provided the subject for obscene comic prints, which saw the spectre of miscegenation between the elevated Wilberforce and his followers as unavoidably funny. Similarly punning and paradox operating around the capacity of black beauty to turn day into night, and black into white, had been a staple of parodic love lyrics since William Dunbar's 'Ane Blake Moire'. Wordsworth's response to Madame Christophe, who is in reality a tragic refugee, is very different from that he felt contemplating a lone black victim on the Calais packet in 1807.

In the end when Wordsworth wanted to celebrate a hero of slavery it was to white abolition leaders, and not the slave revolutionaries of the Diaspora, that he turned. The sonnet 'To Thomas Clarkson' shows the completely orthodox parameters of Wordsworth's vision of slavery. As a poem celebrating the abolition of the English slave trade this work is typical in its usurpations. It focuses exclusively upon the labour and suffering of the white political agitator, who is a metaphoric, and unintentionally ironic, slave figure: the 'pure yoke-fellow of Time'. The slaves are typically excluded from the whole process.

To Toussaint L'Ouverture

Toussaint, the most unhappy Man of Men!
Whether the rural Milk-maid by her Cow
Sing in thy hearing, or thou liest now
Alone in some deep dungeon's earless den,
O miserable Chieftain! where and when
Wilt thou find patience? Yet die not; do thou
Wear rather in thy bonds a cheerful brow:
Though fallen Thyself, never to rise again,
Live, and take comfort. Thou hast left behind
Powers that will work for thee; air, earth, and skies;
There's not a breathing of the common wind
That will forget thee; thou hast great allies;
Thy friends are exaltations, agonies,
And love, and Man's unconquerable mind.

September 1st, 1802

We had a fellow-Passenger who came
From Calais with us, gaudy in array,
A Negro Woman like a Lady gay,
Yet silent as a woman fearing blame;

Dejected, meek, yea pitiably tame,
She sate, from notice turning not away,
But on our proffer'd kindness still did lay
A weight of languid speech, or at the same
Was silent, motionless in eyes and face.
She was a Negro Woman driv'n from France,
Rejected like all others of that race,
Not one of whom may now find footing there;
This the poor Out-cast did to us declare,
Nor murmur'd at the unfeeling Ordinance.

The Prelude, from Book X (1805)

When to my native land,
(After a whole year's absence) I return'd,
I found the air yet busy with the stir
Of a contention which had been rais'd up
Against the Traffickers in Negro blood,
An effort, which, though baffled, nevertheless
Had call'd back old forgotten principles
Dismiss'd from service, had diffus'd some truths,
And more of virtuous feeling, through the heart
Of the English People. And no few of those,
So numerous—little less in verity
Than a whole Nation crying with one voice—
Who had been cross'd in their just intent
And righteous hope, thereby were well prepared
To let that journey sleep a while, and join
Whatever other Caravan appeared
To travel forward towards Liberty
With more success. For me that strife had ne'er
Fasten'd on my affections, nor did now
Its unsuccessful issue much excite
My sorrow, having laid this faith to heart,
That if France prospered good men would not long
Pay fruitless worship to humanity,
And this most rotten branch of human shame
Object, as seemed, of superfluous pains
Would fall together with its parent tree.

Such was my then belief—that there was one,
And only one, solicitude for all.
And now the strength of Britain was put forth
In league with the [confederated] host;
Not in my single self alone I found,
But in the minds of all ingenuous Youth,
Change and subversion from this hour.

The Prelude, from Book X (1850)

Twice had the trees let fall
Their leaves, as often Winter had put on
His hoary crown, since I had seen the surge
Beat against Albion's shore, since ear of mine
Had caught the accents of my native speech
Upon our native Country's sacred ground.
A Patriot of the world, how could I glide
Into communion with her sylvan shades.
Erewhile my tuneful haunt? It pleased me more
To abide in the great City, where I found
The general Air still busy with the stir
Of that first memorable onset made
By a strong levy of humanity
Upon the Traffickers in Negro blood;
Effort which, though defeated, had recalled
To notice old forgotten principles,
And through the Nation spread a novel heat
Of virtuous feeling. For myself, I own
That this particular strife had wanted power
To *rivet* my affections; nor did now
Its unsuccessful issue much excite
My sorrow; for I brought with me the faith
That, if France prospered, good men would not long
Pay fruitless worship to humanity,
And this most rotten branch of human shame,
Would fall together with its parent tree.
What, then, were my emotions, when in Arms
Britain put forth her free-born strength in league,
Oh, pity and shame! with those confederate Powers!

Not in my single self alone I found,
But in the minds of all ingenuous youth,
Change and subversion from that hour.

To Thomas Clarkson

On the final passing of the Bill for the Abolition of the Slave Trade, March, 1807

Clarkson! it was an obstinate Hill to climb;
How toilsome, ay how dire it was, by Thee
Is known,—by none, perhaps, so feelingly;
But Thou, who, starting in thy fervent prime,
Didst first lead forth this pilgrimage sublime,
Hast heard the constant Voice its charge repeat,
Which, out of thy young heart's oracular seat,
First roused thee.—O pure yoke-fellow of Time
With unabating effort, see, the palm
Is won, and by all Nations shall be worn!
The bloody Writing is for ever torn,
And Thou henceforth shalt have a good Man's calm,
A great Man's happiness; thy zeal shall find
Repose at length, firm Friend of human kind!

Queen and Negress Chaste and Fair!

Queen and Negress chaste and fair!
Christophe now is laid asleep
Seated in a British Chair
State in humbler manner keep
Shine for Clarkson's pure delight
Negro Princess, ebon bright!

Lay thy Diadem apart
Pomp has been a sad Deceiver
Through thy Champion's faithful heart
Joy be poured, and thou the Giver
Thou that mak'st a day of night
Sable Princess, ebon bright!

Let not "Wilby's"[1] holy shade
Interpose at Envy's call,
Hayti's shining Queen was made
To illumine Playford Hall[2]
Bless it then with constant light
Negress excellently bright!

Thomas Moore (1779–1852), from 'To the Lord Viscount Forbes from the City of Washington', in *Poems Relating to America* (1806), reprinted in *The Poetical Works of Thomas Moore, Complete in One Volume* (1846)

Moore was one of the most celebrated poets of the Romantic age, and his popularity was rivalled only by Byron and Scott, while he massively outsold those poets now considered the major Romantics. Byron indeed became a friend and admirer of 'Tom's' and entrusted Moore with the manuscript of his highly controversial memoirs, which Moore eventually destroyed, having sold them to a publisher and then bought them back. The publication within two years of each other of the *Irish Melodies* (1815) and *Lalla Rookh* (1817), his Orientalist epic, rocketed Moore to truly international stardom, and made him for a short time the most famous English-speaking poet in the world. More did not see Atlantic slavery in isolation but was also interested in exposing what he considered the enslavement of the Irish by the English. Even within *Lalla Rookh* critics noticed that it was the passages of lament over a lost and ruined homeland which held most power, because they were thinly veiled elegies on the plight of contemporary Ireland.

In his mid-twenties Moore undertook a short tour of the United States, and confronted American plantation slavery first hand in Virginia and Washington. Moore's antipathy to American slavery remained inveterate, and he is perhaps unique in setting up connections between American slavery and the plight of the Irish peasantry. The lines to Lord Viscount Forbes below indicate Moore's tendency to see slavery as a comparative phenomenon, stretching from ancient Rome to the Russian serf.

[1] A mocking reference to William Wilberforce, parliamentary spearhead for the abolition movement. Mary Wordsworth wrote in the margin of her letter of 24 Oct. 1821 to Catherine Clarkson, 'Mrs Wilberforce calls her husband by that pretty diminutive—"Wilby"—you must have heard her.'

[2] Mary Wordsworth, letter of 24 Oct, 1821, explained the poem's genesis in the 'lively picture I shaped myself of the sable Queen with her sable daughters beside you on the sofa in my dear little Parlour at Playford'.

from *To Lord Viscount Forbes*[1]
from the City of Washington

Oh! Freedom, Freedom, how I hate thy cant!
Not Eastern bombast, not the savage rant
Of purpled madmen, were they number'd all
From Roman Nero down to Russian Paul,[2]
Could grate upon my ear, so mean, so base,
As the rank jargon of that factious race,
Who, poor of heart and prodigal of words,
Formed to be slaves, yet struggling to be lords,
Strut forth, as patriots, from their negro-marts,
And shout for rights, with rapine in their hearts.

Who can, with patience, for a moment see
The medley mass of pride and misery,
Of whips and charters, manacles and rights,
Of slaving blacks and democratic whites,
And all the piebald polity that reigns
In free confusion o'er Columbia's plains?
To think that man, thou just and gentle God!
Should stand before thee with a tyrant's rod
O'er creatures like himself, with souls from thee,
Yet dare to boast of perfect liberty;
Away, away—I'd rather hold my neck
By doubtful tenure from a sultan's beck,
In climes, where liberty has scarce been nam'd,
Nor any right but that of ruling claim'd,
Than thus to live, where bastard Freedom waves
Her fustian flag in mockery over slaves;
Where—motley laws admitting no degree
Betwixt the vilely slav'd and madly free—
Alike the bondage and the licence suit,
The brute made ruler and the man made brute.

---

[1] George John, Viscount Forbes (1785–1836).
[2] Tsar Paul I of Russia (1750–1801) fought to curb the powers of the nobility and liberate the serfs.

John Thelwall (1764-1834),
'The Negro's Prayer' (1807)

Thelwall is chiefly remembered now for his activities as a radical reformer. Together with Thomas Hardy and John Horne Tooke he was one of the famous victims of the 1794 Treason Trials, and consequently one of the popular heroes of London radicalism on his acquittal. Thelwall was an autodidact with huge abilities. He wrote political pamphlets, edited and contributed to mainstream radical periodicals, and wrote large amounts of rather terrible Romantic poetry. Overcoming a speech impediment he turned himself into one of the most popular orators of the early nineteenth century. He lectured initially on contemporary politics and he remained a heroic enemy of Pittite policy during the French wars. Thelwall later switched to lecturing on speech theory and specialized in the cure of speech impediments. He even opened his own clinic.

Throughout his varied career Thelwall remained an uncompromising enemy of slavery and the slave trade. The arguments he used in various prose publications to attack pro-slavery advocates were brilliant in their subversive subtleties. Above all it needs to be stressed that Thelwall was most unusual among radicals in his uncompromising vision of poor white and poor black labour as equally exploited by the nascent forms of capitalism. From mid-1795 until the end of the century there appear to be no radical publications, apart from Thelwall's *Tribune*, which attempt detailed comparison between the aims and exploited status of the poor white labourer in England and the black slave in the Caribbean. Thelwall stood out against the Negrophobe orthodoxies of English radicalism. Where leading radical theorists including Cobbett saw abolition concerns over black suffering as an attempt to deflect attention from the plight of the English labourer, Thelwall saw the white and black as victims of the same system. This was uniquely forward looking for the late eighteenth century. Unlike the majority of radicals engaged in grass-roots activism Thelwall was not a political pragmatist over questions of race and Empire, but remained a profound idealist. The Thelwall who emerges from the great speeches and open letters of the mid-1790s is a figure who hated all social and political injustice with an intensity and uncompromising absolutism that put him, as a disciple of Godwin's *Political Justice*, next to Shelley, and nowhere near Cobbett.

When Thelwall came to compose 'The Negro's Prayer', his commemorative verse celebrating the 1807 abolition bill, he typically refused to bow to abolition expectations. The black narrational persona prays to a 'Great Spirit' who is clearly different from the Christian God demanded by abolition orthodoxy. The repeated request by the narrator is that Africa be liberated from all contact with the European running of the slave trade, and only in this way will Africa be free. This is a very different agenda from the majority of abolition polemic in verse or prose. Even Equiano argued at the end of the *Interesting Narrative* that it would be in Africa's interests to allow Europe to develop both free trade and Christianity in Africa during the post-emancipation era. Thelwall keeps things solidly Afrocentric and unchristian.

The Negro's Prayer

O spirit! that rid'st in the whirlwind and storm,
  Whose voice in the thunder is fear'd,—
If ever from man, the poor indigent worm,
  The prayer of affliction was heard,—
If black man, as white, is the work of thy hand—
  (And who could create him but Thee?)
    Ah give thy command,—
    Let it spread thro' each land,
That Afric's sad sons shall be free!—

If, erst, when the man-stealer's treacherous guile
  Entrap'd me, all thoughtless of wrong,—
From my Nicou's dear love, from the infantine smile
  Of my Aboo, to drag me along;—
If then, the wild anguish that pierced thro' my heart,
  Was seen in its horrors by thee,
    O ease my long smart,
    And thy sanction impart,
That Afric, at last, may be free!—

If while in the Slave Ship, with many a groan,
  I wept o'er my sufferings in vain;
While hundreds around me, reply'd to my moan,
  And the clanking of many a chain;—
If then, thou but deign'dst, with a pitying eye,
  Thy poor shackled creature to see;
    O thy mercy apply
    Afric's sorrows to dry,
And bid the poor Negro be free!

If here, as I faint in the vertical sun,
  And the scourge goads me on to my toil,—
No hope faintly soothing, when labour is done,
  Of one joy my lorn heart to beguile;—
If thou view'st me, Great Spirit! as one thou hast made,
  And my fate as dependant on thee;—
    O impart thou thy aid,
    That the scourge may be stay'd,
And the Black Man, at last, may be free.

Thus pray'd the poor Negro; with many a groan,
   Whole nations re-echo'd the prayer;—
Heaven bent down its ear,—and the fiat is known,
   Which Britain, in thunder shall bear.—
Yes hear it, ye Isles of the Westering deep!
   The Lords of the Ocean maintain,
     No traffic of blood
     Shall pollute the green flood,
And freedom, for Afric shall reign.

James Field Stanfield (d. 1824), *The Guinea Voyage in Three Books* (1807)

Stanfield's *The Guinea Voyage* finally came out in 1807, the year of slave trade abolition. Stanfield had written the poem in the mid-1780s as a contribution to the abolition propaganda machine, but it was agreed by the abolition committee that Stanfield would do more for the cause if he submitted an account of his slaving experiences in prose; the poem was seen as too problematic a piece of evidence—fact and fancy were greatly at odds. Stanfield duly wrote up his memories in more factual form in a series of letters. In 1788 Stanfield published *Observations on a Guinea Voyage in a Series of Letters Addressed to the Rev. Thomas Clarkson*. Like John Newton, Stanfield worked as a sailor on slave ships and also as a factor in the slave factories of the African coast. His *Observations* is an unremitting catalogue of the hardships and brutality on board slave ships. The majority of it is, however, not concerned with the slaves but is given over to descriptions of the punishments and diseases of the sailors. In other words it is rhetorically directed at the destruction of the myth that slavery was a nursery of British seamanship. One suspects Clarkson's influence in changing the emphasis, given that the attack on slave crew mortality rates was the central concern of the majority of testimony he collected.

Stanfield's poem *The Guinea Voyage* had put a very different emphasis on slave suffering. The first part of the poem does give a more or less poeticized version of the prose descriptions of the manning and outfitting of a slaver. Yet the third and final part of the poem gives a detailed account of the middle passage. In this section, and in the poem as a whole, the adoption of Popean couplets and of a parodic epic machinery that seems in competition with the *Rape of the Lock* leads to a weird tension between the horror of what is being narrated and the form in which it is packaged. Even more than Grainger's *Sugar Cane* (pp. 7–29) this poem draws into hideously sharp focus the aesthetic contradictions inherent in the act of trying to turn the inheritance of the slave trade into fashionable art.

The Guinea Voyage

Book the First

The direful Voyage to Guinea's sultry shore,
And Afric's wrongs, indignant Muse! deplore.
.   .   .   .

Assist to paint the melancholy view,
The dismal, the disgraceful track pursue,
And with the Eagle-eye of Truth pervade
All the dark mazes of th' *inhuman trade*.

   Whilst awful pause marks the advancing ill
Whose gathering horrors the scar'd fancy fill,
Like *Afric's* own *Tornado*,—must its rise
Be view'd, portentous, staining *British* skies?
Can the full storm, that blackens in its course,
From *British* climes derive its fated source?
From *British* climes, alas! the Demon springs,
On whose polluted form and horrid wings
Hangs, of dire Slavery, the collected store,
Which, hapless *Afric*, on thy injur'd shore
Shall, in its fulness of destruction, fall,
Outraging, desolating, whelming all!
   At length th' unfeeling colleagues close combine,
And midnight council broods the black design;
Strikes the first link of the tremend'ous chain,
Whose motion vibrates thro' the realms of pain.
Th' insatiate thirst of av'rice to supply,
Or fill the pomp of fancy's changing eye;
For vice, intemp'rance, passion, to provide,
To dress up folly, or to pamper pride,
Th' infernal *traffic's* plann'd.   Now busy care
Furrows each face, and clamours rend the air.
The sounding anvil shakes the distant main,
Forging with pond'rous strokes th' accursed chain.
Th' attractive *Outfit* claims each bustling hand:
Confusion works, and uproar gives command.
   Th' undaunted souls, whose manly bosoms dare
The tempest's fury, or the nation's war,

Whose unsuspecting hearts no dangers scan,
Fall the first victims of th' enormous plan.
Round them, nefarious agents spread the wing,
And o'er unconscious youth their poisons fling.
Polluted dens of infamy they throng,
With painted vice, to raise the Syren-song;
With specious arts subdue th' unwary mind,
Close their limed web, their feeble victims bind.
Fictitious debts, false oaths, undue arrests,
Crowd the wrong'd prison with illegal guests.
Immur'd from friendship's aid, unnerv'd by grief,
Hopeless of justice—no disclos'd relief.—
One only portal opes the gloomy road;
One dire condition bursts the drear abode.
Slav'ry's dark genius heaves the iron door.
And, grinning ghastly, points to *Guinea*'s shore—
Some few, the voluntary woe embrace.
Sore from false friends, or undeserv'd disgrace;
Subdu'd by pow'r, by fell misfortune worn,
Or by the pangs of hopeless passion torn;
Weary of griefs no patience can endure.
They seek the *Lethe*[1] of a mortal curc.

.   .   .   .   .   .

Book the Second

.   .   .   .   .   .

And now the Bark, advancing o'er the main,
Drags her disastrous store of guilt and pain—
Approaches, baneful, spreads her dazzling snares,
Her glaring instruments of woe prepares,
To catch, malign, with many a practic'd wile,
And all the mazes of Delusion's guile,
The impious native, whom Corruption's hand
Has led to desolate his injur'd land.

Wide o'er the soil dire agents wing their way
Insatiate prowl for the devoted prey.
Unfeeling Avarice deals the galling wound,
Destructive hurls the flaming brand around.

---

[1] A river of the underworld causing forgetfulness in all who drank from it. Oblivion.

See—his fell torches spread devouring fires!
The peaceful village in the blaze expires.
Sunk in the terrors of their burning rage,
Lie helpless *infancy* and feeble *age:*
And *vigour*—flying the consuming ray,
'Scapes—to more poignant ills the wretched prey,
To drag,—in tears, and chains his lingering day.

    The harmless cultivator of the soil,
Returning from the task of pleasing toil,
Torn from the shelter of his kindred grounds,
Is dragg'd to bonds, to stripes, and smarting wounds.
Meanwhile his anxious wife, with eager eye,
Looks on the homeward path, and evening sky.
Children, bereft, the nightly boon require,
And anxious call their slow-returning sire.
Ne'er shall returning sire his children bless—
Ne'er shall the weeping wife her husband press—
Destruction bursting ev'ry tender band,
Sweeps, like a deluge, thro' the hapless land!

    Slow to the shores now march the fetter'd crowd,
Tugging huge chains, or bent beneath the load.
Torn from all kindred ties dismay'd they stand,
While prying cruelty's insulting hand,
Minutely vigilant, with butcher skill,
Turns the examin'd wretch at savage will,
And (ev'ry limb and ev'ry joint survey'd)
Completes the practice of the brutal trade.

    The gloomy ship, in sable terror drest
Receives the burthen of the wretched guest;
Torn as his bosom is, still wonder glows
As on the vast machine attention grows.
Wonder, commix'd with anguish, shakes his frame,
At the strange sight his language cannot name.
Ropes, tackles, spars and ponderous engines seem
As racking instruments, prepar'd for him:
And, as his doom new horrors seem t' await,
His manly heart sinks at th' uncertain fate.
The yawning deck now opes the dreary cell;
Hot mists exhale in many a putrid smell.

Loaded with chains, at length the hapless slave,
Plung'd in the darkness of the floating cave,
With horror sees the hatch way close his sight—
His last hope leaves him with the parting light!

    Now from the embattled pests that cloud the shore,
And hovering wait the ripe, avenging hour,
Their icy Leader calls a blood-nurs'd fiend—
Hell ne'er saw direr from her womb ascend!
Perch'd on a sack he held his ruthless stand;
A scorpion scourge wav'd in his wither'd hand;
Snaky his locks—his eye balls roll'd in flame;
Sin's second born and *Cruelty* his name.

    Him to the trading mast the vengeful King,
Precursive sends, with many a venom'd sting;
For, *here*, ere Death the slacken'd heart-string tears,
Still savage Cruelty the wound prepares.

    With flaggy wing th' infected air he wounds,
'Till hovering o'er the vessel's murky bounds,
The *master's* kindred form he cowering spies—
Swift through the sanguin'd eye rapacious hies
To the congenial mansion rushes prone,
And on the willing heart erects his throne.

    Then Tyranny inflam'd stalks uncontrol'd,
And raging Furies their sharp stores unfold.
Pallid or *black*—the *free* or *fetter'd* band,
Fall undistinguish'd by the ruffian hand.
Nor age's awe, nor sex's softness charm;
Nor law, nor feeling, wrest the blood-steep'd arm.
While, skill'd in ev'ry torture that can rend,
O'er gasping heaps exults the rav'ning fiend.

    Mark, how in hellish wantonness, he calls
Yon trembling innocent—the sight appals!
The weeping sacrifice, with nervless pace,
Obeys the mandate—while his infant face
The butcher seizing, with infernal hold,
Fastens his gripe in lacerating fold;
In his torn mouth the wounded passage finds,
And thro' the mangled cheeks his fingers winds.

Convolv'd in pangs, that rev'rend form survey
Beneath his country's wars and commerce grey,
Now writhes his tortur'd frame! The scourges ply—
And from the lash the quiv'ring morsels fly.
Invention next, from her exhaustless stores,
O'er the bare bones the venom'd lotion pours,
Whose acrid salts in searching conflict dart,
With pungent anguish barbing ev'ry smart:
The tortur'd fibres their last feeling strain,
And life just vibrates on the strings of pain!
Nor this the close: between his toothless jaws
The furious monster the thwart iron draws—
The poor relief to wail his fate deny'd,
And the hot gore sent down in choaking tide,
Unnaturally return'd with horrid force,
Dire meal! again to throb its wasted course!

But while new tortures raise the piercing cry,
And wound with dreadful sight the wearied eye,
Th' avenging hour arrives—in dreadful din
The troops of wan *Disease* their march begin.
With fervid eye they trace the fatal road
Their agent *Cruelty* had mark'd with blood.

Now droops the head in faint dejection hung,
Now raging thirst enflames the dry-parch'd tongue;
In yellow films the rayless eye is set,
With chilling dews the loaded brow is wet;
Fierce thro' the burning roads of purple life,
The acrid venoms rush with mortal strife,
Their poisons thro' th' intestine mazes bear,
The viscous linings from their channels tear;
Pour with corroding deluge thro' the frame,
And whelm the vitals in the liquid flame.

Th' infected air, upon her loaded wings,
Thro' the warm ship the green contagion brings.
Strew'd o'er the filthy deck, the fever'd lie,
And for cool moisture raise the feeble cry;
The pitying messmate brings the cheering draught
And, in the pious act, the venom'd shaft,

Repays the charity with barb ingrate,
And whelms the soother in the kindred fate.

.   .   .   .   .   .

Book the Third

.   .   .   .   .   .

The hateful purchase made—compressive stow'd,
The floating dungeon with th' unnatural load
Is cramm'd profane: immers'd in deadly gloom,
The shackled sufferers wait th' ambigious doom,
Till the bark, glutted with the purchas'd gore,
Hoists the full sail, and quits the wasted shore.

Now from the scanty crew the goblins dire
Avert awhile the dart: the fiends require
A fuller carnage. On the hapless train,
T' avenge whose wrongs they left the burning plain,
They turn insatiate; and with recreant rage,
On the chain'd sufferers wars atrocious wage.

Soon as umbrageous night on raven-wings
O'er the sad freight her dewy opiates flings,
Pack'd in close misery, the reeking crowd,
Sweltering in chains, pollute the hot abode.
In painful rows with studious art comprest,
Smoking they lie, and breathe the humid pest:

Moisten'd with gore, on the hard platform ground,
The bare-rub'd joint soon bursts the painful bound;
Sinks in th' obdurate plank with racking force,
And ploughs—dire task, its agonizing course!
Nor can they turn to an exchange of pains,
Prest in their narrow cribs, and whelm'd with chains,
Th' afflictive posture all relief denies,
Recruiting sleep the squalid mansion flies,
One long sad groan the feeble throng unite;
One strain of anguish wastes the dismal night.

With broad'ning disk, and slow increasing ray,
Up from old ocean climbs the orb of day.
Then the drear hatchway morning hands disclose,
And point the sufferers to a change of woes.

Soon as the gorged cell of dim disease
Opes the sick passage to a quicker breeze,
From the rank maw, belched up in morbid stream
The hot mist thickens in the side-long beam;
When from the noisome cave, the drooping crowd
In fetter'd pairs, break through the misty cloud
With keen despair they eye the morning's glow
And curse the added day that swells their woe.
Wet with foul damps, behold the sad array
Disclose their misery to th' unpitying day.
What deep dejection presses yonder face?
Grief's dusky shade, and sad Reflection's trace.
His fellow—see—from orbs of blood-shot ire,
On his pale tyrants dart th' indignant fire!

Striving with feeble force to press the grate,
Yon struggling suff'rer heaves a pond'rous weight.
Stripes from the sounding lash, fierce drawn, succeed,
To give the fainting trembler hapless speed.
Alas! the sounding lash applies in vain;
For close united by the fest'ring chain,
His dead companion up th' untoward height,
(Struck by the mortal ministers of night)
The living victim tugs with painful throes;
Himself, less blest, reserv'd for keener woes.

Now hot black clouds in spreading volumes rise:
Now culinary uproar shakes the skies.
Spread through the venom'd ship, with bustling care,
A joyless meal the surly mates prepare.
Marshal'd around th' unwish'd for mess they lie,
And the strange nutriments discons'late eye.
Sunk with dejection, some the viands spare,
Some with keen scorn reject the profer'd fare,
Keep the superior pride, that nerves the brave,
Nor, free-born, taste the portion of a slave.
Then flies the scourge, sparing nor sex nor age,
Stripe follows stripe, in boundless, brutal rage.
Then the vile engines in the hateful cause
Are plied relentless; in the straining jaws

The wrenching instruments with barbarous force
Give the detested food th' unwilling course.

.   .   .   .   .   .

   Hark! from yon lodge in many a wounding groan
A labouring victim raise the feeble moan!
Swift to the darksome cell the females fly,
To still the tumult of the conscious cry:
Join the deep woe with sad combin'd exclaim;
As pangs maternal shake her drooping frame.
Heav'ns! what a mansion for the tender woes,
The painful travail partial nature throws
Upon the gentler sex—when lenient art
And soothing care should cheer the fainting heart.
Here, with dejected wretchedness enclos'd,
To brutal hands and impious eyes expos'd,
Her sacred sorrows the sad crisis press,—
Occurrent horrors, premature distress,
Spread with foul clouds the inauspicious ray,
That opes the new-born victim's doleful day!
   Behold her bending o'er her infant charge,
Hear the laments her copious grief enlarge.
'Ill-fated innocent,' (she wailing cries)
'Thou joy and anguish of these aching eyes,'
Of parent misery the hapless heir,
Thy mother gives the welcome of despair;
Greets thy unconscious smile with throbbing fears;
Repays thy fondness with presageful tears.
Where now the joys should light the holy bow'r?
Where the sweet hopes that wing the natal hour?
Nor hope's blest dawn shall e'er thy fancy warm;
Nor joy's sweet smile illume thy abject form.
No grateful sire hails thee with conscious pride;
Thy future worth no flattering friends decide:
A wretched mother press'd by tyrant fate,
Can yield no succour to thy helpless state:
The spoiler's chains, that load her languid frame,
By spoiler's right thy fetter'd service claim.
Has o'er this pallid race a mother's love
E'er bent in fondness?—Could they ever prove

A wife's soft transport, as she gently prest
The smiling stranger to a father's breast?
Ah, sure the soft remembrance would have pow'r
T' attone the sex, and sooth this mournful hour!'

.   .   .   .   .   .

Fainting, with such a course of loathsome views,
And length of horrors, the dejected Muse
Spreads her tir'd wings, and with desponding mein,
Weeps o'er the close of the destructive scene;
Sees the dire bark 'midst direr regions steer;
Hears the plung'd anchor tell grim Slavery near;
Beholds the fell Receivers fiercely pour,
In savage swarms, upon the blood-stain'd shore,
Sees their abhorr'd approach—with harsher chains,
To load (curst act!) oppression's weak remains.

Now o'er the gloomy ship, in villain guise,
The shrouding canvass drawn, shuts out the skies.
The pitchy curtain throws a shade unclean;
Meet apparatus for the horrid scene.
Marshal'd with fatal skill, in abject bands—
Forbearing heaven!—the *human purchase* stands.
Now rush the trading fiends; and, with fell sway
Fasten rapacious on the shuddering prey.
What shrieks of terror pierce the sickening skies—
What floods of anguish burst their wounded eyes!
As strife tumultuous shakes the *scrambling*[2] *brood*—
Scrambling for *human flesh*—for *kindred blood!*

Richard Mant (1776-1848), 'The Slave', in *The Slave and Other Poetical Pieces* (1807)

Mant was an ambitious and successful ecclesiastical careerist, and a prolific author, whose works related closely to his career moves. His slavery writings are a significant reminder of the extent to which many ruthless political operators, especially within the Church, saw abolition as a perfect stage on which to develop their ambition. Mant

---

[2] Once the slaves arrived in port they were often set out on deck and the planters or their representatives would rush in and grab the likeliest looking bargains. This was known as a scramble.

worked his way up through the British Church. By 1820 he had gained the ear of the notoriously corrupt Liverpool administration and was personally nominated for an Irish bishopric. As a British minor bishop in a Catholic stronghold Mant set out his stall immediately by importing an entire English domestic household. Enraged local residents soon forced him to ship his servants back to the mainland. Yet Mant maintained his harsh Anglocentricism and continually voted against Catholic emancipation throughout the 1830s. As a reward he was moved up north to Belfast, and set about transforming it into the Protestant loyalist stronghold it remains. Not long before his death he became one of the most powerful men in Ireland; as Bishop of Down, Connor, and Dromore he had control of a diocese which covered one fifteenth of the country. In 1840 Mant published the highly influential *History of the Church in Ireland* which became the orthodox defence of the Protestant-inspired rape of Ireland and the Irish. The work is a chillingly readable justification of one of the most iniquitous areas of British imperial depravity.

Mant would have been aware of the remarkable moral groundswell which had launched abolition in the 1780s as an Anglo-American movement. Yet 'The Slave' was, typically, published once the fight was over. Mant sets himself up as the omniscient overseer narrating at third hand the vision which abolitionist orthodoxy had established. Africa is an unreal place which veers crazily between a godless and unproductive chaos and a sort of pre-lapsarian natural idyll. The poem takes an idealizing nationalist line on every issue. So comparisons between the Caribbean slave and British labourer set up the British labour force as an ideal protected by Christianity and aristocracy. The Haytian revolution is called up as a terrible warning to England, but Mant remains supremely confident that 'Divine Compassion' spread by the English Church and vaunted British liberty will prevent revolution in the British sugar islands. Crucially however Mant never goes so far as to lay down outright emancipation as a cure to the evils of slavery. Again there is a retreat into the familiar position that if the African can be given ultimate freedom in the form of 'the dew of heaven'ly love' then mere political definitions of slavery and liberty cease to be that important. The black Jacobins who led the Haytian revolution had a rather different analysis of political freedom within the slave Diaspora.

The Slave

If there be aught on this terrestrial sphere
May claim from virtue's eye the generous tear,
With shame and grief the swelling heart inspire,
With pity melt, with indignation fire;
'Tis Man, created by his Maker free,
Torn by his fellow man from liberty;
To endless hopeless servitude consign'd;
His body shackled, and debas'd his mind;

And his high soul, ordain'd to soar the sky,
Sunk to a level with the beasts that die.
Be he my theme. I ask no fabled aid,
Nor Delian seer, nor Heliconian maid.[1]
But thou, pure partner of the eternal throne,
O Justice, rigid to thyself alone;
And Love, beside th' abandon'd stranger found,
Soothing with oil and wine his burning wound;
And Faith with lifted hand, and kindling eye,
Which scorning things below anticipates the sky:
If e'er from Britain's senate, where ye hung
With holy joy on Wilberforce's tongue,
To the green vale of gentle Ouse[2] retir'd,
Ye caught the numbers, which yourselves inspir'd,
While, as your Cowper's[3] fingers lightly flew,
Sounds half-prophetic from the harp he drew:
O grant another humbler bard to hear
Your accents warbled in his nightly ear,
Then strike the answering chords, and wake a strain so clear.

And Thou, among the nations seated high,
Queen of the lion-heart and eagle-eye,
Who form'st thy sons to scorn a tyrant's frown,
And deem the sorrows of the slave their own;
If Briton-born, and nurtur'd at thy breast,
True to the lore on all thy race imprest,
A man, I suffer when my brethren bleed;
A free-man, freedom's outrag'd rights I plead;
And dare assert, in injur'd Afric's cause,
Of heav'nly Truth the violated laws:
Think not with foul and parricidal art
I aim the dagger at a parent's heart;
Nor blame the hand, which strikes, the slave to free,
E'en tho' the stroke, my country, light on thee.

Alas for Afric! By the western flood
Long had she sat in melancholy mood.

---

[1]   Delian, relating to Delos in the Aegean Sea, the supposed birthplace of Apollo and Artemis; Heliconian, relating to Helicon, a mountain range in Boeotia, which was famed as the haunt of the Muses.
[2]   A river in England; the source is in Northamptonshire, whence it flows out through the Fens to the Wash. The river is celebrated in Cowper's poem 'The Poplar Field'.
[3]   For William Cowper's role as an abolition poet see pp. 81–93 above.

Appall'd she listen'd to the fearful sound
Of warriors' shouts, and monsters prowling round:
With wishful look she eyed the distant main;
At hand she gaz'd on many a sandy plain,
On many a deep morass, and tangled wood,
Loud howling waste, and shapeless solitude.
She heard not Law her heav'nly descant sing:
She saw not Science plume her golden wing:
She view'd the sun, the ocean, and the sky;
Ah! wherefore view'd? unable to descry
Him, in the hollow of his ample hand
Who weigh'd the waters, and the mountains spann'd,
Bade the fair moon the brow of eve adorn,
And op'd the radiant eyelid of the morn.

What then avail'd the stamp divine imprest,
His Maker's image, on her offspring's breast?
Ah! what avail'd the spark of heav'nly flame,
The gentle spirit, and the manly frame?
What, her rich gums from fragrant groves distill'd,
With teeming herds her palmy mountains fill'd,
The ivory stores her pathless woods infold,
Ambrosial gales, and streams that flame with gold?

But tho' involv'd in gloom, and unrefin'd
The native graces of the Negro's mind,
Fair breaks its lustre on the pensive eye;
Like gleams of sunshine in an April sky,
Or flow'rs, at random thrown by nature's hand
To deck with beauty a neglected land.

If foes assail him, his the soul to dare;
Beset with torments, his the strength to bear;
And his, when hush'd the storms of danger cease,
The smile of friendship and the voice of peace.
Fierce as th' Atlantic waves, when tempests sweep;
Or placid, as the slumber of the deep:
Or like the mighty elephant, that reigns,
Mildest of beasts, in wide Kaarta's[4] plains.

---

[4] Most northern part of the highland region of Senegambia, north of upper Senegal.

Dear is the hut, in which his childhood play'd;
And dear the shelter of his plantain shade:
('Twas here he laid his father's bones to rest;
'Twas here he clasp'd his consort to his breast;
'Twas here, reclining on her neck, his child
Reach'd to its sire its little arms, and smil'd:)
But dear o'er all the land which gave him breath,
His joy, while living; and his hope in death.
From her and freedom torn, he pines away
In dreams by night, in frantic grief by day,
Disdaining life, and obstinate to die:
Then to lov'd scenes of transport will he fly;
Again with many a lost companion rove
The fragrant walks of Zara's orange grove;
Through Manding's[5] wilds the antelope pursue;
Down Lagos' current guide the light canoe;
Bound to the harp in Fantyn's martial dance,
Swell the loud hymn, and poise the ebon lance;
At ease by Gambia's golden flood recline;
Or quaff on Ambris'[6] banks the palmy wine.

    Yet can he feel the sacred ties, that bind
The scatter'd brotherhood of human kind;
And when the rains descend, and whirlwinds rave,
Round Sego's[7] walls by Niger's ample wave,
Can welcome to his hospitable door
The wand'ring stranger, shelterless and poor;
Nor heed the colour of his guest; but spread
The cocoa board, and strew the rushy bed;
Beside the couch his midnight vigil keep,
And lull with plaintive song the white man's sleep.

O prospect bright, and heav'nly fair, to see
The white man quit his debt of charity!
O glorious boast for England! more divine
Than all the laurels, which her brows intwine!
For Afric's wrongs the pitying thought to feel;
Her woes to solace; and her wounds to heal;

---

[5] Manding, region inhabited by the Mandingo people in Senegambia and the upper eastern Niger.
[6] Ambris, or Ambriz, Portuguese Guinea, an area at the mouth of the Loje river.
[7] Sego, or Segor, a river running through Algeria and the Sahara.

To rear the peopled city's tow'ring pile;
To bid in peace the shelter'd hamlet smile;
With plenty clothe the vale and mountain's head;
The decent joys of social life to spread;
To bind her sons in order's golden chain;
To wake from heathen tongues the rapturous strain
Of praise and holy comfort; and abroad
Spread the glad tidings of the Saviour God.

Is this her triumph? O'er the swarming coast
Does grateful Afric pour her sable host,
To greet fair Albion's long-expected sails;
To lead the strangers to their peaceful vales;
And, while with kindling zeal their bosoms glow,
To bless the men, from whom their blessings flow?

Is this her triumph? Ah! no joyous hail
From grateful Afric greets fair Albion's sail:
No sable nations throng the echoing shore:
No peaceful valleys spread their friendly store:
But groans instead, and curses deep resound,
And death and desolation gloom around.

On Congo's or Angola's spicy shore,
Or Koromantyn's [8] sands of golden ore,
Or northward, where to swell th' Atlantic deep
Majestic floods thro' Senegambia[9] sweep,
Before them horrour, and despair behind,
Speed to their task the stealers of mankind.
Their's is the honied tongue, and specious smile;
The open outrage; and the covert wile:
'Tis their's to quench the intellectual light,
And whelm the negro's mind in grosser night:
'Tis their's to rend with impious force apart
The ties, which nature winds around his heart:
But most 'tis their's to spread the woes afar,
The crimes and horrours of intestine war!
Not with more sweepy sway, or more deform,
O'er Afric breaks the equinoctial storm;
When from the south the mad tornadoes rise,
Unlock the springs, and burst the flood-gates of the skies.

---

[8] See p. 71 n. 1.   [9] An area on the west coast of Africa.

O, bear me to sequester'd coverts, plac'd
Deep, deep amid the solitary waste!
There, distant from the commerce-haunted shore,
There where their streams no sail-clad rivers pour,
Fair fertile spots the culturing hand confess,
Secur'd within the sandy wilderness,
Like verdant islands in a stormy sea;
There peace and plenty dwell, for man is free,
And innocence is there, and cheerful industry.

Ah! gentle tribes, in safe seclusion blest,
May never Europe violate your rest!
Be never your's by fatal proof to know
Your brethren's lot of infamy and woe!
Nor envy ye, whom trackless wilds restrain,
Their fairer station by the neighb'ring main;
Their richer meads; and streams profound, that lave
More ample vales with fertilizing wave.
In vain o'er seas (by Providence design'd
In bonds of amity to knit mankind,
To waft inventive art from zone to zone,
And bless the climes with treasures not their own)
Its freight to *them* the gallant vessel bears;
And richer meads in vain, and fruitful streams are their's.
Darkness and woe beset the cheerless strand,
And commerce visits, but to blast, the land.

Mark! where their baneful arts the spoilers shed,
O'er every clime is devastation spread!
Hark to the sounds of woe, that echo wide!
By Saara's[10] sands, on Komri's[11] mooned side,
Mid vales, where Niger rolls his secret flood,
Intent on rapine, prodigal of blood,
Thine Av'rice, Europe, preys on lands unknown;
Thy bribes prevail; and Afric's millions groan.
Kings, lur'd by thee, forget their people's claim,
And yield a father's, for a traitor's, name:
While rous'd by mutual wrongs to mutual rage,
In open war contiguous tribes engage;

[10] Alternative old spelling of Sahara, the desert region of North Africa between Sudan and Barbary.
[11] Mountain range stretching in a high unbroken chain across Africa.

Or, couch'd in foul and midnight ambuscade,
With flames the slumb'ring hamlet's rest invade,
Surprize their weak and unsuspecting prey,
And tear from scenes of former bliss away;
Far from the charm of each domestic tie;
Far from the pity of a kindred eye;
Beneath a tyrant's lawless scourge to mourn,
Inthrall'd by terror, and repaid with scorn.
Ye cooling streams; ye waving palms, that spread
Your broad-leav'd umbrage o'er the captive's shed;
O hills; O valleys; and thou sacred well,
Sweet to his lip as liquid honey, tell;
How sad along the melancholy air
He breath'd his groans in agony of pray'r;
How oft he lifted to the conscious skies
(Alas! he could no more) his burning eyes.
But nought his groans, that load the mournful gale,
And nought his eyes, for mercy rais'd, avail
To melt the ruthless spoiler. O, accurst
Of baleful gold the heart-perverting thirst!
That rend'st the freeman from his native plain,
Wind'st round his struggling limbs the galling chain,
Nor heed'st the anguish of a father's pray'r,
The orphan's cries, the widow's dumb despair.
But tho' from country, home, and kindred torn;
Of hope, the wretch's privilege, forlorn;
Denied in woe to clasp his infant race;
Denied the comfort of a last embrace;
And doom'd to tremble at a tyrant's nod,
Writhe at the lash, and kiss the vengeful rod:
Yet Mercy, mindful whence his griefs began,
Bends o'er the form of the degraded man,
Wipes with soft touch his sorrows, as they start,
And whispers solace to his bleeding heart.
Is such thy thought? Ah! turn thy streaming eye,
Where in yon bark the countless victims lie;
Where rank infection broods with venom'd breath,
And bathes their temples in the dews of death.
There many a carcase, fest'ring in its gore;
And many a heart, that soon shall throb no more:

And here in horrid fellowship are laid,
Link'd in one chain, the living and the dead.

Peace to the dead! his mortal course is done!
To other climes th' immortal part is flown.
High rapt perchance upon an angel's wing,
It soars where seraphs touch the golden string,
In heav'nly bliss, a spirit pure, to glow,
And find that mercy, man denied below.
But O for them, who still survive to bear
The pangs and griefs of comfortless despair.
In vain they strive their shackled hands to wring:
In vain the piteous sons of sorrow sing:
Or gaze where Afric's vanish'd pleasures dwell,
And weep with straining eyes a last farewell:
Or, starting wild from short and broken sleep,
Howl to the hollow murmur of the deep:
Or plunge indignant in the circling wave,
Where pain can vex no more, nor man enslave.
But lo! smooth-swelling from the billowy tide
Jamaica's mountains rise in azure pride:
And o'er the shadowy clouds, that round them sweep,
Wave the tall woods on Cuba's ridgy steep.

Now raise thy head, desponding captive; free
From all the horrours of the sultry sea,
Fly to the grassy vale, the cedar hill;
Catch the fresh breeze, and quaff the bounding rill;
Or to the wide Savanna haste away,
Where golden Autumn wears the bloom of May.
For thee th' anana[12] springs: for thee shall bleed
The liquid amber of the dulcet reed:
The humming bird, to charm thy wond'ring eyes,
Bright to the sun shall show his rainbow dies:
To veil the streaming splendour o'er thine head,
His grove of leaves the smooth palmetto spread:
Cool gales of evening fragrance round thee move,
And glist'ning fire-flies light thee to thy love.
No! cease the hope; the loathsome voyage o'er,
Severer horrors circle thee on shore.

[12] See p. 24 n. 68.

For ever doom'd an exile to remain;
For ever doom'd to drag the slavish chain;
Driv'n to the crowded mart; for sordid gold
Thyself and all thy future offspring sold;
There (shame to manhood!) shall a tyrant's hand
Stamp on thy naked breast the burning brand.
Ere to bright morn the shadowy twilight yield,
The sounding conch shall warn thee to the field,
Slave of a slave! To chide each short delay.
On thy torn limbs the knotted whip shall prey.
Fann'd by no gale, where plains unshelter'd lie,
Beat by the fervour of a blazing sky,
'From morn till noon, from noon till dewy eve,'[13]
No comfort cheer thee, and no rest relieve,
Unblest, unfriended: till the pitying sun,
Who rising saw thy livelong task begun,
With purple light array the golden west,
And faint dismiss thee to distemper'd rest.
Then shall thy limbs confess the tort'ring smart:
Then shall the iron enter in thy heart:[14]
Or if for one short hour oblivious sleep
In balmy dews thy aching temples steep,
And waft thee back to Afric's distant shore,
And gild the dream with bliss, ah! thine no more;
Scar'd by the echo of the morning shell
Again shall fade the visionary spell,
And leave thee to the horrours of despair,
The sad reality of waking care.

Not such the rest Britannia's peasant knows,
Whose willing labour leads to calm repose.
Tho' few the pleasures of his humble cot,
Tho' plain his fare, and toilsome be his lot,
Yet blest in conscious liberty he lives;
Yet law secures the rights, which nature gives;
And still, as breaking from the smiling east,
Beams the glad day of consecrated rest,

---

[13] Milton, *Paradise Lost*, 1, 744.
[14] In Psalm 105 Joseph's bitter experience of enslavement in Egypt, having been sold by his brothers, is described through the phrase 'and the iron entered into his soul'.

Religion wakes the fires, that slumb'ring lie,
Refines his heart, and lifts his soul on high.

But thou, degraded Afric's abject son,
Drear is the course of sorrow, thou must run.
Thy plaints by foul misshapen justice tried,
Thy feelings question'd, and thy rights denied,
If pity, shame, or selfishness impart
Repose or comfort to thy drooping heart,
Thy scanty pittance of precarious joy
The hand, which proffers, shall at will destroy;
The voice, which bids the lash its fury stay,
At will shall give suspended vengeance way:
While, form'd for heav'n and heav'nly thoughts in vain!
The ceaseless weight of the reproachful chain
Shall quell each nobler purpose of thy mind;
Benumb thy feelings, and thy reason blind;
Down to the earth thy tow'ring spirit draw;
Defeat thy Maker's will, reverse his law:
Till thy immortal nature it imbrute,
Thy earthly frame's celestial attribute;
Forbid thy soul superiour worlds to scan;
Displace, degrade thee in creation's plan;
And leave a worthless form, the semblance of a man.

So shall at length thy nobler part be broke,
Cleave to the ground, and hug the slavish yoke:
Or proudly spurning at the name of slave,
Too fierce to yield, yet impotent to save,
A willing victim to the tomb go down:
Or, leagu'd with high-born spirits, like thine own,
Rise in wild vengeance o'er the trembling foe,
Repay the wrong, and lay th' oppressor low.

Thus o'er Jamaica's pallid isle of late
Hung the black cloud, with ruin charg'd and fate:
Thus rolling on with gather'd fury, shed
Its night of tempest on Domingo's head.
Thron'd on the storm, and all his soul on flame,
A thirst for vengeance, Afric's Genius came.
His sons beheld him, tow'ring in his might;
And clank'd their chains with horrible delight;

Wav'd the red banner o'er the murmuring flood;
And yell'd to war; and bath'd the land in blood.
Nor rest; nor respite: death to death succeeds:
The negro triumphs, and the white man bleeds.
E'en Europe trembled, as she heard from far
The sounding march of injur'd Afric's war;
While bleeding Gaul her ravish'd empire mourn'd,
And bow'd to freemen, whom as slaves she scorn'd.

Britannia, watch! the spreading tempest stay,
Ere o'er thy trembling isles it burst its way;
With timely pity hear the Negro's pray'r,
Or, if unmov'd by pity, dread despair!

But rather, let divine Compassion plead,
Swell at the heart, and sanctify the deed.
And, O! if He, whose breath thy offspring form'd,
With kindred blood the Negro's heart hath warm'd:
If his dread voice in thunder hath assign'd
Woe to the thieves and murderers of mankind,
And in soft strains of mercy whisper'd peace
To those who bid the captive's sorrows cease:
If His right hand in bounty from above
Sheds on thy sons the dew of heav'nly love:
If He with corn thy waving valleys fills;
And spreads thy cattle o'er a thousand hills;
And gives thy fleets in awful pomp to sweep
Majestic o'er the bosom of the deep;
And, while He round thee flings the girding sea,
Stamps on the face of thy white cliffs, "Be free:"
O, spread thy blessings: be the glory thine,
The first in mercy, as in pow'r, to shine;
Till not a spot Britannia's ermine stain,
And not a captive wear Britannia's chain;
Till Freedom's voice the song of gladness pour
From Niger's flood to western India's shore;
And Afric, starting from her Pagan dream,
Behold the day-spring break, and bless the heav'nly beam.

Mrs Amelia Opie (1769-1853), 'The Lucayan's Song' (1808); 'The Negro Boy's Tale', in *Poems by Mrs. Opie* (1811); *The Black Man's Lament; or, How to Make Sugar* (1826)

Opie had little formal education, but by the age of 18 had already become a favourite in fashionable social circles in Norwich. She performed her own ballads, and even wrote a short tragedy *Adelaide*, in which she took the leading role when it was performed as an evening entertainment. She maintained a deep love of parties and performance throughout her life, which gave rise to a good deal of sniping after her Quaker conversion. She inherited strong radical political opinions, and in 1794 visited London during the famous Treason Trials of Thomas Hardy, Thomas Holcroft, Horne Tooke, and John Thelwall. When Tooke was acquitted she theatrically crossed the court and publicly kissed him. Amelia was something of a smash hit in radical intellectual circles in London in the ensuing months; she became close to William Godwin and Mary Wollstonecraft. After marriage to the painter John Opie she began to devote herself to writing seriously for the first time. She stuck at the profession and was prolific as an author of highly charged sentimental novels, and equally lachrymose periodical fiction and verse, although she stopped writing novels once she became a Quaker in 1822. Much like Harriet Martineau, Opie was committed to a great array of philanthropic and political causes during her long life, including hospital and prison reform. Slavery and emancipation remained a central concern.

In 'The Lucayan's Song' Opie writes within the conventions of the late eighteenth-century ballad, and the work suggests the influence of Thomas Mallet. In taking as her narrational slave subject an indigenous Caribbean rather than an African black Opie is also working within another fictional tradition, the well-rehearsed conventions of the Spanish Black Legend. The tragic lament of the idealized Indian, forced to endure a brutal slavery at the hands of the treacherous Spanish, was a popular way of attacking Spanish imperial expansion in the sixteenth century. The demonizing of Spain and implicit celebration of benevolent British colonization was popular with pro-slavery British rhetoricians. Indeed Bryan Edwards's *History . . . of the West Indies*, from which Opie took both the Robertson anecdote and the subsequent prefatory paragraph on the laments of the enslaved Lucayans, was a bedrock of pro-slavery historiography. In taking a tragic anecdote concerning an Indian from Robertson's *History of South America* and working it up into a poetic lament Opie took precisely the same path that Tennyson did over two decades later in his *Anacoana* (pp. 313–16).

Opie wrote several other slavery poems: the most popular of these were designed for the rapidly developing children's book market. 'The Negro Boy's Tale' was another pathetic ballad, this time with the slave/narrator's diction set in a particularly crude attempt at Caribbean patois. More unusual, and more elaborate, was Opie's 1826 *The Black Man's Lament; or, How to Make Sugar*. Opie is writing nearly twenty years after the abolition of the British slave trade, and six years before the slave emancipation in the British Caribbean. The poem is consequently an attempt to bring the realities of Caribbean sugar production before children and their parents in the run-up to slavery abolition in the British colonies. Opie published the poem with the successful children's book specialists Harvey and Darnton who had developed a new form of dramatically illustrated and hand-coloured children's book. Opie adapts her narrative style effectively to work with the shallow space and bold outlines of the plates. The narrative cleverly balances a factual account of sugar production against the incidental sufferings it causes for the slave. When comparisons are drawn between the slave and the British labourer they consequently have some force; black slave labour is no longer a distant and mysterious process.

The Lucayan's Song

Hail, lonely shore! hail, desert cave!
To you, o'erjoyed, from men I fly,
And here I'll make my early grave....
For what can misery do but *die*?

Sad was the hour when, fraught with guile,
Spain's cruel sons our valleys sought;
Unknown to us the Christian's wile,
Unknown the dark deceiver's thought.

They said, that here, for ever blest,
'Our loved forefathers lived and reigned,
And we, by pious fondness prest,
Believed the flattering tales they feigned.

But when we learnt the mournful truth....
No, I'll the horrid tale forbear:
For on our trusting, blighted youth,
My brethren, who will drop a tear!

Thou treasure of these burning eyes,
Where wave thy groves, dear native isle?
Methinks where yon blue mountains rise,
'Tis there thy precious valleys smile!

Yes.... Yes.... these tears of joy that start,
The softly-soothing truth declare:
Thou whisperest right, my beating heart....
My loved regretted home is there!

But then its trees that wave so high,
The glittering birds that deck each grove,
I cannot, cannot hence descry,
Nor, dearer far, the forms I love.

Yet still the winds that cool my brow,
And o'er these murmuring waters come,
A joy that mocks belief bestow;
For sure they lately left my home.

Then deeply I'll the breeze inhale,
To life it yet imparts one joy,
Methinks your breath has filled the gale,
My faithful love, my prattling boy!

My prattling boy, my beauteous wife!
Say, do you still my name repeat,
And only bear the load of life
In hopes that we once more may meet!

My love! in dreams thou still art nigh,
But changed and pale thou seemest to be;
Yet still the more thou charmest my eye,
I think thee changed by love for me:....

While oft, to fond remembrance true,
I see thee seek the sparkling sand,
In hopes the little bark to view
That bears me to my native land.

But never more shall Zama's eye
Her loved returning husband see,
Nor more her locks of ebon dye
Shall Zama fondly braid for me.

Yet still, with hope chastised by fear,
Watch for my bark from yonder shore,
And still, my Zama, think me near,
When this torn bosom throbs no more.

Yet surely hope, each day deceived,
At length to daring deeds will fire;
The Spaniard's tale no more believed,
My fate will fearful doubts inspire.

And then, blest thought! across the main
Thou'lt haste, thy injured love to find,
All danger scorn, all fears disdain,
And gladly trust the waves and wind.

Ha! even now the distant sky
Seems by one spot of darkness crost;
Yes, yes, a vessel meets my eye!....
Or else I gaze in phrensy lost!

It hither steers!........ No.... beating breast,
Too well I see what bade thee glow;
The sea-bird hastening to its nest,
To taste a joy I ne'er shall know.

Moment of hope, too bright to last,
Thou hast but deepened my despair;
But woe's severest pangs are past,
For life's last closing hours are near.

'Twas morn when first this beach I sought,
Now evening's shadows fill the plain;
Yet here I've stood entranced in thought,
Unheeding thirst, fatigue or pain.

'Tis past.... I faint.... my throbbing brow
Cold clammy drops I feel bedew;
Dear native shore! where art thou now?....
Some Spaniard shuts thee from my view.

Monster, away! and let me taste
That joy in death, in life denied!
Still let me o'er the watery waste
Behold the hills which Zama hide!

Alas! I rave! no foe is near;
'Tis death's thick mist obscures my sight;
Those precious hills, to memory dear,
No more shall these fond eyes delight!

But sent from thee, my native shore,
Again that precious breeze is nigh....
Zama, I feel thy breath once more,
And now content, transported, die!

The Negro Boy's Tale

'Haste! hoist the sails! fair blows the wind:
Jamaica, sultry land, adieu!
Away! and loitering Anna find!
I long dear England's shores to view.'

The sailors gladly haste on board,
Soon is Trevannion's voice obeyed,
And instant, at her father's word,
His menials seek the absent maid.

But where was 'loitering Anna' found?....
Mute, listening to a Negro's prayer,
Who knew that sorrow's plaintive sound
Could always gain her ready ear;....

Who knew, to sooth the slave's distress
Was gentle Anna's dearest joy;
And thence, an earnest suit to press,
To Anna flew the Negro boy.

'Missa,' poor Zambo cried, 'sweet land
Dey tell me dat you go to see,
Vere, soon as on de shore he stand,
De helpless Negro slave be free.

'Ah! dearest missa, you so kind!
Do take me to dat blessed shore,
Dat I mine own dear land may find,
And dose who love me see once more.

'Oh! ven no slave, a boat I buy,
For me a letel boat vould do,
And over wave again I fly
Mine own loved negro land to view.

'Oh! I should know it quick like tink,
No land so fine as dat I see,
And den perhaps upon de brink
My moder might be look for me!....

'It is long time since lass ve meet,
Ven I vas take by bad vite man,
And moder cry, and kiss his feet,
And shrieking after Zambo ran.

'O missa! long, how long me feel
Upon mine arms her lass embrace!
Vile in de dark, dark ship I dwell,
Long burn her tear upon my face.

'How glad me vas she did not see
De heavy chain my body bear;
Nor close, how close ve crowded be,
Nor feel how bad, how sick de air!

'Poor slaves!.... but I had best forget.
Dey say (but teaze me is deir joy)
Me grown so big dat ven ve meet
My moder vould not know her boy.

'Ah! sure 'tis false! But yet if no,
Ven I again my moder see,
Such joy I at her sight vould show
Dat she vould tink it must be me.

'Den, kindest missa, be my friend;
Yet dat indeed you long become;
But now one greatest favour lend,....
O find me chance to see my home!

'And ven I'm in my moder's arms,
And tell de vonders I have know,
I'll say, Most best of all de charms
Vas she who feel for negro's woe.

'And she shall learn for you dat prayer
Dey teach to me to make me good;
Though men who sons from moders tear,
She'll tink, teach goodness never could.

'Dey say me should to oders do
Vat I vould have dem do to me;....
But, if dey preach and practise too,
A negro slave me should not be.

'Missa, dey say dat our black skin
Be ugly, ugly to de sight;
But surely if dey look vidin,
Missa, de negro's heart be vite.

'Yon cocoa-nut no smooth as silk,
But rough and ugly is de rind;
Ope it, sweet meat and sweeter milk
Vidin dat ugly coat ve find.

'Ah missa! smiling in your tear,
I see you know what I'd impart;
De cocoa husk de skin I vear,
De milk vidin be Zambo's heart.

'Dat heart love you, and dat good land
Vere every negro slave be free,....
Oh! if dat England understand
De negro wrongs, how wrath she be!

'No doubt dat ship she never send
Poor harmless negro slave to buy,
Now vould she e'er de wretch befriend
Dat dare such cruel bargain try.

'O missa's God! dat country bless!'
(Here Anna's colour went and came;
But saints might share the pure distress,
For Anna blushed at other's shame.)

'But, missa, say; shall I vid you
To dat sweet England now depart,
Once more mine own good country view,
And press my moder on my heart?'

Then on his knees poor Zambo fell,
While Anna tried to speak in vain:
The expecting boy she could not tell
He'd ne'er his mother see again.

But, while she stood in mournful thought,
Nearer and nearer voices came;
The servants 'loitering Anna' sought,
The echoes rang with Anna's name.

Ah! then, o'ercome with boding fear,
Poor Zambo seized her trembling hand,
'Mine only friend,' he cried, 'me fear
You go, and me not see my land.'

Anna returned the artless grasp:
'*I* cannot grant thy suit,' she cries;
'But I my father's knees will clasp,
Nor will I, till he hears me, rise.'

But woe betides an ill-timed suit:
His temper soured by her delay,
Trevannion bade his child be mute,
Nor dare such fruitless hopes betray.

'I know,' she cried, 'I cannot free
The numerous slaves that round me pine;
But one poor negro's friend to be,
Might, (blessed chance!) might now be mine.'

But vainly Anna wept and prayed,
And Zambo knelt upon the shore;
Without reply, the pitying maid
Trevannion to the vessel bore.

Mean while, poor Zambo's cries to still,
And his indignant grief to tame,
Eager to act his brutal will,
The negro's scourge-armed ruler came.

The whip is raised.... the lash descends....
And Anna hears the sufferer's groan;
But while the air with shrieks she rends,
The signal's given.... the ship sails on.

That instant, by despair made bold,
Zambo one last great effort tried;
He burst from his tormentor's hold....
He plunged within the foaming tide.

The desperate deed Trevannion views,
And all his weak resentment flies:
'See, see! the vessel he pursues!
Help him, for mercy's sake!' he cries:

'Out with the boat! quick! throw a rope!
Wretches, how tardy is your aid!'
While, pale with dread, or flushed with hope,
Anna the awful scene surveyed.

The boat is out,.... the rope is cast,....
And Zambo struggles with the wave;....
'Ha! he the boat approaches fast!
O father, we his life shall save!'

'But low, my child, and lower yet
His head appears;.... but sure he sees
The succour given.... and seems to meet
The opposing waves with greater ease:....

See, see! the boat, the rope he nears;
I see him now his arm extend!....
My Anna, dry those precious tears;
My child shall be *one negro's friend*!'

Ah! Fate was near, that hope to foil:....
To reach the rope poor Zambo tries;....
But, ere he grasps it, faint with toil,
The struggling victim sinks, and dies.

.   .   .   .   .   .

Anna, I mourn thy virtuous woe;
I mourn thy father's keen remorse;
But from my eyes no tears would flow
At sight of Zambo's silent corse:....

The orphan from his mother torn,
And pining for his native shore,....
Poor tortured slave.... poor wretch forlorn....
Can I his early death deplore?....

I pity those who live, and groan:
Columbia countless Zambos sees;....
For swelled with many a wretch's moan
Is Western India's sultry breeze.

Come, Justice, come! in glory drest,
O come! the woe-worn negro's friend,....
The fiend-delighting trade arrest,
The negro's chains asunder rend!

The Black Man's Lament

Come, listen to my plaintive ditty,
    Ye tender hearts, and children dear!
And, should it move your souls to pity,
    Oh! try to *end* the griefs you hear.

There is a *beauteous plant*,[1] that grows
    In western India's sultry clime,
Which makes, alas! the Black man's woes,
    And also makes the White man's crime.

For know, its tall gold stems contain
    A sweet rich juice, which White men prize;
And that they may this *sugar* gain,
    The Negro toils, and bleeds, and *dies.*

But, Negro slave! *thyself* shall tell,
    Of past and present wrongs the story;
And would all British hearts could feel,
    To *end* those wrongs were *Britain's glory.*

Negro speaks.
First to our own dear Negro land,
    His ships the cruel White man sends;
And there contrives, by armed band,
    To tear us from our homes and friends;

From parents, brethren's fond embrace;
    From tender wife, and child to tear;
Then in a darksome ship to place,
    Pack'd close, like bales of cotton there.

Oh! happy those, who, in that hour,
    Die from their prison's putrid breath!
Since they escape from White man's pow'r,
    From toils and stripes, and lingering death!

---

[1] The sugar cane, *Sacharum officinarum*, a thick, woody type of grass, from the juice of which sugar is refined.

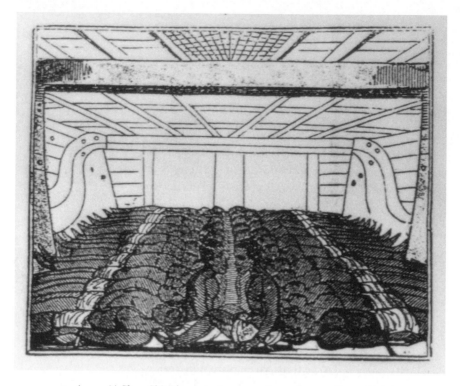

3. Anon., 'A Slave-Ship' (copper-plate engraving and watercolour, 1826), in
Amelia Opie, *The Black Man's Lament; or, How to Make Sugar*.

For what awaited us on shore,
    Soon as the ship had reach'd the strand,
Unloading its degraded store
    Of freemen, forc'd from Negro land?

See! eager White men come around,
    To choose and claim us for their slaves;
And make us envy those who found
    In the dark ship their early graves.

They bid black men and women stand
    In lines, the drivers in the rear:
Poor Negroes hold a *hoe* in hand,
    But they the wicked cart-whip bear.

Then we, in gangs, like beasts in droves,
    Swift to the cane-fields driven are;
There first our toil the weeds removes,
    And next we holes for plants prepare.

But woe to all, both old and young,
    Women and men, or strong or weak,
Worn out or fresh, those gangs among,
    That dare the toilsome line to break!

As holes must all *at once* be made,
    Together we must work or stop;
Therefore, the whip our strength must aid,
    And lash us when we pause or drop!

When we have dug *sufficient space,*
    The bright-eye top of many a cane,
Lengthways, we in the trenches place,
    And *then* we trenches dig again.

We cover next the plants with mould;
    And e'en, ere fifteen days come round,
We can the slender sprouts behold,
    Just shooting greenly from the ground.

The weeds about them clear'd away,
    Then mould again by hand we throw;
And, at no very distant day,
    Here Negroes plough, and there they hoe.

But when the crops are ripen'd quite,
    'Tis then begin our saddest pains;
For then we toil both day and night,
    Though fever burns within our veins.

When 18 months complete their growth,
    Then the tall canes rich juices fill;
And we, to bring their liquor forth,
    Convey them to the bruising-mill.

That mill, our labour, every hour,
    Must with fresh loads of canes supply;
And if we faint, the cart-whip's power,
    Gives force which *nature's* powers *deny.*

Our task is next to catch the juice
    In leaden bed, soon as it flows;
And instant, lest it spoil for use,
    It into boiling vessels goes.

4. Anon., 'Boiling and Cooling the Sugar' (copper-plate engraving and watercolour, 1826),
in Amelia Opie, *The Black Man's Lament; or, How to Make Sugar.*

Nor one alone: four vessels more
   Receive and clear the sugar-tide.
Six coolers next receive the store;
   Long vessels, shallow, wooden, *wide.*

While cooling, it begins to grain,
   Or form in crystals white and clear;
Then we remove the whole again,
   And to the *curing-house* we bear.

Molasses there is drain'd away;
   The liquor is through hogsheads pour'd;
The scum falls through, the crystals stay;
   The casks are clos'd, and soon on board.

The ships to English country go,
   And bear the hardly-gotten treasure.
Oh! that good Englishmen could know
   How Negroes suffer for their pleasure!

Five months, we, every week, alas!
    Save when we eat, to work are driven:
Six days, three nights; then, to each class,
    Just twenty hours of rest are given.

But when the Sabbath-eve comes round,
    That eve which White men sacred keep,
Again we at our toil are found,
    And six days more we work and weep.

"But, Negro slave, some men must toil.
    The English peasant works all day;
Turns up, and sows, and ploughs the soil.
    Thou wouldst not, sure, have Negroes play?"

"Ah! no. But Englishmen can work
    Whene'er they like, and stop for breath;
No driver dares, like any Turk,
    Flog peasants on almost to death.

"Who dares an English peasant flog,
    Or buy, or sell, or steal away?
Who sheds his blood? treats him like dog,
    Or fetters him like beasts of prey?

"He has a cottage, he a wife;
    If child he has, that child is free.
I am depriv'd of married life,
    And my poor child were *slave* like *me*.

"Unlike his home, ours is a shed
    Of pine-tree trunks, unsquar'd, ill-clos'd;
Blanket we have, but not a bed,
    Whene'er to short, chill sleep dispos'd.

"Our clothing's ragged. All our food
    Is rice, dried fish, and Indian meal.
Hard, scanty fare! Oh, would I could
    Make White men Negroes' miseries feel!"

"But could you not, your huts around,
    Raise plants for food, and poultry rear?
You might, if willing, till your ground,
    And then some wants would disappear."

"Work for ourselves and others too?
　　When all our master's work is o'er,
How could we bear our own to do?
　　Poor, weary slaves, hot, scourg'd, and sore!

"Sometimes, 'tis true, when Sabbath-bell
　　Calls White man to the house of pray'r,
And makes poor blacks more sadly feel
　　'Tis thought *slaves* have no *business* there:

"Then Negroes try the earth to till,
　　And raise their food on Sabbath-day;
But Envy's pangs poor Negroes fill,
　　That we must *work* while others *pray*.

"Then, where have we *one* legal right?
　　White men may bind, whip, torture slave.
But oh! if we but strike one White,
　　Who can poor Negro help or save?

"There are, I'm told, upon some isles,
　　Masters who gentle deign to be;
And there, perhaps, the Negro *smiles*,
　　But *smiling* Negroes *few* can see.

"Well, I must learn to bear my pain;
　　And, lately, I am grown more calm;
For Christian men come o'er the main,
　　To pour in Negro souls a balm.

"They tell us there is one above
　　Who died to save both bond and free;
And who, with eyes of equal love,
　　Beholds White man, and *humble me*.

"They tell me if, with patient heart,
　　I bear my wrongs from day to day,
I shall, at death, to realms depart,
　　Where God wipes every tear away!

"Yet still, at times, with fear I shrink;
　　For, when with sense of injury prest,
I burn with rage! and *then* I think
　　I ne'er can *gain* that place of rest."

He ceas'd; for here his tears would flow,
    And ne'er resum'd his tale of *ruth*.
Alas! it rends my heart to know
    He only told a *tale of truth*.

Mary Lamb (1764–1847), 'Conquest of Prejudice' (1809)

Mary Lamb was criminally insane. On 22 September 1796, having been irritated by the behaviour of a small apprentice girl who had been hired to look after her brother Charles, Mary, and their mother, she grabbed a knife and chased the servant round the room. Mary's mother attempted to protect the defenceless girl and Mary stabbed her mother to death. She was thereafter placed under the protection of her brother. They led an itinerant and precarious life, but both Charles and Mary continued writing. Mary wrote her 'Conquest of Prejudice' in 1809 near the end of the period that she and Charles had been encouraged to write children's books of various sorts for the great radical philosopher William Godwin, who had set himself up as a children's publisher. In 1807 the Lambs' joint masterpiece *Tales from Shakespeare* had been published. In her 'Conquest of Prejudice' Mary Lamb takes an unusual subject, racism in the classroom. When the head boy cannot tolerate having a black in his class the teacher's solution is to lock him and the black 'Juba' in solitary confinement together for a month. Food is passed through a skylight in their cell and the teacher waits to see what happens. The absurd finale, where the head boy Orme now wishes all the other children to respect Juba because Orme has been locked up in a cage with the black and enjoyed the resulting conversation, leaves a strange taste in the mouth. Orme's negrophiliac 'conversion' becomes the sole subject, and Juba exists only as an abstract proof of the young white male's capacity to express enlightenment. Juba does not speak in the poem, and does not do anything; he is simply a passive symbol of blackness. He even seems to accept as an unproblematic *fait accompli* his own totally unjust punishment, namely being locked in a room with a racist for a month on the grounds that the racist hates him.

Conquest of Prejudice

Unto a Yorkshire school was sent
    A Negro youth to learn to write,
And the first day young Juba went
    All gazed on him as a rare sight.

But soon with altered looks askance
    They view his sable face and form,
When they perceive the scorning glance
    Of the head boy, young Henry Orme.

He in the school was first in fame:
    Said he, 'It does to me appear
To be a great disgrace and shame
    A black should be admitted here.'

His words were quickly whispered round,
    And every boy now looks offended;
The master saw the change, and found
    That Orme a mutiny intended.

Said he to Orme, 'This African
    It seems is not by you approved;
I'll find a way, young Englishman,
    To have this prejudice removed.

'Nearer acquaintance possibly
    May make you tolerate his hue;
At least 'tis my intent to try
    What a short month may chance to do.'

Young Orme and Juba then he led
    Into a room, in which there were
For each of the two boys a bed,
    A table, and a wicker chair.

He locked them in, secured the key,
    That all access to them was stopt;
They from without can nothing see;
    Their food is through a sky-light dropt.

A month in this lone chamber Orme
    Is sentenced during all that time
To view no other face or form
    Than Juba's parched by Afric clime.

One word they neither of them spoke
    The first three days of the first week;
On the fourth day the ice was broke;
    Orme was the first that deigned to speak.

The dreary silence o'er, both glad
   To hear of human voice the sound,
The Negro and the English lad
   Comfort in mutual converse found.

Of ships and seas, and foreign coast,
   Juba can speak, for he has been
A voyager: and Orme can boast
   He London's famous town has seen.

In eager talk they pass the day,
   And borrow hours ev'n from the night;
So pleasantly time passed away,
   That they have lost their reckoning quite.

And when their master set them free,
   They thought a week was sure remitted,
And thanked him that their liberty
   Had been before the time permitted.

Now Orme and Juba are good friends;
   The school, by Orme's example won,
Contend who first shall make amends
   For former slights to Afric's son.

James Montgomery (1771–1854), from *The West Indies: A Poem in Four Parts* (1809); 'Inscription under the Picture of an Aged Negro Woman' (1826), 'Abolition of Colonial Slavery' (1834); 'The Negro is Free' (1833), in *The Collected Poetical Works of James Montgomery* (1841)

Montgomery's parents were ardent Moravian missionaries. They placed him as a boy in a Moravian school in England, while they went as missionaries to the Caribbean; his mother died in 1790 of yellow fever in Tobago, and the next year his father met the same fate in Barbados. While at school Montgomery showed a passion for verse and had composed two strange religious epics in the late 1780s. Determined to forge his own career as a poet and journalist he moved to Sheffield in 1792 to work on the *Sheffield Register*, owned and run by the radical John Gales. Gales fled to America during the persecution of radicals surrounding the 1794 Treason Trials and Montgomery became the editor. Although he was a moderate supporter of the radical cause state paranoia had reached such extremities by the mid-1790s that Montgomery was twice prosecuted and imprisoned for libel for republishing works sympathetic to the early stages of the French Revolution. Montgomery continued to be a prolific poet but it was only in 1806 that he became famous for his poem *The Wanderer in Switzerland*, which took the unusual theme of describing Switzerland under Napoleon. As a result of this he was commissioned by the publisher Bowyer to write a poem commemorating the abolition of the slave trade and *The West Indies* was the result. It was one poem in a lavish, and beautifully illustrated, anthology celebrating abolition; the book came out in 1809, but the poem only became a best-seller when published separately in 1810.

The poem is a condensation of arguments, attitudes, and fictions which had developed during the preceding two decades of abolition polemic, and which were to remain an orthodoxy. It has a carefully orchestrated colonial and nationalist agenda and opens by reciting a fully inflated version of the Spanish Black Legend. Columbus is constructed as an idealist betrayed by subsequent Spanish depredations; Bartolomco de las Casas, 'the saviour of the Indians', is sanctified as the protector of the indigenous peoples (despite the fact that he was the first apologist for, and a great instigator of, African slavery in the Americas) who are presented as beautiful and doomed innocents. Africa is shown as savage, the Africans as exotic heathens; yet once captured they are shown in every stage of slavery as utterly passive in their unending victimhood. Slavery is shown as a force of evil outside Britain which must be condemned and destroyed by the activities of a band of selfless and heroic white gentlemen philanthropists. The pantheon of the leaders of abolition is then dutifully recited. The Creole planters are singled out as the rotten and corrupted heart of slavery: the males are shown as cruelty incarnate, the females as indolent, sensuous, and corrupt. The poem ends with a paean to the healing powers of Christianity, and argues that the double-pronged advance of European commerce and religion provides the only hope for African freedom. Montgomery's work provides a chilling distillation of the manner in which abolition propaganda seamlessly incorporated the theme of the missionary 'liberation' of a subjugated Africa as the price which the 'dark Continent' had to pay for its liberation from the European slave trade.

from *The West Indies*

PART I

ARGUMENT

Introduction; on the Abolition of the Slave Trade.—The Mariner's Compass.— Columbus.—The Discovery of America.—The West Indian Islands.—The Charibs.—Their Extermination.

"Thy chains are broken, Africa, be free!"
Thus saith the island-empress of the sea;
Thus saith Britannia.   O, ye winds and waves!
Waft the glad tidings to the land of slaves;
Proclaim on Guinea's coast, by Gambia's side,
And far as Niger rolls his eastern tide,
Through radiant realms, beneath the burning zone,
Where Europe's curse is felt, her name unknown,
Thus saith Britannia, empress of the sea,
"Thy chains are broken, Africa, be free!"

. . . . .

Let nobler bards in loftier numbers tell
How Cortez conquer'd, Montezuma fell;
How fierce Pizarro's ruffian arm o'erthrew
The sun's resplendent empire in Peru;
How, like a prophet, old Las Casas[1] stood,
And raised his voice against a sea of blood,
Whose chilling waves recoil'd while he foretold
His country's ruin by avenging gold.
—That gold, for which unpitied Indians fell,
That gold, at once the snare and scourge of hell,
Thenceforth by righteous Heaven was doom'd to shed
Unmingled curses on the spoiler's head;
For gold the Spaniard cast his soul away,—
His gold and he were every nation's prey.

But themes like these would ask an angel-lyre,
Language of light and sentiment of fire;
Give me to sing, in melancholy strains,
Of Charib martyrdoms and Negro chains;
One race by tyrants rooted from the earth,
One doom'd to slavery by the taint of birth!

Where first his drooping sails Columbus furl'd
And sweetly rested in another world,
Amidst the heaven-reflecting ocean, smiles
A constellation of elysian isles;

---

[1] Bartolomeo de las Casas (1474–1566), Spanish missionary and humanitarian during the early stages of the Spanish conquest of the Americas. He fought for the rights of the indigenous peoples, and wrote brilliant propaganda attacking the enormities of the colonial Spanish. He also supported the use of African labour as an alternative to that of indigenous Americans.

Fair as Orion[2] when he mounts on high,
Sparkling with midnight splendour from the sky:
They bask beneath the sun's meridian rays,
When not a shadow breaks the boundless blaze;
The breath of ocean wanders through their vales
In morning breezes and in evening gales:
Earth from her lap perennial verdure pours,
Ambrosial fruits, and amaranthine flowers;
O'er the wild mountains and luxuriant plains,
Nature in all the pomp of beauty reigns,
In all the pride of freedom.—NATURE FREE
Proclaims that MAN was born for liberty.
She flourishes where'er the sunbeams play
O'er living fountains, sallying into day;
She withers where the waters cease to roll,
And night and winter stagnate round the pole:
Man too, where freedom's beams and fountains rise,
Springs from the dust, and blossoms to the skies;
Dead to the joys of light and life, the slave
Clings to the clod; his root is in the grave:
Bondage is winter, darkness, death, despair;
Freedom the sun, the sea, the mountains, and the air!

In placid indolence supinely blest,
A feeble race these beauteous isles possess'd;
Untamed, untaught, in arts and arms unskill'd,
Their patrimonial soil they rudely till'd,
Chased the free rovers of the savage wood,
Insnared the wild-bird, swept the scaly flood;
Shelter'd in lowly huts their fragile forms
From burning suns and desolating storms;
Or when the halcyon sported on the breeze,
In light canoes they skimm'd the rippling seas;
Their lives in dreams of soothing languor flew,
No parted joys, no future pains they knew,
The passing moment all their bliss or care;
Such as their sires had been the children were,
From age to age; as waves upon the tide
Of stormless time, they calmly lived and died.

---

[2] A constellation of seven really bright stars, three of which are supposed to form Orion's belt.

Dreadful as hurricanes, athwart the main
Rush'd the fell legions of invading Spain;
With fraud and force, with false and fatal breath,
(Submission bondage, and resistance death,)
They swept the isles.   In vain the simple race
Kneel'd to the iron sceptre of their grace,
Or with weak arms their fiery vengeance braved;
They came, they saw, they conquer'd, they enslaved,
And they destroy'd;—the generous heart they broke,
They crush'd the timid neck beneath the yoke;
Where'er to battle march'd their fell array,
The sword of conquest plough'd resistless way;
Where'er from cruel toil they sought repose,
Around the fires of devastation rose.
The Indian, as he turn'd his head in flight,
Beheld his cottage flaming through the night,
And, midst the shrieks of murder on the wind,
Heard the mute blood-hound's death-step close behind.

The conflict o'er, the valiant in their graves,
The wretched remnant dwindled into slaves;
Condemn'd in pestilential cells to pine,
Delving for gold amidst the gloomy mine.
The sufferer, sick of life-protracting breath,
Inhaled with joy the fire-damp blast of death:
—Condemn'd to fell the mountain palm on high,
That cast its shadow from the evening sky,
Ere the tree trembled to his feeble stroke,
The woodman languish'd, and his heart-strings broke;
—Condemn'd in torrid noon, with palsied hand,
To urge the slow plough o'er the obdurate land,
The labourer, smitten by the sun's quick ray,
A corpse along the unfinish'd furrow lay.
O'erwhelm'd at length with ignominious toil,
Mingling their barren ashes with the soil,
Down to the dust the Charib people pass'd,
Like autumn foliage withering in the blast:
The whole race sunk beneath the oppressor's rod,
And left a blank among the works of God.

END OF THE FIRST PART

PART II

ARGUMENT

The Cane.—Africa.—The Negro.—The Slave-Carrying Trade.—The Means and Resources of the Slave Trade.—The Portuguese,—Dutch,—Danes,—French,— and English in America.

Among the bowers of paradise, that graced
Those islands of the world-dividing waste,
Where towering cocoas waved their graceful locks,
And vines luxuriant cluster'd round the rocks;
Where orange-groves perfum'd the circling air,
With verdure, flowers, and fruit for ever fair;
Gay myrtle-foliage track'd the winding rills,
And cedar forests slumber'd on the hills;
—An eastern plant, ingrafted on the soil,
Was till'd for ages with consuming toil;
No tree of knowledge with forbidden fruit,
Death in the taste, and ruin at the root;
Yet in its growth were good and evil found,—
It bless'd the planter, but it cursed the ground;
While with vain wealth it gorged the master's hoard,
And spread with manna his luxurious board,
Its culture was perdition to the slave,—
It sapp'd his life, and flourish'd on his grave.

When the fierce spoiler from remorseless Spain
Tasted the balmy spirit of the cane,
(Already had his rival in the west
From the rich reed ambrosial sweetness press'd,)
Dark through his thoughts the miser purpose roll'd
To turn its hidden treasures into gold.
But at his breath, by pestilent decay,
The Indian tribes were swiftly swept away;
Silence and horror o'er the isles were spread,
The living seem'd the spectres of the dead.
The Spaniard saw; no sigh of pity stole,
No pang of conscience touch'd his sullen soul:
The tiger weeps not o'er the kid;—he turns
His flashing eyes abroad, and madly burns
For nobler victims, and for warmer blood:
Thus on the Charib shore the tyrant stood,

Thus cast his eyes with fury o'er the tide,
And far beyond the gloomy gulph descried
Devoted Africa: he burst away,
And with a yell of transport grasp'd his prey.

    .   .   .   .   .   .

    In these romantic regions man grows wild:
Here dwells the Negro, nature's outcast child,
Scorn'd by his brethren; but his mother's eye,
That gazes on him from her warmest sky,
Sees in his flexile limbs untutor'd grace,
Power on his forehead, beauty in his face;
Sees in his breast, where lawless passions rove,
The heart of friendship and the home of love;
Sees in his mind, where desolation reigns,
Fierce as his clime, uncultur'd as his plains,
A soil where virtue's fairest flowers might shoot,
And trees of science bend with glorious fruit;
Sees in his soul, involved with thickest night,
An emanation of eternal light,
Ordain'd, midst sinking worlds, his dust to fire,
And shine for ever when the stars expire.
Is he not *man*, though knowledge never shed
Her quickening beams on his neglected head?
Is he not *man*, though sweet religion's voice
Ne'er made the mourner in his God rejoice?
Is *he* not man, by sin and suffering tried?
Is *he* not man, for whom the Saviour died?
Belie the Negro's powers:—in headlong will,
Christian! *thy* brother thou shalt prove him still:
Belie his virtues; since his wrongs began,
His follies and his crimes have stampt him Man.

    The Spaniard found him such:—the island-race
His foot had spurn'd from earth's insulted face;
Among the waifs and foundlings of mankind,
Abroad he look'd, a sturdier stock to find;
A spring of life, whose fountains should supply
His channels as he drank the rivers dry:
That stock he found on Afric's swarming plains,
That spring he open'd in the Negro's veins;
A spring, exhaustless as his avarice drew,
A stock that like Prometheus' vitals grew

Beneath the eternal beak his heart that tore,
Beneath the insatiate thirst that drain'd his gore.
Thus, childless as the Charibbeans died,
Afric's strong sons the ravening waste supplied;
Of hardier fibre to endure the yoke,
And self-renew'd beneath the severing stroke;
As grim oppression crush'd them to the tomb,
Their fruitful parent's miserable womb
Teem'd with fresh myriads, crowded o'er the waves,
Heirs to their toil, their sufferings, and their graves.

Freighted with curses was the bark that bore
The spoilers of the west to Guinea's shore;
Heavy with groans of anguish blew the gales
That swell'd that fatal bark's returning sails;
Old Ocean shrunk as o'er his surface flew
The human cargo and the demon crew.
—Thenceforth, unnumber'd as the waves that roll,
From sun to sun, or pass from pole to pole,
Outcasts and exiles, from their country torn,
In floating dungeons o'er the gulph were borne;
—The valiant, seized in peril-daring fight;
The weak, surprised in nakedness and night;
Subjects by mercenary despots sold;
Victims of justice prostitute for gold;
Brothers by brothers, friends by friends betray'd;
Snared in her lover's arms the trusting maid;
The faithful wife by her false lord estranged,
For one wild cup of drunken bliss exchanged;
From the brute-mother's knee, the infant-boy,
Kidnapp'd in slumber, barter'd for a toy;
The father, resting at *his* father's tree,
Doom'd by the son to die beyond the sea:
—All bonds of kindred, law, alliance broke,
All ranks, all nations crouching to the yoke;
From fields of light, unshadow'd climes, that lie
Panting beneath the sun's meridian eye;
From hidden Ethiopia's utmost land;
From Zaara's[3] fickle wilderness of sand;
From Congo's blazing plains and blooming woods;
From Whidah's[4] hills, that gush with golden floods;

[3] Old spelling of Sahara, desert region in North Africa.   [4] Ouidah.

Captives of tyrant power and dastard wiles,
Dispeopled Africa, and gorged the isles.
Loud and perpetual o'er the Atlantic waves,
For guilty ages, roll'd the tide of slaves;
A tide that knew no fall, no turn, no rest,
Constant as day and night from east to west;
Still widening, deepening, swelling in its course,
With boundless ruin and resistless force.

Quickly by Spain's alluring fortune fired,
With hopes of fame, and dreams of wealth inspired,
Europe's dread powers from ignominious ease
Started; their pennons stream'd on every breeze:
And still where'er the wide discoveries spread,
The cane was planted, and the native bled;
While, nursed by fiercer suns, of nobler race,
The Negro toil'd and perish'd in his place.

First, Lusitania,[5]—she whose prows had borne
Her arms triumphant round the car of morn,
—Turn'd to the setting sun her bright array,
And hung her trophies o'er the couch of day.

Holland,—whose hardy sons roll'd back the sea,
To build the halcyon-nest of liberty,
Shameless abroad the enslaving flag unfurl'd,
And reign'd a despot in the younger world.

Denmark,—whose roving hordes, in barbarous times,
Fill'd the wide North with piracy and crimes,
Awed every shore, and taught their keels to sweep
O'er every sea, the Arabs of the deep,
—Embark'd, once more to western conquest led
By Rollo's[6] spirit, risen from the dead.

Gallia,—who vainly aim'd, in depth of night,
To hurl old Rome from her Tarpeian[7] height,

---

[5] Portugal.

[6] Rollo, or Hrolf (*c*.860–932), was the Viking founder of the duchy of Normandy. He was the leader of a band of mercenary Vikings pillaging France in 911. After laying siege to Chartres he eventually made peace with King Charles III and was offered Normandy in exchange for agreeing to become Charles's vassal. Rollo was reportedly too enormous for any horse to carry him, hence his name of Rollo the 'ganger' (walker).

[7] Meaning 'of Tarpeia', a Roman soldier's daughter. She betrayed Rome to the Sabines and was executed and buried under a rock on the Capitoline hill. The 'Tarpeian rock' became a place from which criminals were thrown.

(But lately laid, with unprevented blow,
The thrones of kings, the hopes of freedom low,)
—Rush'd o'er the theatre of splendid toils,
To brave the dangers and divide the spoils.

Britannia,—she who scathed the crest of Spain,
And won the trident sceptre of the main,
When to the raging wind and ravening tide
She gave the huge Armada's scatter'd pride,
Smit by the thunder-wielding hand that hurl'd
Her vengeance round the wave-encircled world;
—Britannia shared the glory and the guilt,—
By her were Slavery's island-altars built,
And fed with human victims;—while the cries
Of blood demanding vengeance from the skies,
Assail'd her traders grovelling hearts in vain,
—Hearts dead to sympathy, alive to gain,
Hard from impunity, with avarice cold,
Sordid as earth, insensible as gold.

Thus through a night of ages, in whose shade
The sons of darkness plied the infernal trade,
Wild Africa beheld her tribes, at home,
In battle slain; abroad, condemn'd to roam
O'er the salt waves, in stranger-isles to bear,
(Forlorn of hope, and sold into despair,)
Through life's slow journey, to its dolorous close,
Unseen, unwept, unutterable woes.

PART III

.   .   .   .   .   .

When the loud trumpet of eternal doom
Shall break the mortal bondage of the tomb;
When with a mothers's pangs the expiring earth
Shall bring her children forth to second birth;
Then shall the sea's mysterious caverns, spread
With human relics, render up their dead:
Though warm with life the heaving surges glow,
Where'er the winds of heaven were wont to blow,
In sevenfold phalanx shall the rallying hosts
Of ocean slumberers join their wandering ghosts,

Along the melancholy gulph, that roars
From Guinea to the Charibbean shores,
Myriads of slaves, that perish'd on the way,
From age to age the shark's appointed prey,
By livid plagues, by lingering tortures slain,
Or headlong plunged alive into the main,[8]
Shall rise in judgment from their gloomy beds,
And call down vengeance on their murderers' heads.

   Yet small the number, and the fortune blest,
Of those who in the stormy deep found rest,
Weigh'd with the unremember'd millions more,
That 'scaped the sea, to perish on the shore,
By the slow pangs of solitary care,
The earth-devouring anguish of despair,[9]
The broken heart, which kindness never heals,
The home-sick passion which the Negro feels,
When toiling, fainting in the land of canes,
His spirit wanders to his native plains;
His little lovely dwelling there he sees,
Beneath the shade of his paternal trees,
The home of comfort:—then before his eyes
The terrors of captivity arise.
—'Twas night:—his babes around him lay at rest,
Their mother slumber'd on their father's breast:

[8] 'On this subject the following instance of almost incredible cruelty was substantiated in a court of justice: "In the year (1783), certain underwriters desired to be heard against Gregson and others of Liverpool, in the case of the ship Zong, Captain Collingwood, alleging, that the captain and officers of the said vessel threw overboard one hundred and thirty-two slaves alive into the sea, in order to defraud them, by claiming the value of the said slaves, as if they had been lost in a natural way. In the course of the trial, which afterwards came on, it appeared that the slaves on board the Zong were very sickly; that sixty of them had already died; and several were ill, and likely to die, when the captain proposed to James Kelsal, the mate, and others to throw several of them overboard, stating, 'that if they died a natural death, the loss would fall upon the owners of the ship, but that if they were thrown into the sea it would fall upon the underwriters.' He selected accordingly, one hundred and thirty-two of the most sickly of the slaves. Fifty-four of these were immediately thrown over board, and forty-two were made to be partakers of their fate on the succeeding day. In the course of three days afterwards the remaining thirty-six were brought upon deck, to complete the number of victims. The first sixteen submitted to be thrown into the sea, but the rest, with a noble resolution, would not suffer the officers to touch them, but leaped after their companions and shared their fate . . .". Clarkson's *History of the Abolition &c.* pp. 95–7.' [Montgomery]

[9] 'The Negroes sometimes in deep and irrecoverable melancholy, waste themselves way, by secretly swallowing large quantities of earth. It is remarkable that "earth-eating" as it is called is an *infectious* and even a *social* malady: plantations have been occasionally almost depopulated by the slaves, with one consent, betaking themselves to this strange practice, which speedily brings them to a miserable and premature end.' [Montgomery]

A yell of murder rang around their bed;
They woke; their cottage blazed; the victims fled;
Forth sprang the ambush'd ruffians on their prey,
They caught, they bound, they drove them far away;
The white man bought them at the mart of blood;
In pestilential barks they cross'd the flood;
Then were the wretched ones asunder torn,
To distant isles, to separate bondage borne,
Denied, though sought with tears, the sad relief
That misery loves,—the fellowship of grief.
The Negro, spoil'd of all that nature gave
To freeborn man, thus shrunk into a slave,
His passive limbs, to measured tasks confined,
Obey'd the impulse of another mind;
A silent, secret, terrible control,
That ruled his sinews, and repress'd his soul.
Not for himself he wak'd at morning-light,
Toil'd the long day, and sought repose at night;
His rest, his labour, pastime, strength, and health,
Were only portions of a master's wealth;
His love—O, name not love, where Britons doom
The fruit of love to slavery from the womb!
Thus spurn'd, degraded, trampled, and oppress'd,
The Negro-exile languish'd in the West,
With nothing left of life but hated breath,
And not a hope except the hope in death,
To fly for ever from the Creole-strand,
And dwell a freeman in his father-land.

Lives there a savage ruder than the slave?
—Cruel as death, insatiate as the grave,
False as the winds that round his vessel blow,
Remorseless as the gulph that yawns below,
Is he who toils upon the wafting flood,
A Christian broker in the trade of blood;
Boisterous in speech, in action prompt and bold,
He buys, he sells,—he steals, he kills, for gold.
At noon, when sky and ocean, calm and clear,
Bend round his bark, one blue unbroken sphere;
When dancing dolphins sparkle through the brine,
And sunbeam circles o'er the waters shine;

He sees no beauty in the heaven serene,
No soul-enchanting sweetness in the scene,
But, darkly scowling at the glorious day,
Curses the winds that loiter on their way.
When swoln with hurricanes the billows rise,
To meet the lightning midway from the skies;
When from the unburden'd hold his shrieking slaves
Are cast, at midnight, to the hungry waves;
Not for his victims strangled in the deeps,
Not for his crimes the harden'd pirate weeps,
But grimly smiling, when the storm is o'er,
Counts his sure gains, and hurries back for more.

   Lives there a reptile baser than the slave?[10]
—Loathsome as death, corrupted as the grave,
See the dull Creole, at his pompous board,
Attendant vassals cringing round their lord:
Satiate with food, his heavy eyelids close,
Voluptuous minions fan him to repose;
Prone on the noonday couch he lolls in vain,
Delirious slumbers rock his maudlin brain;
He starts in horror from bewildering dreams;
His bloodshot eye with fire and frenzy gleams:
He stalks abroad; through all his wonted rounds,
The Negro trembles, and the lash resounds,
And cries of anguish, shrilling through the air,
To distant fields his dread approach declare.
Mark, as he passes, every head declined;
Then slowly raised,—to curse him from behind.
This is the veriest wretch on nature's face,
Own'd by no country, spurn'd by every race;
The tether'd tyrant of one narrow span,
The bloated vampire of a living man;
His frame,—a fungous form, of dunghill birth,
That taints the air, and rots above the earth;

---

[10] 'The character of the Creole planter here drawn is justified both by reason and fact: it is no monster of imagination, though, for the credit of human nature, we may hope that it is a monster as rare as it is shocking. It is the double curse of slavery to degrade all who are concerned with it, *doing or suffering*. The slave himself is the lowest in the scale of human beings,—except the slave dealer. Dr. Pinkard's *Notes on the West Indies*, and Captain Stedman's *Account of Surinam* afford examples of the cruelty, ignorance, sloth and sensuality of Creole planters, particularly in Dutch Guiana, which is fully equal to the epitome of vice and abomination exhibited in these lines.' [Montgomery]

His soul;—has *he* a soul, whose sensual breast
Of selfish passions is a serpent's nest?
Who follows, headlong, ignorant, and blind,
The vague brute instinct of an idiot mind;
Whose heart, 'midst scenes of suffering senseless grown,
E'en from his mother's lap was chill'd to stone;
Whose torpid pulse no social feelings move;
A stranger to the tenderness of love,
His motley haram charms his gloating eye,
Where ebon, brown, and olive beauties vie;
His children, sprung alike from sloth and vice,
Are born his slaves, and loved at market price:
Has *he* a soul?—With his departing breath,
A form shall hail him at the gates of death,
The spectre Conscience,—shrieking through the gloom,
"Man, we shall meet again beyond the tomb."

.   .   .   .   .   .

PART IV

ARGUMENT

*The Advocates of the Negroes in England.—Granville Sharpe,—Clarkson,—
Wilberforce,—Pitt,—Fox,—The Nation itself.—The Abolition of the Slave
Trade.—The future State of the West Indies,—of Africa,—of the Whole World.—
The Millennium.*

Was there no mercy, mother of the slave!
No friendly hand to succour and to save,
While commerce thus thy captive tribes oppress'd,
And lowering vengeance linger'd o'er the west?
Yes, Africa! beneath the stranger's rod
They found the freedom of the sons of God.

.   .   .   .   .   .

  Meanwhile, among the great, the brave, the free,
The matchless race of Albion and the sea,
Champions arose to plead the Negro's cause;
In the wide breach of violated laws,
Through which the torrent of injustice roll'd,
They stood:—with zeal unconquerably bold,
They raised their voices, stretch'd their arms to save
From chains the freeman, from despair the slave;

The exile's heart-sick anguish to assuage,
And rescue Afric from the spoiler's rage.
She, miserable mother, from the shore,
Age after age, beheld the barks that bore
Her tribes to bondage:—with distraction wrung,
Wild as the lioness that seeks her young,
She flash'd unheeded lightnings from her eyes;
Her inmost deserts echoing to her cries;
Till agony the sense of suffering stole,
And stern unconscious grief benumb'd her soul.
So Niobe,[11] when all her race were slain,
In ecstasy of woe forgot her pain:
Cold in her eye serenest sorrow shone,
While pitying Nature soothed her into stone.

  Thus Africa, entranced with sorrow, stood,
Her fix'd eye gleaming on the restless flood:
—When Sharpe,[12] on proud Britannia's charter'd shore,
From Libyan limbs the unsanction'd fetters tore,
And taught the world, that while she rules the waves,
Her soil is freedom to the feet of slaves:
—When Clarkson his victorious course began,
Unyielding in the cause of God and man,
Wise, patient, persevering to the end,
No guile could thwart, no power his purpose bend;
He rose o'er Afric like the sun in smiles,—
He rests in glory on the western isles:
—When Wilberforce, the minister of grace,
The new Las Casas of a ruin'd race
With angel-might opposed the rage of hell,
And fought like Michael, till the dragon fell:[13]

[11] Niobe was an embodiment of human despair. The daughter of Tantalus, she was the proud mother of seven sons and seven daughters. She boasted of her superiority on this count to Leto. Leto's children Apollo and Artemis consequently killed all Niobe's children. Their mother's ceaseless weeping in reaction to the tragedy led her to turn into a stone column on Mount Sipylus.

[12] 'Granville Sharpe Esq. After a struggle of many years, against authority and precedent, established in our courts of justice the *law of the constitution, that there are no slaves in England,* and that the fact of a Negro being found in this country is of itself a proof that he is a freeman.' [Montgomery]

[13] In Revelation 12: 9 Satan is termed 'the great dragon . . . that old serpent' who was 'cast out of the earth' along with the angels who followed him. In Psalm 91: 13 'the Saints shall trample the dragon under their feet'. The greatest of the angels, Michael (St Michael), is the angel who is most commonly represented slaying the dragon in art and poetry.

—When Pitt,[14] supreme amid the senate, rose
The Negro's friend, among the Negro's foes;
Yet while his tones like heaven's high thunder broke,
No fire descended to consume the yoke:
—When Fox,[15] all-eloquent, for freedom stood,
With speech resistless as the voice of blood,
The voice that cries through all the patriot's veins,
When at his feet his country groans in chains;
The voice that whispers in the mother's breast,
When smiles her infant in his rosy rest;
Of power to bid the storm of passion roll,
Or touch with sweetest tenderness the soul.
He spake in vain;—till, with his latest breath,
He broke the spell of Africa in death.

 . . . . . .

 High on her rock in solitary state,
Sublimely musing, pale Britannia sate:
Her awful forehead on her spear reclined,
Her robe and tresses streaming with the wind;
Chill through her frame foreboding tremors crept;
The Mother thought upon her sons, and wept
—She thought of Nelson in the battle slain,
And his last signal beaming o'er the main;[16]
In Glory's circling arms the hero bled,
While Victory bound the laurel on his head;
At once immortal, in both worlds, became
His soaring spirit and abiding name;
—She thought of Pitt, heart-broken on his bier;
And, "O my country!" echoed in her ear;
—She thought of Fox;—she heard him faintly speak,
His parting breath grew cold upon her cheek,
His dying accents trembled into air;
"Spare injured Africa! the Negro spare!"

 . . . . . .

[14]   William Pitt 'the younger' (1759–1806), second son of the Earl of Chatham, British Prime Minister during the period climaxing with the Battle of Trafalgar in 1805.
[15]   Charles James Fox (1749–1806), great English liberal and notorious political opponent of Pitt. He was initially enthusiastic about the French Revolution, and later put himself at the forefront of the attempts to impeach Warren Hastings for his corrupt administration of colonial India.
[16]   'England Expects Every Man to do his Duty.' [Montgomery] Nelson's original message was more trusting and read 'England Confides that Every Man Will do his Duty', but the message was too long, and an officer changed it into its famous form.

Unutterable mysteries of fate
Involve, O Africa! thy future state.
—On Niger's banks, in lonely beauty wild,
A Negro-mother carols to her child:
"Son of my widow'd love, my orphan joy!
Avenge thy father's murder, O my boy!"
Along those banks the fearless *infant* strays,
Bathes in the stream, among the eddies plays;
See the *boy* bounding through the eager race;
The fierce *youth*, shouting foremost in the chase,
Drives the grim lion from his ancient woods,
And smites the crocodile amidst his floods:
To giant strength in unshorn *manhood* grown,
He haunts the wilderness, he dwells alone.
A tigress with her whelps to seize him sprung;
He tears the mother, and he tames the young
In the drear cavern of their native rock:
Thither wild slaves and fell banditti flock;
He heads their hordes; they burst, like torrid rains
In death and devastation o'er the plains;
Stronger and bolder grows his ruffian band,
Prouder his heart, more terrible his hand,
He spreads his banner: crowding from afar,
Innumerable armies rush to war;
Resistless as the pillar'd whirlwinds fly
O'er Libyan sands revolving to the sky,
In fire and wrath through every realm they run,
Where the noon-shadow shrinks beneath the sun;
Till at the Conqueror's feet, from sea to sea,
A hundred nations bow the servile knee,
And throned in nature's unreveal'd domains,
The Jenghis Khan[17] of Africa he reigns.

Dim through the night of these tempestuous years
A Sabbath dawn o'er Africa appears;
Then shall her neck from Europe's yoke be freed,
And healing arts to hideous arms succeed;

---

[17] Jenghis (or Genghis) Khan (*c*.1162–1227), Mongol warrior king and conqueror of territories which finally gave him a vast Asian empire stretching from the Black Sea to the Pacific, and taking in much of China and Russia. His name has become synonymous with ruthless nomadic military expansion.

At home fraternal bonds her tribes shall bind,
Commerce abroad espouse them with mankind;
While Truth shall build, and pure Religion bless,
The Church of God amidst the wilderness.

Nor in the isles and Africa alone
Be the Redeemer's cross and triumph known:
Father of Mercies! speed the promised hour;
Thy kingdom come with all-restoring power;
Peace, virtue, knowledge, spread from pole to pole,
As round the world the ocean-waters roll!
—Hope waits the morning of celestial light;
Time plumes his wings for everlasting flight;
Unchanging seasons have their march begun;
Millennial years are hastening to the sun;
Seen through thick clouds, by Faith's transpiercing eyes,
The New Creation shines in purer skies.
—All hail!—the age of crime and suffering ends;
The reign of righteousness from heaven descends;
Vengeance for ever sheathes the afflicting sword;
Death is destroy'd, and Paradise restored;
Man, rising from the ruins of his fall,
Is one with GOD, and God is All in All.

Inscription under the Picture of an Aged Negro Woman

Art thou a *woman*?[1]—so am I; and all
That woman can be, I have been, or am;
A daughter, sister, consort, mother, widow.
Whiche'er of these *thou* art, O be the friend
Of one who is what thou canst never be!
Look on thyself, thy kindred, home and country,
Then fall upon thy knees, and cry "Thank GOD,
An English woman cannot be a SLAVE!"

---

[1] Echoes the slogan 'Am I not a woman and a sister' put on the female version of the seal of the Society for Effecting the Abolition of the Slave Trade. The words also anticipate the famous 'Aren't I a woman?' aphorism of the great North American ex-slave activist Sojourner Truth, see p. lx.

Art thou a *man*?—Oh! I have known, have loved,
And lost, all that to woman man can be;
A father, brother, husband, son, who shared
My bliss in freedom, and my woe in bondage.
—A childless widow now, a friendless slave,
What shall I ask of thee, since I have nought
To lose but life's sad burthen; nought to gain
But heaven's repose?—these are beyond thy power;
Me thou canst neither wrong nor help;—what then?
Go to the bosom of thy family,
Gather thy little children round thy knees,
Gaze on their innocence; their clear, full eyes,
All fix'd on thine; and in their mother, mark
The loveliest look that woman's face can wear,
Her look of love, beholding them and thee:
Then, at the altar of your household joys,
Vow one by one, vow altogether, vow
With heart and voice, eternal enmity
Against oppression by your brethren's hands:
Till man nor woman under Britain's laws,
Nor son nor daughter born within her empire,
Shall buy, or sell, or hold, or be, a slave.

Abolition of Colonial Slavery

Hymn for the First of August, 1834

Ages, ages have departed,
    Since the first dark vessel bore
Afric's Children, broken hearted,
    To the Caribbean shore,
        She, like Rachael,[1]
Weeping, for they were no more.

---

[1] Personified Africa is identified with the biblical Rachel. Rachel's lost children represented the Israelites in Babylonian exile (Jeremiah 31: 15) and also came to be applied to describe the Massacre of the Innocents (Matthew 2: 18). It is consequently logical that a grieving mother Africa, lamenting the loss of her 'children' into Atlantic slavery, should take on identification with Rachel and its ramification in biblical typology.

Millions, millions have been slaughter'd
    In the fight, and on the deep;
Millions, millions more have water'd,
    With such tears as Captives weep,
      Fields of travail,
Where their bones till Judgment sleep.

Mercy, mercy vainly pleading,
    Rent her garments, smote her breast,
Till a Voice, from heaven proceeding,
    Gladden'd all the gloomy West,
      "Come, ye weary,
Come, and I will give you rest."

Satan, Satan heard and trembled,
    And, upstarting from his throne,
Bands of Belial's[2] sons assembled,
    Fired with rancour all his own,
      Madly swearing,
"Christ to Slaves shall NOT be known."

Tidings, tidings of Salvation!
    Britons rose with one accord,
Swept the plague-spot from our nation,
    Negroes to their rights restored;
      Slaves no longer,
Free-men,—free-men of the Lord!

The Negro is Free

Imitated from Moore's Sacred Melody, "Sound the loud
timbrel o'er Egypt's dark sea."[1]

Blow ye the trumpet abroad o'er the sea,
Britannia hath triumphed, the Negro is free;

---

[2] A great fallen angel often equated with Satan. Milton associates him explicitly with lewdness: 'Belial came last; than whom a Spirit more lewd | Fell not from Heav'n, or more gross to love | Vice it self . . .' *Paradise Lost*, I. 110–12.

[1] A famous and revolutionary lyric of Moore's in which the Hebrew women celebrate the violent destruction of Pharaoh's army in the Red Sea.

Sing, for the pride of the tyrant is broken,
　　His scourges and fetters, all clotted with blood,
Are wrenched from his grasp;—for the word was but spoken,
　　And fetters and scourges were sunk in the flood;
Blow ye the trumpet abroad o'er the sea,
Britannia hath triumphed, the Negro is free.

Hail to Britannia, fair Liberty's isle!
Her frown quailed the tyrant, the slave caught her smile;
Fly on the winds to tell Afric the story;
　　Say to the Mother of mourners, "Rejoice!"
Britannia went forth in her beauty, her glory,
　　And slaves sprang to men at the sound of her voice:
Praise to the GOD of our fathers,—'twas HE,
Jehovah, that triumphed, my Country, by THEE.

Percy Bysshe Shelley (1792–1822), 'Similes for Two Political Characters of 1819' (written 1819, published 1832); from *A Vision of the Sea* (1820); from *Prometheus Unbound*, Act I (1820)

Shelley, with his passionate hatred of all forms of tyranny and enslavement, engaged with the subject of Atlantic slavery with typical originality. Of all the major Romantic poets, Shelley is the one who has spoken to the descendants of slaves in the Diaspora most directly. The uncompromising energy of his libertarian diction has remanifested itself in some unpredictable contexts. The great dub poet Mikey Smith, a few months before he was stoned to death in Kingston, Jamaica, performed Shelley's *Song to the Men of England* in Westminster Abbey, and was filmed by the BBC. Smith's gorgeous performance showed that slavery and tyranny are excoriated by Shelley in a language which maintains transparent power for the oppressed ex-slave populations of the Diaspora.

Yet the extent to which Shelley directly addressed Atlantic slavery in his major work has been questioned. Alan Richardson recently suggested that Shelley made his 'opposition to colonial slavery clear' although he never wrote a 'poem against slavery per se', and suggests that Shelley's *Prometheus* may relate to abolition literature (Duncan Wu (ed.), *Companion to Romanticism* (Blackwell, 1992), 465). In fact Prometheus was a central symbolic figure not only for Blake, Southey, Byron, and Shelley, but for the anti-slavery movement. Montgomery's *Prometheus Delivered* is a good example of how abolition appropriated the Promethean myth. (For the text of *Prometheus Delivered* see

Basker, *Amazing Grace*, pp. 662–4. Basker gives the poem as 'Anonymous', but it was written by James Montgomery and appeared accompanying an elaborate emblematic engraving that constituted the frontispiece to the *Poems on the Abolition of the Slave Trade* (London, 1809). See also Marcus Wood, *Slavery, Empathy, and Pornography* (Oxford University Press, 2002), pp. 244–9.) Back in the 1790s Romantic poetry had already played a series of imaginative variations on the slave body as Promethean. For example one of Southey's 1797 sonnets on the slave trade presented the punishment of a rebel slave in Promethean terms (see p. 218).

Shelley's analysis of slavery and liberty in *Prometheus Unbound* is very different from these precursors. The engagement of *Prometheus Unbound* with slavery is, first and foremost, an abstract meditation on the tendency of power to enslave the powerful, and more horrifically those who make themselves dependent on the powerful. Act I of *Prometheus Unbound* considers how power corrupts and how power manifests itself in violence. It is Jupiter's enslavement to his own tyranny, and not the consequent suffering of the humans he has enslaved, or the torture of the enslaved Prometheus, which is Shelley's primary moral concern. With a typical loftiness Shelley reveals the great slave to be Jupiter, who, no matter what he does, is consequently to be pitied, not hated. While *Prometheus Unbound* constitutes Shelley's central meditation on slavery in the context of human ethics, he did write other verse which is more intimately involved in the rhetoric of the abolition debates.

Shelley's 'Similes for Two Political Characters of 1819' (1819) and *A Vision of the Sea*, which was significantly published in the 1820 volume *Prometheus Unbound . . . with Other Poems*, both confront the slave trade directly. 'Similes' is one of the poems which Shelley wrote in 1819 in a state of politicized indignation after he had heard about the Peterloo massacre. The poem is a grim satire aimed at Sidmouth and Castlereagh, two leading Cabinet members in the hated Liverpool administration. Having compared the two politicians to ravens and 'gibbering night-birds', in the third stanza Shelley brings in a reference to the slave trade, turning the men into fish. The image of the shark following the slave ship hoping for corpses to be thrown overboard was introduced into English poetry by James Thompson, in a justly celebrated passage of the *Seasons* (see Wood, *Slavery, Empathy, and Pornography*, pp. 250–1).

A Vision of the Sea is a neglected poem which has so far been seen by Shelley critics to have no central subject. It is in fact a poem about a slave insurrection on the middle passage. *A Vision* describes the violent destruction of a guilty ship laden with a furious and oppressed living cargo. The main events of the poem run as follows. At the opening the ship is torn about by a series of violent forces which constitute a virtual inventory of the natural signs of divine retribution catalogued in the anti-slavery verse of Thompson, Cowper, and Hannah More. At the point of its destruction two chained tigers burst from the hold. There is then an account of how the 'populous vessel' was becalmed, and of how most of the crew died of disease, and were thrown to the fish. As the ship is about to go down a single lovely woman, with her child, is seen at the helm. The woman is terrified, but the child is delighted both by the fury of the storm, and by the tigers. As the ship is finally ripped apart the tigers dive overboard. One is destroyed in a violent conflict with a giant sea snake. The other is executed by marksmen who arrive in a ship's boat. As the wreck goes down the beautiful woman clings to her child, who is still fearless.

It is in the introduction of the slave presence as an energized revolutionary force, the tigers, that the most confrontational aspect of Shelley's poem emerges. Tigers are of course Asian, not African, in origin, but this had not prevented them from being used as the symbol of slave vengeance and rebellion in earlier poetry. Blake's destruction of the slave power, the sons and daughters of Mystery, which forms the climax to *Vala* describes 'ramping tygers play in the jingling traces' of the carts which draw the victims to destruction (see pp. 147–50 above). In the 1790s Bryan Edwards, the Jamaican planter and at times strangely ambivalent pro-slavery rhetorician, had written an 'Ode on Seeing a Negro Funeral'. In this poem the ghost of the slave Omalco is presented as an inspirational force bringing joy to the bereaved. The mourners at his funeral do not lament his death but celebrate it. They envision Omalco flying over the ocean to his ancestors to rouse 'Africk's god' to vengeance. The god looses 'Africk's ruthless rage' in the form of a horde of ravening tigers (see p. 71 above). Shelley's magnificent tigers plunge into the ocean, and meet destruction, but they go out fighting with convulsive energy. The tigers' rebellion may lead to inevitable death, but it is a glorious assertion of freedom in which nature conjoins in a spectacular fusion of destruction and celebration. The combination of innocence and vengeful fury which Shelley articulates as the essence of the revolutionary spirit in this poem is formulated in the meeting between the 'bright child' and the tigers.

Similes for Two Political Characters of 1819

I

As from an ancestral oak
Two empty ravens sound their clarion,
Yell by yell, and croak by croak,
When they scent the noonday smoke
Of fresh human carrion:—

II

As two gibbering night-birds flit
From their bowers of deadly yew
Through the night to frighten it,
When the moon is in a fit,
And the stars are none, or few:—

III

As a shark and dog-fish wait
Under an Atlantic isle,
For the negro-ship, whose freight
Is the theme of their debate,
Wrinkling their red gills the while—

IV

Are ye two, vultures sick for battle,
Two scorpions under one wet stone,
Two bloodless wolves whose dry throats rattle,
Two crows perched on the murrained cattle,
Two vipers tangled into one.

from *A Vision of the Sea*

'Tis the terror of the tempest.   The rags of the sail
Are flickering in ribbons within the fierce gale:
From the stark night of vapours the dim rain is driven,
And when lightning is loosed, like a deluge from Heaven,
She sees the black trunks of the waterspouts spin
And bend, as if Heaven was ruining in,
Which they seemed to sustain with their terrible mass
As if ocean had sunk from beneath them: they pass
To their graves in the deep with an earthquake of sound,
And the waves and the thunders, made silent around,
Leave the wind to its echo.   The vessel, now tossed
Through the low-trailing rack of the tempest, is lost
In the skirts of the thunder-cloud: now down the sweep
Of the wind-cloven wave to the chasm of the deep
It sinks, and the walls of the watery vale
Whose depths of dread calm are unmoved by the gale,
Dim mirrors of ruin, hang gleaming about;
While the surf, like a chaos of stars, like a rout
With splendour and terror the black ship environ,
Of death-flames, like whirlpools of fire-flowing iron,
Or like sulphur-flakes hurled from a mine of pale fire
In fountains spout o'er it. In many a spire
The pyramid-billows with points of brine

In the cope of the lightning inconstantly shine,
As piercing the sky from the floor of the sea.
The great ship seems splitting! it cracks as a tree,
While an earthquake is splintering its root, ere the blast
Of the whirlwind that stripped it of branches has passed.
The intense thunder-balls which are raining from Heaven
Have shattered its mast, and it stands black and riven.
The chinks suck destruction. The heavy dead hulk
On the living sea rolls an inanimate bulk,
Like a corpse on the clay which is hungering to fold
Its corruption around it. Meanwhile from the hold,
One deck is burst up by the waters below,
And it splits like the ice when the thaw-breezes blow
O'er the lakes of the desert! Who sit on the other?
Is that all the crew that lie burying each other,
Like the dead in a breach, round the foremast? Are those
Twin tigers, who burst, when the waters arose,
In the agony of terror, their chains in the hold;
(What now makes them tame, is what then made them bold;)
Who crouch, side by side, and have driven, like a crank,
The deep grip of their claws through the vibrating plank:—
Are these all? Nine weeks the tall vessel had lain
On the windless expanse of the watery plain,
Where the death-darting sun cast no shadow at noon,
And there seemed to be fire in the beams of the moon,
'Till a lead-coloured fog gathered up from the deep,
Whose breath was quick pestilence; then the cold sleep
Crept, like blight through the ears of a thick field of corn,
O'er a populous vessel. And even the morn,
With their hammocks for coffins the seamen aghast
Like dead men the dead limbs of their comrades cast
Down the deep, which closed on them above and around,
And the sharks and the dogfish their grave-clothes unbound,
And were glutted like Jews with this manna rained down
From God on their wilderness.[1] One after one

---

[1] Manna was the food miraculously provided to feed the Israelites in the wilderness during the Exodus. Hence the word carries the association of anything delicious, wonderful, or heaven sent. Yet Shelley is doing something very strange with the metaphoric application of manna in these lines. The shark and dogfish are compared to the Israelites under Moses. In a hideous upending of the myth, the rotten and diseased corpses of the perpetrators of the British slave trade feed Shelley's deeply strange marine representatives of liberated slavery.

the mariners died; on the eve of this day,
When the tempest was gathering in cloudy array,
But seven remained. Six the thunder has smitten,
And they lie black as mummies on which time has written
His scorn of the embalmer; the seventh, from the deck
An oak-splinter pierced through his breast and his back.
And hung out to the tempest, a wreck on the wreck.
No more? At the helm sits a woman more fair
Than heaven, when, unbinding its star-braided hair,
It sinks with the sun on the earth and the sea.
She clasps a bright child on her upgathered knee;
It laughs at the lightning, it mocks the mixed thunder
Of the air and the sea, with desire and with wonder
It is beckoning the tigers to rise and come near,
It would play with those eyes where the radiance of fear
Is outshining the meteors; its bosom beats high,
The heart-fire of pleasure has kindled its eye
While its mother's is lustreless: 'Smile not, my child,
But sleep deeply and sweetly, and so be beguiled
Of the pang that awaits us, whatever that be,
So dreadful since thou must divide it with me!
Dream, sleep! this pale bosom, thy cradle and bed,
Will it rock thee not, infant? 'Tis beating with dread!
Alas! what is life, what is death, what are we,
That when the ship sinks we no longer may be?
What! to see thee no more, and to feel thee no more?
To be after life what we have been before?
Not to touch those sweet hands? Not to look on those eyes,
Those lips, and that hair,—all the smiling disguise
Thou yet wearest, sweet Spirit, which I, day by day,
Have so long called my child, but which now fades away
Like a rainbow, and I the fallen shower?'—Lo! the ship
Is settling, it topples, the leeward ports dip;
The tigers leap up when they feel the slow brine
Crawling inch by inch on them; hair, ears, limbs, and eyne,
Stand rigid with horror; a loud, long, hoarse cry
Bursts at once from their vitals tremendously,
And 'tis borne down the mountainous vale of the wave,
Rebounding like thunder, from crag to cave,
Mixed with the crashing of the lashing rain
Hurried on by the might of the hurricane.

from *Prometheus*[1] *Unbound*

From Act I

SCENE: A *Ravine of Icy Rocks in the Indian Caucasus.* PROMETHEUS *is discovered bound to the Precipice.* PANTHEA *and* IONE *are seated at his feet. Time, Night. During the Scene, Morning slowly breaks.*

PROMETHEUS.   Monarch of Gods and Daemons,[2] and all Spirits
　　But One, who throng those bright and rolling Worlds
　　Which Thou and I alone of living things
　　Behold with sleepless eyes! regard this Earth
　　Made multitudinous with thy slaves, whom thou
　　Requitest for knee-worship, prayer and praise,
　　And toil, and hecatombs[3] of broken hearts,
　　With fear and self contempt and barren hope;
　　Whilst me, who am thy foe, eyeless in hate,
　　Hast thou made reign and triumph, to thy scorn,
　　O'er mine own misery and thy vain revenge.—
　　Three thousand years of sleep-unsheltered hours
　　And moments—aye divided by keen pangs
　　Till they seemed years, torture and solitude,
　　Scorn and despair,—these are mine empire:—
　　More glorious far than that which thou surveyest
　　From thine unenvied throne, O Mighty God!
　　Almighty, had I deigned to share the shame
　　Of thine ill tyranny, and hung not here
　　Nailed to this wall of eagle-baffling mountain,
　　Black, wintry, dead, unmeasured; without herb,
　　Insect, or beast, or shape or sound of life.
　　Ah me, alas, pain, pain ever, forever!

　　No change, no pause, no hope!—Yet I endure.
　　I ask the Earth, have not the mountains felt?
　　I ask yon Heaven—the all-beholding Sun,

---

[1] Prometheus was one of the Titans. He stole fire from heaven (in some versions of the myth in order to give it to humans) and as a result Jove had Prometheus riveted on a mountainside where vultures eternally preyed upon him. For European romanticism Prometheus became a central metaphor for the spirit of the selfless artist revolutionary. The Promethean myth was developed by Blake, Byron, Shelley, Goethe, and Beethoven.

[2] See p. 21 n. 52.

[3] A large public sacrifice, any event involving a huge number of victims.

Has it not seen? The Sea, in storm or calm,
Heaven's ever-changing Shadow, spread below—
Have its deaf waves not heard my agony?
Ah me, alas, pain, pain ever, forever!

The crawling glaciers pierce me with the spears
Of their moon-freezing chrystals; the bright chains
Eat with their burning cold into my bones.
Heaven's winged hound, polluting from thy lips
His beak in poison not his own, tears up
My heart; and shapeless sights come wandering by,
The ghastly people of the realm of dream,
Mocking me: and the Earthquake-fiends are charged
To wrench the rivets from my quivering wounds
When the rocks split and close again behind;
While from their loud abysses howling throng
The genii of the storm, urging the rage
Of whirlwind, and afflict me with keen hail.
And yet to me welcome is Day and Night,
Whether one breaks the hoar frost of the morn,
Or starry, dim, and slow, the other climbs
The leaden-coloured East; for then they lead
Their wingless, crawling Hours, one among whom
—As some dark Priest hales the reluctant victim—
Shall drag thee, cruel King, to kiss the blood
From these pale feet, which then might trample thee
If they disdained not such a prostrate slave.
Disdain? Ah no! I pity thee.—What Ruin
Will hunt thee undefended through wide Heaven!
How will thy soul, cloven to its depth with terror,
Gape like a Hell within! I speak in grief,
Not exultation, for I hate no more,
As then, ere misery made me wise.—The Curse
Once breathed on thee I would recall. Ye Mountains,
Whose many-voiced Echoes, through the mist
Of cataracts, flung the thunder of that spell!
Ye icy Springs, stagnant with wrinkling frost,
Which vibrated to hear me, and then crept
Shuddering through India! Thou serenest Air,
Through which the Sun walks burning without beams!
And ye swift Whirlwinds, who on poised wings

Hung mute and moveless o'er yon hushed abyss,
As thunder louder than your own made rock
The orbed world! If then my words had power
—Though I am changed so that aught evil wish
Is dead within, although no memory be
Of what is hate—let them not lose it now!
What was that curse? for ye all heard me speak.

.   .   .   .   .   .

PHANTASM

Fiend, I defy thee! with a calm, fixed mind,
    All that thou canst inflict I bid thee do;
Foul Tyrant both of Gods and Humankind.
    One only being shalt thou not subdue.
        Rain then thy plagues upon me here,
        Ghastly disease and frenzying fear;
        And let alternate frost and fire
        Eat into me, and be thine ire
Lightning and cutting hail and legioned forms
Of furies, driving by upon the wounding storms.

Aye, do thy worst. Thou art Omnipotent.
    O'er all things but thyself I gave thee power,
And my own will. Be thy swift mischiefs sent
    To blast mankind, from yon etherial tower.
        Let thy malignant spirit move
        Its darkness over those I love:
        On me and mine I imprecate
        The utmost torture of thy hate
And thus devote to sleepless agony
This undeclining head while thou must reign on high.

But thou who art the God and Lord—O thou
    Who fillest with thy soul this world of woe,
To whom all things of Earth and Heaven do bow
    In fear and worship—all-prevailing foe!
        I curse thee! let a sufferer's curse
        Clasp thee, his torturer, like remorse,
        Till thine Infinity shall be,
        A robe of envenomed agony;[4]

[4] Recalling the story of the poisoned shirt which the centaur Nessus gave to Hercules; when he put it on, it consumed his flesh.

And thine Omnipotence a crown of pain
To cling like burning gold round thy dissolving brain.

Heap on thy soul by virtue of this Curse
  Ill deeds, then be thou damned, beholding good,
Both infinite as is the Universe,
    And thou, and thy self-torturing solitude.
      An awful Image of calm power
      Though now thou sittest, let the hour
      Come, when thou must appear to be
      That which thou art internally.
And after many a false and fruitless crime
Scorn track thy lagging fall through boundless space and time.

                  [*The Phantasm vanishes.*]

PROMETHEUS. Were these my words, O Parent?
THE EARTH.   They were thine.
PROMETHEUS. It doth repent me: words are quick and vain;
  Grief for awhile is blind, and so was mine.
  I wish no living thing to suffer pain.

THE EARTH

    Misery, O misery to me,
    That Jove at length should vanquish thee.
    Wail, howl aloud, Land and Sea,
    The Earth's rent heart shall answer ye.
  Howl, Spirits of the living and the dead,
  Your refuge, your defence lies fallen and vanquished.

FIRST ECHO

Lies fallen and vanquished?

SECOND ECHO

           Fallen and vanquished!
Fear not—'tis but some passing spasm,
  The Titan is unvanquished still.
  .   .   .   .   .

FURY. Behold, an emblem—those who do endure
  Deep wrongs for man, and scorn and chains, but heap
  Thousand-fold torment on themselves and him.
PROMETHEUS. Remit the anguish of that lighted stare—
  Close those wan lips—let that thorn-wounded brow
  Stream not with blood—it mingles with thy tears
  Fix, fix those tortured orbs in peace and death

So thy sick throes shake not that crucifix,
So those pale fingers play not with thy gore.—
O horrible! Thy name I will not speak,
It hath become a curse. I see, I see
The wise, the mild, the lofty and the just,
Whom thy slaves hate for being like to thee,
Some hunted by foul lies from their heart's home,
An early-chosen, late-lamented home,
As hooded ounces cling to the driven hind,[5]
Some linked to corpses in unwholesome cells:
Some—hear I not the multitude laugh loud?—
Impaled in lingering fire: and mighty realms
Float by my feet like sea-uprooted isles
Whose sons are kneaded down in common blood
By the red light of their own burning homes.
FURY. Blood thou canst see, and fire; and canst hear groans;
    Worse things, unheard, unseen, remain behind.
PROMETHEUS. Worse?
FURY.   In each human heart terror survives
    The ravin it has gorged: the loftiest fear
    All that they would disdain to think were true:
    Hypocrisy and custom make their minds
    The fanes[6] of many a worship, now outworn.
    They dare not devise good for man's estate
    And yet they know not that they do not dare.
    The good want power, but to weep barren tears.
    The powerful goodness want: worse need for them.
    The wise want love, and those who love want wisdom;
    And all best things are thus confused to ill.
    Many are strong and rich,—and would be just,—
    But live among their suffering fellow men
    As if none felt: they know not what they do.[7]
PROMETHEUS. Thy words are like a cloud of winged snakes
    And yet, I pity those they torture not.
FURY. Thou pitiest them? I speak no more!   *[Vanishes.]*
PROMETHEUS.   Ah woe!
    Ah woe! Alas! pain, pain ever, forever!
    I close my tearless eyes, but see more clear

---

[5] Ounces are leopards; a hind is a deer.   [6] Temples.
[7] Echoing Christ's words, Luke 23: 24: 'Forgive them, father, for they know not what they do.'

Thy works within my woe-illumed mind,
Thou subtle Tyrant! . . . Peace is in the grave—
The grave hides all things beautiful and good—
I am a God and cannot find it there,
Nor would I seek it: for, though dread revenge,
This is defeat, fierce King, not victory.
The sights with which thou torturest gird my soul
With new endurance, till the hour arrives
When they shall be no types of things which are.

PANTHEA. Alas! what sawest thou?

PROMETHEUS.   There are two woes:
To speak and to behold; thou spare me one.
Names are there, Nature's sacred watchwords—they
Were borne aloft in bright emblazonry.
The nations thronged around, and cried aloud
As with one voice, "Truth, liberty and love!"
Suddenly fierce confusion fell from Heaven
Among them—there was strife, deceit and fear;
Tyrants rushed in, and did divide the spoil.
This was the shadow of the truth I saw.

THE EARTH. I felt thy torture, Son, with such mixed joy
As pain and Virtue give.—To cheer thy state
I bid ascend those subtle and fair spirits
Whose homes are the dim caves of human thought
And who inhabit, as birds wing the wind,
Its world-surrounding ether;[8] they behold
Beyond that twilight realm, as in a glass,
The future—may they speak comfort to thee!

Robert Wedderburn (1762–1834?), 'The Desponding Negro', 'The Negro Boy Sold for a Watch', in *The Axe Laid to the Root no. 2* (1817)

In London in 1824 Wedderburn published an autobiographical pamphlet, *The Horrors of Slavery*. Its remarkable title page shows, despite the ironic dedication to Wilberforce, just how unlike the work of respectable Clapham sect abolitionists this writing

---

[8] The clear upper air, a medium not matter, and assumed when Shelley was writing to fill all space and to emit electromagnetic waves.

was: *Dedicated to W. WILBERFORCE M. P. THE HORRORS OF SLAVERY EXEMPLIFIED IN The Life and History of the Rev. Robert Wedderburn, V.D.M. (Late a Prisoner in His Majesty's Gaol at Dorchester, for Conscience-Sake,) Son of the late JAMES WEDDERBURN, ESQ. Of Inveresk, Slave-Dealer, by one of his Slaves in the Island of Jamaica . . . IN WHICH IS INCLUDED . . . Remarks on, and Illustrations of the Treatment of the Blacks, AND A VIEW OF THEIR DEGRADED STATE, AND THE DISGUSTING LICENCIOUSNESS OF THE PLANTERS.* Under the guise of an abolition pamphlet, dedicated to the most internationally renowned abolition leader who ever lived, Wedderburn launches an attack on the Plantocracy, and his father in particular, in which the main theme is the sexual abuse of slaves.

Wedderburn tells how he was born in Jamaica, the child of a union between a slave woman belonging to Lady Douglas, and a Scottish planter, James Wedderburn, 'whom I am compelled to call by the name of father'. Wedderburn describes in detail the underhand manner in which his father obtained possession of his mother and then installed her in his house 'full of female slaves, all objects of his lusts; amongst whom he strutted like Solomon in his grand seraglio'. He then goes on to tell of the horrific abuse of his mother, and of his own destitute predicament, as his father refused at any point to acknowledge him. Brought up by his grandmother he eventually, after a spell as a sailor, made it to England as a penniless and self-educated immigrant. He initially supported himself as a tailor. Wedderburn spent the rest of his life mixing with, and contributing to, the ultra-radical underground. Like Equiano and Marrant (pp. 150–67) he was employed in the British navy for a while and like them underwent a violent conversion experience, but unlike them felt no desire to channel his religious feelings into any respectable avenue. To use Iain McCalman's wonderful term Wedderburn was and remained completely 'unrespectable' and in this sense he differs from all other black British authors of the 1760–1820 period. He joined the ultra-radical Spencean Philanthropists, and the details of his subversive activities in London only survive because of the extensive government reports filed at the Home Office by the spies, informants, and *agents provocateurs* who observed him. He was eventually imprisoned on a charge of blasphemous libel for two years.

Unlike the majority of white radicals Wedderburn was throughout his life passionate about the status of blacks and the effects of slavery. He saw reform in Britain and emancipation in Jamaica as of equal importance. *The Axe Laid to the Root* significantly carried the subtitle *A Fatal Blow to Oppressors, Being an Address to the Planters and Negroes of the Island of Jamaica.* The poems included in this volume strike a very different tone from anything else in this collection. 'The Desponding Negro' is in metrical terms very rough indeed. It is set out in the form of an ironic begging plea by a starving Negro boy on a British street. It talks of the destitution, loneliness, and isolation of the poor black in Britain, culturally suspended between Britain and the Caribbean. Its focus on the horror of migrant consciousness puts it closer to Jimmy Cliff's desolate and beautiful 'Many Rivers to Cross' than the complacent emotionalism of white abolition poems on a similar theme (see pp. 266–70). 'The Negro Boy Sold for a Watch' is technically a far tighter production. The poem is clever in the way in which it suspends the racial character of the speaker. The narrator tells us that they have taken a black child from his parents, and sold him for a watch. We cannot tell, however, whether it is a black African slave trader or a white European who is talking.

The Desponding Negro

On Afric's wide plains where the lion now roaring,
When freedom stalks forth the vast desert exploring,
I was dragg'd from my hut and enchain'd as a slave,
In a dark floating dungeon upon the salt wave.

CHORUS

Spare a half-penny, spare a half penny,
O spare a half-penny to a poor Negro boy.

Toss'd on the wide main, I all wildly despairing
Burst my chains, rush'd on deck with my eye balls wide, glaring,
When the light'ning's dread blast, struck the inlets of day,
And its glorious bright beam sent for ever away.

Spare, etc.

The despoiler of man his prospect thus losing
Of gain by my sale, not a blind bargain chusing,
As my value compar'd with my keeping was light,
Had me dash'd overboard in the dead of the night.

Spare, etc.

And, but for a bark, to Britannia's coast bound then,
All my cares by that plunge in the deep had been drown'd then,
But by moonlight deferred was dash'd from the wave,
And reluctantly robb'd of a watery grave.

Spare, &c.

How disastrous my fate, freedom's ground though I tread now,
Torn from home, wife and children, I wander for bread now,
While seas roll between us which ne'er can be cross'd,
And hope's distant glimmering in darkness is lost.

Spare, &c.

The Negro Boy Sold for a Watch

When thirst of gold enslaves the mind,
　And selfish views alone bear sway,
Man turns a savage to his kind,
　　And blood and rapine mark the way,
　　　Alas! for this poor simple toy,
　　　I sold the weeping negro boy.

His father's hope, his mother' pride,
　Tho' black, yet comely to their view,
I tore him helpless from their side,
　　I gave him to a ruffian crew,
　　　To fiends that Afric's coast annoy,
　　　I sold the weeping negro boy.

In isles that deck the western waves,
　The unhappy youth was doom'd to dwell,
A poor forlorn insulted slave.
　　A beast that Christians buy and sell,
　　　And yet for this same simple toy,
　　　I sold the weeping negro boy.

May he who walks upon the wind,
　Whose voice in thunder's heard on high,
Who doth the raging tempest bind,
　　And wings the lightening thro' the sky,
　　　Forgive the wretch, who, for a toy,
　　　Could sell the guiltless negro boy.

Alfred, Lord Tennyson (1809–82), *Anacaona* (1828)

Tennyson (1809–92), who remains *the* embodiment of the poetical spirit of Victorian Britain, is not customarily thought of as a poet confronting imperial themes or the history of slavery. In fact he wrote several poems addressing these issues of which the late *Columbus* is the most extended. *Anacaona* is very early, and shows him ingeniously recasting history as imperial mythology with a heavy anti-Hispanic bias: the poem develops out of the tropes of abolition poetry dealing with the natives of Hispaniola. Samuel Whitchurch, in his 1804 epic poem *Hispaniola*, had already used the San Domingue rebellion to set up a bloody assault not only on Bonaparte, but on Spanish colonialism as well. The first third of the poem describes Spanish atrocities against the native Indians. The tricking and murder of the Indian princess Anacaona is a central episode (see pp. 171–5). The spirit of the murdered princess curses all future colonial invaders. Tennyson, however, takes a far more oblique approach to the princess's story.

Tennyson's *Anacaona* was an unpublished poem of 1828, which Tennyson was obdurate about not putting into print. In 1837 the publisher Milnes tried to get him to publish the poem in *The Tribute*, a request which elicited a letter which shows Tennyson to have had, to put it mildly, a light-hearted and less than committed approach to the plight of his subject: 'See now whether I am not doing my best for you, and whether you had any occasion to threaten me with that black b— Anacaona and her cocoa-shadowed *coves* of niggers—I cannot have her strolling about the land in this way—it is neither good for her reputation or for mine.'

Anacaona

A dark Indian maiden,
   Warbling in the bloomed liana,[1]
Stepping lightly flower-laden,
   By the crimson-eyed anana,[2]
Wantoning in orange groves
   Naked, and dark limbed, and gay,
Bathing in the slumbrous coves,
In the cocoa-shadowed coves,
   Of sunbright Xaraguay,[3]
Who was so happy as Anacaona,
   The Beauty of Espagnola,
   The golden flower of Hayti?

All her loving childhood
   Breezes from the palm and canna[4]
Fanned this queen of the green wildwood,
   Lady of the green Savannah:
All day long with laughing eyes,
   Dancing by a palmy bay,
In the wooded paradise,
The cedar-wooded paradise,
   Of still Xaraguay:
None were so happy as Anacaona,
   The beauty of Espagnola,
   The golden flower of Hayti!

---

[1] A climbing woody plant festooning tropical forests.   [2] Pineapple tree.
[3] A native province of Hayti, ruled by Anacaona.   [4] Cotton grass.

In the purple island,
    Crowned with garlands of cinchona,[5]
Lady over wood and highland,
    The Indian queen, Anacaona,
Dancing on the blossomy plain
    To a woodland melody:
Playing with the scarlet crane,
    Beneath the papao tree!
Happy, happy was Anacaona,
    The beauty of Espagnola,
The golden flower of Hayti!

Many an emerald flyer
    Through the snow-white thicket flitting
Glanced, and birds plume-flecked with fire
    In the lustrous woodland sitting
Looked with bright eyes across
    The glooming ebony tree:
Only came the Albatross
The shadow of the Albatross
    Floating down the sea.
Happy, happy, was Anacaona,
    The beauty of Espagnola,
    The golden flower of Hayti!

The white man's white sail, bringing
    To happy Hayti the new-comer,
Over the dark sea-marge springing,
    Floated in the silent summer:
Then she brought the guava fruit,
    With her maidens to the bay:
She gave them the yuccaroot,[6]
Maizebread and the yuccaroot,
    Of sweet Xaraguay:
Happy, happy Anacaona,
    The beauty of Espagnola,
    The golden flower of Hayti!

Naked, without fear, moving
    To her Areyto's mellow ditty,

[5] Type of tropical tree from the bark of which quinine is obtained.   [6] Cassava.

Waving a palm branch, wondering, loving,
    Carolling 'Happy, happy Hayti!'
She gave the white men welcome all,
    With her damsels by the bay;
For they were fair-faced and tall,
They were more fair-faced and tall,
    Than the men of Xaraguay,
And they smiled on Anacaona,
    The beauty of Espagnola,
The golden flower of Hayti!

Following her wild carol
    She led them down the pleasant places,
For they were kingly in apparel,
    Loftily stepping with fair faces.
But never more upon the shore
    Dancing at the break of day,
In the deep wood no more,—
By the deep sea no more,—
    No more in Xaraguay
Wandered happy Anacaona,
    The beauty of Espagnola,
    The golden flower of Hayti!

Thomas Pringle (1789–1834), 'The Forester of the Neutral Ground', in *The Bow in the Cloud; or, The Negro's Memorial: A Collection of Original Contributions in Prose and Verse Illustrative of the Evils of Slavery and Commemorative of its Abolition in the British Colonies* (1834)

Pringle was a Scot, educated at Edinburgh University; he became a friend of Walter Scott. Despite knowing literary figures in Edinburgh he had little money and decided to emigrate as a government-sponsored settler to South Africa in 1820. After a couple of years attempting to establish a settlement he moved to the Cape and became librarian in the public library in Cape Town. He became involved in local politics and was particularly interested in the South African slave trade. His essays published on the subject in British journals brought him to the attention of leading abolitionists Zachary Macaulay and Sir Thomas Fowell Buxton. He was invited to become secretary of the Anti-Slavery Society and came back to Britain to take the job in 1827. For the next five years he was instrumental in overseeing the propaganda drive leading up to the final emancipation of slaves in the British colonies. His *African Sketches* was published in 1834 and was very well received. Coleridge considered 'Afar in the Desert' one of the three most perfect lyrics in English. Several of the poems dealt with themes related to African slavery. 'The Forester of the Neutral Ground' is unusual in dealing with racism within South Africa, and in criticizing the Boer's practices of slavery.

The Forester of the Neutral Ground

We met in the midst of the Neutral Ground,
'Mong the hills where the buffalo's haunts are found;
And we joined in the chase of the noble game,
Nor asked each other of nation or name.

The buffalo bull wheeled suddenly round,
When first from my rifle he felt a wound;
And before I could gain the Umtoka's bank,
His horns were tearing my courser's flank.

That instant a ball whizzed past my ear,
Which smote the beast in his fierce career;
And the turf was drenched with his purple gore,
As he fell at my feet with a bellowing roar.

The stranger came galloping up to my side,
And greeted me with a bold huntsman's pride;
Full blithely we feasted beneath a tree;—
Then out spoke the forester, Arend Plessie.

"Stranger! We now are true comrades sworn;
Come pledge me thy hand while we quaff the horn;
Thou'rt an Englishman good, and thy heart is free,
And 'tis therefore I'll tell my story to thee.

"A Heemraad of Camdeboo was my sire;
He had flocks and herds to his heart's desire,
And bondmen and maidens to run at his call,
And seven stout sons to be heirs of all.

"When we had grown up to man's estate,
Our father bade each of us choose a mate,

Of Fatherland blood, from the *black* taint free,
As became a Dutch burgher's of proud degree.

"My brothers they rode to the Bovenland,
And each came with a fair bride back in his hand;
But *I* brought the handsomest bride of them all—
Brown Dinah, the bondmaid who sat in our hall.

"My father's displeasure was stern and still;
My brothers flamed forth like a fire on a hill;
And they said that my spirit was mean and base,
To lower myself to the African race.

"I bade them rejoice in their herds and flocks,
And their pale faced spouses with flaxen locks;
While I claimed for my share, as the youngest son,
Brown Dinah alone with my horse and gun.

"My father looked black as a thunder-cloud,
My brothers reviled me and railed aloud,
And their young wives laughed with disdainful pride,
While Dinah in terror clung close to my side.

"Her ebon eyelashes were moistened with tears,
As she shrunk abashed from their venomous jeers;
But I bade her look up like a Burgher's wife—
Next day to be *mine* if God granted life.

"At dawn brother Reolof came galloping home
From the pastures—his courser all covered with foam;
''Tis the Bushmen!' he shouted; 'haste, friends, to the spoor!
Bold Arend! Come help with your long-barrelled *roer*.'[1]

"Far o'er Bruintjes-hoogtè we followed—in vain:
At length surly Reolof cried, 'Slacken your rein;
We have quite lost the track.' —Hans replied with a smile.—
Then my dark-boding spirit suspected their guile.

"I flew to our father's. Brown Dinah was sold!
And they laughed at my rage as they counted the gold.
But I leaped on my horse, with my gun in my hand,
And sought my lost love in the far Bovenland.

---

[1] A long-barrelled rifle used by the South African Boers for big game hunting.

"I found her; I bore her from Gautritz' fair glen,
Through lone Zitzikamma, by forest and fen
To these mountains at last like wild-pigeons we flew
Far, far from the cold hearts of proud Camdebóo.

"I've reared our rude shieling[2] by Gola's green wood,
Where the chase of the deer yields me pastime and food:
With my Dinah and children I dwell here alone,
Without other comrades—and wishing for none.

"I fear not the Bushman from Winterberg's fell,
Nor dread I the Caffer from Kat-Riever's dell:
By justice and kindness I've conquered them both,
And the sons of the desert have pledged me their troth.

"I fear not the leopard that lurks in the wood,
The lion I dread not, though raging for blood:
My hand it is steady—my aim it is sure—
And the boldest must bend to my long-barrelled *roer*.

"The elephant's buff-coat my bullet can pierce;
And the giant rhinoceros, headlong and fierce,
Gnu, eland, and buffalo furnish my board,
When I feast my allies like an African lord.

And thus from my kindred and colour exiled,
I live like old Ismael,[3] Lord of the Wild—
And follow the chase with my hounds and my gun;
Nor ever regret the bold course I have run.

"But sometimes there sinks on my spirit a dread
Of what may befall when the turf's on my head;
I fear for poor Dinah—for brown Rodomond
And dimple-faced Karel, the sons of the *bond*.

"Then tell me, dear stranger, from England the free
What good tidings brings't thou for Arend Plessie?
Shall the Edict of Mercy be sent forth at last,
To break the harsh fetters of Colour and Caste?"

---

2 Shepherd's primitive hut.
3 Ismael (or Ishmael), an Old Testament Israelite, the son of Abraham by Hagar, the Egyptian hand-maid of his wife Sarah. He is considered the progenitor of the Arab peoples. Muhammad claimed that he was descended from Ishmael.

Josiah Conder (1789–1855), 'The Last Night of Slavery' (written 1834, published 1837)

Conder was a bookseller, publisher, journalist, and author. In the 1830s he worked for the Anti-Slavery Society who commissioned him to write a long pamphlet arguing for the superiority of wage labour over slavery in the Caribbean. The resultant *Wages or the Whip* was mass produced at the recommendation of Anti-Slavery leaders Thomas Babington Macaulay and Thomas Fowell Buxton, and distributed nationally. With the coming of emancipation Conder clearly felt he had earned the right to create a hymn of triumph for the slaves. This poem is typical of the mass of effusive writings which the emancipation moment generated in Britain. The imagined slave who chants this anthem is ecstatic; slavery simply disappears in a blaze of light and Christianity. Of course what was actually happening in the British slave colonies was rather different. By the time Conder published his triumphant vision of the end of slavery the Anti-Slavery Society had very serious anxieties about black exploitation. Eyewitness accounts were making it increasingly plain that the so-called 'apprentice system', brought in to smooth over the transition to a free market, was not working. Former slave owners had nothing to lose by working their ex-slaves to death in the short time that they maintained power over them. The following passage is a minute of 23 June 1835, from the 'Minutes of the Committee of the Anti-Slavery Society of Great Britain', and summarized the situation in bleak terms:

> after an attentive examination of the Acts passed by the Jamaica Legislature to carry into effect the Imperial Act for the abolition of Colonial Slavery it is the opinion of the Committee that many of their provisions are calculated and intended to defeat the benevolent intentions of the Mother Country. That especially the frequent use of the whip, for the punishment of offences of a trifling character, and even for preferring complaints of ill-treatment, the severity with which that punishment is allowed to be inflicted extending to 39 lashes even for the uncertain offence of 'insolence', the establishment of penal gangs, the arbitrary appropriation of the Negro's time, the rigorous restraints on his personal freedom during that time and the unsatisfactory and vague protection afforded against cruelty and injustice on the part of the Master lead to the conclusion, that it has been the desire of the Legislature of Jamaica, to retain under the system of Apprenticeship, as much of the character of slavery as is possible.

So much for Conder's last night of slavery. But by the time his happy poem was published the British public was heartily sick of the subject of slavery. Conder's readers were only too eager to believe the self-aggrandizing fictions which the official celebrants of British emancipation laid over the memory of their nation's involvement in the slavery holocaust.

The Last Night of Slavery

Let the floods clap their hands!
Let the mountains rejoice!
From our own native sands
Breathes the jubilant voice:
The sun that now sets on thy waves, Caribbee!
Shall gild with his rising *the Isles of the Free.*

Let the islands be glad,
For their King in his might,
Who his glory has clad,
With a garment of light,
In the waters the beams of his chambers hath laid,
And in the great waters his pathway has made.

No more shall the deep
Lend its awe-stricken waves
In their caverns to steep
Its wild burden of slaves:
The Lord sitteth King;—sitteth King on the flood.
He heard, and hath answered the voice of their blood.

Oh, what of the night?
Doth the Crucifix bend?
When shall glimmer the light
This gross darkness to end?
Deep in the Pacific has sunk the last gleam
That o'er the dark horrors of bondage might stream.

Brief, brief is the night
Of the tropical zone,
Ere a balance of light
Shall the darkness atone;
And thus for black ages may brightness return,
Nor fail till the dawn of eternity burn.

The sunlight must glance
On OUR freedom-girt shore,
Ere its splendours advance
Their blest ransom to pour.
Our rivers and vales must reflect the *first* glow,
That captives shall, freed from captivity, know.

Now fades on our sphere
The last vigilant star:
From moorland and mere
Rolls the mist-cloud afar;
And springs from the Levant a life-teeming ray,
To chase deeper shadows than midnight's away.

Dispel the blue haze,
Golden fountain of morn!
With meridian blaze
The wide ocean adorn!
The sunlight has touched thy glad shores, Caribbee!
And day *now* illumines *the Isles of the Free!*

Three Chartist poems: 'The Slaves' Address to British Females', *Northern Star and General Leeds Advertiser* (17 Feb. 1838); Dr Arbington, 'The Land of Freedom', *Chartist Circular* (27 June 1840); 'The Black and the White Slave', *Chartist Circular* (7 June 1840)

Historians of British radicalism argued in the 1960s that abolition, from its first rise to attention as a mass movement in 1788, and then on through the first half of the nineteenth century, exerted a decided influence on the development of popular radicalism in Britain. This view has now been heavily qualified to be replaced by a lot of evidence that radicals, and Chartists in particular, became increasingly suspicious of organized abolitionism in the first three decades of the nineteenth century. Popular radical demagogues and journalists including Henry Hunt and Henry Hetherington, as well as Cobbett, singled out the anti-slavery movement, and Wilberforce in particular, because of its increasing connection with emergent bourgeois political economy, and because of its strong links with a type of establishment Evangelicalism which the radicals had come to associate with support for the political repression of the poor. There was particular fury over the way in which prominent abolitionists, with Lord Brougham at their head, contributed to, and supported, the Poor Law. Chartists developed this anti-black inheritance with vigour, and even got to the stage of regarding the violent disruption of anti-slavery meetings as an act of radical solidarity and class consciousness.

As the nineteenth century progressed blacks were increasingly figured in terms of a potentially dangerous diversion. They came to represent an emotional vacuum sucking attention away from the exploitation of the new factory labour forces in big British cities. White suffering upon the killing floors of the British factories increasingly held centre stage. This expanding empathetic space not only equalized, but finally obliterated any obligation to think through the inheritance of Atlantic slavery for the white working man or woman. Recent work by race and post-colonial theorists points up the frequent parallels in Victorian literatures between European industrial pauper masses (and particularly factory child labour) and slaves or colonized blacks. Yet what is not emphasized, particularly within the context of working-class race dialectic, is that the slave and the factory worker do not occupy a common rhetorical ground. Popular radical race theorists, with Cobbett at their head, put forward arguments which stressed an absolute difference between white labour in Britain and black labour in the slave colonies. These arguments were founded in race(ist) distinction, rather than similarity, and this difference becomes most pronounced in the representation of violence.

The slave, and after 1834 ex-slave, populations are shown as idle, fallen, passive, and debased. Their suffering, when it is presented, exists in a different physical sphere from that of the white labourer. The mass success of abolition in its heyday in the late 1780s as a focus for the sentimental projection of the philanthropic public had demonstrated a phenomenal national capacity for empathy with an abstract black suffering. For British radicals the lesson to be learned was simple: bring that sympathy home and change its colour. Yet this domestication of pity was to be achieved at the price of objectifying the black slave and ex-slave populations. Increasingly the black slave is set up beside, but cannot compete with, the suffering labour force of the British factories. Chartist literatures are shot through with sentimentally fraught illustrations of this statement. 'The Black and the White Slave' is a poem which encapsulates, in extreme form, an argument whereby the black male slave exists as a privileged backdrop for the depiction of the suffering of the white freeborn Briton, or here, freeborn white girl. The initial move is an orthodox Cobbettian levelling antithesis; the black slave is in heaven and the white English slave in hell: a 'negro sky . . . lit with the hues of Heaven', and a 'spinner's room' which is 'a hell of gloom'. The poem continues in a familiar vein, while the black man, who is built for the ordeal, is beaten crisply with a whip that 'cracks', the sound that the 'strap' makes on infant white female flesh is peculiarly muffled and is a 'sickening sound'. The inference is clear: the pistol shot of the cow hide on a burly black man is almost attractive; but within the divisive dynamic of this verse there is not space for the sound of the whip on the absent bodies of black women and children. The central stimulant behind this verse is one of paranoid competition—the desperate desire to prove that *we* (ultimately in the form of the little white girl) suffered more than *them*.

The same basic argument is advanced in the humorous if bitter little satire 'The Land of Freedom'. Although composed in 1840, some six years after emancipation, this poem is set back in a hypothetical slave age Caribbean. The abstracted black slave 'Mohab' is presented according to well-established comparative stereotypes as 'light-hearted and glad, though a slave'. He manages to get to Britain to see the land of liberty only to find that sailors are impressed and soldiers are tortured worse than the slaves. A final sight of the extremities of suffering in an English poorhouse convinces the black that he is far better off heading home to benevolent Caribbean slavery. Again this is primarily a poem about white suffering in England; yet the claims for white suffering cannot be made except at the expense of the black slave. Chartist poetry which takes in Caribbean slavery exhibits an almost pathological compulsion to belittle the inherited traumatic history of Atlantic slavery. It is as if white pain can only be real when it is proved that the traumatic histories of Atlantic slavery are ridiculous.

The Slaves' Address to British Females

Natives of a land of glory
Daughters of the good and brave,
Hear the injured Negroes' story,
Hear and help the fetter'd Slave!

Think how nought but death can sever
 Your lov'd children from your hold.
  Still alive, but lost for ever,
 Ours are parted, bought and sold!

Seize, O seize, the favouring season,
 Scorning censure or applause;
Justice, Truth, Religion, Reason,
 Are our leaders in our cause.

Follow, faithful, firm, confiding
Spread our wrongs from shore to shore;
 Mercy's God your efforts guiding
 Slavery shall be known no more.

The Land of Freedom

Beneath Afric's hot sun, Mohab toil'd thro' the day,
 Light-hearted and glad, though a slave;
For Mohab could eat—to his God he could pray;
And at night, on his pallet, he grateful would say,
 He liv'd by the labour he gave.

But the white man had told him that there was a shore
 Where the poor and the stranger were free—
Where the stern hand of justice indignantly tore
Every fetter which man for his fellow-man bore:
 Mohab wished that that land he might see.

Soon a ship bound for Britain his native home passed,
    In whose captain a patron he found;
From his master he fled—the trim vessel sail'd fast,
And Mohab beheld England's white cliffs at last,
    And he sprung a free man—on free ground.

"What large vessels," he ask'd of his patron, "are those,"
    They fill me with feelings of wonder?"
"They are war-ships, by which we for ever oppose
All attempts of invaders; and liberty's foes
    Full well know the force of their thunder."

"And what's that dark vessel, unlike all the rest?"
    He inquired, and was told 'twas "The Tender,"
And that, when the war vessels for men were distress'd,
On board that dark hulk many persons were press'd,
    Whom their country compell'd to defend her.

"But come to the barracks," the Englishman cried,
    For our army you yet have to see:
A brave army is ever a nation's best pride,
And our soldier's in battle have often been tried,
    And are worthy the land of the free!"

And they saw a deserter dragg'd forth from his cell,
    And by force to the triangles bound,
And they heard the loud shriek, and the heart-thrilling yell
'Till the mangled and shivering sufferer fell
    Senseless, covered with blood, on the ground.

Then the African said, "That's like slavery's thong,"
    And the Briton replied, "I confess
There are some little errors our blessings among;
But we have a relief from oppression and wrong
    In the voice of our free British Press."

"I'll examine your journals," the African thought,
    And he found, when enabled to read 'em,
That the rich man by bribes venal journalists bought,
And by libel indictments vile ministers sought
    To crush the true struggles for freedom.

And he saw a huge poor-house, By Liberals plann'd,
    And a man with sunk eyes and parch'd tongue,

On whom famine had laid her cold withering hand;
A poor starving wretch in a plentiful land,
   But his kindred around him still clung!

They from him his wife and his little ones tore,
   And to separate dungeons conveyed:
Mohab heard him in accents most piteous implore
For a morsel of bread; he was spurn'd from the door,
   With hunger's sharp pangs unallay'd.

"Then, farewell!" Mohab cried, "to the land praised so high
   As the home of wealth, freedom, and bravery:
Tho' the truth of your boasting I dare not deny,
Yet I thank the great God of my fathers that I
   Am a child of the regions of slavery!"

The Black and the White Slave

I had a dream of slavery,
   A vision of the night;
And methought I saw, on either hand,
   The victims—black and white.

I glanced my eye to the negro sky,
   And I looked to the spinner's room;
And one was lit with the hues of Heaven,
   And one was a hell of gloom.

There were fruitful, bright, and shining fields,
   and the sun was all above,
And there was something in the air
   That even a slave might love.

And there was the quick incessant whirl
   Of wheels revolving fast,
And there was the rank and moted air—
   Like a siroc's[1] deadly blast.

---

[1] An abbreviated form of sirocco, a hot, dry, gusty, and dusty wind blowing from North Africa across southern Italy. It stands generically for any fierce, dry wind.

Then the negro's shell and the factory bell
    For brief relief rang out—
Some ran to the shade where the blue stream played,
    Some raised the revel shout.

But as for yon poor sickly child,
    When her mid day was come,
She still abode in that region wild,
    She could not reach her home.

There was no gladdening stream for her,
    Albeit her tender years;
The stream that strayed, in that horrid shade,
    Was the factory infant's tears.

Aye! tears direct from the throbbing heart—
    Hot drops from burning brain—
Yet no relief from that shower of grief—
    Her tyrant came again.

Then I heard the crack of the sounding whip
    Ring sharply through the air;
But the slave was a huge and hardy man,
    That well the lash might bear.

The next was the dull and sickening sound
    Of the "strap" in that vale of tears;
I saw no man, save the wretch who struck
    The child of tender years.

He smote the infant o'er the face,
    The neck, the trembling breast;
And the words that fell from his brutal tongue
    But made her the more distressed.

And still as the blood came creeping down
    Towards the crime stained floor,
Still on was urged that little slave,
    Till her hateful task was o'er.

While the "man" slave sat at his cottage door,
    Or lay in the plaintain shade,
That worn-out child crept sadly home,
    Where her bed of chaff was laid,

Yet aye in her sleep the infant hears
  That every chaunting chime,
And she starts from her healthless rest and calls
  "Oh! Mother! is it time?"

Then I knelt me down, in that vision wild,
  And raised my hands to God:
I breathed a prayer for the man and child
  Who groan 'neath the tasker's rod.

Great God! like thy pure and balmy sir,
  Let all thou hast made be free,
And blot from thy fair and beauteous world
  The ban of slavery.

Robert Browning [RB] (1812–89), 'The Runaway Slave', from *Sordello* (1840); 'Slave Market', from *Cleon* (1855); 'Caliban upon Setebos; or, Natural Theology in the Island', in *Dramatis Personae* (1864)

Browning shares with Blake and Shelley the capacity to come at slavery in indirect and unsettling ways. Unlike his wife (pp. 353–68), a far more obviously politically engaged artist, he wrote no straightforward poetry about Atlantic slavery. Yet he produced 'Caliban upon Setebos', a poem which is the most terrifying meditation upon the psychological effects of enslavement which the nineteenth century was to throw up. The long metaphoric vignette unpacking the curious state of mind of the runaway slave in *Sordello*, and the intriguing presentation of the 'one white she-slave' standing amidst the chequer-work of black and white slaves in *Cleon*, are both fragments which bear testament to RB's long-standing and wide-ranging interest in the psychology of the enslaved. The central treatment of this theme in his work is, however, 'Caliban'.

   This poem is RB's only direct reinterpretation of a Shakespearian character through dramatic monologue. Caliban, the strangely suspended character he chose for this experiment, has emerged in the twentieth century as the most spectacularly contested canonic hot spot within post-colonial and slavery studies. Caliban has spawned a series of theatrical, poetic, dramatic, theoretical, and artistic adaptations which have been produced across North and South America, Africa, the Caribbean, and Europe. It can be argued that it is not in the work of European literary theory but in the work of creative artists and poets, including George Lamming, Robert Marquez, and Taban lo Liyong, who are working in Latin America, the Caribbean, and Africa, that is, within the slave

Diaspora, that the most exciting reinterpretations of Shakespeare's engagement with colonialism have re-emerged. In other words post-colonial theory is being practised on Caliban in artistic contexts within cultures where the inheritance of colonialism, the trauma of colonialism, the paradoxes of post-colonial identity, and the continuing damage of a colonialist inheritance have a constant, immediate, and ungainsayable impact on the ways in which these cultures construct or reconstruct Western literature.

Yet 'Caliban upon Setebos' is a constant reminder that new-historicist and post-colonial interpretations of Caliban and of *The Tempest* are not the first interpretations to foreground the complicated operations of colonialist and slave-power thought in the context of the play. 'Caliban upon Setebos' is arguably the most extreme piece of Caliban criticism ever written. RB imagines an intoxicated Caliban lying down and letting his mind play around with ideas concerning his origin and his present position. RB's Caliban presents a consciousness which in its colonized state can only envisage liberty in terms of a series of parodies of the tyranny to which Prospero has subjected it. In one horrific passage Caliban attempts to imagine what motivates his master, Prospero. Caliban is shown to have tried to understand his master and the operations of colonial power by trying to reproduce them in terms of his abuse of the natural creatures on the island which he can dominate.

There are necessary limits to the robust and sensually sadistic consciousness which RB has created. He has extracted and expanded on only a small part of Shakespeare's Caliban, but it is the part most damaged by colonialism, the part which has been closed down and perverted by colonialism, the part which can only see freedom as the desire to re-enact the behaviour of its master. It also creates a new imaginative history for the character which reflects on Victorian imperialist paradigms for expansion and control. In the end RB's interpretation, as with all Shakespearian interpretation, closes the original Caliban down, and in the imaginative brutality he presents shuts out one of the most disturbing aspects of Shakespeare's original—his extraordinarily gorgeous lyric gifts with language, when he comes to talk of his relationship with his own island.

from *Sordello* (IV. 864–85)[1]

As, shall I say, some Ethiop, past pursuit
Of all enslavers, dips a shackled foot
Burnt to the blood, into the drowsy black
Enormous watercourse which guides him back

---

[1] This long poem is set in early 13th-century Italy in the context of the struggles between the Guelphs and the Ghibellines. Sordello is a troubadour poet torn between his artistic calling and his political responsibilities. The poem was notorious for its obscurity: Tennyson is reported to have stated that on reading it he understood only the first and last lines, stating that Sordello's tale would be told, and had been told, and that these two lines were lies.

To his own tribe again, where he is king;
And laughs because he guesses, numbering
The yellower poison-wattles on the pouch
Of the first lizard wrested from its couch
Under the slime (whose skin, the while, he strips
To cure his nostril with, and festered lips,
And eyeballs bloodshot through the desert blast)
That he has reached its boundary, at last
May breathe;—thinks o'er enchantments of the South
Sovereign to plague his enemies, their mouth
Eyes, nails, and hair; but, these enchantments tried
In fancy, puts them soberly aside
For truth, projects a cool return with friends,
The likelihood of winning mere amends
Ere long; thinks that, takes comfort silently,
Then, from the river's brink, his wrongs and he,
Hugging revenge close to their hearts, are soon
Off-striding for the Mountains of the Moon.

from *Cleon*[1] (ll. 7–18)

The master of thy galley still unlades
Gift after gift; they block my court at last
And pile themselves along its portico
Royal with sunset like a thought of thee:
And one white she-slave from the group dispersed
Of black and white slaves (like the chequer-work
Pavement, at once my nation's work and gift
Now covered with this settle-down of doves),
One lyric woman, in her crocus vest
Woven of sea-wools, with her two white hands
Commends to me the strainer and the cup
Thy lip hath bettered ere it blesses mine.

[1] Cleon was an Athenian politician. He introduced a new style of demagoguery, winning support through charismatic speeches to the courts and the Assembly. He was renowned for ruthless policies relating to Athenian expansion and the suppression of revolts.

Caliban upon Setebos;[1] or, Natural Theology[2] in the Island

"Thou thoughtest that I was altogether such a one as thyself."

['Will sprawl, now that the heat of day is best,
Flat on his belly in the pit's much mire,
With elbows wide, fists clenched to prop his chin.
And, while he kicks both feet in the cool slush,
And feels about his spine small eft-things course,
Run in and out each arm, and make him laugh:
And while above his head a pompion-plant,
Coating the cave-top as a brow its eye,
Creeps down to touch and tickle hair and beard,
And now a flower drops with a bee inside,
And now a fruit to snap at, catch and crunch,—
He looks out o'er yon sea which sunbeams cross
And recross till they weave a spider-web
(Meshes of fire, some great fish breaks at times)
And talks to his own self, howc'er he please,
Touching that other, whom his dam called God.
Because to talk about Him, vexes—ha,
Could He but know! and time to vex is now,
When talk is safer than in winter-time.
Moreover Prosper and Miranda sleep
In confidence he drudges at their task,
And it is good to cheat the pair, and gibe,
Letting the rank tongue blossom into speech.]

Setebos, Setebos, and Setebos!
'Thinketh, He dwelleth i' the cold o' the moon.[3]

'Thinketh He made it, with the sun to match,
But not the stars; the stars came otherwise;
Only made clouds, winds, meteors, such as that:
Also this isle, what lives and grows thereon,
And snaky sea which rounds and ends the same.

---

[1] Setebos is the name of the god whom Caliban's mother Sycorax worshipped in *The Tempest*.
[2] The belief that knowledge of God can be achieved through exercise of the reason, not divine revelation.
[3] This line developed out of *The Tempest*, II. ii. 136–8, 'Caliban: Hast thou not dropped from heaven? Stefano: Out o'th'moon, I do assure thee. I was the man i'th' moon when time was.'

'Thinketh, it came of being ill at ease:
He hated that He cannot change His cold,
Nor cure its ache. 'Hath spied an icy fish
That longed to 'scape the rock-stream where she lived,
And thaw herself within the lukewarm brine
O' the lazy sea her stream thrusts far amid,
A crystal spike 'twixt two warm walls of wave;
Only, she ever sickened, found repulse
At the other kind of water, not her life,
(Green-dense and dim-delicious, bred o' the sun)
Flounced back from bliss she was not born to breathe,
And in her old bounds buried her despair,
Hating and loving warmth alike: so He.

'Thinketh, He made thereat the sun, this isle,
Trees and the fowls here, beast and creeping thing.
Yon otter, sleek-wet, black, lithe as a leech;
Yon auk, one fire-eye in a ball of foam,
That floats and feeds; a certain badger brown
He hath watched hunt with that slant white-wedge eye
By moonlight; and the pie with the long tongue
That pricks deep into oakwarts for a worm,
And says a plain word when she finds her prize,
But will not eat the ants; the ants themselves
That build a wall of seeds and settled stalks
About their hole—He made all these and more,
Made all we see, and us, in spite: how else?
He could not, Himself, make a second self
To be His mate; as well have made Himself:
He would not make what he mislikes or slights,
An eyesore to Him, or not worth His pains:
But did, in envy, listlessness or sport,
Make what Himself would fain, in a manner, be—
Weaker in most points, stronger in a few,
Worthy, and yet mere playthings all the while,
Things He admires and mocks too,—that is it.
Because, so brave, so better though they be.
It nothing skills if He begin to plague.
Look now, I melt a gourd-fruit into mash,
Add honeycomb and pods, I have perceived,
Which bite like finches when they bill and kiss,—

Then, when froth rises bladdery, drink up all,
Quick, quick, till maggots scamper through my brain;
Last, throw me on my back i' the seeded thyme,
And wanton, wishing I were born a bird.
Put case, unable to be what I wish,
I yet could make a live bird out of clay:
Would not I take clay, pinch my Caliban
Able to fly?—for, there, see, he hath wings,
And great comb like the hoopoe's to admire,
And there, a sting to do his foes offence,
There, and I will that he begin to live,
Fly to yon rock-top, nip me off the horns
Of grigs high up that make the merry din,
Saucy through their veined wings, and mind, me not.
In which feat, if his leg snapped, brittle clay,
And he lay stupid-like,—why, I should laugh;
And if he, spying me, should fall to weep,
Beseech me to be good, repair his wrong,
Bid his poor leg smart less or grow again,—
Well, as the chance were, this might take or else
Not take my fancy: I might hear his cry,
And give the mankin three sound legs for one,
Or pluck the other off, leave him like an egg,
And lessoned he was mine and merely clay.
Were this no pleasure, lying in the thyme,
Drinking the mash, with brain become alive,
Making and marring clay at will? So He.

'Thinketh, such shows nor right nor wrong in Him,
Nor kind, nor cruel: He is strong and Lord.
'Am strong myself compared to yonder crabs
That march now from the mountain to the sea;
'Let twenty pass, and stone the twenty-first,
Loving not, hating not, just choosing so.
'Say, the first straggler that boasts purple spots
Shall join the file, one pincer twisted off;
'Say, this bruised fellow shall receive a worm,
And two worms he whose nippers end in red;
As it likes me each time, I do: so He.

Well then, 'supposeth He is good i' the main,
Placable if His mind and ways were guessed,

But rougher than His handiwork, be sure!
Oh, He hath made things worthier than Himself,
And envieth that, so helped, such things do more
Than He who made them! What consoles but this?
That they, unless through Him, do nought at all,
And must submit: what other use in things?
'Hath cut a pipe of pithless elder-joint
That, blown through, gives exact the scream o' the jay
When from her wing you twitch the feathers blue:
Sound this, and little birds that hate the jay
Flock within stone's throw, glad their foe is hurt:
Put case such pipe could prattle and boast forsooth
"I catch the birds, I am the crafty thing,
"I make the cry my maker cannot make
"With his great round mouth; he must blow through mine!"
Would not I smash it with my foot? So He.

But wherefore rough, why cold and ill at ease?
Aha, that is a question! Ask, for that,
What knows,—the something over Setebos
That made Him, or He, may be, found and fought,
Worsted, drove off and did to nothing, perchance.
There may be something quiet o'er His head,
Out of His reach, that feels nor joy nor grief,
Since both derive from weakness in some way.
I joy because the quails come; would not joy
Could I bring quails here when I have a mind:
This Quiet, all it hath a mind to, doth.
'Esteemeth stars the outposts of its couch,
But never spends much thought nor care that way.
It may look up, work up,—the worse for those
It works on! 'Careth but for Setebos
The many-handed as a cuttle-fish,
Who, making Himself feared through what He does,
Looks up, first, and perceives he cannot soar
To what is quiet and hath happy life;
Next looks down here, and out of very spite
Makes this a bauble-world to ape yon real,
These good things to match those as hips do grapes.
'Tis solace making baubles, ay, and sport.
Himself peeped late, eyed Prosper at his books

Careless and lofty, lord now of the isle:
Vexed, 'stitched a book of broad leaves, arrow-shaped,
Wrote thereon, he knows what, prodigious words;
Has peeled a wand and called it by a name;
Weareth at whiles for an enchanter's robe
The eyed skin of a supple oncelot;
And hath an ounce[4] sleeker than youngling mole,
A four-legged serpent he makes cower and couch,
Now snarl, now hold its breath and mind his eye,
And saith she is Miranda and my wife:
'Keeps for his Ariel a tall pouch-bill crane
He bids go wade for fish and straight disgorge;
Also a sea-beast, lumpish, which he snared,
Blinded the eyes of, and brought somewhat tame,
And split its toe-webs, and now pens the drudge
In a hole o' the rock and calls him Caliban;
A bitter heart that bides its time and bites.
'Plays thus at being Prosper in a way,
Taketh his mirth with make-believes: so He.

His dam held that the Quiet made all things
Which Setebos vexed only: 'holds not so.
Who made them weak, meant weakness He might vex.
Had He meant other, while His hand was in,
Why not make horny eyes no thorn could prick,
Or plate my scalp with bone against the snow,
Or overscale my flesh 'neath joint and joint,
Like an orc's armour? Ay,—so spoil His sport!
He is the One now: only He doth all.
'Saith, He may like, perchance, what profits Him.
Ay, himself loves what does him good; but why?
'Gets good no otherwise. This blinded beast
Loves whoso places flesh-meat on his nose,
But, had he eyes, would want no help, but hate
Or love, just as it liked him: He hath eyes.
Also it pleaseth Setebos to work,
Use all His hands, and exercise much craft,
By no means for the love of what is worked.
'Tasteth, himself, no finer good i' the world

----

[4] Originally the lynx, but applied to any fairly large wild cat.

When all goes right, in this safe summer-time,
And he wants little, hungers, aches not much,
Than trying what to do with wit and strength.
'Falls to make something: 'piled yon pile of turfs,
And squared and stuck there squares of soft white chalk,
And, with a fish-tooth, scratched a moon on each,
And set up endwise certain spikes of tree,
And crowned the whole with a sloth's skull a-top,
Found dead i' the woods, too hard for one to kill.
No use at all i' the work, for work's sole sake;
'Shall some day knock it down again: so He.

'Saith He is terrible: watch His feats in proof!
One hurricane will spoil six good months' hope.
He hath a spite against me, that I know,
Just as He favours Prosper, who knows why?
So it is, all the same, as well I find.
'Wove wattles half the winter, fenced them firm
With stone and stake to stop she-tortoises
Crawling to lay their eggs here: well, one wave,
Feeling the foot of Him upon its neck,
Gaped as a snake does, lolled out its large tongue,
And licked the whole labour flat: so much for spite.
'Saw a ball flame down late (yonder it lies)
Where, half an hour before, I slept i' the shade:
Often they scatter sparkles: there is force!
Dug up a newt He may have envied once
And turned to stone, shut up inside a stone.
Please Him and hinder this?—What Prosper does?
Aha, if He would tell me how! Not He!
There is the sport: discover how or die!
All need not die, for of the things o' the isle
Some flee afar, some dive, some ran up trees;
Those at His mercy,—why, they please Him most
When . . when . . well, never try the same way twice!
Repeat what act has pleased, He may grow wroth.
You must not know His ways, and play Him off,
Sure of the issue. 'Doth the like himself:
Spareth a squirrel that it nothing fears
But steals the nut from underneath my thumb,
And when I threat, bites stoutly in defence:

Spareth an urchin[5] that contrariwise,
Curls up into a ball, pretending death
For fright at my approach: the two ways please.
But what would move my choler more than this,
That either creature counted on its life
To-morrow and next day and all days to come,
Saying, forsooth, in the inmost of its heart,
"Because he did so yesterday with me,
And otherwise with such another brute,
So must he do henceforth and always."— Ay?
Would teach the reasoning couple what "must" means!
Doth as he likes, or wherefore Lord? So He.

Conceiveth all things will continue thus,
And we shall have to live in fear of Him
So long as He lives, keeps His strength: no change,
If He have done His best, make no new world
To please Him more, so leave off watching this,—
If He surprise not even the Quiet's self
Some strange day,—or, suppose, grow into it
As grubs grow butterflies: else, here are we,
And there is He, and nowhere help at all.

'Believeth with the life, the pain shall stop.
His dam held different, that after death
He both plagued enemies and feasted friends:
Idly! He doth His worst in this our life,
Giving just respite lest we die through pain,
Saving last pain for worst,—with which, an end.
Meanwhile, the best way to escape His ire
Is, not to seem too happy. 'Sees, himself,
Yonder two flies, with purple films and pink,
Bask on the pompion-bell above: kills both.
'Sees two black painful beetles roll their ball
On head and tail as if to save their lives:
Moves them the stick away they strive to clear.

---

[5] A hedgehog. Browning's Caliban is especially generous in sparing this hedgehog in that the original
Caliban in Shakespeare's *Tempest* is tortured by Prospero using urchins: 'for this be sure . . . urchins |
Shall for that vast of night that they may work, | All exercise on thee: thou shall be pinch'd.'

Even so, 'would have Him misconceive, suppose
This Caliban strives hard and ails no less,
And always, above all else, envies Him;
Wherefore he mainly dances on dark nights,
Moans in the sun, gets under holes to laugh,
And never speaks his mind save housed as now:
Outside, 'groans, curses. If He caught me here,
O'erheard this speech, and asked "What chucklest at?"
'Would, to appease Him, cut a finger off,
Or of my three kid yearlings burn the best,
Or let the toothsome apples rot on tree,
Or push my tame beast for the orc to taste:
While myself lit a fire, and made a song
And sung it, "*What I hate, be consecrate*
To celebrate Thee and Thy state, no mate
For Thee; what see for envy in poor me?"
Hoping the while, since evils sometimes mend,
Warts rub away and sores are cured with slime,
That some strange day, will either the Quiet catch
And conquer Setebos, or likelier He
Decrepit may doze, doze, as good as die.

[What, what? A curtain o'er the world at once!
Crickets stop hissing; not a bird—or, yes,
There scuds His raven that has told Him all!
It was fool's play, this prattling! Ha! The wind
Shoulders the pillared dust, death's house o' the move,
And fast invading fires begin! White blaze—
A tree's head snaps—and there, there, there, there, there,
His thunder follows! Fool to gibe at Him!
Lo! 'Lieth flat and loveth Setebos!
'Maketh his teeth meet through his upper lip,
Will let those quails fly, will not eat this month
One little mess of whelks, so he may 'scape!]

S. Sanford, from 'Poem on Seeing Biard's Picture of a Slave Mart', in *The National Anti-Slavery Bazaar* (Boston, 1846)

Sanford's poem is a meditation on, and narrative extrapolation of, a painting by the French artist Auguste-François Biard. His *Scene on the African Coast* (Plate 5) had caused a sensation when it was hung in the Royal Academy summer exhibition in 1840. It had met with universal applause from the critics, many of whom had lambasted Turner's *Slavers Throwing Overboard the Dead and Dying*. Turner's painting hung near Biard's in the same show and dealt in a far more difficult manner with England's slave trade inheritance. The novelist and Negrophobe William Makepiece Thackeray wrote the most fulsome review of the Biard, in *Fraser's Magazine* for June 1840, and was drawn to its sadistic and pornographic elements. He began: 'The scene is laid upon the African coast. King Tom or King Boy has come with troops of slaves down the Quorra, and sits in the midst of his chiefs and mistresses (one a fair creature, not much darker than a copper tea-kettle) bargaining with a French dealer.' He was particularly excited by the detail of the torture of a naked young woman:

> Yonder is a poor woman kneeling before a Frenchman; her shoulder is fizzing under the hot iron with which he brands her; she is looking up shuddering, and wild, yet quite mild and patient: it breaks your heart to look at her. I never saw anything so exquisitely pathetic as that face. God bless you Monsieur Biard, for painting it! It stirs the heart more than a hundred thousand tracts, reports or sermons: it must convert every man who has seen it. You British government who have given twenty million to the freeing of this hapless people, give yet a couple of thousand more to the French painter and don't let his work go out of the country, now that it is here. Let it hang alongside the Hogarths in the National Gallery; it is as good as the best of them.

Like Thackeray Sanford is compulsively drawn to this detail and also to the figure just below, a young mother who is traumatized at the death of her infant. Sanford feels that she has an absolute right to fantasize the suffering of these figures, who are themselves the fantasies of a white French academic painter, packaging slave sale and the middle passage for a mid-nineteenth-century art-loving audience. Her poem constitutes part of the popular dissemination of Biard's image, and testifies to the vulgar emotionalism with which, by the middle of the nineteenth century, the British public fed off the memory of the middle passage. Biard's work was, as Thackeray demanded, bought for the nation and presented to the Anti-Slavery Society. It now hangs on the main staircase in Wilberforce House, Hull. The work was also mass produced in engraved and woodcut forms. When she wrote the poem in 1846 it is most likely that Sanford would have gained access to the image though a woodcut such as the one reproduced here.

5. Anon., after Auguste-François Biard, 'Scene on the African Coast' (wood engraving, [1840] 1860), in Richard Drake, *Revelations of a Slave Smuggler*.

from *Poem on Seeing Biard's Picture of a Slave Mart*

·   ·   ·   ·   ·   ·

Meanwhile, upon the heaving of the sea,
(With sails now faintly in the faint breeze flapping,
Now with loose fold the steady masts enwrapping,)
The anchored vessel vibrates languidly;
Hot comes the breath from Afric's burning sand.
As for her destined freight she waiteth patiently.

And with as calm a patience, on the strand
Tarry her masters yet, their traffic ending.
Appeased is now the tumult of contending;
And they are gathered all, a quiet band,
The sellers, and the buyers, and the bought;
Accomplished is the scheme with such deep wisdom planned.

The doubtful, bloody battle has been fought,
But not by them, the fair-skinned Christian strangers;
They stirred the strife, but wisely shunned its dangers;
And now the booty to their feet is brought;
To give some gold, some trinkets, is their part;
And then the prey is theirs, for which these shores they sought.

So many limbs, to labor and to smart;
So many sinews, strung for long-enduring,
And healthful organs, length of life ensuring;—
So many pulses of the human heart;—
So many brains, whose thoughts shall ne'er unfold;—
Such is the merchandise of that renowned mart.

Ay, scan your victim; leave no bone untold,
No muscle, ere your barter be completed;
Yet hath your subtlety itself defeated;
The *soul* lies crushed within its hollow mould.
Ye think, perchance to buy a man; but learn,
'Tis but a clay-machine, though rarely wrought, ye hold.

But scarce perhaps as yet; he still can spurn
Insult, half-understood; still, still rebelleth
Th' instinctive manhood in his breast that swelleth,
Which shall wane from him, never to return.

And thou, poor victim! dost thou writhe to feel
Into thy living flesh the branding-iron burn?

Thou must endure, when time *this* wound shall heal,
Within thy soul the cankered fetters crushing,
Till thy dark cheek forget the sense of blushing,
Thy woman's pulses quick to woe or weal,
Calmed by despair, beat sullenly and slow,
Unmoved by hope, or love, or pity's soft appeal.

But envy *her*, yon mother, bent in woe
O'er her slain child; how blest is her complaining;
When others moan beneath the whip-stroke's paining,
She 'll feel no smart, for joy that *he* lies low;
That his soft limbs and childish spirits gay,
Can meet no word unkind, no driver's scoring blow.

And now, ye Christian strangers, go your way;
Go, fitting traces of your presence leaving,
Ye, in the covenant of love believing;
Those whom their savage nature taught to slay,
You, proud instructors of humanity,
Have taught the subtler arts, to ensnare and to betray.

The vessel sailed:—but then a thrilling cry
Rang startlingly beneath the cloudless heaven,
In anguish not to mortal bosoms given;
So moans the forest in its agony,
When struggling wildly from its night-mare sleep
Beneath the ghastly hush of tempest-laden sky.

Back to their rest those woe-struck wanderers sweep;
But a deep voice o'ertook them: "Earth will purge
The foul stain from her! From the gloomy vision
Turn your pure gaze, until in deep contrition
We expiate the past! The good will urge
Their prayers and labors, till earth's utmost verge
With Love and Truth be girt, as with the booming surge."

Anon., *The Political Life of Cornelius Cuffey Esq. Patriot* (1848)

This anti-Chartist and anti-black satire ridicules one of the leading lights of Chartist demagoguery, William Cuffay. Cuffay was an artisan; he was also a mulatto of West Indian origin. Like Wedderburn (pp. 310–13) he emigrated to London and mixed in ultra-radical political circles, where he became a renowned political orator. He would probably have been flattered to find himself a big enough threat to be singled out within a full-blown parody of *The Rime of the Ancient Manner*.

Poor Coleridge: neither pro- nor anti-slavery propaganda treated him kindly. As if the parodic liberties which Southey took with the *Rime* in the late 1790s were not enough (pp. 219–22) Coleridge finds his masterpiece the formal vehicle of mid-century Negrophobe anti-radicalism. One of the repeated premisses of this poem is the idea that as a black from the colonies Cuffey has no business talking politics to English whites. Consequently Cuffey's political parameters are shown as out of place. He is presented as an ignorant megalomaniac who looks at political action in terms of slave revolt and whose ambitions are dictatorial: 'Cut your own canes! Dat done de vorld will be Cuffey's.' The poem describes Cuffey's disastrous attempts to address a mass Chartist rally, which end in flight from a police inspector and pelting from the crowd. He returns a broken man to 'her dat lubs him' and also returns to his job as a washerman, turning a mangle. This is self-contented Victorian middle-class racism in full-blown form. White Chartist leaders can be taken seriously, but a black immigrant talking the language of freedom is seen as of its essence a ridiculous phenomenon. Thomas Carlyle would have heartily approved.

The Political Life of Cornelius Cuffey Esq. Patriot

> This pretty lad will prove our country's bliss:
> His looks are full of peaceful majesty;
> His head by nature framed to wear a crown,
> His hand to wield a sceptre—and himself
> Likely, IN TIME, to bless a regal throne.
> Make much of him, my lords!—*Shakspere*.[1]

---

[1] Shakespeare, *3 Henry VI*, IV. vii. 70–5.

I

The Preparation

An ancient Washerman prepareth an oration on the rights of himself in the broadest point of view.

It is an ancient Washerman:
   And he scratcheth for a speech;
"By thy woolly pate and thy beer-shot eye,
   Now what is 't thou would'st teach?"[2]

His ancient wife inquireth the cause of his energy and thinketh of reasoning with him,

So spake unto that Washerman
   His ancient Washerwife,
His other dearer life in life;
And, but she feared to rouse a strife
Which nought save blood could quell,
She would have said: " 'T would be as well,
"Dear Cuff, if thou thy pike shouldst sell,
   And, making somewhat less uproar,
   Shouldst turn thy native mangle more!"

but is deterred by his terrible aspect—nathless she hazardeth a remark.

His brow was dusk: his voice was husk:
   His eyes were all aflame:
And his wool stood straight and at frightful rate
   Green blushes went and came:
He was a fearful thing to see,
   Leering, leering horribly!
At last forth spake that Washerman:
   "We all are Slaves!"—quoth she:
"La now, my Cuff, my nigger loon,
   "It's me am Slaves to thee."

The Washerman deserteth his wife and native mangle for the parliament in John St. assembled.

The Washerman right quickly ran
   Away from wife and Southwark,
And tow'rds John Street did flap his feet,
   For he longed to ply his mouth-work.

And after due encouragement expatiateth on the wrongs of himself.

Soon sprang he forth above the mass,
   Out of the crowd leap't he;
And he raised his wrist-
Bands and shook his fist,
And his lips grew pale,
And he seized the rail,
   And his watch-chain dangled free;

---

[2] Parody of the first quatrain of the *Rime of the Ancient Mariner*: 'It is an ancient Mariner, | And he stoppeth one of three | "By thy long grey beard and glittering eye, | Now wherefore stopp'st thou me?"'

And it came to pass
When he'd gulped his glass
Of Bass's[3] best, that then
His eloquence flowed, and for nearly ten
Hours roared he of wrongs of Washermen.

II

The Speech

The Speech according to the authorized version;

"Britons, Washermen, and Chartists!
Broders in pikes, my witriolic friends!
Pray, sit ye still, and listen to my 'peech;
Or, if ye vill not, hear at least ven I
Proclaim to all de vorld, leastways to *you*,
De all-important objeck of my mission.
Plain vashing done at home by Mrs. Cuffey,
De money paid beforehand—and N.B.
A mangle kept—vot! can it be, dat ve,
De honly lawful sauces of true power,
Is sunk to mangling, wile de rich man sucks
De taxes from our wittals? tyrannous
De hate of all 'gainst niggers—aye, by'r Jug,
Our 'andsome face dey laughs at—come vot may,
Freedom is freedom, dat is, I am I."
      The Washer-man here drained the can,
      And gloomily thus continued:—
"Awake, harise, or be for ever [hear, hear]
Ye chosen few, deputed here by all
Who love demselves alone, or p'raps, as I,
Sent by de stim'lus of a vife, who owns,
Dat, come a scramble, ve shall get de pickings—
Blow, fire! burn, hail! cats! dogs! and pitchforks! Chartists!

The Speaker laying claim to the presidency is interrupted by his hearers, and reduced to the level of private Cuffeyism.

Expiflicate vot e'er is not yourselves:
And, if ye be de patriots dat ye boast,
Cut your own canes! dat done, de vorld vill be
Cuffey's! and he de president and . . ."
      [hiss-s-s-s-s].

---

[3] A famous brand of English bitter beer.

III

The Presidency

The assembly roused by the speech forgetteth its dignity.

"No President! No government!
  "No nuffin! down with Cuffey!"
So howl'd they all within that hall,
  The members somewhat huffy.

But soon the sublime unselfishness of the members stands out in the brightest colours.

"Up Mob—down law—away with every thing!—
  "Pikes for third parties, self for self alone!
"Hurrah! Hear, hear! Hiss, hiss! Hurrah! don't cheer!"
  The Parliament a Bear-garden[4] has grown.

The Muse in more solemn tone inquireth how the hero fared.

But where is Cuffey now amid the crush
Of fraternizing free Philosophers?
Poor Cuffey sank adown before the rush,
And found a resting-place between two chairs;
There might you see him writhing, ere he dares
To lift aloft his presidential form:
Alas! that thus in hunting for a Mare's-
Nest[5] he should meet so lucklessly with storm,
And from his height divine descend into a worm.

And describeth his pleasant visions of "the coming man."

Sweet were his dreamy visions of the throne
Whose ruddy velvet was to bear his weight:
Sweet the bag-wig: and passing sweet the tone
Of dreamt-of voices calling "Mr. State
Commissioner of Safety,"—"Mr. (late
Ex-washerman) First Consul," and the cry
Of "long live Cuffey! Cuffey live the Great!"
Ah! when he found his plans were all awry,
He scarce could smoke his pipe, tears gathered to his eye.

And sheweth where he met his recent fall and whence, on his recovery, he started in procession.

There stands a house in John Street, famed afar
For scientific teas and Politics
(Albeit the latter savoured more of war
Than thinking): there, whoe'er was in a fix
For sundry little sums to pay his ticks,

---

[4] An enclosure for bear-baiting, an obsolete sport where hunting dogs are set on a bear, and bets placed on the outcome of the fight.

[5] A supposed discovery that turns out to have no reality.

Met to excogitate the wisest way
(Omitting legal forms and such vain cricks)
Out of his neighbour's purse the same to pay,
And thus from social Night to extricate the Day.

IV

The Procession

The terrified people prepare for the Cuffey-ian invasion.

Noon-day—and not a pen
From inkstand drew the essence of a Brief—
Noon-day—(to tell the truth, 't was just at ten)
And all the specials went to the relief
    Of the A and the B and the C,
    And the D and the F and the E,
(Rhyme makes me dock the E
Of its proper and due priority),
And the soldiers, &c., &c.,
Stood ready and willing to fetter a
    Wicked design to enstall
    King Uproar and open the ball
Of anarchical humbug and riot.

The hero for a considerable space is not forthcoming.

But why stands Cuffey idly now,
Dark John Street, on thine airy brow?
Why sinks the banner of his fame?
Why hear we not the Cuffey's name
    Ring from a thousand tongues?
It cannot be the hero shrinks
Back from his path of pride and blinks
Before two million souls this day,
Encased in glory, to display
    The virtue of his lungs.

At last he cometh amid banners and body-guards.

Hark! heard ye not that roar of dreadful note?
Sounds not the tramp of thousands in the street?
Saw ye not whom the special's truncheon smote?
Saw ye not Cuffey planting firm his feet,
    And daring in proud confidence to meet
    No opposition on his way across
The Bridges? high in air his banners greet

The morning coolness, and abroad they toss
"Freedom, Equality, and Brotherhood" (what dross!!!)

"We have waited long—we have waited long—
   A weary time"—they cry:
"But now that the Cuffey is come, we are strong,
Let us break forth with the Cuffey's song—
   Old Clo: Old Clo: Old Clo:
Then move we on boldly and lo! and lo!
The world will be ours for weal or for woe
   In the twinkling of an eye.
The people of England are now thrice ten
Millions, but we of available men
Can reckon a billion or two at the least,
And so for our patent invincible feast
Of reason and freedom and equal fraternity
Come we, bold Cuffey, and fight to eternity!
   Bold Cuffey, Bold Cuffey, so, so,
   Cuffey's a fine dog, tally-ho, tally-ho!"[6]

V

The Meeting

Lo, where the waggon on the common stands,
Its madcap inmates smiling to the ranks
Of half-deluded Innocents, whose hands
Are almost ready to perform the pranks
Those knaves (Heaven send a horsewhip to their flanks)
Shall point to:—see! Lord Humbug at their feet,
Hard by Chief Baron Nonsense seats his shanks,
For on this morn the Cuffeys all do meet
To shed before their Judge the Cant he deems most sweet.

Did ye not see it? No, 't was but the wind,
Or the strange shaking of the waggon's floor;
Not so: Hah! Cuffey—look, aye, look behind;
Policemen's staves are now for thee in store—
Arm, Arm, it is, it is the Inspector's roar—
His thunders cease—his knees together smite,
His ducal wool will bear his hat no more,

---

[6] The shout announced on an English fox hunt when the quarry is sighted.

His eyes take leave of everything but fright,
His lips and nose are blanched—he IS a startled wight.

He urgeth his friends
stand firm and allow
n to retreat.

Yet spake he in his hour of terror—so—
"Good countrymen, let ME depart alone—
And, for my sake, stay here with Feargus O'
Connor,[7] to grace his triumph and his throne:
Yea, for the love of home-brew'd, ere a stone
By our permission is allowed to start,
Let ME be vanished—be your goodness shown;
I do entreat you, not a man depart,
Save me alone"—Alas, the Inspector scales the cart.

VI

The Conflict

The hero essayeth to
e, but his pursuer,
ertaking him as he
mbeth the rail,

In vain our hero clomb the rail—
Fate fought against him—his coat-tail
Caught firmly on a tressel-nail:
His shoe stuck fast between the bars,
Certes, he looked a wondrous Mars!
His ensign-scarf sank down behind,
'T is said some pickpocket unkind
    Annex'd his vast repeater:
His darling flag-staff dropp'd beneath,
He hung, as though 'tween life and death,
And still, tho' gasp succeeded gasp,
Clung to the coping-rail his grasp:
    While fleeter now and fleeter,
    And nearer too and nearer
The fierce Inspector came upon his prey,
To mar the imagined bliss of that stupendous day.

Poketh him severely
th the regulation staff.

Ill fared it then with Cuffey bold,
That to the waggon-rail his hold
Still held—for from advantage ground
His practised enemy did wound
    His shoulders with the staff:
For, trained in Scotland Yard to wield
That staff as spear and sword and shield,

[7] Fiery Irish demagogue and leader of the Chartist movement in London. He was elected Member of Parliament in 1847, and was declared insane in 1852. The two events are not necessarily connected.

The Inspector knew the important point,
What limb to bruise, which arm, what joint;
And then he brought his skill to bear,
To teach dark Cuffey to beware
How henceforth against England's laws,
Enclothed in plumage of the daws,
(Peacocks, I mean, but verse confined
Won't let my pen confess my mind,)
He venture to uphold a strife
To benefit himself and wife,
    And turn to gold his chaff.
Three times the Inspector poked his side,
And thrice the avenging staff replied
    Unto the hero's gibes—
He writhed and roll'd to make him free,
And whispering asked his foe, if he
    Were capable of bribes:
Till at the last his coat gave way,
His shoe came out and sent a ray
    Of hope into his heart,

Finally the hero escapeth and fleeth.

And then he heard the Inspector say:—
"Good friend, you've had your fill to-day,
    You'd better far depart."

VII

The Flight

He fleeth amid a miraculous rain which aideth in covering his escape.

Away, away, his fears and he,
    Upon the pinions of the wind,
    The treacherous waggon left behind;
He sped, like meteor, through the sea
Of Kennington humanity—
And, though most laughed, yet none thought right
To stay the progress of his flight;
Only he felt some wondrous showers
    Of carrots, cabbages, and rats,
      Come sweeping o'er his head;
A dark storm-cloud above him lowers!
    Nay—'t is the blest ghost of a cat's
      Ill-fated offspring dead—

And a low breeze crept moaning by,
He answered with a deep-drawn sigh,
For well he knew that breeze portended
That, ere his race for life be ended,
The stains of embryo-chickenhood
Should mix with the heroic blood
    Now mantling on his cheek:
(Ah, that Free Trade should grant the way
For Gallic nest-eggs to dismay
    A Patriot so—meek:)
Never—oh, never more, I ween,
The Cuffey's coat will bear the sheen
    Of newness which it bore that day,
Never—oh—never more the care
Of "she dat lubs him" can repair
    The wreckings of that fray.

His strength faileth him, but the distant sight of his "washus" stimulateth him to increased speed.

Onward he went—but slack and slow—
    His energies well nigh o'erspent;
His head droop'd melancholy low;
    His gaze was on yon "washus" bent;
It was the merest speck of white,
Far distant; but in Cuffey's sight
It was a city of salvation,
Fit to secure him from the Station-
    House of the B police.
The sigh re-nerved the hero's feet,
No Arab courser e'er more fleet
    To make the space decrease
Which severs him from wished-for spot,
Than Cuffey to regain his cot,
There, for a few more hours content to bear his lot.
A moment, and his goal was won,
A moment, he was not alone,
    Mrs. before him stood!

The Muse refuseth to reveal the secrets of the meeting between the ex-President and his quean.

The veil must hide her crushing grief,
Respect will lend a covering leaf,
Nor will we blazon forth her pain,
Nor say, how flowed her tears in rain,
    The scold she gave, how good.

Suffice it, they made friends at tea
And sipped in peace the light bohea,
SHE quaffed new courage from her can,
    HE was of hope forlorn;
A sadder, not a wiser man,
    He rose the morrow morn.

VIII

The Dome

The warrior's repose

By the washing tub at rest
    We found the warrior lying—
Of shears and patterns re-possessed,
    His needle sternly plying—
        Dark and grim
        SHE looked at him,
To cleanse an egg-stained mantle vainly trying.

is broken in upon by an
order for a new coat,
when he declareth his
recent losses in trade.

We went with words of cheer,
    A new coat to bespeak;
He sighed and said, it must be dear,
    So had his costly freak
        Drained his purse,
        And what was worse
His lady-quean had had no washing for the week.

and saith his wife's time
is devoted to stitching
his tattered uniform.

"What laves she now?" we said—
    "Call'st thou that mountain nought?"
"Woe's me"—he smote his woolly head—
    "The robes wherein I fought—
        "Fiercely he
        "Did batter me,
"That terrible Inspector in his foul onslaught."

Stung by the speak-
er's questions,

"What mean'st thou now to do?
    "Thou may'st not be a king,"
We asked—he, meditating, drew
    His needle out—"Go bring
        "Freedom's sword."
        And at his word
The tearful lady brought down stairs
        th'ancestral thing.

e proposeth suicide—
recommended to fol-
w that course.

"I cannot live disgraced!
  "Ho—mark a Cuffey die!
"For Cuffey's fame is now defaced!"
  We said, "Thou'dst better try."—
    Silently
    And slowly he
Dropped the expectant blade and eke began to cry.

'he curtain falleth.

His public life is o'er:
  His private life before him—
Of Freedom now he'll say no more,
  We trust, and so restore him,
    All renowned
    But never crowned,
  To turn his native mangle round,
For ever and amen to turn his native mangle round.

Elizabeth Barrett Browning [EBB] (1806–61),
The Runaway Slave at Pilgrim's Point (written 1846,
published 1848); 'Hiram Power's Greek Slave'
(written 1847, published 1850); from *Aurora Leigh*
(1856); 'A Curse for a Nation' (1857)

EBB was fortunate in being educated at home alongside her brother. She consequently, and unusually for a British woman at this period, became fluent in Latin and Greek,
and later learned Hebrew as well. In 1840 her brother was drowned in a sailing acci-
dent. He was only staying on the coast in order to keep Elizabeth company during a
convalescence, and he went out sailing following an argument with her. She was traumatized by an event that she saw as the result of her own selfishness. Her subsequent
poetry was to be shot through with an intense sensitivity to the psychological operation
of the processes of guilt and mourning.

EBB secretly married Robert Browning [RB] in 1846, having (famously) eloped with
him. The couple settled in Italy, making their base in Florence from 1847 to 1861 where
they entertained and were entertained by a rich mixture of European and American
artists and intellectuals. They are the most genuinely cosmopolitan and cross-cultural
of Victorian poets, and both wrote poetry which addressed a vast historical and geographical range of subjects. In the last thirty years EBB's formal ambition and intense
engagement with contemporary international affairs has begun to be acknowledged.

She wrote unusual poetry about both the Greek and Italian independence struggles. She also composed the vastly influential proto-feminist epic *Aurora Leigh*, which has been rediscovered in the last twenty years. The poem thinks about male power and the debasement of British women with unprecedented boldness. The poem includes Aurora's passionate outburst, reprinted below, on the perverse appropriativeness of fashionable women. She presents the vision of a privileged white female elite who support the status quo while pretending they can enter the trauma of the plantation slave or the factory worker. EBB ruthlessly lays bare the corrupted operation of an insatiable white female sentimentality capable of understanding suffering only within the confines of its own narrow solipsism.

EBB was deeply interested in the artistic dilemma of how it was possible to render the mind of the traumatized slave, and she became passionate about the cause of North American abolition. Her involvement in anti-slavery must relate in deep ways to her family background, which had been intimately attached to the fortunes of British West Indian plantation slavery. Her father had inherited an enormous estate in Jamaica from his maternal grandfather. This was ruined in the wake of emancipation in Jamaica in 1833, and to make good the debts the family had to sell its estate in Hertfordshire. EBB, while completely acknowledging the ruin emancipation had brought on many of the planters, and the hardships that had descended on her own family, still maintained that emancipation was necessary. Shortly after the emancipation of the British sugar colonies she stated in a letter of September 1833: 'the late Bill has ruined the West Indians. That is settled. The consternation here is very great. Nevertheless I am glad, and always shall be, that the Negroes are—virtually—free' (*The Letters of Elizabeth Barrett Browning*, ed. F. G. Kenton, 2 vols. (Macmillan, 1898), i. 23). EBB maintained her interest in slavery, and was swept up in the sudden resurgence of abolition activity which Harriet Beecher Stowe's *Uncle Tom's Cabin* both reflected and encouraged. When Stowe toured Europe in 1853 she stayed with the Brownings in Italy. EBB wrote to the iconographer Mrs Jameson in passionate terms about the book: 'Not read Mrs. Stowe's book. *But you must....* Oh, and is it possible that you think a woman has no business with questions like the question of slavery? Then she had better use a pen no more. She had better subside into slavery and concubinage herself.... A difficult question—yes! All virtue is difficult. England found it difficult. France found it difficult. But we did not make ourselves an armchair of our sins. As for America I honour America much; but I would not be an American for the world while she wears that shameful scar upon her brow' (*Letters*, ii. 110).

EBB's interest in American abolition fed directly into her art, and she composed two major poems on slavery, the first of which came out several years before the publication of *Uncle Tom's Cabin*. *The Runaway Slave at Pilgrim's Point*, her slavery masterpiece, and one of the great nineteenth-century poems on slavery, was contributed to the 1848 abolition anthology *The Liberty Bell*, edited by Lydia Maria Child (pp. 472–82) and published for the Boston Anti-Slavery Bazaar. The poem in fact goes a lot further than Stowe's novel in confronting the unspeakable enormities which women had to endure under the slave systems. Using the poetic form so brilliantly developed by RB she wrote an extended dramatic monologue on the state of mind of a murderer in the wake of the terrible crime of infanticide. *The Runaway Slave* is clearly indebted at points to RB's 'Porphyria's Lover'. The poem is, however, unique among nineteenth-century abolition verse by whites in taking on the themes of slave mother infanticide, and the rape of slave women, and in attempting to provide a detailed psychological profile of the victim's state of mind. It is a testament to EBB's stern artistic vision that it was not until Toni Morrison's *Beloved* (1984) that a great female author was to take the still taboo subject of slave mother infanticide into darker and even more extended territory.

EBB continued to think about American slavery in ways which avoid the typical charges of hypocrisy which saturate so much English writing against the continuation of the American plantation system. Her 1850 meditation on the sculpture *The Greek Slave* exemplifies this open-mindedness. The American sculptor Hiram Power's wonderfully executed, and blatantly erotic, sculpture *The Greek Slave* caused a sensation when it was shown at the Great Exhibition in London in 1850. Yet the typical reaction of the English public was to see the work as a wonderful opportunity to criticize the Union for allowing the continuance of slavery.

Punch, a central mouthpiece of Victorian culural opinion, returned to Power's sculpture on a number of occasions in order to make crude accusations. The article 'America in Crystal' (vol. 20, p. 209) opened with a sarcastic reference to the enormous crystal eagle which dominated the American exhibit. The satire continues: 'A very little consideration might have given us the American Eagle, with the treasures of America gathered below its hovering wings. Why not have sent some choice specimens of slaves? We have the Greek Captive in dead stone, why not the Virginian slave in living ebony?' The same issue of *Punch* (vol. 20, p. 236) developed the suggested sculpture in woodcut. *Virginian Slave Intended as a Companion to Power's 'Greek Slave'* took the form more of a mock monument than a statue. The base of the pedestal carried the 'E Pluribus Unum' motto, while the pedestal itself is ornamented with scourges, ropes, and chains. A topless black woman slave leans against a whipping post draped in the stars and stripes; she is manacled at wrists and ankles, and stares out with an expression of exaggerated and passive hopelessness. EBB's interpretation of Power's statue is far more radical, seeing in the neoclassical white perfection of the statue an assault on white delusions of power.

'A Curse for a Nation', although not as powerful as *The Runaway Slave*, is a final indication of Browning's determination to work against the grain of English moral triumphalism over American slavery. The prologue is a variation on the dialogue between self and soul. EBB, instructed by a guardian angel to write a curse against America for its perpetuation of slavery, counters the angel's arguments with statements about the slavery and poverty in England, before turning in the second half of the poem to attack America.

Textual note: For the complicated publishing history of the different editions of both *The Runaway Slave* and 'A Curse for a Nation' see Andrew M. Stauffer, *English Language Notes*, 34/4 (1997), 29–49. The texts reproduced here are *The Runaway Slave*, *The Liberty Bell*, Dec. 1847, and 'A Curse for a Nation', *The Liberty Bell*, Dec. 1856.

The Runaway Slave at Pilgrim's Point

I

I stand on the mark, beside the shore,
  Of the first white pilgrim's bended knee;[1]
Where exile changed to ancestor,
  And God was thanked for liberty.
I have run through the night—my skin is as dark—
I bend my knee down on this mark—
  I look on the sky and the sea.

II

O, pilgrim-souls, I speak to you:
  I see you come out proud and slow
From the land of the sprits, pale as dew,
  And round me and round me ye go.
O, pilgrims, I have gasped and run
All night long from the whips of one
  Who, in your names, works sin and woe!

III

And thus I thought that I would come
  And kneel here where ye knelt before,
And feel your souls around me hum
  In undertone to the ocean's roar;
And lift my black face, my black hand,
Here in your names, to curse this land
  Ye blessed in Freedom's, heretofore.

IV

I am black, I am black,
  And yet God made me, they say:
But if he did so—smiling, back
  He must have cast his work away
Under the feet of His white creatures,
With a look of scorn, that the dusky features
  Might be trodden again to clay.

---

[1] Plymouth Rock is the symbolic spot where the *Mayflower* pilgrims first disembarked in south-east Massachusetts at a place they named Plymouth in 1620.

V

And yet He has made dark things
    To be glad and merry as light;
There's a little dark bird sits and sings,
    There's a dark stream ripples out of sight;
And the dark frogs chant in the safe morass,
And the sweetest stars are made to pass
    O'er the face of the darkest night.

VI

But we who are dark, we are dark!
    O God, we have no stars!
About our souls, in care and cark[2]
    Our blackness shuts like prison-bars!
And crouch our souls so far behind,
That never a comfort can they find,
    By reaching through the prison-bars.

VII

Howbeit God's sunshine and His frost,
    They make us hot, they make us cold,
As if we were not black and lost;
    And the beasts and birds, in wood and wold,
Do fear us and take us for very men;—
Could the whippoorwill[3] or the cat of the glen
    Look into my eyes and be bold?

VIII

I am black, I am black!—
    And once I laughed in girlish glee;
For one of my colour stood in the track
    Where the drivers drove, and looked at me:
And tender and full was the look he gave!
A Slave looked so at another Slave,—
    I look at the sky and the sea.

IX

And from that hour our spirits grew
    As free as if unsold, unbought;
We were strong enough, since we were two,
    To conquer the world, we thought.

   [2] Anxiety.   [3] Bird, a species of goatsucker.

The drivers drove us day by day:
　We did not mind; we went one way,
　　And no better a liberty sought.

X

In the open ground, between the canes,
　He said "I love you," as he passed:
When the shingle-roof rang sharp with the rains,
　I heard how he vowed it fast.
While others trembled, he sate in the hut
As he carved me a bowl of the cocoa-nut,
　Through the roar of the hurricanes.

XI

I sang his name instead of a song;
　Over and over I sang his name:
Backward and forward I sang it along,
　With my sweetest notes it was still the same!
But I sang it low, that the slave girls near
Might never guess, from ought they could hear,
　That all the song was a name.

XII

I look on the sky and the sea!
　We were two to love, and two to pray,—
Yes, two, O God, who cried on Thee,
　Though nothing didst thou say.
Coldly thou sat'st behind the sun,
And now I cry, who am but one,—
　Thou wilt not speak to-day!

XIII

We were black, we were black,
　We had no claim to love and bliss—
What marvel, ours was cast to wrack?
　They wrung my cold hands out of his—
They dragged him—why, I crawled to touch
His blood's mark in the dust—not much,
　Ye pilgrim-souls,—though plain as THIS!

XIV

Wrong, followed by a deeper wrong!
　Grief seemed too good for such as I;

So the white men brought the shame ere long
   To stifle the sob in my throat thereby.
They would not leave me for my dull
Wet eyes!—it was too merciful
   To let me weep pure tears, and die.

XV

I am black, I am black!
   I wore a child upon my breast,–
An amulet that hung too slack,
   And, in my unrest, could not rest!
Thus we went moaning, child and mother,
One to another, one to another,
   Until all ended for the best.

XVI

For hark! I will tell you low—low—
   I am black, you see;
And the babe, that lay on my bosom so,
   Was far too white—too white for me.
As white as the ladies who scorned to pray
Beside me at church but yesterday,
   Though my tears had washed a place for my knee.

XVII

And my own child—I could not bear
   To look in his face, it was so white:
I covered him up with a kerchief rare;
   I covered his face in, close and tight!
And he moaned and struggled as well as might be,
For the white child wanted his liberty,—
—Ha, ha! he wanted his master's right.

XVIII

He moaned and beat with his head and feet—
   His little feet that never grew!
He struck them out as it was meet
   Against my heart to break it through.
I might have sung like a mother mild—
But I dared not sing to a white-faced child
   The only song I knew.

XIX

And yet I pulled the kerchief close:
    He could not see the sun, I swear,
More then, alive, than now he does
    From between the roots of the mangles[4]—where?
I know where!—close!—a child and mother
Do wrong to look at one another,
    When one is black and one is fair.

XX

Even in that single glance I had
    Of my child's face,—I tell you all,—
I saw a look that made me mad,—
    The master's look, that used to fall
On my soul like his lash,—or worse,—
Therefore, to save it from my curse,
    I twisted it round in my shawl.

XXI

And he moaned and trembled from foot to head,—
    He shivered from head to foot,—
Till, after a time, he lay, instead,
    Too suddenly still and mute;
I felt, beside, a creeping cold,—
I dared to lift up just a fold,
    As in lifting a leaf of the mango fruit.[5]

XXII

But MY fruit! ha, ha!—there had been
    (I laugh to think on't at this hour!)
Your fine white angels,—who have seen
    God's secret nearest to His power,—
And gathered my fruit to make them wine,
And sucked the soul of that child of mine,
    As the humming bird sucks the soul of a flower.

---

[4] Mangroves, the roots of which form the swamp.
[5] Adapted from the following lines in RB' s 'Porphyria's Lover' as the narrator examines the corpse of the woman he has just strangled: 'As a shut bud that holds a bee, | I warily op'd her lids: again . . .'

XXIII

Ha, ha! for the trick, of the angels white!
  They freed the white child's spirit so;
I said not a word,[6] but day and night
  I carried the body to and fro;
And it lay on my heart like a stone—as chill;
The sun may shine out as much as he will—
  I am cold, though it happened a month ago.

XXIV

From the white man's house and the black man's hut
  I carried the little body on;
The forest's arms did round us shut,
  And silence through the trees did run!
They asked no question as I went,—
They stood too high for astonishment,—
  They could see God rise on his throne.

XXV

My little body, kerchiefed fast,
  I bore it on through the forest—on—
And when I felt it was tired at last,
  I scooped a hole beneath the moon.
Through the forest-tops the angels far,
With a white fine finger in every star,
  Did point and mock at what was done.

XXVI

Yet when it was all done aright,
  Earth twixt me and my baby strewed,—
All, changed to black earth,—nothing white,—
  A dark child in the dark,—ensued
Some comfort, and my heart grew young;
I sate down smiling there, and sung
  The song I told you of, for good.

XXVII

And thus we two were reconciled,
  The white child and black mother, thus;
For, as I sang it,—soft and wild,
  The same song, more melodious,

---

[6] Echoes the final line of 'Porphyria's Lover': 'And yet God has not said a word.'

Rose from the grave whereon I sate!
It was the dead child singing that,
   To join the souls of both of us.

XXVIII

I look on the sea and the sky!
   Where the Pilgrims' ships first anchored lay,
The free sun rideth gloriously!
   But the pilgrim-ghosts have slid away
Through the first faint streaks of the morn!
My face is black, but it glares with a scorn
   Which they dare not meet by day.

XXIX

Ah, in their stead, their hunter sons!
   Ah, ah! they are on me!—they form in a ring!
Keep off,   I brave you all at once,—
   I throw off your eyes like a noisome thing!
You have killed the black eagle at nest, I think;
Did you never stand still in your triumph, and shrink
   From the stroke of her wounded wing?

XXX

(Man, drop that stone you dared to lift!—)
   I wish you, who stand there, seven abreast,
Each, for his own wife's grace and gift,
   A little corpse as safely at rest,
As mine in the mangles!—Yes, but *she*
May keep live babies on her knee,
   And sing the song she liketh best.

XXXI

I am not mad,—I am black!
   I see you staring in my face,—
I know you, staring, shrinking back,—
   Ye are born of the Washington race!
And this land is the Free America,—
And this mark on my wrist,—(I prove what I say)
   Ropes tied me up here to the flogging place.

XXXII

You think I shrieked then? Not a sound!
  I hung as a gourd hangs in the sun;[7]
I only cursed them all around,
    As softly as I might have done
My own child after. From these sands
Up to the mountains, lift your hands
    O Slaves, and end what I begun.

XXXIII

Whips, curses! these must answer those!
  For in this UNION, ye have set
Two kinds of men in adverse rows,
    Each loathing each! and all forget
The seven wounds[8] in Christ's body fair;
While He sees gaping everywhere
    Our countless wounds that pay no debt.

XXXIV

Our wounds are different—your white men
  Are, after all, not gods indeed,
Nor able to make Christs again
    Do good with bleeding. *We* who bleed—
(Stand off!)—we help not in our loss,—
We are too heavy for our cross,
    And fall and crush you and your seed.

XXXV

I fall,—I swoon,—I look at the sky!
  The clouds are breaking on my brain:
I am floated along, as if I should die
    Of Liberty's exquisite pain!
In the name of the white child waiting for me
In the deep black death where our kisses agree,—
White men, I leave you all curse-free,
In my broken heart's disdain!

---

[7] Echoes RB' s 'A Loose Woman': 'And she,—she lies in my hand as tame | As a pear late basking over a wall.' Also a reference to the gourd which grows above Jonah, see Jonah, 4.

[8] An obscure number; usually the five wounds are referred to, one on each hand and foot, and the spear wound in Christ's side. The seven wounds also include the crown of thorns, and finally the shoulder wound which was revealed to Bernard of Clairvaux.

Hiram Power's Greek Slave

They say Ideal beauty cannot enter
The house of anguish. On the threshold stands
An alien Image with enshackled hands,
Called the Greek Slave! as if the artist meant her
(That passionless perfection which he lent her,
Shadowed not darkened where the sill expands)
To, so, confront man's crimes in different lands
With man's ideal sense. Pierce to the centre,
Art's fiery finger!—and break up ere long
The serfdom of this world! appeal, fair stone,
From God's pure heights of beauty against man's wrong!
Catch up in thy divine face, not alone
East griefs but west,—and strike and shame the strong,
By thunders of white silence overthrown.

from *Aurora Leigh* (II. 183–209)

Can women understand... The human race
To you means, such a child, or such a man,
You saw one morning waiting in the cold,
Beside that gate, perhaps. You gather up
A few such cases, and when strong sometimes
Will write of factories and of slaves, as if
Your father were a negro, and your son
A spinner in the mills. All's yours and you,
All, coloured with your blood, or otherwise
Just nothing to you. Why, I call you hard
To general suffering. Here's the world half blind
With intellectual light, half brutalized
With civilization having caught the plague
In silks from Tarsus, shrieking east and west
Along a thousand railroads, mad with pain
And sin too!... does one woman of you all
(You who weep easily) grow pale to see
This tiger shake his cage?—does one of you

Stand still from dancing, stop from stringing pearls,
And pine and die because of the great sum
Of universal anguish?

A Curse for a Nation

PROLOGUE

I heard an angel speak last night,
    And he said, "Write!
Write a nation's curse for me,
And send it over the western sea."

I faltered, taking up the word—
    Not so, my lord!
If curses must be, choose another
To send thy curse against my brother.

"For I am bound by gratitude,
    In love and blood,
To brothers of mine across the sea,
Who have stretched out kindly hands to me."

"Therefore," the voice said, "shalt thou write
    My curse to-night!
From the summits of love a curse is driven,
As lightning from the tops of heaven."

"Not so! " I answered. "Evermore
    My heart is sore
For my own land's sins! for the little feet
Of children bleeding along the street.

"For parked-up honours, that gainsay
    The right of way!
For almsgiving through a door that is
Not open enough for two friends to kiss.

"For an oligarchic parliament,
    And classes rent.
What curse to another land assign,
When heavy-souled for the sins of mine?"

"Therefore," the voice said, "shalt thou write
    My curse to-night!
Because thou hast strength to see and hate
An ill thing done within thy gate."

"Not so!" I answered once again—
    "To curse, choose men;
For I, a woman, have only known
How the heart melts and the tears run down."

"Therefore," the voice said, "shalt thou write
    My curse to-night!
There are women who weep and curse, I say,
(And no one marvels) night and day.

"And thou shalt take their part to-night—
    Weep and write!
A curse from the depths of womanhood,
Is very salt, and bitter, and good."

So thus I wrote, and mourned indeed,
    What all may read;
And thus, as was enjoined on me,
I send it over the western sea.

The Curse

I

Because ye have broken your own chain
    With the strain
Of brave men climbing a nation's height,
Yet thence bear down with chain and thong
On the souls of others,—for this wrong
    This is the curse—write!

Because yourselves are standing straight
    In the state
Of Freedom's foremost acolyte,
Yet keep calm footing all the time
On writhing bondslaves,—for this crime
    This is the curse—write!

Because ye prosper in God's name,
    With a claim

To honour in the whole world's sight,
Yet do the fiend's work perfectly
On babes and women—for this lie
   This is the curse—write!

II

Ye shall watch while kings conspire
Round the people's smouldering fire,
   And, warm for your part,
Shall never dare—O shame!
To utter the thought into flame
   Which burns at your heart.
      This is the curse—write!

Ye shall watch while nation's strive
With the bloodhounds—die or survive,—
   Drop faint from their jaws,
Or throttle them backward to death,
And only under your breath
   Shall ye bless the cause.
      This is the curse—write!

Ye shall watch while strong men draw
The nets of feudal law
   To strangle the weak;
Ye shall count the sin for a sin,
But your soul shall be sadder within
   Than the word which ye speak.
      This is the curse—write!

Ye shall watch while rich men dine,
And poor men hunger and pine
   For one crust in seven;
But shall quail from the signs which present
God's judgment as imminent
   To make it all even.
      This is the curse—write!

When good men are praying erect
That Christ may avenge his elect
   And deliver the earth,
The prayer in your ears, said low,
Shall sound like the tramp of a foe

That's driving you forth.
This is the curse—write!

When wise men give you their praise,
They shall pause in the heat of the phrase,
    And sicken afar;
When ye boast your own charters kept true,
Ye shall blush!—for the thing which ye do
    Derides what ye are.
        This is the curse—write!

When fools write taunts on your gate,
Your scorn ye shall somewhat abate
    As ye look o'er the wall;
For your conscience, tradition, and name
Strike back with a deadlier blame
    Than the worst of them all.
        This is the curse—write!

Go! while ill deeds shall be done,
Plant on your flag in the sun
    Beside the ill-doers;
And shrink from clenching the curse
Of the witnessing universe,
    With a curse of yours!
        This is the curse—write!

Anon., 'King Cotton Bound; or, The Modern Prometheus', *Punch* (1861)

The American Civil War generated, in Britain, almost no poetry, and certainly very little verse of any quality, on the subject of slavery. 'King Cotton Bound; or, The Modern Prometheus', together with its accompanying graphic satire, are a good example of English response to the South during the war. Referring to the effect of the North's blockade of Southern ports the print shows the cotton interest as a Promethean monarch made of a patchwork of textiles and wearing a crown. He is stapled to a huge block, with an iron band marked 'blockade'. An eagle with the Union flag on its wings tears at his liver. Yet it is very much the aristocratic, patriarchal white South which is metaphorically portrayed here. The slaves are not included in the process of

6.   Anon., 'King Cotton Bound; or, The Modern Prometheus'
(wood engraving, 1861), in *Punch*.

martyrology. This comes out clearly in the poem, which carries the same title and also
carries a sophisticated commentary on the effects of the blockade on the English textile
industry. It is very revealing of the nationalistic and self-serving attitudes which typify
English public response to the war. The victims of King Cotton's Promethean torments
under the cotton blockade are presented not as Americans, let alone as black slaves, but
as English factory workers. Prometheus, who as in the classical myth is shown suffering
for mankind, does not hear the screaming of the American Eagle which tortures him,
but the sounds of starvation from England. In the final section the poem moves on to

conclude that English military intervention in breaking the blockade would be a blessing. Intriguingly all moral issues relating to slavery and the war are suspended: when English suffering is the subject it seems as ever that the normal moral rules do not apply.

King Cotton Bound; or, The Modern Prometheus[1]

Far across Atlantic waters
    Groans in chains a Giant King;
Like to him, whom Ocean's daughters
    Wail around in mournful ring,
In the grand old Grecian strains
Of PROMETHEUS in his chains!

Needs but Fancy's pencil pliant
    Both to paint till both agree;
For King Cotton is a giant,
    As PROMETHEUS claimed to be.
Each gave blessings unto men,
Each dishonour reaped again.

From the gods to sons of clay
    If PROMETHEUS brought the flame,
Who King Cotton can gainsay,
    Should he equal honour claim?
Fire and life to millions giving,
That, without him, had no living.

And if they are one in blessing,
    So in suffering they are one;
Both, their captive state confessing,
    Freeze in frost and scorch in sun:
That, upon his mountain chain,
This, upon his parching plain.

Nor the wild bird's self is wanting—
    Either giant's torment sore;
If PROMETHEUS writhed, while panting
    Heart and lungs the vulture tore.
So Columbia's eagle fierce,
Doth King Cotton's vitals pierce.

[1] See p. 305 n. 1.

On those wings so widely sweeping
   In its poise the bird to keep,
See, if you can see for weeping,
   "North" and "South" are branded deep—
On the beak all reeking red,
On the talons blood-bespread!

But 'tis not so much the anguish
   Of the wound that rends his side,
Makes this fettered giant languish,
   As the thought how once, in pride,
That great eagle took its stand,
Gently on his giant hand!

How to it the meat he'd carry
   In its mew[2] to feed secure;
How he'd fling it on the quarry,
   How recall it to the lure,
Make it stoop, to his caresses,
Hooded neck and jingling jesses.

And another thought is pressing,
   Like hot iron on his brain—
Millions that would fain be blessing,
   Ban, e'en now, King Cotton's name.
Oh, that here those hands are bound,
Which should scatter wealth around!

"Not this Eagle's screaming smothers
   That sad sound across the sea—
Wailing babes and weeping mothers,
   Wailing, weeping, wanting me.
Hands that I would fain employ,
Hearts that I would fill with joy!

"I must writhe—a giant fettered,—
   While those millions peak and pine;
By my wealth their lot unbettered,
   And their suffering worse than mine.
For *they* know that I would fain
Help their need, were 't not my chain!

        [2] Hiding place.

"But *I* know not where to turn me
   For relief from bonds and woe;
Frosts may pinch and suns may burn me,
   But for rescue—none I know,
Save the millions I have fed,
Should they rise for lack of bread—

"Saying, 'We will brook no longer,
   That King Cotton bound should be:
Be his gaolers strong, *we*'re stronger,
   In our hunger over sea—
More for want, than love, uprisen,
We are come to break his prison!'

"Welcome even such releasing,
   Fain my work I'd be about:
Soon would want and wail be ceasing,
   Were King Cotton once let out—
Though all torn and faint and bleeding,
Millions still I've strength for feeding."

Anti-Slavery Verse for Children

**Broadsides, songsheets, paper-games, and handouts:
'Little Benny', 'I Thank the Goodness and the Grace',
'A Child's Evening Hymn', 'The Poor Little Negro',
'Slaves Set Free' (undated handbills, printed in Leeds,
for the Leeds Anti-Slavery Society, 1820-33);
'Alphabet of Slavery', 'The Young Catechist',
'Anti-Slavery Dial'**

Abolition was a broad-based popular coalition which from the first thought tactically about reaching the widest audience possible. The involvement of so many leading female intellectuals and educationalists meant that the children's market was targeted from an early stage. Hannah More, Amelia Opie, and Anna Barbauld all wrote for children as well as adults and all included slavery in their children's works. Several relevant poems are included elsewhere in the anthology (see pp. 48–53, 110–16, 278–9). The work included in this section is representative of the manner in which poetry was used as an element in popular single-sheet ephemera which were handed out, often for free, to children.

The first five of the following juvenile publications are all taken from a single series. These were little coloured handbills approximately five inches by three, mass produced and given out on the street by members of the Leeds Anti-Slavery Society in the 1820s and early 1830s and published under the general the title of The Leeds Anti-Slavery Juvenile Series.

Each handbill is printed on both sides, so the poems create a sort of dialogue with each other. On the back of 'Little Benny' is printed the notorious abolition hymn 'I thank the Goodness and the Grace'. The poem is based on the premiss that the state of every English child is blessed and the extent of the blessedness is defined by placing it within the context of three miserable states, the first that of being a heathen African, the second that of being a kidnapped slave, the third that of being a slave on the middle passage. All three are linked causally: there is an inference that enslavement is the natural result of not being a Christian; for those who 'pray a useless prayer to blocks of wood and stone' slavery is perhaps inevitable. The concept of prayer is therefore bound up in a utilitarian logic. Heathen prayer is useless because God does not hear it and the African gods to whom it is directed do not exist. The tone and the thought are complacent and gloating. It is not enough to enjoy one's privileged white Christian status in England; this blessed state has to be defined through its opposite, the suffering and spiritually blind status of the black slave child. The last stanza is the most sinister with its hint of a predeterministic interpretation of slavery. If the good, free life of the white Christian child is deliberately 'plann'd' by God, then so must be the state of enslavement of the black child. Such logic is a very short step away from justifying slavery as a divine institution rather than simply a human one.

'A Child's Evening Hymn' creates variations around the central premisses of entrapment established in the previous hymn; the argument runs: the blessed and domestically stable life of the white English child is an exact opposite of the state of the slave. The slave may only be freed by the Christianizing of his master; once God has 'touched the flinty heart' of the slave owner then the slave can be freed. With emancipation comes gratitude and the child will instantaneously thank God for his freedom.

'The Poor Little Negro' and 'Slaves Set Free' are again printed on opposite sides of the same little handbill. This pair of poems are written in a nursery rhyme mode. The first concerns a 'blackamoor' begging, presumably in the streets of a large industrial city, having been shipped over and left at some point. The poem turns on the simple antithesis of carefree savage/miserable slave. The degraded animality of 'little blacks' comes out in the comparison with the 'water-rat'. In 'Slaves Set Free' emancipation is presented as the direct result of Christian petitioning, and petitioning letters are seen as sent initially to the King, then to Parliament.

The last three items in this section show how the newly expanding market for children's games and rhymes was used by the abolitionists. 'Alphabet of Slavery' takes up the ancient form of the Battledore, or ABC, and attaches an abolition aphorism to each letter. The form remained popular: an American variation is included in the following section (pp. 675–7). 'The Young Catechist' provides a new take on the child's catechism. Here the black male slave is catechized by the pure white Christian missionary girl, the implication being that black slaves are below white children in their ductability. The poem both serves to keep the black in his place and to celebrate white female missionary calling. Uncle Tom and Eva were to provide the mid-nineteenth-century *locus classicus* for this scenario. The final item, the anti-slavery sundial, uses a combination of poetic explanation and board game, to allow white children to project themselves into the mental world of the slave on the other side of the globe, at any time of the day or night.

Little Benny

I will tell you a story of poor little Benny,
A slave-boy who lived in the state of Virginny.[1]
When but seven years old he was sold from his mother,
His father, and Dickie, his dear little brother;
Poor fellow! He cried and he begged hard to stay,
But they pitied him not and they forced him away;
No kind ones went with him, his kind heart to cheer,
The voices so loved he will never more hear!

Do you wonder poor Benny then wished he might die?
Just think little boys, if 'twere you or 'twere I!
What if some one to-day with a purse full of gold,
Should come to our home and *we* too should be sold,
Never more to behold the dear face of our mother—
To receive the fond kiss of a father or brother.
Sold just like a dog, or an ox or a cow
To toil all our life long, it matters not how!

Now if it is wrong to make *Yankee* boys slaves,
Are not those who steal negro boys also base knaves?
Do you think that our father in heaven will say,
"You may make slaves of *negroes* but *whites* shall be free"?

---

[1] Virginia, notorious as the slave 'breeding' state for the Southern plantations.

I Thank the Goodness and the Grace

I thank the goodness and the grace,
   Which on my birth have smil'd,
And made me, in these Christian days,
   A happy English child.

I was not born, as thousands are,
   Where God was never known,
And taught to pray a useless prayer
   To blocks of wood and stone.

I was not born a little slave,
   To labour in the sun,
And wish I were but in the grave,
   And all my labour done.

I was not stolen from my home,
   And sent across the sea;
And forc'd in distant lands to roam,
   And wish that I was free.

My God, I thank Thee, who hast plann'd
   A better lot for me;
And plac'd me in this happy land,
   Where I can hear of Thee.

A Child's Evening Hymn

Father while the daylight dies,
Hear our grateful voices rise:
For the blessing that we share;
For thy kindness and thy care;
For the joy that fills our breast;
And the love that makes us blest—
   We thank Thee, Father!

For an earthly father's arm
Shielding us from wrong and harm—
For a mother's watchful cares,
Mingled with her many prayers—

For the happy kindred band,
'Midst whose peaceful lands we stand—
　　We bless Thee, Father!

Yet, while 'neath the evening skies,
Thus we bid our thanks arise,
Father! still we think of those
Who are bowed with many woes—
Whom no earthly parent's arm
Can protect from wrong or harm—
　　The poor slaves, Father!

Ah! while we are richly blest,
They are wretched and distrest;
Outcasts in their native land,
Crushed beneath oppression's hand;
Scarcely knowing even Thee,
Mighty Lord of earth and sea!
　　O save them, Father!

Touch the flinty hearts that long
Have, remorseless, done them wrong;
Ope the eyes that long have been
Blinded to each guilty scene,
That the slave—a slave no more—
Grateful thanks to thee may pour,
　　And bless Thee, Father!

The Poor Little Negro

Ah! the poor little blackamoor,
　　See there he goes,
And the blood gushes out
　　From his half-frozen toes;
And his legs are so thin
　　You may almost see the bones,
And he goes shiver, shiver,
　　All along upon the stones.

He was once a negro boy,
　　And a merry boy was he,

Playing outlandish plays
　　By the tall palm-tree,
Or bathing in the river
　　Like a brisk water-rat,
And at night sleeping soundly
　　On a little piece of mat.

But there came some wicked people,
　　And they stole him far away,
And then good-bye to palm tree tall,
　　And merry, merry play;
For they took him from his house and home,
　　And everybody dear,
And now, poor little negro boy,
　　He's come a begging here.

And fie upon the wicked folks
　　Who did this cruel thing!
I wish some mighty nobleman
　　Would go and tell the king;
For to steal him from his house and home
　　Must be a crying sin,
Though he was a little negro boy,
　　And had a sooty skin.

Slaves Set Free

I've heard a little story,
　　And I'll tell it you, my dear,—
'Tis true as well as beautiful,
　　And does one good to hear,
About the little negro boy,
　　And many, many more,
But not about the cruel things
　　I told you of before.

For thousands upon thousands
　　Of good people in the land,
Did write some pretty letters,
　　That the king might understand;

And sent them up to parliament,
　　To beg that they would do—
As Jesus Christ had told them—
　　"As they would be done unto."

They prayed them just to make a law
　　That no such thing might be,
That everybody—white or black—
　　Should after that be free;
For God hath made us all alike,
　　And all to him belong;
And stealing men and women,
　　We are certain must be wrong.

So on the first of August,
　　Eighteen hundred and thirty-four,
We told the poor black people
　　We would serve them so no more;
"We did as we'd be done to,"
　　Which is so very clear;
And that's the pleasant story
　　Which it does one good to hear.

Alphabet of Slavery

A　Is an AFRICAN torn from his home.
B　Is a BLOODHOUND to catch all that roam.
C　Is the COTTON PLANT Slaves pick and hoe.
D　Is the DRIVER who makes their blood flow.
E　Is for ENGLAND which Slaves long to see,
　　Her daughter, fair Canada, whither they flee.
F　Is a FUGITIVE—hide him by day!
　　The North Star at midnight will show him the way.
G　Is for GAMBLER both drunken and wild,
　　Stakes money and bowie-knife, mother and child.
H　Is SLAVE HUNTER with horses and gun,
　　The ugliest monster that's under the sun.
I　Is for INFANT at mother's breast found,
　　Was sold at an auction one guinea a pound.

J   Is the JOURNEY when many Slaves die,
    Their grave the deep waters, their shroud the blue sky.
K   Was a KIDNAP' who stole a poor man,
L   Was the LAWYER who joined in the plan,
M   Was the MERCHANT who bartered for gold,
N   The poor NEGRO like pig or horse sold.
O   Is OHIO, the train starts from here
    Of that underground railway the slaveholder's fear.
P   Are some PREACHERS with Slaves like the rest,
    They buy them, and whip them, then pray to be blest.
Q   Stands for QUAKER, who helps the poor slave,
    A hero of hero's both peaceful and brave.
R   Is the RICE SWAMP, a sickening place,
    Where ague and fever soon finish the race.
S   Is for SUGAR—Slavegrown—and shrewd sages
    Declare 'twould be better if Negros had wages.
T   Is TOBACCO—I don't like the weed—
    To sow it and dress it the Negros oft bleed.
U   Is that UNION of stripes and of stars,
    The Slaves get the stripes, yes! and plenty of scars.
V   Is VIRGINIA where Uncle Tom's wife
    With Children and home were the joy of his life.
W   Is the WHIP, which with paddle and chain,
    Stocks, thumbscrew, and bell give them terrible pain.
X   Ends the REFLEX of every ones mind,
    The better for all men when gentle and kind.
Y   Is for YOUTH, and wherever you be
Z   ealously labour to set the Slaves free

The Young Catechist

Q   While this tawny Ethiop prayeth
    Painter,[1] who is she that stayeth
    By, with skin of brightest lustre;
    Sunny locks a shining cluster;
    Saint like seeming to direct him

[1] The poem appears beneath an engraving of the picture it describes, which is captioned 'Painted and Engraved by Henry Meyer, Great Russell Street'. Meyer may have commissioned the poem, or even have written it himself.

> To the Power that must protect him?
> Is she of the Heav'n born Three
> Meek Hope, strong Faith, sweet Charity?
> Or some cherub?
> A   They you mention
> Far transcend my weak invention.
> Tis a simple Christian child,
> Missionary young and mild,
> From her stock of scriptural knowledge,
> Bible-taught without a college,
> Which by reading she could gather,
> Teaches him to say 'Our Father'
> To the common Parent, who
> Colour not respects nor hue.
> White and black in Him have part
> Who looks not to the skin but heart.

Anti-Slavery Dial

This Dial is intended to shew the relative time of day at London, and in those parts of the World where Slavery exists. From an inspection of the Dial it may be at once ascertained in what circumstances of Labor or Rest the Negro Slaves are placed at any period of British Time. It will thus be seen that when we are enjoying the domestic comforts of an evening fireside, they are toiling in the field or the plantation under the oppressive heat of a tropical sun. It will also appear that there are Negro Slaves at work in the British Colonies during nearly the whole of every 24 hours. The labor of the Slaves ceases about 9 o'clock in the evening and soon after those in Jamaica have retired to rest, the lash of the driver's whip is sounding in the Mauritius to rouse the unhappy Negroes from their slumbers, to another day of hardship, toil and SLAVERY.

> To him who wastes his hours, when all
>   That words can do, is done—
> Yet heedless lets his talents fall
>   His moments idly run:
> To mark the Dial's shadow glide
>   Around the silent plate,
> Or hear a clock when none beside
>   May warn him of his fate

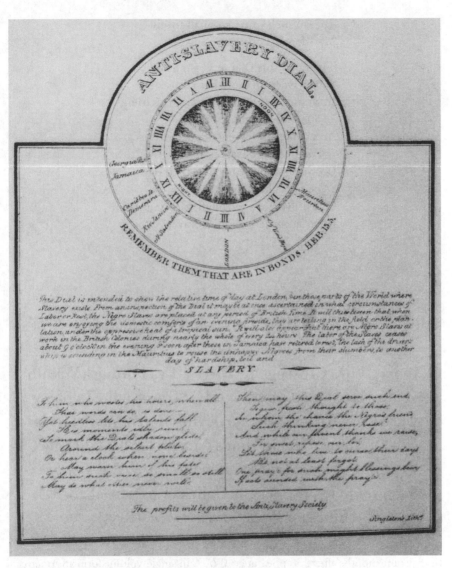

7. Anon., 'The Anti-Slavery Dial' (copper-plate engraving, n.d.).

To him such voice, so small so still
May do what others never will.

Then may this Dial serve such end
    To give fresh thought to those
In whom, tho' chance the Negro's friend,
    Such thinking never rose.
And while our fervent thanks we raise,
    For sweet repose, our lot,
Let those who live to curse their days
    Be not at least forgot.
One prayer for such might blessings bear,
If acts accorded with the prayer.

Songs and Poems Based on *Uncle Tom's Cabin* (*UTC*)

Anon., 'Eliza Crossing the River', 'Eva Putting a Wreath of Flowers Round Tom's Neck', 'Topsy at the Looking Glass', in *Pictures and Stories from Uncle Tom's Cabin* (1853); Anon., 'Uncle Tom's Lament for the Old Folks at Home', 'The Slave Auction', in *Uncle Tom's Cabin Songster* (*c.*1852–3); Dante Gabriel Rossetti (1828–82), 'Lines on *Uncle Tom's Cabin*' (1853)

In 1852 nine months after the appearance of *UTC* in single-volume form an American reviewer wrote:

> One of our newspaper critics compares the Uncle Tomific, which the reading world is now suffering from, to the yellow fever, which does not strike us a very apt comparison, because the yellow fever is confined wholly to tropical climes, while *Uncle Tom*, like the cholera, knows no distinction of climate or race. He is bound to go; and future generations of the Terra-del-Fuegans and Esquimaux will be making Christmas presents at this season of the year, of *Uncle Tom's Cabin* in holiday bindings. It is in England where *Uncle Tom* has made his deepest mark. Such has been the sensation produced by the book there and so numerous

have been the editions published that it is extremely difficult to collect the statistics of its circulation.... We have seen it stated that there were thirty different editions published in London, within six months of the publication of the work here. (Charles Briggs, repr. in Marcus Wood, *Blind Memory* (Manchester University Press, 2000), 145)

UTC constituted perhaps the first, and certainly the most significant, nineteenth-century example of the public appropriation of a text in a world where political propaganda could utilize the leisure and entertainment industries, and techniques of consumer mass production. During the second half of the nineteenth century the text, in a bewildering variety of printed forms, including serials, illustrated editions, songsters, song sheets, and children's books, evolved and proliferated all over the world. Stowe's book had become so well assimilated into the mainstream of sentimental children's fiction that editions of Anna Sewell's *Black Beauty* sponsored by the humane societies bore the title 'Black Beauty: His Grooms and Companions; the "Uncle Tom's Cabin" of the Horse'. The fragmentations and adaptations of the text in England were endless. There was abolition stationery with envelopes featuring illustrative cycles of all the main scenes, there were *UTC* jigsaw puzzles, and even board and card games in which players represented characters from the novel and had to decide how to act at key moments in the plot; in one of these games, Justice, the winner was inevitably the player holding Eva, Uncle Tom, and Justice. From 1853 until this day *UTC* remains a children's classic effortlessly adapting to changing racial and moral emphases and to different styles of illustration. English editions of *UTC* muse upon the irony of the American Declaration of Independence in the context of the survival of the 'peculiar institution'. *UTC* was used as a stick with which to beat the Americans and particularly the American constitutional claim to 'life, liberty, and the pursuit of happiness'. This line comes out strongly in the earliest of the children's adaptations. Partridge and Oakey's threepenny books of 1853 *All about Poor Little Topsy* and *All about Little Eva* carry prefaces emphatically stating that English children will:

think of realities when they learn—

'I'm glad I was not made a slave
To labour in the sun;
To wish I were not in my grave
And all my labour done.'   [See above, p. 375.]

Thus poor little Topsy's history will insensibly impress on their susceptible minds a sense of their own privileges—that they were born Free—of Free parents—in a Free Country.

And the front cover and the title page proudly bear the quatrain:

I thank the goodness and the grace,
That on my birth have smiled;
And made me in these happy days,
A little English child.

Darton and Company's *True Stories from Uncle Tom's Cabin* of 1853 provides the most succinct summary of this tendency: 'In England we have no Slaves. All men are born free. Those who work, are paid for their labour, and if they do not like their master, may go away, and hire themselves to another. But in America it is not so. For there it is lawful to keep slaves.' Clearly one of the easiest ways to gut the book for its essentials for the juvenile market lay in writing short poems about each central character or event, which were then combined with an illustration. The first three poems are taken from one of the most popular of such collections. The next two poems are extracted from *The Uncle Tom's Cabin Songster*, which in fact carried few poems directly about the novel and rehashed favourite old songs on any subject.

The final example shows how one of the most elevated figures within the artistic and literary English establishment responded to the books' success in flagrantly racist terms. Rossetti, the charismatic Pre-Raphaelite painter and poet, exhibited little interest in abolition or colonial slavery in his work. Yet he did respond to the popularity of Stowe's *UTC* in several ways, all of which are parodic and suggest unease. Characters from *UTC* which were absorbed into theatrical low comedy could be readapted within the context of his own clowning and buffoonery with his young Pre-Raphaelite disciples. Rossetti envisioned the notoriously tousled William Morris as the comic black slave girl Topsy, a sobriquet which once invented was rapidly adopted as a group nickname when the second generation of Pre-Raphaelites, under Rossetti's leadership, painted the roof of the Oxford University Students' Union. Morris's pursuit of Jane Lipscombe, later to be Janey Morris, was ridiculed in doggerel which equates Morris's artistic clumsiness with Topsy's illiteracy: 'Poor Topsy has gone | To make a sketch of Miss Lipscombe, | But he can't draw the head | And don't know where the hips come.' All good fun no doubt but the substitutions involved are not harmless—Morris, real, rich, white, free, amorous, and male, becomes Topsy, fictional, destitute, black, enslaved, unsexual, and female. Rossetti's poetical burlesque of Uncle Tom produced below takes the form of a parody of a popular black-face minstrel song, 'Old Ned', which begins, 'Dere was an old nigger, and him name was Uncle Ned | And him died long long ago . . .' The basis of Rossetti's racism is a feigned carelessness about colour. His brother describes his views on blacks as founded in a terrible flippancy: 'My brother had no very settled ideas about negroes, their rights and wrongs: he knew, and was much tickled by, Carlyle's "Occasional Discourse on the Nigger Question".' Of course this tells us that Rossetti did indeed have very precise ideas about black people, their rights and wrongs. Educated society in mid-nineteenth-century Britain and the Northern states of America was outraged and disgusted by Carlyle's scandalous assault on the effects of black emancipation in the English sugar colonies. The Southern states were delighted by a text that seemed to legitimize the continuation of slavery as a necessary and benevolent patriarchy. Rossetti does not much care either way, he is 'tickled'. (All quotations taken from Wood, *Blind Memory*, 143–50.)

Eliza Crossing the River[1]

From her resting-place by the trader chased,
Through the winter evening cold,
Eliza came with her boy at last,
Where a broad deep river rolled.

Great blocks of the floating ice were there,
And the water's roar was wild,
But the cruel trader's step was near,
Who would take her only child.

Poor Harry clung around her neck,
But a word he could not say,
For his very heart was faint with fear,
And with flying all that day.

Her arms about the boy grew tight,
With a loving clasp, and brave;
"Hold fast! Hold fast, now, Harry dear,
And it may be God will save."

From the river's bank to the floating ice
She took a sudden bound,
And the great block swayed beneath her feet
With a dull and heavy sound.

So over the roaring rushing flood,
From block to block she sprang,
And ever her cry for God's good help
Above the waters rang.

And God did hear that mother's cry,
For never an ice-block sank;
While the cruel trader and his men
Stood wondering on the bank.

A good man saw on the further side,
And gave her his helping hand;

---

[1]   The subject for this poem is the famous climax to chapter 8 of *Uncle Tom's Cabin*. Eliza's desperate escape over the ice with her baby was more widely adapted in plays, film, and children's literature than any other single scene.

So poor Eliza, with her boy,
Stood safe upon the land.

A blessing on that good man's arm,
On his house, and field, and store;
May he never want a friendly hand
To help him to the shore!

A blessing on all that make such haste,
Whatever their hands can do!
For they that succour the sore distressed,
Our Lord will help them too.

Eva Putting a Wreath of Flowers Round Tom's Neck [1]

Poor Tom is far from his cottage now,
From his own good wife, and children three,
Where coffee, and rice, and cedars grow,
By a wide old river like the sea.

And he has a master rich and kind,
With all that his heart can well desire,
But homeward still goes the negro's mind,
To the curly heads by his cottage fire.

He the gentle Eva's life did save,
When over the great ship's side she fell,
And brought her up from the drowning wave,—
So Eva had grown to love him well.

She will read to Tom for hours on hours,
And sit with him on the grass all day;
You see she is wreathing pretty flowers,
About his neck, in her pleasant play.

Different in colour and in years
Are the negro man and that fair child's face;
But a likeness in God's sight appears,
For both are the children of his grace.

---

[1] This famous scene occurs in 'Kentuck', chapter 21 of *Uncle Tom's Cabin*, shortly before Eva's death: 'Tom and Eva were seated on a little mossy seat, in an arbour, at the foot of the garden. It was Sunday evening and Eva's bible lay open on her knee.'

Topsy at the Looking Glass[1]

See little Topsy at the glass quite gay,
Her mistress has forgot the keys to-day,
So she has rummaged every drawer, and dressed
Herself out in Miss Feely's very best.

Mark where she stands! the shawl of gorgeous red
Wound like a Turk's great turban round her head;
A finer shawl far trailing on the floor,
Just shews her bare black elbows, and no more.

With what an air she flaunts the ivory fan,
And tries to step as stately as she can,
Mincing fine words to her own shadow, "Dear!
How very ungenteel the folks are here!"

But while that shadow only Topsy sees,
Back comes the careful lady for her keys,
And finds her in her grandeur all arrayed—
Poor Topsy will be punished, I'm afraid.

Now it is wrong, as every reader knows,
To rummage people's drawers, and wear their clothes;
But Topsy is a negro child, you see,
Who never learned to read like you and me.

A child whom bad men from her mother sold,
Whom a harsh mistress used to cuff and scold,
Whom no one taught or cared for all her days,
No wonder that the girl had naughty ways.

No home, no school, no Bible she had seen,
How bless'd beyond poor Topsy we have been!
Yet boys and girls among ourselves, I've known
Puffed up with praise for merits not their own.

---

[1] This scene, focused on the antics of the comic slave girl Topsy, occurs in 'Topsy', chapter 20 of *Uncle Tom's Cabin*: 'she would . . . dress the bolster up in Miss Ophelia's night clothes, and enact various scenic performances with that,—singing and whistling, and making grimaces at herself in the looking-glass.'

8. Anon., 'Topsy at the Looking Glass' (wood engraving, 1853), in
Pictures and Stories from Uncle Tom's Cabin.

The copy by some clever school-mate penned,
The witty saying picked up from a friend,
Makes many a miss and master look as fine,
As if they coined the words or penned the line.

But none can keep such borrowed plumes as these,
For some one still comes back to find the keys,
And so they are found out, it comes to pass,
Just like poor Topsy at the looking-glass.

Uncle Tom's Lament for the Old Folks at Home

Though from five hundred miles, or nearly,
    Brought far away,
Dere's a little spot dat I lub dearly,
    Down where de old folks stay.
Men in cruel chains may bind me,
    Fancy will roam,
When thinking of those left behind me,
    Down wid de old folks at home.

CHORUS
All to me is sad and gloomy,
    Eb'ry ting does come,
And bring de good old times unto me,
    Spent wid de old folks at home.

Den I dream ob de old farm yonder,
    Where when a child,
Round de fields I used to wander,
    Down where de fruits grew wild.
Oh! how I lubb'd dat old plantation!
    Lubb'd eb'ry tree—
Now nothing in de whole creation
    Brings such a joy to me.

Time dat will for no man tarry,
    Quickly had flown;
And at last I came to marry,
    Had children ob my own.

Oh! what kind words den were spoken,
    Here nebber known;
I feel my heart is nearly broken,
    Now I am left alone.

So I sit and watch de ember—
    Fire dies away,
And feel my heart is like December,
    Which once was blythe as May.
When shall I hear my children's prattle,
    When see dere mudder come?
Oh! a slave dey only call a chattel,
    And such is Uncle Tom!

But; whilst all looks dark and gloomy,
    Dreams seem to come,
And bring back olden times unto me,
    Pass'd wid de old folks at home.

The Slave Auction

Hark! midst the roar of an eager crowd,
    For one dark purpose blending,
The cry of a helpless multitude
    Is thence in pray'r ascending;
And negro forms are gather'd round,
    Their cheeks with hot tears streaming,
Their limbs in iron shackles bound,
    Their minds as fetter'd seeming.

CHORUS
'O! give us back our Rights,' they pray,
    'That man from man has riven,
That Freedom which is yours to-day,
    Our Birth-right, held from Heaven!'
'O! give us but our Rights,' they pray,
    'That man from man has riven;
Man—born unfetter'd as the day—
    Free as the air from Heaven!'

The sale is on—and men begin
  To sell their fellow creatures;
Yet He who made the whiter skin
  Made those with darker features.
A premium on the stout and strong,
  A tax on bone and sinew;
O! men with human hearts, how long
  Shall this foul trade continue.

A child is from its mother torn,—
  Hark! hear that shriek distressing!
A helpless girl is left to mourn
  A parent's nightly blessing.
Another!—and the tendrest ties
  Of life are rent asunder;—
Hath Heaven, in eacho to those cries,
  No crime avenging thunder?

The sale proceeds—a loving wife
  They from her husband sever;
But, ere the bargain's seal'd, a knife
  Annuls the bond for ever!
The man, self slaughter'd, yields his breath—
  The wife dies broken-hearted?
Far happier to be join'd in death,
  Than both in slav'ry parted.

'Who bids?' none care—the shrieks are drown'd
  Beneath the auction's clamour;
They reach not those who hear no sound
  Beyond the sales-man's hammer;
Still louder grows the din around,
  The biddings follow faster,
Till ev'ry slave at last has found
  A tyrant, call'd a master.

O! let us hope the day is near,
  The dawn of brighter ages,
When slaves and slav'ry shall appear
  But names in hist'ry's pages;
That man 'gainst man may ne'er combine,
  In this inhuman manner,
And ev'ry star shall brighter shine
  Upon the spangled banner!

'O! give us back our Rights,' they pray,
  'That man from man has riven,
That Freedom which is yours to-day,
  Our Birth-right, held from Heaven!'
Yes, let us hope that we pray
  To us may soon be given;
When all men shall be free as day,
  That freely flows from Heaven!

Lines *on* Uncle Tom's Cabin

Dere was an old nigger, and him name was Uncle Tom,
  And him tale was rather slow;
  Me try to read the whole but me only read some,
Because me found it no go.
    Den hang up de auther Mrs Stowe,
      And kick de volume wid your toe—
    And dere's no more public for poor Uncle Tom,
      He am gone where de trunk lining go.

Him tale dribbles on and on widout a break,
  Til you hab no eyes for to see;
When I reached Chapter 4 I had got a headache,
  So I had to let chapter 4 be.
    Den Hang up, etc.

De demand one fine morning for Uncle Tom died,
  De tears down Mrs. Stowe's face ran like rain;
For she knew berry well, now dey'd laid him on de shelf,
  Dat she'd neber get a publisher again.
    Den hang up, etc.

PART II

American Poems

Contents of Part II

Selections from plantation songs and spirituals: 'Go Down, Moses', 'No More Auction Block', 'There's a Better Day a Coming', 'Swing Low, Sweet Chariot', 'Mary, Don't You Weep', in William Francis Allen, Charles Packard Ware, and Lucy McKim Garrison (eds.), *Slave Songs of the United States* (1867)

The songs created by the slaves on the Southern plantations hold a unique and central place for an Anglo-American anthology of the poetry of slavery. If you stand in the crowd at an international rugby match and watch the English fans singing 'Swing Low, Sweet Chariot', the song they have adopted as 'their' anthem, you are listening to a white rendition of the slave poetry of America. The poetic songs generated by the slaves are still alive, still thriving and developing in global culture white and black, from the recordings of Mahalia Jackson and Paul Robeson to the terraces of Twickenham. The spirituals have become absorbed into American and European cultures in deep, indeed unfathomable ways. They are the most influential and intense poetry to have been generated by the slave systems of the Americas. In terms of their cultural transmission they have no beginning and no end. Indentured African labour began in the Southern tobacco plantations in the second decade of the seventeenth century. Black slaves were thinking, dancing, singing, telling stories, and, later, occasionally writing about their experiences from then on until the Civil War. When they came in contact with the narratives of the Old Testament they saw in these stories a ready-made mythology with which to critique and subvert the power dynamics of the plantations. The work songs and later the spirituals which they developed constitute not only the earliest but the most powerful and revolutionary anthems created by the slaves. These works are emotionally complicated, conjoining extreme expressions of sadness, loss, and suffering with extreme joy at the prospect of deliverance.

Obviously this material is primarily oral: it has no specific authors, and no firm compositional dates which scholars can fix, yet it is hardly contentious to posit that the first poetry created about slavery was slave songs. As early as 1801 some of the songs were anthologized in printed form. The big anthologies of African-American literature which broke through at the end of the last millennium (the Norton appeared in 1997, the Riverside in 1998) include substantial selections from the songs and spirituals, which are termed part of the *vernacular* tradition of slave literature. I felt it was important to register their presence at the opening of the American section of this book because from a surprisingly early date a consolidated canon of this work had become widely accepted and embraced across Europe and North America. The spirituals consequently existed both as printed texts, poetic texts, and as songs to be performed.

Walking into a minute bookshop in the tiny town of Kenmare on the wild coast of southern Ireland in 1995 I bought a book, printed in London in 1885, J. B. T. Marsh,

The Story of the Jubilee Singers with their Songs (Hodder & Stoughton), which stated it was 'a new edition completing one hundred and fifth thousand': that is a lot of books to sell in the United Kingdom at the end of the nineteenth century. Opposite the title page is a photograph showing eleven impeccably dressed African Americans; they look in age range to be about 30 to 50. The men are in black tail coats, white shirt, and black tie, the women in full-length elaborately brocaded black gowns. Both men and women have straightened hair, the men with arrow-straight partings. They all stare straight out at the camera, and now at us, with expressions so intense as to be indecipherable. These ex-slaves were big transatlantic celebrities who, less than twenty years after the cessation of the American Civil War, had toured the Northern states of America and the principal nations of Europe leaving white audiences stunned and weeping. They had performed before the major statesmen and aristocracy of central Europe including William Gladstone, at a private breakfast, and Queen Victoria. Their performances consisted of harmonic renditions of the slave songs of the Southern plantations. They had a repertoire of 130 songs. They made a fortune of $100,000 in three years in order to endow their own school, Fisk University in Tennessee.

The texts and the music of the spirituals were lastingly injected into what we like to term Western culture from top to bottom. When the Jubilee Singers performed in Brooklyn, New York, one Dr Cuyler reported: 'the wild melodies of these emancipated slaves touched the fount of tears and grey haired men wept like little children.' He went on to describe these performers as 'the living representatives of the only true native school of American music', and set them against the degraded traditions of 'nigger minstrelsy': 'we have long enough had its coarse caricatures in corked faces; our people can now listen to the genuine soul-music of the slave cabins, before the Lord led his children "out of the land of Egypt, out of the house of bondage!"' (Marsh, *Story of the Jubilee Singers*, 31). English musical theorists could not comprehend how or why these works had the effect they did on English audiences: 'They come from no musical cultivation whatever, but are the simple, ecstatic utterances of wholly untutored minds. From so unpromising a source we could reasonably expect only such a mass of crudities as would be unendurable to the cultivated ear. On the contrary, however, the cultivated listener confesses to a new charm, and to a power never before felt' (ibid. 122). English and North American audiences were powerless to defend their intellects against the traumatic emotional impact of this art of the plantations, and finally acculturated these beautiful yet terrifying songs by projecting a normalizing pietism onto their religious content. Yet for the slaves who sung these works, not in churches but throughout the diurnal cycles of slave life, they meant something very different. Many of the songs, and certainly the majority of the spirituals, were not merely another sort of Evangelical hymn, but were some of the first artworks of a black liberation theology; they took the religion of the masters and ran with it. Recent scholarship has convincingly established that the spirituals did not develop primarily out of the imitation of extant forms of Eurocentric religious lyric, song, or hymnology, but African oral traditions of heroic epic. Slaves took their heroes and narratives from the Old Testament and adapted them to African-evolved narrative, performative, and linguistic structures. They also used Old Testament typology and applied it to their own situation. Pharaoh is also the slave power, Egypt is also the slave South, and as the refrain of 'Oh Mary, Don't You Weep' states delightedly again, and again, and again, and again: 'Pharaoh's army got drownded.'

Go Down, Moses

Go down, Moses,
Way down in Egyptland
Tell old Pharaoh
To let my people go.

When Israel was in Egyptland
Let my people go
Oppressed so hard they could not stand
Let my people go.

Go down, Moses,
Way down in Egyptland
Tell old Pharaoh
"Let my people go."

"Thus saith the Lord," bold Moses said,
"Let my people go;
If not I'll smite your first-born dead
Let my people go.

"No more shall they in bondage toil,
Let my people go;
Let them come out with Egypt's spoil,
Let my people go."

The Lord told Moses what to do
Let my people go;
To lead the children of Israel through,
Let my people go.

Go down, Moses,
Way down in Egyptland,
Tell old Pharaoh,
"Let my people go!"

No More Auction Block

No more auction block for me,
No more, no more,
No more auction block for me,
Many thousand gone.

No more peck of corn for me,
No more, no more,
No more peck of corn for me,
Many thousand gone.

No more pint of salt for me,
No more, no more,
No more pint of salt for me,
Many thousand gone.

No more driver's lash for me,
No more, no more,
No more driver's lash for me,
Many thousand gone.

There's a Better Day a Coming

A few more beatings of the wind and rain,
Ere the winter will be over—
   Glory, Hallelujah!
Some friends has gone before me,—
I must try to go and meet them—
   Glory, Hallelujah!
A few more risings and settings of the sun,
Ere the winter will be over—
   Glory, Hallelujah!
There's a better day a coming—
There's a better day a coming—
   Oh, Glory, Hallelujah!

Swing Low, Sweet Chariot

Swing low, sweet chariot,
Coming for to carry me home,
Swing low, sweet chariot,
Coming for to carry me home.

I looked over Jordan[1] and what did I see
Coming for to carry me home,
A band of angels, coming after me,
Coming for to carry me home.

If you get there before I do,
Coming for to carry me home,
Tell all my friends I'm coming too,
Coming for to carry me home.

Swing low, sweet chariot,
Coming for to carry me home,
Swing low, sweet chariot,
Coming for to carry me home.

Oh Mary, Don't You Weep

Oh Mary, don't you weep, don't you moan,
Oh Mary, don't you weep, don't you moan,
Pharaoh's army got drownded,[1]
Oh Mary, don't you weep.

One of dese mornings, bright and fair,
Take my wings and cleave de air,
Pharaoh's army got drownded,
Oh Mary, don't you weep.

One of dese mornings, five o'clock,
Dis ole world gonna reel and rock,

---

[1] The great river of Palestine, also used figuratively to mean death, as a passage to the promised land.

[1] Referring to Exodus 13: 27–8: 'and the Lord overthrew the Egyptians in the midst of the sea. And the waters returned and covered the chariots, and the horsemen, and all the host of Pharaoh that came into the sea after them: there remained not so much as one of them.'

Pharaoh's army got drownded,
Oh Mary, don't you weep.

Oh Mary, don't you weep, don't you moan,
Oh Mary, don't you weep, don't you moan,
Pharaoh's army got drownded,
Oh Mary, don't you weep.

Phyllis Wheatley (1753?-1784), 'To the University of Cambridge in New England', 'On Being Brought from Africa to America', 'To the Right Honourable William, Earl of Dartmouth, His Majesty's Principal Secretary of State for North America, &c.', 'To S.M. a Young African Painter, on Seeing his Works', in *Poems on Various Subjects Religious and Moral* (1773)

In 1973, to mark the bicentennial of the publication of Phyllis Wheatley's poems, eighteen leading African-American women poets held the 'Wheatley Poetry Festival' in Jackson, Mississippi. This landmark event symbolically marked a massive shift of attention towards early British and American black slave authors, and Wheatley has remained at the heart of this canonic move. Prior to the mid-1970s Phyllis Wheatley was unknown outside a tiny coterie of scholars interested in the early slave authors within the Diaspora. Wheatley is now one of the most celebrated of the early African-American authors, and holds an iconic place within the Anglo-American literatures of the slave Diaspora. There is, however, intense and continuing debate over both the literary status of her work, and the extent to which it is engaged with a critique of slavery in ways which would now be considered politically cogent.

Certainly a large part of Wheatley's notoriety comes out of the dramatic and sentimental aspects of her biography. Born, probably, in 1753, Wheatley was kidnapped into slavery as an infant on the West African slave coast. She was shipped to America and bought by the relatively wealthy Wheatleys of Boston in 1761. Mary, the Wheatleys' daughter, took the fragile black girl under her wing, and gave her a remarkably advanced education in literature and the classics. Wheatley not only read the English classics but became fluent in Latin and Greek. Wheatley, unlike the majority of white British and American women, and come to that *men*, achieved the amazing step of mastering the secret languages of Anglo-American aristocratic patriarchy. By the mid-1760s Wheatley was writing fluent letters in English and composing her first

9. Anon., 'Phyllis Wheatley' (copper-plate engraving, 1773), frontispiece to
Phyllis Wheatley, *Poems on Various Subjects Religious and Moral*.

neoclassical verse. By 1772 she had written enough verse for her mistress to contemplate publishing a volume through subscription. Unable to get financial backing for the
venture in New England the Wheatleys sent their young protégée to London in 1773,
under the protection of their son Nathaniel. In London she was rapidly converted into
a literary prodigy, and was taken up by leading figures in the nascent British abolition
movement. Sir James Thornton, head of the Clapham sect Evangelicals, introduced

Wheatley to European and American abolitionist and radical intellectuals in London. Wheatley's work was enthusiastically, if often patronizingly, reviewed in all areas of the British press, and she was a sensation in fashionable circles. From these heady literary and social heights Wheatley returned to America and a life of tragic decline. Three years after returning to America she was given her freedom. She married a free black man called John Peters, who seems to have been something of an ambitious failure in business. She and her three children slipped into increasingly dire poverty. When Wheatley died in 1784 she had been unable to find backers for two subsequent volumes of poetry and she and her one surviving child died in destitution.

Wheatley had to encounter and to negotiate a colonial British, and then a British literary, culture which was not sure whether it admired her for her literary accomplishments or whether it was fascinated by a freakish phenomenon, a black African-American slave girl who could write like a female Alexander Pope. In many ways the original social limitations and uncertainties surrounding Wheatley's literary status persist. The goalposts may have been shifted slightly, but the questions remain: is the poetry really any good, and would anyone read it if the circumstances of Wheatley's biographical history were not known? The relation between biographical history and literary quality in any individual œuvre is different in every example, and is always a question of unique complexity. The charged historiography which the 'Wheatley phenomenon' has generated around itself in the last quarter-century has made it particularly difficult to separate her life from her work. And yet, as more close literary studies of the poetry emerge, it is becoming increasingly evident that the formal and technical range of Wheatley's poetry is quite exceptional. Wheatley is also emerging as a delicate and conscious ironist, who turns the tools of her classical education back on her white readership. Her critique of the psychological and physical depredations of Atlantic slavery lacks the crudity and bravura of subsequent abolition verse. Yet Wheatley's delicate subversions are a terribly important part of the poetic slave archive. It is the very vulnerability and loquacious fragility of this voice which embody its final and beautiful strength. In this sense, as a critic of Atlantic slavery, she finds an artistic sister in Jane Austen, the Jane Austen who so darkly unpicked the workings of the slave economy in *Mansfield Park*.

To the University of Cambridge in New England

> While an intrinsic ardor prompts to write,
> The muses promise to assist my pen;
> 'Twas not long since I left my native shore
> The land of errors, and *Egyptian* gloom:[1]
> Father of mercy, 'twas thy gracious hand
> Brought me in safety from those dark abodes.

---

[1] Exodus 10: 22: 'And Moses stretched forth his hand toward Heaven, and there was a thick darkness over the land of Egypt, even the darkness which may be felt.'

Students, to you 'tis giv'n to scan the heights
Above, to traverse the ethereal space,
And mark the systems of revolving worlds.
Still more, ye sons of science ye receive
The blissful news by messengers from heav'n,
How *Jesus'* blood for your redemption flows.
See him with hands out-stretcht upon the cross;
Immense compassion in his bosom glows;
He hears revilers, nor resents their scorn:
What matchless mercy in the Son of God!
When the whole human race by sin had fall'n,
He deign'd to die that they might rise again,
And share with him in the sublimest skies,
Life without death, and glory without end.

Improve your privileges while they stay,
Ye pupils, and each hour redeem, that bears
Or good or bad report of you to heav'n.
Let sin, that baneful evil to the soul,
By you be shunn'd, nor once remit your guard;
Suppress the deadly serpent in its egg.
Ye blooming plants of human race devine,
An *Ethiop*[2] tells you 'tis your greatest foe;
Its transient sweetness turns to endless pain,
And in immense perdition sinks the soul.

On Being Brought from Africa to America

'Twas mercy brought me from my *Pagan* land,
Taught my benighted soul to understand
That there's a God, that there's a *Saviour* too:
Once I redemption neither sought nor knew.
Some view our sable race with scornful eye,
"Their colour is a diabolic die."
Remember, *Christians*, *Negros*, black as *Cain*,
May be refin'd, and join th' angelic train.

---

[2] Ethiop and Ethiopian were both used at this time as generic terms for African and African-American people.

To the Right Honourable William, Earl of Dartmouth,[1] His Majesty's Principal Secretary of State for North America, &c.

Hail, happy day, when, smiling like the morn,
Fair *Freedom* rose *New-England* to adorn:
The northern clime beneath her genial ray,
Dartmouth, congratulates thy blissful sway:
Elate with hope her race no longer mourns,
Each soul expands, each grateful bosom burns,
While in thine hand with pleasure we behold
The silken reins, and *Freedom's* charms unfold.
Long lost to realms beneath the northern skies
She shines supreme, while hated *faction* dies:
Soon as appear'd the *Goddess*[2] long desir'd,
Sick at the view, she lanquish'd and expir'd;
Thus from the splendors of the morning light
The owl in sadness seeks the caves of night.

No more, *America*, in mournful strain
Of wrongs, and grievance unredress'd complain,
No longer shalt thou dread the iron chain,
Which wanton *Tyranny* with lawless hand
Had made, and with it meant t' enslave the land.

Should you, my lord, while you peruse my song,
Wonder from whence my love of *Freedom* sprung,
Whence flow these wishes for the common good,
By feeling hearts alone best understood,
I, young in life, by seeming cruel fate
Was snatch'd from *Afric's* fancy'd happy seat:
What pangs excruciating must molest,
What sorrows labour in my parent's breast?
Steel'd was that soul and by no misery mov'd
That from a father seiz'd his babe belov'd:
Such, such my case. And can I then but pray
Others may never feel tyrannic sway?

---

[1] William Legge (1731–1801), 2nd Earl of Dartmouth, was Secretary of State for the American colonies until 1775.
[2] Freedom.

For favours past, great Sir, our thanks are due,
And thee we ask thy favours to renew,
Since in thy pow'r, as in thy will before,
To sooth the griefs, which thou did'st once deplore.
May heav'nly grace the sacred sanction give
To all thy works, and thou for ever live
Not only on the wings of fleeting *Fame*,
Though praise immortal crowns the patriot's name,
But to conduct to heav'ns refulgent fane,[3]
May fiery coursers sweep th' ethereal plain,
And bear thee upwards to that blest abode,
Where, like the prophet,[4] thou shalt find thy God.

To S.M.[1] a Young African Painter, on Seeing his Works

To show the lab'ring bosom's deep intent,
And thought in living characters to paint,
When first thy pencil did those beauties give,
And breathing figures learnt from thee to live,
How did those prospects give my soul delight,
A new creation rushing on my sight?
Still, wond'rous youth! each noble path pursue,
On deathless glories fix thine ardent view:
Still may the painter's and the poet's fire
To aid thy pencil, and thy verse conspire!
And may the charms of each seraphic theme
Conduct thy footsteps to immortal fame!
High to the blissful wonders of the skies
Elate thy soul, and raise thy wishful eyes.
Thrice happy, when exalted to survey
That splendid city, crown'd with endless day,
Whose twice six gates on radiant hinges ring:
Celestial *Salem*[2] blooms in endless spring.

[3] 'Heav'ns refulgent fane' means 'Heaven's light-filled temple'.
[4] The prophet Elijah who ascended to heaven in a fiery chariot.

[1] Almost certainly the young local artist Scipio Moorhead, a black slave belonging to the Revd John Moorhead.
[2] Jerusalem.

Calm and serene thy moments glide along,
And may the muse inspire each future song!
Still, with the sweets of contemplation bless'd,
May peace with balmy wings your soul invest!
But when these shades of time are chas'd away,
And darkness ends in everlasting day,
On what seraphic pinions shall we move,
And view the landscapes in the realms above?
There shall thy tongue in heav'nly murmurs flow,
And there my muse with heav'nly transport glow:
No more to tell of *Damon's*[3] tender sighs,
Or rising radiance of *Aurora's*[4] eyes,
For nobler themes demand a nobler strain,
And purer languge on th' ethereal plain.
Cease, gentle muse! the solemn gloom of night
Now seals the fair creation from my sight.

Jupiter Hammon (1711–1806), *An Address to Miss Phillis Wheatly* [sic], *Ethiopian Poetess in Boston, who Came from Africa at Eight Years of Age* (1778)

Hammon's first poem appeared in 1760, making him the first published slave poet of North America. The only known slave poet to pre-date him is Lucy Terry, whose *Bars Fight* was written in 1746, although not published until 1895. He was born into slavery on the Manor House estate on Long Island. The owner Henry Lloyd allowed the slaves to attend a primitive school he set up on the plantation. Hammon bought a Bible from his master when he was in his early twenties and his resulting writings are all intensely religious in their focus. Yet the evidence of Hammon's sermons, and to an extent his verse, show that he did a lot more than simply recirculate the regulatory pietism of the slave power. His sermons discuss the heroic role of black slaves during the English war, and he goes so far as to introduce the subject of slave petitions for freedom. Hammon in his poetry and prose is, like Phyllis Wheatley, playing a dangerous game. Given the standard slave power line on slave literacy, and intelligence, Hammon must present himself as passive, a good Christian, and grateful to be able to write at all. He must also present himself as quite exceptional to the slave population as a whole, because the

---

[3] Damon was a stock character used in pastorals, a singing rustic.
[4] Personification of sunrise, or dawn.

notion that all slaves might teach themselves to read and write and then become theorists of social revolution was a little too frightening to be borne. Yet within the structures of literary policing in which he was required to express himself he is constantly playing challenging games with the conventions he uses. As with Wheatley's work it is up to the reader to decide where mimicry ends and sarcasm begins. Can Hammon's insistence on prefacing each of his published works with the details of his 'three generations of servitude' to the Lloyd family be entirely unironic? Then again the intensely moving dedication of the *Address* to 'Miss Phillis Wheatly, Ethiopian Poetess in Boston, who came from Africa at eight years of age' might have appeared amusingly over-elevated to contemporary white readers who saw the diction of literary gentility applied to a young black female slave. Yet, one might ask, who gets the last laugh? In describing Phyllis's experience of the horrors of the middle passage as a little girl in the laconic statement that she 'came from Africa at eight years of age' is Hammon being ironic or obtuse? The *Address* with its obsessive harping upon how Phyllis has been set free by Christianity— 'God's tender mercy set thee free . . . The blessed Jesus set thee free . . . His tender mercies still are free'—can be read as the emphatic assertion of a conventional gratitude for the gift of 'Grace'. Then again when does the emphatic become overemphatic; when does Brutus cease to be 'an honourable man'? Hammon's assertions can be seen as an acidic articulation of the fact that while God offers freedom as an option, the slave owner emphatically does not. The fact that the only freedom on offer in this poem comes through Christ's sacrifice, when both the poet and his subject are in reality slaves, can be powerfully constructed as a critique of the American slavery institutions. That Hammon had a deep understanding of the double standards whites applied over the definition of freedom comes out with an unusual frankness in his *An Address to the Negroes in the State of New York*: 'That liberty is a great thing we may know from our own feelings, and we may likewise judge so from the conduct of the white people in the late war. How much money has been spent and how many lives have been lost to defend their liberty! I must say that I have hope that God would open their eyes, when they were so much engaged for liberty, to think of the state of the poor blacks and to pity us.' This is not the voice of a broken spirit upholding the status quo.

An Address to Miss Phillis Wheatly [sic], Ethiopian Poetess in Boston, who Came from Africa at Eight Years of Age

I

O come you pious youth! adore
The wisdom of thy God,
In bringing thee from distant shore,
To learn His holy word.
Eccles. xii.

II

Thou mightst been left behind
    Amidst a dark abode;
God's tender mercy still combin'd,
    Thou hast the holy word.
      Psal. cxxxv, 2, 3.

III

Fair wisdom's ways are paths of peace,
    And they that walk therein,
Shall reap the joys that never cease,
    And Christ shall be their king.
      Psal. i, 1, 2; Prov. iii, 7.

IV

God's tender mercy brought thee here;
    Tost o'er the raging main;
In Christian faith thou hast a share,
    Worth all the gold of Spain.
      Psal. ciii, 1, 3, 4.

V

While thousands tossed by the sea,
    And others settled down,
God's tender mercy set thee free,
    From dangers that come down.
      Death.

VI

That thou a pattern still might be,
    To youth of Boston town,
The blessed Jesus set thee free,
    From every sinful wound.
      2 Cor. v. 10.

VII

The blessed Jesus, who came down,
    Unvail'd his sacred face,
To cleanse the soul of every wound,
    And give repenting grace.
      Rom. v. 21.

VIII

That we poor sinners may obtain,
   The pardon of our sin;
Dear blessed Jesus now constrain,
   And bring us flocking in.
     Psal. xxxiv, 6, 7, 8.

IX

Come you, Phillis, now aspire,
   And seek the living God,
So step by step thou mayst go higher,
   Till perfect in the word.
     Matth. vii, 7, 8.

X

While thousands mov'd to distant shore,
   And others left behind,
The blessed Jesus still adore,
   Implant this in thy mind.
     Psal. lxxxix, 1.

XI

Thou hast left the heathen shore;
   Thro' mercy of the Lord,
Among the heathen live no more,
   Come magnify thy God.
     Psal. xxxiv, 1, 2, 3.

XII

I pray the living God may be,
   The shepherd of thy soul;
His tender mercies still are free,
   His mysteries to unfold.
     Psal. lxxx, 1, 2, 3.

XIII

Thou, Phillis, when thou hunger hast,
   Or pantest for thy God;
Jesus Christ is thy relief,
   Thou hast the holy word.
     Psal. xiii, 1, 2, 3.

XIV

The bounteous mercies of the Lord,
  Are hid beyond the sky,
And holy souls that love His word,
  Shall taste them when they die.
    Psal. xvi, 10, 11.

XV

These bounteous mercies are from God,
  The merits of His Son;
The humble soul that loves His word,
  He chooses for His own.
    Psal. xxxiv, 15.

XVI

Come, dear Phillis, be advis'd,
  To drink Samaria's[1] flood;
There nothing that shall suffice
  But Christ's redeeming blood.
    John iv, 13, 14.

XVII

While thousands muse with earthly toys;
  And range about the street,
Dear Phillis, seek for heaven's joys,
  Where we do hope to meet.
    Matth. vi, 33.

XVIII

When God shall send his summons down,
  And number saints together,
Blest angels chant, (triumphant sound),
  Come live with me forever.
    Psal. cxvi, 15.

XIX

The humble soul shall fly to God,
  And leave the things of time,
Start forth as 'twere at the first word,
  To taste things more divine.
    Matth. v, 3, 8.

---

[1] In the relevant passage from the Gospel of John, the woman of Samaria is drawing water at a well, when Jesus asks her for a drink. In the ensuing discussion of her refusal to give him a drink Jesus teaches her that the water of faith is something which once taken will cure thirst eternally.

XX
Behold! the soul shall waft away,
   Whene'er we come to die,
And leave its cottage made of clay,
   In twinkling of an eye.
    Cor. xv, 51, 52, 53

XXI
Now glory be to the Most High,
   United praises given,
By all on earth, incessantly,
   And all the host of heav'n.
    Psal. cl, 6.

Phillip Frenau (1752–1832), 'To Sir Toby' (1792) [alternatively titled *The Island Free Negro* in some versions]

Frenau, nicknamed 'The Poet of the Revolution', was one of the hardest-hitting American satirists of the eighteenth century. He wrote a mass of scathing and genuinely popular satires attacking the British and was particularly vitriolic at the expense of the British officials in New England. Writing at a time when there simply was not a big enough reading public in the colonies for a poet to make a decent living out of writing poetry alone, Frenau did a variety of jobs including schoolteacher, newspaper editor, and sailor. The fact that he had lived in the West Indies, Charleston, Carolina, Philadelphia, New Jersey, and New York meant that he had a very wide breadth of experience to draw on when he came to write about social issues. He was intensely interested in the developing culture of post-war America. Frenau was, in terms of form and content, the most ambitious and talented of the early American poets. The range of his gifts, particularly as a Romantic lyricist of genuine quality, is only now being recognized. 'To Sir Toby' is an accomplished satire in the late Popean mode. As narrational persona Frenau takes the moral high ground, and the tone of outraged hauteur which typifies the Pope of the *Moral Epistles*. 'To Sir Toby' is in many ways Frenau's version of the superb 'Timon's Villa' passage from Pope's 'Epistle to Richard Boyle, Earl of Burlington' on 'the use of Riches'. Frenau's unremitting sarcasm is at points in danger of ridiculing the slave victim at the same time that he lambastes the slave owner. Yet overall Frenau manages to attack the cruelty of the plantations with an incredulous ferocity which finds no match in the anti-slavery verse being written in Britain during the early

1790s. It is possible his directness emanates from the fact he had been an eyewitness to acts of torture on plantations in the Caribbean and the American South.

To Sir Toby

A Sugar Planter in the interior parts of Jamaica, near the City of San Jago de la Vega, (Spanish Town) 1784

> *"The motions of his spirit are black as night,*
> *And his affections dark as Erebus."*
>   —SHAKESPEARE[1]

If there exists a hell—the case is clear—
Sir Toby's slaves enjoy that portion here:
Here are no blazing brimstone lakes—'tis true;
But kindled Rum too often burns as blue;
In which some fiend, whom nature must detest,
Steeps Toby's brand, and marks poor Cudjoe's[2] breast.
Here whips on whips excite perpetual fears,
And mingled howlings vibrate on my ears:
Here nature's plagues abound, to fret and tease,
Snakes, scorpions, despots, lizards, centipees—
No art, no care escapes the busy lash;
All have their dues—and all are paid in cash—
The eternal driver keeps a steady eye
On a black herd, who would his vengeance fly.
But chained, imprisoned, on a burning soil,
For the mean avarice of a tyrant, toil!
The lengthy cart-whip guards this monster's reign—
And cracks, like pistols, from the fields of cane.
Ye powers! who formed these wretched tribes, relate,
What had they done, to merit such a fate!
Why were they brought from Eboe's[3] sultry waste,
To see that plenty which they must not taste—
Food, which they cannot buy, and dare not steal;
Yams and potatoes—many a scanty meal!—

---

[1] *Merchant of Venice*, v. i. 87: in this speech Lorenzo is talking of the evil and treacherous nature of any human who does not love music. Erebus is a place of darkness between Earth and Hades.

[2] Generic slave name, popular in the British Caribbean and Surinam.

[3] Eboe was a name applied in the West Indies and North America to any slave who had originated from Benin.

One, with a gibbet wakes his Negro's fears,
One to the windmill nails him by the ears;
One keeps his slave in darkened dens, unfed,
One puts the wretch in pickle ere he's dead:
This, from a tree suspends him by the thumbs,
That, from his table grudges even the crumbs!

O'er yond' rough hills a tribe of females go,
Each with her gourd, her infant, and her hoe;
Scorched by a sun that has no mercy here,
Driven by a devil, whom men call overseer—
In chains, twelve wretches to their labors haste,
Twice twelve I saw, with iron collars graced!—

Are such the fruits that spring from vast domains?
Is wealth, thus got, Sir Toby, worth your pains!—
Who would your wealth on terms, like these, possess,
Where all we see is pregnant with distress—
Angola's[4] natives scourged by ruffian hands,
And toil's hard product shipp'd to foreign lands.

Talk not of blossoms, and your endless spring;
What joy, what smile, can scenes of misery bring?—
Though Nature, here, has every blessing spread,
Poor is the laborer—and how meanly fed!—

Here Stygian paintings light and shade renew,
Pictures of hell, that Virgil's[5] pencil drew:
Here, surly Charons[6] make their annual trip,
And ghosts arrive in every Guinea ship,[7]
To find what beasts these western isles afford,
Plutonian[8] scourges, and despotic lords:—

Here, they, of stuff determined to be free,
Must climb the rude cliffs of the Liguanee;[9]
Beyond the clouds, in skulking haste repair,
And hardly safe from brother traitors there.—

---

[4] Now specifically a part of West Africa but in the 18th century a generic term for Africa.

[5] Great Latin poet and author of the *Georgics* and most relevantly of the *Aeneid* with its celebrated description of the underworld.

[6] Charon was the ferry master who carried the souls of the dead to Hades across the river Styx. He is reputedly very ill tempered.

[7] Slave ship, so called because they travelled to the Guinea (African) coast.

[8] Relating to Pluto, terrifying god of the underworld.

[9] Liguanee, the liguanea swamps, near the isle of Pines, Cuba.

Timothy Dwight (1752–1817), from *Greenfield Hill* (1794)

Dwight was a pillar of Connecticut society, and hugely respected as an intellectual and theologian. As the president of Yale he came to represent the social and intellectual status quo of New England in the late eighteenth and early nineteenth centuries. He was considered, at least within Yale, to be a poet of genius. As a thinker Dwight became deeply conservative, and a good deal of his voluminous published work was dedicated to destroying the ideas coming over from Europe, whether in the form of the thinking of the *Philosophes*, and Voltaire in particular, or the new British radicalism of Dr Priestley. Yet Dwight had not always been such a stodgy character.

Dwight began his literary career as an idealist supporter of the American Revolution and all it stood for. His poem 'African Address' and his 1794 anti-slavery speech which he made to the Connecticut Society for the Promotion of Freedom emphasize his apparent concerns over slavery. Yet in the same year he published his long poem *Greenfield Hill*. This work is significant for this anthology because it nicely articulates the moral fence-sitting over the continuance of slavery which was increasingly becoming a Northern trait in the years immediately following the Revolutionary War. This really is a deeply troubled analysis of slavery systems which in the end idealizes North American slave holding both in the South and in those East Coast states where it is still legal. Yet this vision of a gentle and loving domestic slavery in America is set against Dwight's vision of sadism and corruption in the West Indies, which constitutes one of the most extreme sadistic fantasies within the poetry of slavery. Both pictures are necessary within Dwight's overall polemic. His argument is constructed via the time-honoured method of setting up a league table of atrocity. British writings on slavery invariably defend British practices by setting the domestic slave system against the depredations of the Spanish. Dwight simply fills different names into the blanks. East Coast slave holders are seen as ideal masters, while West Indian slavery is excoriated as a living hell. We are dealing with white political agendas, and the whitewashing of the new republic. Slaves are incidental within this framework, a fact emphasized by Dwight's dismissive picture of the African slave.

from *Greenfield Hill*

PART II

THE FLOURISHING VILLAGE

THE ARGUMENT

African appears—State of Negro Slavery in Connecticut—Effects of Slavery on the African, from his childhood through life—Slavery generally characterized—West-Indian Slavery—True cause of the calamities of the West-Indies.

But hark! what voice so gaily fills the wind?
Of care oblivious, whose that laughing mind?
'Tis yon poor black, who ceases now his song,
And whistling, drives the cumbrous wain[1] along.
He never, dragg'd, with groans, the galling chain;
Nor hung, suspended, on th' infernal crane;[2]
No dim, white spots deform his face, or hand,
Memorials hellish of the marking brand!
No scams of pincers, scars of scalding oil;
No waste of famine, and no wear of toil.
But kindly fed, and clad, and treated, he
Slides on, thro' life, with more than common glee.
For here mild manners good to all impart,
And stamp with infamy th' unfeeling heart;
Here law, from vengeful rage, the slave defends,
And here the gospel peace on earth extends.

He toils, 'tis true; but shares his master's toil;
With him, he feeds the herd, and trims the soil;
Helps to sustain the house, with clothes, and food,
And takes his portion of the common good;
Lost liberty his sole, peculiar ill,
And fix'd submission to another's will.
Ill, ah, how great! without that cheering sun,
The world is chang'd to one wide, frigid zone;
The mind, a chill'd exotic, cannot grow,
Nor leaf with vigour, nor with promise blow;
Pale, sickly, shrunk, it strives in vain to rise,
Scarce lives, while living, and untimely dies.

See fresh to life the Afric infant spring,
And plume its powers, and spread its little wing!
Firm is its frame, and vigorous is its mind,
Too young to think, and yet to misery blind.
But soon he sees himself to slavery born;
Soon meets the voice of power, the eye of scorn;
Sighs for the blessings of his peers, in vain;
Condition'd as a brute, tho' form'd a man.

---

[1] A wagon usually for hay or agricultural produce.
[2] A common form of slave punishment in the Caribbean was to suspend slaves in an iron cage in a public place and to leave them to starve or die of thirst.

Around he casts his fond, instinctive eyes,
And sees no good, to fill his wishes, rise:
(No motive warms, with animating beam,
Nor praise, nor property, nor kind esteem,
Bless'd independence, on his native ground,
Nor sweet equality with those around;)
Himself, and his, another's shrinks to find,
Levell'd below the lot of human kind.
Thus, shut from honour's paths, he turns to shame,
And filches the small good, he cannot claim.
To sour, and stupid, sinks his active mind;
Finds joys in drink, he cannot elsewhere find;
Rule disobeys; of half his labour cheats;
In some safe cot, the pilfer'd turkey eats;
Rides hard, by night, the steed, his art purloins;
Serene from conscience' bar himself essoins;[3]
Sees from himself his sole redress must flow,
And makes revenge the balsam of his woe.

Thus slavery's blast bids sense and virtue die;
Thus lower'd to dust the sons of Afric lie.
Hence sages grave, to lunar systems given,
Shall ask, why two-legg'd brutes were made by HEAVEN;
HOME seek, what pair first peopled Afric's vales,
And nice MONBODDO[4] calculate their tails.
O thou chief curse, since curses here began;
First guilt, first woe, first infamy of man;
Thou spot of hell, deep smirch'd on human kind,
The uncur'd gangrene of the reasoning mind;
Alike in church, in state, and household all,
Supreme memorial of the world's dread fall;
O slavery! laurel of the Infernal mind,
Proud Satan's triumph over lost mankind!

See the fell Spirit mount his sooty car!
While Hell's black trump proclaims the finish'd war;
Her choicest fiends his wheels exulting draw,
And scream the fall of GOD's most holy law.

---

[3] An excuse for not appearing in court.
[4] Lord Monboddo, an eccentric 18th-century British race theorist, who considered the orang-utan to be a type of man.

In dread procession see the pomp begin,
Sad pomp of woe, of madness, and of sin!
Grav'd on the chariot, all earth's ages rolls,
And all her climes, and realms, to either pole.
Fierce in the flash of arms, see Europe spread!
Her jails, and gibbets, fleets, and hosts, display'd!
Awe-struck, see silken Asia silent bow!
And feeble Afric writhe in blood below!
Before, peace, freedom, virtue, bliss, move on,
The spoils, the treasures, of a world undone;
Behind, earth's bedlam millions clank the chain,
Hymn their disgrace, and celebrate their pain;
Kings, nobles, priests, dread senate! lead the van,
And shout "Te-Deum!"[5] o'er defeated man.

Oft, wing'd by thought, I seek those Indian isles,
Where endless spring, with endless summer smiles,
Where fruits of gold untir'd Vertumnus[6] pours,
And Flora[7] dances o'er undying flowers.
There, as I walk thro' fields, as Eden gay,
And breathe the incense of immortal May,
Ceaseless I hear the smacking whip resound;
Hark! that shrill scream! that groan of death-bed sound!
See those throng'd wretches pant along the plain,
Tug the hard hoe, and sigh in hopeless pain!
Yon mother, loaded with her sucking child,
Her rags with frequent spots of blood defil'd,
Drags slowly fainting on; the fiend is nigh;
Rings the shrill cowskin; roars the tyger-cry;
In pangs, th' unfriended suppliant crawls along,
And shrieks the prayer of agonizing wrong.

Why glows yon oven with a sevenfold fire?
Crisp'd in the flames, behold a man expire!
Lo! by that vampyre's hand, yon infant dies,
Its brains dash'd out, beneath its father's eyes.
Why shrinks yon slave, with horror, from his meat?
Heavens! 'tis his flesh, the wretch is whipp'd to eat.

---

[5] *Te Deum*, a hymn devoted to God the Father and Son; the earliest version is ascribed to St Augustine.
[6] Autumn.   [7] Spring.

Why streams the life-blood from that female's throat?
She sprinkled gravy on a guest's new coat!

    .   .   .   .   .   .

   Why croud those quivering blacks yon dock around?
Those screams announce; that cowskin's shrilling sound.
See, that poor victim hanging from the crane,
While loaded weights his limbs to torture strain;
At each keen stoke, far spouts the bursting gore,
And shrieks, and dying groans, fill all the shore.
Around, in throngs, his brother-victims wait,
And feel, in every stroke, their coming fate;
While each, with palsied hands, and shuddering fears,
The cause, the rule, and price, of torment bears.

   Hark, hark, from morn to night, the realm around,
The cracking whip, keen taunt, and shriek, resound!
O'ercast are all the splendors of the spring;
Sweets court in vain; in vain the warblers sing;
Illusions all! 'tis Tartarus[8] round me spreads
His dismal screams, and melancholy shades.
The damned, sure, here clank th' eternal chain,
And waste with grief, or agonize with pain.
A Tartarus new! inversion strange of hell!
Guilt wreaks the vengeance, and the guiltless feel.
The heart, not form'd of flint, here all things rend;
Each fair a fury, and each man a fiend;
From childhood, train'd to every baleful ill,
And their first sport, to torture, and to kill.

   Ask not, why earthquakes rock that fateful land;
Fires waste the city; ocean whelms the strand;
Why the fierce whirlwind, with electric sway,
Springs from the storm, and fastens on his prey,
Shakes heaven, rends earth, upheaves the cumbrous wave,
And with destruction's besom fills the grave:
Why dark disease roams swift her nightly round,
Knocks at each door, and wakes the gasping sound.

   Ask, shuddering ask, why, earth-embosom'd sleep
The unbroken fountains of the angry deep:

---

[8] Hell, in Homer a black abyss as far below Hades as Earth is below Heaven.

Why, bound, and furnac'd, by the globe's strong frame,
In sullen quiet, waits the final flame:
Why surge not, o'er yon isles its spouting fires,
'Till all their living world in dust expires.
Crimes sound their ruin's moral cause aloud,
And all heaven, sighing, rings with cries of brother's blood.

Thomas Branagan (b. 1774), from *Avenia; or, A Tragical Poem on the Oppression of the Human Species, and Infringement on the Rights of Man. In six books, with notes explanatory and miscellaneous written in imitation of Homer's Iliad*, Book V (1805)

Thomas Branagan was, in terms of his preparedness to incorporate new print technology, by far the most ambitious of the abolitionists working in North America in the period 1780–1810. Branagan was America's John Newton (pp. 77–80), compulsively concerned to mythologize, narrate, and re-examine his youthful experiences working in slave systems from a perspective of agonized self-righteousness. He produced a wide range of publications including many long, indeed over-long, poems. He was also prepared to use copper-plate engraving and woodcut (both only developing arts in the American colonies) in order to give his publications maximum impact. Branagan came to abolition, uniquely for an American abolitionist poet, via extensive experience both within the Atlantic slave trade and as a chief overseer on Caribbean plantations.

The first edition of *The Penitential Tyrant* carries 'Compendious Memoirs of the Author'. The overstrained humility of the prose, and egocentricity of the argument, give a good sense of how clever Branagan was at marketing his own relatively sensational experience as an abolition package in which the slave is a means rather than an end. Branagan states that he was born and grew up in Dublin, a self-confessed dunce at school; his mother died when he was 5. He was brought up a Roman Catholic and against his father's desires became a merchant sailor, travelling to Seville, St Petersburg, and Copenhagen. After a quarrel with his father he fled to Liverpool and took his first job in the slave trade 'on board the Ellen, a Guineaman'. He then joined the Dutch merchant fleet and worked in Surinam for a short time, before becoming a pirate on an English privateer cruising off San Domingue. He left this employment in disgust and went back to Bermuda, before sailing to Antigua. It was at this stage that his work within the plantation systems began. He started as an assistant overseer on a large plantation called the Villa and soon advanced to become chief overseer of the entire set-up. Branagan's self-serving account of his time in slavery shows him making great personal sacrifices on moral grounds. He describes himself as finally leaving the trade in order to live out the idealistic edicts regarding slavery set out in Cowper's famous lines in *The Task* (see p. 87):

> After being impressed with a sense of the villainy and barbarity of keeping human beings in such deplorable conditions as I often saw the slaves reduced to, I resolved to relinquish the situation I then held, though lucrative and advantageous. I was solicited very warmly by a number of religious friends in particular, and my acquaintances generally, to continue; but being necessitated from conscientious motives, I gave up my situation, without any prospect of another, relying entirely on that Providence whom I endeavored to please and obey. And I then resolved that
>
> > I would not have a slave to till my ground...
> > To carry me... to fan me while I sleep,
> > And tremble when I wake... for all the wealth
> > That sinews bought and sold have ever earn'd
> > No;... dear as freedom is, and in my heart's
> > Just estimation priz'd above all price;
> > I had much rather be myself the slave
> > And wear the bonds than fasten them on him
> > > (*The Penitential Tyrant: or, Slave Trader*
> > > *Reformed: A Pathetic Poem, in Four Cantos*
> > > (2nd edn. Samuel Wood, 1807), 19)

He then moved back to Dublin, but was persecuted for having relinquished Catholicism, and so left for Philadelphia and arrived in the United States destitute. It was while working on a sloop at New Providence that Branagan underwent a conversion experience. He dreamed that he was taken to the 'temple of God' where the deity appeared to him 'like a mighty flame of golden light'. He believed, in a manner very similar to John Newton, that his past sins had led God to seek him out as a special object of his amazing grace: 'I seemed dissolved in joy, love and gratitude, with the ecstasies of which I awoke. From that to the present period the sprit of God has never left striving with me in a peculiar manner' (*Penitential Tyrant*, 26). After his conversion the contrite Branagan began to devote himself to writing prose and poetry concerning slavery. In 1805 he published *Serious Remonstrances: Addressed to the Citizens of the Northern States, and their Representatives; being an appeal to their natural feelings and common sense: consisting of speculations and animadversions, on the recent revival of the slave trade in the American republic* (T. Stiles). Again the preface contained extensive biographical self-analysis. Branagan's bragging accounts of his financial self-sacrifice in leaving the trade descend to new levels of bathos in this work, yet of more interest is his attitude to the rise of slavery within the Union. Branagan displays a conventional pity for the slaves as victims but considers them to be a dangerous problem that must literally be removed from white Northern civilization. Having set up comparisons between American and classical slavery systems Branagan warns that the slaves in the United States are an insurrectionary time bomb. His solution is to develop a form of apartheid, whereby all slaves will be rounded up and then kept within a giant compound in the Louisiana swamps: 'The new state might be established upwards of 2,000 miles from our population. It is asserted that the most distant part of Louisiana is farther from us than some parts of Europe' (*Serious Remonstrances*, 22). Within the imaginative world of Branagan's abolition the North is a land of hope and the South a vicious terrain beyond the moral pale. The following account, with its weirdly unworkable incorporation of Pilate, and its megalomaniac interpretation of the North's attitude to slavery through Branagan's own experiences as a pirate and overseer, suggests the limitless nature of his triumphalism. Branagan, at this early date, sets up a total divide between the essential moral nature of North and South based on their relative attitudes to slavery:

> Our Southern brethren are like a profligate, bent on his own ruin; duplicity and vanity are so interwoven with their politics, that the recent scenes exhibited in Hispaniola, does not in the least alarm their fears. Our prospects and politics are as different from theirs as light is from darkness. It would be as absurd to reason with them in this manner, or cause them to forego their slaves, as it would be to attempt by argument to prevail on a lion to forego his mangled prey. We have like true Christians and patriots, relinquished our ill gotten slaves; we have made them free virtually, but not politically: let us then from motives of generosity, as well as self preservation, make them free and happy in every sense of the word, in a republic of their own; seeing it is impracticable to make them such amongst ourselves; and thus, like Pilate, let us wash our hands and shake their blood from our garments. I remember when I was a minor, while a privateering on board the brig Lamp of Bermuda, the first cruise I went, I saw such palpable villainy in the business, that I relinquished all my prize money, and at the same time left the privateer and her piratical crew; and in the same manner and from the same conscientious motives, I relinquished a lucrative establishment in Antigua, as planter. The citizens of the North, have thus relinquished the wages of unrighteousness; like me let them likewise separate from those who their avarice formerly subjected and make them ample amends for interior injustice by subsequent acts of kindness and benevolence: and the only way to do this, is by making them free and independent citizens of America, in a separate state of their own. (*Serious Remonstrances*, 23–4)

His writings sometimes get a mention in standard histories of American abolition, but because of their length and frequent stylistic ungainliness, he has slipped into oblivion. Branagan's unfortunate insistence on attempting to present his anti-slavery arguments in the form of epic poems, given his spectacular lack of poetic ability, is definitely a stumbling block. If, however, he is analysed not as a literary cripple but as a propagandist of energy and formal ambition, he emerges as a highly significant figure. What he wrote is not, perhaps, as important as the manner in which he published it. In the context of the abolitionists' later use of graphic methods Branagan was innovative, and his most significant contribution to the abolition movement was his ability to show the uses to which wood engraving could be put as both a satiric and a didactic tool.

Avenia was an enormous poem with substantial footnotes in which Branagan excoriated the United States and warned in apocalyptic tones of the inevitably destructive effects of slavery on the morals and economy of the nation. Branagan here showed a capacity for plain speaking and argument, drawing on proverbial wisdom in a manner which suggests that he was familiar with the writings of Tom Paine: 'The idea of a slave holder being a good legislator or governor, is as inconceivable as to suppose a wolf would be a good shepherd, and defend, not devour the sheep; or a fox would protect, not destroy, the poultry.' If only Branagan had been capable of such proverbial concision in his poetry he might be read more today.

from *Avenia*

BOOK V

ARGUMENT

At the first dawn the slavers wiegh their anchors and sail for the West Indies—Dissipation of the mariners, and wretchedness of the slaves contrasted—A tornado overtakes them—Admiral's ship with three others founder and all hands perish, the remainder steer for Grenada, where they arrive after a passage of fifty-six days—Distress of the slaves at seeing the town—They are landed, and whipped in droves to market. Relatives sold to different purchasers: are violently separated, never to see each other again—Arrive on the plantations—Their labour—Food—Wretched habitations—AVENIA is violated by her master—Her lamentations—She commits suicide, by plunging from a high rock into the ocean.

> Now had the stars, diminish'd, fled away,
> Before the glories of the dawning day,
> When the commander of the Christian host,
> The signal gave to leave the flaming coast.
> Soon as Aurora[1] rob'd in purple light,
> Pierc'd with her golden shaft, the rear of night,
> And ere bright Sol[2] from ocean's briny bed,
> Uprais'd his glorious radiated head,
> Mounted above the re-illumin'd main,
> And darted o'er the lawn, his horizontal beam;
> The sailors toil, their anchors all atrip,
> A gallant breeze, impels each tilting ship,
> And now unmoor'd the tyrants launch to sea,
> And pale with guilt, commence their wat'ry way.

[1] The dawn, the sunrise.   [2] The sun.

As in her nest within some cavern hung,
The dove sits brooding[3] o'er her callow young,
Till rous'd at last by some impetuous shock,
She starts surpriz'd, and beats around the rock;
Then to the open fields for refuge flies,
And the free bird expatiates in the skies;
Her pinions pois'd, thro' liquid air she springs,
And smoothly glides, nor moves her level wings,
So did the vessels their swift course pursue,
And gain'd new force and swiftniss as they flew.
Swift as they sail, the waters fly before,
And dash'd beneath the ships the surges roar;
The tars[4] in haste their topsails all unbind,
Then sheet them home, and stretch them to the wind;
High o'er the roaring waves the spacious sails,
Bow the tall masts and swell before the gales,
Each crooked stem the parting surge divides,
And to the stern retreating roll the tides.
They now their flags, their crimson flags unbind
To tow'r a loft and swell before the wind;
The long proud pendants with the mikwhite sails,
From thc high masts, invite the swelling gales;
Past sight of shore, along the surge they bound,
And all above is sky, and ocean all around.
The cann of grog[5] the boy obsequious brings,
To tars more welcome than translucent springs,
Luxurious now they feast, observant round,
Gay stripling youths, the brimming bumpers crown'd,
The purple vintage now allures their taste,
They quaff the wine, and then devour the feast.
In deep debauch they drown their guilty fears,
And bury in oblivion all their cares.

And now th' imperious hypocritic croud,
With insolence, and wine elate and loud,
Give three proud cheers, denoting victory,
And fill again "To Heav'n and liberty."

---

[3] A reference to Milton's celebrated description of God's state of mind during Creation, *Paradise Lost*, I. 20–2: 'with mighty wings outspread | Dove-like sat'st brooding on the vast abyss | And mad'st it pregnant.'
[4] British sailors.
[5] The strong liquor, usually rum, served to British sailors as part of their daily ration.

Stemm'd by the ships, the foaming surges rise,
And with their shouts, the sailors rend the skies.
While peals of loud applause from ev'ry side
The navy flew, and shot along the tide.
Enslav'd humanity, the sacred load!
The sons of Adam, who's the son of God!
Oppress'd with anguish, pain and mighty woe,
Down their black cheeks, the briny riv'lets flow;
Their hopes, their joys, all prematurely gone!
Wretched, alas, abandon'd, and undone.
Of friends, of peace, of smiling comforts left,
And all their dear delights on earth bereft;
While here, for shady groves and verdant bow'rs,
For pleasant walks, and beds of fragrant flow'rs:
They find a floating dungeon on the main,
Chains, hunger, whips, contagion, woe and pain:
Instead of music's sweet melodious sound,
Repeated yells and deadly groans go round;
The mighty scourge, and mightier voice of pain,
The iron fetter and the clanking chain.
And for the joyful faces of their friends,
They see, in human forms, terrific fiends.
A thousand nameless terrors, lag behind,
Despair, confusion, frenzy sieze the mind.
A maid amongst the captives, *Lama*, nam'd,
For beauty much, but more for virtue fam'd,
While down her cheeks the copious sorrows flow,
In loud laments, thus deprecates her woe:
   "No more my friends, we'll view the flow'ry field,
Enjoy the various scents the meadows yield:
Farewel ye forests, vales and verdant hills,
Ye sylvan bowers, and ye tinkling rills;
Ye scented groves, to which I us'd to run,
And find a shelter from the burning sun;
Ye fields alas, my native fields, adieu!
Whose charming flow'rs my early labours knew,
   Where, when an infant, I was wont to stray,
And gather daisies at the call of day;
These fragrant fields I see, or think I see,
Like willows weep, or seem to weep, for me;
The warbling linnet, too forgets to sing,

And the sweet gold finch flags the painted wing.
No more I'll bless the incense breathing gale,
Nor gaze enchanted on the enamell'd vale.
Nor spend the joyful and the dancing hours,
By silver streams, or in ambrosial bow'rs."
Thus those indulge their lusts, and these their woe,
And here the tears, and there the bumpers flow.
Ten guilty hours the mariners employ,
In impious feasting, and unhallow'd joy;
The twelfth arriv'd, and lo! the immortal God,
With anger view'd them on the briny flood.
He bade the whirlwinds rise, the thunders roll,
The forked lightnings flash'd from pole to pole.
The clouds o'ercharg'd with checquer'd darkness spread,
Black'ning the floods, and gath'ring o'er the head.
In haste the mariners now reef[6] the sail,
While the sea whitens with the rising gale:
Now here, now there, the giddy ships are borne,
And all the rattling shrouds in fragments torne.
The night now far advanc'd her gloomy reign,
And setting stars roll'd down the azure plain.
Fierce and more fierce the dreadful whirlwinds rise,
Black clouds, and double darkness veil the skies.
The moon, the stars, the bright æthereal host,
Seem as extinct, and all their splendors lost,
The furious tempest blows with horrid sound,
The lightnings flash and thunders roar profound.
The sails now furl'd, the sailors freeze with fears,
And ghastly death on ev'ry wave appears;
And while they mourn, the western blast prevails,
Breaks the firm topmasts, rends the flying sails,
Round go the ships, the vessels leave their sides.
Bare to the working waves, and roaring tides;
While in huge heaps the gathering surges spread,
And hang in mountains o'er proud *Hawkin's*[7] head:
Fierce on his ship descends the furious blast,
Howls thro' the shrouds, and rends them from the mast.
The mast gives way, and cracking as it bends,
Tears up the deck, and all at once descends.

---

[6] To reduce the exposed surface of a sail.   [7] See pp. xxv, 134 n. 3 for Hawkins.

Back to the stern retreating surges flow,
And with the surge the shatter'd topmasts go;
The helmsman by the tumbling ruin slain,
Dash'd from his post, falls headlong in the main.
Loud and more loud God bids his thunders roll,
The vived lightnings flash from pole to pole.
And now at *Hawkin's* head a bolt he aims,
And hissing, the fell bolt descends in flames,
Full on the ship it falls, now high, now low,
Toss'd and retoss'd, she heels beneath the blow;
At once into the main the crew she shook,
And steams sulphureous rose, and smoth'ring smoke.
As from a hanging rock, tremendous height,
The sable crows with intercepted flight,
Drop endlong, scar'd, and black with sulph'rous hue.
So from the deck arc hurl'd the guilty crew
Now midst the angry waves they sink, they rise,
Now lost, now seen, with shrieks and dreadful cries,
They strive to gain the ship, but heav'n denies;
The low'ring heav'ns o'er the waves impend.
And swell'd with vengeance on three ships descend;
The decks are white with foam, the winds aloud,
Howl o'er the ships, and sing thro' ev'ry shroud.
Now on a tow'ring arch of waves they rise,
Heav'd on the bounding billows to the skies,
Then as the roaring surge retreating falls:
They shoot down headlong as to hell's dark walls.
Thrice the wild waves rebellow as they rise,
Thrice mount the foaming floods, and dash the skies.
Above the sides of three gay ships ascends,
A watry deluge, and their ribs it rends;
The waves dissolve their well compacted sides,
Which drink, at many a leak, the briny tides.
The vessels by the surge toss'd round and round,
Sunk in the whirling gulf, devour'd and drown'd:
Two from the dark abyss emerge again,
Boats, planks and treasures float along the main;
Vengeance o'ertakes them in their wooden wall,
And mounting billows overwhelm them all:
Thus four ships sink, their crews to death consign'd,
In tumbling billows, and a war of wind.

During the dire event, each slave remains
Seasick, oppress'd with grief, and bound in chains
Twice twenty by the hand of death set free,
And twelve, half starv'd were launch'd into the sea.
The rest promiscuously[8] to heav'n complain;
And strive to breathe the wholesome [air] in vain.
Down in the stinking hold they vent their woe,
And down each sable cheek the sorrows flow:
ANGOLA[9] to his countrymen imparts,
A ray of hope, and thus revives their hearts;
    "Friends we have seen more toils than now we know,
By long experience exercis'd in woe,
And soon to these disasters shall be given,
A certain period by relenting heav'n.
Think how you saw these Christians on our shore,
And how your friends lay welt'ring in their gore:
Dismiss your fears, on those misfortunes past,
Your minds with pleasure may reflect at last.
With manly patience bear your present state,
And with firm courage wait a better fate."
The injur'd youth thus strove some hope t'impart,
And hid the secret anguish of his heart.
    Mild winds succeed the storm, the sailor train,
Rigg their tall jury masts, and plow the main.
Each captain orders, and th' obedient band,
With due observance, wait the stern command.
With speed the masts they rear, with haste unbind,
The spacious sails, and stretch them to the wind,
High o'er the frothy waves the milkwhite sails
Drive on the ships, and swell before the gales;
The ships now rigg'd, and fill'd with human store,
Intent to voyage to the Christian shore;
The sailors swill the grog, a cruel train,
And heedless shoot along th' indignant main.
Now pay the debt to craving nature due.
Their jaded strength with balmy rest renew:
Now interrupted slumbers vail their eyes,
Their cares dissolve in visionary joys.

[8] Indiscriminate, mixed together with no order.
[9] Angola here personifies all slaves from the Angolan area; see p. 417 n. 4.

Not so the slaves: the downy bands of sleep
Too soon relax'd, they wake again to weep.
A gloomy pause ensues of dumb despair,
And then th' invoke th' immortal powers with prayer
All stifled with effluvia, and with heat,
Half starv'd, they mourn their melancholy fate.
Full six and fifty days the Christian crew,
They hateful course along the main pursue,
Safe thro' the level seas they force their way,
The steersmen govern, and the ships obey.
The sun now rises, beauteous to behold,
And tips each lofty wave with gleams of gold
And as they rudely stem the briny tide,
And tilting o'er the sea impetuous ride;
Like distant clouds the mariner descries,
Grenada's high emerging hills arise:
The steersmen keep them in the liquid road,
And plow the various windings of the flood.
Clear, and more clear the swelling shore they spy,
See the thin smokes that melt into the sky,
And blueish hills just op'ning to the eye.
At eve the ships approach the fatal land,
And in the winding bay they anchor on the sand.
Close to the town a spacious port appears
Belonging to king George[10] whose name it bears;
Two lofty mounts projecting to the main,
The roaring winds tempestuous rage restrain,
Within, the waves in softer murmurs glide,
The ships secure within the harbour ride.
AVENIA now, o'ercome with black despair,
Address'd to heav'n her agonizing prayer:
   "Oh, Jove, this fated moment, heave thy dart,
And ease the torture of my aching heart!
Oh snatch me far from this bloodthirsty race,
Toss'd thro' the vast illimitable space,
Or oh! let thunder from some hov'ring cloud,
Transfix me, or let briny seas enshroud.
Ah, my Angola, 'tis for thee I groan,
By day I weep, by night I make my moan;

[10] Georgetown, named after King George III, then King of England although periodically deranged.

How would I welcome any fav'ring death
To ease me of the burden of my breath;
For ah! the worst of ills is still behind,
The brutal conduct of the Christian kind.
Sure nature first in anger did intend
A plague of monsters o'er the world to send,
Cast from her hand the brutish offspring men,
And turn'd each house into a savage den.
In this rapacious species we may find
All that's destructive in the preying kind,
Lion, wolf, tiger, bear and crocodile,
Strong to devour and cunning to beguile.
But beasts are led to prey by appetite,
And that once pleas'd, no more in blood delight,
Christians, like hell, have an insatiate thirst,
And still are keen, tho' they be like to burst.
Lust fills the world with loud alarms of war,
And turns each plowshare to a hostile spear."

 The sounds assault Angola's wakeful ear,
Misjudging of the cause, a sudden fear,
Of her distress and pain the youth alarms,
He thinks some foe is rushing to her arms;
Upspringing with his chains in active haste,
He plung'd alas, into the watry waste;
Nor saw his folly, "whose untutor'd mind,
Saw God in waves, or heard him in the wind.[11]
Yet simple nature to his hope had giv'n,
Beyond the briny deep an humble heav'n.
Some safer world with depths of wood embrac'd,
Some happier island in the watry waste,
Where slaves once more their native land behold,
No fiends torment, no Christians thirst for gold,
He thinks, admitted to that equal sky,
His injur'd wife will bear him company."
He looks toward his consort as he dies.

 "Farewel, a long, a last farewel," he cries,
And closes on the world his dying eyes,
Which glance, expiring, at his native shore,
Then round his head the waves redounding roar.

---

[11] See Alexander Pope's 1733 *An Essay on Man*, ll. 99–102. See also Whitchurch, *Negro Convert*, n. 1, above, for another use of the same lines.

Thus died Angola, while his dearer part,
Unconscious of his fate, now vents her bursting heart.
Tow'rd her lov'd coast she casts her eyes in vain,
They fail with looking, and with grief they stream:
In her foul prison she consumes the day,
While horrors wear the heavy night away.
To some kind friend she'd feign her wants disclose.
Now doom'd to meet unutterable woes;
But all around are curst with hearts of steel,
Without the sense to pity or to feel.
The land approach'd, the slaves with wild affright,
Behold the town and sicken at the sight;
While the proud planters view the ships around,
In haste they rush along the landing ground,
Flush'd at the sight, they haste at early dawn,
Precipitate and bounding o'er the lawn,
To purchase slaves then to the ship repair,
And view the product of the fatal war.
The slaves beheld them in that dreadful hour,
And inly shudder'd at their barb'rous pow'r.[12]
Their cruel trade! who live in heav'ns despite,
Contemning laws, and trampling human right;
Untaught to work, to turn the glebe, or sow,
They all their riches to their neighbours owe.
The tyrants now prepare their slaves to land,
All shorn and trimm'd, upon the yellow sand;
Now forc'd into the boat with wild affright,
A sudden horror struck their aching sight.
The sailors catch the word, their oars they sieze,
And sweep, with equal strokes the smoking seas;
Clear of the ships the impatient longboats fly,
While silent tears flow from each captive's eye.
Within a long recess, a bay there lies,
Edg'd round with clifts, high pointing to the skies;
The jutting shores that swell on either side,
Contract its mouth, and break the rushing tide.
The eager sailors sieze the fair retreat,
And bound within the port the little fleet;

---

[12] The preceding six lines describe the phenomenon of a slave 'scramble', a favourite way of selling a slave cargo in Jamaica.

For here retir'd the sinking billows sleep,
And smiling calmness silvers o'er the deep.
With earnest hearts the joyful sailors press,
Their friends whose transports glow at their success;
But the sad fate that did their men destroy,
Cool'd ev'ry heart, and damp'd the rising joy.
The shackled captives in their tyrant's sight,
Dejected stand, and shake with wild affright;
Their fate bewail, while to the hated land,
Their masters drive, and range them on the sand,
In droves, unhappy matrons, maids and men,
Are driv'n promiscuous from the imprison'd den.
Like flocks of sheep, alas! they move along,
Scourg'd to the market with the knotted thong.
With red hot irons now they brand the crew,
While from their galled eyes the tears descend anew.
Their sparkling tears the want of words supply,
And the full soul bursts copious from each eye.
They strive their tyrant's pity to command,
The ruffians hear but will not understand,
To what submissions, in what low degree,
Are mortals plac'd, dirc avarice, by thee!
They try their suppliant arts, and try again,
To move their pity, but alas in vain.
In body tortur'd, and distress'd in mind,
No hope the poor unhappy creatures find.
They curse their natal and their nuptial hour,
Tears flow amain in one unceasing shower.
And peals of groans in mighty columns rise,
Ascend the heav'ns and echo in the skies.
Pierc'd with the noise the wretch'd babes, in vain,
With tender cries, repeat the sound again,
And at the mournful call the mothers press'd,
Their starting infants screeching to the breast.
And now, a matron wearied heav'n with pray'r,
Just on the precipice of black despair,
Embrac'd, in arms of wretchedness, her son,
And thus in broken accents she begun:
    "And have I borne thee with a mother's throes,
To suffer thus, nurs'd thee for future woes?
How short the space allow'd my boy to view!

How short, alas! and fill'd with anguish too."
They view their fate, and sicken at the sight,
In bitterness of soul they long for night.
Again she cries, "These floods of grief restrain,
Vengeance will soon o'ertake the impious train.
Let us be patient and our hearts prepare,
To move great Jove, our heavenly sire, by prayer.
Our woes to him are known, to him belongs,
The strangers cause, and the revenge of wrongs;
When friendly death our toil-worn frames shall free,
And take our abject souls from misery;
Our ghosts, for injur'd blood, shall daily cry,
To heav'n, for vengeance, and shall pierce the sky.
If we, for latent guilt, be doom'd to woes,
Our crimes we learned from our Christian foes.
Our vengeful spirits shall enhance their hell,
Enjoy their torments, as enchain'd they dwell."
The scramble o'er, the horrid sale now done,
The slaves but find their sorrows just begun;
Babes to their parents cling with close embrace,
With kisses wander o'er each tearful face;
To seperate the hapless, weeping throng,
The cowskin hero wields the knotted thong,
And as he wields, applies the dreadful blow,
While streams of blood in purple torrents flow.
Smit with the sign, which all their fears explain,
The children still embrace, their knees sustain
Their feeble weight no more; their arms alone
Support them, round their bleeding parents thrown.
They faint, they sink, by cruel woes oppress'd,
Each heart weeps blood, and anguish rends each breast.
Now, stain'd with blood, a weeping mother press'd
Her dear, dear trembling infant to her breast,
Then shrieking, to her wretched husband sprang,
A moment snatch'd on his lov'd neck to hang;
Kissing his lips, his cheeks, his swollen eyes,
While tears descend to earth, and groans ascend the skies.
Now furious rage the mournful chief inspires,
And all his soul just indignation fires;
Amid his hapless family he stands,
And lifts to heav'n his eyes and spreading hands.

Oppress'd with grief, and raving with despair,
Groaning he lifts to heav'n his mental pray'r.
Now motionless he stands, in grief profound,
Fixing his eyes with anguish on the ground.
Behold, and blush, ye first born of the skies.
Behold the complicated villanies,
Practis'd by Christian hyprocrites, unjust,
Full of rage, rapine, cruelty and lust,
Who, smooth of tongue, in purpose insincere,
Hide fraud in smiles, while death is harbor'd there.
They proffer peace, yet wage unnat'ral war,
From tender husbands, weeping wives they tear:
And still they hope, heav'n winks at their deceit,
And call their cruelties the crimes of fate.
Unjust mankind, whose will's created free,
Charge all their guilt on absolute decree.
The Christian rulers in their ruin join,
And truth is scorn'd by all the perjur'd line.
Their crimes transcend all crimes since Noah's flood[13]
But all their glory soon shall set in blood.
Shall heav'n be false, because revenge is slow?
No—it prepares to strike the fiercer blow,
Sure is its justice. They shall feel their woe.
The day shall come, that great avenging day,
When all their honours in the dust shall lay.
God will himself pour judgments on their land,
Thus hath he said—and what he saith must stand
Their cruelty for justice daily cries,
And pulls reluctant vengeance from the skies.
Their dreadful end will wing its fatal way,
Nor need their rage anticipate the day.
And tho' they charge on heav'n their own offence,
And call their woes the crimes of providence;
Yet they themselves their misery create,
They perish by their folly, not their fate.
And now th' unhappy exiles mournful stand,
Men, babes and dames, a miserable band,
A wretched train of shrieking mothers bound,
Behold their captive children trembling round.

---

[13] In Genesis God decides to flood the earth because of the sins of all humans, Noah and his family alone being spared.

And oft they strive to ease each other's pain,
But still repeat the moving theme in vain.
Scarce can the whip release the mournful band,
Like sculptur'd monumental grief they stand;
Compassion now touch'd *my tyrannic soul*,
And down *my* cheek the tear *unusual* stole;
Then, nor till then I pitied! tho' their foe,
Struck with the sight of such unequall'd woe.
Parental *tenderness*, and *kindred blood*!
Your force, till now, I little understood.

    Now parted by the whip, in doleful sound,
The children speak their agonies profound.
Dissolv'd in tears they round their parents hung,
And their young arms in early sorrows wrung.
And each complains with moving tears and cries,
And begs for aid with eloquence of eyes.
Lash'd with the thong, the bleeding youths in vain,
Fly back for refuge to their sires again;
Lost to the soft endearing ties of life,
The social names of daughter, parent, wife.
The frantic mother hears the well known sound—
    "Can no redress, oh graciou's heav'n, be found?
Ye savage Christians, now your rage is spent,
Your malice can no greater pains invent.
Oh that the base tyrannic Christian band,
Had never touch'd my dear paternal land,
Oh that I were some monster of the wood,
Or bird of air, or fish that swims the flood,
Unthoughtful then, my sorrows I could bear,
Nor sin, nor groan, no[r] weep, nor sigh, nor fear.
Immortal Sire! shall christians still prevail?
And shall thy promise to thy creatures fail?
And shall they, shall they still encrease our woe,
And dye our lands with purple as they go?
Rise in thy wrath, almighty maker rise,
Behold our grievous wrongs, with gracious eyes.
Oh save my valiant friends, the bold, the brave,
Their wives abus'd, their bleeding infants save!
See wives and daughters serve promiscuous lust,
Their sires and husbands bite the bloody dust."
Depriv'd alas; the priv'lege to complain,

The ruffians whip her from the place again.
Lo! tyrants thus administer relief,
Add wrong to wrong, and wretchedness to grief.
Give ear ye tyrants, distant nations hear,
And learn the judgments of high heaven to fear!
Your children yet unborn shall blush to see,
Their predecessor's guilt and villany,
Their impious thirst for gold, while fierce in arms,
Their cruel breasts no tender pity warms;
Should heathens but one virtuous Christian find,
Name but the slave trade; they will curse your kind.
Deceitful gold! how high will Christians rise,
In flagrant guilt to gain the glittering prize!
Hence sacred faith, and public trust are sold,
And villains barter Adam's sons for gold.
Shall the oppressed race of human kind,
From heav'n above, or earth no justice find.
Can brutal carnage please Jehovah's sight,
Or flaming war reflect a grateful light?
Impell'd by love, he promis'd to the poor,
To hear their prayers, nor drive from mercy's door.
Compell'd by truth he will his word fulfil,
Save the oppress'd, and do his sov'reign will.
He will redress his creature's wrongs, tho' late;
Thus has he spoke, and what he speaks is fate.
Then shall the tyrants of their species bend,
Their honours vanish and their glories end.
For come it will, that dreadful day, replete
With righteous judgment, with tremendous fate,
Then despots, tho' on golden thrones, shall bleed,
And reap the wages to their crimes decreed;
While tyrants govern with an iron rod,
Oppress, destroy—their dreadful scourge is God:
    And ev'n the sons of freedom prove unjust,
Alike in cruelty, alike in lust!
Them shall the muse to infamy consign,
Despis'd, abhorr'd, the theme of tragic rhyme.
Those bastard freemen spread consuming death,
The name of freedom withers at their breath;
Virtue disrob'd, infernal vice aspires,
And weeping liberty and truth retires;

Laurels that should fair virtue deck alone,
To systematic hypocrites are thrown;
Their nature and their nation they disgrace,
Aud stamp with sable signatures their race;
Wide o'er the world their character has spread,
Disgrac'd their country, and disgrac'd the dead,
Who fought for freedom, and for freedom, bled.
Their hypocritic villany proclaim,
Oh, sing their guilt, my muse—inglorious fame!
For yet more woes their tragic acts inspire,
To attune with energetic verse the mournful lyre.
     Now to th' estate the slaves are driv'n like lambs[14]
Bound to the butchers, sever'd from their dams.
With beating hearts, and solemn steps, and slow,
They move along, while tears in torrents flow.
Time here would fail us, did we pause to view,
The various torments of the sable crew,
And as to the plantation they advance,
Take of the hapless drove a transient glance;
Who view, the moment they approach th' estate,
Their countrymen in chains, their own dire fate.
The person who beholds their pains, nor can
Feel pity, is a monster not a man.
No mortal eloquence can paint their woes,
Depict their wrongs, the malice of their foes.
Not *Milton's* pen, not *Shakespear's* tragic lyre,
Not *Homer's* flame, nor *Pope's* poetic fire,
To count their wrongs, demands immortal tongues,
A throat of brass, and adamantine[15] lungs.
Their fate, alas, is dismal and severe,
Their lamentations still assault my ear:
If a poor slave from servitude has ran,
They lacerate and lop away the man;
When they have caught, they trim with brazen shears
The wretched slave, and rob him of his ears!
And if impell'd by hunger, he should steal, ⎫
Or strike his cruel master and rebel,   ⎬
His arm is sure the vengeful knife to feel   ⎭

[14] This association of the slave victim is a commonplace of sentimental abolition verse; see p. 93 above.
[15] Unbreakable, impregnable, impenetrable.

Nocturnal stars their constant wailings know,
And blushing Phoebus[16] witnesses their woe.
No Christian views them with a tender tear,
They find no mercy, no, nor hope to cheer;
And when their toil is o'er, like hogs repair,
To wretched dens, and far more wretched fare.
All day they tend the canes, and as they grow,
Their tears to water them incessant flow:
Their scanty pittance when their work is done,
Is half devour'd e'er it is well begun;
And while their limbs each hour, are like to fail,
Ah! how they long for ev'n this scanty meal.
Slow seems the sun to move, the hours to roll,
Their native home, deep imag'd in each soul
As the tir'd plowman spent with stubborn toil,
Whose horses long have torn the furrow'd soil,
Sees with delight the sun's declining ray,
When home with feeble knees he bends his way;
To late repast, the day's sad labour done,
So to the slaves, thus welcome sets the sun:
But he departs to joyful friends and rest,
And these to wretchedness with grief oppress'd.
Their bodies scourg'd, and stiff with clotted gore,
The wounds renew'd that were receiv'd before
Their lacerated limbs oppress'd with chains,
Their minds, alas! with more than mortal pains.
And when the toil of each sad day is o'er,
They sink to sleep, and wish to wake no more.
Here might I cease, nor further paint their woe,
Too horrid for the sons of men to know.
The pond'rous earth would roll her annual way,
E'er I could half their miseries display;
The woodland monsters would with tears bewail,
And ev'n *Apollyon*[17] shudder at the tale:
But yet *Avenia's* fate demands my song,
For her, my muse, the tragic strain prolong;
The captives on th' estate arriv'd, and there
Compell'd to drudge in chains, and deep despair

---

[16]   Phoebus Apollo, the sun god.
[17]   The destroyer or devil, a spirit who appears in the Book of Revelation.

The planter views his new bought slaves, while foul.
Unhallow'd passions, kindle in his soul;
In depth of grief he hears *Avenia* cry,
For pity to the sov'reign of the sky,
The unfeeling tyrant, bent on wickedness,
Eager beheld her, in her keen distress;
He calls his slave.... the sable princess hears,
And with obedient reverence appears;
Her fate unknown. To speak she makes essay;
But her tongue faultering, ceases to obey:
He bids her follow where he leads the way.
And as they to the place prepar'd, proceed,
The lustful ruffian meditates the deed,
Which stamps for ever poor Avenia's fate;
And the chaste muse now blushes to relate:
At length arriv'd, and preparation made,
His brutal purpose he forthwith display'd.
In vain the sable captive lifts her hand,
In vain she strives his pity to command;
Invokes her lov'd Angola, tears her hair,
And lifts to heav'n her unavailing prayer!
And oh, what various passions struggling, rise
Swell her vex'd bosom, and inflame her eyes;
What sobs of anguish, what hysteric screams,
What shrieks of frenzy, in their fierce extremes!
The monster braves them all, by wild lust driv'n,
And violates the dame, in face of heav'n!
Cease my indignant muse, by shame suppress'd,
Let tears and burning blushes speak the rest.
But this, ev'n this, is nothing to the shame
And nameless crimes of the tyrannic train.
Nor dare I paint what prudence must conceal,
Nor half their studied villanies reveal.
    Methinks I see each sentimental fair,
With tender sorrow wipe the trickling tear,
While shame and horror thro' their bosoms rush,
Swell ev'ry vein, and spread th' indignant blush.
Ah, let your quick and kindred spirits form
A vivid picture of the fatal storm;
In which she labour'd, and whose force to paint;
The muses' strongest tints appear too faint:

In sympathetic thought her sufferings see,
But oh, forever from her wrongs be free.
    'Twas on the evening of the following day,
In solemn silence all creation lay;
The injur'd captive, weary of her woe,
And loathing her existence here below
Thrice in her anguish tore her sable hair,
Thrice beat her breast in madness of despair.
And oft repeated her Angola's name,
And view'd his image in the fleeting dream:
In thought she sees him, but a transient guest,
Pants on his lips, and murmurs on his breast,
Raptur'd she contemplates his sable charms,
And clasps the phantom in her loving arms;
She calls aloud, his fleeting course to stay,
In vain she calls—the phantom glides away.
To her paternal home, now trav'lling on,
In thought, abandon'd, desolate, alone;
She treads, or seems to tread, a dismal plain,
And seeks her lover thro' the waste in vain.
Now from her troubled sleep the princess starts,
While the dear vision from her view departs:
And raising toward heav'n her frenzy'd eyes,
Implores compassion on her miseries:
Bewails her own and her Angola's woe,
Whom now she paints as murder'd by the foe;
Frantic she rushes o'er the distant plain,
Ascends a rock projecting o'er the main;
Intent on death, above the flood she stands,
And bath'd in tears, and with uplifted hands,
The poor insane now loves and hates by turns,
With grief now maddens, now with fury burns;
Now looks toward her dear paternal plain,
Now lifts her streaming eyes to heaven again.
    "Ah me! Why view I yet the hated light,
Hence let me hasten for I loathe the sight,
Life has no charms for me, then let me go,
And meet my husband in the shades below;
He's gone, while I beneath the load of life,
Am left to bear unutterable grief."
Now the deep flood she views with native fear,

And wrings her hands, envelop'd in despair.
Her piercing shriek the distant region rends,
The woods re-echo with the voice she sends;
The hills reverberate, the vales rebound,
And to the heav'ns convey the mournful sound.
Now near the fatal precipice she flies,
Reviews the torrent with her streaming eyes,
From the rough rock projecting o'er the main
Whose giddy prospect turn'd her tortur'd brain.
Sharp are the rocks, loud roars the surge beneath,
She shudders at the thought of instant death;
And as she hears the briny billows roar,
And sees the foaming waves ascend the shore;
Back from her stand, in haste she starts aghast,
While tow'rd her native land her eyes are cast.
     "And must I die, the shudd'ring princess cries
Thus unreveng'd. Thou ruler of the skies.
And must I die! then let me fearless go,
And 'scape forever my base christian foe."
Then as a vulture from the rocky height,
Her carrion seen, impetuous at the sight,
Forth springing, instant darts herself from high,
Shoots on the wing, and rushes down the sky;
So plung'd precipitate the hapless dame,
Down from the craggy brow, into the foaming main.
The pointed rocks her tender body tore,
And the white surf was purpled with her gore.
     The moon just rising blush'd to see her doom,
And seem'd to prophesy of woes to come;
With dusky redness veil'd her silver light,
And back revolving left the earth in night.
The foaming billows, mounting to the shore,
High on the rock the mangled body bore;
There in the craggy bason, long it lay,
To ev'ry wind, and rav'nous bird, a prey.
Hapless Avenia! whither art thou gone;
Launch'd in a moment to a world unknown.
No more, alas, for thee the chaunting train,
Shall join harmonious on the verdant plain;
No more, with grace superior to the rest,
Shalt thou inflame the wond'ring hero's breast;

For thee no more awake the tuneful strings;
No more to charm thee thy Angola sings;
No more shall Philomel,[18] the plaintive bird,
To soothe thee in thy native woods be heard;
The feather'd tribes shall cease their notes to sound,
The smiling landscape sadden all around;
While the hoarse breathings of the hollow wind,
With deep resounding waves in concert join'd;
Shall day and night repeat their ceaseless moan,
In plaints responsive for AVENIA gone.

Joel Barlow (1754–1812), from *The Vision of Columbus* (1787); from *The Columbiad*, Book VIII (1809, an extended and reworked version of *The Vision*)

For some bizarre reason Barlow is now principally remembered as the author of the rather silly mock-heroic poem *The Hasty Pudding*, inspired by a yearning to return to New England. Yet both as a writer and political propagandist he was a significant figure for his American, British, and French contemporaries. Barlow led an astonishingly full life and lived out his revolutionary ideals to the full. Educated at Yale he acted as a chaplain in the ranks of the Revolutionary Army for three years during the American War. After the war he was the centre of a literary coterie called the Hartford wits, whose principal desire was to create an elevated national literature for the new nation. Barlow's *Vision of Columbus* was a contribution to this movement, and was a big hit, not only in the ex-colonies but in Britain. Barlow published it just as the British abolition movement was really taking off. A lot of the poem's success in Britain can be put down to the spirited way in which Barlow tears into the Spanish conquest of the Americas, retelling the Spanish Black Legend in poeticized and essentialized form. The greatest British abolition poet, William Cowper (see pp. 81–93), when reviewing Barlow's poem, singled out for his longest quotation the character assassination of Cortez, and sees this passage as a suitable goad to young British poets to attempt an imperial epic. This passage constitutes the first extract below.

From 1788 to 1802 Barlow was in Europe and became sucked into revolutionary politics. He published several radical essays and pamphlets in England including the extremely revolutionary *Advice to the Privileged Orders*, and in 1792 was made a French citizen in recognition of his contributions to the revolutionary cause. He was a close friend of Tom Paine and managed to get Paine's brilliant, outrageous, and hilarious

---

[18] The nightingale.

assault on state religion *The Age of Reason* published, while Paine languished in a Parisian prison. After several years of diplomatic manoeuvring in Tripoli, Algiers, and Tunis Barlow returned to the United States in 1805. He then set about revising *The Vision of Columbus* into the longer and dramatically more ambitious *Columbiad* of 1809. Although he worked the style of the poem up into what is at times an almost impenetrable periphrastic jungle the poem took a strong liberal line on many areas of contemporary American politics. The passage included here is an extended assault on the continued existence of slavery in America. The attack opens in the form of a majestic address spoken by the god Atlas on behalf of Africa and the African slaves. Barlow chooses Atlas as a representative of Africa because he was said to have been transformed into the eponymous mountain range in Africa. Atlas concludes by warning Europe and America that they will be destroyed by natural cataclysms unless slavery and the slave trade are ended. Barlow's discussion of slavery ends with an intelligent analysis of the manner in which European approaches to power had provided an intellectual justification of, and practical models for, American slavery. Roman political power structures based in the enslavement of conquered peoples are seen to bleed into European power structures: 'modern Europe with her feudal codes, | Serfs, villains, vassals, nobles, kings.' His conclusion that slavery continues in America because too much of European thought and culture has been transplanted to the Americas is stern but fair.

Barlow re-entered international diplomacy in 1811 when he became US plenipotentiary to France. After a bizarre wild goose chase into Russia, in an attempt to gain an audience with the French Minister of Foreign Affairs, the Duc de Bassano, Barlow was caught up in the retreat of French troops from Moscow. After nearly freezing to death Barlow died of pneumonia in Poland on Christmas eve 1812.

from *The Vision of Columbus*

> Now see, from yon fair isle, his[1] murdering band
> Stream o'er the wave and mount the fated strand;
> On the wild shore behold his fortress rise,
> The fleet in flames ascends the darken'd skies,
> The march begins; the nations, from afar,
> Quake in his sight, and wage the fruitless war;
> O'er the rich provinces he bends his way,
> Kings in his chain, and kingdoms for his prey;
> While, robed in peace, great Montezuma[2] stands,
> And crowns and treasures sparkle in his hands,

---

[1] Cortez's.

[2] Montezuma II (1466–1520), the last Aztec emperor of Mexico, succeeded to the throne in 1502. He died during the early stages of the Spanish conquest of Mexico, as a result of the policy of Hernando Cortez.

Proffers the empire, yields the scepter'd sway,
Bids vassal'd millions tremble and obey;
And plies the victor, with incessant prayer,
Thro' ravaged realms the harmless race to spare.
But prayers, and tears, and sceptres plead in vain,
Nor threats can move him, or a world restrain;
While blest religion's prostituted name,
And monkish fury guides the sacred flame:
O'er fanes[3] and altars, fircs unhallow'd bend,
Climb o'er the wall and up the towers ascend,
Pour, round the lowering skies, the smoky flood,
And whelm the fields, and quench their rage in blood.
The Hero heard; and with a heaving sigh,
Dropp'd the full tear that started in his eye:
'Oh hapless day!' his trembling voice reply'd,
'That saw my wandering streamer mount the tide!
Oh! had the lamp of heaven, to that bold sail,
Ne'er mark'd the passage nor awak'd the gale,
Taught eastern worlds these beauteous climes to find,
Nor led those tygers forth to curse mankind,
Then had the tribes, beneath those bounteous skies,
Seen their wall widen and their spires arise;
Down the long tracts of time their glory shone,
Broad as the day and lasting as the sun:
The growing realms, beneath thy shield that rest,
O hapless monarch still thy power had blest,
Enjoy'd the pleasures that surround thy throne,
Survey'd thy virtues and sublimed their own.
Forgive me, prince; this impious arm hath led
The unseen storm that blackens o'er thy head;
Taught the dark sons of slaughter where to roam,
To seize thy crown and seal thy nation's doom.'

---

[3] See p. 309 n. 6.

from *The Columbiad*[1]

BOOK VIII

ARGUMENT

Atlas,[2] *the guardian Genius of Africa, denounces to Hesper the crimes of his people in the slavery of the Africans. The Author addresses his countrymen on that subject, and on the principles of their government.*

My friends, I love your fame, I joy to raise
The high toned anthem of my country's praise;
To sing her victories, virtues, wisdom, weal,
Boast with loud voice the patriot pride I feel;
Warm, wild I sing; and, to her failing blind,
Mislead myself, perhaps mislead mankind.
Land that I love! is this the whole we owe?
Thy pride to pamper, thy fair face to show;
Dwells there no blemish where such glories shine?
And lurks no spot in that bright sun of thine?
Hark! a dread voice, with heaven-astounding strain,
Swells like a thousand thunders o'er the main,
Rolls and reverberates around thy hills,
And Hesper's heart with pangs paternal fills.
Thou hearst him not; 'tis Atlas, throned sublime,
Great brother guardian of old Afric's clime;
High o'er his coast he rears his frowning form,
O'erlooks and calms his sky-borne fields of storm,
Flings off the clouds that round his shoulders hung,
And breaks from clogs of ice his trembling tongue;
While far thro space with rage and grief he glares,
Heaves his hoar head and shakes the heaven he bears:
—Son of my sire! Oh latest brightest birth
That sprang from his fair spouse, prolific earth!
Great Hesper, say what sordid ceaseless hate
Impels thee thus to mar my elder state.
Our sire assign'd thee thy more glorious reign,
Secured and bounded by our laboring main;

---

[1]   The epic of America.
[2]   The classical Titan who carried the heavens on his shoulders; because he was finally transformed into the Atlas mountains in Africa, he carries African associations.

That main (tho still my birthright name it bear)
Thy sails o'ershadow, thy brave children share;
I grant it thus; while air surrounds the ball,
Let breezes blow, let oceans roll for all.
But thy proud sons, a strange ungenerous race,
Enslave my tribes, and each fair world disgrace,
Provoke wide vengeance on their lawless land,
The bolt ill placed in thy forbearing hand.—
Enslave my tribes! then boast their cantons[3] free,
Preach faith and justice, bend the sainted knee,
Invite all men their liberty to share,
Seek public peace, defy the assaults of war,
Plant, reap, consume, enjoy their fearless toil,
Tame their wild floods, to fatten still their soil,
Enrich all nations with their nurturing store,
And rake with venturous fluke each wondering shore.—
Enslave my tribes! what, half mankind imban,[4]
Then read, expound, enforce the rights of man![5]
Prove plain and clear how nature's hand of old
Cast all men equal in her human mould!
Their fibres, feelings, reasoning powers the same,
Like wants await them, like desires inflame.
Thro former times with learned book they tread,
Revise past ages and rejudge the dead,
Write, speak, avenge, for ancient sufferings feel,
Impale each tyrant on their pens of steel,
Declare how freemen can a world create,
And slaves and masters ruin every state.—
Enslave my tribes! and think, with dumb disdain,
To scape this arm and prove my vengeance vain!
But look! methinks beneath my foot I ken[6]
A few chain'd things that seem no longer men;
Thy sons perchance! whom Barbary's[7] coast can tell
The sweets of that loved scourge they wield so well.
Link'd in a line, beneath the driver's goad,
See how they stagger with their lifted load;

[3] A division of territory; in Switzerland a canton is independent, having its own government.
[4] To curse.
[5] The great English revolutionary Thomas Paine published the two-part *The Rights of Man* in 1791–2.
[6] Know, recognize.
[7] Barbary coast is that part of Mediterranean coast of North Africa between the Strait of Gibraltar and Cape Bon.

Fling far the bursting fragments, scattering wide
Rocks, mountains, nations o'er the swallowing tide.
Plunging and surging with alternate sweep,
They storm the day-vault and lay bare the deep,
Toss, tumble, plough their place, then slow subside,
And swell each ocean as their bulk they hide;
Two oceans dasht in one! that climbs and roars,
And seeks in vain the exterminated shores,
The deep drencht hemisphere. Far sunk from day,
It crumbles, rolls, it churns the settling sea,
Turns up each prominence, heaves every side,
To pierce once more the landless length of tide:
Till some poized Pambamarca[8] looms at last
A dim lone island in the watery waste,
Mourns all his minor mountains wreck'd and hurl'd,
Stands the sad relic of a ruin'd world,
Attests the wrath our mother kept in store,
And rues her judgments on the race she bore.
No saving Ark around him rides the main,
Nor Dove weak-wing'd her footing finds again;
His own bald Eagle[9] skims alone the sky,
Darts from all points of heaven her searching eye,
Kens, thro the gloom, her ancient rock of rest,
And finds her cavern'd crag, her solitary nest.
      Thus toned the Titan[10] his tremendous knell,
And lash'd his ocean to a loftier swell;
Earth groans responsive, and with laboring woes
Leans o'er the surge and stills the storm he throws.
      Fathers and friends, I know the boding fears
Of angry genii and of rending spheres
Assail not souls like yours; whom Science bright
Thro shadowy nature leads with surer light;
For whom she strips the heavens of love and hate,
Strikes from Jove's hand the brandisht bolt of fate,
Gives each effect its own indubious cause,
Divides her moral from her physic laws,
Shows where the virtues find their nurturing food,

8 Or Pambambaca, formerly an area of Portuguese West Africa.
9 Symbol of the United States of America.
10 A son, daughter, or direct descendant of Uranus and Gaea, a race of giants. Hence Titan can be applied to anything huge or gigantic.

And men their motives to be just and good.
　　You scorn the Titan's threat; nor shall I strain
The powers of pathos in a task so vain
As Afric's wrongs to sing; for what avails
To harp for you these known familiar tales?
To tongue mute misery, and re-rack the soul
With crimes oft copied from that bloody scroll
Where Slavery pens her woes; tho 'tis but there
We learn the weight that mortal life can bear.
The tale might startle still the accustom'd ear,
Still shake the nerve that pumps the pearly tear,
Melt every heart, and thro the nation gain
Full many a voice to break the barbarous chain.
But why to sympathy for guidance fly,
(Her aids uncertain and of scant supply)
When your own self-excited sense affords
A guide more sure, and every sense accords?
Where strong self-interest, join'd with duty, lies,
Where doing right demands no sacrifice,
Where profit, pleasure, life-expanding fame
League their allurements to support the claim,
Tis safest there the impleaded cause to trust;
Men well instructed will be always just.
　　From slavery then your rising realms to save,
Regard the master, notice not the slave;
Consult alone for freemen, and bestow
Your best, your only cares, to keep them so.
Tyrants are never free; and, small and great,
All masters must be tyrants soon or late;
So nature works; and oft the lordling knave
Turns out at once a tyrant and a slave,
Struts, cringes, bullies, begs, as courtiers must,
Makes one a god, another treads in dust,
Fears all alike, and filches whom he can,
But knows no equal, finds no friend in man.
　　Ah! would you not be slaves, with lords and kings,
Then be not masters; there the danger springs.
The whole crude system that torments this earth,
Of rank, privation, privilege of birth,
False honor, fraud, corruption, civil jars,
The rage of conquest and the curse of wars,

Pandora's[11] total shower, all ills combined
That erst o'erwhelm'd and still distress mankind,
Box'd up secure in your deliberate hand,
Wait your behest, to fix or fly this land.
    Equality of Right is nature's plan;
And following nature is the march of man.
Whene'er he deviates in the least degree,
When, free himself, he would be more than free,
The baseless column, rear'd to bear his bust,
Falls as he mounts, and whelms him in the dust.
    See Rome's rude sires, with autocratic gait,
Tread down their tyrant and erect their state;
Their state secured, they deem it wise and brave
That every freeman should command a slave,
And, flusht with franchise of his camp and town,
Rove thro the world and hunt the nations down;
Master and man the same vile spirit gains,
Rome chains the world, and wears herself the chains.
    Mark modern Europe with her feudal codes,
Serfs, villains, vassals, nobles, kings and gods,
All slaves of different grades, corrupt and curst
With high and low, for senseless rank athirst,
Wage endless wars; not fighting to be free,
But *cujum pecus*,[12] whose base herd they'll be.
    Too much of Europe, here transplanted o'er,
Nursed feudal feelings on your tented shore,
Brought sable serfs from Afric, call'd it gain,
And urged your sires to forge the fatal chain.
But now, the tents o'erturn'd, the war dogs[13] fled,
Now fearless Freedom rears at last her head
Matcht with celestial Peace,—my friends, beware
To shade the splendors of so bright a pair;
Complete their triumph, fix their firm abode,
Purge all privations from your liberal code,
Restore their souls to men, give earth repose,
And save your sons from slavery, wars and woes.

[11] Pandora's curiosity led her to open a forbidden box, which released all evils and diseases of the world; only hope was left at the bottom.

[12] Virgil, 'dic mihi cujum pecus', 'tell me whose sheep they are'.

[13] The Portuguese were notorious, certainly within the Iberian Black Legend, for their use of mastiffs or 'war dogs' in their early slaving expeditions to Africa.

Robert Y. Sydney, 'Anthem', in *An Oration Commemorative of the Abolition of the Slave Trade* (1809)

British abolition of the slave trade in 1807 was taken up as a celebratory focus by the black communities of New England. This poem was introduced into a prose oration and sung as part of the celebration for the 'National Jubilee of the Abolition of the Slave Trade' on 1 January 1809. Sydney's verses express the conventional line that the blacks should give thanks to God for abolition as a sign of his special favour to the 'sons of Afric'. The hymn cannot help but carry a political punch—if Britain can abolish the slave trade, then why cannot America abolish slavery?

Anthem

Dry your tears, ye sons of Afric,
God has shown his gracious power;
He has stopt the horrid traffic,
That your country's bosom tore.
See through clouds he smiles benignant.
See your nation's glory rise;
Though your foes may frown indignant,
All their wrath you may despise.

Chorus
Dry your tears ye hapless nation,
    Banish all your cares away;
God has given great salvation,
    On this ever glorious day.

Solo
O raise to heaven a grateful voice,
Through every age rejoice, rejoice.

Recitative
What objects meet the piteous eye,
    What passions fill the soul of man,
To see a hapless nation rise,
    And all its various actions scan,
In deep disgrace, depriv'd of peace,

And every blessing dear,
Now blest with peace, rais'd up in fame,
And free from every fear.

Thus the clouds the light obscuring,
Vainly try to veil the day:
Thus shall you all toils enduring,
See your troubles pass away.
Though the clouds of night have hover'd,
On your nation's hapless head;
See the blushing morn discover'd,
See the dawn of glory shed.

See each science round you blooming,
Like the flowers at dawn of day,
With their sweets the air perfuming,
With their beauties cheer the way.
See with eagle wings expanded,
See each hidden talent rise;
See each slavish fear disbanded,
See your genius mount the skies.

Chorus

Peter William (1780–1840), 'Hymn', in *An Address to the New York Academy* (1809)

Williams's hymns were performed the day after the anthem of Sydney at the same celebration two years after the passage of the British slave trade abolition bill (pp. xlii,
297–9, 320–2). Again, on the surface, they constitute a pietist and conventional black
response to the anniversary, but again demonstrate how the black community on the
East Coast could use developments in Britain to accuse Americans over slavery.
Williams reiterates the propaganda agenda of British abolition. He thanks the
Christian God for the gift of freedom, he presents the enslaved Africans as passive
objects of pity, 'A harmless race', and abolition is described as the result of the actions
of white philanthropists, whose actions are blessed by God.

Hymn

I

To the Eternal Lord,
By saints on earth ador'd
   And saints above.
Let us glad honors rear,
In strains of praise and pray'r
His glorious name declare,
   The God of Love.

II

When the oppressor's hands
Bound us in iron bands
   Thou didst appear.
Thou saw our weeping eyes,
And list'ning to our cries,
In mercy didst arise,
   Our hearts to cheer.

III

Thou did'st the trade o'erthrow,
The source of boundless woe,
   The world's disgrace,
Which ravag'd Afric's coast,
Enslaved its greatest boast,
A happy num'rous host,
   A harmless race.

IV

In diff'rent parts of earth
Thou called the Humane forth,
   Our rights to plead,
Our griefs to mitigate,
And to improve our state,
An object truly great,
   Noble indeed.

V

Thou didst their labours bless,
And gave them great success,
   In Freedom's cause.

They prov'd to every sight
By truth's unerring light,
All men are free by right
Of Nature's laws.

VI
They to insure our bliss,
Taught us that happiness
Is from above.
That it is only found
On this terrestrial ground,
Where virtuous acts abound
And Mutu'l Love.

Sarah Wentworth Morton (1759–1846), 'The African Chief' (1823)

Morton wrote a considerable number of essays on a wide variety of social issues, as well as being a prolific poet. She usually wrote under the pseudonym of 'Philenia', and her most successful publication, in commercial terms, was *My Mind and its Thoughts* (1823). 'The African Chief' was her most widely reproduced abolition poem. The work's popularity results from the manner in which Wentworth succinctly reworks a number of motifs relating to the conventions of middle passage abolition propaganda and sentimentalism. The African chief is a figure of elevated and aristocratic abstraction. His inability to bear separation from his wife and her subsequent abuse are present as the motives which lead him to rebellious action. His violence, however, is descriptively contained, and presented through the filters of a series of classical comparisons. His rebellion ends in capture and the revolting torture of being broken upon the wheel. Morton of course draws a discreet veil over this scene in order not to affront her polite Boston readership.

The African Chief

See how the black ship cleaves the main,
  High bounding o'er the dark blue wave,
Remurmuring with the groans of pain,
  Deep freighted with the princely slave!

Did all the Gods of Afric sleep,
    Forgetful of their guardian love,
When the white tyrants of the deep
    Betrayed him in the palmy grove?

A chief of Gambia's[1] golden shore,
    Whose arm the band of warriors led,
Or more—the lord of generous power,
    By whom the foodless poor were fed.

Does not the voice of reason cry,
    Claim the first right that nature gave,
From the red scourge of bondage fly,
    Nor deign to live a burdened slave?

Has not his suffering offspring clung,
    Desponding round his fettered knee;
On his worn shoulder, weeping hung,
    And urged one effort to be free?

His wife by nameless wrongs subdued,
    His bosom's friend to death resigned;
The flinty path-way drenched in blood,
    He saw with cold and frenzied mind.

Strong in despair, then sought the plain,
    To heaven was raised his steadfast eye,
Resolved to burst the crushing chain,
    Or mid the battle's blast to die.

First of his race, he led the band,
    Guardless of danger, hurling round,
Till by his red avenging hand,
    Full many a despot stained the ground.

When erst Messenia's[2] sons oppressed
    Flew desperate to the sanguine field,
With iron clothed each injured breast,
    And saw the cruel Spartan[3] yield,

---

[1] One of the smallest states of Africa, on the west coast.
[2] A region of Peloponnesus in ancient Greece. During the 350s BC Sparta made concerted efforts to regain control of the area.
[3] Referring to Sparta's final failure to regain Messenia.

Did not the soul to heaven allied,
　　With the proud heart as greatly swell,
As when the Roman Decius[4] died,
　　Or when the Grecian victim[5] fell?

Do later deeds quick rapture raise,
　　The boon Batavia's[6] William won;
Paoli's[7] time-enduring praise,
　　Or the yet greater Washington?

If these exalt thy sacred zeal,
　　To hate oppression's mad control,
For bleeding Afric learn to feel,
　　Whose Chieftain claimed a kindred soul.

Ah, mourn the last disastrous hour,
　　Lift the full eye of bootless grief,
While victory treads the sultry shore,
　　And tears from hope the captive chief.

While the hard race of pallid hue,
　　Unpracticed in the power to feel,
Resign him to the murderous crew,
　　The horrors of the quivering wheel,

Let sorrow bathe each blushing cheek,
　　Bend piteous o'er the tortured slave,
Whose wrongs compassion cannot speak,
　　Whose only refuge was the grave.

[4] Gaius Decius (249–51), who was notorious for his organized and empire-wide persecution of the early Christians.

[5] 'Leonidas.' [Morton] Referring to the heroic defence of the pass at Thermopylae by the Spartan King Leonidas, against the invading Persian forces led by Xerxes.

[6] A city in the state of New York, settled by the Dutch in the late 18th century. In 1826 William Morgan, who was interested in exposing the secrets of the Masons, disappeared there.

[7] Pasquali di Paoli (1725–1807), a notorious contemporary Corsican patriot and nationalist.

William Cullen Bryant (1794–1878), 'The African Chief' (first printed *Literary Gazette*, Dec. 1826)

Bryant was a hugely influential cultural commentator and personality in nineteenth-century New York, and his life and times are exhaustively examined in the excellent Charles H. Brown biography *William Cullen Bryant* (Scribner, 1971). To his contemporaries he emerged as one of the great philanthropic spokesmen for human rights, including those of the slave. In David W. Bartlett's almost insanely enthusiastic *Modern Agitators; or, Pen Portraits of Living American Reformers* (Miller, Orton & Mulligan, 1855) 'The African Chief' is one of only two poems which Bartlett quotes as Bryant's masterpieces. He concludes: 'The poem is one of the most beautiful and pathetic ever written by an American bard. Its simplicity is striking yet it is one of its beauties ... In this little poem the poet preaches a more eloquent anti slavery sermon, that was ever preached from the pulpit' (Bartlett, *Modern Agitators*, 190). In fact 'The African Chief' is profoundly conventional in theme and treatment. As has been seen elsewhere the figure of the wronged African aristocrat separated from his beloved, and refusing to endure slavery because of his noble nature, had been done to death in the wake of Behn's *Oroonoko* and Thomas Southerne's late seventeenth-century stage adaptation of this (p. xviii). Bryant takes this literary inheritance to a sentimental extreme, and in doing so maintains the disempowering tropes reserved for the presentation of wronged African male nobility. The rules are that the black male be allowed to fight furiously for his liberty and then be captured, like a great wild beast. Indeed Bryant makes it explicit that this chief is like 'a lion'. Yet having been captured he just pines away and dies, long before he can do any real insurrectionary damage either on the middle passage or on the plantation.

Bryant actually wrote little poetry explicitly about slavery, and in his development as a thinker on slavery he followed a fairly common path. Although always against slavery in the abstract he showed himself initially pragmatic on some issues. In some of his earlier journalism he took a fairly detached position on the free-soil debate, stating that it was up to the individual pioneers in the new lands to decide their personal politics. As with so many abolitionists it was the Kansas Nebraska Act, and then the Fugitive Slave Law, which turned him to a more radical stance on abolition.

The African Chief

Chained in the market-place he stood,
    A man of giant frame,
Amid the gathering multitude,
    That shrunk to hear his name—
All stern of look and strong of limb,

His dark eye on the ground:—
And silently they gazed on him,
As on a lion bound.

Vainly, but well that chief had fought,
He was a captive now,
Yet pride, that fortune humbles not,
Was written on his brow.
The scars his dark broad bosom wore
Showed warrior true and brave;
A prince among his tribe before,
He could not be a slave.

Then to his conqueror he spake:
"My brother is a king;
Undo this necklace from my neck,
And take this bracelet ring,
And send me where my brother reigns,
And I will fill thy hands
With store of ivory from the plains,
And gold dust from the sands."

"Not for thy ivory nor thy gold
Will I unbind thy chain;
That bloody hand shall never hold
The battle-spear again.
A price that nation never gave
Shall yet be paid for thee;
For thou shalt be the Christian's slave,
In lands beyond the sea."

Then wept the warrior chief, and bade
To shred his locks away;
And one by one, each heavy braid
Before the victor lay.
Thick were the platted locks, and long,
And closely hidden there
Shone many a wedge of gold among
The dark and crisped hair.

"Look, feast thy greedy eye with gold
Long kept for sorest need;
Take it—thou askest sums untold—
And say that I am freed.

Take it—my wife, the long, long day,
    Weeps by the cocoa-tree,
And my young children leave their play,
    And ask in vain for me."

"I take thy gold, but I have made
    Thy fetters fast and strong,
And ween that by the cocoa-shade
    Thy wife will wait thee long."
Strong was the agony that shook
    The captive's frame to hear,
And the proud meaning of his look
    Was changed to mortal fear.

His heart was broken—crazed his brain:
    At once his eye grew wild;
He struggled fiercely with his chain,
    Whispered, and wept, and smiled;
Yet wore not long those fatal bands,
    And once, at shut of day,
They drew him forth upon the sands,
    The foul hyena's prey.

George Moses Horton (1797?–1883?), 'The Slave's Complaint', 'On Liberty and Slavery', in *The Hope of Liberty* (1829); 'Division of an Estate', 'Troubled with the Itch, and Rubbing with Sulphur', in *The Poetical Works of Thomas M. Horton the Colored Bard of North Carolina* (1845)

Horton was born a slave in Northampton County, North Carolina, and only gained his freedom at the end of the Civil War. His owner moved to Chatham County when Horton was still an infant, yet this move was to be the event which gave him the chance to become a poet. The nearby University of Chapel Hill became the focus for his adolescent life. Horton got permission to work as a cleaner at the university and, having taught himself to read, and compose extempore verse, he soon found a ready market amongst the students for writing love poetry. Horton was then taken up by Caroline Lee Hentz, the wife of a professor. Hentz was from Massachusetts and had abolitionist sympathies. She not only taught Horton to write but sent some of his poems which criticized slavery to news-papers. Horton's work first appeared in the local *Lancaster Gazette*, but was subse-quently published in leading national abolition papers. In 1829 Horton, now something of a minor celebrity known locally as 'the slave poet', saw his first volume of poetry *The Hope of Liberty* appear. The volume had been organized by sympathetic whites as a sub-scription volume, and it was hoped the profits would buy Horton's freedom. Although Horton never succeeded in writing himself into freedom his verse was a success: *The Hope of Liberty* was reprinted twice and he brought out two further volumes.

Horton's poetry directly addressing the issue of slavery is conventional and rather flat, reiterating in a tired late Romantic diction the libertarian platitudes of mid-nineteenth-century Anglo-American abolition verse. The poem 'Division of an Estate' has more power than the other slavery poems. Here Horton uses blank verse instead of his custom-ary lyric or balladic models. A curious tension results when the confused everyday busi-ness of the separation of livestock, including the slaves, is described in the elevated terms of Miltonic parody. It is, however, perhaps in some of the shorter, more colloquial poems when he takes a tangential approach to slavery that Horton is at his most distinctive, and subtle, as a critic of slavery. 'Troubled with the Itch, and Rubbing with Sulphur' for ex-ample is an odd, comic little piece until the last verse brings home the terrifying idea that this force 'Which oft deprives me of my sleep | And plagues me to the heart' may not be a simple itch, but a brilliantly down-to-earth metaphor for the condition of enslavement.

The Slave's Complaint

Am I sadly cast aside,
On misfortune's rugged tide?
Will the world my pains deride
        Forever?

Must I dwell in Slavery's night,
And all pleasure take its flight,
Far beyond my feeble sight,
        Forever?

Worst of all, must hope grow dim,
And withhold her cheering beam?
Rather let me sleep and dream
        Forever!

Something still my heart surveys,
Groping through this dreary maze;
Is it Hope?—then burn and blaze
        Forever!

Leave me not a wretch confined,
Altogether lame and blind—
Unto gross despair consigned,
      Forever!

Heaven! in whom can I confide?
Canst thou not for all provide?
Condescend to be my guide
      Forever:

And when this transient life shall end,
Oh, may some kind, eternal friend
Bid me from servitude ascend,
      Forever!

On Liberty and Slavery

Alas! and am I born for this,
    To wear this slavish chain?
Deprived of all created bliss,
    Through hardship, toil, and pain!

How long have I in bondage lain,
    And languished to be free!
Alas! and must I still complain—
    Deprived of liberty.

Oh, Heaven! and is there no relief
    This side the silent grave—
To soothe the pain—to quell the grief
    And anguish of a slave?

Come, Liberty, thou cheerful sound,
    Roll through my ravished ears,
Come, let my grief in joys be drowned,
    And drive away my fears.

Say unto foul oppression, Cease:
    Ye tyrants rage no more,
And let the joyful trump of peace,
    Now bid the vassal soar.

Soar on the pinions of that dove
   Which long has cooed for thee,
And breathed her notes from Afric's grove,
   The sound of Liberty.

Oh, Liberty! thou golden prize,
   So often sought by blood—
We crave thy sacred sun to rise,
   The gift of nature's God!

Bid Slavery hide her haggard face,
   And barbarism fly:
I scorn to see the sad disgrace
   In which enslaved I lie.

Dear Liberty! upon thy breast,
   I languish to respire;
And like the Swan unto her nest,
   I'd to thy smiles retire.

Oh, blest asylum—heavenly balm!
   Unto thy boughs I flee—
And in thy shades the storm shall calm,
   With songs of Liberty!

Division of an Estate

It well bespeaks a man beheaded, quite
Divested of the laurel robe of life,
When every member struggles for its base,
The head; the power of order now recedes,
Unheeded efforts rise on every side,
With dull emotion rolling through the brain
Of apprehending slaves. The flocks and herds,
In sad confusion, now run to and fro,
And seem to ask, distressed, the reason why
That they are thus prostrated. Howl, ye dogs!
Ye cattle, low! ye sheep, astonish'd, bleat!
Ye bristling swine, trudge squealing through the glades,
Void of an owner to impart your food!
Sad horses, lift your heads and neigh aloud,
And caper frantic from the dismal scene;

Mow the last food upon your grass-clad lea,
And leave a solitary home behind,
In hopeless widowhood no longer gay!
The trav'ling sun of gain his journey ends
In unavailing pain; he sets with tears;
A king sequester'd sinking from his throne,
Succeeded by a train of busy friends,
Like stars which rise with smiles, to mark the flight
Of awful Phoebus[1] to another world;
Stars after stars in fleet succession rise
Into the wide empire of fortune clear,
Regardless of the donor of their lamps,
Like heirs forgetful of parental care,
Without a grateful smile or filial tear,
Redound in rev'rence to expiring age.
But soon parental benediction flies
Like vivid meteors; in a moment gone,
As though they ne'er had been. But O! the state,
The dark suspense in which poor vassals stand,
Each mind upon the spire of chance hangs fluctuant;
The day of separation is at hand;
Imagination lifts her gloomy curtains,
Like ev'ning's mantle at the flight of day,
Thro' which the trembling pinnacle we spy,
On which we soon must stand with hopeful smiles,
Or apprehending frowns; to tumble on
The right or left forever.

Troubled with the Itch, and Rubbing with Sulphur[1]

'Tis bitter, yet 'tis sweet,
Scratching effects but transient ease;
Pleasure and pain together meet,
And vanish as they please.

[1] Phoebus Apollo, the sun god.

[1] Also known as brimstone, a yellow non-metallic element, very brittle and inflammable. Because of its spectacular performance in chemical reactions, and its easy conversion into sulphuric acid, it is inevitably associated with the Devil and hell.

My nails, the only balm,
To ev'ry bump are oft applied,
And thus the rage will sweetly calm
Which aggravates my hide.

It soon returns again;
A frown succeeds to ev'ry smile;
Grinning I scratch and curse the pain,
But grieve to be so vile.

In fine, I know not which
Can play the most deceitful game,
The devil, sulphur, or the itch;
The three are but the same.

The devil sows the itch,
And sulphur has a loathsome smell,
And with my clothes as black as pitch,
I stink where'er I dwell.

Excoriated deep,
By friction play'd on ev'ry part,
It oft deprives me of my sleep,
And plagues me to my heart.

Noah Calwell Cannon (d. 1850), 'Hymn 12: Of the Christian's Barbarity', in *The Rock of Wisdom: An Explanation of the Sacred Scriptures, By the Rev. N. C. Cannon, (A Man of Color) To which are added several Interesting Hymns* (1833)

Cannon's prose and verse are marked out by a straightforward ability to talk about racial discrimination in the North. In his preface to *The Rock* Cannon makes a passionate plea that his work not be dismissed on the grounds of his colour, stating that he is 'well aware of the particular prejudice that still seems to exist from some whites towards that nation of people which is called Ethiopians'. In writing a practical spiritual guide based on his own experiences Cannon is only too aware that he is moving into a domain dominated by the white clerical power elite. His preface goes on to defend himself from the imagined attacks of critics and warns them not to focus on the weakness of his text, and states: 'if there is anything that is not beneficial throw it away and do not stumble over it and go down to hell, for I love your souls although I am of Ethiopian race, and never had the chance of being taught in the Colleges or Academies.' The hymn reproduced below is the only one which explicitly tackles the subject of slavery. While the ultimate theme of the poem is the hypocrisy of white slave holders who profess the Christian faith his hymn sets up a powerful tension between the suffering slave masses and his own consciousness as a free black divine in New York. The first quatrain of each stanza introduces stark imagery of general slave suffering, while the last two lines operate as a refrain. In these lines Cannon moves from objective observation to the inclusion of himself as one of the victims of slavery.

Hymn 12: Of the Christian's Barbarity

Was stolen and sold from Africa,
Imported to America:
Like the brute beasts at market sold,
To stand the heat and bear the cold.
    When will Jehovah hear our cries!
    And free the sons of Africa.

They bear the lash—endure the pain—
Forced through frost, hail, snow and rain,
And often-night sleep on the ground,
No freedom till, the grave is found,
    We pray Jehovah will hear our cries,
    And relieve the sons of Africa.

Working all day and half the night,
And up before the morning light;
Exposed to hardships, heat and cold,
And if they beg they meet with scold.
    We pray Jehovah to plead our cause,
    And put in force his righteous laws.

Their skins are dark, their hair is short:
Shall dying men make them trade and sport!
In sorrow dragging iron chains;
Depriv'd of all the rights of men.
    O, great Redeemer, view their wrong,
    And grant them aid e'er it be long.

> But He that rides upon the storms,
> Whose voice in thunder rolls along:
> In his own time will make a way
> To relieve the oppressed of Africa.
>   O, Prince of Glory be their friend!
>   And keep them faithful to the end.

Jones Very (1813–80), 'Lines Written on Reading Stuart's Account of the Treatment of Slaves in Charleston' (1833), 'The Plagues of Egypt' (1839), 'The Abolition of Serfdom in Russia' (1861), in Jones Very, *The Complete Poems*, ed. Helen Reese (University of Georgia Press, 1993)

Very grew up in Salem, and after a patchy education owing to the early death of his father he finally ended up at Harvard where he became intensely interested in theology. By 1843 he was licensed as a Unitarian preacher, although his extreme shyness prevented him from ever taking up the calling. He returned to Salem and became something of a literary recluse, walking the hills and writing a large amount of poetry. He became increasingly convinced that he had a mystical calling and that he was in contact with the divine spirit in all his acts. The intensity of his mysticism led his sanity to be questioned and he was committed for a time to a lunatic asylum in 1838. He believed his poetry to be a direct and personal gift from God to himself. Although primarily remembered as a religious poet of great intensity Very wrote many poems on contemporary political issues, including slavery.

Very's slavery verse is unusual in its methods and its message. 'The Plagues of Egypt' takes the biblical story most beloved of slave literatures and central to many of the spirituals, namely God's punishment of the Egyptians for the enslavement of the Israelites. In this poem Very adopts an extreme prophetic stance, and a diction of peculiar vividness: the image of the lice eating human flesh as if it is rust is particularly memorable. 'The Aboliton of Serfdom in Russia' is an unusual poem in attacking American slavery indirectly through the celebration of legal abolition of the serf system in Russia.

Lines Written on Reading Stuart's Account of the Treatment of Slaves in Charleston

Oh slavery! thou bane of human kind;
Thou tyrant o'er the body and the mind;
To all that's just, to all that's right a foe,
Thou fill'st the world with misery and woe.
Ah! many a wretch by thee is caused to mourn;
From friend, from relative, from country torn,
From all the joys that e'er his soul held dear,
Beneath thy cruel scourge is doomed to fear.
By curs't desire of gain, by thirst for gold,
The unhappy victim of thy crime is sold.
Is sold? to whom? would I could hide the shame!
To man; O traffic base, disgraceful to the name;
To man, with reason and with freedom blest,
O'er all creation placed the first, and best;
Alas! how fallen from that station he,
Who, blest with reason, proud in being free,
Can from his proper sphere a being draw,
Deprive of rights, of liberty, and law;
Deprive, (what's far more cruel than the rest,)
Of all the gifts with which himself is blest.
Would that my lips the tale could never tell,
The tale of horror, known, alas! too well.
Would that the world had never seen the day,
When man his fellow man should thus betray,
Would rather every ship that sailed the main,
For such base traffic, such degrading gain,
Had sunk with all beneath the raging sea,
Where they from slavery ever would be free:
Free from a tyrant's power, who often rends
Parent from children, friend from dearest friend;
Free from a life of wretchedness and woe,
Free from all toil and suffering here below.
Ah! who could read the story of that woe?
And who if reading half their sorrow know?
Would that by me their wrongs could half be told,
Would that their sufferings I could half unfold.

Before our God and theirs those sufferings rise,
He sees their wrongs, he hears their helpless cries:
Soon may those wrongs and sufferings have an end,
Man be not foe to man, but friend.

The Plagues of Egypt[1]

I see them spreading o'er the land,
    The swarming locust fly;
More numerous than the small-grained sand,
    They speed them from on high.

O'er golden crops that gallant waved,
    O'er groves with foliage green;
They march; not e'en the grass is saved,
    Nor hill nor flood can screen.

And lice within men's dwellings creep,
    More small than finest dust;
Their kneading troughs, and where they sleep;
    They eat their flesh like rust.

Repent! e'er yet your eldest born,
    Be stricken at your side;
Repent! e'er yet ye see the morn,
    The wave with blood be dyed.

For He who lives will Israel call,
    From out their bondage sore;
And Egypt's pride again shall fall,
    And Egypt's sons deplore.

---

[1] The seven plagues of Egypt were afflictions sent upon the Egyptians as signs of God's displeasure after Pharaoh had refused to listen to Moses' plea that his people, the Israelites, be allowed their freedom. The plagues were frogs, lice, flies, boils, hail, locusts, and darkness.

The Abolition of Serfdom in Russia

From the great, imperial city[1]
　　Has gone forth the fixed decree,
That the Russian serf forever
　　From oppression shall be free![2]

Through a long, long night of bondage,
　　He has felt the oppressor's rod;
Bought and sold by haughty boyars,[3]
　　Held for life to till the sod.

The increasing light of knowledge
　　Still denied to heart and mind;
He for ages has toiled onward
　　To its cheering radiance blind.

With a nature thus degraded,
　　His own good he scarce has known;
While, in lands by Freedom favored,
　　Man to manhood's height has grown.

But the day at length is dawning
　　O'er the dark and frozen North;
Now the trumpet's voice proclaimeth
　　Man's true dignity and worth.

That to all the right belongeth,
　　To the strong and to the weak,
To the noble, and the peasant,
　　Knowledge, happiness to seek.

Unto Russia's Czar be honor,
　　For his brows the laurel twine;
His a nobler crown and kingdom,
　　Than the greatest of his line.

---

[1] St Petersburg.

[2] Russian serfs performed servile labour for the Russian landowners under conditions which amounted to slavery. Serfdom was finally ended in Russia in 1861, under the rule of Tsar Alexander II.

[3] The boyars were the old Russian aristocracy, next in rank to the controlling princes. They were dismantled and supplanted during the reforms of Peter the Great, who was responsible in many ways for a cultural revolution whereby Russia embraced European culture and economic policy.

Lydia Maria Child (1802–80), 'The Slave Trader', 'The Runaway', in *The Oasis* (1834); Mary Howitt (1799–1888), 'The Hedgehog', 'The Devil's Walk in Washington', in Child (ed.), *National Anti-Slavery Standard* (1/50 (20 May 1841), 200; 2/11 (18 Aug. 1841), 44)

Child did not write very much anti-slavery poetry of importance herself, yet was probably among the most gifted and influential of the American abolition authors. She was a propagandist of genius, infiltrating every publicity avenue then in existence. Child was a well-known literary figure before she entered the anti-slavery crusade. She had written two successful novels by the time she was 23, one of them, *Hobomok*, dealing with the marriage between a young Puritan woman and an indigenous American. After her financially disastrous marriage to David Child she needed money and wrote a series of practical domestic guides for women, the most popular being *The Frugal Housewife*. Coming under the direct influence of Garrison (pp. 536–40) in the early 1830s she became a convinced abolitionist. She edited the *National Anti-Slavery Standard* 1841–3, and published an unusual variety of slavery verse in the paper's poetry column, including the first substantial printing of William Blake's poetry in North America (pp. 142–4). She also brought out a huge variety of books and pamphlets on slavery: there was an anti-slavery catechism, several children's books, a biography of the Quaker abolitionist Isaac Hopper which contained a series of mini-biographies of fugitive slaves he had helped, and a series of anthologies. While John Brown was held in jail awaiting execution Child wrote and then published the popular *Correspondence between Lydia Maria Child, and Gov. Wise of Virginia*, in which she celebrated Brown as a martyr. The selections below are two ballads which appeared in her 1834 miscellany *The Oasis*.

Child also introduced a mass of poetry to an American readership in the pages of the *National Anti-Slavery Standard*. She was particularly astute in recognizing the ways in which sensitive poetry about the rights of all living things to liberty could be harnessed to the cause. Consequently she might be dangerously close at times to equating slave and animal suffering. Child included much of Mary Howitt's verse in the *Standard*, stating that: 'Anything which excites the tenderness of the human heart, and directs it toward heartless customs and cruel prejudices is doing the work of a missionary in the world's redemption, though it be in the forms of a little child like poem. Who can estimate the blessed influence of Mary Howitt on future generations! The small seeds she plants with such living diligence, will grow into spreading trees and nations rest in their shade. Hear her pleas for the persecuted Hedge hog.'

The Slave Trader

The following lines are founded upon the history of one of the writer's townsmen, who in his youth was engaged in the African Slave Trade. A short time after his return to his native place, he was stricken with insanity;—and it became necessary to confine his limbs. A pair of shackles which he had brought from Africa, but whose former use none of his family had suspected, were used on the occasion. Just before his death, he started up suddenly—gazed on his chains, and making a desperate effort to free himself exclaimed, *"Oh, my God!—the very fetters of my slaves."*

'T is long ago—the grass is green,
  Where once a cheerful dwelling rose;
And where the frequent step hath been,
  The thistle now untrampled grows.

Ay—long ago—since on that spot,
  A lighted hearth, and voice of prayer,
From those who now are half forgot,
  Told of a human dweller there.

Full eighty years have pass'd, since there,
  His numerous household band beside,
A kneeling man with thin gray hair,
  Offer'd his prayer at even-tide.

How fervent was that father's prayer,
  For those whose cherish'd love was dear
To Him, who hath a father's care
  For all his lowly children here!

With earnest voice, and upraised eye,
  His wrestling spirit rose above,
Asking for blessings, trustingly,
  On him who bore his name and love.

A journeyer on the Ocean's breast,
  His best beloved—his elder born,
Dove-like, from home's dear ark of rest,
  Long weary years before had gone.

And ever had that wanderer's name
    Been breathed, as in the evening prayer.
The father's voice uprose the same,
    As it had risen when he was there.
   .   .   .   .   .   .

Night fell on Teemboo's[1] heated bay,
    Its breeze the heavy palm-tops fann'd—
Quiet and cool the dew-drops lay
    Upon the parch'd and burning land!

Abroad upon the earth that night,
    The solemn veil of moonlight fell—
Each low-walled dwelling rose in light,
    And tree and flowret slumber'd well!

Pure, dove-like peace watch'd o'er the scene,
    And breathed upon the balmy air—
Had human hearts as holy been,
    Bright angels might have worshipp'd there!

Casting her shadow on that bay,
    Where all beside was waveless light,
Anchor'd, a stranger vessel lay,
    With Afric's slumbering world in sight.

Her leader—oh!—why *was* he there?
    Forgetful of his childhood's love,
Of home, where still for him in prayer,
    A father's spirit rose above?

From that dark vessel to the land,
    A crowded boat was swiftly sped—
The forms it bore were on the sand,
    With serpent eye and stealthy tread.

They bound their captives;—and the oar
    Moved lightly for the ship again—
While from the water and the shore,
    Arose wild shrieks of grief and pain!

---

[1] Formerly an area of Africa adjoining Sierra Leone, through which the Senegal river flowed.

Out sea-ward in the rising breeze,
    That vessel's sails were stretching far—
What power should guard her o'er the seas?
    What light should be her guiding star.

   .   .   .   .   .

Again his foot is on the spot,
    So often press'd in childhood's hours—
All is the same—all unforgot—
    The same green trees, the same bright flowers.

Again at home—as some young vine,
    Torn rudely from its loved embrace,
Restored again will fondly twine,
    Around its earlier resting-place—

So should the kindly heart return,
    Though long and wearily estranged;
And still that heart's own altar burn
    With light and incense all unchanged.

Not so with him:—the guilty heart,
    Might never thrill with joy again,
Nor the stung conscience bear a part,
    In anything save sin and pain.

In vain he struggled to conceal,
    Beneath a stern and gloomy air,
Feelings that scorched like burning steel,
    Till reason yielded to despair.

In sleep the weary sufferer lay,
    With fever'd brow and fetter'd limb—
Madness had worn his life away—
    Another world awaited him.

Sleep pass'd away:—no longer burn'd
    The fire of madness on his brain,
The blessed light of mind return'd,
    And for a moment shone again!

"Why have ye bound me?"—and his eye
    Fell quickly on his fetter'd hands,—
One glance—one shriek of agony—
    One struggle to unloose his bands!

Visions of blood, and stormy waves,
  Swept wildly o'er his clouded brain—
"Oh God!—the fetters of my slaves!
  Take off—take off the negro's chain!"

Kind hands had loosed each fetter'd limb,
  As painful came the sufferer's breath,
But other chains were binding him,
  The colder, heavier chains of death!

The Runaway

A TRUE STORY

Behind the hills the setting sun
  Has hidden now his golden light;
There stood a slave, his labor done,
  Watching the slow approach of night.

To be a slave—this thought press'd deep
  Upon his spirit, free and brave;
And often, when alone, he'd weep
  To think that he was born a slave.

But then his faithful Nanny's smile,
  Or little Willy's merry voice,
His soul would of its grief beguile—
  And William's heart would half rejoice.

His children climbing on his knees,
  The watchful kindness of his wife,
Brought to his wounded spirit ease,
  And help'd him bear the load of life.

And now you hear his fervent prayer,
  As before God he bends the knee,
"My wife and children bid them spare,
  And lay their burthens all on me."

His master died; for he was old,
  And nature still must have her due:
William, and all his slaves were sold,
  With other goods and cattle too.

He in the market-place was sold.
    His wife and children—where are they?
How can the dreadful tale be told!—
    They tore them from his arms away.

They heard his agonizing groans,
    They heard his little children's cries,
They heard his wife's heart-breaking tones
    Piercing the hollow, silent skies.

They heard them all, and turn'd away;
    They heeded not the negro's pain.
If God is just, there is a day
    When they must hear those sounds again.

Like a wild beast poor William then
    Was chain'd, and by a whip was driven;
One of a drove of slaves, of men,
    Whom Jesus came to lead to Heaven.

Time pass'd away—as pass it will,
    Though cruel sorrow mark each day;
Through joy and wo[e], through good and ill,
    The sands flow on, and pass away.

Who at the midnight hour is he,
    Creeping along upon the ground,
Hiding behind each bush and tree,
    And starting at the faintest sound?

'T is he—he 's near the river's side,
    He's safe within the boat;
A friend is there, to help him hide;
    Poor William! he may yet be free.

They offer'd food—he turn'd away;
    And then he quickly seized the knife,
And ere they could his purpose stay,
    He tried to end his hated life.

His master now, with cruel scorn,
    Laugh'd at his poor slave's frantic wo[e];
"What makes you, Bill, look so forlorn?
    Why did you cut your jacket so?

"I bade them give you food enough,
　And I'll forgive you for this trip;
I see you're made of right good stuff;
　I think you'll go without the whip.

"My negroes all are happy dogs,
　They never have too much to do;
My driver very seldom flogs;
　And why can't you be happy too?"

"I'm not a dog; I am a man;
　My wife and children, where are they?
Be happy! that I never can—
　They've taken all I love away."

" 'T is all pretence, you silly loon;[1]
　You lead a very happy life:
You will feel better very soon;
　I'll give you, Bill, another wife."

"Pity the creature thou hast made,
　Almighty God!" the negro cried,
"On whom the load of life is laid,
　Whilst all its blessings are denied.

"My wife and children—God does know
　They're living in this breaking heart;
And when compell'd from them to go,
　He saw how bitter 't was to part.

"But soon will cease these cruel pains;
　There 's one kind hand will set me free.
Death will strike off these hateful chains—
　Death will restore my liberty."

And now again in silent grief
　He look'd up at the boundless sky;
And not one tear, with sad relief,
　Moisten'd his glazed and bloodshot eye.

They reach'd the shore; and each one goes
　Where pleasure or where duty calls;
All but the slave—his burning woes
　Are hidden by his dungeon walls.

---

[1] A simple-minded or eccentric person, a rascal.

Hidden from men—but not from Him
    Whose eye of light is everywhere;
That light which darkness cannot dim,
    That eye of mercy, it was there.

They who could dare to take the name
    Of him who came from Heaven to save—
On them the sin! on them the shame!
    They made a heathen of the slave.

He thought that he was free to die;
    He never tasted food again.
He utter'd not another cry;
    He spoke not of his burning pain.

And thus he burst his prison door;
    And thus he set his spirit free.
The negro's misery is o'er—
    Death *has* restored his liberty.

The Hedgehog

The poor little English Porcupine,
What a harassed and weary life is thine!
And thou art a creature meek and mild,
And would'st not harm a sleeping child.

Thou scarce can stir from thy tree-root
But thy foes are up in hot pursuit;
Thou might be a horned asp or snake,
Thou poor little martyr of the brake![1]

Thou scarce can'st put out that nose of thine;
Thou can'st not show a single spine,
But the urchin rabble are in a rout,
With terrier curs to hunt thee out.

The poor hedge-hog! one would think he knew
His foes so many, his friends so few;
For when he comes out he's in a fright,
And hurries again to be out of sight.

[1] A woodland thicket.

How unkind the world must seem to him
Living under the thicket dusk and dim,
And getting his living among the roots,
Of the insects small and dry hedge fruits.

How hard it must be to be kicked about
If by a chance his prickly back peep out;
To be all his days misunderstood,
When he could not harm us if he would!

He's an innocent thing, living under the blame
That he merits not, of an evil name;
He is weak and small,—and all he needs
Lies under the hedge, among the weeds.

He robs not man of rest nor food
And all that he asks is quietude;
To be left by him as a worthless stone,
Under the dry hedge bank alone!

Oh, poor little English porcupine,
What a troubled and weary life is thine!
I would that my pity thy foes could quell,
For thou art ill used, and meanest well.

The Devil's Walk in Washington

"From his brimstone bed, at break of day,
  A walking the devil is gone,
To visit his snug little farm the earth,
  And see how his stock went on"
                                    Coleridge[1]

The Devil was tired of all his old haunts,
  And he longed to gang a new way;
So one morning he said, as he drew on his pants,
  "I'll to Washington to-day!"

---

[1] Coleridge's early satire 'The Devil's Thoughts', of which this quotation is the first stanza, was published in the *Morning Post*, 6 Sept. 1799. It is a powerful laconic satire on the corruption of the Church, the law, and the repression of radical reformers in England.

He stopped in the principal Avenue,
    And shook off the brimstone perfume,
And coiled up his tail; he always knew
    What phase it is best to assume.

'Twas cool for him, so he opened his vest,
    And gaily he twirled a light cane,
As other fops do, when they sport their best,
    And, perhaps, feel a little vain.

He saw two coaches conveying out
    Two duellists,[2] going to fight;
"Aye, aye" Quoth he "I'll turn me about,
    That will be a pleasant sight!"

He afterwards passed the market place,
    Where cattle and men were bought;
And the Devil exclaimed, "Ye angels of grace!
    Here's humanity's story, self taught!"'

He stood up to see them buy and sell,
    Bidding mortals off under the hammer;
And he chuckled to hear the mothers' yell,
    And their children's delightful clamor.

He examined the thumb-screws, the chains, and the lash,
    And took patterns to carry to Hell;
He watched all the men who took the cash,
    And observed that they spent it well.

Some went to the "coffee-house," some to dice,
    And some to run horses to death;
Fools call such places "abodes of vice"—
    But he grinned and held his breath.

A mob demolished a house on a hill,
    Because its owner drew the latchet;
"Ah!" said he "so they here make laws with a quill,
    And break them with club and hatchet."

---

[2] Duelling had come to be associated by the abolitionists with the decadence and violence of the Southern plantocracy.

The Devil bethought him he would walk
　　Towards the Capitol, in style;
To hear the nation's guardians talk,
　　And encourage them with his smile.

So he dressed him in a priestly coat,
　　That he might not shame his friends,
And went up to see the members vote,
　　And shape the country's ends.

He heard all the honorable gentlemen
　　Speak freely of his home,
And swear and argue, and swear again,
　　That 'twas time a war should come.

One member rose to offer a bill;
　　The Devil admired his phiz,
For he always likes purple, and always will—
　　The Devil has reason for this.

The bill too, he liked, for that provided
　　That those should be plunged in the waves,
Who owned the soil, while this was divided
　　To white men with gangs of slaves.

An orator made a brilliant speech
　　And the Devil made him show it,
To compare with one he was led to preach,
　　Reported by Milton,[3] the poet.

Just then a Senator's honor was sounded
　　By something said in debate,
Whereat the chamber with words resounded
　　That stunned even the Devil's pate.

He said to himself "They're too hot for me,
　　These men of this upper air;
I'll get me back to my sulphur sea,
　　And be ready to meet them there!"

---

[3] This reference could be alluding to any number of sophistical speeches by Satan, who emerges in many ways as the hero, or at least anti-hero, of Milton's *Paradise Lost* and who is even more wily in *Paradise Regained.*

Maria Weston Chapman (1806–85) (ed.), Henry Hart Milman (1791–1868), 'Christian Hymn of Triumph', in *Songs of the Free and Hymns of Christian Freedom* (1836)

Chapman was both an anti-slavery and women's rights activist. She established herself at the heart of Boston abolition, and in the 1830s among her myriad organizational activities was editing *The Liberty Bell*, the lavishly produced annual anthology which the Boston Female Anti-Slavery Society brought out to seduce sympathetic Bostonians into their ranks. Chapman was active in soliciting many leading British women writers to contribute to abolition publications including Elizabeth Barrett Browning (pp. 353–68) and Harriet Martineau. She had a profound belief in women's efficacy as political activists. She had no time for the reactionary approach of many East Coast males to the political commitment of female abolitionists, and wrote poems satirizing male timidity. When male abolition leaders objected to the public lectures of the Grimke sisters Chapman published the following lines in the 1839 *Liberty Bell*. Addressing a male anti-slavery counterpart she argues that in the long run women's grass-roots activism for the cause might well be as effective as debates in the exclusively male Congress: 'O would eternal Providence | Enlarge his soul—increase his sense, | To see that on this mole-hill earth, | A congress and a sewing meeting, | May each to like events give birth.' For her abolition was completely justified on religious grounds; it was quite literally a holy war. Her philosophy is plainly set out in her 'Editor's Advertisement' to *Songs of the Free*: 'Those who are labouring for the freedom of the American slave . . . feel that the spiritual warfare in which they are engaged, requires the exercise of all the faculties; and they cannot allow the opponents of their principles the selection of the moral and intellectual powers with which it shall be carried on,—not though this free use of their own souls should occasion men to call them agitators and fanatics. In giving man imagination and affections, God has furnished him with powers that ennoble him to follow the dictates of reason and revelation; and he should not do otherwise than cultivate and sanctify ALL the faculties, subduing them to the obedience that is in Christ Jesus, by gladly acknowledging through them all the fraternity of the whole human race.' Abolition is 'spiritual warfare', a divine battle against slavery/Satan, and the rhetorical weaponry claimed is that of the language of divine revelation, the prophetic, the irrational, the inspired. Viewed from outside abolition this is the language, as Chapman admits, of 'agitators and fanatics'. Intriguingly Chapman turns to English Civil War martyrological models in order to defend American abolitionism from the charge of fanaticism.

Chapman's selections in the influential *Songs of the Free* exhibit the same political intelligence that she showed in compiling *The Liberty Bell*. Her tactical nous as a poetry editor is discussed in more general terms in the introduction above (pp. xxx–xxxii). The poem selected here has been chosen because of the emphatic way in which it foregrounds the peculiar martyrological fusions generated within East Coast abolition during the 1830s. If Chapman is to defend her fellow abolition bards and activists from charges of extremism then she requires a martyrological tradition in which to set them. Chapman constantly seeks to justify the combination of the hortatory and sacrificial which dominates the volume, through reference to a tradition of radical martyrdom growing out of British tyranny. The Pilgrim Fathers provide the central American example, and this is not surprising. One constant in abolition writing of all sorts, at all periods, is the criticism of contemporary American corruption via comparison with the unblemished purity of the sacred Plymouth brethren. What is different, and what separates Chapman's martyrological verse from later abolition writing, is the constant insertion, alongside her American martyrs, of unusual and unfamiliar accounts of seventeenth-century British political and religious martyrs in the form of extended footnotes. These notes run in parallel to many of the poems creating a textual counterpoint. Henry Hart Milman's 'Christian Hymn of Triumph' is a good example. Milman's poem, in all its late Romantic metaphoric extremity, coexists with the unadorned and outraged prose of the Scottish martyr Marion Harvey, whose 'dying testimony' is quoted at length. At this stage American martyrs cannot stand on their own poetic feet but require the extensive prose crutch of seventeenth-century British gallows martyrology.

Christian Hymn of Triumph[1]

Sing to the Lord! let harp, and lute, and voice,
Up to the expanding gates of heaven rejoice,
    While the bright martyrs to their rest are borne!
Sing to the Lord! their blood-stained course is run,

---

[1] '"Now let not the frowns of men, and their flatteries, put you from your duty. *Keep up your societies, and the assembling of yourselves together*, for there is much profit to be found in it."
                                                                                                    Marion Harvie.

'In reading and singing hymns of triumph and martyrdom, our minds receive a general idea of something high and heroic: it would be well if our ideas of the *why* were more definite, and that we looked on such actions more as matters of simple duty, than with an idle admiration, which might have been positive condemnation had they been performed in our own day. I have always derived benefit from reading the dying testimony of Marion Harvie, who suffered for the truth in Scotland in 1681, and subjoin a few extracts here, because the book in which I find it is a very rare one in America:—

'"Christian friends and acquaintance, I being to lay down my life on Wednesday next, January 26, 1681, I thought fit to let it be known to the world *wherefore* I lay down my life; and to let it be seen that I die not as a fool, or as an evil doer, or as a busy body in other men's matters. No; It is for adhering to the truths of Jesus Christ, and avowing *him* to be King in Zion, and head of his Church; and the testimony against the ungodly laws of men, and their robbing Christ of his right and usurping his prerogative royal, which I durst not but testify against; and I bless his holy name that ever he called me to bear witness against the sins of the times, and the defections of ministers and professors. I leave my testimony against all the bloodshed and massacres of the Lord's people, either on scaffolds or in fields. I protest against banishings, and finings, and cruel murderings. I leave my testimony against the professors who say this is not the truth of God for which I suffer, and call the way of God delusion, and make it their business to make me deny Christ, and betake myself to the ungodly laws of men, and call the truths of God delusions, which I am to seal with my blood: and I rejoice that ever he counted me worthy so to do. Which truths

And every head its diadem hath won,
    Rich as the purple of the summer morn—
Sing the the triumphant champions of their God,
While burn their mountain feet along their skyward road.

Sing to the Lord! for her, in beauty's prime,
Snatched from this wintry earth's ungenial clime,
    In the eternal spring of paradise to bloom;
For her the world displayed its brightest treasure,
And the airs panted with the songs of pleasure.
    Before earth's throne she chose the lowly tomb,
The vale of tears with willing footsteps trod,
Bearing her cross with thee, incarnate Son of God.

Sing to the Lord! it is not shed in vain,
The blood of martyrs! from its freshening rain
    High springs the church, like some fount-shadowing palm:
The nations crowd beneath its branching shade,
Of its green leaves are kingly diadems made,
    And, wrapt within its deep, embosoming calm,
Earth sinks to slumber like the breezeless deep,
And war's tempestuous vultures fold their wings and sleep.

Sing to the Lord! no more the angels fly
Far in the bosom of the stainless sky—
    The sound of fierce, licentious sacrifice.
From shrined alcove and stately pedestal,
The marble gods in cumbrous ruin fall;
    Heedless, in dust, the awe of nations lies;
Jove's thunder crumbles in his mouldering hand,
And mute as sepulchres the hymnless temples stand.

ministers and professors have counted it prudence to disown and deny, for which the land will be made to mourn and merely to smart, e'er all be done. I desire all those that are endeavoring to contend for Christ and his truths, that they would be faithful in their witnessing for him, and eschew the least appearance of sin. For I, a dying witness of Christ, attest you, as ye will answer when you stand before him in the day of your appearance, that you be faithful in owning him in all his truths, and not yield a hoof to ungodly, per-jured, bloody, and excommunicated tyrants; for there is much advantage to be had in faithfulness to Christ. *That* I verify set my seal to the truth of; and I think he is taking a narrow view of his followers at this time; for there are few that yield a hair-breadth of the truths of God, that readily win to their feet again; yet go from one degree of defection to another. And again I desire to bless and magnify the Lord. I bless him that the thoughts of death are not terrible to me. And now ye that are his witnesses, be not afraid to adventure upon the cross of Christ. *They said there was but a few of us for these principles*. I said *they* had the fault of it; and it was most bitter to us, that our *ministers* had spoken against these truths, and, indeed, I think they had not been so cruel to me, were it not for these ministers; and so I think these ministers are not free of our blood; for when *they* spoke *against and the* WAY, [measures?] *it hardened these bloody traitors, and emboldened them to take our lives.*"' [Chapman]

Sing to the Lord! from damp, prophetic cave
No more the loose-haired Sybils burst and rave:
   Nor watch the augurs pale the wandering bird:
No more on hill or in the murky wood,
Mid frantic shout and dissonant music rude,
   In human tones are wailing victims heard;
Nor fathers, by the reeking altar stone,
Cowl their dark heads to escape their children's dying groan.

Sing to the Lord! no more the dead are laid
In cold despair beneath the cypress shade,
   To sleep the eternal sleep, that knows no morn:
There, eager still to burst death's brazen bands,
The angel of the resurrection stands;
   While, on its own immortal pinions borne,
Following the breaker of the imprisoning tomb,
Forth springs the exulting soul, and shakes away its gloom.

Sing to the Lord! the desert rocks break out,
And the thronged cities in one gladdening shout,—
   The farthest shores by pilgrim step explored;
Spread all your wings, ye winds, and waft around,
Even to the starry cope's pale waning bound,
   Earth's universal homage to the Lord;
Lift up thine head, imperial capitol,
Proud on thy height to see the bannered cross unroll.

Sing to the Lord! when time itself shall cease,
And final Ruin's desolating peace
   Enwrap this wide and restless world of man;
When the Judge rides upon the enthroning wind,
And o'er all generations of mankind
   Eternal Vengeance waves its winnowing fan;
To vast infinity's remotest space,
While ages run their everlasting race,
Shall all the beatific hosts prolong,
Wide as the glory of the Lamb, the Lamb's triumphant song.

A Looker On (pseud.), from *Slavery Rhymes Addressed to the Friends of Liberty throughout the United States* (1837)

The year 1837 saw the publication of another volume of anti-slavery verse that employed a framework of martyrological reference centred on the English Civil War, English radicalism, and the example of the Pilgrim Fathers. *Slavery Rhymes* is an attempt to write a religious epic on the subject of abolition. The preface echoes Chapman (p. 483) in discussing slavery and the commitment to abolition in terms of a religious mission, although the rhetoric is far more extravagant.

Slavery Rhymes takes the form of a loosely jointed epic of slavery which is nothing if not ambitious. Written in heroic couplets it provides an allegorized global history of the battle between slavery and abolition which draws heavily on *Paradise Lost* for its machinery, particularly its expansive metaphors, and, surprisingly, as heavily on Pope's youthful parodic epic *The Rape of the Lock* for its metrics and tone. The resulting ungainly hybrid possesses a combination of stridency and literary precociousness that in its scale and unabashedness could only have come out of mid-century America.

The poem is finally not about the necessity of abolishing slavery so much as providing a mythic transatlantic coalition, a grand fiction which conjoins American abolition with the emergence of a Nonconformist universal philanthropy in nineteenth-century England. Slavery appears near the poem's opening as an extended personification, a monster ultimately revealed to find its ancestor in that nadir of Semitic depravity as imagined by the Puritans, Milton's Moloch, but presented initially in couplets which bear the trappings of the seventeenth-century emblem books still popular with American Puritan readers:

> Slavery! foul child of cruelty and vice,
> Cherish'd and nursed by grinding avarice—
> Guarded by brutal violence, that spurns
> Truth, justice, mercy—heaven and earth by turns;
> Its emblems, torturing whips, the galling chain,
> Brands, racks and gibbets, in an endless train;
> Pregnant with every ill—devoid of good,
> Its stands complete all guilt, all tears, all blood! ...
> ... Thou modern Moloch! At thy impious shrine,
> Lust, tyranny and avarice combine
> In fearful orgies, millions victims bleed,
> While Christian voices justify the deed;
> And bring God's sacred book to feed the fire
> On which thy human hecatombs expire.   (p. 15)

Moloch was to be adopted by Whittier in 1851 to personify the Fugitive Slave Law in 'Moloch in State Street'. In the opening sections of *Slavery Rhymes* the monster is shown trampling through European history. It first appears in the familiar guise of Portuguese and Spanish colonialism in the Americas. The English abolition narratives of the Spanish Black Legend (see pp. 36–48, 53–7, 86–8, 150–4, 168–80, 279–96) are duly rehearsed. The extract below starts at the point where British domination of Atlantic slavery is then excoriated. This attack, unsurprisingly, finds no equivalent in British abolition verse, and shows America getting one back for the interminable charges of hypocrisy which British abolitionists aimed at America in the wake of the 1834 emancipation bill. The poem then moves on to discuss the overthrow of colonial slavery in Britain but makes a definite swerve from the accepted British version of this history. The overthrow of slavery in Britain is interpreted not as the achievement of the abolition deities of Wilberforce and Clarkson, who are not mentioned by name, but in terms of the activities of the radical Nonconformist and millenarian activist of the 1780s Granville Sharp. Sharp does not feature in British abolition verse, but here he is credited with bringing about Lord Mansfield's legal ruling over the Sommerset case which was widely believed to mean that no person could be a slave once they set foot on British soil. Sharp was not only a pioneering abolitionist but a supporter of radical parliamentary reform and general social reform in Britain. By setting him centre stage abolition is placed in the context of the birth of a general politicized and Dissenting philanthropy. Slavery is only one among many evils, and Sharp is celebrated beside the prison reformer John Howard, and not, as in British mid-nineteenth-century histor-iography, as a small star in the constellation of Clapham sect abolition. Abolition is seen to follow this generalized philanthropic impetus, and indeed is a final flowering of a Nonconformist drive for moral regeneration.

The poem's ostensible subject is almost buried at this point by the recapitulation of an eccentric British history. If the narrative and dramatic impact of the epic is to be resuscitated personified slavery must be revived and presented as a worthy opponent of the victor philanthropists. The poetic solution chosen to bring this about is massively awkward. An analogy is attempted between the fall of Satan in *Paradise Lost* and the fall of Slavery in Britain. Slavery/Satan and Abolition/God is a difficult conflation to carry through in the context of the narrative of *Paradise Lost*. Who or what is to be Adam and Eve, and is there not a danger that Slavery will now steal the show, as Milton's Satan did for Blake and most twentieth-century readers? In answer to the first question, the insti-tutionalization of slavery in America after the War of Independence is presented as the equivalent of the fall. In answer to the second, slavery does not fire the imagination of 'A Looker On' quite as richly as Satan fired Milton's. Columbia is overrun by Satan, but by a Satan denied a language of rage or celebration. Columbia can only become a 'para-dise regained' through the crusade of abolition; abolition then performs the narrative role of Milton's Christ. Blake's famous aphorism in *The Marriage of Heaven and Hell*, 'The reason Milton wrote in fetters when he wrote of angels and God, and at liberty when of devils and Hell, is because he was a true poet, and of the Devil's party without knowing it,' indicates why *Slavery Rhymes* fails as art. The trouble is that the poet seems so remarkably unexcited in describing the works and the thought of his Devil, the slave power. The language used to describe evil is worn out, where the abolitionist of the 1790s would at least have enjoyed the task of denunciation. Indeed a radical of the 1790s would have drawn upon the language of prophecy and the comparison of the American South with Babylon, in order to describe the evils to be overthrown.

The poem fails in educative ways. In its contradiction and tediousness it pinpoints the difficulties which face the author who attempts to produce a serious and elevated poetics of abolition by composing epic. Is it possible to aggrandize the quest of the abolitionist without aggrandizing, ennobling, and imaginatively expanding the role of the slave power? Confused it may be, but in its energy and ambition this poem is more impressive than anything which came out of British abolition in the 1830s.

Slavery Rhymes (pp. 15–30)

Slavery! foul child of cruelty and vice,
Cherish'd and nursed by grinding avarice—
Guarded by brutal violence, that spurns
Truth, justice, mercy—heaven and earth by turns;
Its emblems, torturing whips, the galling chain,
Brands, racks, and gibbets, in an endless train;
Pregnant with every ill—devoid of good,
Its stands complete all guilt, all tears, all blood!

Mark well the monster's course: beneath his tread
All human virtue, joy, and hope are dead.
Where'er he breathes, the pestilential air
Is fill'd with groans and echoes of despair;
Whene'er he speaks, 'tis in the withering tone
Of tyrants, utter'd from a heart of stone;
Where'er he moves, his track is stain'd with blood,
Deep human misery forms his daily food!
Thou modern Moloch![1] at thy impious shrine,
Lust, tyranny, and avarice, combine
In fearful orgies; millions of victims bleed,
Whilst Christian voices justify the deed;
And bring God's sacred Book to feed the fire
On which thy human hecatombs[2] expire.

High on the list, swift in the guilty race,
Proud England reap'd pre-eminent disgrace.

[1] A Semitic god to whom children are sacrificed as food.
[2] A great public sacrifice; any event involving a large number of victims.

As the bright sun of freedom first arose
O'er her horizon, Britain joined its foes,
And, struggling for her rights, with maniac hands
Forged chains and manacles for other lands:
Freedom, with blighted hope and gathering frown,
Withdrew her cheering beams—her sun went down;
Whilst coming ills their lengthening shadows threw,
And tyranny's dark night commenced anew.

Amidst the fiendish scourges of their race,
The name of HAWKINS[3] holds conspicuous place,
Basely enroll'd the first of England's sons
Leading the van of Slavery's myrmidons:[4]
Cut-throat and pirate—murderer—despot—all
Combined, condensed, sublimed, that can appal
The stoutest heart, or make the tenderest bleed—
All ages execrate his name and deed!

Man's better nature startled for a time,
Rebuked the atrocious act, denounced the crime:
Humanity, all bleeding and distress'd,
Wept o'er her children, kidnapp'd and oppress'd,
And plead the sufferers' cause with fervent zeal,
That made e'en hearts of stone their wrongs to feel.
But Mammon, bold, insatiate, grasp'd his prize—
Held forth large golden baits—recoin'd his lies—
Moved earth and hell to draw within his toils
The opposing elements, and keep his spoils:
Complete was his success: the public mind
First wink'd at guilt, and soon became stone-blind;
Slurr'd o'er the felon wrong, then shared its gains,
Till mighty Britain stood herself in chains,
And Slavery stretch'd his desolating wand
O'er freedom's grave, in freemen's chosen land!

As when foul leprosy man's frame invades,
Swift through his veins the circling poison speeds,
Transforming beauty, health, and gracefulness,
To hopeless sickness—loathsome rottenness;

[3] John Hawkins, purportedly the first English slaving captain, who led three slaving expeditions during the reign of Elizabeth the first.
[4] One of a tribe of warriors who followed Achilles to Troy. Hence it has come to mean anyone prepared to follow another's orders, no matter how extreme, without fear or pity.

So nations, smit by Slavery's poisonous breath,
By sure transitions pass to moral death:
All honor, justice, purity, and peace,
Beneath its reptile touch must ever cease.
There never has, there never will be found
True Liberty where slaves and chains abound:
Perish the monstrous thought! darkness with light—
Water with fire—can easier far unite,
Than Freedom's pure, benign, and holy reign,
Acceptance meet in Slavery's foul domain.
'Twas thus with Britain: Slavery struck its roots
Deeply, and fill'd her land with noxious fruits.
Ridden by kings and priests, what scenes of wo,
Through long and dreary years, her annals show!
Religion, clad in pure and heavenly grace—
Philosophy, in grave and serious face;
Science, with piercing eye—and law divine,
And human too, all bent at Slavery's shrine:
Each race of men, the polish'd and the rude,
By its seductive wiles alike subdued,
Nurtured and guarded with a jealous eye
This sin of sins—Hell's foulest progeny!
Recreant to freedom, heaven in justice sent
With base apostacy due punishment:
Shadows of tyranny portentous gloom'd,
Whose gath'ring blackness spoke a nation doom'd,
Whilst Britons, Samson-like, were shorn of might,
To smite the oppressor, and maintain the right.
In vain her patriots toil'd, and strove to raise
The noble spirit of her earlier days,
When Magna Charta's[5] glorious roll appear'd,
(A splendid monument to freedom rear'd!)
Speaking a tyrant's fears, a people's might,
Wrought out and raised in England's deepest night;
In vain the glorious scenes of Eighty-eight[6]

---

[5]   In Latin literally 'the great charter', Magna Carta is the most significant document of English constitutional history. It was issued by King John in 1215 under compulsion of the English barons. The charter was initially produced as a check on the excessive and arbitrary exercise of royal power, but came to be seen as a document protecting the basic civil rights of all communities and 'freeborn Englishmen'.

[6]   The events transpiring in England in 1688–9 came to be known as the 'Glorious Revolution' when James II was deposed and King William and Queen Mary took his place. Mary and William were invited over from Holland by a powerful Whig and Tory coalition, and upon their arrival James's army deserted

Revived the waning fortunes of the state,
Radiant with cheering hopes of liberty,
To England's millions, panting to be free:
The spirit of Slavery, like malignant fate,
Chased every generous purpose from the state,—
Through every rank diffused its loathsome leaven,
With'ring and wasting like a blight from heaven,—
Fell like a canker on the nation's heart,
Spreading corruption vile through every part,
Till Britain's boasted freedom gasp'd for breath,
And struggled in the agonies of death.
In that dark hour of England's gloom and shame,
There shone in glory bright one honor'd name,
Raised, qualified, and led by heavenly grace,
That gloom to dissipate, that shame to efface.
On Britain's soil SHARP[7] heard the clanking chain
Of Negro servitude—nor heard in vain.
The hapless bondman in that brother found
Warm sympathy, as though himself were bound.
His country's honor and his brother's good
He nobly pleaded, and his foes withstood;
Nor ceased, until he spread the blessed sound
From Britain's sea-girt shores through earth around,
That ev'ry slave was free who touch'd her hallow'd ground!

O blessed era! hope's bright jubilee,
Thenceforth one spot of earth at least was free!
One place of refuge stands, wherein the oppress'd
Of every caste and clime may safely rest;
One sacred nook, where bond and free can raise
Altars to Liberty, and chaunt her praise!

Amidst thy sons, Philanthropy benign!
Two kindred sainted spirits brightly shine—
HOWARD[8] and SHARP undying honors claim,
Embalm'd in purest, holiest, endless fame.
One age produced them both—their bosoms fired
To noblest deeds—the purest zeal inspired.

and he fled. William and Mary accepted the 'Bill of Rights' which ensured royal power would be sub-
sidiary to parliamentary power.

[7] See Montgomery, *The West Indies*, n. 8, above.

[8] John Howard (1726–90) the great Evangelical British reformer of the prison systems.

The poor, oppress'd, forsaken, and forlorn,
Bereft of all of earth except its scorn,
Whom priests and pharisees swept proudly by,
To rescue such these Christian heroes fly.
Howard the white man's prison-house explored,
Which law, divorced from mercy, thickly stored;
The abyss of human suffering deeply guaged,
Its sorrows lighten'd, and its woes assuaged;
Whilst Sharp his sable brethren sought to win
From deeper ills—their only crime their skin!
Chain'd, hunted, brutified, o'erwhelm'd with grief,
He mourn'd their cruel wrongs, and brought relief.
Fragrant are their memorials—ne'er to die,
Their faith and toils are register'd on high!
Theirs are the triumphs that illume the page
Of history, and shed glory on all age:
They are a nation's treasures, rich in gain,
For Heaven's best blessings follow in their train.

And such are England's glories—such the salt
Which purified her state—her hopes exalt
Her days of guilt are past, and now we see
Fruits of repentance crowd her history.
Slavery and priestcraft[9] long had weigh'd her down,
Robb'd her of half her glory, dimm'd her crown;
Repress'd her noblest energies, and threw
O'er all her rising hopes a gloomy hue.
Those shadows all are gone! with quicken'd pace,
Worthy the free, she runs a glorious race;
Breaks every fetter through her wide domains,
And cheers both hemispheres with freedom's strains;
For whips, and manacles, and mental night,
Gives equal laws, and pours instruction's light;
Transforming slaves to freemen, foes to friends,
And curses into praise, where'er her realm extends.

Enshrined in glory is each patriot's name,
Who to the rescue of his country came;
Who, spurning ease, and wealth, and courtly smiles,
The mob's opprobrium, and the devil's wiles,

---

[9] Any policy of the clergy directed purely to earthly ends.

Enter'd the field of strife—defied the foe—
And struck at Slavery's root a mortal blow;
Tore off the monster's law-perverted guise—
Chased him from all his refuges of lies—
Dash'd tyranny's proud fabric to the dust,
And forced reluctant senates to be just.

In vain the combined hosts of hell opposed—
The conflict, long and fierce, was nobly closed:
Oppression, fraud, hypocrisy, vile lust,
(Slavery's allies and props,) all bit the dust;
All fled before truth's penetrating light,
And sought concealment in congenial night.
Most blessed consummation! worthy to bring
Angels to earth again, its joys to sing;
Worthy of note on mercy's roll above—
Bright midst the splendors of those deeds of love!

O'er Slavery, hunted from its fav'rite lair,
Demoniac lamentations rent the air;
All hell was moved this scourge of earth to shield
From threat'ning death, and keep it in the field;
But moved in vain—the powers of darkness quail'd,
Truth in its might and majesty prevail'd;
One mighty empire, disenthrall'd, set free,
Was lost to Satan—gain'd to Liberty!
Banish'd from England's realm, where, long enthroned
Beneath their cruel sceptre, millions groan'd—
Abash'd before the effulgent[10] light of day
Pour'd on their deeds—foul Slavery's legions lay,
Mourning their broken spells—cursing the hour
Which loosed imperial Britain from their power—
Yielding to furious rage and deep despair—
Gnashing at blessings they could never share.
The prince of darkness then address'd his crew
"Arise! dismiss your fears! your zeal renew!
Though much indeed is lost, all is not gone:
Far in the West fresh triumphs may be won.
Thither direct your steps—there glory leads—
Our triumphs there shall shame all former deeds:

---

[10] Beaming or shining forth.

There shall the standard of the pit be rear'd,
Amidst a people for our sway prepared;
Deep in that soil each plant of hell shall grow,
And bear on earth the fruits matured below!"

The Angel of Mercy heard—nor heard in vain:
Swiftly to heaven he bore the impious strain;
Low at the Almighty's footstool bent to plead,
For millions yet unborn to intercede;
Implored a respite for Columbia's race—
A space for penitence—a day of grace!

The Accusing Angel Mercy's suit withstood:
He spake of light abused—of slighted good—
Of tyrants, trampling millions in the dust—
Of rulers, partial, prejudiced, unjust;
Of priests, perverting truth, upholding guilt;
Of churches, by unrighteous mammon[11] built;
Of heavenly truth, by man from man withheld;
Of men by men, to unpaid toil impelled;
God's image rudely spoil'd—immortals driv'n
And bought and sold like beasts before high heav'n;
Of fiendish passion's bearing direful sway—
Grim murder stalking in the face of day;
Deep tragedies of wrong by millions done;
Foul revellings of lust before the sun;
Hand joined in hand, in fierce confederacy,
To crush the rising foes of Slavery—
To bind afresh his adamantine[12] chains,
And urge the monster on by cheering strains!

He ceased, and silence reigned—then from the throne
The solemn fiat came—Let them alone
To reap the harvest which in guilt they've sown!

The angelic pleaders bowed with awe profound:
Amen! amen! in solemn cadence round
Rose through all heaven:—then burst a song of praise,
Holy art thou, O Lord, in all thy ways!
Thy grace abounding hath thy mercy shown;
Thy awful judgments make thy justice known!

[11] Riches, the god of riches.   [12] Unbreakable.

The listening demons heard the fateful strain,
And Slavery's legions rushed across the main—
Where Lust, Hypocrisy, Oppression, Fraud,
Stretched their vile wings and spread themselves abroad—
Blighting all grace and virtue—quickening vice,
In monstrous forms—not Egypt's plague of lice,
Nor frogs, nor murrain, nor the avenger's rod,
Gave signs so fearful of an angry God!

John Greenleaf Whittier (1807–92), 'The Hunters of Men', 'The Slave Ships', 'Toussaint L'Ouverture', in *Poems Written During the Progress of the Abolition Question* (1837); 'The Branded Hand' (1846, handbill); 'Ichabod' (1850), in *Complete Poetical Works* (1894)

Of the canonic nineteenth-century American poets Whittier was the one who committed himself most emphatically to abolition, and specifically Garrisonian immediatism, throughout the quarter-century preceding the Civil War. As a Quaker Whittier was passionately aware of the long-standing and effective anti-slavery history of his sect. The poetry he wrote on slavery stretches over a mighty range of subjects and chronologically begins in the early 1830s and ends with his poetic tribute to America's leading white abolitionist, written in 1879 and simply entitled *Garrison*. A good quarter of Whittier's enormous poetic output falls under the specific designation of 'anti-slavery', and was fervently propagandistic and narrowly occasional. Whittier was perfectly aware of the political limitations of this work, and stated in 1888 that most of the slavery poems 'were written with no expectation that they would survive the occasions which called them forth: they were protests, alarm-signals, trumpet-calls to action, words wrung from the writer's heart, forged at white heat.' Whittier created poetry on every major episode which marked the progress of the anti-slavery crusade. He was a founding member of the American anti-slavery society in 1833; he provided spirited contributions to the 'martyr complex' verse celebrating the persecution of pioneer abolitionists. He wrote about the Texas annexation and resulting war in relation to the expansion of slavery, Webster Clay and the notorious Missouri Compromise, the iniquity of the Fugitive Slave Law, the free-soil debate in the Kansas Territory, and finally the horrors of the Civil War, which for Whittier was a war about slavery. He also wrote a host of poems about Caribbean slavery. His prose writings are equally committed and varied, and his superb address 'What is Slavery' given to the Liberty Party Convention, New Bedford, in the autumn of 1843 remains one of the most lucid definitions, and simultaneous denunciations, of American chattel slavery. It is difficult to know what to select, but I have chosen verse which emphasizes the range of his style and interests.

'Toussaint L'Ouverture' provides an unusual take on the Toussaint myth. The poem is not frightened to deal directly, and rather sensually, with black rape of white women during the insurrection, or to present Toussaint as violent and vengeful. The account of the manner in which he effected the escape of his master's family is sentimentalized and inaccurate, yet the enthusiastic take on black revolutionary violence is bold for its time. Harriet Martineau's romantic novel on Toussaint, *The Hour and the Man*, gives the more typical mid-nineteenth-century abolition fiction which reconstructs Toussaint as a blancophile pacifist. The first edition of Whittier's *Poems Written During the Progress of the Abolition Question* printed Wordsworth's famous sonnet to Toussaint (see pp. 231–3) as a footnote to Whittier's poem, but Wordsworth's Toussaint is an altogether more abstract entity. 'The Slave Ships' is a fine melodramatic ballad which uses an atrocious historical anecdote connected with the middle passage as the basis for a moral fable. The poem cleverly operates a metaphorics of blindness. The disease which spreads indiscriminately through the slaves and the white slavers describes the moral blindness which inevitably contaminates all involved in the power dynamics of slavery. 'The Branded Hand' is perhaps the most perfect example of martyrological hagiography in the whole of aboliton poetry. The poem brilliantly reinvents Jonathan Walker as a martyr, and was reproduced in the form of a folding handbill headed by a large engraving of Walker's hand with its brand of SS (slave stealer). Walker handed these sheets out to the mass crowds who attended his lectures, and the version below is reproduced from one of the originals. 'Ichabod' is one of the greatest of Whittier's occasional slavery poems. Whittier's prefatory note explains the circumstances surrounding the poem's composition fully. Contextually it is worth adding that 'Ichabod' is Hebrew for 'inglorious'. The opening stanza alludes to Satan's astonished response to seeing his fellow devil Beelzebub in his fallen state for the first time: 'oh how fall'n! how chang'd | From him who, in the happy realms of light, | Cloth'd with transcendent brightness didst outshine | Myriads though bright!' Whittier's precise exploitation of Milton is a good deal more successful than that of 'A Looker On' (see pp. 494–6). What makes this poem so unusual is the manner in which it refuses to demonize the slave power. Webster is presented as a tragic loss to America and humanity, not as a demon. Slavery consequently emerges as an impossibly complicated political reality which it is up to each individual to respond to.

The Hunters of Men

These lines were written when the orators of the American Colonization Society[1] were demanding that the free blacks should be sent to Africa, and opposing Emancipation unless expatriation followed. See the report of the proceedings of the society at its annual meeting in 1834.

[1] The American Colonization Society involved many American abolitionists who believed that the solution to the slavery question lay in 'repatriating' all blacks to Africa. The movement was at its most

Have ye heard of our hunting, o'er mountain and glen,
Through cane-brake and forest,—the hunting of men?
The lords of our land to this hunting have gone,
As the fox-hunter follows the sound of the horn;
Hark! the cheer and the hallo! the crack of the whip,
And the yell of the hound as he fastens his grip!
All blithe are our hunters, and noble their match,
Though hundreds are caught, there are millions to catch.
So speed to their hunting, o'er mountain and glen,
Through cane-brake and forest,—the hunting of men!

Gay luck to our hunters! how nobly they ride
In the glow of their zeal, and the strength of their pride!
The priest with his cassock flung back on the wind,
Just screening the politic statesman behind;
The saint and the sinner, with cursing and prayer,
The drunk and the sober, ride merrily there.
And woman, kind woman, wife, widow, and maid,
For the good of the hunted, is lending her aid:
Her foot's in the stirrup, her hand on the rein,
How blithely she rides to the hunting of men!

Oh, goodly and grand is our hunting to see,
In this 'land of the brave and this home of the free.'[2]
Priest, warrior, and statesman, from Georgia to Maine,
All mounting the saddle, all grasping the rein;
Right merrily hunting the black man, whose sin
Is the curl of his hair and the hue of his skin!
Woe, now, to the hunted who turns him at bay!
Will our hunters be turned from their purpose and prey?
Will their hearts fail within them? their nerves tremble, when
All roughly they ride to the hunting of men?

Ho! alms for our hunters! all weary and faint,
Wax the curse of the sinner and prayer of the saint.
The horn is wound faintly, the echoes are still,
Over cane-brake and river, and forest and hill.
Haste, alms for our hunters! the hunted once more
Have turned from their flight with their backs to the shore:

forceful in the early 1830s and led to a violent extremist abolition backlash led most flamboyantly by
Garrison.
    [2] The final line of 'The Star Spangled Banner'.

What right have they here in the home of the white,
Shadowed o'er by our banner of Freedom and Right?
Ho! alms for the hunters! or never again
Will they ride in their pomp to the hunting of men!

Alms, alms for our hunters! why will ye delay,
When their pride and their glory are melting away?
The parson has turned; for, on charge of his own,
Who goeth a warfare, or hunting, alone?
The politic statesman looks back with a sigh,
There is doubt in his heart, there is fear in his eye.
Oh, haste, lest that doubting and fear shall prevail,
And the head of his steed take the place of the tail.
Oh, haste, ere he leave us! for who will ride then,
For pleasure or gain, to the hunting of men?

The Slave Ships

'That fatal, that perfidious bark,
Built i' the eclipse, and rigged with curses dark.'
MILTON'S *Lycidas*.[1]

'The French ship Le Rodeur, with a crew of twenty-two men, and with one hundred and sixty negro slaves, sailed from Bonny, in Africa, April, 1819. On approaching the line, a terrible malady broke out,—an obstinate disease of the eyes,—contagious, and altogether beyond the resources of medicine. It was aggravated by the scarcity of water among the slaves (only half a wine-glass per day being allowed to an individual), and by the extreme impurity of the air in which they breathed. By the advice of the physician, they were brought upon deck occasionally; but some of the poor wretches, locking themselves in each other's arms, leaped overboard, in the hope, which so universally prevails among them, of being swiftly transported to their own homes in Africa. To check this, the captain ordered several, who were stopped in the attempt, to be shot, or hanged, before their companions. The disease extended to the crew; and one after another were smitten with it, until only *one* remained unaffected. Yet even this dreadful condition did not preclude calculation: to save the expense of supporting slaves rendered unsalable, and to obtain grounds for a claim against the underwriters, *thirty-six of the negroes, having become blind, were thrown into the*

---

[1] Milton wrote *Lycidas* in 1638 as an elegy on the death of his young friend Edward King, drowned at sea. The quoted lines refer to the fatal ship on which King last sailed.

sea and drowned!'—Speech of M. Benjamin Constant, in the French Chamber of Deputies, June 17, 1820.

In the midst of their dreadful fears lest the solitary individual whose sight remained unaffected should also be seized with the malady, a sail was discovered. It was the Spanish slaver, Leon. The same disease had been there; and, horrible to tell, all the crew had become blind! Unable to assist each other, the vessels parted. The Spanish ship has never since been heard of. The Rodeur reached Guadaloupe on the 21st of June; the only man who had escaped the disease, and had thus been enabled to steer the slaver into port, caught it in three days after its arrival.—*Bibliothèque Ophthalmologique* for November, 1819.

'All ready?' cried the captain;
　'Ay, ay!' the seamen said;
'Heave up the worthless lubbers,—
　The dying and the dead.'
Up from the slave-ship's prison
　Fierce, bearded heads were thrust:
'Now let the sharks look to it,—
　Toss up the dead ones first!'

Corpse after corpse came up,—
　Death had been busy there;
Where every blow is mercy,
　Why should the spoiler spare?
Corpse after corpse they cast
　Sullenly from the ship,
Yet bloody with the traces
　Of fetter-link and whip.

Gloomily stood the captain,
　With his arms upon his breast,
With his cold brow sternly knotted,
　And his iron lip compressed.
'Are all the dead dogs over?'
　Growled through that matted lip;
'The blind ones are no better,
　Let's lighten the good ship.'

Hark! from the ship's dark bosom,
　The very sounds of hell!
The ringing clank of iron,
　The maniac's short, sharp yell!
The hoarse, low curse, throat-stifled;

The starving infant's moan,
The horror of a breaking heart
  Poured through a mother's groan.

Up from that loathsome prison
  The stricken blind ones came:
Below, had all been darkness,
  Above, was still the same.
Yet the holy breath of heaven
  Was sweetly breathing there,
And the heated brow of fever
  Cooled in the soft sea air.

'Overboard with them, shipmates!'
  Cutlass and dirk were plied;
Fettered and blind, one after one,
  Plunged down the vessel's side.
The sabre smote above,
  Beneath, the lean shark lay,
Waiting with wide and bloody jaw
  His quick and human prey.

God of the earth! what cries
  Rang upward unto Thee?
Voices of agony and blood,
  From ship-deck and from sea.
The last dull plunge was heard,
  The last wave caught its stain.
And the unsated shark looked up
  For human hearts in vain.

.   .   .   .   .   .

Red glowed the western waters,
  The setting sun was there,
Scattering alike on wave and cloud
  His fiery mesh of hair.
Amidst a group in blindness,
  A solitary eye
Gazed, from the burdened slaver's deck,
  Into that burning sky.

'A storm,' spoke out the gazer,
  'Is gathering and at hand;
Curse on 't, I'd give my other eye

For one firm rood of land.'
And then he laughed, but only
   His echoed laugh replied,
For the blinded and the suffering
   Alone were at his side.

Night settled on the waters,
   And on a stormy heaven,
While fiercely on that lone ship's track
   The thunder-gust was driven.
'A sail!—thank God, a sail!'
   And as the helmsman spoke,
Up through the stormy murmur
   A shout of gladness broke.

Down came the stranger vessel,
   Unheeding on her way,
So near that on the slaver's deck
   Fell off her driven spray.
'Ho! for the love of mercy,
   We're perishing and blind!'
A wail of utter agony
   Came back upon the wind:

'Help us! for we are stricken
   With blindness every one;
Ten days we've floated fearfully,
   Unnoting star or sun.
Our ship's the slaver Leon,—
   We've but a score on board;
Our slaves are all gone over,—
   Help, for the love of God!'

On livid brows of agony
   The broad red lightning shone;
But the roar of wind and thunder
   Stifled the answering groan;
Wailed from the broken waters
   A last despairing cry,
As, kindling in the stormy light,
   The stranger ship went by.

.   .   .   .   .

In the sunny Guadaloupe[2]
  A dark-hulled vessel lay,
With a crew who noted never
  The nightfall or the day.
The blossom of the orange
  Was white by every stream,
And tropic leaf, and flower, and bird
  Were in the warm sunbeam.

And the sky was bright as ever,
  And the moonlight slept as well,
On the palm-trees by the hillside,
  And the streamlet of the dell:
And the glances of the Creole
  Were still as archly deep,
And her smiles as full as ever
  Of passion and of sleep.

But vain were bird and blossom,
  The green earth and the sky,
And the smile of human faces,
  To the slaver's darkened eye;
At the breaking of the morning,
  At the star-lit evening time,
O'er a world of light and beauty
  Fell the blackness of his crime.

Toussaint L'Ouverture

Toussaint L'Ouverture, the black chieftain of Hayti, was a slave on the plantation 'de Libertas,' belonging to M. Bayou. When the rising of the negroes took place, in 1791, Toussaint refused to join them until he had aided M. Bayou and his family to escape to Baltimore. The white man had discovered in Toussaint many noble qualities, and had instructed him in some of the first branches of education; and the preservation of his life was owing to the negro's gratitude for this kindness.

In 1797, Toussaint L'Ouverture was appointed, by the French government, General-in-Chief of the armies of St. Domingo, and, as such, signed the

---

[2] Now an overseas department of France in the West Indies, it was an important sugar-producing island during the period of French colonial slavery.

Convention with General Maitland for the evacuation of the island by the British. From this period until 1801 the island, under the government of Toussaint, was happy, tranquil, and prosperous. The miserable attempt of Napoleon to re-establish slavery in St. Domingo, although it failed of its intended object, proved fatal to the negro chieftain. Treacherously seized by Leclerc,[1] he was hurried on board a vessel by night, and conveyed to France, where he was confined in a cold subterranean dungeon, at Besançon, where, in April, 1803, he died. The treatment of Toussaint finds a parallel only in the murder of the Duke D'Enghien.[2] It was the remark of Godwin,[3] in his Lectures, that the West India Islands, since their first discovery by Columbus, could not boast of a single name which deserves comparison with that of Toussaint L'Ouverture.

It was night. The tranquil moonlight smile
　With which Heaven dreams of Earth, shed down
Its beauty on the Indian isle,—
　On broad green field and white-walled town;
And inland waste of rock and wood,
In searching sunshine, wild and rude,
Rose, mellowed through the silver gleam,
Soft as the landscape of a dream.
All motionless and dewy wet,
Tree, vine, and flower in shadow met:
The myrtle with its snowy bloom,
Crossing the nightshade's solemn gloom,—
The white cecropia's[4] silver rind
Relieved by deeper green behind,
The orange with its fruit of gold,
The lithe paullinia's[5] verdant fold,
The passion-flower, with symbol holy,
Twining its tendrils long and lowly,
The rhexias[6] dark, and cassia tall,
And proudly rising over all,
The kingly palm's imperial stem,
Crowned with its leafy diadem,

---

[1] One of the deputies sent over from Paris to try and reinstate French control of the island of San Domingue (late Hayti) during the slave revolution there.

[2] Louis Henri Antoine de Bourbon, Duc d'Enghien (1772–1804); during the French Revolution he led the émigré vanguard. He moved to Baden and settled there in 1801 yet continued to be a thorn in Napoleon's side. Napoleon invaded Baden in 1804 and d'Enghien was shot dead in his castle moat.

[3] William Godwin (1756–1836), brilliant English radical intellectual and author of *Political Justice*.

[4] A tropical American tree of the mulberry variety.

[5] Variant spelling of Paulownia, shrubs and trees with showy bell-shaped purple flowers.

[6] Also known as meadow beauty or deer grass; a North American perennial herb.

Star-like, beneath whose sombre shade,
The fiery-winged cucullo[7] played!
How lovely was thine aspect, then,
   Fair island of the Western Sea!
Lavish of beauty, even when
Thy brutes were happier than thy men,
   For they, at least, were free!
Regardless of thy glorious clime,
   Unmindful of thy soil of flowers,
The toiling negro sighed, that Time
   No faster sped his hours.
For, by the dewy moonlight still,
He fed the weary-turning mill,
Or bent him in the chill morass,
To pluck the long and tangled grass,
And hear above his scar-worn back
The heavy slave-whip's frequent crack:
While in his heart one evil thought
In solitary madness wrought,
One baleful fire surviving still
   The quenching of the immortal mind,
   One sterner passion of his kind,
Which even fetters could not kill,
The savage hope, to deal, erelong,
A vengeance bitterer than his wrong!
Hark to that cry! long, loud, and shrill,
From field and forest, rock and hill,
Thrilling and horrible it rang,
   Around, beneath, above;
The wild beast from his cavern sprang,
   The wild bird from her grove!
Nor fear, nor joy, nor agony
Were mingled in that midnight cry;
But like the lion's growl of wrath,
When falls that hunter in his path
Whose barbëd arrow, deeply set,
Is rankling in his bosom yet,
It told of hate, full, deep, and strong,
Of vengeance kindling out of wrong;

---

[7] Shrub with hood-shaped flower; hence the name, from *cuculla*, Latin for 'hood'.

It was as if the crimes of years—
The unrequited toil, the tears,
The shame and hate, which liken well
Earth's garden to the nether hell—
Had found in nature's self a tongue,
On which the gathered horror hung;
As if from cliff, and stream, and glen
Burst on the startled ears of men
That voice which rises unto God,
Solemn and stern,—the cry of blood!
It ceased, and all was still once more,
Save ocean chafing on his shore,
The sighing of the wind between
The broad banana's leaves of green,
Or bough by restless plumage shook,
Or murmuring voice of mountain brook.

Brief was the silence. Once again
    Pealed to the skies that frantic yell.
Glowed on the heavens a fiery stain,
    And flashes rose and fell;
And painted on the blood-red sky,
Dark, naked arms were tossed on high;
And, round the white man's lordly hall,
    Trod, fierce and free, the brute he made;
And those who crept along the wall,
And answered to his lightest call
    With more than spaniel dread,
The creatures of his lawless beck,
Were trampling on his very neck!
And on the night-air, wild and clear,
Rose woman's shriek of more than fear;
For bloodied arms were round her thrown,
And dark cheeks pressed against her own!

Then, injured Afric! for the shame
Of thy own daughters, vengeance came
Full on the scornful hearts of those,
Who mocked thee in thy nameless woes,
And to thy hapless children gave
One choice,—pollution or the grave!

Where then was he whose fiery zeal
Had taught the trampled heart to feel,
Until despair itself grew strong,
And vengeance fed its torch from wrong?
Now, when the thunderbolt is speeding;
Now, when oppression's heart is bleeding;
Now, when the latent curse of Time
    Is raining down in fire and blood,
That curse which, through long years of crime,
    Has gathered, drop by drop, its flood,—
Why strikes he not, the foremost one,
Where murder's sternest deeds are done?

He stood the aged palms beneath,
    That shadowed o'er his humble door,
Listening, with half-suspended breath,
To the wild sounds of fear and death,
    Toussaint L'Ouverture!
What marvel that his heart beat high!
    The blow for freedom had been given,
And blood had answered to the cry
    Which Earth sent up to Heaven!
What marvel that a fierce delight
Smiled grimly o'er his brow of night,
As groan and shout and bursting flame
Told where the midnight tempest came,
With blood and fire along its van,[8]
And death behind! he was a Man!
Yes, dark-souled chieftain! if the light
    Of mild Religion's heavenly ray
Unveiled not to thy mental sight
    The lowlier and the purer way,
In which the Holy Sufferer trod,
    Meekly amidst the sons of crime;
That calm reliance upon God
    For justice in His own good time;
That gentleness to which belongs
Forgiveness for its many wrongs,
Even as the primal martyr, kneeling
For mercy on the evil-dealing;

[8] Shortened form of vanguard, the front line of an army.

Let not the favored white man name
Thy stern appeal, with words of blame.
Has he not, with the light of heaven
    Broadly around him, made the same?
Yea, on his thousand war-fields striven,
    And gloried in his ghastly shame?
Kneeling amidst his brother's blood,
To offer mockery unto God,
As if the High and Holy One
Could smile on deeds of murder done!
As if a human sacrifice
Were purer in His holy eyes,
Though offered up by Christian hands,
Than the foul rites of Pagan lands!
.   .   .   .   .   .

Sternly, amidst his household band,
His carbine grasped within his hand,
    The white man stood, prepared and still,
Waiting the shock of maddened men,
Unchained, and fierce as tigers, when
    The horn winds through their caverned hill.
And one was weeping in his sight,
    The sweetest flower of all the isle,
The bride who seemed but yesternight
    Love's fair embodied smile.
And, clinging to her trembling knee,
Looked up the form of infancy,
With tearful glance in either face
The secret of its fear to trace.

'Ha! stand or die!' The white man's eye
    His steady musket gleamed along,
As a tall Negro hastened nigh,
    With fearless step and strong.
'What ho, Toussaint!' A moment more,
His shadow crossed the lighted floor.
'Away!' he shouted; 'fly with me,
The white man's bark is on the sea;
Her sails must catch the seaward wind,
For sudden vengeance sweeps behind.

Our brethren from their graves have spoken,
The yoke is spurned, the chain is broken;
On all the hills our fires are glowing,
Through all the vales red blood is flowing!
No more the mocking White shall rest
His foot upon the Negro's breast;
No more, at morn or eve, shall drip
The warm blood from the driver's whip:
Yet, though Toussaint has vengeance sworn
For all the wrongs his race have borne,
Though for each drop of Negro blood
The white man's veins shall pour a flood:
Not all alone the sense of ill
Around his heart is lingering still,
Nor deeper can the white man feel
The generous warmth of grateful zeal.
Friends of the Negro! fly with me,
The path is open to the sea:
Away, for life!' He spoke, and pressed
The young child to his manly breast,
As, headlong, through the cracking cane,
Down swept the dark insurgent train,
Drunken and grim, with shout and yell—
Howled through the dark, like sounds from hell.
Far out, in peace, the white man's sail
Swayed free before the sunrise gale.
Cloud-like that island hung afar,
   Along the bright horizon's verge,
O'er which the curse of servile war
   Rolled its red torrent, surge on surge;
And he, the Negro champion, where
   In the fierce tumult struggled he?
Go trace him by the fiery glare
Of dwellings in the midnight air,
The yells of triumph and despair,
   The streams that crimson to the sea!
Sleep calmly in thy dungeon-tomb,
   Beneath Besançon's[9] alien sky.

---

[9] Region of France where Toussaint was imprisoned.

Dark Haytien! for the time shall come,
      Yea, even now is nigh,
When, everywhere, thy name shall be
Redeemed from color's infamy;
And men shall learn to speak of thee
As one of earth's great spirits, born
In servitude. and nursed in scorn,
Casting aside the weary weight
And fetters of its low estate
In that strong majesty of soul
      Which knows no color, tongue, or clime,
Which still hath spurned the base control
      Of tyrants through all time!
Far other hands than mine may wreathe
The laurel round thy brow of death,
And speak thy praise, as one whose word
A thousand fiery spirits stirred,
Who crushed his foeman as a worm,
Whose step on human hearts fell firm:
Be mine the better task to find
A tribute for thy lofty mind,
Amidst whose gloomy vengeance shone
Some milder virtues all thine own,
Some gleams of feeling pure and warm,
Like sunshine on a sky of storm,
Proofs that the Negro's heart retains
Some nobleness amid its chains,—
That kindness to the wronged is never
      Without its excellent reward,
Holy to human-kind and ever
      Acceptable to God.

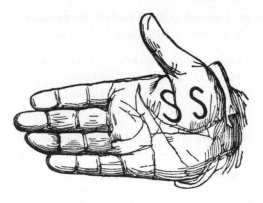

10. Anon., *Walker's Branded Hand* (wood engraving).

The Branded Hand

Captain Jonathan Walker, of Harwich, Mass., was solicited by several fugitive slaves at Pensacola, Florida, to carry them in his vessel to the British West Indies. Although well aware of the great hazard of the enterprise he attempted to comply with the request, but was seized at sea by an American vessel, consigned to the authorities at Key West, and thence sent back to Pensacola, where, after a long and rigorous confinement in prison, he was tried and sentenced to be branded on his right hand with the letters 'S.S.' (slave-stealer) and amerced in a heavy fine.

Welcome home again, brave seaman! with thy thoughtful brow and gray,
And the old heroic spirit of our earlier, better day;
With that front of calm endurance, on whose steady nerve in vain
Pressed the iron of the prison, smote the fiery shafts of pain!

Is the tyrant's brand upon thee? Did the brutal cravens aim
To make God's truth thy falsehood, His holiest work thy shame?
When, all blood-quenched, from the torture the iron was withdrawn,
How laughed their evil angel the baffled fools to scorn!

They change to wrong the duty which God hath written out
On the great heart of humanity, too legible for doubt!
They, the loathsome moral lepers, blotched from footsole up to crown,
Give to shame what God hath given unto honor and renown!

Why, that brand is highest honor! than its traces never yet
Upon old armorial hatchments[1] was a prouder blazon[2] set;

---

[1] In heraldry the arms of a deceased person shown within a black lozenge shape.
[2] In heraldry a coat of arms; hence it carries the associated meaning of showing publicly and ostentatiously.

And thy unborn generations, as they tread our rocky strand,
Shall tell with pride the story of their father's branded hand!

As the Templar[3] home was welcome, bearing back from Syrian wars
The scars of Arab lances and of Paynim[4] scimitars,
The pallor of the prison, and the shackle's crimson span,
So we meet thee, so we greet thee, truest friend of God and man.

He suffered for the ransom of the dear Redeemer's grave,
Thou for His living presence in the bound and bleeding slave;
He for a soil no longer by the feet of angels trod,
Thou for the true Shechinah,[5] the present home of God!

For, while the jurist, sitting with the slave-whip o'er him swung,
From the tortured truths of freedom the lie of slavery wrung,
And the solemn priest to Moloch, on each God-deserted shrine,
Broke the bondman's heart for bread, poured the bondman's blood for wine;

While the multitude in blindness to a far-off Saviour knelt,
And spurned, the while, the temple where a present Saviour dwelt;
Thou beheld'st Him in the task-field, in the prison shadows dim,
And thy mercy to the bondman, it was mercy unto Him!

In thy lone and long night-watches, sky above and wave below,
Thou didst learn a higher wisdom than the babbling schoolmen know;
God's stars and silence taught thee, as His angels only can,
That the one sole sacred thing beneath the cope of heaven is Man!

That he who treads profanely on the scrolls of law and creed,
In the depth of God's great goodness may find mercy in his need;
But woe to him who crushes the soul with chain and rod,
And herds with lower natures the awful form of God!

Then lift that manly right-hand, bold ploughman of the wave!
Its branded palm shall prophesy, 'Salvation to the Slave!'[6]
Hold up its fire-wrought language, that whoso reads may feel
His heart swell strong within him, his sinews change to steel.

Hold it up before our sunshine, up against our Northern air;
Ho! men of Massachusetts, for the love of God, look there!

<hr/>

[3] Knights Templars were members of a military and religious order founded in 1119 for the protection of the Holy Sepulchre in Jerusalem.

[4] Heathendom; a heathen, a non-Christian.   [5] Hebrew for the divine presence.

[6] Walker's hand was branded with SS, the standard acronym for slave stealer in the Southern states; Whittier is reinventing the acronym for abolition.

Take it henceforth for your standard, like the Bruce's heart of yore,
In the dark strife closing round ye, let that hand be seen before!

And the masters of the slave-land shall tremble at that sign,
When it points its finger Southward along the Puritan line:
Can the craft of State avail them? Can a Christless church withstand,
In the van of Freedom's onset, the coming of that hand?

Ichabod[1]

This poem was the outcome of the surprise and grief and forecast of evil consequences which I felt on reading the seventh of March speech of Daniel Webster in
support of the 'compromise,' and the Fugitive Slave Law. No partisan or personal enmity dictated it. On the contrary my admiration of the splendid personality
and intellectual power of the great Senator was never stronger than when I laid
down his speech, and, in one of the saddest moments of my life, penned my
protest. I saw, as I wrote, with painful clearness its sure results,—the Slave Power
arrogant and defiant, strengthened and encouraged to carry out its scheme for the
extension of its baleful system, or the dissolution of the Union, the guaranties of
personal liberty in the free States broken down, and the whole country made the
hunting-ground of slave-catchers. In the horror of such a vision, so soon fearfully fulfilled, if one spoke at all, he could only speak in tones of stern and sorrowful
rebuke.

But death softens all resentments, and the consciousness of a common inher-
itance of frailty and weakness modifies the severity of judgment. Years after, in
The Lost Occasion, I gave utterance to an almost universal regret that the great
statesman did not live to see the flag which he loved trampled under the feet of
Slavery, and, in view of this desecration, make his last days glorious in defence of
'Liberty and Union, one and inseparable.'

> So fallen! so lost! the light withdrawn
> Which once he wore!
> The glory from his gray hairs gone
> Forevermore!
>
> Revile him not, the Tempter hath
> A snare for all;

---

[1] A name meaning 'the glory is departed', from 1 Samuel 4: 21: 'And she [Phineas's wife] named the child Ichabod, saying the glory is departed from Israel'; hence the name is associated with fallen grandeur generally.

And pitying tears, not scorn and wrath,
 Befit his fall!

Oh, dumb be passion's stormy rage,
 When he who might
Have lighted up and led his age,
 Falls back in night.

Scorn! would the angels laugh, to mark
 A bright soul driven,
Fiend-goaded, down the endless dark,
 From hope and heaven!

Let not the land once proud of him
 Insult him now,
Nor brand with deeper shame his dim,
 Dishonored brow.

But let its humbled sons, instead,
 From sea to lake,
A long lament, as for the dead,
 In sadness make.

Of all we loved and honored, naught
 Save power remains;
A fallen angel's pride of thought,
 Still strong in chains.

All else is gone; from those great eyes
 The soul has fled:
When faith is lost, when honor dies,
 The man is dead!

Then, pay the reverence of old days
 To his dead fame;
Walk backward, with averted gaze,
 And hide the shame!

Southern Nabob (pseud.), reported by Philo Fidelitas (pseud.), *Slavery Vindicated; or, The Beauty and Glory of the 'Patriarchal System' Illustrated: A Poetical Oration* (1839)

The challenge of writing an American satiric epic on the subject of slavery was taken up by the pseudonymous Philo Fidelitas. This 'poetical oration by a Southern Nabob' again attempts the heroic couplet, and although no *MacFlecnoe* does at least employ some of the form's potential for Drydenesque vainglorious bombast. The poet also shows some skill in conducting an argument over several verse paragraphs. The rehearsal of Southern defences of slavery, in terms of the benign nature of the institution when set against the way white workers are treated under Northern industrialization, is effective because barely exaggerated, indeed it closely anticipates not only the logic but the tone of later pro-slavery writings and satire, most notoriously George Fitzhugh's *Cannibals All*. The arguments about the condition of the labouring poor and Northern hypocrisy are directly inherited from the tradition of anti-abolition radical reform in Britain, the most extreme and complete manifestation of which was William Cobbett's writings attacking the Clapham sect abolitionists. The tradition was then crudely expanded in the Negrophobe brutalism of Thomas Carlyle's late work. This position became a staple of American pro-slavery defence in the 1830s and was not limited to criticisms of the Northern industrialized cities but frequently returned to Britain and to London for its evidence.

It is a bold satiric ruse to allow your fictional opponent to play devil's advocate at your own expense. If the opponent's arguments are too powerful the satirist can shoot himself in the foot. Philo Fidelitas here manages to discredit the argument not through refutation but by showing how it grows out of, and is involved in, a corrupt and violent network of defensive thought which in the end depends on sentiment, violence, and intimidation. The Southern Nabob expounds a set of attitudes which combine 'see for yourself, leave us alone, and watch out if you come South' in a single ultimately incoherent monologue. The satire works because the Northern reader, who is the intended audience, is presented with only a slightly caricatured version of every argument with which the South familiarly met criticisms of its policies on slavery.

Slavery Vindicated

What madness to think our republic can stand,
If the *Slavery-System* be swept from the land!
'Tis the cap-stone of Freedom—'tis Chivalry's guard;—
Yet traitors and fools would the blessing discard!

Can they point out a way how the nation coud be,
Without it, one hour independent and free?
Our ebony chattels—God knows that we need 'em,
To grace and embellish the Temple of Freedom.
Yet the meddlesome North would their burdens unbind,
And give them a rank with the rest of mankind!
Heaven's thunderbolts blast the fanatics outright!
How dare they the maxims of Jefferson[1] cite?
How dare they presume, quoting chapter and verse,
The rights of the slave from the Bible rehearse?
Can Negroes be freeborn? Who think so, are blind;
'Tis a thought which ne'er came into Jefferson's mind;
"All men are born equal" his writings may teach,
But he merely design'd it a flourish of speech;
And as for the Bible, we find that of late,
Men deem its authority quite out of date.
Down! sturdy fanatics! ye only are fit
For the brimstone and fire of the bottomless pit;
Your insolent preaching though blackguards may relish.
As yours is, no project was ever so hellish.

In Chivalry's eye if the system have charms,
Let the South, Mr. President, STAND TO HER ARMS!
Our slaves are our chattels—and we have a right
To the labor of black men, because—we are white.
Shall we, noble Southrons, submit to the shame
Of toil, who the glory of Chivalry claim?
No—Heaven ordain'd we should live at our ease,
In pomp and in luxury just as we please;
And that negroes for nothing should toil till they die.
Whatever our wishes require, to supply.
And Heaven ordain'd that, for Chivalry's good,
We should prudently deal them coarse raiment and food.
Heaven, too, put the whip into Chivalry's hand,
And we flog the delinquent by Heaven's command.
Moreover, to prove that the blacks are a race
Inferior to white men, and abject and base,

---

[1] Thomas Jefferson (1743–1826), third American President and Governor of Virginia; he also drafted the Declaration of Independence. Recently there has been much interest over Jefferson's ambivalent position over slavery, and over the children he fathered with his female slaves.

We keep them in ignorance as much as we can,—
Supernatural wisdom has taught us the plan.
Thus, the slave-institution is plainly divine,
And in perfect accordance with Heaven's design.

What *would* the fanatics, if clothed with the power?
They would *sunder the Union* the very next hour!
To bring *that* about is their ultimate aim,
Whate'er be the motives they plausibly claim.
We are friends to the Union— provided that we
Through the slave-power can govern the States that are free:
Our prerogative still to bear absolute sway,
Born to rule, as the rest of mankind to obey.
The union of States is a glorious bond;—
But the slave-institution we prize far beyond.
We value the least link of Slavery's chain,
More precious than all from the Union we gain.
Let the insolent, browbeating zealots beware,
Ere their crusade arrive at a serious affair!
Let them cease with their neighbors a quarrel to pick—
Of the high game they strike for they soon will be sick!
Let it come to the issue, whate'er may ensue—
Their vile interference they'll bitterly rue;
The base, craven creatures, though vaunting of power,
To our metal and might will ingloriously cower.
We will stand to our arms—we will never surrender
The rights we inherit—the means of our splendor;
Yes, every slaveholder will fight to the last—
Let the tocsin be sounded, and long be the blast!

Cowards! let them be seen at the South—holding forth
The damnable doctrines they preach at the North;
Circulating their papers, and pictures, and tracts,
And moulding the hearts of the negroes like wax;
To excite discontent and rebellion—to change
Their servile submission to direful revenge!—
Ay, once let the miscreant cowards come here,
If their love be so perfect it casteth out fear,[2]
And their labor of love straight among us begin—
In no enviable plight will they find themselves in.

[2] 1 John 4: 18: 'There is no fear in love; but perfect love casteth out fear: because fear hath torment. He that feareth is not made perfect in love.'

Prompt pay shall be theirs for each blow that they strike,
Though perchance in a coin they would rather dislike;
To wit, deepest hatred and purest contempt,
Judge Lynch's embrace and a necklace of hemp.[3]

Ere the cursed fanatics their crusade begun,
How quiet our beautiful system went on!
Patriarchal and mild is the system throughout,
To the people of color a blessing no doubt.
The beams of its glory fanatics may hate,
And about the injustice of slavery prate;
Ay, pour if they please their mock sympathy forth,
To enlist in their crusade the fools of the North;
Yet we of the South can clear evidence show,
That the system's a blessing, as all of us know.
Denounce it who will, 'tis a beautiful thing;
What else either safety or comfort could bring
To the African race? If to-day they were free,
The Lord knows how sad their condition would be!
And fudge to the tale that so often is told,
Concerning the scenes when at auction are sold
To different buyers, the husband and wife,
With their children—thence forcibly parted for life.
Though fondly together they seemingly cling,
Can feeling belong to a *chattel*, or *thing*?
And fudge to the tale, that our rule is to urge
Our slaves to hard labor by plying the scourge;
Though truly, when some sturdy fellow is slack,
The soft oil of whip we apply to his back.
We are known the world o'er to be gentle, refin'd,
Nor can otherwise be than indulgent and kind.
Protection, subsistence, we grant to our negroes,—
While the poor of the North are like vagabond beggars,
Who toil for a pittance, most wretched of slaves,
Ground down by aristocrats, plundered by knaves.
Just look at the Factories! slavery there
Is too horribly galling for nature to bear;
Poor children, for scanty subsistence and pay,
Are there doom'd to toil *sixteen hours* in a day!

---

[3] A hangman's rope.

While the slaves of *New England* are groaning with want,
It befits you, fanatics, to whine out your cant—
Weep crocodile tears o'er the poor *Southern* slave,
And about *our* injustice unceasingly rave!

'Tis the case the world over, deny it who will,
That the poor man must bow to the opulent still—
Yield the fruits of his toil to his betters, and be
The slave of the rich, though he claim to be free.
The nominal slave is the best off by half,
He may dance, he may sing, play the fiddle and laugh;
When his few hours of moderate labor are past,
To his own merry hut he may joyfully haste;
With no thought of the morrow, his wants all supplied,—
A boon to the poor Northern packhorse denied.
Our slaves are protected, and sure of a home,
But often, in want, Northern laborers roam.
The rich—the rich only have rights, we allow,
And slaves, black or white, in submission should bow
To the opulent lords of the land; yet the poor
Who are nominal slaves, are most safe and secure.
Let the poor talk of rights—but their claim is all null,
Who sees not the fact in perception is dull;
But slaves may have lenity shown them and grace,
And that ours are *most favor'd*, is clearly the case.
Go, lovers of justice—philanthropists pure,
And remember the wrongs which *your* drudges endure;
Humanity's duties fulfill nearer home,
Nor here let your thoughts *sentimentally* roam.

Abolition! the project is passing absurd;
It is treason, rank treason, to utter the word.
'Tis a question the North has no right to debate,
At the fireside, in Congress, in church or in state;
No right has the North, not the least, to petition
On what ev'n remotely concerns Abolition.
But they force it upon us the gag to apply,—
So we pass resolutions the right to deny:
No member of Congress dares open his mouth,
Without the consent of the sovereign South:
Our prerogative, also, to muzzle the Press;—
And let none dare infringe on the rights we possess!

Abolish the slave-system! Better essay
To abolish the Sun at meridian day!
Ridiculous effort! the *crow*[4] too would soar
Aloft like the eagle—but wanted the power.
Never madmen so foolish a project devised;
Yet the chiefs of the crusade are all idolized,
By silly old women, and children, and priests,
By fools and fanatics as ignorant as beasts.
O, what an oracular being is Garrison![5]
In wisdom and worth he exceeds all comparison;
And John Quincy Adams[6] is more than a sage—
The glory, the lion, the light of the age—
Deserving a sceptre without any doubt,
For the part he has acted *in* Congress and *out*.
(Though the wily old fellow is full of his tricks,
And 'tis said that he frequently flounders and kicks;
And *some* Abolitionists shrewdly discover
He fills up the milkpail, and then—kicks it over.)
While zealots are tossing their firebrands round,
Thus fools to applaud them, in plenty are found.
How glorious the slave-system flourish'd of old,
We are oft in the pages of history told.
In fair classic Greece and republican Rome,
The system was cherish'd, the slave found a home;
For those noblest States of antiquity knew
That the most of their greatness from Slavery grew.
The sweat of the slave gave them riches and power,
And brighten'd the tints of fair liberty's flower.
Their highborn and rich lived in dignified ease,
And bask'd in a freedom becoming grandees—
Which they ne'er could have done in an equal degree,
Had the bondmen of Rome and of Athens been free.
The Jews, too, had slaves—in abundance, no doubt;
Old Abraham had lots of them, sturdy and stout—

---

[4] Because of its blackness the crow had become associated with blacks; the association gained in popularity in the wake of the popular late 18th-century black entertainer and slave holder 'Jim Crow'.

[5] For Garrison see pp. 536–40.

[6] John Quincey Adams was an ex-President of the United States who in his old age became strongly associated with slave rights, most notoriously in the leading role he took over the *Amistad* case. Following a slave revolt the Spanish ship *Amistad* was finally taken to New York and the surviving slaves became the focus for a historic court case in which Adams argued for their rights.

Else ne'er had he been half so mighty and rich,
Nor had risen his fame to so lofty a pitch.
No crime was it deem'd by the chosen of God,
To hold men in bondage by dint of the rod
Of power, which at pleasure the master might wield
To quicken the tame, make the obstinate yield.
Yet the slave-institution, so truly sublime,
Is by Northern fanatics regarded a crime!
They see not the evidence, fools that they are,
By that sure indication, the skin which they wear,
That the darkies are merely for servitude made,
Or nature had given 'em a different shade.
It is nature herself has committed the sin,
In giving the blacks an unfashionable skin:
That the fault is not ours is notoriously plain;
We would whitewash them all, *we* would wipe off the stain.
The process of bleaching we've practiced long since,
As facts in abundance will clearly evince—
And with ample success; Mr. Senator Clay[7]
Has not the least doubt, if we hold on our way,
Two centuries at most will suffice to erase
The ebony hue and the woolly disgrace;
When pure *Anglo-Saxon* will be the whole nation,
The glorious result of Amalgamation.[8]

The sordid and grovelling sons of the North,
Who affect to disdain the distinctions of birth;
Who dream of nought nobler than shillings and pence,
Yet set up the claim of superior sense;
Whose cold villain blood runs reluctant and slow—
Boors that never yet felt noble chivalry's glow,
Dead to honor, may deal out their calumny vile,
Full of plausible slang, and all mischief and guile;—
We reck not, we fear not—resolv'd to maintain
Our rights, and in bondage our slaves to retain.
Wo, wo to the hell-hounds who dare interfere
With the wise institutions we value so dear!
We will firmly defend what our fathers adored—
Nor shrink from our duty—by dint of the sword.

---

[7] Senator Henry Clay, staunch and ingenious pro-slavery advocate.
[8] A blending of different elements, here explicitly a mixture of the races.

Shall *we*, all chivalrous, and noble of soul,
Submit to the scandal of Northern control?
And tamely our rights and our riches surrender,
Because some pretend they have consciences tender,
And think that our beautiful darkies should be,
(O monstrous!) like ladies and gentlemen, free?
Ye harpies![9] away with your insolent stuff,
Of your taunts and palaver we've had quite enough;
Cease, cease from your browbeating—dictate no more;
The South you would humble—but where is your power?
Our sires wouldn't pay ev'n a three-penny tax,
But Tyranny's tree they consigned to the axe;
And think you, that we are so passive and tame
We will quietly yield to your arrogant claim,
Surrender our wealth at *your pious* command,
And with *negroes* on ground of equality stand?

Let the whole clan of crusaders timely beware,
And prudently cease Southern vengeance to dare!
There's a cell in each bosom where vengeance long pent,
Restrain'd by forbearance, now struggles for vent,
And forth, like the bolt from the cloud, let it burst,
And wither at once the fanatics accurst!
Mr. President!—no—we will ne'er shrink from slaughter—
For the present, I'm done—now some brandy and water.

Eliza Lee Follen (1787–1860), 'Children in Slavery', 'For the Fourth of July', in *Poems* (1839); 'The Slave Boy's Wish', in George W. Clark (ed.), *The Liberty Minstrel* (1845)

Follen came from a large and powerful Boston family, her father being a wealthy businessman. After his death Follen showed her independence by setting up a Sunday school. She married a German political refugee, Charles Follen, and the couple increasingly committed themselves to extreme abolitionism in the 1830s. Following his

---

[9] Rapacious and filthy monsters, half woman, half bird.

death in 1840 Follen became one of the most revered figures in Boston anti-slavery. She combined her interests in children's education and in abolition to stunning effect in her poetry.

Follen shared Maria Weston Chapman's (pp. 483–6) belief that women should be allowed a public role in political reform. In an essay entitled 'Women's Work' in Chapman's *Liberty Bell* she went so far as to argue that women were better qualified to work as abolitionists than men because they had not been irreparably corrupted by access to power. She concludes: 'The abolition of slavery is indeed woman's work . . . Let neither fathers, nor brothers, nor husbands, nor false or weak friends keep us back from it.' One of Follen's particular gifts lay in her abilities as an educationalist; her interest in the moral education of children led her to edit first *The Christian Teachers Manual* and then *The Child's Friend*. But although these were both Sunday school publications, and although she was a deeply religious woman, she took a joyful and celebratory approach to teaching children. She was not grim or pietistic and had an almost Blakean delight in, and reverence for, the visionary qualities of childish imagination. Her wonderful 'Lines on Nonsense' bluntly attack 'stupid reason, That stalking, ten-foot rule' and are an enduring and passionate plea for the life-enhancing effects of creative unreason. Follen is at her very best as a slavery poet when she seems to speak as a child to children. The little poem 'Children in Slavery' has an economy and a lyric intensity that are genuinely close to Blake's *Songs of Innocence and of Experience*. The contrasting of childish joy and childish despair in two eight-line stanzas has great power, and Follen uses the simple ballad stanza, which is her staple lyric form, with great artistry. I take a deep breath when I say this, but 'Children in Slavery' is one of the few nineteenth-century American lyrics which can compete with Blake and Wordsworth at their best. It must not be forgotten that Follen was a genuine intellectual heavyweight who worked hard to achieve the utter simplicity of her best lines. The same woman who wrote 'Yes! Nonsense is a treasure, | I love it with my heart' also translated and published large amounts of Fénelon's most challenging work, believing that the French proto-revolutionary theorist 'apostle of interior inspiration' had a lot to say to nineteenth-century America.

Children in Slavery

When children play the livelong day,
  Like birds and butterflies;
As free and gay, sport life away,
  And know not care nor sighs:
Then earth and air seem fresh and fair,
  All peace below, above:
Life's flowers are there, and everywhere
  Is innocence and love.

When children pray with fear all day,
    A blight must be at hand:
Then joys decay, and birds of prey
    Are hovering o'er the land:
When young hearts weep as they go to sleep,
    Then all the world seems sad:
The flesh must creep, and woes are deep
    When children are not glad.

For the Fourth of July

My country, that nobly could dare
    The hand of oppression to brave,
O, how the foul stain canst thou bear,
    Of being the land of the slave?

His groans, and the clank of his chains
    Shall rise with the shouts of the free,
And turn into discord the strains
    They raise, God of mercy, to thee.

The proud knee at his altar we bend,
    On God as our Father we call:
We call him our Father and Friend,
    And forget he's the Father of all.

His children he does not forget;
    His mercy, his power can save;
And, sure as God liveth, he yet
    Will liberty give to the slave.

O talk not of freedom and peace!
    With the blood of the slave on our sod:
Till the groans of the negro shall cease,
    Hope not for a blessing from God.

He asks,—am not I a man?
    He pleads,—am not I a brother?
Then dare not, and hope not you can
    The cry of humanity smother.

'T will be heard from the south to the north,
    In our halls, and in poverty's shed:
It will go like a hurricane forth,
    And wake up the living and dead.

The dead whom the white man has slain,
    They cry from the ground and the waves:
They once cried for mercy in vain,
    They plead for their brothers the slaves.

O! let them my country be heard!
    Be the land of the free and the brave!
And send forth the glorious word,
    This is not the land of the slave!

The Slave Boy's Wish

I wish I was that little bird,
    Up in the bright blue sky;
That sings and flies jut where he will,
    And no one asks him why.

I wish I was that little brook,
    That runs so swift along;
Through pretty flowers and shining stones,
    Singing a merry song.

I wish I was that butterfly,
    Without a thought or care;
Sporting my pretty, brilliant wings,
    Like a flower in the air.

I wish I was that wild, wild deer
    I saw the other day;
Who swifter than an arrow flew
    Through the forest far away.

I wish I was that little cloud,
    By the gentle south wind driven
Floating along, so free and bright
    Far, far up into heaven.

I'd rather be a cunning fox,
    And hide me in a cave;
I'd rather be a savage wolf,
    Than what I am—a slave.

My mother calls me her good boy
    My father calls me brave;
What wicked action have I done
    That I should be a slave.

I saw my little sister sold,
    So will they do to me;
My Heavenly Father, let me die,
    For then I shall be free.

Joseph L. Chester (1821–82), 'Farewell Address to Joseph Cinque', *National Anti-Slavery Standard*, 12/29 (16 Dec. 1841), 112

This is an occasional poem, the occasion being the point when the African leader of the *Amistad* rebellion Joseph Cinque, and the other slaves who had taken part in the uprising and resultant legal disputes in New York, were finally allowed to return to Sierra Leone. Although Cinque sails to freedom, and escapes imprisonment, there is much in the hortatory tone and the oppressive imperatives of this poem that recalls the tone of Wordsworth's 'To Toussaint L'Ouverture' (pp. 231–3). There is also the feeling that although Cinque has finally gained his freedom the abolitionist author cannot bear to let him out of his sight. Even Cinque's reunion with his family does not escape the shadow of abolitionist envy. As the intensity of the slave's suffering cannot be matched by the abolitionist martyr, so the intensity of the slave's joy is something beyond the experience of Joseph Chester, who categorically states: 'Of pleasures here I would an age resign | That for a day I might unite in thine.'

Farewell Address to Joseph Cinque

Once more upon the water! Whither now,
Brave Cinque! do thy anxious wanderings tend?
The gallant ship! Say, doth her gilded prow
Again her way to climes of bondage wend?

Art thou once more in chains, and borne along
To regions where thy fetters will be strong?

Ah no! thou art a freeman now! The air
You breathe is but the breath of Liberty!
No more of sorrow or of dark despair
Shall press thy noble heart. Ay, *thou art free!*
And even now, far o'er the trackless main,
The good ship flies to bear thee home again.

Home! Home! thy soul must kindle at the word!
Thou art a *husband* and thy doting wife
Will greet thee with a heart whose throbs are heard
Thou art a *father*; thou hast given life
To those who soon will cling around thy knee,
And shout for joy their sire again to see.

Oh! might I then an unseen witness stand,
And see the greetings of thy kindred there—
The wild embrace—the grasping of the hand—
And hear the shouts that then will rend the air—
Of pleasure here I would an age resign,
That for a day I might unite in thine!

I charge you now, forget not those whose hand
And hearts were opened at your tale of grief:
Forget not him—that brave old man[1]—who stands
A noble monument to your relief:
Forget not any who have lent you aid,
And for their welfare let your prayers be made.

And most of all, forget not Him, whose name
Ye now have heard aright: Him whose strong hand
Gave impulse to the helm when first ye came,
Heav'n-guided, to this portion of our land:
Him who hath raised up friends to plead your cause,
And judges who have rightly read our laws.

Go, tell your kindred of the white man's God,
By whom your faces once again they see!
How he hath freed you from th'oppressor's rod,
And how His Truth hath made you doubly free:

---

[1] John Quincey Adams; see p. 520 n. 6.

And should the memory of your *friends* grow dim,
I charge you, on your souls, *forget not Him!*

And now farewell! My spirit with you flies,
And Hope's bright eye looks far beyond the sea:
I seem to see your native hills arise,
And all your kindred gathered on the lea.
One prayer I breathe, ere yet you leave our strand—
God bless thee Cinque and thy native land!

Henry Wadsworth Longfellow (1807–82), 'The Slave in the Dismal Swamp', 'The Warning', 'The Witnesses', in *Poems on Slavery* (1842)

Longfellow's slavery compositions could hardly have been created under conditions more different from those of Whittier. Having written almost no verse even touching on slavery Longfellow found himself returning from a health trip to Europe in 1842. In a letter to a friend he described how the Atlantic crossing in cramped and unpleasant conditions led him to meditate upon the ordeal of the middle passage and to create a sudden explosion of slavery poetry:

> I was in the forward part of the vessel, where all the great waves struck and broke with voices of thunder. There, 'cribbed, cabined, and confined,' I passed fifteen days. During this time, I wrote seven poems on slavery; I meditated upon them in the stormy, sleepless nights, and wrote them down with a pencil in the morning. A small window in the side of the vessel admitted light into my berth, and there I lay on my back and soothed my soul with songs.

Consequently these poems are one of the most literal examples of a white sympathetic consciousness attempting to appropriate the suffering of the slave through a process of emotional mimicry.

Longfellow published these works together with the earlier 'The Warning' as *Poems on Slavery* in 1842. The poems are unremitting in their Gothic horror, and in their presentation of the slave as passive victim. 'The Witnesses' is one of the few poems about the middle passage to think about how not only the remains of slaves, but the sea itself, might be seen to constitute an eternal memorial to, and witness of, the horror of the middle passage. By far the most popular of the collection was 'The Slave in the Dismal Swamp' which takes the image of the desolate runaway slave striving against a hostile nature to new extremes of sublime horror. Longfellow takes up the overused abolition trope which compares the freedom of wild animals with the captivity of the slave. Yet the appropriation has a curious edge given that the slave himself is effectively animalized when described as a 'wild beast' in the third stanza. 'The Warning' which concludes the volume is the only one of the poems to raise the spectre of slave insurrection. Longfellow begins by using the biblical comparison of contemporary America with the Philistines, and ends by making the bold association of Samson with the slave population. Consequently it is implied, although never explicitly stated, that the dormant and abused slave body will rise and destroy North and South with the sanction of an angry God. In many ways that is what happened.

The Slave in the Dismal Swamp[1]

In dark fens of the Dismal Swamp
    The hunted Negro lay;
He saw the fire of the midnight camp,
And heard at times a horse's tramp
    And a bloodhound's distant bay.

Where will-o'-the-wisps[2] and glow worms shine,
    In bulrush and in brake;
Where waving mosses shroud the pine,
And the cedar grows, and the poisonous vine
    Is spotted like the snake;

Where hardly a human foot could pass,
    Or a human heart would dare,
On the quaking turf of the green morass
He crouched in the rank and tangled grass,
    Like a wild beast in his lair.

A poor old slave, infirm and lame;
    Great scars deformed his face;
On his forehead he bore the brand of shame,
And the rags, that hid his mangled frame,
    Were the livery of disgrace.

---

[1] A vast swampland which spanned the boundary between Virginia and North Carolina, where fugitive slave communities were rumoured to exist. Harriet Beecher Stowe entitled her sequel to *Uncle Tom's Cabin, Dred: A Tale of the Great Dismal Swamp*, and her eponymous hero is supposed to live there.

[2] The *ignis fatuus*, the light caused by the combustion of marsh gas, and more widely any elusive person or phenomenon.

All things above were bright and fair,
    All things were glad and free;
Lithe squirrels darted here and there,
And wild birds filled the echoing air
    With songs of Liberty !

On him alone was the doom of pain,
    From the morning of his birth;
On him alone the curse of Cain
Fell, like a flail on the garnered grain,
    And struck him to the earth!

The Warning

Beware! The Israelite of old,[1] who tore
    The lion in his path,—when, poor and blind,
He saw the blessed light of heaven no more,
    Shorn of his noble strength and forced to grind
In prison, and at last led forth to be
A pander to Philistine revelry,—

Upon the pillars of the temple laid
    His desperate hands, and in its overthrow
Destroyed himself, and with him those who made
    A cruel mockery of his sightless woe;
The poor, blind Slave, the scoff and jest of all,
Expired, and thousands perished in the fall!

There is a poor, blind Samson in this land,
    Shorn of his strength and bound in bonds of steel,
Who may, in some grim revel, raise his hand,
    And shake the pillars of this Commonweal,
Till the vast Temple of our liberties
A shapeless mass of wreck rubbish lies.

[1] Samson.

The Witnesses

In Ocean's wide domains,
  Half buried in the sands,
Lie skeletons in chains,
  With shackled feet and hands.

Beyond the fall of dews,
  Deeper than plummet lies,
Float ships, with all their crews,
  No more to sink nor rise.

There the black Slave-ship swims,
  Freighted with human forms,
Whose fettered, fleshless limbs
  Are not the sport of storms.

These are the bones of Slaves;
  They gleam from the abyss;
They cry from yawning waves,
  'We are the Witnesses!'

Within Earth's wide domains
  Are markets for men's lives;
Their necks are galled with chains,
  Their wrists are cramped with gyves.[1]

Dead bodies, that the kite
  In deserts makes its prey;
Murders, that with affright
  Scare school-boys from their play!

All evil thoughts and deeds;
  Anger, and lust, and pride;
The foulest, rankest weeds,
  That choke Life's groaning tide!

These are the woes of Slaves;
  They glare from the abyss;
They cry from unknown graves,
  'We are the Witnesses!'

---

[1] Fetters.

Daniel Mann, from *The Virginia Philosopher; or, A Few Lucky Slave Catchers: A Poem by Mr. Latimer's Brother* (1843)

The preface states that the 'Poem commenced as a parody of Watts *Indian Philosopher* as a means of immortalising the persons and their abettors who were engaged in the business of re-enslaving George Latimer'. The poem was inspired by the notorious events surrounding the sensational capture, imprisonment, and spectacular release of Latimer. On 19 October 1842 Latimer was arrested in Boston for larceny, although the charge was a pretext for his capture as a fugitive slave. Latimer's arrest generated riots, led by Boston free blacks, outside the prison in which he was being held. Chief Justice Shaw at this point ruled that legally he had to send Latimer back to his owner, one Gray in Norfolk, Virginia. Gray was given two weeks to prove his ownership of the slave, and Latimer meanwhile remained in prison, although he was no longer charged with any crime. Mass riots were generated by the abolitionists, and in the rising hysteria Gray panicked and readily agreed to sell Latimer to a Boston abolitionist consortium for $400. Latimer was duly bought and set free amid celebrations.

The satire is supposedly spoken by an enthusiastic Northerner spelling out with high irony the advantages of the slave laws. The section here is effective as the narrator runs through the gamut of slave tortures, urging constraint so that the market value of the slave is not damaged. This is a very rare instance of the parodic mimicry of the voice of the slave power as sadistic fantasy. Unlike British abolition verse Americans are reluctant to use ironic humour to describe the torture of slaves.

The Virginia Philosopher; or, A Few Lucky Slave Catchers

·   ·   ·   ·   ·

XLIX

Then shall Virginia, now deprest,
Arise, in native beauty drest,
    As in her virtuous youth;
Then waving fields of yellow grain,
And flocks and herds shall fill the plain,
And cities rise with towering fane,[1]
    Sacred to God and truth.

---

[1] See p. 309 n. 6.

L

Here ceased the vision and the strain,
O then, cried I, from this 'tis plain
    What course for us were wise,
Since times grow harder every day,
And bankrupt rogues refuse to pay,
Let one new scheme without delay
    Be tried as I advise.

LL

Good Mayor and Council *do* provide,
Of constables an ample tribe,
    Like some we've now on hand,
With blood-hound noses skilled to catch,
Handcuff and gag the flying wretch,
    Or swear upon the stand.

LII

Yet ere you loose the blood-hound crew,
Teach them the game they should pursue,
    And rules of this new trade;
That slaves henceforward shall be known,
Not by the color's doubtful tone,
But by their slavish souls alone,
    For slavish uses made.

LIII

Then Tally-Ho![2] on every side
Brisk business echoes far and wide;
See where the hunted wretches hide,
    And where the dogs pursue!
See one that counting room explore,
Where rum pipes load the yielding floor,
And bales of cotton block the door,
    Poor wretch—'twill never do.

LIV

See to his lawyer's office one
Slave-hunting, hunted rascal run,
    Vain now his quip and quirk;
See to the pulpit that one turn,

---

[2] The shout let out when the quarry is sighted on a fox hunt.

Ah, Rev'rend slave soul! soon you'll learn
Another kind of work.

LV

Now good slave-catcher do be kind,
And let these poor white serviles find
   Their former notions right—
That "slaves are better off than we,
Enough to eat, from trouble free,
Their day glides onward merrily,
   And peacefully their night."

LVI

Ah, lightly wield that sounding lash
And not too deep imprint the gash
   On backs till now unscarred;
And though cat-hauling[3] is not wrong,
Let pussy's claws be not *too* long,
Nor let the brine be *very* strong,
   Nor rub the wounds *too* hard.

LVII

Twist not those thumb-screws *quite* so tight,
Nor let those hounds *too fiercely* bite,[4]
   They tear a JUDGE's skin;
Ah, master, don't brand that one *there*,
He, once a godly PRIEST, took care
To keep his cheek exceeding fair,[5]
   And smooth his dimpled chin.

---

[3] '"*Cathauling*" is one of the ingenious modes of torture which slaveholding ingenuity (mostly employed in that direction) has invented. The victim being bound upon a log, with the face downward, a vigorous cat is dragged by the tail over the naked back. The animal, in its efforts to escape, thus accomplishes the driver's purpose, in tearing up and lacerating the sufferer's skin, which, to complete the horrid work, is then rubbed with brine.' [Mann]

[4] '"*Nor let the hounds too fiercely bite.*" Blood-hounds are kept not only to track and *pull down* fugitives, but also as a terrible means of punishment to slaves, and of revenge or amusement to the whites. When they attack a negro even by mistake, it is a maxim that they must be made to conquer him, to keep up their courage and ferocity. Terrible instances are recorded of this mode of cruelty practised upon those who have stolen food, or secreted themselves to escape other punishment, and often by the overseers of other plantations, who have taken this means of revenge upon their neighbors, by maiming and injuring their HUMAN PROPERTY.' [Mann]

[5] 'The use of the thumb-screw and branding-iron are pretty well known, the *latter* through the frequent advertisements in the Southern papers describing fugitive slaves by letters branded upon the cheeks. The deformity caused by this cruel operation will hardly be taken into account in estimating the hardships of negroes, by those who consider them destitute of human feelings, but will probably be considered an aggravated item when inflicted upon the smooth cheeks of our modern Scribes and Pharisees.' [Mann]

LVIII

When wife and babes you sell away,
Send off the husband for a day,[6]
   'Twill save a useless noise;
Then for a season let him fret,
While tears his bursting bosom wet,
Poor fool—he's not "*used to it*" yet,
   As are your nigger boys.

XLIX

Ah, happy Massachusetts! tell
What merchandize thou hast to sell,
   Thy human cattle count;
Then be Virginia's boasting done,
Two slaves have we where she has one,
And each must fetch a handsome sum
   To swell the gross amount.

LX

Some blood-hound villain tell me where
Handcuffs are sold—full many a pair—
   And whips with many a lash;
Quick, ere the knell of slavery tolls,
I'll drive a gang of slavish souls
To where the free Potomac[7] rolls,
   And turn them into cash.

[6] 'When a planter chooses to sell the wife or children of one of his slaves, the unsuspecting husband and father is usually sent upon some pretence to a distant town or plantation, for a day or two. In the mean time the slavetrader takes off his family, leaving the deserted and empty hut to tell the well understood tale of bereavement to the wretched parent. Cases have occurred in which the unhappy victims of separation have, in their frantic grief, committed suicide, or pined (in planter's phrase, "sulk'd") to death.' [Mann]

[7] A river on the border of Virginia.

William Lloyd Garrison (1805–79), 'Song of the
Abolitionist', 'The Kneeling Slave', 'To Isaac T. Hopper',
in *Sonnets and Other Poems* (1843); 'The Triumph
of Freedom' (printed as conclusion in
Frederick Douglass, *What to the Slave is the
Fourth of July* (1852))

Garrison was the most famous, and frequently infamous, white male abolitionist to be
involved in the slavery debates. He was also a brilliant propagandist and self-promoter
and carefully cultivated his own martyrological myth from early on in his career. Garrison grew up in Massachusetts under the influence of a deeply pious mother. By 1819 he
had finally settled down to become a printer and journalist. His early writings were passionate interventions in just about every area of social reform, including Greek independence, universal education, temperance, woman's rights, and slavery. The great Quaker
abolitionist Benjamin Lundy took him under his wing and got him to edit the *Genius*. By
1830 Garrison had managed to get himself imprisoned for libelling a slave trader, and
made brilliant capital out of his ordeal, publishing his own sensational and self-serving
account of his trial. After his release he set up the paper with which he and the abolition
movement were to become synonymous, the *Liberator*. Garrison renounced the Colonization Society, which supported an agenda for the 'repatriation' of African Americans to
Africa. By 1833 Garrison was the most extreme and widely read of the abolition journalists, and managed to get himself selected as agent to the New England Anti-Slavery
Society. He was sent to Britain to whip up support for the American movement and met
every leading British abolitionist. He managed to be in the cortège at Wilberforce's
funeral, walking beside the abolition demagogue George Thompson. He arranged for
Thompson to come to the United States on a lecture tour in 1834. In 1835 Garrison was
attacked by a mob who were after Thompson, and had to be imprisoned for his own
safety. From then on his status as the central focus for a radical abolition platform, connected to general reform and women's rights, was assured. To many, especially the
conventional clergy, Garrison appeared a weird fanatic, and there were also suspicions
at the manner in which he acted as a magnet for 'aristocratic' and gentrified extreme supporters of reform including Wendell Phillips and Maria Weston Chapman. Garrison
took an extreme prophetic rhetorical stance, and in his prose for the *Liberator* could
sound more like a radical enthusiast of 1790s London than a mainstream New England
abolition printer and journalist in the mid-nineteenth century. He fulminated against the
sins of America which merited 'an avalanche of wrath, hurled from the Throne of God,
to crush us into annihilation'. By the late 1830s he was increasingly attracting eccentrics
and political curiosities. In his desire to stay at the centre of abolition publicity, he
appears more like Andy Warhol than William Wilberforce.

The histrionic and solipsistic approach which typified Garrison's anti-slavery feeds into his poetry. Yet the poetry seems far more concerned to fantasize over the suffering and potential suffering of white abolitionists than it does to try and approach the trauma of the slaves in any way. Garrison is, to put it kindly, a pedestrian technician, whose verse reiterates self-righteous platitudes usually centred upon the activities of himself and his circle. In 1843 he published his *Sonnets and Other Poems* which stands out for the way in which the poems prioritize the ordeals of abolitionists. 'Song of the Abolitionist' and 'Hopper' typify the Garrisonian approach to slavery verse. The first is a hymn celebrating the martyrdom of those who take up the cause of abolition. The sufferings of the white opponent of slavery are the only subject, the slave an absent and convenient catalyst for abolition suffering. Similarly 'Hopper' only mentions slaves in a single line, while the main body of the poem consists of a weird comparison between Hopper and Napoleon, as physical doubles, but moral anti-types. 'The Kneeling Slave' is one of the few poems which purport to treat the figure of the slave directly. Significantly the poem is a meditation upon the iconic image manufactured in 1789 as the seal of the British Anti-Slavery Society (Pl. 11). The headpiece to Garrison's *Liberator* carried the image

11. Josiah Wedgwood, *Am I Not a Man and a Brother* (cameo in jasper, 1788).

which showed a bowed and chained kneeling African imploring a white audience to answer the question 'Am I not a man and a brother?' The poem is really about Garrison's intensely personal, and sentimental, reactions as he looks at the image. Garrison takes it upon himself to answer 'Yes' to both elements of the question, yet seems oblivious to the irony of placing himself in a position of total domination over the black. Garrison's poetry is an extreme demonstration of the extent to which abolition verse could end up being about the Christological sacrifices of the white abolitionists. The ostensible subjects of slavery and slave emancipation are squeezed out to the point of invisibility.

Song of the Abolitionist

I

I am an Abolitionist!
　I glory in the name;
Though now by SLAVERY's minions hissed,
　And covered o'er with shame:
It is a spell of light and power—
　The watchword of the free:—
Who spurns it in the trial-hour,
　A craven soul is he!

II

I am an Abolitionist!
　Then urge me not to pause;
For joyfully do I enlist
　In FREEDOM's sacred cause:
A nobler strife the world ne'er saw,
　Th' enslaved to disenthral;
I am a soldier for the war,
　Whatever may befall!

III

I am an Abolitionist!
　Oppression's deadly foe;
In God's great strength will I resist,
　And lay the monster low;
In God's great name do I demand,
　To all be freedom given,
That peace and joy may fill the land,
　And songs go up to heaven!

IV

I am an Abolitionist!
   No threats shall awe my soul—
No perils cause me to desist—
   No bribes my acts control;
A freeman will I live and die,
   In sunshine and in shade,
And raise my voice for liberty,
   Of nought on earth afraid.

V

I am an Abolitionist—
   The tyrant's hate and dread—
The friend of all who are oppressed—
   A price is on my head!
My country is the wide, wide world,
   My countrymen mankind:—
Down to the dust be Slavery hurled!
   All servile chains unbind!

The Kneeling Slave

'Am I not a man and a brother?'

My heart is sad as I contemplate thee,
   Thou fettered victim of despotic sway;
   Driven, like a senseless brute, from day to day,
Though equal born, and as thy tyrant free.
With hands together clasped imploringly,
   And face upturned to Heaven, (Heaven shall repay!)
   For liberty and justice thou dost pray,
In piteous accents, and on bended knee.
Thy exclamation, 'AM I MOT A MAN?
   A BROTHER?' thrills my soul! I answer—YES!
Though placed beneath an ignominious ban,
   That thou art both, all shall at last confess:
To rescue thee incessantly I'll plan,
   And toil and plead, thy injuries to redress.

To Isaac T. Hopper

HOPPER! thou venerable friend of man,
  In heart and spirit young, though old in years;
  The tyrant trembles when thy name he hears,
And the slave joys thy countenance to scan.
A friend more true and brave, since time began,
  HUMANITY has never found:—her fears
  By thee have been dispelled, and wiped the tears
Adown her sorrow-stricken cheeks that ran.
If like Napoleon's appears thy face,[1]
  Thy soul to his bears no similitude;
He came to curse, but thou to bless our race—
  Thy hands are white—in blood were his imbrued:
His memory shall be covered with disgrace,
  But thine embalmed among the truly great and good!

John Pierpont (1785–1866), 'The Fugitive Slave's Apostrophe to the North Star' (written 1839), 'Slave Holder's Address to the North Star' (written 1840), 'The Chain' (written 1839), in *The Anti-Slavery Poems of John Pierpont* (1843)

Pierpont emerges as one of those mid-nineteenth-century American *characters*, impractical but brimming with energy and idealism. He came from a famous and powerful New England family, which was to become also fantastically rich following the career of John's grandson J. P. Morgan. John Pierpont graduated from Yale in 1804 and then worked in South Carolina for five years as a private tutor. Morgan's attempted careers in the law, business, and the Church were not very successful.

  It was during the period 1819–45 when he worked as pastor at the famous Hollis Street Chapel, Boston, that he produced his major reform work. He vehemently supported and preached upon a broad-based reform agenda that in its amplitude was almost Garrisonian. He was consequently far too radical for a large proportion of his

---

[1] 'The resemblance of this venerable Philanthropist, in person and features, to Napoleon, is said, by Joseph Bonaparte, to be most remarkable.' [Garrison]

congregation, who, after years of plotting, succeeded in getting him fired in 1845. It was during this year that he published *The Anti-Slavery Poems*, his second volume of poetry after the well-received 1816 *Airs of Palestine*. He subsequently became a fanatical supporter of spiritualism, yet his finest hour, or at least fortnight, was when he insisted at the age of 76 on joining the 22nd Massachusetts Infantry, where he intended to work during the Civil War as chaplain. He explained with moving simplicity in a letter of 19 September 1861 that he was fighting 'against that infernal power that has been so long serving the devil . . . if indeed the slave power is not the very devil itself'. Unfortunately he was too frail and had to resign after two weeks.

The poetry is not great art, but it is most effective propaganda. Much of it takes the very Garrisonian stance of attempting to whip the abolition reader into a state where she or he is desperate to undergo martyrological sacrifice ('The Tocsin' and 'Plymouth Rock' are typical). 'The Chain' is an interesting poem in that its central argument relates to the differentiation of the suffering of slaves and martyrs. The poem ends by pointing out that the slave has no choice but to endure violence and abuse. The slave's sufferings may outwardly resemble those of Christ and the martyrs, but the horror lies in the fact that the suffering is not volitional, but the result of the fact that to the slave owner the slave is just an animal. The two 'North Star' poems play clever games with diction: while the slave is imagined speaking in a polite elevated literary diction (although his or her grasp of Queen Elizabeth's role in British slavery is way off mark), the slave holder is given a coarse, colloquial racist language. When William Wells Brown (pp. 570–6) wrote of his journey to freedom he described how he and his fellow slaves looked for the North Star. In order to describe the effect of finally seeing the star he quotes extensively from Pierpont's 'North Star'. Brown's moving quotation is an indication of both the popularity and emotional strength which this verse was felt to have at the time.

The Fugitive Slave's Apostrophe to the North Star

Star of the North! though night-winds drift
    The fleecy drapery of the sky,
Between thy lamp and me, I lift,
    Yea, lift with hope, my sleepless eye,
To the blue heights wherein thou dwellest,
And of a land of freedom tellest.

Star of the North! while blazing day
    Pours round me its full tide of light,
And hides thy pale but faithful ray,
    I, too, lie hid, and long for night:
For night;—I dare not walk at noon,
Nor dare I trust the faithless moon,—

Nor faithless man, whose burning lust
　　For gold hath riveted my chain;
No other leader can I trust,
　　But thee, of even the starry train;
For, all the host around thee burning,
Like faithless man, keep turning, turning.

I may not follow where *they* go:
　　Star of the North, I look to thee,
While on I press; for well I know
　　Thy light and truth shall set me free;—
Thy light, that no poor slave deceiveth;
Thy truth, that all my soul believeth.

They of the East beheld the star
　　That over Bethlehem's manger glowed;
With joy they hailed it from afar,
　　And followed where it marked the road,
Till, where its rays directly fell,
They found the hope of Israel.

Wise were the men, who followed thus
　　The star that sets man free from sin!
Star of the North! thou art to us,—
　　Who 're slaves because we wear a skin
Dark as is night's protecting wing,—
Thou art to us a holy thing.

And we are wise to follow thee!
　　I trust thy steady light alone:
Star of the North! thou seem'st to me
　　To burn before the Almighty's throne,
To guide me, through these forests dim
And vast, to liberty and HIM.

Thy beam is on the glassy breast
　　Of the still spring, upon whose brink
I lay my weary limbs to rest,
　　And bow my parching lips to drink.
Guide of the friendless negro's way,
I bless thee for this quiet ray!

In the dark top of southern pines
　　I nestled, when the driver's horn
Called to the field, in lengthening lines,
　　My fellows, at the break of morn.
And there I lay, till thy sweet face
Looked in upon 'my hiding-place.'

The tangled cane-brake,—where I crept,
　　For shelter from the heat of noon,
And where, while others toiled, I slept,
　　Till wakened by the rising moon,—
As its stalks felt the night-wind free,
Gave me to catch a glimpse of thee.

Star of the North! in bright array,
　　The constellations round thee sweep,
Each holding on its nightly way,
　　Rising, or sinking in the deep,
And, as it hangs in mid heaven flaming,
The homage of some nation claiming.

This nation to the Eagle cowers;
　　Fit ensign! she 's a bird of spoil;—
Like worships like! for each devours
　　The earnings of another's toil.
I've felt her talons and her beak,
And now the gentler Lion seek.

The Lion, at the Virgin's feet,
　　Couches, and lays his mighty paw
Into her lap!—an emblem meet
　　Of England's Queen and English law:—
Queen, that hath made her Islands free!
Law that holds out its shield to me!

Star of the North! upon that shield
　　Thou shinest!—O, for ever shine!
The negro, from the cotton-field,
　　Shall then beneath its orb recline,
And feed the Lion couched before it,
Nor heed the Eagle screaming o'er it!

Slave Holder's Address to the North Star

Star of the North, thou art not bigger
    Than is the diamond in my ring;
Yet every black, star-gazing nigger
    Stares at thee, as at some great thing !
Yes, gazes at thee, till the lazy
And thankless rascal is half crazy.

Some Quaker scoundrel must have told 'em
    That, if they take their flight tow'rd thee,
They 'd get where 'massa' cannot hold 'em;
    And, therefore, to the North they flee.
Fools! to be led off, where they can't earn
Their living, by thy lying lantern.

Thou 'rt a cold water star, I reckon,
    Although I 've never seen thee, yet,
When to the bath thy sisters beckon,
    Get even thy golden sandals wet;
Nor in the wave have known thee dip,
In our hot nights, thy finger's tip.

If thou *wouldst*, nightly, leave the pole,
    To enjoy a regular ablution
In the North Sea, or Symmes's hole,[1]
    Our 'Patriarchal Institution,'
From which thou findest many a ransom,
Would, doubtless, give thee something handsome.

Although thou 'rt a cold water star,
    As I have said, I think, already,
Thou 'rt hailed, by many a tipsy tar,
    Who likes thee just because thou 'rt steady,
And hold'st the candle for the rover,
When he is more than 'half seas over.'

But, while Ham's seed,[2] our land to bless,
    'Increase and multiply' like rabbits,

---

[1] Probably a reference to Miami; John Cleves Symmes was responsible for the Miami Purchase.

[2] One of the biblical sanction arguments for slavery was that blacks were the sons of Ham, who had been cursed by God for looking on their father Noah naked. Ham was consequently turned black as a mark of divine disfavour.

We like thee, Yankee Star, the less,
    For thy bright eye, and steady habits.
Pray waltz with Venus, star of love,
Or take a bout with reeling Jove.

Thou art an abolition star,
    And to my wench wilt be of use, if her
Dark eye should find thee, ere the car
    Of our true old slave-catcher, 'Lucifer,'[3]
Star of the morning,' upward rolls,
And, with its light, puts out the pole's.

On our field hands thou lookest, too—
    A sort of nightly overseer—
Canst find no other work to do?
    I tell thee, thou 'rt not wanted here;
So, pray, shine only on the oceans,
Thou number one of 'Northern notions.'

Yes, northern notions,—northern lights!
    As hates the devil holy water,
So hate I all that Rogers[4] writes,
Or Weld,[5] that married Grimkè's daughter:—[6]
So hate I all these northern curses,
From Birney's[7] prose to Whittier's[8] verses.

'Put out the light!'[9] exclaimed the Moor—
    I think they call his name Othello—
When opening his wife's chamber door
    To cut her throat—the princely fellow!
Noblest of all the nigger nation!
File leader in amalgamation!

---

[3] 'Light Giver', an angel who has been associated with Satan.

[4] Nathaniel P. Rogers, follower of Garrison, and also a courageous abolition activist.

[5] Theodore Dwight Weld, great Boston abolitionist and author of the hugely influential propaganda pamphlet *American Slavery as it is; or, Testimony of a Thousand Witnesses*.

[6] Angelina Grimké, a Southerner who married Weld and moved North to become a brilliant and tireless abolition propagandist together with her sister Sarah.

[7] James G. Birney, seminal abolition figure, and one of the masterminds behind the great abolition postal campaign in the early 1830s.

[8] See pp. 496–514.

[9] The famous exclamation of Othello when he contemplates the sleeping form of Desdemona, just before he murders her.

'Put out the light!' and so say I
    Could 'I quench *thee*, thou flaming minister,'
No longer, in the northern sky,
    Should blaze thy beacon-fire so sinister.
North Star, thy light's unwelcome—*very*—
We 'll vote thee 'an incendiary.'

And, to our 'natural allies'—
    Our veteran Kinderhook Invincibles,[10]
Who do our bidding, in the guise
    Of 'northern men, with southern principles,'—
Men who have faces firm as dough,[11]
And, as we *set* their noses, go—

To these, we 'll get some scribe to write,
    And tell them not to let thee shine—
Excepting of a cloudy night—
    Any where, south of Dixon's line.[12]
If, beyond that, thou shin'st, an inch,
We 'll have thee up before Judge Lynch:—

And when, thou abolition star,
    Who preachest freedom, in all weathers,
Thou hast got on a coat of tar,
    And, over that, a cloak of feathers,[13]
That thou art 'fixed' shall none deny,
If there 's a fixed star in the sky.

The Chain

Is it his daily toil, that wrings
    From the slave's bosom that deep sigh?
Is it his niggard fare, that brings
    The tear into his down-cast eye?

---

[10] A group of free-state mercenaries operating in Kinderhook, central Missouri, during the period of the free-soil struggles.

[11] 'Dough-face' was a popular expression for Northerners who supported extreme Southern policies in the ante-bellum period. The word was coined by John Randolph of Virginia in contempt for Northern members of the House of Representatives who would not oppose the extension of slavery to Missouri.

[12] The Mason Dixon line which divided the free from the slave states according to the Missouri Compromise.

[13] A reference to the Southern practice of tarring and feathering abolitionists.

O no; by toil and humble fare,
    Earth's sons their health and vigor gain;
It is because the slave must wear
        His chain.

Is it the sweat, from every pore
    That starts, and glistens in the sun,
As, the young cotton bending o'er,
    His naked back it shines upon?

Is it the drops that, from his breast,
    Into the thirsty furrow fall,
That scald his soul, deny him rest,
    And turn his cup of life to gall?

No;—for, that man with sweating brow
    Shall eat his bread, doth God ordain;
This the slave's spirit doth not bow;
        It is his chain.

Is it, that scorching sands and skies
    Upon his velvet skin have set
A hue, admired in beauty's eyes,
    In Genoa's[1] silks, and polished jet?

No; for this color was his pride,
    When roaming o'er his native plain;
Even here, his hue can he abide,
        But not his chain.

Nor is it, that his back and limbs
    Are scored with many a gory gash,
That his heart bleeds, and his brain swims,
    And the MAN dies beneath the lash.

For Baäl's[2] priests, on Carmel's[3] slope,
    Themselves with knives and lancets scored,
Till the blood spirted,—in the hope
    The god would hear, whom they adored;—

---

[1] Capital of Ligua in north-west Italy, it became an influential port in the Renaissance and famous for imported Eastern silks.

[2] Originally a Phoenician god, but came to stand for any false god.

[3] Sacred mountain in Palestine.

And Christian flagellants[4] their backs,
   All naked, to the scourge have given;
And martyrs to their stakes and racks
   Have gone, of choice, in hope of heaven;—

For here there was an inward WILL!
   Here spake the spirit, upward tending;
And o'er Faith's cloud-girt altar, still,
   Hope hung her rainbow, heavenward bending

But will and hope hath not the slave,
   His bleeding spirit to sustain:—
No,—he must drag on, to the grave,
   His chain.

Frederick Douglass [slave name Frederick Augustus Washington Bailey] (1817/1818?–1895), 'A Parody', printed as appendix to *Narrative of the Life of Frederick Douglass, an American Slave* (1845)

The literature on Douglass is now vast, and there are many standard accounts of his remarkable life. Born to a slave mother, and never sure who his father was, he grew up on the coast of Maryland and was taught to read and write by his mistress. The trauma of his slave life, and the manner in which his mental world evolved as a result of this horror, are set out in the *Narrative*, one of the great books of the nineteenth century. In 1838 he managed, using forged documents, to escape to the North. He was taken up and encouraged by Garrison (see pp. 536–40). By 1845, with the publication of his *Narrative*, he was a focus for the cause of African Americans in the North. He moved to England for two years returning in 1847, his freedom having been officially purchased by the British abolitionists. Differing from Garrison on many issues he moved to Rochester, New York, and began publication of the magnificent *North Star*, which ran from 1847 to 1865 and was a focus for radical black journalism, and which was not restricted to anti-slavery issues. Rather the paper worked at exposing inequality in many areas and opened up a new intellectual agenda for thinking about the role of African Americans in North America. Douglass was both an idealist and a pragmatist. His consultations with John Brown led him to the conviction that only a military invasion of the South could end slavery, although he clearly saw that Brown's catastrophic Harper's Ferry

---

[4] Extreme Christian sects who flagellate themselves as part of their religious rituals.

raid was never going to inaugurate the process. Douglass earned the respect of Lincoln and his circle of advisers and was one of the people who finally convinced the wavering President that he had to draw up the Emancipation Proclamation which finally went through on 1 January 1863. Of much greater practical effect on future policy towards African Americans, he was instrumental in forcing through the Fourteenth and Fifteenth Amendments. He kept fighting for black and women's rights to his death, and indeed collapsed and died after leaving the stage having made a speech for women's suffrage.

Douglass is never talked about as a poet. Yet with a typically dark playfulness he chose to end his masterpiece, the *Narrative,* with the following parody of a popular Southern hymn. Douglass, with a bitter irony, claims that the poem was the work of a Northern minister, but a source has never been found, and there is little doubt that Douglass wrote the piece and that the false attribution adds yet another layer to the satire. The poem itself is a masterpiece of incensed hilarity; it has an almost mad energy within its irony, and a superb economy of expression: the picture of the fashionable young slave holders 'Who dress as sleek as glossy snakes' brilliantly combines natural observation, social satire, and Satanic typology. The stanza form with its pounding four-line repeat-rhyme, followed by the staccato refrain, achieves a cumulative power. This is one of the great abolition protest lyrics; its sarcastic disgust at the appropriation of religion is reminiscent of, though a deal sharper than, Bob Dylan's 'God on our Side'.

A Parody

"Come, saints and sinners, hear me tell
How pious priests whip Jack and Nell,
And women buy and children sell,
And preach all sinners down to hell,
   And sing of heavenly union.

"They'll bleat and baa, dona like goats,
Gorge down black sheep, and strain at motes,
Array their backs in fine black coats,
Then seize their negroes by their throats,
   And choke, for heavenly union.

"They'll church you if you sip a dram,
And damn you if you steal a lamb;
Yet rob old Tony, Doll, and Sam,
Of human rights, and bread and ham;
   Kidnapper's heavenly union.

"They'll loudly talk of Christ's reward,
And bind his image with a cord
And scold, and swing the lash abhorred,
And sell their brother in the Lord
    To handcuffed heavenly union.

"They'll read and sing a sacred song,
And make a prayer both loud and long,
And teach the right and do the wrong,
Hailing the brother, sister throng,
    With words of heavenly union.

"We wonder how such saints can sing,
Or praise the Lord upon the wing,
Who roar, and scold, and whip, and sting,
And to their slaves and mammon cling,
    In guilty conscience union.

"They'll raise tobacco, corn, and rye,
And drive, and thieve, and cheat, and lie,
And lay up treasures in the sky,
By making switch and cowskin fly,
    In hope of heavenly union.

"They'll crack old Tony on the skull,
And preach and roar like Bashan bull,
Or braying ass, of mischief full,
Then seize old Jacob by the wool,
    And pull for heavenly union.

"A roaring, ranting, sleek man-thief,
Who lived on mutton, veal, and beef,
Yet never would afford relief
To needy, sable sons of grief,
    Was big with heavenly union.

" 'Love not the world,' the preacher said,
And winked his eye, and shook his head;
He seized on Tom, and Dick, and Ned,
Cut short their meat, and clothes, and bread,
    Yet still loved heavenly union.

"Another preacher whining spoke
Of One whose heart for sinners broke:

He tied old Nanny to an oak,
And drew the blood at every stroke,
    And prayed for heavenly union.

"Two others oped their iron jaws,
And waved their children-stealing paws;
There sat their children in gewgaws;
By stinting negroes' backs and maws,
    They kept up heavenly union.

"All good from Jack another takes,
And entertains their flirts and rakes,
Who dress as sleek as glossy snakes,
And cram their mouths with sweetened cakes;
    And this goes down for union."

Jessee Huchinson Junior, *The Fugitive's Song* (song sheet, 1845)

Following the celebrity which accrued to Douglass with the publication of his *Narrative*, he became a public figure and the subject of popular songs. Huchinson's lyrics are supposedly put in the mouth of the fleeing Douglass, who is shown as a classic fugitive slave with bundle on stick, on the front cover of the song sheet (Pl. 12). The platitudes which the fictional Douglass is imagined to sing here could hardly have been further from the ruthlessly truthful vision of both Northern and Southern racism which Douglass expressed in his own work.

The Fugitive's Song

I'll be free! I'll be free! and none shall confine,
With fetters and chains this free spirit of mine;
From my youth have I vow'd in my God to rely,
And despite the oppressor gain Freedom or die.
Tho my back is all torn by the merciless rod,
Yet firm is my trust In the right arm of God
In his strength I'll go forth and for ever will be,
'Mong the hills of the North where the Bond-man is Free.
'Mong the hills of the North where the Bond-man is Free.

12. Anon., *The Fugitive's Song* (song sheet cover, stone lithograph, 1845).

Let me go! Let me go! to the land of the brave,
Where shackles must fall from the limbs of the Slave,
Where freedom's proud Eagle screams wild thro' the sky;
And the sweet mountain birds in glad notes reply.
I'll flee to New England where the Fugitive finds,
A home 'mid her mountains and deep forest winds,
And her hill-tops shall ring of the wrongs done to me;
'Till responsive they sing, "Let the Bond-man go Free!"
'Till responsive they sing, "Let the Bond-man go Free."

New England! New England! thrice blessed and free,
The poor hunted slave finds a shelter in thee,
Where no bloodthirsty hounds ever dare on his track;
At thy stern voice, New England! the monsters fall back!
Go back! then ye blood-hounds, that howl on my path,
In the Land of New England I'm free from your wrath,
And the Sons of the Pilgrims my deep scars shall see,
Till they cry with one voice "Let the Bondmen go free."

That voice shall roll on, 'mong the hills of the North,
In murmurs more loud 'till its thunders break forth;
On the wings of the wind shall its deep echoes fly,
Swift as Lightning above, from sky e'en to sky;
Nor Charters nor Unions its mandates shall choke,
'Twill cry in God's Name, "Go Break every Yoke"
Like the tempests of Heaven, shaking mountain and sea,
Shall the North tell the South, "Let the Bondmen go free!"

Great God! hasten on the glad jubilee,
When my brothers in Bonds shall arise and be Free;
And our blotted escutcheon be wash'd from its stains,
Now the scorn of the world,—Three Millions in Chains!
Oh! then shall Columbia's proud flag be unfurl'd,
The glory of Freemen, and pride of the World,
While Earth's struggling millions point hither in glee,
"To the Land of the Brave, and the Home of the Free!"

Ralph Waldo Emerson (1803–82), *Ode Inscribed to W. H. Channing* (1847)

As one of America's first real literary founding fathers and celebrities Emerson's life and works are well researched and documented, yet a detailed study of the full ambiguities of his shifting positions over slavery still needs to be produced.

During the long course of his literary and journalistic career Emerson wrote of slavery repeatedly, and, as with so many of the major nineteenth-century Americans, inconsistently. When he was 19 he wrote a series of long journal entries on 6, 8, and 14 November 1822 on Africans and slavery. The first was a dream vision which presented blacks on the African coast as idealized 'noble savages' violently seized by corrupt Europeans. The latter two entries philosophize about slavery in America, and although they do not support slavery they do exhibit a belief that Africans are an inferior species. In 1837 Emerson went so far in a public speech to announce that the 'black race' had caused its 'own degradation'. Emerson is finally against slavery in principle, but incapable of moving beyond a vision of the black as an abstracted object of suffering. This tendency to abstract black suffering and pacify black personality comes out in essentialized form in his account of slave behaviour during West Indian emancipation. The slave populations of the Caribbean are presented listening to the clock strike twelve: 'on their knees, the silent weeping assembly became men; they rose and embraced each other; they cried, they sung, they prayed, they were wild with joy, but there was no riot, no feasting.' Emerson, like so many educated Northerners, was finally forced to take an extreme stance over slavery and abolition by the passage of the 1850 Fugitive Slave Law, which legally implicated the North in the perpetuation and expansion of the Southern slave systems. After this he wrote in support of abolition, yet his most passionate responses were restricted to outrage at the treatment of white abolitionists, whether the beating of Senator Sumner or the execution of John Brown.

The *Ode* is a good example of Emerson's extraordinary, and international, range as a critic of social abuse. The energetically varied rhyme, and almost spasmodic lineation and metre, mime the exploratory thought of the poet's mind. The poem is also however an articulation of Emerson's indeterminate stance over slavery and white power. While the North is criticized for tolerating the existence of slave hunters, the 'jackals of the negro-holder', it is finally difficult to work out what Emerson is saying about the global processes of imperialization which he gestures towards, and of which slavery is an element. Those crucial lines 'The over-god | Who marries Right to Might, | Who peoples, unpeoples,— | He who exterminates | Races by stronger races, | Black by white faces,— | Knows to bring honey | Out of the lion' need careful analysis. Surely these words articulate with a terrible lucidity the attitudes which would make Emerson such a firm favourite with Europe's two most influential proto-fascists, the Negrophobe Thomas Carlyle and Friedrich Nietzsche. Emerson here seems to be arguing that his *Übermensch* or 'over-god', who presides not only over slavery but over the imperial genocide whereby whites destroy blacks because they are black, is eventually going to produce something sweet, beautiful, and healthy out of the processes of destruction, 'honey | Out of the lion'.

Ode Inscribed to W. H. Channing

Though loath to grieve
The evil time's sole patriot,
I cannot leave
My honied thought
For the priest's cant,
Or statesman's rant.

If I refuse
My study for their politique,
Which at the best is trick,
The angry Muse
Puts confusion in my brain.

But who is he that prates
Of the culture of mankind,
Of better arts and life?
Go, blindworm, go,
Behold the famous States
Harrying Mexico
With rifle and with knife!

Or who, with accent bolder,
Dare praise the freedom-loving mountaineer?
I found by thee, O rushing Contoocook![1]
And in thy valleys, Agiochook![2]
The jackals of the negro-holder.

The God who made New Hampshire
Taunted the lofty land
With little men;—
Small bat and wren

---

[1] Native American name for a river in New Hampshire.
[2] Native American name for the White Mountains of New Hampshire.

House in the oak:—
If earth-fire cleave
The upheaved land, and bury the folk,
The southern crocodile would grieve.
Virtue palters; Right is hence;
Freedom praised, but hid;
Funeral eloquence
Rattles the coffin-lid.

What boots thy zeal,
O glowing friend,
That would indignant rend
The northland from the south?
Wherefore? to what good end?
Boston Bay and Bunker Hill
Would serve things still;—
Things are of the snake.

The horseman serves the horse,
The neatherd serves the neat,
The merchant serves the purse,
The eater serves his meat;
'T is the day of the chattel,
Web to weave, and corn to grind;
Things are in the saddle,
And ride mankind.

There are two laws discrete,
Not reconciled,—
Law for man, and law for thing;
The last builds town and fleet,
But it runs wild,
And doth the man unking.

'T is fit the forest fall,
The steep be graded,
The mountain tunnelled,
The sand shaded,
The orchard planted,
The glebe tilled,
The prairie granted,
The steamer built.

Let man serve law for man;
Live for friendship, live for love,
For truth's and harmony's behoof;
The state may follow how it can,
As Olympus follows Jove.[3]

    Yet do not I implore
The wrinkled shopman to my sounding woods,
Nor bid the unwilling senator
Ask votes of thrushes in the solitudes.
Every one to his chosen work;—
Foolish hands may mix and mar;
Wise and sure the issues are.
Round they roll till dark is light,
Sex to sex, and even to odd;—
The over-god
Who marries Right to Might,
Who peoples, unpeoples,—
He who exterminates
Races by stronger races,
Black by white faces,—
Knows to bring honey
Out of the lion;[4]
Grafts gentlest scion
On pirate and Turk.

The Cossack eats Poland,[5]
Like stolen fruit;
Her last noble is ruined,
Her last poet mute:
Straight, into double band

The victors divide;
Half for freedom strike and stand—
The astonished Muse finds thousands at her side.

---

[3] Jove traditionally lives on top of Mount Olympus, together with the other twelve Olympian gods. It is the highest mountain peak in Greece.

[4] Reference to Samson's famous riddle to the Philistine, Judges 14: 8–14: 'Out of the eater came forth meat, and out of the strong came forth sweetness'; Samson had earlier seen a lion's carcass with a bee's nest and hence honey inside it.

[5] A reference to the recent efforts of Russia brutally to subjugate Poland.

James Russell Lowell (1819–91), 'The Present Crisis' (1843); 'No. V: The Debate in the Sennit', 'No. IX: A Third Letter from B. Sawin, Esq.', in *The Biglow Papers* [1846](1848)

Lowell had a varied career the public highlights of which were in 1855 when he was appointed professor of literature at Harvard, and in the 1870s and 1880s when he was consecutively Foreign Minister to Spain and then Britain. He began his career as a lawyer, but constantly wrote poems and essays for many of the leading East Coast literary journals.

Lowell's importance both as a journalist and poet on slavery lies in the breadth of his attack on colour prejudice. Lowell could fall into the prescribed modes of thinking about African-American slaves: they can be seen as degenerate 'niggers', or as abstracted ideals of suffering –black Christ substitutes. But where Lowell was unique among contemporary critics of race was in his ability to reveal how Northern hypocrisy operated. He attacked the colour prejudice directed against free blacks in the North and was particularly virulent in his criticisms of the Church's role in perpetuating prejudice.

In 1843 Lowell became a committed abolitionist and during this year wrote a series of uplifting popular poems on the subject, including 'Stanzas on Freedom', 'Wendell Phillips', and the lastingly and widely popular 'The Present Crisis'. The latter poem, with its mesmeric metre, switching on the last foot from tetrameter to the unusual trimetric *amphimacer* (an emphatic stress-unstress-stress u-x-u), cries out for declamation and was a favourite with pubic abolition orators. The poem climaxes with what is the most violent and ecstatic summarization of the abolition drive to martyrdom. The verse at points calls forth the imagery of Foxe's *Book of Martyrs* and the accounts of the Marian persecutions: 'Far in front the cross stands ready and the crackling faggots burn.' The conclusion reiterates the standard abolition argument that the same sacrifice and religious idealism which took the Pilgrim Fathers to America must be reinvented in the hearts of abolitionists. If abolition had a single poetic anthem then this was it.

In 1846 however Lowell took an unexpected turn in his poetic development. In this year the Boston *Courier* began publishing a sequence of poems in extreme Yankee colloquial dialect, which purported to be written by Hosea Biglow. The poems were collected and published in 1848 as 'First Series' of the famous *Biglow Papers*. In book form the poems were surrounded by an ornate parodic apparatus including mock and mostly outraged press reviews, letters commenting on the verse, and notes by a fictional editor, the Revd Homer Wilbur. Lowell explained his satiric strategy in linguistic terms, stating that he 'needed on occasion to rise above the level of mere *patois*, and for this purpose conceived the Rev. Mr. Wilbur who should express the more cautious element of New England character and its pedantry, as Mr. Biglow should serve for its homely common-sense vivified and heated by conscience' (*The Writings of James Russell*

Lowell in Ten Volumes (Houghton Mifflin & Co., 1890), viii. 155–6). The immediate subject of *The Biglow Papers* was the Mexican War, which for Lowell is an event centrally connected to the extension of Southern slavery into new territory. 'The Debate in the Sennit' is an attack on the great defender of slavery and expansionist John C. Calhoun, and after the prefatory letter the poem is set in the popular parodic form of a mock children's nursery rhyme. In the later poems Lowell introduced the character of the itinerant soldier 'Birdofredum Sawin' whose letters home Hosea translates into verse. It is from one of these poems that the extracts below on slavery are taken, giving Birdofredum's ill-fated and nefarious activities in the Mexican War.

Lowell deserves pride of place in this anthology because *The Biglow Papers* were enormously popular in Britain as well as America. From 1848 to 1860 they were among the most successful transatlantic abolition writing, and were only to be superseded in mass public response in Britain by Stowe's 1852 *Uncle Tom's Cabin* (for poetic versions of Stowe see pp. 382–92). A measure of their popularity is indicated by the fact that the first English edition was illustrated by George Cruikshank, the most famous graphic artist in the world. Yet the plates show Cruikshank applying the same Negrophobe stereotypes to the depiction of blacks as he was to use in his equally popular plates to *Uncle Tom's Cabin*.

The Present Crisis

WHEN a deed is done for Freedom, through the broad earth's
    aching breast
Runs a thrill of joy prophetic, trembling on from east to west,
And the slave, where'er he cowers, feels the soul within him climb
To the awful verge of manhood, as the energy sublime
Of a century bursts full-blossomed on the thorny stem of Time.

Through the walls of hut and palace shoots the instantaneous throe,
When the travail of the Ages wrings earth's systems to and fro;
At the birth of each new Era, with a recognizing start,
Nation wildly looks at nation, standing with mute lips apart,
And glad Truth's yet mightier man-child leaps beneath
    the Future's heart.

So the Evil's triumph sendeth, with a terror and a chill,
Under continent to continent, the sense of coming ill,
And the slave, where'er he cowers, feels his sympathies with God
In hot tear-drops ebbing earthward, to be drunk up by the sod,
Till a corpse crawls round unburied, delving in the nobler clod.

For mankind are one in spirit, and an instinct bears along,
Round the earth's electric circle, the swift flash of right or wrong;
Whether conscious or unconscious, yet Humanity's vast frame
Through its ocean-sundered fibres feels the gush of joy or shame;—
In the gain or loss of one race all the rest have equal claim.

Once to every man and nation comes the moment to decide,
In the strife of Truth with Falsehood, for the good or evil side;
Some great cause, God's new Messiah, offering each the bloom or blight,
Parts the goats upon the left hand, and the sheep upon the right,
And the choice goes by forever 'twixt that darkness and that light.

Hast thou chosen, O my people, on whose party thou shalt stand,
Ere the Doom from its worn sandals shakes the dust against our land?
Though the cause of Evil prosper, yet 't is Truth alone is strong,
And, albeit she wander outcast now, I see around her throng
Troops of beautiful, tall angels, to enshield her from all wrong.

Backward look across the ages and the beacon-moments see,
That, like peaks of some sunk continent, jut through Oblivion's sea;
Not an ear in court or market for the low foreboding cry
Of those Crises, God's stern winnowers, from whose feet
    earth's chaff must fly;
Never shows the choice momentous till the judgement hath passed by.

Careless seems the great Avenger; history's pages but record
One death-grapple in the darkness 'twixt old systems and the Word;
Truth forever on the scaffold, Wrong forever on the throne,—
Yet that scaffold sways the future, and, behind the dim unknown,
Standeth God within the shadow, keeping watch above his own.

We see dimly in the Present what is small and what is great,
Slow of faith, how weak an arm may turn the iron helm of fate,
But the soul is still oracular; amid the market's din,
List the ominous stern whisper from the Delphic[1] cave within,—
'They enslave their children's children who make compromise with sin.'

Slavery, the earth-born Cyclops,[2] fellest of the giant brood,
Sons of brutish Force and Darkness, who have drenched the
    earth with blood,

---

[1] Relating to Delphi a town of ancient Greece, and to its famous oracle, hence oracular.
[2] One of a fabled race of giants, who were supposed mainly to inhabit Sicily; they were distinguished by having only a single eye, in the middle of the forehead.

Famished in his self-made desert, blinded by our purer day,
Gropes in yet unblasted regions for his miserable prey;—
Shall we guide his gory fingers where our helpless children play?

Then to side with Truth is noble when we share her wretched crust,
Ere her cause bring fame and profit, and 't is prosperous to be just;
Then it is the brave man chooses, while the coward stands aside,
Doubting in his abject spirit, till his Lord is crucified,
And the multitude make virtue of the faith they had denied.

Count me o'er earth's chosen heroes,—they were souls that stood alone,
While the men they agonized for hurled the contumelious stone,
Stood serene, and down the future saw the golden beam incline
To the side of perfect justice, mastered by their faith divine,
By one man's plain truth to manhood and to God's supreme design.

By the light of burning heretics Christ's bleeding feet I track,
Toiling up new Calvaries[3] ever with the cross that turns not back,
And these mounts of anguish number how each generation learned
One new word of that grand *Credo*[4] which in prophet-hearts hath burned
Since the first man stood God-conquered with his face to heaven upturned.

For Humanity sweeps onward: where to-day the martyr stands,
On the morrow crouches Judas with the silver in his hands;
Far in front the cross stands ready and the crackling fagots burn,
While the hooting mob of yesterday in silent awe return
To glean up the scattered ashes into History's golden urn.

'T is as easy to be heroes as to sit the idle slaves
Of a legendary virtue carved upon our fathers' graves,
Worshippers of light ancestral make the present light a crime;—
Was the Mayflower launched by cowards, steered by men
  behind their time?
Turn those tracks toward Past or Future, that make
  Plymouth Rock sublime?

They were men of present valour, stalwart old iconoclasts,
Unconvinced by axe or gibbet that all virtue was the Past's;
But we make their truth our falsehood, thinking that hath made us free,
Hoarding it in mouldy parchments, while our tender spirits flee
The rude grasp of that great Impulse which drove them across the sea.

---

[3] The name of the place where Jesus was crucified.
[4] Literally 'I believe'; the Credo is the formal set of Christian beliefs.

They have rights who dare maintain them; we are traitors to our sires,
Smothering in their holy ashes Freedom's new-lit altar-fires;
Shall we make their creed our jailer? Shall we, in our haste to slay,
From the tombs of the old prophets steal the funeral lamps away
To light up the martyr-fagots round the prophets of to-day?

New occasions teach new duties: Time makes ancient good uncouth;
They must upward still, and onward, who would keep abreast of Truth;
Lo, before us gleam her camp-fires! we ourselves must Pilgrims be,
Launch our Mayflower, and steer boldly through the desperate winter sea,
Nor attempt the Future's portal with the Past's blood rusted key.

No. V: The Debate in the Sennit[1]

SOT TO A NUSRY RHYME

[The incident which gave rise to the debate satirized in the following verses was the unsuccessful attempt of Drayton and Sayres to give freedom to seventy men and women, fellow-beings and fellow-Christians. Had Tripoli, instead of Washington, been the scene of this undertaking, the unhappy leaders in it would have been as secure of the theoretic as they now are of the practical part of martyrdom. I question whether the Dey of Tripoli is blessed with a District Attorney so benighted as ours at the seat of government. Very fitly is he named Key,[2] who would allow himself to be made the instrument of locking the door of hope against sufferers in such a cause. Not all the waters of the ocean can cleanse the vile smutch of the jailer's fingers from off that little Key. *Ahenea clavis*,[3] a brazen Key indeed!

Mr. Calhoun, who is made the chief speaker in this burlesque, seems to think that the light of the nineteenth century is to be put out as soon as he tinkles his little cow-bell curfew. Whenever slavery is touched, he sets up his scarecrow of dissolving the Union. This may do for the North, but I should conjecture that something more than a pumpkin-lantern is required to scare manifest and

---

[1] The debate in question relates to a series of recent events. In 1848 Captain Edward Sayres and Daniel Drayton had attempted to smuggle seventy-six slaves out of Washington to freedom on a boat. They were captured and arrested. Gamiliel Bailey, editor of the extreme abolitionist newspaper the *National Era*, was suspected of being involved in the escape plan and his offices were attacked by a mob. Following the attack Senator John Hale of New Hampshire tried to get a bill through which would give Bailey compensation; the Southern Senators were up in arms and a spectacularly vitriolic debate ensued.

[2] Philip Barton Key, son of Francis Key, author of 'The Star-Spangled Banner'.

[3] A learned pun: *ahenea clavis* is a brass key; Lowell is using the adjective brazen to mean both 'made of brass' and 'impudent', in other words to say that Key is an impudent man.

irretrievable Destiny out of her path. Mr. Calhoun cannot let go the apron-string of the Past. The Past is a good nurse, but we must be weaned from her sooner or later, even though, like Plotinus,[4] we should run home from school to ask the breast, after we are tolerably well-grown youths. It will not do for us to hide our faces in her lap, whenever the strange Future holds out her arms and asks us to come to her.

But we are all alike. We have all heard it said, often enough, that little boys must not play with fire; and yet, if the matches be taken away from us and put out of reach upon the shelf, we must needs get into our little corner, and scowl and stamp and threaten the dire revenge of going to bed without our supper. The world shall stop till we get our dangerous plaything again. Dame Earth, meanwhile, who has more than enough household matters to mind, goes bustling hither and thither as a hiss or a sputter tells her that this or that kettle of hers is boiling over, and before bedtime we are glad to eat our porridge cold, and gulp down our dignity along with it.

Mr. Calhoun has somehow acquired the name of a great statesman, and, if it be great statesmanship to put lance in rest and run a tilt at the Spirit of the Age with the certainty of being next moment hurled neck and heels into the dust amid universal laughter, he deserves the title. He is the Sir Kay[5] of our modern chivalry. He should remember the old Scandinavian mythus. Thor was the strongest of gods, but he could not wrestle with Time, nor so much as lift up a fold of the great snake which bound the universe together; and when he smote the Earth, though with his terrible mallet, it was but as if a leaf had fallen. Yet all the while it seemed to Thor that he had only been wrestling with an old woman, striving to lift a cat, and striking a stupid giant on the head.

And in old times, doubtless, the giants *were* stupid, and there was no better sport for the Sir Launcelots and Sir Gawains than to go about cutting off their great blundering heads with enchanted swords. But things have wonderfully changed. It is the giants, now-a-days, that have the science and the intelligence, while the chivalrous Don Quixotes of Conservatism still cumber themselves with the clumsy armour of a by-gone age. On whirls the restless globe through unsounded time, with its cities and its silences, its births and funerals, half light, half shade, but never wholly dark, and sure to swing round into the happy morning at last. With an involuntary smile, one sees Mr. Calhoun letting slip his pack-thread cable with a crooked pin at the end of it to anchor South Carolina upon the bank and shoal of the Past—H.W.]

---

[4] The famous Neo-platonic philosopher; the story about his quest for breast milk was recounted by one of his students.

[5] One of the knights of the Round Table, he is Arthur's foster-brother and distinguished by his boastfulness.

TO MR. BUCKENAM.

MR. EDITER, As i wuz kinder prunin round, in a little nussry sot out a year or 2 ago, the Dbait in the sennit cum inter my mine An so i took & Sot it to wut I call a nussry rime. I hev made sum onnable Gentlemun speak thut dident speak in a Kind uv Poetikul lie sense the seeson is dreffle backerd up This way

ewers as ushul

HOSEA BIGLOW.

"HERE we stan' on the Constitution, by thunder!
It 's a fact o' wich ther 's bushils o' proofs;
Fer how could we trample on 't so, I wonder,
Ef 't worn 't thet it 's ollers under our hoofs?"
Sez John C. Calhoun, sez he;
"Human rights haint no more
Right to come on this floor,
No more 'n the man in the moon," sez he.

"The North haint no kind o' bisness with nothin',
An' you 've no idee how much bother it saves;
We aint none riled by their frettin' an' frothin',
We 're *used* to layin' the string on our slaves,"
Sez John C. Calhoun, sez he;—
Sez Mister Foote,
"I should like to shoot
The holl gang, by the gret horn spoon!"[6] sez he.

"Freedom's Keystone is Slavery, thet ther 's no doubt on,
It's sutthin' thet 's—wha' d' ye call it?—divine,—
An' the slaves thet we ollers *make* the most out on
Air them north o' Mason an' Dixon's line,"
Sez John C. Calhoun, sez he;—
"Fer all thet," sez Mangum,
" 'T would be better to hang 'em,
An' so git red on 'em soon," sez he.

"The mass ough' to labor an' we lay on soffies,
Thet's the reason I want to spread Freedom's aree;
It puts all the cunninest on us in office,
An' reelises our Maker's orig'nal idee,"

---

[6] 'By the great horn spoon' was a general term for a completely ludicrous oath.

Sez John C. Calhoun, sez he;—
    "Thet 's ez plain," sez Cass,
    "Ez thet some one's an ass,
It's ez clear ez the sun is at noon," sez he.

"Now don't go to say I 'm the friend of oppression,
    But keep all your spare breath fer coolin' your broth,
Fer I ollers hev strove (at least thet 's my impression)
    To make cussed free with the rights o' the North,"
        Sez John C. Calhoun, sez he;—
            "Yes," sez Davis o' Miss.,
            "The perfection o' bliss
        Is in skinnin' thet same old coon."[7] sez he.

"Slavery's a thing thet depends on complexion,
    It's God's law thet fetters on black skins don't chafe;
Ef brains wuz to settle it (horrid reflection!)
    Wich of our onnable body 'd be safe?"
        Sez John C. Calhoun, sez he;—
            Sez Mister Hannegan,
            Afore he began agin,
        "Thet exception is quite oppertoon," sez he.

"Gen'nle Cass, Sir, you need n't be twitchin' your collar,
    Your merit's quite clear by the dut on your knees,
At the North we don't make no distinctions o' color;
    You can all take a lick at our shoes wen you please,"
        Sez John C. Calhoun, sez he;—
            Sez Mister Jarnagin,
            "They wunt hev to larn agin,
        They all on 'em know the old toon," sez he.

"The slavery question aint no ways bewilderin'.
    North an' South hev one int'rest, it 's plain to a glance;
No'thern men, like us patriarchs, don't sell their childrin,
    But they *du* sell themselves, ef they git a good chance,"
        Sez John C. Calhoun, sez he;—
            Sez Atherton here,
            "This is gittin' severe,
        I wish I could dive like a loon," sez he.

---

[7] In America at this time the racoon was used as an epithet denoting slyness.

"It 'll break up the Union, this talk about freedom,
      An' your fact'ry gals (soon ez we split) 'll make head,
An' gittin' some Miss chief or other to lead 'em,
      'll go to work raisin' permiscoous Ned,"[8]
            Sez John C. Calhoun, sez he;—
                  "Yes, the North," sez Colquitt,
                  "Ef we Southeners all quit,
            Would go down like a busted balloon," sez he.

"Jest look wut is doin', wut annyky 's brewin'
      In the beautiful clime o' the olive an' vine,
All the wise aristoxy 's a tumblin' to ruin,
      An' the sankylots[9] drorin' an' drinkin' their wine,"
            Sez John C. Calhoun, sez he;—
                  "Yes," sez Johnson, "in France
                  They're beginnin' to dance
            Beelzebub's own rigadoon,"[10] sez he.

"The South's safe enough, it don't feel a mite skeery,
      Our slaves in their darkness an' dut air tu blest
Not to welcome with proud hallylugers[11] the ery
      Wen our eagle kicks yourn from the naytional nest,"
            Sez John C. Calhoun, sez he;—
                  "O," sez Westcott o' Florida,
                  "Wut treason is horrider
            Then our priv'leges tryin' to proon?" sez he.

"It 's 'coz they 're so happy, thet, wen crazy sarpints
      Stick their nose in our bizness, we git so darned riled;
We think it 's our dooty to give pooty sharp hints,
      Thet the last crumb of Edin on airth shan't be spiled,"
            Sez John C. Calhoun, sez he;—
                  "Ah," sez Dixon H. Lewis,
                  "It perfectly true is
            Thet slavery 's airth's grettest boon," sez he.

---

[8] 'To raise merry/promiscuous Ned' meant 'to stir up trouble'.
[9] A Yankee dialect spelling of the loanword 'sansculottes', adopted into English during the French Revolution. In the Revolution this was the court party nickname for the democrats, meaning apparently wearing long trousers as opposed to knee-breaches (culottes). The term had come to stand for any extreme political revolutionary or radical by the time Lowell adopted it.
[10] A lively jig type of dance, performed by a single couple, or the music for the dance.
[11] Hallelujahs.

[It was said of old time, that riches have wings; and, though this be not applicable in a literal strictness to the wealth of our patriarchal brethren of the South, yet it is clear that their possessions have legs, and an unaccountable propensity for using them in a northerly direction. I marvel that the grand jury of Washington did not find a true bill against the North Star for aiding and abetting Drayton and Sayres. It would have been quite of a piece with the intelligence displayed by the South on other questions connected with slavery. I think that no ship of state was ever freighted with a more veritable Jonah[12] than this same domestic institution of ours. Mephistopheles[13] himself could not feign so bitterly, so satirically sad a sight as this of three millions of human beings crushed beyond help or hope by this one mighty argument,—*Our fathers knew no better!* Nevertheless, it is the unavoidable destiny of Jonahs to be cast overboard sooner or later. Or shall we try the experiment of hiding our Jonah in a safe place, that none may lay hands on him to make jetsam of him? Let us, then, with equal forethought and wisdom, lash ourselves to the anchor, and await, in pious confidence, the certain result. Perhaps our suspicious passenger is no Jonah after all, being black. For it is well known that a superintending Providence made a kind of sandwich of Ham[14] and his descendants, to be devoured by the Caucasian race.

In God's name, let all, who hear nearer and nearer the hungry moan of the storm and the growl of the breakers, speak out! But, alas! we have no right to interfere. If a man pluck an apple of mine, he shall be in danger of the justice; but if he steal my brother, I must be silent. Who says this? Our Constitution, consecrated by the callous consuetude of sixty years, and grasped in triumphant argument by the left hand of him whose right hand clutches the clotted slave-whip. Justice, venerable with the undethronable majesty of countless æons, says,—SPEAK! The Past, wise with the sorrows and desolations of ages, from amid her shattered fanes and wolf-housing palaces, echoes,—SPEAK! Nature, through her thousand trumpets of freedom, her stars, her sunrises, her seas, her winds, her cataracts, her mountains blue with cloudy pines, blows jubilant encouragement, and cries,—SPEAK! From the soul's trembling abysses, the still, small voice not vaguely murmurs,—SPEAK! But, alas! the Constitution and the Honorable Mr. Bagowind, M. C., say,—BE DUMB!]

---

[12] Jonah, the biblical prophet, attempted to flee the Lord by getting onto a ship, but the boat was then afflicted with foul weather and the sailors, feeling Jonah to be the cause, threw him overboard where he was swallowed by the whale.

[13] Literally 'he who loves not the light'; a fallen angel, one of the seven great angels of hell. In secular literature Mephistopheles is either a minion of Satan or a stand-in for Satan, but is not the devil himself.

[14] See p. 544 n. 2.

No. IX: A Third Letter from B. Sawin, Esq.

.   .   .   .   .   .

Ez fer the niggers, I 've ben South, an' thet hez changed my min';
A lazier, more ongrateful set you could n't nowers fin'.
You know I mentioned in my last thet I should buy a nigger,
Ef I could make a purchase at a pooty mod'rate figger;
So, ez there 's nothin' in the world I 'm fonder of 'an gunnin',
I closed a bargin finally to take a feller runnin'.
I shou'dered queen's-arm an' stumped out, an', wen
    I come t' th' swamp,
'T worn't very long afore I gut upon the nest o' Pomp;
I come acrost a kin' o' hut, an', playin' round the door,
Some little woollyheaded cubs, ez many 'z six or more.
At fust I thought o' firin', but *think twice* is safest ollers;
There aint, thinks I, not one on 'em but 's wuth his twenty dollars,
Or would be, ef I hed 'em back into a Christian land,—
How temptin' all on 'em would look upon an auctionstand!
(Not but wut *I* hate Slavery in th' abstract, stem to starn,—
I leave it ware our fathers did, a privit State consarn.)
Soon 'z they see me, they yelled an' run, but Pomp wuz out ahoein'
A leetle patch o' corn he hed, or else there aint no knowin'
He would n't ha' took a pop at me; but I hed gut the start,
An' wen he looked, I vow he groaned ez though he 'd broke his heart;
He done it like a wite man, tu, ez nat'ral ez a pictur,
The imp'dunt, pis'nous hypocrite! wus 'an a boy constrictur.
"You can't gum *me*, I tell ye now, an' so you need n't try,
I 'xpect my eye-teeth every mail, so jest shet up," sez I.
"Don't go to actin' ugly now, or else I 'll let her strip,
You 'd best draw kindly, seein' 'z how I 've gut ye on the hip;
Besides, you darned ole fool, it aint no gret of a disaster
To be benev'lently druv back to a contented master,
Ware you hed Christian priv'ledges you don't seem quite aware on,
Or you 'd ha' never run away from bein' well took care on;
Ez fer kin' treatment, wy, he wuz so fond on ye, he said
He 'd give a fifty spot right out, to git ye, 'live or dead;
Wite folks aint sot by half ez much; 'member I run away,
Wen I wuz bound to Cap'n Jakes, to Mattysqumscot bay;
Don' know him, likely? Spose not; wal, the mean ole codger went
An' offered—wut reward, think? Wal, it worn't no *less* 'n a cent."

Wal, I jest gut 'em into line, an' druv 'em on afore me,
The pis'nous brutes, I 'd no idee o' the illwill they bore me;
We walked till som'ers about noon, an' then it grew so hot
I thought it best to camp awile, so I chose out a spot
Jest under a magnoly tree, an' there right down I sot;
Then I unstrapped my wooden leg, coz it begun to chafe,
An' laid it down 'long side o' me, supposin' all wuz safe;
I made my darkies all set down around me in a ring,
An' sot an' kin' o' ciphered up how much the lot would bring;
But, wile I drinked the peaceful cup of a pure heart an' min',
(Mixed with some wiskey, now an' then,) Pomp he snaked up behin',
An', creepin' grad'lly close tu, ez quiet ez a mink,
Jest grabbed my leg, an' then pulled foot, quicker 'an you could wink,
An', come to look, they each on 'em hed gut behin' a tree,
An' Pomp poked out the leg apiece, jest so ez I could see,
An' yelled to me to throw away my pistils an' my gun,
Or else thet they 'd cair off the leg an' fairly cut an' run.
I vow I did n't b'lieve there wuz a decent alligatur
Thet hed a heart so destitoot o' common human natur;
However, ez there worn't no help, I finally give in
An' heft my arms away to git my leg safe back agin.
Pomp gethered all the weapins up, an' then he come an' grinned,
He showed his ivory some, I guess, an' sez, "You 're fairly pinned;
Jest buckle on your leg agin, an' git right up an' come,
'T wun't du fer fammerly men like me to be so long frum hum."
At fust I put my foot right down an' swore I would n't budge,
"Jest ez you choose," sez he, quite cool, "either be shot or trudge."
So this blackhearted monster took an' act'lly druv me back
Along the very feetmarks o' my happy mornin' track,
An' kep' me pris'ner 'bout six months, an' worked me, tu, like sin,
Till I hed gut his corn an' his Carliny taters in;
He made me larn him readin', tu, (although the critter saw
How much it hut my morril sense to act agin the law,)
So 'st he could read a Bible he 'd gut; an' axed ef I could pint
The North Star out; but there I put his nose some out o' jint,
Fer I weeled roun' about sou'west, an', lookin' up a bit,
Picked out a middlin' shiny one an' tole him thet wuz it.
Fin'lly, he took me to the door, an', givin' me a kick,
Sez,—"Ef you know wut's best fer ye, be off, now, double quick;
The wintertime's acomin' on, an', though I gut ye cheap,
You 're so darned lazy, I don't think you 're hardly wuth your keep;

Besides, the childrin's growin' up, an' you aint jest the model
I 'd like to hev 'em immertate, an' so you 'd better toddle!"

Now is there any thin' on airth 'll ever prove to me
Thet renegader slaves like him air fit fer bein' free?
D' you think they 'll suck me in to jine the Buff 'lo chaps, an' them
Rank infidels thet go agin the Scriptur'l cus o' Shem?
Not by a jugfull! sooner 'n thet, I 'd go thru fire an' water;
Wen I hev once made up my mind, a meet'nhus aint sotter;
No, not though all the crows thet flies to pick my bones wuz cawin',—
I guess we're in a Christian land,—

Yourn,

BIRDOFREDUM SAWIN.

William Wells Brown (1814?-1884), 'Jefferson's Daughter', in *The Anti-Slavery Harp* (1848); 'Oh Master', 'See These Poor Souls from Africa?', in *Narrative of William W. Brown Fugitive Slave* (1848); 'To William Wells Brown, the American Fugitive Slave, by E. S. Mathews', in *The American Fugitive in Europe* (1854)

Although he wrote little significant anti-slavery verse himself Brown was the most able and ambitious ex-slave anti-slavery propagandist. As a textual strategist of abolition he stands beside the other two great multi-media abolitionists Lydia Maria Child (pp. 472–82) and Elizur Wright. Brown wrote a great number of works in many different forms, including an anti-slavery novel, two anti-slavery plays (one of them lost), a narrative of his life, and books concerning his life and travels in Europe and America. He also wrote a mass of journalism and was a keen early scholar and collector of African-American and ex-slave authors and activists producing important early anthologies and biographical compendia. As an abolition anthologist his work is of the first importance. The poems selected here are from three sources, his classic *Narrative*, his celebratory but edgy take on European travel literature *The American Fugitive in Europe*, and his hymn and poetry anthology *The Anti-Slavery Harp*.

Brown's corpus has now generated a hefty critical literature, but it has not been noticed that of all the ex-slave authors his work is more heavily steeped in poetical quotation than any other. Both the *Narrative* and the *American Fugitive* weave poetry in and out of the text; poetic citation is used as a sort of shorthand to describe certain extreme emotional states, or to essentialize moral arguments. Brown is also prepared to quote the poetry of slaves. The following short extract from the *Narrative* shows Brown's sophisticated pastiche approach to the use of poetic resources. The prose describes with a detached exactitude the horrific separation of slave mother and child, as one incident during the journey of a slave coffle. Yet Brown isolates the event and then comments upon it, first through the quotation of a melodramatic and even sentimental abolition ballad. This is then followed by another short burst of detached prose providing another horrific detail, and following this Brown quotes a rearranged version of a slave song, which deals with ultimate pain in terms of a biblical language tending towards typological abstraction. Brown emerges as a literary craftsman who is capable of using different poetic resources within the larger structures of the slave narrative.

In the preface to *The Anti-Slavery Harp* Brown argues for the effectiveness of song as an anti-slavery publicity form, and states that he has drawn on two earlier anthologies, Jairus Lincoln's *Anti-Slavery Melodies* and George W. Clark's *The Liberty Minstrel*. Although he drew very heavily on these collections, including the lyrics but leaving out the music, he added many more poems and songs gleaned from anti-slavery newspapers.

Overall the collection was an intriguing gallimaufry of what was known and not so well known. Poems by Whittier, Garrison, and Lowell are included, as might be expected, and also Pierpont's satiric 'Slave holder's Address to the North Star' (see pp. 544–6). Brown also included the satiric 'Colonization Song to the Free Colored People', another poem which ironically reiterates anti-black arguments in parodic form. It was unusual to include such bitter satire in a popular abolition songster. It is also indicative of Brown's radicalism, especially given that at this point he claimed to be a Garrisonian pacifist, that there are two fairly bloodthirsty poems by women. Mrs G. G. Carter's 'Ye Sons of Freemen' was to be sung to the tune of the sanguineous 'La Marseillaise', and Mrs Sarah Towne's 'On to Victory' to the no less violent tune of Burns's 'Scots wha ha'e wi' Wallace bled'. Most revolutionary of all, however, was Brown's inclusion of one of his own poems focused on the sale of a slave woman supposed to be the bastard slave daughter of Thomas Jefferson. 'Jefferson's Daughter' had appeared nine years before in *Tait's Edinburgh Magazine*, July 1839, and then again in Garrison's *Liberator*, 26 May 1848. The prefatory statement regarding the sale was reproduced from the earlier printings. Brown, whose work systematically attacks American hypocrisy over the War of Independence, given the history of slavery in North and South, singled out this detail from Jefferson's biography as the basis for a novel, *Clotel; or, The President's Daughter*. His verse treatment is again a satire, but it moves, with its rousing anapaestic metre, from the satiric accusation of the opening to straightforward outrage by the end.

Jefferson's Daughter

"It is asserted, on the authority of an American Newspaper, that the daughter of Thomas Jefferson, late President of the United States, was sold at New Orleans for $1,000."—Morning Chronicle

Can the blood that, at Lexington,[1] poured o'er the plain,
When the sons warred with tyrants their rights to uphold,
Can the tide of Niagara wipe out the stain?
No! Jefferson's child has been bartered for gold!

Do you boast of your freedom? Peace, babblers—be still;
Prate not of the goddess who scarce deigns to hear;
Have ye power to unbind? Are ye wanting in will?
Must the groans of your bondman still torture the ear?

The daughter of Jefferson sold for a slave!
The child of a freeman for dollars and francs!
The roar of applause, when your orators rave,
Is lost in the sound of her chain, as it clanks.

Peace, then, ye blasphemers of Liberty's name!
Though red was the blood by your forefathers spilt,
Still redder your cheeks should be mantled with shame,
Till the spirit of freedom shall cancel the guilt.

But the brand of the slave is the tint of his skin,
Though his heart may beat loyal and true underneath;
While the soul of the tyrant is rotten within,
And his white the mere cloak to the blackness of death.

Are ye deaf to the plaints that each moment arise?
Is it thus ye forget the mild precepts of Penn,—[2]
Unheeding the clamor that "maddens the skies,"
As ye trample the rights of your dark fellow-men?

When the incense that glows before Liberty's shrine,
Is unmixed with the blood of the galled and oppressed,—
O, then, and then only, the boast may be thine,
That the stripes and stars wave o'er a land of the blest.

---

[1] Opening battle of the War of Independence. British troops marched from Boston to seize colonial stores from Concord and met colonial militia at Lexington; the British then opened fire.
[2] William Penn (1644–1718), English Quaker who became the leader and founder of the Pennsylvania colony in America, which was established as a utopia for the English Quakers.

Narrative of William W. Brown

. . . . .

We put up at night with an acquaintance of Mr. Walker, and in the morning, just as we were about to start, the child again commenced crying. Walker stepped up to her, and told her to give the child to him. The mother tremblingly obeyed. He took the child by one arm, as you would a cat by the leg, walked into the house, and said to the lady,

"Madam, I will make you a present of this little nigger; it keeps such a noise that I can't bear it."

"Thank you, sir," said the lady.

The mother, as soon as she saw that her child was to be left, ran up to Mr. Walker, and falling upon her knees, begged him to let her have her child; she clung around his legs, and cried, "Oh, my child! my child! master, do let me have my child! oh, do, do, do! I will stop its crying if you will only let me have it again." When I saw this woman crying for her child so piteously, a shudder—a feeling akin to horror—shot through my frame. I have often since in imagination heard her crying for her child:—

> "O, master, let me stay to catch
>   My baby's sobbing breath,
> His little glassy eye to watch,
>   And smooth his limbs in death.
>
> And cover him with grass and leaf,
>   Beneath the large oak tree:
> It is not sullenness, but grief—
>   O, master, pity me!
>
> The morn was chill—I spoke no word,
>   But feared my babe might die,
> And heard all day, or thought I heard,
>   My little baby cry.
>
> At noon, oh, how I ran and took
>   My baby to my breast!
> I lingered—and the long lash broke
>   My sleeping infant's rest.
>
> I worked till night—till darkest night,
>   In torture and disgrace;
> Went home and watched till morning light,
>   To see my baby's face.

> Then give me one little hour—
>> O! do not lash me so!
> One little hour—one little hour—
>> And gratefully I'll go."

Mr. Walker commanded her to return into the ranks with the other slaves. Women who had children were not chained, but those that had none were. As soon as her child was disposed of she was chained in the gang.

The following song I have often heard the slaves sing, when about to be carried to the far south. It is said to have been composed by a slave.

> "See these poor souls from Africa
> Transported to America;
> We are stolen, and sold to Georgia—
> Will you go along with me?
> We are stolen, and sold to Georgia—
> Come sound the jubilee!
>
> See wives and husbands sold apart,
> Their children's screams will break my heart;—
> There's a better day a coming—
> Will you go along with me?
> There's a better day a coming,
> Go sound the jubilee!
>
> O, gracious Lord! when shall it be,
> That we poor souls shall all be free?
> Lord, break them slavery powers—
> Will you go along with me?
> Lord, break them slavery powers,
> Go sound the jubilee!
>
> Dear Lord, dear Lord, when slavery 'll cease.
> Then we poor souls will have our peace;—
> There's a better day a coming—
> Will you go along with me?
> There's a better day a coming,
> Go sound the jubilee!"

We finally arrived at Mr. Walker's farm. He had a house built during our absence to put slaves in. It was a kind of domestic jail.

To William Wells Brown, The American Fugitive Slave, by E. S. Mathews

Brother, farewell to thee!
　His blessing on thee rest
Who hates all slavery
　And helps the poor oppressed.

Go forth with power to break
　The bitter, galling yoke;
Go forth 'mongst strong and weak,
　The aid of all invoke.

O, thou wilt have much woe,
　Tossed on a sea of strife,
Hunted by many a foe
　Eager to take thy life.

Perchance thou'lt have to brook
　The taunts of bond and free.
The cold, disdainful look
　of men—less men than thee.

We feel thy soul will rise
　Superior to it all;
For thou hast heard the cries,
　And drained the cup of gall.

Thine eyes have wept the tears
　Which tyrants taught to flow,
While craven scorn and sneers
　Fell with the shameful blow.

And now that thou art come
　To Freedom's blessed land,
Thou broodest on thy home
　And Slavery's hateful brand.

Thou thinkest thou canst hear
　Three million voices call;
They raise to thee their prayer,—
　Haste, help to break their thrall!

Say, wilt thou have, thy steps to guard,
    Some powerful spell or charm?
Then listen to thy sister's word,
    Nor fear thou hurt or harm.

When shines the North Star, cold and bright,
    Cheer thou thy heart, lift up thy head!
Feel, as thou look'st upon its light,
    That blessings on its beams are shed!
For rich, and poor, and bond, and free,
Will also gaze and pray for thee.

James Cruikshanks (b. 1828), 'The Fugitive Slave Law of 1850', 'Lex Fugitiva' (translated by Norman Vance), in *A Bouquet of Flowers from the Garden of Paradise* (1851)

Cruikshanks was an obscure *littérateur* who worked in New York in the mid-nineteenth century. His value for this anthology lies in the way he represents the frivolous reaction of some members of the Northern intellectual elite to the passage of the Fugitive Slave Law in 1850. The law was greeted by the abolition press in the North with general fury, and many white cultural figures shifted from ambivalence over the slavery issue to a sudden radicalism. The law generated a new wave of extreme anti-slavery publication, and directly led to some of the most effective abolition publications, including *Uncle Tom's Cabin*. The extremity of Northern reaction did not, however, go unmolested and in its turn generated some satiric responses even in the free states. The doom-laden rhetoric which greeted the passage of the law was considered a suitable subject for two of Cruikshanks's parodic squibs in *A Bouquet of Flowers*. This lightweight literary pastiche published in 1851 generally steered clear of politics, restricting its humour to rather arcane stylistic jokes. The parodic prefatory biography facetiously singled out the poem 'The Fugitive Slave Law of 1850/The American Congress Unmasked' as the central example of a new poetic primitivism and realism. 'The Fugitive Slave Law' quite cannily catches the fulminating bluster which greeted the passage of the Act, a diction which attempts condemnatory grandeur complete with classical comparison, and achieves a befuddled grumpiness suggestive of bad stump oratory.

The question of the appropriate diction in which to express the anguish and fury let loose by the passage of the bill is taken up later in the volume in a remarkably recondite poem entitled 'Lex Fugitiva.' This is entirely composed in dog Latin, and accompanied with a fully fledged scholarly apparatus of variant editorial translations and disquis-itions on the metrical felicities of the piece. Where the earlier poem performed an empty vulgarity the second displays an erudite frivolity. The message of 'Lex Fugitiva' is relayed via an initial synopsis, and a running commentary, while the main text destroys classical metre and grammar in order to apply the most basic English rhyme scheme. As the synopsis brutally reveals, the slave does not feature at all. The parody is clever in places, particularly in the exploitaton of the phoney footnotes. At one point, in their commentary (see n. 8), the mythical editors are even made to come up with the advanced notion that linguistic confusion and the obliteration of grammat-ical structure might be considered the only legitimate poetic response to the institu-tional ramifications of the slavery question. Cruikshanks's work suggests that there is an erudite, but unserious, readership in the early 1850s capable of enjoying the debates over the legal status of fugitives as a subject for frivolous parody.

The Fugitive Slave Law of 1850

The American congress unmasked

The law has passed, the crowning act is done.
The most nefarious beneath the sun;
Yes, men the authors—once the nation's prop,
Begun, alas! God knows where they will stop.
There's ********, and a host of men as great,
Have now revealed to us their awful fate.
O vile intruders! fiends adorned in white!
Sprung from hell's legions to destroy heaven's light!
Exaggeration has no station here!
Ye demagogues may speak, we've nought to fear!—
Ye may let loose your friends from lowest hell,—
Lay waste, destroy, yea more, your country sell;
Fight on, ye party men, I say, fight on!
You may succeed, the nation to dethrone,
To thrust it down, yea e'en to depths more deep
Than those, where Greece and Athens soundly sleep.
But "stop and think," ye cowards—traitors all,
You are the great, we know, and we the small,
But "stop and think," I say; sure as God lives,
While you he conquers, us the vict'ry gives.

Lex Fugitiva[1]

SYNOPSIS

The Author expresses his joy on being permitted to stand before the people in the temple. He first entreats them to be attentive, in order that they may hear. Secondly, he points out the means adopted to destroy our country. Thirdly, states that liberty is in danger, and warns the people to be cautious. Fourthly, predicts that speedily the sun, moon and stars will be changed into blood. Fifthly, foretells that the stars will fall. Sixthly, these convulsions are wholly confined to the earth.

Gratulor vos omnes;[2] laetor
Compelare[3] nunc, et feror
Supra meum expectatum,
Sto dum ante vos in fanum.[4]
Capite, et mea dicta

---

[1] 'This is written in ungrammatical and unidiomatic dog Latin. The notes, pretending otherwise, parody the editorial notes in editions of classical texts, sometimes reducing impossible Latin to near-impossible English of the kind manufactured by desperate schoolboys called upon to construe Latin. The non-classical metre recalls the rhymed accentual verse of medieval Latin poems such as the *Dies Irae*, also in rhymed octosyllabics. What follows is an attempt to represent the kind of rough sense the author probably intended Latinate readers to derive from these lines, though sense is often sacrificed to rhythm and rhyme.

"I congratulate you all; I am delighted to address you now, and I am moved beyond expectation as I stand before you in the temple. Take to your minds my unfeigned words. Listen! I shall say what can be ascertained about the fugitive law. First, then, look at the way in which it has been abused by men, plundering and laying waste your country to pacify it. Secondly, there is also zeal for public affairs which needs to be consulted in relation to institutions which are to be despoiled whether triumphantly or in sorrow. Liberty [is] now in danger! Citizens! Go, beware lest destruction should scatter you far and wide and toss you about, all you patricians and people who are on the way to encountering illumination. I fear for [the time] when moon and sun will turn to blood and the stars also will fall to earth and there will be murders, battles, slaughter; earth and the heavens will lie beyond the sea of war."' [Note on style, and literal prose translation, by Norman Vance.]

'This poem is beyond all description. Its beauties can only be appreciated by the careful student, and no translation can do justice to the ideas. We have therefore contented ourselves with a few annotations, and with a brief synopsis taken from the original English manuscript of the Author, to which we are much indebted, as the dialectic variations, and the principle of continuous scansion, in which the Latin poem is written would otherwise, in some cases, have left the ideas obscure.

'In this piece the effusions of Virgil are far outdone—a new element is added, that of rhyme, which the ancients had not the talent to apply. The success of this attempt proves how deficient they were in this respect. We have no doubt but this poem will take its appropriate place among the immortal productions of the Augustan age.

'Auctor requiescat in pace.' [Cruikshanks]

[2] '"Vos omnes:" the Accusative is here used for the Dative, Antiptozis; to give roundness, and beauty to the verse.' [Cruikshanks]

[3] '"Compelare:" for "compellare", metri gratia.' [Cruikshanks]

[4] '"In fanum:" in the temple. What temple is referred to, is uncertain: most however have considered it to be the temple of fame. The idea of tendency towards, resulting from the Author's having just entered, deserves notice.' [Cruikshanks]

Vestros animos,[5] non ficta!
Audite![6] quam inventuram,
Lege fugitiva, dicam!
Primum, tunc, videte modum![7]
Quod hominibus abusum
Populare, et vastare,
Vestram patriam, pacare!
Deinde,[8] etiam, et rerum
Studium, et consultandum:
Instituta gloriose!
Et rapienda luctuose!
Libertas nunc in pericla!
Civites! ite! cavento!
Ne exitia[9] sparserint
Late, longe, et volverint
Patricii, et plebes, omnes
Inventurae clarae dies![10]
Ego vereor, quum luna,
In sanguinem, et sol, sit versa![11]
Astra, quoque, occiderint

---

[5] '"Vestros animos:" some have regarded this as a mere poetic substitution for "vestris animis;" others supply "et," etc. The best natural construction is, that "capio" is followed by two Accusatives, thus: "take [consider] my unfeigned words as your minds".' [Cruikshanks]

[6] '"Audite:" this passage has been rendered, "hear what I am about to say will take place in consequence of this fugitive law" obviously, a construction the Latin will not permit. Let "legem" be supplied before "quam," as its antecedent, and "inventuram" be rendered actively, and the sense is plain: "hear the law, which I say [not positive assertion] on account of this fugitive law, shall bring to pass." It is designedly left incomplete; and the sudden transition, leaving every one to his own conclusions, adds sublimity to force.' [Cruikshanks]

[7] '"Modum—quod." A masculine noun of the second declension [perhaps from its ending] takes a neuter relative: "which has abused men to plunder, to lay waste, to tranquillize your country".' [Cruikshanks]

[8] '"Deinde—luctuose:" this is a very difficult sentence. Critics differ much in translating it. Some supply what they suppose to be intentional omissions; Davidson reads for "et consultandum," "est consultandum," thus: "in the next place, also, the desire of power must be consulted in regard to the institutions to be destroyed both gloriously, and mournfully:" while Dr. Trapp suggests that viewing the chaos arising from the demolition of ancient institutions, in a moment of intense excitement, the author expressed his feelings in these disjointed, and unconnected exclamations.' [Cruikshanks]

[9] '"Ne exitia:" "lest destruction should scatter far and wide, and toss about all of you; O Patricians, and renowned Plebeians! about to receive light!"' [Cruikshanks]

[10] '"Dies = lucem:" reference is here made to the educating and enlightening of the common people.' [Cruikshanks]

[11] '"Sit versa:" for "sit versus," or "sint versi," for the sake of the rhyme, which in this species of poetry takes precedence of all grammatical principles.' [Cruikshanks] The imagery is from Revelation 6: 12–13.

Super terram, et fuerint
Neces, pugnae, cedes; belli[12]
Ultra mare, terra, caeli!!

Henry 'Box' Brown (b. 1816), 'Psalm 40' (extemporized version), 'Song in Commemoration of my Fate in the Box; Air: "Uncle Ned"', in *Narrative of the Life of Henry Box Brown, Written by Himself* (1851, English edition)

In 1848 Brown was working as a slave in a tobacco factory in Richmond, Virginia, when he was suddenly informed that his master had sold his wife and three children to a Methodist minister. This was too much for him and Brown determined on flight. His method was both novel and sensational. He was mailed north to Philadelphia and freedom in a packing case, by Adams Express. Brown's journey took twenty-seven hours, during which time he was several times turned up the wrong way and nearly suffocated. Brown was eventually received and liberated in Philadelphia by James McKim and the black abolitionist William Still.

Brown and the abolitionists saw the publicity potential of this eccentric mode of escape. He kept the famous box and toured the abolition lecture circuit with it. On occasions he would begin a lecture by leaping out of it. Brown's story developed an even more sensational twist when, in the autumn of 1850, as a direct result of the passage of the new Fugitive Slave Law, an attempt was made by slave catchers to kidnap him. Brown left for Britain. He toured the British Isles for four years, lecturing, singing, and showing his enormous painted 'Panorama' of scenes from slave life, concluding with his own escape. Brown's performances in Britain, and his refusal to succumb to the established norms for black ex-slave performers on the abolition lecture circuit, led to racist reports about him in the press. He challenged the accepted framework for the presentation of the ordeal of the runaway. He fought attempts to close down the languages and images in which he decided to narrate his experiences at both a textual and a performative level. Brown had spirit, in the true gospel sense, and his religious interpretation of his escape was reverent and awe-filled, but also full of joy and even a certain element of low comedy. His gifts as a self-dramatist, and his ability to draw on linguistic and artistic resources unique to North American slave culture, come out clearly in the two types of poetry reproduced below. Brown's first extended response on coming out of his box was to break into his own gospel rendition of the fortieth psalm. The compulsive reiteration, using emphatic repetitions, reinvents the psalm as a hymn of heartbreaking innocence: Brown is singing at the coming of a personal jubilee. He had

---

[12] '"Belli:" connect this with the preceding clause, and all difficulty is removed: "beyond the sea of war, there shall be the earth and heavens:" i.e., the mighty revolution shall affect only what, lying beneath the heavens, the earth contains; and not the heaven and the earth themselves.' [Cruikshanks]

chosen this text because in its original version the theme of resurrection from the pit had a precise relevance: 'I waited patiently for the Lord; and he inclined unto me and heard my cry. He brought me up as of an horrible pit, out of the miry clay, and set my feet upon a rock and established my goings. And he hath put a new song in my mouth even praise unto our God.' Brown certainly does create a 'new song'; he takes a creative approach to his source, seizing on key phrases and extemporizing.

There are several other examples of Brown's determination to reinvent his experience using vernacular forms and language which were beyond the pale for white abolitionists. The main text of his 1851 *Narrative* concludes with the retelling of his escape in the form of a popular ballad which he composed himself. Above all Brown had the confidence to embrace the bathetic elements of the tale. A man shipped in a box, turned on his head, tumbling out ruefully having tricked the entire force of the slave-holding South, *is*, at one level, the stuff of slapstick. But it is the potent slapstick of the triumphant underdog: Brown is a kind of Brer Rabbit figure, with his nose in exuberant performance and his tail in African and African-American folklore. He is a cunning, as well as a heroic, ex-slave. He did not have to run away; he used the most advanced high-tech machinery and travelled, as his delighted italics announce, '*express*'; now there will be no more 'Slave work', he will work for himself.

Psalm 40

I waited patiently, I waited patiently for the Lord, for the Lord;
And he inclined unto me, and heard my calling:
I waited patiently, I waited patiently for the Lord,
And he inclined unto me, and heard my calling:
And he hath put a new song in my mouth,
Even a thanksgiving, even a thanksgiving, even a thanksgiving
    unto our God.
Blessed, Blessed, Blessed, Blessed is the man, Blessed is the man,
Blessed is the man that hath set his hope, his hope in the Lord;
[torn page] my God, Great, Great, Great,
Great are the wondrous works which thou hast done.
Great are the wondrous works which thou hast done, which
    thou hast done:
If I should declare them and speak of them, they would be more,
    more, more than I am able to express.
I have not kept back thy loving kindness and truth from
    the great congregation.
I have not kept back thy loving kindness and truth from
    the great congregation.

Withdraw not thou thy mercy from me,
Withdraw not thou thy mercy from me, O Lord;
Let thy loving kindness and thy truth always preserve me,
Let all those that seek thee be joyful and glad,
Let all those that seek thee be joyful and glad, be joyful, and
    glad, be joyful and glad, be joyful, be joyful, be joyful, be joyful,
    be joyful and glad—be glad in thee.
And let such as love thy salvation,
And let such as love thy salvation, say, always,
The Lord be praised,
The Lord be praised.
Let all those that seek thee be joyful and glad,
And let such as love thy salvation, say always,
The Lord be praised,
The Lord be praised,
The Lord be praised.

Song in Commemoration of my Fate in the Box;
Air: 'Uncle Ned'

I

Here you see a man by the name of Henry Brown,
Ran away from the South to the North;
Which he would not have done but they stole all his rights,
But they'll never do the like again.

Chorus—Brown laid down the shovel and the hoe,
Down in the box he did go;
No more Slave work for Henry Box Brown,
In the box by Express he did go.

II

Then the orders they were given, and the cars did start away;
Roll along—roll along—roll along,
Down to the landing, where the steamboat lay,
To bear the baggage off to the north.
CHORUS.

III

When they packed the baggage on, they turned him on his head,
There poor Brown liked to have died;

THE RESURRECTION OF HENRY BOX BROWN AT PHILADELPHIA.
Who escaped from Richmond Va. in a Box. 3 feet long 2½ ft. deep and 2 ft wide.

13. Anon., *The Resurrection of Henry Box Brown at Philadelphia* (stone lithograph, 1850).

There were passengers on board who wished to sit down,
And they turned the box down on its side.
CHORUS.

IV

When they got to the cars they threw the box off,
And down upon his head he did fall,
Then he heard his neck crack, and he thought it was broke,
But they never threw him off any more.
CHORUS.

V

When they got to Philadelphia they said he was in port,
And Brown then began to feel glad,
He was taken on the waggon to his final destination,
And left, "this side up with care."
CHORUS.

VI

The friends gathered round and asked if all was right,
As down on the box they did rap,
Brown answered them, saying; "yes all is right!"
He was then set free from his pain.
CHORUS.

James Monroe Whitfield (1822/3?–1871), 'America', 'To Cinque', in *America and Other Poems* (1853)

Whitfield was 28, and a free black from Exeter, New Hampshire, when Frederick Douglass 'discovered' him, working in the basement of a barber's shop in Buffalo, New York. Finding that Whitfield wrote poetry Douglass encouraged him, and published his poems in the *North Star* and *Frederick Douglass' Paper*; poems also appeared in Garrison's *Liberator*. By 1853 Whitfield had assembled a sufficient number of poems for the volume *America*. This book gave him enough of a public reputation to leave his job and work full time on the abolition circuit. He became a strong advocate of recolonization, supporting the idea that blacks should be allowed to set up their own colonies in Central and South America. In 1854 he attended the National Emigration Convention, and thereafter entered into public debate with Douglass over the pros and cons of recolonization. His poetic output fell off markedly once he was involved in black rights and abolition debate.

Whitfield, at his most effective as a political poet, shares with Joseph Holly (pp. 589–94) the ability to express a genuine outrage at white racism and hypocrisy on the part of the post-revolutionary North. He also has a sardonic humour which comes out forcefully in the harsh parody of 'America', where a popular New England hymn forms the model for the satire. 'America' also uses Old Testament typology in significant ways. Respectable white abolition poetry does not confidently employ the Egyptian and Babylonian imagery used here to describe the depravity of Southern slavery. Yet Whitfield in calling upon the Babylonian inheritance looks back to the imagery employed by extreme millenarians and revolutionaries in 1790s Britain and America to describe slave systems. The poem 'To Cinque' although not as tightly written is important in the way it shows a black rights activist taking up a contemporary news story to create a new black slave hero. Joseph Cinque became a celebrity in America and to an extent England when he emerged as the leader of the rebel slaves during the *Amistad* mutiny, and the subsequent and protracted New York court case (pp. 526–8).

America

America, it is to thee,
Thou boasted land of liberty,—
It is to thee I raise my song,
Thou land of blood, and crime, and wrong.
It is to thee, my native land,
From whence has issued many a band
To tear the black man from his soil,
And force him here to delve and toil;
Chained on your blood-bemoistened sod,
Cringing beneath a tyrant's rod,
Stripped of those rights which Nature's God
    Bequeathed to all the human race,
Bound to a petty tyrant's nod,
    Because he wears a paler face.
Was it for this, that freedom's fires
Were kindled by your patriot sires?
Was it for this, they shed their blood,
On hill and plain, on field and flood?
Was it for this, that wealth and life
Were staked upon that desperate strife,
Which drenched this land for seven long years
With blood of men, and women's tears?
When black and white fought side by side,
    Upon the well-contested field,—
Turned back the fierce opposing tide,
    And made the proud invader yield—
When, wounded, side by side they lay,
    And heard with joy the proud hurrah
From their victorious comrades say
    That they had waged successful war,
The thought ne'er entered in their brains
That they endured those toils and pains,
To forge fresh fetters, heavier chains
For their own children, in whose veins
Should flow that patriotic blood,
So freely shed on field and flood.
Oh no; they fought, as they believed,
    For the inherent rights of man;

But mark, how they have been deceived
   By slavery's accursed plan.
They never thought, when thus they shed
   Their heart's best blood, in freedom's cause.
That their own sons would live in dread,
   Under unjust, oppressive laws:
That those who quietly enjoyed
   The rights for which they fought and fell,
Could be the framers of a code,
   That would disgrace the fiends of hell!
Could they have looked, with prophet's ken,
   Down to the present evil time,
   Seen free-born men, uncharged with crime,
Consigned unto a slaver's pen,—
Or thrust into a prison cell,
With thieves and murderers to dwell—
While that same flag whose stripes and stars
Had been their guide through freedom's wars
As proudly waved above the pen
Of dealers in the souls of men!
Or could the shades of all the dead,
   Who fell beneath that starry flag,
Visit the scenes where they once bled,
   On hill and plain, on vale and crag,
By peaceful brook, or ocean's strand,
   By inland lake, or dark green wood,
Where'er the soil of this wide land
   Was moistened by their patriot blood,—
And then survey the country o'er,
   From north to south, from east to west,
And hear the agonizing cry
Ascending up to God on high,
From western wilds to ocean's shore,
   The fervent prayer of the oppressed;
The cry of helpless infancy
   Torn from the parent's fond caress
By some base tool of tyranny,
   And doomed to woe and wretchedness;
The indignant wail of fiery youth,
   Its noble aspirations crushed,
Its generous zeal, its love of truth,

Trampled by tyrants in the dust;
The aerial piles which fancy reared,
   And hopes too bright to be enjoyed,
Have passed and left his young heart scared,
   And all its dreams of bliss destroyed.
The shriek of virgin purity,
   Doomed to some libertine's embrace,
Should rouse the strongest sympathy
   Of each one of the human race;
And weak old age, oppressed with care,
   As he reviews the scene of strife,
Puts up to God a fervent prayer,
   To close his dark and troubled life.
The cry of fathers, mothers, wives,
   Severed from all their hearts hold dear,
And doomed to spend their wretched lives
   In gloom, and doubt, and hate, and fear;
And manhood, too, with soul of fire,
And arm of strength, and smothered ire,
Stands pondering with brow of gloom,
Upon his dark unhappy doom,
Whether to plunge in battle's strife,
And buy his freedom with his life,
And with stout heart and weapon strong,
Pay back the tyrant wrong for wrong,
Or wait the promised time of God,
   When his Almighty ire shall wake,
And smite the oppressor in his wrath,
And hurl red ruin in his path,
And with the terrors of his rod,
   Cause adamantine[1] hearts to quake.
Here Christian writhes in bondage still,
   Beneath his brother Christian's rod,
And pastors trample down at will,
   The image of the living God.
While prayers go up in lofty strains,
   And pealing hymns ascend to heaven,
The captive, toiling in his chains,
   With tortured limbs and bosom riven,
Raises his fettered hand on high,

---

[1] Unbreakable.

And in the accents of despair,
To him who rules both earth and sky,
   Puts up a sad, a fervent prayer,
To free him from the awful blast
   Of slavery's bitter galling shame—
Although his portion should be cast
   With demons in eternal flame!
Almighty God! 'tis this they call
   The land of liberty and law;
Part of its sons in baser thrall
   Than Babylon or Egypt saw—
Worse scenes of rapine, lust and shame,
   Than Babylonian ever knew,
Are perpetrated in the name
   Of God, the holy, just, and true;
And darker doom than Egypt felt,
May yet repay this nation's guilt.
Almighty God! thy aid impart,
And fire anew each faltering heart,
And strengthen every patriot's hand,
Who aims to save our native land.
We do not come before thy throne,
   With carnal weapons drenched in gore,
Although our blood has freely flown,
   In adding to the tyrant's store.
Father! before thy throne we come,
   Not in the panoply of war,
With pealing trump, and rolling drum,
   And cannon booming loud and far;
Striving in blood to wash out blood,
   Through wrong to seek redress for wrong;
For while thou'rt holy, just and good,
   The battle is not to the strong;
But in the sacred name of peace,
   Of justice, virtue, love and truth,
We pray, and never mean to cease,
   Till weak old age and fiery youth
In freedom's cause their voices raise,
And burst the bonds of every slave;
Till, north and south, and east and west,
The wrongs we bear shall be redressed.

To Cinque

All hail! thou truly noble chief,
    Who scorned to live a cowering slave;
Thy name shall stand on history's leaf,
    Amid the mighty and the brave:
Thy name shall shine, a glorious light
    To other brave and fearless men,
Who, like thyself, in freedom's might,
    Shall beard the robber in his den.
Thy name shall stand on history's page,
    And brighter, brighter, brighter glow,
Throughout all time, through every age,
    Till bosoms cease to feel or know
"Created worth, or human woe."
Thy name shall nerve the patriot's hand
    When, 'mid the battle's deadly strife,
The glittering bayonet and brand
    Are crimsoned with the stream of life:

When the dark clouds of battle roll,
And slaughter reigns without control,
Thy name shall then fresh life impart,
And fire anew each freeman's heart.
Though wealth and power their force combine
    To crush thy noble spirit down,
There is above a power divine
    Shall bear thee up against their frown.

Joseph Cephas Holly (1825–54), 'Freedom's Champions', 'Injustice—not Law', in *Freedom's Offering: A Collection of Poems* (1853)

Holly, an African-American ex-slave, published this volume with an apology 'To the Public'. This short statement sets the author out as a humble black with no literary pretensions: 'the author is aware of the many defects contained therein. Indeed it is not as a competitor to Whittier, Lowell, Longfellow, Bryant, or Willis that he appears before you; but as the unlearned representative of an oppressed race, who have been denied the capacity for anything intellectual—and indeed as a humble member than as a representative of that race.' Holly justifies his volume not on the grounds of any literary merit, but simply because it is written by a black. He goes on to explain that he began writing the poems at the age of 15, and that he had no formal education of any kind and virtually no books to read or consult as models. The volume is divided into three parts: the first part contains love poems, nature poems, and elegies. The second, making up about half the collection, contains poems around the theme of slavery, and the third and shortest section consists of temperance poems. For the most part Holly lives up to the introduction he has provided for himself, mimicking in metrically and linguistically primitive ways the late Romantic American canonic models mentioned in the apology. It is only in the poems on slavery that he allows a distinctive voice to emerge. The poems are at their strongest when dealing with the implications of the recently passed Fugitive Slave Law, and with the hypocrisy of the North which he feels has been revealed. In 'Freedom's Champions' for example he opens with a long paean to the stars of the English abolition movement Sharpe, Wilberforce, Clarkson, Fox, and more surprisingly given their shifting positions Burke and Pitt, in order to point the finger at American attitudes to slavery after the heroics of the War of Independence. This is well-tried terrain for abolition verse (see pp. xlvi, 483–95, 584–9, 618–23, 641–59). 'Injustice—not Law', printed in full below, takes the charges of betrayal and hypocrisy a good deal further. Holly achieves a tone of fury from the outset which the poem sustains through the unbridled use of exclamatory and imperative forms. The poem is unusual in breaking out beyond the charge that the ideals of the Revolution have been betrayed, to talk about Northern race prejudice as the real explanation for the passing of the Fugitive Slave Law. This is an uncompromised statement of outrage.

Freedom's Champions

All honor to the illustrious dead,
    Who toiled in freedom's sacred cause;
The glorious chieftains brave, who led
    Chivalrous hearts in all its wars,
First noble Sharpe the banner rears,
    And waves aloft for Afric's rights,
His soul bows to no coward fears,
    While in the cause of man he fights.
And thou, great Clarkson, who did rise
    In freedom's ranks with might and mind,
Unmasked the scenes to Britton's eyes;
    The bruised, the maimed, the halt, the blind,
The sighs, the groans, the sobs, the shrieks,

Of babes and mothers reft apart,
The the tears that rolled down manly cheeks,
    Of inward grief which breaks the heart.
And these in England's proud domain,
    Beneath her sovereign's sceptre's sway,
She who when dared the haughty Dane
    Whom lust of power had lead stray,
To think that on her sea-girt land,
    He'd plant his power in steel array;
She who with Alfred's patriot band.
    Drove the invader far away.
Could she remain deaf to the note,
    Cold unrelenting to the crimes,
Which in each eastward breeze that float,
    Grate on her ear from India's climes?
Her Wilberforce in silence bound,
    Her Fox, O'Connell, Chatham, Burke,[1]
In Parliament, while all around
    The Bondman's groans and sighs did lurk.
Could freedom's champions, thus like stone,
    All wrapped in silence coldly stand,
Pour forth no sound that shake the throne,
    Reverberating through the land?
For Afric's bleeding sons who toil
    Beneath the sun from day to day,
Far o'er the waves on British soil,
    With gyves and chains, and stripes for pay.
No—true to freedom they did raise,
    Their voices bold, in lofty strains,
Till British hearts warmed with the blaze,
    Struck from his limbs the bondman's chains.
Eight hundred thousand freemen stout,
    As if by magic of a wand,
From chattled slaves beneath the knout,
    Erect in manly stature stand.
And shall old England loud proclaim
    To all around that thou art free,
While sons whose fathers, in the name

---

[1] All the figures named in this and the preceding line were, at different points in their careers, central to the abolition movement.

Of God, fought hard for liberty?
Shall offspring of that pilgrim band,
Who pledged their lives, their fortunes too,
Their sacred honor they would stand
In freedom's cause forever true,
Prove false to every solemn vow,
Their fathers offered on the shrine
Of liberty? Their sacred trow
Be trampled on like pearls by swine?
Shall slaves breathe in the sacred land,
Where Bunkerhill's[2] proud martyrs stood,
To meet oppressions hired band,
And sealed their freedom with their blood?
The memory of the noble men,
Who stood on Flatbush's bloody plains,
Led on by Putnam, Sullivan.[3]
Dishonored be by slavery's chains,
And Trenton, too, where Washington
Led on oppression's deadliest foes,
The gory fields of old Princeton,
Be cursed by slavery's crying woes.
Old Germantown, in the land of Penn,[4]
Augment the mother's parting cry,
Where fell one thousand patriot men,
And where their sacred ashes lie.
In Camden, Cowpens, and Eutaw,[5]
Where southmen, freedom's battles fought,
Shall wrong be sanctioned by the law,
And men and women there be bought?
Shall Yorktown's[6] glorious battle ground,

---

[2] The Battle of Bunker Hill took place on 17 June 1775: the colonial militia defended the height against the British General William Howe, until their powder gave out. This heroic defence was a massive boost to American morale.

[3] Israel Putnam (1718–90), general in the War of Indpendence, integral to the planning of Bunker Hill; Major General John Sullivan: his most famous battle involved a massive defeat of the Loyalist 'Indian' forces in 1779.

[4] Germantown was established in Pennsylvania in 1719 and during the 18th century became a strictly religious centre for German immigrant communities.

[5] The Battle of Cowpens was a battle in the War of Independence in which 2,000 revolutionaries, including many blacks, fought off the British. Camden and Eutaw Springs were also independence battles.

[6] General Cornwallis finally surrendered the English troops to the rebellious colonies on 17 October 1781 at Yorktown, and the American War of Independence ended.

Where freedom triumphed in the strife,
  Be cursed by cries of those who 're bound,
    Of husband parted from the wife?
The glorious spirit which led on
  Our fathers in the fierce contest,
In valley deep, hill top upon,
  Is slumbering from east to west.
Freedom shall triumph! God will save
  His people from oppression's yoke,
And by his power the bleeding slave,
  Shall see his chains and fetters broke.
Then will our noble country be,
  Land of the free—home of the brave;
When monarchs far beyond the sea,
  Dare not upbraid us with the slave.
Sons of the pilgrims, oh, prove true
  To fathers' deeds and memory;
Devote and pledge yourselves anew,
  To human rights and liberty!

Injustice—not Law

I said that it would be very bad for the free colored people, and through them for their race if they hate us. They are already jealous of us—we are already useless to them; and we shall become more and more so, until they shall see us taking the open, and decided, and honest ground, that slavery, whether it be for blacks or whites, cannot take shelter in law—cannot be clothed with the dignity and power of law.

—*Gerrit Smith's speech, at Pittsburgh Convention, August, 1852.*

Ye hypocrites! whose fathers scorned
  To bear the menace of a chain,
Stand forth unvarnished, unadorned,
  Your boasted love of right is vain.
When George the Fourth, by legal right,
  O'erran your land with martial band,
Ye dared to meet them in the fight,
  And scattered them like ropes of sand.
Your vaunted freedom we despise,

Whilst trampling on our injured race—
  A sepulchre of whited lies,
    We throw your parchment in your face.
"Our Father's compact;" how dare they
  To barter off their brother men;
By what great charter tell us pray;
  The manner given, how and when?
Methinks an edict, turning loose
  Foul man-hunters, your babes the game,
Claiming obedience, ye would choose,
  To trample on in heaven's name.
We hold that life, and liberty,
  The right our fortune's to persue;
Ordained of God for you, and me,
  No argument can make more true;
No sophistry can contravene,
  No constitution take away,
No "father's compact" go between,
  They are as plain as light of day.
Then how can we believe your true,
  When freedom's champion's ye proclaim,
While millions of your bondmen sue
  For freedom to your country's shame?
And ye abuse, proscribe and hate,
  Your brother of a darker hue;—
Tho' raised above a slave's estate—
  False friends of freedom, he scornes you.

S. R. Philips, from *Nebraska* (1854)

Philips's *Nebraska* was an attempt to write a noble anti-slavery epic around recent politics of settlement and expansion. The period 1853–4 saw tensions mounting to a head over the issue of slavery and free-soil settlement of the vast new territories of the American West. The ambitious Senator Stephen A. Douglas thought he could step in and find a way of ending the bitter disputes that were opening up in Congress over the issue. He proposed a bill that would establish two territories, Kansas and Nebraska. Under the terms of the bill slavery would be technically legitimized in Nebraska, although as far as Douglas and his followers were concerned this was purely a symbolic gesture to placate the slave power. In the wake of the fugitive slave bill this was hardly how the development was seen in the north-east. There was an eruption of public sentiment over the issue in the North and suddenly the extent of public fury over the extension of the slave power became evident. As Douglas rushed back to Illinois to try and save his political position in the forthcoming elections he famously stated: 'I could travel from Boston to Chicago by the light of my own effigy . . . All along the Western Reserve of Ohio I could find my effigy on every tree we passed.' The results of Douglas's ill-judged initiative were to be the emergence of Lincoln at the head of a distinctive Northern political party. The political polarization of North and South was taking an extreme form and Civil War was becoming inevitable.

Philips's *Nebraska*, although now completely forgotten, was an attempt to respond to some of these momentous events in a big political poem. This is a long and ambitious work which deserves reprinting and studying in its entirety. *Nebraska* is a pretty fair stab at Miltonic blank verse, and Philips certainly had a sense of occasion, realizing that the momentous nature of recent events merited the very grandest of models. The selections below open with a harsh satiric portrait of Douglas and then move on to consider the implications of the Kansas Nebraska Act for the North. The conclusion is stark, Douglas's initiative is seen as releasing a plague of slave-owning and slave-catching frogs in the North, while the politicians with Douglas at their head are men who 'for place or pay would now enslave | Nebraska, Kansas, and New England, too!' *Nebraska* is impressive in its technical range, opening out into narrative set pieces where appropriate (as in the vignette of the fugitive slave) and introducing various lyric interludes, a notable example being the hymn against the Fugitive Slave Law.

from *Nebraska*

PART IV

> The blushing sun hid its indignant face
> Behind the free hills of the blooming west.
> It seemed red with the human blood absorbed
> From lands soaked with the sweat and tears of slaves,
> Where canes grow for the toiler's aching back
> And sugar sweetens the proud tyrant's cup;
> Where the white cotton blooms like mimic snow,
> Not for the naked negro's bleeding loins,
> But for the lily lords who will not toil
> Nor spin, though Solomon was not arrayed
> Like them in all his glory and his pomp.[1]

---

[1] Solomon, a great and wealthy king of Israel in the 10th century BC. For Solomon as the epitome of splendour see Matthew 6: 28–9.

And when the waves of light had ebbed away
The tide of night flowed in and filled the land,
And covered up the fresh and bleeding wounds
That plead like piteous lips for liberty.
God heard the blood that shrieked to Heaven for help,
And held the flaming north star in his hand,
And sent an angel down to tell the slave
To follow where the torch of Freedom led.
The negro from his humble cabin crept
While echo slumbered and the dogs were dumb:
The north star crowned the lofty hills he climbed
And watched his weary footsteps o'er the plain.
Day broke and found him in the forest shade,
Where the low bushes fed him with their fruit
And the soft moss invited him to rest,
While cheerful birds sang songs to Liberty.
In vain with horse, and hound, and murderous gun
Pale pirates scoured the land for miles about.
    The panting fugitive had reached the shores
Of a free state and dreamed that he was free.
But he, alas! was seized by human hounds,
And, like a felon, dragged before the judge,
Charged with the crime of seeking liberty,
(Unpardonable sin in this free land!)
He and the judge were brothers in the church,
Sang the same songs, indorsed the same belief,
At the same altar bowed, and hoped to end
Life's dreary march in the same heaven at last.
That judge had power to heal his wounds and wipe
The tears which ploughed deep channels in his cheeks;
But he betrayed his brother for a vote,
And scorned the holy charter God had signed,
Sealed, and delivered to the race of man.
He might have made the young West blush with pride,
And twined a laurel round her lovely brow;
He might have thrilled a nation's heart with joy,
And with brave Ingraham shared the honest fame
Bestowed by an appreciating world.
But he, a timid and timeserving man,
Feared the proud south more than he loved his God.
He rent the stripes from Freedom's starry flag,

And scourged his brother in the courts of law.
With his white hands that morning clasped in prayer
He locked the clanking chains upon the slave;
With knees that bowed before the throne of Heaven
He knelt upon a Christian's heaving breast
Until his broken heart oozed out in tears;
With lips that asked a blessing on his meal
He doomed the black to hopeless servitude.
Yes; he would send all Afric's sable sons
Back into bondage were they brought to him;
And all her dusky daughters, were they pure
As his own children fair, he would return
To the slave driver's harem at the south.
Out of such facts Nebraska's chains were forged:
May God ordain that they shall not be worn!
Old Massachusetts proudly said, the slave
Will find asylums in the Old Bay State.
This was her loudest boast; just hear her song:—

 Shall the poor bondman, from oppression flying,
Be hunted here with bloodhounds on his track,
O'er valleys where our fathers' bones are lying,
  Because he's black?

Shall priest and statesman climb the tapering steeple
 At Concord to behold the wondrous chase,
To see black Kossuth[2] and our own white people
  Running a race?

And when the slave is bleeding in their clutches,
 Shall we light bonfires for the men so brave,
And crown with laurel they who did as much as
  Catch a poor slave?

God bless old Massachusetts! She will never
 Hunt panting negroes o'er her classic plains;
She's true to Freedom, and she will forever
  Spurn bribes and chains.

---

[2] Kossuth was the charismatic and oratorically flamboyant leader of the Hungarian revolution of 1848; he served as President of the new Hungarian republic for only six months in 1849 before the Russians moved in and forced him into exile.

    Her free-born sires, brave sons, and angel daughters
        Speak from the rocky hill and rolling wave,
    In tones loud as Niag'ra's stormy waters,
        God speed the slave!

    Here man's more sacred than the constitution;
        Tyrants and traitors now are blanched with fear
    Because the spirit of the revolution
        Still lingers here.

    An armless hand is writing on the plaster;
        Belshazzar[3], drunken, cannot read the sign.
    Meanwhile the sable slave outwits his master,
        Who's steeped in wine.

    We have a Daniel[4] to translate the letters
        Which burn like lightning on the southern wall,
    While their false prophets now are forging fetters
        For those who fall.

    The footsore slave, sad, battered, and heartbroken,
        Finds freedom and a safe asylum here,
    And gentle words from pleasant faces spoken,
        And friends sincere.

    Such was her song; but when the negro came
    They hunted him through Boston's classic streets
    Until the stones beneath his feet cried "Shame!"
    Descendants of white slaves[5] like dogs pursued
    The fugitive and harnessed him with steel;
    He asked for freedom, and they gave him chains.
    That was a dark day in our history;
    The sun of Freedom was in black eclipse;
    But then, thank God, the brightest stars shone out,
    And scared Conservatism's bats and owls!

---

[3] Belshazzar was the last king of Babylon before its capture by the Persian monarch Cyrus, remembered for his spectacular downfall as narrated in the Book of Daniel. During a sumptuous feast a hand writes mysterious words on the wall of Belshazzar's banquet hall, stating, 'Thou art weighed in the balance and found wanting.'

[4] Belshazzar is unable to read the writing on the wall until Daniel is sent for and tells him the terrible truth.

[5] Massachusetts had, in the later 17th and 18th centuries, imported large numbers of white indentured 'servants' from Europe, who worked out their terms of contract as white slaves.

O that the constant ticking clock of Time
Could be turned back, or that sad day be struck
Forever from the records of past!
Why, drizzling Friday at a hanging time,
Or even starless Night, alive with ghosts,
Would be fair weather and fine scenery
Contrasted with that ill-born imp of Time!
Two dozen guilty hours skulked slowly by;
Each one was sixty wicked minutes long;
Each moment was a traitor and a thief.
That day fair Liberty was cloven down
Beneath the shadow of old Fanueil Hall![6]
The Court House, even, wore a zone of chains,
While jailer, jurymen, and learned judge
Bowed down and crawled like cravens under it.
That was the chain which held the Union fast—
Let Curtis[7] wear it as his coat of arms.
Its links are brightened for Nebraska's use!
Methinks the bust of Adams[8] in the hall
Cried "Shame!" until the very plaster cracked,
Thus opening mouths for other tongues to shout.
Methinks the portraits shook their gilded frames,
And pointed at the hateful scene with scorn.
Who did not hear their withering rebuke?
I will repeat it in unpolished rhyme:—

Have ye been rocked in Fanueil Hall,
    The famous "cradle" of the free?
And will ye hear your brother call
    For help, and never heed his plea?
Ye heap the granite to the skies
    O'er heroes' graves on Bunker's Hill;
But if the sleepers there could rise,
    While men are slaves, would *they* be still?

---

[6] Famous centre of abolition debate in Boston.

[7] Justice Benjamin Curtis, famous as one of the two justices who bravely provided historically based arguments to counter Justice Taney's notorious ruling over the Dred Scott decision, implying that blacks could not be citizens.

[8] John Adams (1735–1836), second President of the United States and father of John Quincey Adams (see p. 520 n. 6); he helped organize and then signed the Declaration of Independence.

They would again renew their vows
   To wipe away a nation's stain;
And Warren's[9] thrilling voice would rouse
   The iron will of mighty men;
They would relight their beacon fires
   On old Wachusett's[10] naked brow,
And clang the bells in all their spires,
   While trumpets bray and torches glow!

Where are the sons of sires who cast
   The taxéd tea chests in the sea?
Where is the spirit of the past
   Which moved the deep of sympathy?
Would not oppression have been driven
   Away, as sunshine drives the dew,
If, when your fathers went to heaven,
   Their falling mantles fell on you?

Descendants of the Pilgrim stock,
   By all the free blood in your veins;
By all the prayers at Plymouth Rock,
   Strike off the bondman's galling chains!
By all the blood your fathers shed,
   By all the laurels they have won,
Stand up for freedom as they did
   At Concord and at Lexington!

Freedom invites her armies forth,
   And waves a flag of spotless white:
Up, freemen! from your couch of sloth,
   And forthwith harness for the fight!
By very stripe and every star
   Our banner shows on land or sea,
Let every man list in the war,
   And fight till all mankind are free!

What cared officials for the warning voice?
Their creed was this: First worship gold, then God;
Make sure of wealth, then turn your thoughts to heaven;

---

[9] Joseph Warren (1741–75), anti-British patriot leader, central figure in the Liberty faction during the Stamp Tax crisis.

[10] A grand, solitary mountain peak in north central Massachusetts.

Heed not the "higher law,"[11] but men in power;
Rise, though you stand upon your brother's neck—
The constitution now, and conscience next;
Souls cannot shine through skins of ebon hue,
So slavery is only abstract sin.
Such is the cruel creed of selfish men.
The errors and the vices of mankind
Are thieves which steal away their happiness.
Behold the miser worshipping his gold!
His stingy skin can scarcely hide his bones;
His little eyes begrudge the light he needs;
His toothless gums his hungry stomach starve;
He knows, he fears, he loves no god but gold—
The mighty dollar is his deity!
His sacred Bible is the bank-note list!
The banker and the broker are his priests;
The mint a model of his paradise;
If air cost cash he would refuse to breathe;
He values heaven because the streets are gold;
And, like a grovelling grub, he dies at last
Smothered and starved beneath his yellow dust!
Behold the idiotic, slavering sot!
His parched mouth like a fiery oven burns;
His veins are vipers plunging fevered fangs
Into his blood, which flows like liquid fire;
Day is a demon scourging him with light,
Night a black ghost which scares him with her stars,
Life a dark ocean lashed with angry storms,
Death a deep gulf which terminates in hell!
But the base miser's and the drunkard's sins
Whiten to innocence compared with those
The God-forsaken demagogues commit:
They'd drench a state in rum to gain their end,
Kidnap a negro or betray a friend,
Profess religion or profane the church,
And veto God's commandments for a vote.
I've seen them flock around our Capitol

[11] During the debate on the 1850 slave compromise Senator William H. Seward declared that although the Fugitive Slave Law could be defended as constitutional, there existed a 'Higher Law', namely a real moral sense which would consider all humans equal and slavery wicked.

As thick as Egypt's lice, and frogs, and flies,[12]
Crawling in crowds along the public street,
Buzzing in house and hall, hotel and mart,
Croaking in secret conclave with their clan,
Flying from post to post in search of game;
Heads of departments itched, and scratched them off,
But those which were not crushed crawled on again.
They lit on every officer of state,
And buzzed petitions at their aching ears.
These frogs from bread troughs and from ovens croaked;
Pierce found them in his chamber night and day;
Not even Caleb[13] could have "crushed" them out.
God speed the time when plagues like these shall pass
Away, and ne'er return to plague us more!
These men for place or pay would now enslave
Nebraska, Kansas, and New England, too!

Ellen Watkins Harper (1825–1911), 'The Slave Mother', 'Eliza Harris', in *Poems on Miscellaneous Subjects* (1854); 'Bury Me in a Free Land' (first published in the *Liberator*, 14 Jan. 1864)

Harper was the most prolific and best-selling African-American woman writer of the nineteenth century. She wrote passionately over a very long time on many reform issues beginning with slavery but branching out into temperance and women's rights and suffrage. The populist style of her writing, and its blatant foregrounding of political agendas, caused her to fall into neglect until the current burst of interest in nineteenth-century protest writing by African-Americans led to her rediscovery as a mainstream American author over the last three decades.

The only child of free parents, but orphaned at 3, she grew up with her uncle's family in Baltimore, Maryland (a slave state). When she was 25 she moved North, and became actively involved in anti-slavery work from about 1853. Taking a teaching job in Little York, Pennsylvania, she was frequently exposed to the sight of escaped slaves trying to make it to Canada, and soon became involved in helping the fugitives. The story of her work in this area is covered in her friend and activist comrade William Still's wonderful *The Underground Railroad*. In 1854 she began public lecturing and became

---

[12] Three of the plagues of Egypt sent by God because Pharaoh refused to listen to Moses' demands to set the Israelites free.   [13] A leader of the tribe of Judah during the wandering in the desert.

a noted orator and performer. In one notorious six-week period of 1854 she is recorded having delivered over thirty speeches in over twenty towns. During the lead-up to the Civil War she toured across Massachusetts, Pennsylvania, New York, New Jersey, Ohio, and Maine. Her 'speeches' were delivered without notes, and had a profound effect on audiences; her quiet yet intense spontaneity led one listener to recall: 'The woe of two hundred years sighed through her tones'. Because of the extempore nature of her abolition oratory the speeches have not survived; yet Harper was also a prolific writer, bringing out many volumes of verse, which are formally and in subject unusually varied, four novels, short stories, and a travel book about the deep South. In terms of the chronology of this volume her first publication, the 1854 *Poems on Miscellaneous Subjects*, is of most relevance, but this early work should be seen as part of an evolving and revolutionary body of work spanning the entire second half of the nineteenth century. Her life and work should perhaps be read as a single organic achievement. If her poems are plucked out of the context of her life's work and viewed according to purely aesthetic criteria they appear weak, yet as occasional protest work which catches the spirit of the age they are direct and powerful. Harper shared with John Pierpont (pp. 540–8) the ability to write verse which chimed with the emotional absolutism of popular abolition sentiment.

The Slave Mother

Heard you that shriek? It rose
    So wildly on the air,
It seemed as if a burden'd heart
    Was breaking in despair.

Saw you those hands so sadly clasped—
    The bowed and feeble head—
The shuddering of that fragile form—
    That look of grief and dread?

Saw you the sad, imploring eye?
    Its every glance was pain,
As if a storm of agony
    Were sweeping through the brain.

She is a mother, pale with fear,
    Her boy clings to her side,
And in her kirtle[1] vainly tries
    His trembling form to hide.

---

[1] A mantle, or outer petticoat.

He is not hers, although she bore
    For him a mother's pains;
He is not hers, although her blood
    Is coursing through his veins!

He is not hers, for cruel hands
    May rudely tear apart
The only wreath of household love
    That binds her breaking heart.

His love has been a joyous light
    That o'er her pathway smiled.
A fountain gushing ever new,
    Amid life's desert wild.

His lightest word has been a tone
    Of music round her heart,
Their lives a streamlet blent in one—
    Oh, Father! must they part?

They tear him from her circling arms,
    Her last and fond embrace.
Oh! never more may her sad eyes
    Gaze on his mournful face.

No marvel, then, these bitter shrieks
    Disturb the listening air:
She is a mother, and her heart
    Is breaking in despair.

Eliza Harris[1]

Like a fawn from the arrow, startled and wild,
A woman swept by us, bearing a child;
In her eye was the night of a settled despair,
And her brow was o'ershaded with anguish and care.

---

[1] Eliza Harris, the beautiful quadroon heroine of Harriet Beecher Stowe's *Uncle Tom's Cabin*, features in one of the novel's most widely adapted dramatic vignettes. At the end of chapter 8 Eliza, pursued by the slave catcher Haley, heroically crosses the semi-frozen Ohio river with her infant son, and makes it to safety and freedom on the other side. The scene provided the climax for many of the popular dramatic adaptations of the book.

She was nearing the river—in reaching the brink,
She heeded no danger, she paused not to think!
For she is a mother—her child is a slave—
And she'll give him his freedom, or find him a grave!

It was a vision to haunt us, that innocent face—
So pale in its aspect, so fair in its grace;
As the tramp of the horse and the bay of the hound,
With the fetters that gall, were trailing the ground!

She was nerv'd by despair, and strengthened by woe,
As she leap'd o'er the chasms that yawn'd from below;
Death howl'd in the tempest, and rav'd in the blast,
But she heard not the sound till the danger was past.

Oh! how shall I speak of my proud country's shame?
Of the stains on her glory, how give them their name?
How say that her banner in mockery waves—
Her "star spangled banner"—o'er millions of slaves?

How say that the lawless may torture and chase
A woman whose crime is the hue of her face?
How the depths of the forest may echo around
With the shrieks of despair, and the bay of the hound?

With her step on the ice, and her arm on her child,
The danger was fearful, the pathway was wild;
But, aided by Heaven, she gained a free shore,
Where the friends of humanity open'd their door.

So fragile and lovely, so fearfully pale,
Like a lily that bends to the breath of the gale,
Save the heave of her breast, and the sway of her hair,
You'd have thought her a statue of fear and despair.

In agony close to her bosom she press'd
The life of her heart, the child of her breast:—
Oh! love from its tenderness gathering might,
Had strengthen'd her soul for the dangers of flight.

But she's free—yes, free from the land where the slave
From the hand of oppression must rest in the grave;
Where bondage and torture, where scourges and chains,
Have plac'd on our banner indelible stains.

Did a fever e'er burning through bosom and brain,
Send a lava-like flood through every vein,
Till it suddenly cooled 'neath a healing spell,
And you knew, oh! the joy! you knew you were well?

So felt this young mother, as a sense of the rest
Stole gently and sweetly o'er *her* weary breast,
As her boy looked up, and, wondering, smiled
On the mother whose love had freed her child.

The bloodhounds have miss'd the scent of her way;
The hunter is rifled and foil'd of his prey;
Fierce jargon and cursing, with clanking of chains,
Make sounds of strange discord on Liberty's plains.

With the rapture love and fulness of bliss,
She plac'd on his brow a mother's fond kiss:—
Oh! poverty, danger and death she can brave,
For the child of her love is no longer a slave!

Bury Me in a Free Land

Make me a grave where'er you will,
In a lowly plain, or a lofty hill,
Make it among earth's humblest graves,
But not in a land where men are slaves.

I could not rest if around my grave
I heard the steps of a trembling slave:
His shadow above my silent tomb
Would make it a place of fearful gloom,

I could not rest if I heard the tread
Of a coffle gang to the shambles led,
And the mother's shriek of wild despair
Rise like a curse on the trembling air.

I could not sleep if I saw the lash
Drinking her blood at each fearful gash,
And I saw her babes torn from her breast,
Like trembling doves from their parent nest.

I'd shudder and start if I heard the bay
Of blood-hounds seizing their human prey,
And I heard the captive plead in vain
As they bound afresh his galling chain.

If I saw young girls from their mother's arms
Bartered and sold for their youthful charms,
My eye would flash with a mournful flame,
My death-paled cheek grow red with shame.

I would sleep, dear friends, where bloated might
Can rob no man of his dearest right;
My rest shall be calm in any grave
Where none can call his brother a slave.

I ask no monument, proud and high
To arrest the gaze of the passers-by;
All that my yearning spirit craves,
Is bury me not in a land of slaves.

George Boyer Vashon, from *Vincent Ogé* (1854)

If it is unusual to find Whitfield writing a poem in celebration of Joseph Cinque
(p. 589) it is far more extraordinary to find Vashon writing an extended poem which
presents Vincent Ogé as a revolutionary martyr and hero. Ogé was a mulatto who led an
early insurrection against the massed forces of the *grands* and *petits blancs* in San
Domingue, in the early stages of social upheaval, before the revolution proper broke
out in 1791. Ogé was captured and then sentenced to a horrific death: tortured in
various ways he was finally broken alive upon the wheel before an almost hysterical
white crowd.

When the cultural dust began to settle around the events which the French Revolu-
tion had generated in the Caribbean Toussaint L'Ouverture became the focus first for
English, and subsequently for American, mythologizations of the black hero of San
Domingue (pp. 176–80, 231–3, 503–10). Ogé was virtually written out of the debates
over the slave revolution, and when he was remembered it was in one of two ways.
Either he was seen as a victim of planter barbarity (not as an influential proto-
revolutionary), or he was seen to stand for a frenzied blancophobe extremism. Thomas
Carlyle's *French Revolution* presents Ogé, on the verge of agonizing death, as a figure still
obsessed with the obliteration of all white life: 'when Ogé's signal-conflagrations went
aloft; with the voice of rage and terror. Repressed doomed to die, he took black powder

or seedgrains in the hollow of his hand, this Ogé; sprinkled a film of white ones on the top, and said to his Judges, "Behold they are white;" then *shook* his hand, and said, "Where are the whites, *Où sont les Blancs?*"' (Thomas Carlyle, *Centenary Edition of the Works of Thomas Carlyle in Thirty Volumes* (Chapman & Hall, 1896), iii. 226).

The San Domingue revolution had presented pro-slavery apologists across Europe and the Americas with a golden opportunity to create a counter-mythology to that of the abolitionists. The atrocities which blacks had inflicted upon the planters and their families during the early stages of the insurrection had generated an extravagant atrocity literature which had rapidly spread from Paris across Europe and North America. The image of the black slave as helpless victim and passive innocent, so carefully constructed in sentimental slavery literatures (see pp. 36–53, 92–3, 110–16, 233–4, 262–79, 320–2), suddenly met its nemesis in the imagery of ultra-violence and sexual depravity which was used to describe the exploits of the 'Black Jacobins' in European and American capitals. This poem, written by an African American in Syracuse, New York, some eighty years after Ogé's death, sets about the task of creating a new revolutionary myth. Vashon goes back to the period before the revolution ignited to look at one of the intellectual instigators of early protest. Ogé is presented as an idealist, fighting for freedom and meeting his appalling fate like a latter-day Marian martyr.

Vincent Ogé (ll. 38–55, 86–95, 134–369)

.   .   .   .   .

The waves dash brightly on thy shore,
   Fair island of the southern seas!
As bright in joy as when of yore
   They gladly hailed the Genoese,—
That daring soul[1] who gave to Spain
A world—last trophy of her reign!
Basking in beauty, thou dost seem
A vision in a poet's dream!
Thou look'st as though thou claim'st not birth
With sea and sky and other earth,
That smile around thee but to show
Thy beauty in a brighter glow,—
That are unto thee as the foil
   Artistic hands have featly set
Around Golconda's[2] radiant spoil,
   To grace some lofty coronet,—

---

[1] Columbus.
[2] Ruined city near Hyderabad in India, once famed for diamond cutting and dealing.

A foil which serves to make the gem
The glory of that diadem!

.   .   .   .

And Ogé stands mid this array
 Of matchless beauty, but his brow
Is brightened not by pleasure's play;
 He stands unmoved—nay, saddened now,
As doth the lorn and mateless bird
That constant mourns, whilst all unheard,
The breezes freighted with the strains
Of other songsters sweep the plain,—
That ne'er breathes forth a joyous note,
Though odors on the zephyrs[3] float—

.   .   .   .   .

For the land of the Gaul[4] had arose in its might,
And swept by as the wind of a wild, wintry night;
And the dreamings of greatness—the phantoms of power,
Had passed in its breath like the things of an hour.
Like the violet vapors that brilliantly play
Round the glass of the chemist, then vanish away,
The visions of grandeur which dazzlingly shone,
Had gleamed for a time, and all suddenly gone.
And the fabric of ages—the glory of kings,
Accounted most sacred mid sanctified things,
Reared up by the hero, preserved by the sage,
And drawn out in rich hues on the chronicler's page,
Had sunk in the blast, and in ruins lay spread,
While the altar of freedom was reared in its stead.
And a spark from that shrine in the free-roving breeze,
Had crossed from fair France to that isle of these
And a flame was there kindled which fitfully shone
Mid the shout of the free, and the dark captive's groan;
As, mid contrary breezes, a torch-light will play,
Now streaming up brightly—now dying away.

The reptile slumbers in the stone,[5]
 Nor dream we of his pent abode;
The heart conceals the anguished groan,
 With all the poignant griefs that goad

---

[3] Zephyr is the west wind, a soft, gentle breeze. [4] France.
[5] It was an ancient folk belief that the toad could enter a stone and sleep within it for centuries.

The brain to madness;
Within the hushed volcano's breast,
    The molten fires of ruin lie;—
Thus human passions seem at rest,
    And on the brow serene and high,
        Appears no sadness.
But still the fires are raging there,
Of vengeance, hatred, and despair;
And when they burst, they wildly pour
    Their lava flood of woe and fear,
And in one short—one little hour,
    Avenge the wrongs of many a year.

And Ogé standeth in his hall;
    But now he standeth not alone;—
A brother's there, and friends; and all
    Are kindred spirits with his own;
For mind will join with kindred mind,
As matter's with its like combined.
They speak of wrongs they had received—
Of freemen, of their rights bereaved;
And as they pondered o'er the thought
Which in their minds so madly wrought,
Their eyes gleamed as the lightning's flash,
Their words seemed as the torrent's dash
That falleth, with a low, deep sound,
Into some dark abyss profound,—
A sullen sound that threatens more
Than other torrents' louder roar.
Ah! they had borne well as they might,
    Such wrongs as freemen ill can bear;
And they had urged both day and night,
    In fitting words, a freeman's prayer;
And when the heart is filled with grief,
    For wrongs of all true souls accurst,
In action it must seek relief,
    Or else, o'ercharged, it can but burst.
Why blame we them, if they oft spake
Words that were fitted to awake
The soul's high hopes—its noblest parts—
The slumbering passions of brave hearts,

And send them as the simoom's[6] breath,
Upon a work of woe and death?
And woman's voice is heard amid
   The accents of that warrior train;
And when has woman's voice e'er bid,
   And man could from its hest refrain?
Hers is the power o'er his soul
   That 's never wielded by another,
And she doth claim this soft control
   As sister, mistress, wife, or mother.
So sweetly doth her soft voice float
   O'er hearts by guilt or anguish riven,
It seemeth as a magic note
   Struck from earth's harps by hands of heaven.
And there 's the mother of Ogé,
   Who with firm voice, and steady heart,
And look unaltered, well can play
   The Spartan[7] mother's hardy part;
And send her sons to battle-fields,
   And bid them come in triumph home,
Or stretched upon their bloody shields,
   Rather than bear the bondman's doom.
"Go forth," she said, "to victory;
Or else, go bravely forth to die!
Go forth to fields where glory floats
In every trumpet's cheering notes!
Go forth, to where a freeman's death
Glares in each cannon's fiery breath!
Go forth and triumph o'er the foe;
Or failing that, with pleasure go
To molder on the battle-plain,
Freed ever from the tyrant's chain!
But if your hearts should craven prove,
Forgetful of your zeal—your love
For rights and franchises of men,
My heart will break; but even then,
Whilst bidding life and earth adieu,
This be the prayer I'll breathe for you:

[6]   Hot, oppressive, and violent desert wind.
[7]   The Spartans were frugal, laconic, militaristic, and the women were as tough and unremitting in their adherence to a ruthless military code of honour as the men.

'Passing from guilt to misery,
May this for aye your portion be,—
A life, dragged out beneath the rod—
An end, abhorred of man and God—
As monument, the chains you nurse—
As epitaph, your mother's curse!'"

A thousand hearts are breathing high,
And voices shouting "Victory!"
   Which soon will hush in death;
The trumpet clang of joy that speaks,
Will soon be drowned in the shrieks
   Of the wounded's stifling breath,
The tyrant's plume in dust lies low—
Th' oppressed has triumphed o'er his foe.
But ah! the lull in the furious blast
May whisper not of ruin past;
It may tell of the tempest hurrying on,
To complete the work the blast begun.
In the voice of a Syren,[8] it may whisp'ringly tell
Of a moment of hope in the deluge of rain;
As the shout of the free heart may rapt'rously swell,
While the tyrant is gath'ring his power again.
Though the balm of the leech may soften the smart.
   It never can turn the swift barb from its aim;
And thus the resolve of the true freeman's heart
   May not keep back his fall, though it free it from shame.
Though the hearts of those heroes all well could accord
With freedom's most noble and loftiest word;
Their virtuous strength availeth them nought
With the power and skill that the tyrant brought.
Gray veterans trained in many a field
Where the fate of nations with blood was sealed,
In Italia's vales—on the shores of the Rhine—
Where the plains of fair France give birth to the vine—
Where the Tagus, the Ebro,[9] go dancing along,
Made glad in their course by the Muleteer's song—
All these were poured down in the pride of their might,

---

[8] Also Siren: sea nymphs, part woman and part bird, who lured sailors to their deaths through seductive song.
[9] A river of north-east Spain flowing into the Mediterranean from the Cantabrian Mountains.

On the land of Ogé, in that terrible fight.
Ah! dire was the conflict, and many the slain,
Who slept the last sleep on that red battle-plain!
The flash of the cannon o'er valley and height
Danced like the swift fires of a northern night,
Or the quivering glare which leaps forth as a token
That the King of the Storm from his cloud-throne has spoken.
And oh! to those heroes how welcome the fate
Of Sparta's brave sons in Thermopylae's[10] strait;
With what ardor of soul they then would have given
Their last look at earth for a long glance at heaven!
Their lives to their country—their backs to the sod—
Their heart's blood to the sword, and their souls to their God!
But alas! although many lie silent and slain,
More blest are they far than those clanking the chain,
In the hold of the tyrant, debarred from the day;—
And among these sad captives is Vincent Ogé!

Another day's bright sun has risen,
And shines upon the insurgent's prison;
Another night has slowly passed,
And Ogé smiles, for 'tis the last
He'll droop beneath the tyrant's power—
The galling chains! Another hour,
And answering to the jailor's call,
He stands within the Judgment Hall.
They've gathered there;—they who have pressed
Their fangs into the soul distressed,
To pain its passage to the tomb
With mock'ry of a legal doom.
They've gathered there;—they who have stood
Firmly and fast in hour of blood,—
Who've seen the lights of hope all die,
As stars fade from a morning sky,—
They've gathered there, in that dark hour—
The latest of the tyrant's power,—
An hour that speaketh of the day
Which never more shall pass away,—

---

[10]   Leonidas' tiny Spartan forces attempted to defend the pass of Thermopylae and held out for three days against the massed armies of the Persian king Xerxes.

The glorious day beyond the grave,
Which knows no master—owns no slave.
And there, too, are the rack—the wheel—[11]
The torturing screw—the piercing steel,—
Grim powers of death all crusted o'er
With other victims' clotted gore.
Frowning they stand, and in their cold,
Silent solemnity, unfold
The strong one's triumph o'er the weak—
The awful groan—the anguished shriek—
The unconscious mutt'rings of despair—
The strained eyeball's idiot stare—
The hopeless clench—the quiv'ring frame—
The martyr's death—the despot's shame.
The rack—the tyrant—victim,—all
Are gathered in that Judgment Hall.
Draw we the veil, for 'tis a sight
But friends can gaze on with delight.
The sunbeams on the rack that play,
For sudden terror flit away
From this dread work of war and death,
As angels do with quickened breath,
From some dark deed of deepest sin,
Ere they have drunk its spirit in.
No mighty host with banners flying,
    Seems fiercer to a conquered foe,
Than did those gallant heroes dying,
    To those who gloated o'er their woe;—
Grim tigers, who have seized their prey,
Then turn and shrink abashed away;
And, coming back and crouching nigh,
Quail 'neath the flashing of the eye,
Which tells that though the life has started,
The will to strike has not departed.

[11] Ogé was extradited to San Domingue from Spanish Santo Domingo, after his attempted revolution failed. His fate is described as follows by C. L. R. James in *The Black Jacobins*: 'The whites tortured Ogé and his companions with a trial lasting two months. They condemned them to . . . be led to the parade-ground, and there have their arms, legs and elbows broken on a scaffold, after which they were to be bound on wheels, their faces turned to the sky, to remain thus while it pleased God to keep them alive. Their heads were then to be cut off, and their goods and property confiscated.'

Sad was your fate, heroic band!
Yet mourn we not, for yours' the stand
Which will secure to you a fame,
That never dieth, and a name
That will, in coming ages, be
A signal word for Liberty.
Upon the slave's o'erclouded sky,
    Your gallant actions traced the bow,
Which whispered of deliv'rance nigh—
    The meed of one decisive blow.
Thy coming fame, Ogé! is sure;
Thy name with that of L'Ouverture,
And all the noble souls that stood
With both of you, in times of blood,
Will live to be the tyrant's fear—
Will live, the sinking soul to cheer!

Bella Marsh, 'Fallen among Thieves', 'The Slave's Offering', in *Lays of Liberty* (1854)

In many ways this is a typical and rather mediocre abolition volume of verse from the mid-1850s. Much of the poetry consists of over-the-top verse renditions of incidents from *Uncle Tom's Cabin*. One of Marsh's poems however does something unusual and powerful. 'The Slave's Offering' is a sentimental extrapolation of an anecdote; yet in suggesting that the black slaves in the American South have more humanity than the free British, it makes a charged political point.

Fallen among Thieves

Where e'er the strong man tramples on the weak,
Forgetful that *he* also is a man,
There is the semblance of that traveler lone,
Who amid rugged, forest paths of old,
Encountered thieves. The eye that sees the heart,
That searches the dim secrets of the soul,
Knows well the dire resemblance. Cover up

With splendors as ye may, the deed unjust,
When the dread scroll shall be unrolled at last,
Of human thought and passion, word and deed,
Then shall the truth shine out as clear and strong,
As though engraved with sunbeams on the sky !

And he, who sees the bleeding victim lie,
Lone and forsaken, and unmoved goes on,
As though he saw him not, till slowly fades
The sad idea of that poor suffering one,
Is but a sharer in the spoiler's guilt.
For through all time the Levite and the Priest,
By light divine made visible, stand forth
Unenvied, in their own attire arrayed,
Of selfishness—neglect of other's grief.
    Who e'er thou art, this picture thou hast scanned,
I ween full oft. Thou knowest well the tale.
One more thou seest—that traveler benign,
Who cheered and raised the fallen—so well approved
By God and man upon the sacred page,
His neighbor who had fallen among thieves!

For ages hath a ruthless war been waged,
By many nations with that suffering race,
Known by the dusky brow and lot forlorn.—
The world hath done the work.
                              What realm shall raise
Her hands inviolate, and say, "In this
I have nor part nor lot."
                              It were a deed
Unmatched on earth in high sublimity,
To see a nation rise—a giant power,
Her myriad hearts all beating as but one,
Her myriad voices as the rushing sound
Of many waters; with determined will,
And holy purpose to redeem the fallen,
And he who lies the lowest to rescue first!

Each helping all, with priceless treasures cast
Upon God's altar, to redeem the lost,
To write upon that brow so long debased,
With degradation of a slave's sad lot,

Freedom and manhood.
Who of us shall say,
But in the piercing vision of our God,
What time he spake in symbol beautiful,
To Jewish listeners, there rose not calm,
And brightly mirrored in his soul serene,
As the consummate meaning of his words,
This wide resplendent scene.
Wilt thou not speed
O! Saviour of our race, just such a day!

The Slave's Offering

A PLEASING INCIDENT.—The Raleigh (N. C.) Recorder relates the following incident, showing the general sympathy throughout the country, even, among the oppressed, for the famishing Irish:

"Early in March last, (1847) I met with a Georgia planter in Charleston, who informed me that he had forwarded to that city ninety odd pounds of bacon, as a spontaneous offering from the negroes of his plantation to the perishing Irish. He had read to his family a pitiable account of the sufferings of that devoted people from famine, which was heard by one of his house servants, who communicated it to the mass. On the eve of his departure from home, he proceeded to give the usual allowance of bacon to his negroes, when one of the head men presented himself and said to his master, that having heard of the condition of the poor Irish, he was instructed by his comrades to say that they had all concluded to give, each one half a pound of his allowance, to Ireland. The amount mentioned constituted the aggregate of their donation, which was immediately forwarded."

We have heard the mournful tale,
Widely echoes Famine's wail,
Borne on every breeze that blows,
Comes the note of distant woes;
We our humble offering bring,
We would cheer the famishing,
Bear our tribute o'er the wave,
Take the offering of the Slave!

Bondage is a bitter fate,
Sad are we and desolate,
Bowed beneath another's will,

Yet our hearts are human still,—
Other's griefs to us made known,
In their woes we lose our own;—
Win the starving from the grave,
Take the offering of the Slave!

In a pleasant land we dwell,
Old and young of Freedom tell,
Banners float in fair array,
Gracing many a festive day,
Yet it ne'er on us has dawned,
Long in bondage we have mourned,
Crushed are we, yet this we crave,—
Take the offering of the Slave!

We have heard of heavenly love,
Gift descending from above,
E'en to us a little ray
Cometh from the Star of day,
In our hearts it burneth deep,
Tears of love and joy we weep,
For His sake who died to save,
Take the offering of the Slave!

Gales of love are sweeping past,
Yet our chains are on us fast,
Shall that influence pure and kind,
Every bond but ours unbind?
Words of love we would not mock,
When will they our chains unlock?
Bear our gift beyond the wave,
Take the offering of the Slave!

Elymas Payson Rogers, *A Poem on the Fugitive Slave Law* (1855)

Rogers, like James Monroe Whitfield (pp. 584–9), was capable of adopting a harsh satiric voice. He was a black slavery poet who was fully capable of telling an audience that he had no faith in whites Northern or Southern. His contempt spilled over with the passage of the Fugitive Slave Law. Rogers's poem differs from the majority of the

Northern verse which greeted the passage of the law in turning its outrage more on the North, for its weakness and hypocrisy, than on the South.

Rogers adopts the octosyllable as the line for his satire. This was the metre made famous by Butler in his *Hudibras*, a popular model in America from early on (see Ebenezor Cook, pp. xxvi–xxvii). The octosyllabic couplet was also, however, the verse form which Swift made his own. Turning from the protracted balance and parallelism of the Popean heroic couplet the octosyllabic line allows for a colloquial tone and staccato effects of intimate anger which suit Rogers's cause well. He shifts between a tone of high moral outrage and the knowing cynicism of the lines considering what the effect of a law might be which pays a judge only half his fee if he lets a slave suspect go free. Throughout the poem Rogers reapplies the symbolic inheritance which the North had applied to the South. The clever reiterations of the imagery of the bloodhound (which reach a climax in the last couplet of this extract) show Rogers's rhetorical subversion at its most powerful. This extract ends with Rogers stepping right up to the mark, and then beyond it. This is the only poem against the Fugitive Slave Law which I have come across where homicide is shown as the only response to being confronted by a slave catcher.

A Poem on the Fugitive Slave Law

> Law! what is law? The wise and sage,
> Of every clime and every age,
> In this most cordially unite,
> That 'tis a rule for doing right.
> Great Blackstone, that illustrious sire,
> Whose commentaries all admire,
> And Witherspoon, and Cicero,
> And all distinguished jurists show
> That law is but the power supreme
> To shield, to nurture, or redeem
> Those rights so sacred, which belong
> To man; and to prohibit wrong.
>   .   .   .   .   .
>
> In fifty, Congress passed a Bill,[1]
> Which proved a crude and bitter pill
> At least in many a northern mouth,
> Though sweet as honey at the South.
>
> It was the object of this Act
> (By priests and politicians backed)

---

[1] See 1850 'Fugitive Slave Law' in the Chronology, p. lx above.

That masters might with ease retake
The wretched slaves who chanced to break
Away from servitude thenceforth,
And sought a refuge at the North.

It was the purpose of this Act
To make the Northern States, in fact,
The brutal master's hunting grounds,
To be explored by human hounds
Who would, for shining gold, again
Bind on the bleeding captive's chain.
This Bill most clearly was designed
To prejudice the public mind
In favor of the master's claim,
Howe'er circuitous or lame.

From officers of baser sort,
The Bill sought sanction and support;
And lawyers bought of no repute
And bribed the dough-faced judge to boot,
It gave encouragement to knaves,
It mocked the suff'rings of the slaves
By giving, if the slave went free,
The judge five dollars as his fee.
But if the judge bound on his chains,
He won ten dollars for his pains.

Go to yon Capitol and look
On this free nation's statute book,
And there you'll find the monstrous Bill
Upon the nation's records still.
And dough-faced[2] politicians now
Their rev'rence for the Act avow,
And hundreds impudently say
That all should peacefully obey
The Act, and yield to its demands,
And give back to the master's hands
The poor, dejected, bleeding slave,
This great Confederacy to save.
We scarce can quench our indignation,
Aroused by such an intimation,

[2] See p. 546 n. 11.

For government should man befit,
And not man sacrifice to it.
And if the Union long has stood
Cemented with the bondsman's blood;
If human hearts and human bone
Are truly its chief corner stone;
If State from State would soon divide
If not with negro sinews tied;
Then let th' accursed Union go,
And let her drift, or, sink below,
Or, let her quick in sunder break
And so become a shattered wreck.

And is that vile requirement just
Which tramples manhood in the dust?
Shall we arrest escaping slaves
At every beck of Southern knaves?
Shall Northern freemen heed a few
Of that untoward apostate crew,
And, let them hunt upon their soil
And drag to unrequited toil
A man, however rude or raw,
Because of that nefarious law
Which causes liberty to bleed,
And gravely sanctions such a deed?
Some call it law; but is it so?
A voice within us answers, no!
It conflicts with the counterpart
Of God's own law in every heart.

Who does not sacred freedom love,
Bequeathed to mortals from above?
Who would not breathe pure freedom's air
And all its kindred blessings share?
Who's so unnatural and so base
As to prefer a bondsman's place?
Not one; for every human breast
Of a free spirit is possessed
Which, incensed, from oppression turns
And direful circumscription spurns;
And, what we love and feign would do,
Our neighbor loves to practise too;

And what we heartily despise
Is hateful in our neighbor's eyes.
We loathe oppression's iron heel,
His bleeding heart can also feel.

That Bill a law? some call it so,
But One above us answers, "No:
It conflicts with my firm decree;
A law therefore it cannot be.
I tell this nation, as I told
My servants in the days of old,
That none the wand'ring shall perplex,
Or e'er the honest stranger vex:
Deliver not the refugee
Who from his master flees to thee;
He who escapes his master's hand
Shall dwell among you in the land,
And to him ye shall not refuse
The dwelling place which he shall choose.
He shall dwell where he likes it best,
And neither shall he be oppressed."

    ·   ·   ·   ·   ·   ·

When we behold our flesh and bone
Dragged back to bondage, there to groan
Beneath the huge and bloody lash,
Which there will lacerate their flesh,
Can we endure their doleful moans
And calmly listen to their groans,
As they exclaim for God's sake save
A helpless, wretched, abject slave
From hopeless, though prospective wo,
From heartless, bloody torture too?
No! let the monster be accursed
Who does not then attempt to burst
Their chains, and set the bondsmen free,
And make the heartless tyrant flee.

E'en now I hear each freeman cry,
That human bloodhounds all shall die,
Whene'er the fugitive shall come,
My house shall ever be his home;
When it is truly necessary

To save some poor defenceless Jerry.
And let the worthless wretch beware
Who comes to seize his victim there.
If in his arrogance and pride
My threshhold he shall e'er bestride,
I near to freedom's altar stand,
And lay thereon my solemn hand,
And on that sacred altar swear
His bleeding form shall welter there.

Moses Austin Cartland (1805–63), from *An Epistolary Lament Supposed to have been Written by a Surviving Hunker* (1855)

Another satire on the Fugitive Slave Law. Cartland, like Rogers, attacks the North for abandoning the ideals of the Revolution. The satiric method, however, could hardly be more different. This poem manages to express mounting outrage through an unusual and very effective use of rhythm. Despite the layout of the verse it is written in rhyming heptametric couplets, the last foot consisting of the unusual bachius (an unstress followed by a double stress u-x-x). This allows for emphatic and reiterative conclusions to lines. The style is consequently highly compressed, and tends to squeeze out political minutiae. Cartland's solution is to run a prose commentary alongside the poem through footnotes. His use of a contemporary political shorthand in the verse allows him to expand on key concepts in short prose essays in the notes. There is only space in this anthology to give a short example, but the disquisition on the phrase 'Devil's masterpiece' gives a full sense of the method.

from *An Epistolary Lament Supposed to have been Written by a Surviving Hunker*[1]

We are "crushed out"—a base reward
   For years of pious toiling;
We've licked the dust from Southern feet,
   Our very manhood soiling—
Stood watch-dogs at the despot call,

[1]   A member of the conservative section of the New York Democratic party 1845–8. The origin of the word is unknown, but it came to stand for any sort of extreme political conservative.

While Slavery was extending,
And crouched in loathsome vassalage,
    Our every back-bone bending.

We've trodden down old Pilgrim rights—
    Preached "abolition dying,"
Deceiving free-born, Northern men
    By systematic lying.
We've stood at every gambling haunt,
    Where offices were prizes;
And torn in shreds, at Slavery's beck,
    OLD FREEDOM'S COMPROMISES.

We've panted for the "nigger-hunt,"
    With true four-footed valor;
And flung our manhood's pride away
    For SLAVERY'S iron collar!
A truckling brood of Northern slaves—
    The scorn of Freemen winning—
We louder bawled "Democracy"
    The more that we were sinning.

We've cursed the "higher law"of God,
    Proclaiming man a chattel"—
That curling hair and sable skin
    Mark but "two-legged cattle"—
That selling them on auction blocks,
    Or in the coffle driven,
Is serving two great Gods at once,
    DEMOCRACY—and HEAVEN!

We've sworn, by wholesale, that old "truths"
    Are lying declamation—
That JEFFERSON,[2] the stripling, penned
    A verdant DECLARATION—
That *he* was but a pigmy sage—

[2] 'A prominent "democrat" of this State, to parry the force of the declaration, "*all men are created equal*," lately said that Jefferson penned *that* sentiment ("truth") when he was a *young man (!)* and before his mind had become matured by reflection! It was simply the "rhetorical flourish" of a Virginia stripling; and, as such, entitled to little consideration!

A certain fable tells us that the *Ass* once undertook to criticise the music of the *Nightingale*. Dear reader,

"Many such critics you and I have seen;
            Heaven be our screen!"' [Cartland]

A now discarded "fossil,"
While PETTIT[3] stands "Democracy's"
GREAT LATTER-DAY APOSTLE!

We've bent our backs to every task
    That most disgraces "freemen,"
And sometimes played the hypocrite,
    And sometimes played the demon—
Been SLAVERY's faithful scavengers,
    Whenever we were able,
And made the "Devil's Masterpiece"[4]
    Our democratic Bible!

But all for nought!—the god we served,
    Is but an olden Liar;
And we are swept, like chaff, before
    An all consuming fire.
The storm-track of the People's wrath
    On every wreck is written,
Where FREEDOM, with her stalwart arm,
    Our tyrant host has smitten.

---

[3] 'Hon. John Pettit, late U.S. Senator from Indiana, declared in his place, in the Senate, that "the self-evident truth, 'ALL MEN ARE CREATED EQUAL,' is a *self-evident* LIE!" Great expounder of TRUTH—and "Democracy!" Wonderful philosopher! sitting in judgement on THOMAS JEFFERSON—

"A tom-tit twittering on an eagle's beak!"

However, some credit is due Senator Pettit for his boldness. He only *speaks* what "Democracy" *acts.*' [Cartland]

[4] 'The Fugitive Slave Act of 1850 has been called, "*The Devil's Masterpiece;*" although we are taught that *that* must be obeyed whatever may become of the promptings of Humanity or the teachings of the Bible. That this Man-Hunting *Law*, so called, is truly characterized above, let the following picture, (by an eye-witness,) of the "Marshal's Body Guard," on the occasion of Burns' rendition at Boston, bear witness. None *but* the Evil One would summon *such* an array of dutiful children to his aid. But read:—

"I never saw such a motley crew as this kidnappers' gang collected together, save in the darkest places of London and Paris, whither I went to see how low humanity might go, and yet bear the semblance of man. He raked the kennels of Boston. He dispossessed the stews. He gathered the spoils of brothels; prodigals not penitent, who upon harlots had wasted their substance in riotous living; pimps, gamblers, the *succubus* of slavery; men that the gorged jails had cast out into the streets; men scarred with infamy; fighters, drunkards, public brawlers, convicts that had served out their time, waiting for a second conviction; men whom the subtlety of counsel, or the charity of the gallows, had left unhanged, 'No eye hath seen such scare-crows.' Jailor Andrews, it is said, recognized forty of his customers among them. The publican who fed these locusts of Southern tyranny said that out of the sixty-five, there was but one respectable man; and he kept aloof from all the rest. I have seen courts of justice in England, Holland, Belgium, Germany, France, Italy and Switzerland, and I have seen just such men, *But they were always in the dock, not the servants of the court.*"

Who, in looking upon this terrible array of haggard humanity, could have failed to exclaim, in the language of Scripture—"*Ye are of your father, the Devil;* and verily ye are doing his work!*"' [Cartland]

Walt Whitman (1819–92), from *Leaves of Grass* (1855, 1892)

Whitman's poetry is the most important writing in this book. As Walt Whitman wound up that unprecedented and still bewildering literary phenomenon, the 1855 edition of *Leaves of Grass*, he wrote: 'Great is wickedness . . . I find I often admire it just as much as I admire goodness: | Do you call that a paradox?' (1855, 'Great are the Myths', ll. 61–2). It certainly is a paradox. The awful thing is that he means it. Which is to say that Whitman and conventional notions of a moral or ethical agenda do not sit easily together, and we forget this fact at our cost when trying to approach Whitman on slavery. There is no definitive way to read *Leaves of Grass*, and like Coleridge's *Rime of the Ancient Mariner*, and Blake's *Vala* (pp. 143–4, 147–50), it explodes any narrow political framework which is laid upon it. Whitman wrote extensively of blacks and slavery throughout his literary career, and there have been several fine scholarly studies which tease out the operations, shifts, and contradictions regarding his approach to these subjects in the prose he wrote in the three decades leading up to the Civil War. Those who want literary and historical contexts should read the work of Christopher Beach, and particularly the excellent Martin Klammer. Yet these recent accounts tend to develop along apologetic lines, attempting to separate Whitman's predominantly early, explicitly proslavery fiction and journalism from *Leaves of Grass*. It is as if there is an unavoidable force which requires contemporary commentators to wish, against all the evidence, that somehow Whitman was capable, deep down, of conforming to contemporary academic notions of what constitutes the 'right' way to look at race and slavery. There is also the repeated argument that Whitman on slavery undergoes a sea change due to Emerson's literary influence in the late 1840s. There seems to be a desire among Whitman critics to prove that *Leaves of Grass* in its various forms, if not Whitman the man in his various forms, ultimately constitutes a triumphantly humanitarian defence of the slave. I cannot agree with this verdict, not only because it seems to fly in the face of Whitman's refusal to stake out a completely stable position on any moral or political issues in the 1855 edition, but because it closes down his art. Quite frankly why should the extraordinarily open experimentation of the mature poetry suddenly be seen to subscribe to an abolitionist agenda, or even more troublingly to the politically normalizing agendas which haunt and police today's professional cultural commentators? Whitman's cosmic triumphalism refuses the confines of contemporary political debate and morality, and is more fascinating as a result, in terms of what it can reveal about slavery and the Northern states. That does not always make what Whitman says easy to stomach now, and he certainly is 'racist' in some aspects of his thought and writing, when set against contemporary PC criteria.

And yet, Whitman goes beyond the ideological agenda of ante-bellum, and I would suggest contemporary, slavery debate to look into far more difficult questions. At times he talks idealistically of black–white relations; at others he is prepared to think about the possible irreconcilability of black and white. Whitman's essentially levelling poetic imagination, where beauty is seen in everything including death, disease, poverty, horror, hatred, *and* slavery, may ultimately be an ironic definition of the inevitability of difference, and of our duty to negotiate this inevitablility. Perhaps even more troubling for his critics is the undeniable delight which Whitman takes in bringing out the potential extremes of pleasure and suffering which the absolute power relations of the state of slavery can enable. He flirts with the abusive and pornographic potential of slave systems in a manner which is now reserved for the 'low' art of popular cinema, the plantation flagellation novel, and the whipping and auction pornographies of the World Wide Web. This is murky territory; rather than hide away from this element in his work it is vital to try and understand it. Many of the Whitmanesque paradoxes over slavery are essentialized in the passages from 'I Sing the Body Electric' where Whitman delightedly casts himself as slave auctioneer in order to provide his ultimate inventory of the beauties of the male and female body. To deny that this move is deeply troubling to an orthodox liberal morality now is to deny Whitman his continuing power to shock. In making this move he forces us to question his role as an artist celebrating the beauty of the slave body in the context of a sharpened awareness brought about by the imminent act of purchase: surely a very American perceptive sharpening. But Whitman does more: he puts his reader in the invidious position of the potential buyer. If his high artistic salesmanship is good enough we will buy into his vision of the slave, and he will laugh all the way to the aesthetic bank. He must surely be laughing now. Those who have written on Whitman and slavery observe a uniform tone of sobriety completely at odds with the poet's outrageous cheek and continually celebratory irony. It is well known that Whitman, while in New Orleans in 1846, saw many slave auctions, and he is known to have kept a poster of a slave auction on his walls for many years. These facts however are not of any help at all in reading 'I Sing the Body Electric'. If there is one area in which white cultural historians and literary critics feel uneasy about embracing Whitman's delighted affirmations of his capacity for self-contradiction, then that area is slavery, sexuality, and humour.

In terms of a broad overview of his writing on slavery there appear to be a series of distinct stages. Whitman began writing fundamentally pro-slavery material in his twenties, of which the most extreme example is the bizarre *Franklyn Evans*. This is a paranoid piece of fiction in which Whitman combines temperance literature with an examination of interracial sexuality, focused upon the eponymous hero Evans's obsession with an octoroon slave, whom he marries in an alcohol-induced state of sexual obsession. His immediate response when sober is utter disgust. The novel climaxes with the octoroon's murder of a white rival and her subsequent suicide. Whitman certainly qualified his pro-slavery and Negrophobe position in the 1840s. In a series of editorials he defended the 'free-soil' policy which would prohibit the extension of slavery into the lands newly opened up to the United States by victory in the Mexican War. Yet his political writing on the issue is more strongly dominated by a concern for the effects slavery would have in closing down the potential white labour market than it is with the immorality of slavery. In the late 1840s Whitman increasingly came under the influence of Emerson, and absorbed his enlightened views regarding the status of African Americans. By the early 1850s Whitman certainly seems to be moving towards a position which openly condemned slavery. Yet it is a mistake to see Emerson's political positioning over slavery precisely reflected in Whitman's mature poetry. Exactly what he thought about the intellectual and spiritual status of both slaves and free blacks is less easy to evaluate from the evidence of the poems (see Martin Klammer, *Whitman, Slavery and the Emergence of Leaves of Grass* (Pennsylvania State University Press, 1995), 1–60). By the time he published the 1855 edition of *Leaves of Grass* he had begun to narrativize and mythologize blacks in a number of morally ambiguous ways in the experimental poetry which preceded the publication of his masterpiece. These range from intense patronization and objectification of the black subject, male and female, to an extreme self-identification with the black slave as martyrological victim, or even as Antichrist. Throughout the subsequent decades of his life Whitman then rewrote the key passages dealing with slavery and inserted new passages in later editions of *Leaves of Grass*, and these changes frequently problematize race and slavery to an even greater extent.

Given Whitman's undisputed centrality to America as the most innovative, influential, and energized poet the United States has generated, his writings on slavery in *Leaves of Grass* are of a crucial cultural significance. These passages emerge as explorations of the central tensions and confusions which inhabit the Northern psyche when it deals with the question of Southern slavery, the status of fugitives, and the practice of ownership within the economic nexus of the master–slave relation. In his sarcastic laughter on the auction block, in his envy of the intensity of the tortured slave's suffering, an envy which leads to the final form of flattery, emotional mimesis, Whitman does not give us an easy way of looking at what the inheritance of slavery leaves for the West. When he says, 'The kept-woman, sponger, thief, are hereby invited, The heavy-lipp'd slave is invited, the venerealee is invited; There shall be no difference between them and the rest', what do his equations mean for race theory? When he says, 'The scholar kisses the teacher and the teacher kisses the scholar . . . the wronged is made right, The call of the slave is one with the master's call . . . and the master salutes the slave', where do his equations leave the slave now, where do they leave Whitman, and where do they leave us? Is such a radical articulation of equality in fact an iniquity? Whitman remains an enigma: full of love, hate, and bad taste, unreal sentiment and real unsentimental horror.

Textual note: Given the complexity surrounding the dating of different texts each quotation has the relevant information appended. Passages concerning blacks and slavery are from the unpublished manuscripts, the 1855 first edition, and the 'death bed' edition of 1892.

from *Leaves of Grass* (1855), 'Song of Myself', X. 177–92

I saw the marriage of the trapper in the open air in the far west....
    the bride was a red girl,
Her father and his friends sat near cross-legged and dumbly smoking....
    they had moccasins to their feet and large thick blankets hanging
    from their shoulders;

On a bank lounged the trapper.... he was dressed mostly in skins....
    his luxuriant beard and curls protected his neck,
One hand rested on his rifle.... the other hand held firmly the wrist
    of the red girl,
She had long eyelashes.... her head was bare.... her coarse straight
    locks descended upon her voluptuous limbs and reached to her feet.

The runaway slave came to my house and stopped outside,
I heard his motions crackling the twigs of the woodpile,
Through the swung half-door of the kitchen I saw him limpsey and weak,
And went where he sat on a log, and led him in and assured him,
And brought water and filled a tub for his sweated body and bruised feet,
And gave him a room that entered from my own, and gave him some
    coarse clean clothes,
And remember perfectly well his revolving eyes and his awkwardness,
And remember putting plasters on the galls of his neck and ankles;
He staid with me a week before he was recuperated and passed north,
I had him sit next me at table.... my firelock leaned in the corner.

[A convenient overview of the highly complicated evolution of Whitman's views on race and of the processes of a developing empathy with the idea of the runaway/rebel slave emerges if this final version of 'the hunted slave' fragment is set in the context of the many earlier treatments of the idea. The first version evolved out of a series of attempts to describe the hunted slave as a 'Lucifer' figure, an angel and a devil simultaneously, a threat and an ideal for white society, and for Whitman himself. *Pictures* was a highly experimental unpublished poem written in 1853–4 which gives 150 'pictures' which hang in the poet's head. Two of the pictures contain descriptions of black slaves which anticipate the greedy sympathy of the hunted slave scene in *Leaves of Grass*, and which are predicated upon the Lucifer as denied God concept.]

    And this black portrait—this head, huge, frowning, sorrowful,—
        is Lucifer's portrait—the denied God's portrait.
    But I do not deny him—though cast out and rebellious,
        He is my God as much as any.
                      (quoted Klammer, *Whitman*, 97)

    And there in the midst of a group, a quell'd revolted slave, cowering, |
        See you, the hand-cuffs, the hopple, and the blood stain'd cowhide . . .
                      (quoted Klammer, *Whitman*, 99)

[Whitman's first full draft version of the hunted slave scene attempted to extend this notion of the figure as Lucifer. A cancelled stanza preceding the description runs: 'What Lucifer [del.] felt, [ins.] cursed [ins.] when [on a line above] tumbling from heaven' (version reconstructed in Klammer, *Whitman*, 99) and makes explicit the continuation of the Lucifer identification.]

> The slave that stood could run no longer, and then stood, by the fence,
>   blowing panting and covered with sweat,
> And his eye that burns defiance and desperation hatred
> And the buck shot, were
> And how the twinges that sting like needles his breast and neck
> The murderous buck-shot planted like terrible
> This he not only sees but
> He is the hunted slave
> Damnation and despair are close upon him
> He clutches the rail of the fence
> His blood presently oozes from and becomes thinned with the
>   plentiful sweat
> See how it
> And trickles down the black skin
> He slowly falls on the grass and stones,
> And the hunters haul up close with their unwilling horses,
> And the taunt and curse dark dim and dizzy in his ears
>   (quoted Klammer, *Whitman*, 99–100)

[Another version followed in which Whitman, through an imaginative act of typically colossal egomania, imagines himself as the slave, and by implication Lucifer.]

> The hunted slave who flags in the race at last, and leans up by the fence,
>   blowing and covered with sweat,
> And the twinges that sting like needles his breast and neck
> The murderous buck-shot and the bullets.
> All this I not only feel and see but am.
> I am the hunted slave
> Damnation and despair are close upon me
> I clutch the rail of the fence.
> My gore presently trickles thinned with ooze of my skin as I fall on the
>   reddened grass and stones,
> And the hunters haul up close with their unwilling horses,
> Till taunt and oath swim away from my dim and dizzy ears.
>   (quoted Klammer, *Whitman*, 112)

from *Leaves of Grass* (1855), 'Song of Myself', XIII. 219–25

The negro holds firmly the reins of his four horses.... the block swags
    underneath on its tied-over chain,
The negro that drives the huge dray of the stone-yard.... steady
    and tall he stands poised on one leg on the stringpiece,
His blue shirt exposes his ample neck and breast and loosens over
    his hipband,
His glance is calm and commanding.... he tosses the slouch of his
    hat away from his forehead,
The sun falls on his crispy hair and mustache.... falls on the black
    of his polish'd and perfect limbs.

I behold the picturesque giant and love him.... and I do not stop there,
I go with the team also.

from *Leaves of Grass* (1855), 'Song of Myself', XV. 266–80

The lunatic is carried at last to the asylum a confirmed case,
He will never sleep any more as he did in the cot in his
    mother's bedroom;
The jour printer with gray head and gaunt jaws works at his case,
The malform'd limbs are tied to the anatomist's table,
What is removed drops horribly in a pail;
The Quadroon girl is sold at the stand.... the drunkard nods by
    the barroom stove,
The machinist roles up his sleeves.... the policeman travels his beat....
    the gate keeper marks who pass,
The young fellow drives the express wagon.... I love him, though
    I do not know him;
The half-breed straps on his light boots to compete in the race,
The western turkey-shooting draws old and young.... some lean
    on their rifles, some sit on logs,
Out from the crowd steps the marksman takes his position and
    levels his piece;
The groups of newly-come immigrants cover the wharf or levee,
The woollypates hoe in the sugar field, the overseer views them
    from his saddle;
The bugle calls in the ballroom, the gentlemen run for their partners,
    the dancers bow to each other;

from *Leaves of Grass* (1855), 'Song of Myself',
XIX. 372–5

This is the meal pleasantly set.... this the meat and drink for
    natural hunger,
It is for the wicked just the same as the righteous.... I make
    appointments with all,
I will not have a single person slighted or left away,
The kept woman, sponger, thief, are hereby invited.... the
    heavy-lipped slave is invited.... the venerealee is invited;
There shall be no difference between them and the rest.

from *Leaves of Grass* (1855), 'Song of Myself',
XXXIII. 828–39

I am the man.... I suffered.... I was there.

The disdain and calmness of martyrs,
The mother condemned for a witch, burnt with dry wood,
    and her children gazing on,
The hounded slave that flags in the race and leans by the fence,
    blowing and covered with sweat,
The twinges that sting like needles his legs and neck,
The murderous buckshot and the bullets,
All these I feel or am.

I am the hounded slave.... I wince at the bite of the dogs,
Hell and despair are upon me.... crack and again crack
    the marksmen,
I clutch the rails of the fence.... my gore dribs, thinned with
    the ooze of my skin,
I fall on the weeds and the stones,
The riders spur their unwilling horses and haul close,
They taunt my dizzy ears.... they beat me violently over
    the head with their whip-stocks.

Agonies are one of my changes of garments;

from *Leaves of Grass* (1855), 'I Sing the Body Electric',
VI. 78–82; VII. 83–103; VIII. 104–20

VI

All is a procession,
The universe is a procession with measured and beautiful motion.
Do you know so much that you call the slave or the
    dullfaced ignorant?
Do you suppose you have a right to a good sight.... and
    he or she has no right to a sight?
Do you think matter has cohered together from its diffused float,
    and the soil is on the surface and water runs and vegetation
    sprouts for you.... and not for him and her?

VII

A slave at auction!
I help the auctioneer.... the sloven does not half know
    his business.

Gentlemen look on this curious creature,
Whatever the bids of the bidders they cannot be high
    enough for him,
For him the globe lay preparing quintillions of years without one
    animal or plant,
For him the revolving cycles truly and steadily rolled.

In that head the all baffling brain,
In it and below it the making of the attributes of heroes.

Examine these limbs, red, black or white.... they are very
    cunning in the tendon and nerve;
They shall be stript that you may see them.

Exquisite senses, lifelit eyes, pluck, volition,
Flakes of breastmuscle, pliant backbone and neck, flesh
    not flabby, goodsized arms and legs,
And wonders within there yet.

Within there runs blood.... the same old blood.... the same
    red running blood;
There swells and jets his heart.... There all passions and
    desires.... all reachings and aspirations:

Do you think they are not there because they are not
    expressed in parlors and lecture-rooms?

This is not only one man.... this is the father of those who
    shall be fathers in their turns,
In him the start of populous states and rich republics,
Of him countless immortal lives with countless embodiments
    and enjoyments.

How do you know who shall come from the offspring of his
    offspring through the centuries?
Who might you find you have come from yourself, if you
    could trace back through the centuries?

VIII

A woman at auction,

She too is not only herself.... she is the teeming
    mother of mothers,
She is the bearer of them that shall grow and be
    mates to mothers.
Her daughters or their daughters' daughters.... who knows
    who shall mate with them?
Who knows through the centuries what heroes may
    come from them?

In them and of them natural love.... in them the divine
    mystery.... the same old beautiful mystery.

Have you ever loved a woman?
Your mother.... is she living?.... Have you been much with her?
    and has she been much with you?
Do you not see that these are exactly the same to all in all
    nations and times all over the earth?

If life and the soul are sacred the human body is sacred;
And the glory and sweet of a man is the token of
    manhood untainted,
And in man or woman a clean strong firmfibred body is
    beautiful as the most beautiful face,

Have you seen the fool that corrupted his own live body?
    or the fool that corrupted her own live body?
For they do not conceal themselves, and cannot
    conceal themselves.

from *Leaves of Grass* (1892), Children of Adam; 'I Sing the Body Electric', VII, VIII, IX

VII

A man's body at auction,
(For before the war I often go to the slave-mart and watch the sale,)
I help the auctioneer, the sloven does not half know his business.

Gentlemen look on this wonder,
Whatever the bids of the bidders they cannot be high enough for it,
For it the globe lay preparing quintillions of years without
    one animal or plant,
For it the revolving cycles truly and steadily roll'd.

In this head the all-baffling brain,
In it and below into the makings of heroes.

Examine these limbs, red, black or white, they are cunning
    in tendon and nerve,
They shall be stript that you may see them.
Exquisite senses, life-lit eyes, pluck, volition,
Flakes of breast muscle, pliant backbone and neck, flesh
    not flabby, good-sized arms and legs,
And wonders within there yet.
Within there runs blood,
The same old blood! the same red-running blood!

There swells and jets a heart, there all passions, desires,
    reachings, aspirations,
(Do you think they are not there because they are not
    express'd in parlours and lecture-rooms?)

This is not only one man, this is the father of those who
    will be fathers in their turns,
In him the start of populous states and rich republics,
Of him countless immortal lives with countless embodiments
    and enjoyments.

How do you know who shall come from the offspring of his
    offspring through the centuries?
(Who might you find you have come from yourself, if you could
    trace back through the centuries?)

VIII

A woman's body at auction,
She too is made only of herself, she is the teeming mother of mothers,
She is the bearer of them that shall grow and be mates to the mothers,

Have you ever loved the body of a woman?
Have you ever loved the body of a man?
Do you not see that these are exactly the same to all in all nations and
    times all over the earth?

If any thing is sacred the human body is sacred,
And the glory and sweet of a man is the token of manhood untainted,
And in man or woman a clean, strong, firm-fibred body, is
    more beautiful than the most beautiful face.
Have you seen the fool that corrupted his own live body?
    or the fool that corrupted her own live body?
For they do not conceal themselves, and cannot conceal themselves.

IX

O my body! I dare not desert the likes of you in other men
    and women, nor the likes of the parts of you,
I believe the likes of you are to stand or fall with the likes of the soul
    (and that they are my soul,)
I believe the likes of you shall stand or fall with my poems,
    and that they are my poems,
Man's, woman's, child's, youth's, wife's, husband's, mother's,
    father's, young man's, young woman's poems.
Head, neck hair, ears, drop and tympan of the ears,
Eyes, eye-fringes, iris of the eye, eyebrows, and the waking
    or sleeping of the lids,
Mouth, tongue, lips, teeth, roof of the mouth, jaws, and the jaw-hinges,
Nose, nostrils of the nose, and the partition,
Cheeks, temples, forehead, chin, throat, back of the neck, neck-slue,
Strong shoulders, manly beard, scapula, hind-shoulders,
    and the ample side-round of the chest,
Upper-arm, armpit, elbow-socket, lower-arm, arm-sinews, arm-bones,
Wrists and wrist joints, hand, palm, knuckles, thumb, forefinger,
    finger-joints, finger-nails,
Broad breast-front, curling hair of the breast, breast-bone, breast-side,
Ribs, belly backbone, joints of the backbone,
Hips, hip-sockets, hip-strength, inward and outward round,
    man-balls, man root,

Strong set of thighs, well carrying the trunk above,
Leg-fibres, knee, knee-pan, upper-leg, under-leg,
Ankles, instep, foot-ball, toes, toe-joints, the heel;
All attitudes, all the shapeliness, all the belongings of my or your body or
    of any one's body, male or female,
The lung-sponges, the stomach-sac, the bowels sweet and clean,
The brain in its folds inside the skull-frame,
Sympathies, heart-valves, palate-valves, sexuality, maternity,
Womanhood, and all that is a woman, and the man that comes from woman,
The womb, the teats, the nipples, breast-milk, tears, laughter, weeping,
    love-looks, love-perturbations and risings,
The voice, articulation, language, whispering, shouting aloud,
Food, drink, pulse, digestion, seat, sleep, walking, swimming,
Poise on the hips, leaping, reclining, embracing, arm-curving and
    tightening,
The continual changes of the flex of the mouth, and around the eyes,
The skin, the sunburnt shade, freckles, hair,
The curious sympathy one feels when feeling with the hand the naked
    meat of the body,
The circling rivers the breath, and breathing it in and out,
The beauty of the waist, and thence of the hips, and thence downward
    to the knees,
The thin red jellies within you or within me, the bones and the marrow in
    the bones,
The exquisite realisation of health;
O I say these are not the parts and poems of the body only, but of the soul,
O I say now these are the soul!

Richard Realf (1834–78), 'A Black Man's Answer' (1863?),
in *Poems by Richard Realf* (1898); 'How Long,
Oh Lord, How Long' (1856), in *Richard Realf's
Free State Poems* (1900)

Realf was a charismatic and tragic figure. Born in East Sussex, he showed a precocious interest in verse. As a youth he was taken up by the Brighton literary set including Lady Noel Byron and Harriet Martineau, and they encouraged his interest in American abolition. In 1854 he travelled to New York under something of a cloud because of an amatory scandal involving a lady in the Byron household. In 1856 Realf moved to

Kansas and joined the escort party of a train of Northern emigrants. The party consisted of free-soil settlers who were hoping to advance the cause of abolition within the newly formed state of Kansas. Realf reported on the situation for various Northern journals and newspapers, and published a volume of anti-slavery verse, the *Free State Poems*. At this point Realf met John Brown and joined his guerrilla band in Springdale, Iowa. Realf became an intimate of Brown's and was even named Secretary of State in Brown's putative government outlined at the notorious Chatham Convention. Realf travelled back to Britain in 1858 in order to raise abolition funds, and consequently missed out on the ill-fated Harper's Ferry raid. He was, however, arrested on suspicion of conspiracy on his return and faced investigation in Washington, only to be eventually released.

Realf threw himself into the Civil War which for him was quite clearly a war on slavery. He enlisted in the 88th Illinois Volunteer Infantry and had a distinguished career, fighting valiantly in several major battles. Later in the war he transferred to the 50th Regiment, United States Coloured Infantry, and also worked for the Freedmen's Bureau. Yet despite his ideals Realf's practical relationship with free blacks was not trouble free. Having established a 'coloured school' in Graniteville, South Carolina, he then abandoned the project because of what he described as 'colorphobia'.

Throughout his career Realf continued writing sporadic journalism and verse, and delivering public lectures. Yet his turbulent Romantic life eventually caught up with him. During the years after the war he was increasingly harassed as a result of a bigamous marriage. Under growing pressure from his first wife's blackmailing threats to expose him Realf killed himself in 1878. (Written by Carole Realff.)

A Black Man's Answer

Well, if it be true, as you assert,
That this is a land for the white man's rule,
And not for "niggers," does that import
That our God is the white man's fool?

"Two peoples? The hammers and heats of war
Have forged and fused, like welded links,
The fates of the twain in one; we are
For you, the riddle of the Sphinx.

"And you must solve us, unless again,
Over the burning marl of woe
Where never falleth the blessed rain,
Hell-dragged you want to go.

"When the scythes of slaughter swung in blood
And fair green fields of men were mown,

Did not our black limbs dapple the sod
With streams as red as your own?

"But not for this do we look in your face,
White man, and ask, with hungry eyes,
My brother! give us a little space
To work in under the skies!

"We are not mendicants: we are Souls!
The soul that thrilled in Shakespeare, and
Lit Lincoln's lips with living coals,
Thrills us here where we stand.

"We try to use our wings and fly;
We try to use our limbs to run;
Do you hold mortmain over the sky,
Over the earth and the sun?

"Your apples are of Hesperides;[1]
You give us those of Tantalus;[2]
But what if the Lord should blight your trees
And mock you as you mock us?"

How Long, O Lord, How Long?

How Long, O Lord, how long
Must fettered Freedom writhe beneathe her chains,
And send the wailing of the captive's song
Across the purple plains?

How long, O Lord, how long
Shall Slavery's bloodhounds hold her by the throat,
And her life reel beneath the dripping throng
Of Hell's Iscariot?

How long, O Lord, how long
Shall she be haunted, homeless, through the earth;

---

[1] The Hesperides were sisters who guarded in their delightful gardens the golden apples which Hera on her marriage to Zeus had been given by Gaea.

[2] Tantalus was a son of Zeus; he was punished for revealing the secrets of the gods. His punishment was to stand in water that ebbed away when he wanted to drink, while grapes which hung above his head drew back whenever he reached out for them. His perpetual frustration gave rise to the concept of being 'tantalized'.

Nor thou—Just One—against the crimson wrong
Launch Thy broad lightnings forth?

O, have Thine eyes not seen
With what high trust she bore her bitter shames;
Nor marked how calm and Godlike and serene
She stood amid the flames?

O, have Thine ears not heard
Her long low gasp of inarticulate prayer,
When livid hate, with redly reeking sword,
Has clutched her by the hair?

O, didst Thou not look down
Upon her cruel buffetings of scorn,
And watch her temples stream beneath the crown,
Made of the mocking thorn?

And dost Thou not discern
How the fierce, pitiless rabble casteth lots
For her white robes—alas! so rent and torn,
And smeared with purple spots?

O, when she held the cup
On those wild nights of her Gethsemane;—
Father in Heaven, did she still not look up,
Firm and unmoved—to Thee?

And when the bloody sweat
Oozed from the blue veins of her shuddering limbs,
Was not the burning clasp of agony met
With calm and triumphant hymns?

O, if she be Thy child,
And Thou art God, burst now this dread eclipse,
And let her pass forth free and undefiled
With Thy breath on her lips.

A. G. Meacham, 'Canto IV The Contest', in *Sumner: A Poem* (1856)

Under the Kansas Nebraska Act of 1854 the South was legally able to try and stop the Kansas territory from remaining free soil. If a strong enough slavery presence could be established Kansas might enter the Union as a slavery state. From 1854 to 1856 slave and free-soil settlers were entering the territory in a highly volatile political climate. John Brown was financed by leading abolitionists to 'protect' free-soilers and carried out covert atrocities as he roamed Kansas, including several ritualized and brutal murders. When in 1856 Charles Sumner made a violent speech in the Senate against the slave power and 'the Crime against Kansas', Preston Brooks, the representative from South Carolina, lost his head, and beat Sumner up horrendously with his stick, actually on the Senate floor. Sumner was badly injured and took weeks to recover. Immediately abolition had yet another major martyr and the abolition publicity machine was not slow to mythologize the event. Meacham's *Sumner* attempted to tell the tale of Kansas and the fate of Sumner as a pseudo-Miltonic epic.

The fourth canto of *Sumner* reproduced below illustrated how, in this bellicose narrative, the slave has become very much an incidental player. The main focus of the verse lies in the demonization of the South, presented as a filthy and venomous serpent, and the elevation of Sumner to the status of saint. This poem might stand as the literary apogee of what Hazel Wolf aptly described as the 'abolition martyr complex'. This is disturbing work because at one level it exists in competition with the slave as a figure of innocent victimhood. There is a desire to create white abolition heroes who suffer more for the slave than the slave can ever repay.

Sumner: A Poem

CANTO IV

THE CONTEST[1]

But yet how vainly did our fathers boast
Of victory complete, and polity
Unmixed and free from elements of all
Despotic kind! The reptile[2] which they deemed

---

[1] 'It was the united sentiment of the Convention that formed the Constitution, that slavery should not extend over any territory other than that where it than existed, that the African Slave trade should cease in 1808, and that thus slavery should lie out, slavery is thus personated.' [Meacham]

[2] 'The slave oligarchy, assuming every form to extend its domain. It complains that the free states withheld for it, its dearest rights among which is that of extending slavery over the territories not organized into states.' [Meacham]

As wounded unto death, they saw ere long,
To move his winding folds, and gath'ring strength,
Threw forth himself full length and boistrously
Demanded domnant rule. Most clam'rously
He charged our patriot bands with foul intent,
To fraud and rob him of his rights most dear;
Which to his purpose had been consecrate,
By the great council of the nation held,
Its character to mould, and to transform
And fix the institutions of the realm
Loud boasts of valor and of excellence
Were made. And pompous threats of blood and war,
Amidst the patient hosts were hurled,
With cries of dissolution thundering forth
To terrify the champions of the free,
To yield submission to[3] his base behest.
    Give, g've us, give, was the loud cry that came
Incessant from oppression's land. And to
That greedy cry response was made, anon,
And due submission rendered as enjoined,
In yielding powers, and territory—rights,
Most sacred, consecrate to Freedom's cause,
Till GIVING, all its virtues lost, and vice,
Alone, became. Not satisfied with thus
Receiving rich and valued boons—loud clanked
At once the chains the monster bare, which by
Fredomia's sons had been extended to great length,
And while his deafening howl went forth, he raved,
And tore, and foamed, with contortions fierce,
Writhed frightfully. And deadly venom from
His fiery tongue he spat most spitefully!
In great and pompous words of insolence,
Loud threatenings, belching forth, he assumed the right
"Peculiar institutions" to set up,[4]
With barb'rous cruelties, and rob'ries base,
As their offspring, legitimate and direct,
To 'ngulph the fair and beauteaus domain,
Then free, with wicked, dark, and horrifying

---

[3] 'A demand by the southern states for new slave States to be admitted into the Union.' [Meacham]
[4] 'The threats of the slaveocracy to sever the Union.' [Meacham]

Scenes; and make Fredomia[5] proper tribute
Pay.[6] And tho' with slight murmur it was paid
The "institutions" of "peculiar" mould,
To cherish and sustain, 'twas sadly rued.
To crown the crusade gainst the rights of man
The virgin daughter of Fredomia's made,
A victim to the monster's burning lusts;
Who to compass his ends, athwart her neck
His iron foot he sat and crushed her to the earth
Her name was Kansas. And when this they saw
And when her guttural and half stifled groan,
Was heard, alarm was given, the champions
Of Freedom's bleeding cause came rushing on
His iron arm to break, and at a blow,
To strike him to the earth. But war[7] ensued.
One archer builded his shaft, and smote the foe
He shrieked and reeled. And then another; then,
Another, still. But like the crocodile,
His armor,[8] quite impervious, proved his shield,
Till one of placid mien, composed, and firm,
And self-possessed, withal, evincing naught
'Twas rare, or strange, but fully confident
Within him of success; with dignified
And graceful air, arose. His mighty arm
He nerved[9] his arrow barbed anew; and while
In attitude erect he stood, exact,
And settled aim, he took, and, letting fly
His shaft, smote, deeply 'twixt his eyes, the foe,
Who bounded, reeled, and fell; but sprang erect,
Again, and caught a feeble, fretted, shred,[10]
Decaying fast, and tottering, thus he hung,
    Discomfited, and thus in dire suspense,
The hydre foe, loud lamentation made,
And flounced, and roared, so terribly, as caused

---

[5] 'Freedomia personates the realms of freedom, or the free states.' [Meacham]

[6] 'This refers to the fact that the free states are constantly paying a heavy tax to support slavery in the south, in which they have no interest or concern. Every freeman contributed to it.' [Meacham]

[7] 'This war was in Congress of '55 and '56.—The archers are those who battled against the extension of Slavery into Kansas and Nebraska. In the Senate were Hale, Seward, Sumner, Trumbull and others. In the House were Giddings. Campbell, Grow, Burlingams and many more too numerous to name.' [Meacham]   [8] 'Sumner.' [Meacham]   [9] 'The Slave System.' [Meacham]

[10] 'A "feeble shred" means the assumption of "Squatters Sovereignty" so called; or that Congress has not the power to inhibit slavery in the territories.' [Meacham]

The earth to quake beneath his feet; and in
His citadel confusion reigned, and all
His emissaries took the alarm; and quick
Resort to ev'ry expedent made, their god
To rescue, and their sinking cause to save.
     Inventions deep and cunning were devised.
Compacts were formed, and wealth in large amounts
Profused, in bribe'ry, to retain, and buy
Large swarms of demagogues, and send them forth
To preach false doctrines through the land;
To slander and Blaspheme the God of truth,
And foul calumny spread o'er Freedom's cause.
One fiery friend, moreover, sought to play
Th' assassin's part, and with his teeth hegnashed
On him who with such giant hand had spread
Confusion, wild, o'er all their ranks and caused
To totter to its base, the citadel
Of human chattlehood. Stung to the life,
And filled with deep remorse, raving, he flew,
And dastardly, and brutishly, he smote,
And mangled with repeated strokes and with
The instrument of death, the object whom
He hated, and whose blood he sought to 'venge
The deep and mortal wound that hand had wrought
Deep cowardice crowned the deed. For while
In cogitations deep, and lab'ring for
The public weal, unheeding all around,
Without defence or warning of the intent
Upon his person, sly the ruffian stole,
And felled him to the floor, where in his gore
He struggled to stem his gaping wounds
And life-blood, which profusely flowed,
With the inconscious groan, and meanless stare
Of eye-balls up-turned—in their sockets fixed,
Brought thrills of terror, and grim shriverings o'er
The standers-by, who in deep sympathy around him thronged
To give relief, and strength, and health restore.
All rushed in quick haste to the scene of blood
And each a kindly part to act made due
Intent, with such, alone, excepted, as
Conspired the horrid deed to execute.

Perchance, howe'er the "Pigmy Giant,"[11] ought
Be made exception to the case. For he,
Aloof, e'en like a statue stood, was cold,
And hard as adamant, and like a rock,
Unmoved by kindly sympathizing care.
    Born thence and lodged at his own residence
And placed within the care of masters in
The healing art, his case was hopeful though
The hero prostrate lay, for weeks before
A state of convalescence empire, gained,
And even to his grave the sad results
Of that most horrid deed, will sore afflict,
And wear his spirits down. He lingers still
The culprit sought his deeds to justify,
And the foul oligarchy quick conspired,
His head to shield from storms of burningwrath
That now portentous, seemed the elements
To fill. The mock tribunal overruled
The loud demands of justice, and, the wretch
His freedom gave, with insignificance,
Of mock fine, as an adequate penalty,
But yet upon him, infamy was fixed,
And mark of vile significance clung fast
Upon him wheresoe'r his guilty head
He showed. A by-word and a hissing game
The virtuous and honorable made him.
And his name a "stink" became, with all
The pure, and high refined, in moral excellence

William Hebbard, from *The Night of Freedom* (1857)

Hebbard's verse is the final example in this anthology of poetic response to the Missouri Compromise and Fugitive Slave Law. The poetry takes a scatter-gun approach to the description of the effects of the law and slave suffering. When the temperature rises the poet falls back on chaotic inventory. So for example Hebbard ambitiously calls on Milton, Byron, and Dante as the only bardic voices capable of describing the fugitive law, 'that deed of shame'. He then rejects them as not up to the job and sends them back.

[11] 'S. A. Douglas, author of the Bill that repeated the Missouri Compromise.' [Meacham]

He next calls up, as more appropriate interpreters, a motley assemblage of tyrants and murderers who begin with Tamerlane, run through the worst of the Roman emperors, only to end with Cain. At this point he sends them all back again, realizing, it would seem, that things have gone badly off course. Cain was of course in the context of slavery debates not merely the first murderer but, because of his crime, a marked man. The pro-slavers argued that he was turned black and doomed to perpetual slavery: Cain was a linchpin of biblical-sanction slavery rhetoric.

Hebbard's frantic argumentative waywardness produces a text with no moral core. The poem shows the dangers of uniting enthusiasm with sentiment in the description of trauma. The subject of slave mother infanticide was still taboo and is hardly ever touched upon in nineteenth-century slavery literature (see pp. 354–5) yet Hebbard rushes in where angels fear to tread. He attempts to describe the dark and psychologically indescribable act of a mother's murder of her own child, through a language of pumped-up stump oratory. The murder is seen as unproblematically heroic: 'The blade flashed in the light!—*one* babe was free!' This pat conclusion is then immediately followed up with a three-stanza lyric bemoaning the child's murder as a final blow against the 'Patriot' values of the old Revolutionary North. Neither the child nor the mother is granted any fictional space; they are crude signs in the over-defined emotional landscape of the poem. When Elizabeth Barrett Browning describes a slave mother's murder of her child she does so from the standpoint of the mother's complicated and ruined consciousness (pp. 356–63). Browning shows the enormity of the slave system by showing that finally neither the mother nor the child is memorially 'free' from the effects of the murder.

Hebbard marks the nadir of Northern abolition verse: all his targets are easy, all his metaphors are second or third hand, garish and inaccurate. It is finally the useless exaggeration which kills the work as a political gesture. The South is demonized: a Satanic toad metaphor, then the deadly simoom wind of the African Sahara. On and on it goes; Hebbard's transformative incontinency knows no bounds.

The Night of Freedom (pp. 23–6)

O for a soul of fire, a tongue of flame,
To speak the meanness of that deed of shame![1]
A Milton's jarring trump—a Byron's ire,—
The Muse of Dante, breathing lurid fire—
The mightiest breath that ever swept a Lyre,—
Were insufficient!—Shades of Tamerlane,
Caligula, Comodus, Nero, Cain!—[2]

[1] The opening couplet is roughly a parody of the Chorus's opening two lines in the prologue to *Henry V*: 'O, for a muse of fire, that would ascend | The brightest heaven of invention!'
[2] A list of notorious tyrants and psychopaths.

Avaunt!—back to your kindred shades of night,
Infernal vision!—"spare our aching sight!"

One glimpse along that "line of Compromise:"—[3]
   Of all the shields against her infant's doom,
What like a *Mother's heart?*—see how she flies!
   Room, in thine arms, O Cincinnati, room!
Room in thy *broader* arms, Ohio,[4]—quick!
   Alas! no Cincinnatus[5] heeds the call,
Rome of the mighty West!—and fast and thick
   The "Powers of Darkness" gather round thy fall:
But lo!—what crime is this? That mother's hand,
Nerved with an awful power, the pirate band
Waves back aghast, and holds the fatal knife
Suspended o'er those threads of infant life!
That Mother's heart! that frenzied gaze! that vow!
   O, were old Rome the scene of that despair,
Would not a Cincinnatus leave his plow,
   Unsheath his sword, and guard that mother there?
But see, the hounds press on! their savage yell
Resounds already through her prison cell!—
All hope of Liberty on earth has fled—
"But shall they not be free in heaven?" she plead;
And from that heart by man's oppression riven,
Up went the dread appeal of woe to Heaven:—
"Forgive, O righteous God, if sin it be,
I give these treasures back, unstained, to Thee!"
The blade flashed in the light!—*one* babe was free!

O what *is* tyranny, that it can make
   Infanticide a virtue in our land,
And not content with human hearts to break,
   Enforces crime upon the human hand?
Where *is* "The Patriot's Hope"?—the Patriot's fire,
   The "Golden Rule"—the Christian heart of Love?
Is only judgment left, in awful ire
   And vialed wrath, outpouring from above?

---

[3] The Mason Dixon line, which separated the slave from free territory according to the Missouri Compromise.

[4] To cross the Ohio river was to pass the border from slave territory to free.

[5] Lucius Quinctius Cincinnatus, a figure representing integrity and frugality in the Roman republic. In 458 he was called from the quiet cultivation of his land to deliver the Roman army in its fight against the Aequians. Having done this and then held power for only six days he went back to his farming.

Poor native land! God hear thy Patriots sigh!
 God hear them pour for thee, the heart-wrung prayer,
And stretch some bow of Promise from on high
 To span the storm that 's brooding in the air!

But what is this?—what can it be, that flings
So foul an incense from its unseen wings?
It blights, it withers all that 's bright and fair!
Some fell Lycanthrope[6] from his southern lair?
No eagle surely would thus smite the air!
What is 't?—Ask him who wrote on Paradise,
 What was it, scaling Eden's walls of light,
"*Squat like a toad?*"[7]—and in his low disguise
 Behold the "Squatter Sovereign"[8] here to-night!
More deadly than the Simoon's[9] withering gales,
His pestilential breath sweeps through our vales
Till touched by some Ithurial[10] spear, and lo!
Our spinal nerves, like magic, turn to dough!
"We will subdue you," are his swelling words:—
Slaves of the North, behold your southern lords!
Pluck from the soil of Freedom every flower;—
And let your Senate-heroes feel the power
With which they dare to cope;—light up the flame
Of persecution round *each* hero's name:—
Rob lawyers of their clients—preachers cast
"Among the useless lumber of the Past:"
Let Poets rue the day they dare to fling
The faintest note from Freedom's northern string,—
And if rebel those "gentry of the quill,"
Grind, bolt, and *bag* them in the fogy mill!—
Stop not to plead "the spirit or the letter,"—
A Gutta-percha[11] bludgeon answers better!

---

 [6] A wolf-man, one with the power to change from a human to a wolf.
 [7] Referring to Satan before Eve in Milton, *Paradise Lost* IV. 799–800: 'him there they found | Squat like a toad, close at the ear of Eve.'
 [8] A pun on the Milton quote in the last line, representing 'Squatter Sovereignty' in the disputed territories as Satanic.
 [9] See Vashon, *Vincent Ogé*, n. 6 above.
 [10] Variant spelling of Ithuriel, an angel with the power to make things appear in their real form. Ithuriel most famously appears in Milton's *Paradise Lost*: when Satan squats in the form of a toad beside the ear of Eve Ithuriel touches him with his spear and forces him to appear in his true likeness.
 [11] A substance like rubber but harder; a type of latex coming from Malaysian trees.

Anon., from *The Martyr Crisis* (1861)

John Brown's disastrous Harper's Ferry raid of 16 October 1859 and his subsequent trial and public hanging in Richmond, Virginia, provided the North with an ultimate martyrological focus over slavery. The North was flooded with ecstatic responses to this sacrifice in the form of broadsides, handbills, public letters, sermons, songs, poems, lithographs, wood engravings, etchings, and paintings. The voices of reason, including Lincoln's—he believed Brown to be a criminal who was justly hanged—were drowned out. Most of the 'literature' generated around Brown operated in very basic formal terms (see pp. 662–3). Yet there were ambitious bards in North America who saw in Brown's actions the raw materials for national epic. Perhaps the most recondite and elaborate verse experiment on this theme was *The Martyr Crisis*.

In 1861 in Chicago an anonymous author penned a minor epic of 101 Spenserian stanzas on recent political developments around slavery. The section of the poem reproduced here considers John Brown's career and the Harper's Ferry raid. The poem has an intriguing preface in which the poet attempts to distance himself from the excesses of the cult of abolition martyrology. He sees much abolition verse, which makes explicit comparisons between the persecution of abolitionists and that of Christ, as a disgusting misappropriation of the Passion. The argument climaxes in a powerful quotation from Goethe's *Wilhelm Meister* against the 'damnable audacity . . . to take these mysterious secrets [the Passion] in which the divine depths of sorrow lies hid, and play with them, fondle them, trick them out, and cease not till the most reverend of all solemnities appears vulgar and paltry'. The aim in *The Martyr Crisis* is to pull apart false notions of the contemporary political martyr, and to ironize 'that hackneyed theme, Martyrdom to the Christian Religion'.

Although the verse form used in *The Martyr Crisis* ultimately looks back to Spenser's *Faerie Queene* the poet is also influenced by Byron's devolved appropriation of the Spenserian stanza in *Childe Harold's Pilgrimage*. Byron's vulgar gloom and melodrama somehow fit Brown as a subject. Finally the poem uses Byron's misanthropic and ironic take on the Spenserian model to great effect. Brown's eschatological and Romantic self-delusion are formally embodied in the exhausted echoes of chivalric romance which constitute Byronic Spenserianism. Brown emerges as a fantasist, abolition's Quixotic champion, who reinvents the tortured slave and the slave power in terms of the emblematic absolutes of late medieval allegory. Unlike Quixote, however, his delusions lead to real and brutal actions with real and tragic consequences. This verse is a demonstration of the subtlety with which North American poets could subvert the inheritance of the British poetic canon.

from *The Martyr Crisis*

·   ·   ·   ·   ·

XXIII

There stood a man[1] of roughly Time-scarred brow,
   His scattered locks with hoary rime besprent,
A lip all nerved as 'neath some speechless vow,
   A kindly eye, but flashing stern intent:
    No trace was Fear, though thick around were sent
The viewless Death-shafts, and his little band
   Were fallen pierced and bleeding by. What meant
The fierce affray, the throng on every hand
Swift weaponing at the sudden note of shrill command?

XXIV

Along the lapse of Toil-marked seasons flown,
   That veteran's heart had Sorrow's keenness felt,
Till now Bereavement claimed it as her own,
   And made it at each brother's anguish melt:
    The brave and beauteous ones that fondly knelt
His hearth-shrine round, and proudly called him sire,
   Had sunk 'neath wanton blows by Ruffians dealt;
Behind the smiting hand, a Power more dire
Uprose, and roused within his breast a quenchless fire.

XXV

A fire not fell Retaliation's flame,
   Though fed by Indignations heaped and hot,
As ever to his ear wild tidings came
   Of horrors by that Gorgon[2] power begot.
    Albeit Fiction's tales, he could not blot
Their fatal seal from his o'ermemoried brain,
   And in the impress, his life-missioned lot
A spectral finger painted forth, mid pain
And perils, Perseus-like,[3] the ravage to restrain.

---

[1] John Brown is 'the man'.
[2] One of three fabled monsters, Stheno, Euryale, and Medusa, with wings, and hissing serpents for hair. The gorgan was so horrible in its aspect that looking upon it the viewer would turn to stone. The word came to be applied to any hideans terrifying woman.
[3] Son of Zeus and Danaë who was set the task of bringing back Medusa's head.

XXVI

E'en when to *thee* those phantasm-tales, forsooth,
    The tattling breeze from Southron homes hath borne,
They seemed of Mythland, yet of mourning Truth—
    From bursting breasts the infant's love-smile torn,
    Young wedded hearts forever made forlorn,
Sweet girlhood shrinking o'er the verge of fate,
    And manhood left, through robbery, stripes and scorn,
A branded thing below the brute's estate,—
A reptiled wretch of falsehood, fear and venom hate.

XXIX

The goal of Now: the Future shall remand
    His case against the Slave-power's iron heel;
For not alone in the far Spirit-land
    Hath Earth a grand Hereafter of appeal:
    Posterity hies hither with a seal
That stamps approved no law save Love's: her trump
    Shall sound accordant with the archangel's peal:
Her Truth-line shall yon sophist ne'er o'erjump—
The little sovereign of the demagogic stump.

XXVII

Judge mildly then, the old man's[4] wild belief,
    "Chide but the means and not the righteous end;"
Thou canst not ken the alembic power of Grief,
    Nor wily Fancy that betimes doth bend
    Before proud Reason like a smooth-tongued friend,
And creep apace on her unguarded throne;
    Then, all of Wisdom's years may not forefend
That mad hallucination's spell alone;—
His Thought no death-plot for the monster nursed, save one:

XXVIII

And that, this crazy crusade: thence the crowd
    Of pallid 'Chivalry' rushing breathless round:
Thence came, anon, a living corse low bowed
    In captive thongs, and slashed with many a wound:
    Peace-loving sages' laws could not o'ersound

---

[4] Brown was only 59 when executed, but he looked much older.

The e'erclamoring whisper in his errant soul,
   "Remember those in bonds as with them bound:"
And thence another name in Crime's black scroll,—
The grim foe is his judge, the gibbet is his goal.

Anon., from *The Ballad of the Abolition Blunderbuss* (1861)

Even in 1861, in Boston (the intellectual and literary centre of abolition), this poem shows that there was still significant anti-abolition sentiment. This clumsy but spirited satire took a recent rather exaggerated gesture from an abolition meeting in order to launch an *ad hominem* attack on leading Boston abolitionists. On 26 January 1861 the Governor of Massachusetts made a speech at the State House in Boston. The occasion was a symbolic pledging of the state to support abolition and the Union, and the central symbol was an old gun. The gun had been given to the great abolition leader Theodore Parker, and was supposed to have been used in the War of Independence in the Battle of Lexington. Parker gave the gun to the state and the gift was seen to provide an opportunity for Massachusetts to focus on the ideals of the struggle for independence in preparation for what was to come. The acceptance speech by Governor John A. Jackson was rather over the top, and was rounded off when he emotionally kissed the gun. The event formed the basis for the following satire. The title of the poem is a rather weak pun playing with the idea of the old gun, a 'blunderbuss', and the absurdity of the kiss, 'buss' still being a current word for a hearty smacking kiss.

The satire is interesting in that it does not really address the subject of slavery at all, but is a focused attack upon the failings, foibles, and hypocrisy of abolitionists. The well-tried anti-abolition device of suggesting amorous connections between the abolition leaders and libidinous black women is prominent (see pp. 184–7). It is a measure of his visibility in Boston abolition circles that Emerson is singled out for particular attack. What is more surprising is that he is associated with Whitman as a pro-slavery crackpot poet. Indeed the accompanying wood engraving showing Emerson mounted on an old nag, his earth-bound 'Pegasus', while the ruined beast munches on 'leaves of grass' makes the charge that Emerson is completely under Whitman's shadow. Six years earlier Emerson had been the only literary figure of reputation to respond to Whitman's opportunistic gift of a copy of the 1855 first edition of *Leaves of Grass*. Whitman wasted no time in using the approbatory letter Emerson sent him, in promoting subsequent editions of the poem. *The Abolition Blunderbuss* is a powerful testament of the extent to which the slavery question, right up to the verge of the Civil War, could be effectively reduced to a series of portraits of the fanatical absurdity of the figureheads of abolition.

from *The Ballad of the Abolition Blunderbuss*

Yᴱ General Court

The great Massachusetts General Court,
That always affords such general sport,
Was assembled on business of grave import,
In that sacred place we are wont to call
By the secular name "Representatives' Hall."
Though why they come together at all,
And what the members represent,
Or why such very dull people are sent,
Would puzzle the seven wise men of Greece,
Or the gray-haired knights of Golden Fleece.

. . . . . .

Yᴱ Abolition Mutual Admiration Society

Near Branning was sitting, deny it who can,
One whom the old maids call "that love of a man;"
Pure, holy and gentle, he breathes peace and good will
To all who agree with him,—the rest you may kill.
The South are all blind, and he pities their blindness,
And sends them Sharpe's[1] rifles in brotherly kindness;
He 's a preacher of Christ, and so when John Brown
Invaded by night a peaceable town,
And in cold-blooded murder began his wild raid,
This preacher of Christ for the murderer prayed,
And exhausted his words in trying to paint
The virtues of that anti-slavery saint;
He thinks cotton is wrong, and commerce a sin,
But still, like those gamblers who always can win,
He manages shrewdly to pocket the stakes,
And he preaches only religion that takes;
And his praying and preaching are always *so* funny
That his house is still full, and *he* always makes money;
Low comedy elbows religion away,
And the seats are all taken when he is to play;
Not perhaps what you 'd call a desirable teacher,
Nor perhaps what you 'd call a pure gospel preacher,

---

[1] A particularly efficient new design of large-bore rifle, widely used in the slaughter of bison.

But, better than that, he 's an out and out screecher,
So all the world says of Henry Ward Beecher.[2]
But who shall describe the wonder of wonders,
The grand Boanerges of all Yankee thunders,
Beëlzebub's son and Belial's[3] own cousin,
The one who tells slanders and lies by the dozen;
Abolition Thersites[4] the man from whose lips
Gall and treason aye flow;—in a word Wendell Phillips.[5]
Modern Athens can boast a Zantippe[6] in breeches,
While *he* always boasts of his eloquent speeches;
Though his speeches have neither a head nor a tail,
For he only knows how to slander and rail,
He scolds like a fishwife, a real old Harry's son;
Or, if you would like another comparison,
There 's a four-legged animal, spotted with white,
But whose name can't be mentioned before ears polite,
Which wanders about, though mostly at night,
With a very long tail and very short legs,
Living meanly by stealing and sucking of eggs,
And attacks as he flies, overpowers as he dies,
Enough said—to the wise a word will suffice.
This simile 's stolen from Sumner, you know,
And must therefore be classic and sure to go.

'Tis said the boys meant to mob him and bang him,
And then take him out on the Common and hang him;
But the notion at last was abandoned in *toto*,
When somebody asked, if dead, where he 'd go to,—
If they sent him to hell, not even the devil
Could stand the old scold, who can never be civil.

.   .   .   .   .   .

So Wendell escaped, and there in the Hall,
Like a surly old mastiff, he growled at them all.
In fact, as the boys say, he was cutting a figger:
For there on one side was a big Congo nigger,

---

[2] Clergyman, abolitionist, and father of Harriet Beecher Stowe.
[3] A great fallen angel commonly associated with Satan.
[4] The most querulous and unpleasant of the Greeks during the Trojan War, finally killed by Achilles for laughing at the latter's sorrow over having slain the Queen of the Amazons.
[5] Leading American abolition activist.
[6] Wife of Socrates renowned for her really bad temper.

On the other was sitting a very stout lady,
Whose complexion was what you at least would call shady;
That is to say, without putting too fine a
Point on the question, (as a penny a liner
Remarked at the time,) a black Messalina.[7]
Like a sore-headed dog, that growls in the yard,
He sat in the midst of his sable guard,
While a wicked reporter, who chanced to be by,
Observed with a very queer wink of the eye,
(As wicked reporters will do on the sly,)
That the black body guard might as well keep away,
'Twas a waste of good money to give them their pay;
And Phillips might save his miserly pelf,
For he was a *black guard* entire of himself.
And Ralph Waldo Emerson[8] also was seen,
Author of Brahma, who in poetry shines.
By way of a sample, here are two of his lines:
"The journeying atoms primordial wholes,
Firmly draw, firmly drive, by their animate poles."
There were ministers there of all sorts of schisms,
And withered old maids of all sorts of isms.
There were widows bewitched, table movers and all,
And Mormons and Millerites[9] there in the hall;
Blasphemers and infidels, not a few,
Abolitionists all, a motley crew.
All doing the work (the proverb is true)
Old Nick always finds idle hands to do.

. . . .

In there came, not from the ceiling or floor,
But with great condescension in at the door,—
In at the door, that is to say, at the portal,
Walking much like an overfed mortal,

---

[7] Wife of the Roman Emperor Claudius and notorious for her profligacy and sexual promiscuity.

[8] See pp. 554–8 above.

[9] William Miller (1782–1849), a prophet and leader of the Adventists. A veteran of the War of 1812, Miller emerged as a religious fanatic who, after obsessively studying the Christian prophets, believed he had absolute proof that Christ would return to the earth in 1843. Consequently he attracted an increasingly hysterical following during the 1830s and early 1840s. From March 1843 to the spring of 1844 his followers, numbering some half-million, reached fever pitch, and the expectation of Christ's advent caused serious social unrest in some eastern states. Miller and the Millerites became a byword for religious fanaticism.

The greatest of men, with three or four Aids,
As pretty as pictures, as modest as maids,
Though how they can *aid* him nobody knows,
Unless, perhaps, in brushing his clothes;
Or, perhaps, *they* practised kissing the gun,
And showed the Governor how it was done;
Or, perhaps, they wrote those General Orders,
Which will scare to death the Southern marauders
Whenever they dare to invade our borders.

It is hard to put on a martial stride,
With very short legs that step very wide,
For if you step short it looks like a waddle,
And if you step long it looks like a straddle.
But he tried to do as well as he could,
If he could do more he undoubtedly would.
It must be confessed that he 's rather fat,
But nobody thinks him the worse for that;
And then he wears such a love of a hat,
So in he stalks, with a martial stride,
Stepping too short, and stepping too wide,
Not very martial, but still very rosy,
And all must admit quite belly cosy;
That is spelling it wrong, as all the world knows,
We meant to have written *bellicose*.

Yᴱ Governor's Oration

So when he got in he stood on the floor,
While the pages behind him looked in at the door,
And he looked at the codfish, and he looked at the ceiling.
Till every one saw he was "busting" with feeling;
And then he began to make his oration,
While the women looked on with profound admiration.
He told them about that remarkable fix
Our fathers got into in Seventy-six;[10]
And he pranced about, and acted quite skittish,
As he blazed away at the absent British.

   .   .   .   .   .   .

And then he looked up at the strong-minded ladies;
And the white women wept, and the dark ladie

---

[10] 1776: the year when the American War of Independence really got into full swing.

Who sat by Phillips dropped tears from her e'e,
And beneath her shawl she squeezed his hand,
In a way he could not but understand,
While he looked as meek or meeker than Moses,
And said something sweet about African roses;
Though what African roses are no one can tell,
Unless they are famed for a very sweet smell.

Then the Governor's brow began to grow darker.
As he told them all, about one Mister Parker,
And how he stood on Lexington green
As brave as a lion, while no one was seen;
But when the British came nigher and nigher,
And kinder looked as though they would fire,
How he bravely shouldered this very gun,
And advised his soldiers to cut and run.

.   .   .   .

Y^E Kyssinge of Y^E Gun

Now listen to the story
How the greatest feat was done,
When he crowned himself with glory,
By kyssinge that old gun.

He took the gun in both his hands,
And also there and then,
In the presence of the codfish
And all the other men,
He thus went on: "With trembling lip,"[11]
Likewise with dewy eye,"—
And thereupon the dirty boy
At once began to cry,—
"With trembling pulses in my breast,
Likewise with beating heart,"—
And thereupon the dirty boy
Gave one convulsive start,—
"I part with this great relic
That came from Lexington,

---

[11] '"I present that *simple* musket," &c., "with throbbing heart, and beating pulse, and dewy eye, and trembling lip, and part with this precious relic," "this almost living and speaking witness." "Dear sons of liberty, dear *shades* of our fathers who fell on all the battle fields," &c., "be present always when hearts grow faint and knees grow weak."—*Governor's Oration.*' [Anon.]

I give this simple musket,
This living, speaking gun;
And now come from the battle fields
All ye ancestral hosts,
And if you cannot come yourselves
Just send along your ghosts;
Back up your humble servant
If ever he grows meek,
Especially whenever
His knees get kinder weak;
And if they do, may some weird hand
Take up the tattered drum
That hangs up in the tother room,
And beat like 'kingdom come.'
That 'll stiffen up our Members,
Like Kellogg's patent starch;
And then this ancient musket
Will take up the line of march,—
Lead patriotism and purpose
The Lord alone knows where,
And if I 'm only Governor,
I neither know nor care."

"Here, Mr. Bonney, take it;
Stick to it like a Jew;
And mind you keep it safely,
Whatever else you do.
If you ever try to fire it,
I 'm afraid you 'll miss the mark;
So I guess you 'd better keep it
Stuck up safely in the Ark."

Yᴱ Kysse

So when the great oration
Had all been said and done,
The Governor most solemnly
Did kiss that rusty gun;
But whereabouts he kissed it
There's nobody who knows,—

At least as yet there's nobody
Who dares the fact disclose.

But here 's the fact, we will not tire
Of saying and repeating,
He kissed the gun, the rusty gun,
And kissed it right in meeting.
The pretty Aids, like modest girls,
Looked on in meek surprise,
And when he kissed it, one and all
They wiped their weeping eyes,
Excepting Colonel Ritchie,
Who 's reported to have sniggled,
While some, too, of the younger girls
Irreverently giggled.
Wendell Phillips he looked sneaking,
His dark ladie looked *pale*,
And the Reverend Mr. Beecher
Swears the codfish wagged his tail.
Mr. Higginson, the Minister,
With meekness blew his nose,
Though why he chanced to blow it then
There 's nobody that knows.

Emily Dickinson (1830–86), 'The Lamp Burns
Sure—Within' (1861); 'The Soul has
Bandaged Moments' (1862)

The sparse biographical circumstances surrounding Dickinson's life, and the unusual almost entirely posthumous publishing history of her 'fascicles', are too well known and too widely available to need rehearsing here. What needs to be addressed is the fact that Dickinson's amazing poetry, perhaps more than any other in this anthology, resists crude historicist interpretations. This fact makes the inclusion of her work in an anthology which is explicitly about a historical phenomenon, Atlantic slavery, problematic. Nobody has ever written like Dickinson; that style—compressed, stark, highly cryptic, economic, and frequently ambiguous to the point of glorious incommunicability— does not preach any sort of narrow political or social agenda. And yet, the poetry included here has enough hints in it to let us know that Dickinson is thinking about issues of liberty and slavery during the Civil War. That the Civil War had a major effect on her output seems to be a fact, or an astonishing coincidence: in 1862 she wrote 366 poems, many more than her entire previous output, in 1863 141, in 1864 174, in 1865 85. After 1865 her output declined significantly. The first Union casualty from Amherst affected her deeply, and she wrote to her cousins about the event, describing how the reports of death inspired her, and of how she 'sang off charnel steps'.

Dickinson cannot have been oblivious to the polemics generated by slavery in the North. There are enough straws in the wind to imply a varied exposure to the development of the slavery debates. Her extended friendship with Thomas Wentworth Higginson, whom she initially approached regarding possible publication of her poems, must have put her in touch at some level with the cutting edge of abolition activism. The wonderful and fascinating Higginson might not have had that much insight into the magnitude of Dickinson's creative achievement but he was a heroic abolition activist. He was right at the heart of events when he was one of those leading the 1854 assault on a Boston courthouse to try and free fugitive slave Anthony Burns. He was one of the 'secret six' who helped finance John Brown's infamous Harper's Ferry raid. Higginson also organized and then led the first black regiment to fight in the Civil War, the 1st South Carolina Volunteers. Dickinson's reading also introduced her to some of the most forceful female imaginations to discuss slavery. She had a passionate response to Elizabeth Barrett Browning and to Stowe's *Uncle Tom's Cabin*, and she also responded powerfully in letters to her reading of Charlotte Brontë's *Jane Eyre*. The latter is one of the deepest discussions of the slavery inheritance that the nineteenth century produced.

Yet there is finally no external evidence to indicate what Dickinson really felt about issues of African-American race and slavery, and in her poetry she comes at slavery through a typically meditative approach. 'The Lamp Burns Sure—Within' is the only poem to talk about a 'slave', although Dickinson leaves the figure of the domestic slave open. This 'slave' who tends the lamp has been read literally as a reference to the Irish immigrant servant Margaret O'Brien working in Dickinson's household. Yet the poem is open to much wider interpretation and can be seen as an analysis of the shifting dependencies within the master-slave relationship. Dickinson is thinking about the mentality of the enslaver, incapable of breaking out of the fantasies of power that slavery has engendered, and which cannot be surpassed. Similarly the poem on the soul's captivity has been read as using the metaphorics of escape, terror, and recapture made fashionable by the recent glut of slave narratives in the Northern press. This position has been argued in detail in Keri J. Winter, *Subjects of Slavery, Agents of Change* (University of Georgia Press, 1992), 12–15. There is, however, always a danger of smothering Dickinson's verse in over-specific contexts. If these poems are about slavery then they are coming at it in terms of the anatomization of a very personal horror and anxiety, a general dread of the killing effects of absolute power on the consciousness of both enslaver and enslaved.

The Lamp Burns Sure—Within

The Lamp burns sure—within—
Tho' Serfs—supply the Oil—
It matters not the busy Wick—
At her phosphoric toil!

The Slave—forgets—to fill—
The Lamp—burns golden—on—
Unconscious that the oil is out—
As that the Slave—is gone.

The Soul has Bandaged Moments

The Soul has Bandaged moments—
When too appalled to stir—
She feels some ghastly Fright come up
And stop to look at her—

Salute her, with long fingers—
Caress her freezing hair—
Sip, Goblin, from the very lips
The Lover—hovered—o'er—
Unworthy, that a thought so mean
Accost a Theme—so—fair—

The soul has moments of escape—
When bursting all the doors—
She dances like a Bomb, abroad,
And swings opon the Hours,

As do the Bee—delirious borne—
Long Dungeoned from his Rose—
Touch Liberty—then know no more—
But Noon, and Paradise—

The Soul's retaken moments—
When, Felon led along,
With shackles on the plumed feet,
And staples, in the song,

The Horror welcomes her, again,
These, are not brayed of Tongue—

Anon., 'John Brown's Body' (1861?); Julia Ward Howe (1819–1910), 'Battle Hymn of the Republic', *Atlantic Monthly* (Feb. 1862)

The two great anthems of the Union army stand in this anthology as representative of the mass of popular songs and ballads generated by the war. In many ways they essentialize the martyrological vision which the slavery cause had come to represent for the North. No matter what the political reality, the war was mythologized as a fight for freedom against slavery.

John Brown's Harper's Ferry raid and subsequent death had generated an intense propaganda literature of its own (pp. 649–52). 'John Brown's Body' is a superbly transparent distillation of what, by the outbreak of war, Brown had come to mean and of where the slaves fitted into the spiritual and political equation. Those four blunt sentences, 'John Brown's body lies a-moldering in the grave . . . John Brown died that the slaves might be free, . . . He's gone to be a soldier in the army of the Lord, . . . The stars of heaven are looking kindly down', obliterate all the grey areas. These words tell each soldier the reason why he is fighting (to free the slaves), who he is trying to emulate (John Brown), and how God feels about it (very enthusiastic).

In 1862 Julia Ward Howe had visited a Union camp near Washington with her minister. Returning with a company of soldiers they had joined in singing 'John Brown's Body', and the clergyman asked Howe if she could write another battle hymn to the tune. She tells in her *Reminiscences* (1899) how the lines flooded into her mind as she lay in bed that night, and in a trance-like state she wrote them down. The verses are a triumphant articulation of an ultimate 'union' army, this time merged with the soldiers of God who will carry out the destruction of the Last Judgement. This is extreme millennialist writing. This is not merely a just war, but the Northern soldiers are God's messengers 'trampling out the vintage where the grapes of wrath are stored': they are enacting the Last Judgement. The last line achieves a tricky spiritual manoeuvre in uniting the passive sacrifice of Christ with the violent martial deaths of the soldiers. While Christ dies 'to make men holy' the Union troops sacrifice themselves for the slave and die 'to make men free'. In this song, however, unlike 'John Brown's Body' the slaves are implied, but not named. They have become a conveniently abstracted cause and have ceased to be a corporeal reality.

John Brown's Body

John Brown's body lies a-moldering in the grave,
John Brown's body lies a-moldering in the grave,
John Brown's body lies a-moldering in the grave,
    But his soul goes marching on.

Chorus:
Glory, glory, hallelujah!
Glory, glory, hallelujah!
Glory, glory, hallelujah!
    His soul goes marching on!

John Brown died that the slaves might be free,
John Brown died that the slaves might be free,
John Brown died that the slaves might be free,
    But his soul goes marching on.

He's gone to be a soldier in the army of the Lord,
He's gone to be a soldier in the army of the Lord,
He's gone to be a soldier in the army of the Lord,
    And his soul is marching on.

The stars of heaven are looking kindly down,
The stars of heaven are looking kindly down,
The stars of heaven are looking kindly down,
    On the grave of old John Brown.

Battle Hymn of the Republic

Mine eyes have seen the glory of the coming of the Lord:
He is trampling out the vintage where the grapes of wrath are stored;
He hath loosed the fateful lightning of his terrible swift sword:
    His truth is marching on.

I have seen Him in the watch-fires of a hundred circling camps;
They have builded Him an altar in the evening dews and damps;
I can read His righteous sentence by the dim and flaring lamps.
    His day is marching on.

I have read a fiery gospel, writ in burnished rows of steel:
'As ye deal with my contemners, so with you my grace shall deal;

Let the Hero, born of woman, crush the serpent with his heel,
  Since God is marching on.'

He has sounded forth the trumpet that shall never call retreat;
He is sifting out the hearts of men before his judgment-seat:
Oh! be swift, my soul, to answer Him! be jubilant, my feet!
  Our God is marching on.

In the beauty of the lilies Christ was born across the sea,
With a glory in his bosom that transfigures you and me:
As he died to make men holy, let us die to make men free,
  While God is marching on.

Citizen of Cotton Country (pseud.), from
Southern Chivalry (1864–5)

Written primarily in Hudibrastic octosyllabic couplets *Southern Chivalry* rehearses
the majority of stereotypes which the North brought to bear upon the South in popular
satire. A veneer of gentility is shown to conceal a coarse, uneducated, sadistic, and
sensualist reality. The poem does not only, however, ridicule the Southern slave power,
but also circulates degrading parodic portraits of the slaves.

Southern Chivalry

BOOK II

THE FIRE-EATER

Southern Wrongs to be Righted—Southern "Commercial" Convention—The
Order of the Golden Circle Organized—The First Degree—Tariff—Com-
merce—The Souls of Slaves—Negro Negro-drivers—Choctaw Negro-drivers—
Southern Literature—Non-intercourse with the North—Tickling the
Funny-bone—"Nigger," "Nigger," "Nigger,"—G. Whillikens dubbed Knight-

        Now flap your wings, my flock of Muses,
          And bear me onward in my flight;
        If any one of you refuses,
          I'll dock her tail this very night.

Twenty years of meditation
Whillikens, on his plantation,
Pass'd with Peter.   Hark! he hears,
Within his two uncotton'd ears,
News that the Southern chivalry
Are waking from their lethargy.
"Pete," said our hero, "catch my mare—
My country calls! I'll do my share
By strength of arm, or word of mouth,
To right the wrongs of my dear South."

How Peter put the bridle on,
Be silent, Muse! Our knight had gone
But three days with his trusty Pete,
Before his journey was complete.
Then he beheld the South a-swelling,
To get up something worth the telling.

The upshot of the mighty toil
    Was a "commercial" convocation,
Where "patriarchs" of Southern soil
    Consulted for the Southern nation.
The upshot of the consultation
    Among the stirring chivalry
Was a bran-new organization,
    The Golden Circle, First Degree.

The Order boasted three degrees;
    It had its wheels within its wheels;
It had its cross-bones, swords and keys;
    It had its secret signs and seals.
Woe to the brother who reveals
    The secrets of the sacred order,
Imparted to him, while he kneels
    And curses all beyond its border!
His broad-cloth coat and patent leathers,
Would be exchanged for tar and feathers.

The outer wheel, or first degree,
Proposed to meet "commercially,"
Though it was but a talking meeting.
The members gave each other greeting;
Preached piously about their "duties,"

Silks, calicoes and other beauties;
All simple "customs" they decried,
While Cotton King was deified.
One said, "Free trade, free ships, free state"—
    "Abusing freedom of debate,
And out of order," said the chair.
"It slipped out ere I was aware,"
Explained the member, fighting Kitty,
Who hailed from the Palmetto city.
A Texan said, "We must prepare
A Southern commerce." Then and there,
The members, showing that they knew it,
Raised a committee *just to do it*.

    A preacher, just to show his wit,
Proved negroes slaves by holy writ;
Proved slavery is good—in fine
The institution is divine.

    A doctor, an anatomist,
Spoke of the negro's horny fist,
His gizzard foot, his sable skin,
And his peculiar make within,
And wisely said, upon the whole
He thought the negro had no soul.

    Uprose a colored gentleman,
Black as a stove or frying pan,
With nose ungristled, woolly head,
And with red, mushy lips, he said,
"I'm a slaveholder; I have thirty,
All of them ignorant and dirty.
I hold the negroes, don't you see,
In *my superiority*.
Denounce my race, not as a whole,
But merely say *slaves* have no soul,
And I will advocate, you see,
The doctor's new psychology."

    A gentleman from Arkansas,
Attorney—Counselor-at-law,
New England Poet—Indian Chief,
Rose, promising to be most brief,
But perpetrated, then and there,
A speech as lengthy as his hair,

Which came so far below his jaw,
Some thought the Chief an Indian squaw.
He said th' enlightened Choctaw Nation,
Well understood the slave relation,
Leaving his native home "down East,"
Behind the age, a league at least;
That red-skin negro-drivers made
The best of masters, and would aid
The Southern cause in any strife,
With tomahawk and scalping knife.

     .   .   .   .   .

   Then rose a dozen gents, or more—
Each loudly claimed to have the floor;
And, as the chair cared not a feather,
It let them jabber altogether.
They chattered lovingly as brothers,
Just to tickle one another's
Funny bone. And then they lifted
Up their voices, rarely gifted,
Just to talk of Southern glory.
Then into the second story
Of their eloquence, they clamber'd;
And the air was badly hammer'd
By their claws; while not a single
Word of all they did commingle,
Came to little, big or bigger,
But the sound of "nigger," "nigger,"
   "Nigger," "nigger" everywhere,
Till the sound of "nigger," "nigger,"
Made our Guinea Peter snigger,
   "White folks is oncommon queer"

     .   .   .   .   .

When the dubbing rites were over,
Whillikens became a rover,
O'er the cotton-country trotting,
Talking, cursing, boasting, plotting,
Southern injuries proclaiming,
Southern independence naming,
Northern progress deprecating,
Northern march of mind debating,
Wouldn't hush. It was his mission

To direct the politician;
Teach the noisy demagogue,
Better how to play the dog;
Teach the editors of papers,
Better how to "cut their capers;"
Teach them all to stir the coals
Of strife and hate in Southern souls,
Till, cursing institutions free,
They should e'en boast of slavery,
"The corner stone of liberty."
G. Whillikens was much assisted
By those who had but late enlisted
In the good cause. Men of the North,
Who to the South had journeyed forth,
Out hectored Hector in the rattle
They made in chaining human cattle.
All Southern editors, I know,
Were yankee babies, long ago;
Three-fourths of Southern officers
Were yankee boys in other years:
One half the negro-traders, too,
Were yankee youths with bellies blue;
And many red-mouthed Southern speakers,
Were what they now call "freedom shriekers."
But south of Mason-Dixon's line,[1]
Of yankee sins they loudly whine,
Lest they, perchance, should be suspected,
Or have their early creed detected.

With such good help, you well may guess,
G. Whillikens had much success,
As he, for twenty months or more,
Preached "Southern rights" from shore to shore,
Leading his converts where he chose,
With secret man-hooks in the nose.

Said Peter, "Wonder if de whites
Aint workin' for de niggers' rights!"
There may have been a meaning in it,
But Whillikens did not unskin it.

[1] See p. 546 n. 12.

"A nigger has no rights," he said,
Knocking his comrade on the head;
"You woolly 'abolitionist,'
If you again bruise up my fist,
I'll whip yon till you do confess,
And then I'll hang you for redress."
Pete answered with humility,
"Masser has been too good to me;
A hundred licks is my desert,
I's sorry Masser's fist is hurt."
G. Whillikens was more composed,
And said, "I'll not repeat my blows;
Bat as to 'rights,' don't make pretense:
Niggers are fools—they've got no sense."
"That's so," said Peter, as he coughed,
"We niggers' heads is mighty soft."

Thus Whillikens did illustrate
The negro's blest contented state;
Thus did he seem to prove, at least,
The negro nothing but a beast.

Herman Melville (1819–91), 'The Swamp Angel', in *Battle Pieces and Aspects of War* (1866)

Fortunately this is an anthology of slave poetry and it is consequently not necessary to dive too deeply into the unending ironies and complexities of Melville's treatment of slavery in his earlier novels and novellas. Melville thought about slavery and the problematic nature of making art out of its inheritance very profoundly. Some aspects of his approach to the slavery inheritance are worked out in *Redburn*, particularly those parts of the novel dealing with Liverpool, and then at a far more disturbing and enigmatic level within the sinister beauties of *Benito Cereno*. Melville's attitudes towards slavery and the African-American presence in the Northern states have been traced in detail in the brilliant detective work of Sterling Stuckey, 'The Tambourine in Glory: African Culture and Melville's Art', in *The Cambridge Companion to Herman Melville* (Cambridge University Press, 1998).

It was after he had completed his major prose works, in fact during, and then directly in the wake of, the Civil War, that Melville turned to poetry to try and think through the horror of a war which was, among other things, a war over slavery. Very shortly after the end of hostilities Melville decided to publish *Battle Pieces and Aspects of the War*. The agonized prose supplement to the first edition of the volume is full of meandering uncertainties, and a sense of guilt about making any sort of art out of the horrific recent history of the United States. In this supplement slavery holds a central place and Melville is stern about the threat of slave emancipation for the future stability of the Union. Melville opens by warning the North against triumphalism, and any sort of blanket moral condemnation of the South. He also warns the North first to expect no 'penitence' from the South, summarily concluding: 'it is enough for all practical purposes, if the South have been taught by the terrors of the civil war to feel that Secession, like Slavery, is against Destiny; that both now lie buried in one grave' (260). Slavery and black emancipation are not seen as distinct processes; Melville is saddened and worried, for both blacks and whites, at the legacy of the war. In a passage of some prescience he envisages a situation of race and social tensions around the existence of a free black ex-slave population which neither North nor South really know what to do with:

> The blacks in their infant pupilage to freedom, appeal to the sympathies of every humane mind. The paternal guardianship which for the interval government exercises over them was prompted equally by duty and benevolence. Yet such kindliness should not be allowed to exclude kindliness to the communities who stand nearer to us in nature. For the future of the freed slaves we may well be concerned, but the future of the whole country, involving the future of the blacks, urges a paramount claim on our anxiety.

In other words African Americans, who are for Melville not as close to white Northerners in 'nature' as the white Southerners are, were a problem as slaves and constitute an even bigger problem for the Union now free. The last thing the North must do is to overprotect the new black populations at the expense of humiliating their former white masters. Melville is far more specific about the dangers of privileging legislation for blacks in the South later on, and even goes so far as to tell Northerners that it is their duty to imagine themselves as Southerners: 'In our natural solicitude to confirm the benefit of liberty to the blacks, let us forbear from measures of dubious constitutional rightfulness toward our white countrymen—measures of a nature to provoke, among other of the last evils, exterminating hatred of race toward race. In imagination let us place ourselves in the unprecedented position of the Southerners—their position as regards the millions of ignorant manumitted slaves in their midst, for whom some of us now claim the suffrage.' Melville as moralist wishes harmony for everyone, Melville as political and social realist sees the emancipated black millions as the seeds of future race hatred, and division between North and South. Yet what does it mean when Melville asserts that the North must imaginatively enter the mind of the white South if this fate is to be avoided?

'The Swamp Angel' can be read as a poem which articulates, at the level of extended metaphor, Melville's vision of the abstracted slave and ex-slave masses as a force of horror and division between white North and South. In the notes to the first edition Melville states that the 'Swamp Angel' of the title is a massive gun set up in the swamps by the North during the siege of Charleston. Yet the 'swamp angel' is obviously not just a gun, it is a vastly complex metaphor for the North's relationship to slavery and the slaves. The superb ironies of the first stanza emphasize that within Melville's poetic vision nothing is stable. The North's giant gun, a literal angel of death, is also quite specifically a black African slave, 'a coal black angel | With a thick Africk lip': the rounded rim of the giant cannon barrel slides into Negrophobe stereotyping. Yet beyond this the gun is also a metaphor for the runaway slave, 'the hunted and harried', living, like Harriet Beecher Stowe's idealized slave revolutionary Dred, out in the dismal swamp. The cannon is a fusion of slave fury at centuries of oppression, and the embodiment of the North's belief that it fights with God on its side. This is not an easy poem to read: like much great art it plays a tricky hand and it plays it very close to its chest. The shells which the great gun fires from the swamps below Charleston into the city's heart are converted into a hideously changed vision of the North Star, which led the slaves to freedom and which was celebrated in so much earlier abolition verse (see pp. 541–6). The poem ends with desolation, and the descent into Christian pietistic platitude in the last line is perhaps the blackest irony of all.

The Swamp Angel

There is a coal-black Angel
   With a thick Afric lip,
And he dwells (like the hunted and harried)
   In a swamp where the green frogs dip.
But his face is against a City
   Which is over a bay of the sea,
And he breathes with a breath that is blastment,
   And dooms by a far decree.

By night there is fear in the City,
   Through the darkness a star soareth on;
There's a scream that screams up to the zenith,
   Then the poise of a meteor lone—
Lighting far the pale fright of the faces,
   And downward the coming is seen;
Then the rush, and the burst, and the havoc,
   And wails and shrieks between.

It comes like the thief in the gloaming;
   It comes, and none may foretell
The place of the coming—the glaring;
   They live in a sleepless spell

That wizens, and withers, and whitens;
   It ages the young, and the bloom
Of the maiden is ashes of roses—
   The Swamp Angel broods in his gloom.

Swift is his messengers' going,
   But slowly he saps their halls,
As if by delay deluding.
   They move from their crumbling walls
Farther and farther away;
   But the Angel sends after and after,
By night with the flame of his ray—
   By night with the voice of his screaming—
Sends after them, stone by stone,
   And farther walls fall, farther portals,
And weed follows weed through the Town.

Is this the proud City? the scorner
   Which never would yield the ground?
Which mocked at the coal-black Angel?
   The cup of despair goes round.
Vainly she calls upon Michael[1]
   (The white man's seraph was he),
For Michael has fled from his tower
   To the Angel over the sea.
Who weeps for the woeful City
   Let him weep for our guilty kind;
Who joys at her wild despairing—
   Christ, the Forgiver, convert his mind.

David Claypoole Johnston (1798–1865), 'The Scourge', 'The Slave Driver', 'The Shackles', in *The House that Jeff Built* (1863)

The vastly popular British Regency satirist William Hone produced, from 1816 to 1822, a series of illustrated mock children's books (see p. 675). These works inspired a host of imitations not only in Britain but in the Northern United States. Johnston, the

---

[1]   Michael is greatest of the angels, chief of archangels, prince of the presence, angel of repentance, righteousness, and mercy.

leading American graphic satirist of the nineteenth century, based his most ambitious anti-slavery satire, *The House that Jeff Built*, directly on Hone's style. He combined the famous rhyme 'The House that Jack Built' with emblematic satiric illustration to attack slavery. The key to the success of the satire is that Johnston never moves too far from the power of simple pictographic communication. One unadorned inanimate symbol or ideogram can have more power in the context of a satiric nursery rhyme than any number of overworked figure compositions.

The method appears simple but is anything but. The verse accompanying the sixth image, reproduced here, is a good example. This simply shows a ball and chain, and a set of ankle shackles hanging from a nail on a post, yet the accompanying verse is clever. The key to its success is the way the apparently unruffled simplicity of the verse carries an undercurrent of bitter double meanings. The delicacy of that second line, elaborating, elongating the concept of limbs into the details of fingers and toes, suddenly snaps the reader back to the image of the shackles which fit around wrists and ankles, isolating feet and hands, fingers and toes. The rhyming of 'who suppose' and 'fingers and toes' is possessed of the kind of colloquial freedom perfectly suited to doggerel written in nursery rhyme metre, but its very lightness and absurdity forces home the bitterness of the message. The use of the word 'prone' in the next line occurs in a colloquial clause, 'prone to believe', but involves a bitter pun: the slaves are not only prone in this sense, but shackled and defenceless; they are physically, literally prone. Like much effective political satire this work is formally clean and ideologically certain, yet it leaves interpretative spaces for the viewer/reader to fill. This satire treats a terrible and dark subject with a light economy.

The Scourge

This is the scourge by some call'd the cat,
Stout in the handle, and nine tails to that:
'Tis joyous to think that the time's drawing near
When the cat will no longer cause chattels to fear,
Nor the going, going, gone of that thing call'd a man,
Whose trade is to sell all the chattels he can,
From yearlings to adults of life's longest span
In and out of the house that Jeff built

The Slave Driver

Here the slave driver in transport applies.
Nine tails to his victim nor heeds her shrill cries.

Alas! that a driver with nine tails his own:
Should be slave to a driver who owns only one:
Albeit he owns that thing call'd a man,
Whose trade is to sell all the chattels he can,
From yearlings to adults of life's longest span.
In and out of the house that Jeff built

The Shackles

These are the shackles, for slaves who suppose
Their limbs are their own from fingers to toes;
And are prone to believe, say all that you can,
That they shouldn't be sold by that thing call'd a man,
Whose trade is to sell all the chattels he can,
From yearlings to adults of life's longest span:
In and out of the house that Jeff built.

14. David Claypoole Johnston, 'The Shackles' (etching, 1863) detail
from *The House that Jeff Built.*

Abel Thomas, from *The Gospel of Slavery: A Primer of Freedom* (1864)

Thomas's little volume is a complex hybrid that relates to the alphabet rhyme, the primer, but formally above all to the devolved emblem book tradition. Emblem books had remained very popular in eighteenth- and nineteenth-century Britain and America in ever simplified forms. The complicated adult emblem books of the seventeenth century, which reached their height with the success of the works of Francis Quarles and George Wither, were no longer widely read on either side of the Atlantic by the mid-eighteenth century. Yet simplified versions of these texts were popular as children's books, and in the early nineteenth century the emblem books underwent a big revival in the form of political pamphlet satires. The hugely influential parodic emblem books of William Hone sold in hundreds of thousands in England in the second decade of the nineteenth century. Hone's biggest hit *The Political House that Jack Built* of 1819 (spectacularly illustrated by George Cruikshank, who was later to produce the most popular of all illustrated editions of *Uncle Tom's Cabin*) combined a parody of a children's nursery rhyme with the illustrated emblem book tradition. *The Gospel of Slavery* is a distant cousin of the Hone pamphlets, and is directly related in formal terms to Hone's illustrated pamphlet *The Political A Apple Pie*, each verse sitting beneath an emblematic wood engraving. Yet Thomas's pamphlet also relates to a series of North American print satires in the form of mock alphabet rhymes.

from *The Gospel of Slavery*

A Stands for Adam. Creation began
By giving dominion of Nature to man.
Men differ in color, and stature, and weight,
Nor equal are all in their talent or state,
But *equal in rights* are the great and the small
In sight of the God and Creator of all.
Then *how* comes dominion of brother by brother?
Or how can the one be the lord of the other?
Consider it well—for an answer I crave,
That reaches the question of Master and Slave.

"We hold these truths to be self-evident: That all men are created equal; that they are endowed by their Creator with certain unalienable rights; that among these are life, liberty, and the pursuit of happiness."—*Decl. of Ind.* It is nothing to affirm that the Negro, or Indian, or Arab, is not equal to the white man—namely, in talent and the like. No two *white* men are equal in all respects—but if you deny an equality of *rights*, specify the grounds of such denial.

> B Stands for Bloodhound. On merciless fangs
> The Slaveholder feels that his "property" hangs,
> And the dog and the master are hot on the track,
> To torture or bring the black fugitive back.
> The weak has but fled from the hand of the strong,
> Asserting the right and resisting the wrong,
> While he who exults in a skin that is white,
> A Bloodhound employs in asserting his might.
> —O chivalry-layman and dogmatist-priest,
> Say, which is the monster—the man, or the beast?

How long is it since Southern papers advertised the offers of rival hunters of fugitive Negroes, who claimed that they had the best bloodhounds, &c.? Truly an honorable and manly vocation. Runaway Slaves were advertised as having been torn by the dogs, thus and so, on former occasions of flight, and large rewards were offered for the capture of such ingrates, dead or alive! Shall not specimens of these advertisements be some day included in the literary curiosities of civilization?

.   .   .   .   .   .

> F Stands for Fugitives hasting from wrath,
> And furies are hot on their dangerous path.
> Away from the cabins of slavery pomp,
> A refuge they seek in the hideous swamp;
> Or, haply eluding the hunters of blood,
> They struggle through thicket and perilous flood,
> Till, reaching the lines of the Union Host,
> The echo has died of the scandalous boast,
> "Hurra for the banner that Liberty waves,
> "With stars for the Masters and stripes for the Slaves!"

A history of this Liberty War would be very incomplete without sample-sketches of the patient, shrewd efforts of individuals and families of Slaves in getting away from the house of bondage into the lines of the Union Army. Almost starved, hunted by dogs and men, shot at, some of the party killed,—none but the good Lord knoweth the miseries endured by thousands in escaping from the comfortable, patriarchal, Gospel institution of the South!

.   .   .   .

Q Stands for Query. Inquisitive thought
May lead to conclusions not anxiously sought.
Suppose of Quadroon we a moment should think,
With *one* side of ancestry sable as ink,
The other side claiming complexion as fair
As fatherly planters most commonly wear:
The child of her Master, a Slave-daughter still,
Must bow to the law of his sensual will:
And when he shall sell her, (perhaps very soon)
The Query may follow the chattel Quadroon.

The cry of "amalgamation" as the result of the abolition of Slavery, comes with a very ill grace from Southerners. How many nearly-white children have been sent to the North for an education, or to hide their negro-blood? How many such have been manumitted, to guard against their continuance in bondage by any mishap? How many Quadroons have been sold voluntarily or brought to the block by the pecuniary embarrassments of their father-masters?

.   .   .   .   .   .

W Stands for Woman. In Slavery-life,
Full many are mothers, but no one is wife.
For decency's sake, form of wedding there is,
But the parties are claimed by the master as his;
And the children are sold, and the father is sold
To this or that trader, "to have and to hold;"
And the woman is whipped, for the motherly moan
And the cry of a heart that is left all alone.
O master all monstrous! is conscience amiss
In dooming the sham of a wedding like this!

Certain Southern ladies claimed, not long since, that they care as tenderly for slave mothers as Northern ladies care for poor white mothers. "Possibly that is true," was the reply, "but Northern ladies do not afterwards sell the baby!"— Besides this, it is the *money interest* of Southerners to look well to the increase of their *property*, whereas a true humanity, as a principle, underlies and quickens the charitable attention of Northern ladies, above referred to.

Children's Anti-Slavery Verse

Anon., 'Mr Prejudice', 'Difference of Colour', 'The Tree of Slavery', in *Slave's Friend* (2/8, pp. 115–16; 2/1, p. 2; 3/9, p. 2)

The *Slave's Friend* was a particularly inventive offshoot of the mass of propaganda thrown up by the New York Anti-Slavery Society's 'great postal campaign' of 1835–6, masterminded by the brilliant abolition publicist Elizur Wright. The campaign not only targeted the blossoming adult abolition readership, but ingeniously colonized the burgeoning children's book market in the North. This miniature child's journal ran for several years and sold widely. The magazine, only about two and a half by three inches in size, combined woodcut illustration with a huge formal variety of texts that included biography, parable, letters, short stories, games, quizzes, dialogues, and poetry. The three poems here suggest something of the variety of verse that the pages of this publication contained. The two poems on race prejudice also indicate that the editors are intent on addressing issues that do not only relate to slavery and the South. Colour prejudice was, in many ways, more extreme and more prevalent in the North than in the South. For Northerners who had little experience of living in physical proximity to blacks physical aversion, and fear, could be insurmountable, as Harriet Beecher Stowe so vividly argued in her characterization of Miss Ophelia in *Uncle Tom's Cabin*. 'The Tree of Slavery' is a more conventional demonization of slavery as the root of all evil within the Union, yet it achieves its effects with an unstinting reiterative intensity.

Mr Prejudice

Pray who is Mr. Prejudice,
    We hear so much about,
Who wants to spoil our pleasant songs,
    And keep the white folks out?

They say he runs along the streets,
    And makes a shocking noise,
Scolding at little colored girls,
    And whipping colored boys.

This wizard we have never met—
    Although our mothers say

That colored folks, both old and young,
   He torments every day.

The colonizers tell us all
   They hate this wicked man—
Yet ask him every day to dine,
   And flatter all they can.

He must be very tall and stout—
   Quite dreadful in a rage—
For strongest colored men, they say,
   He 'll toss out of a stage.

We wish that we could catch him *here!*
   We think he'd hold his tongue,
If he should see our smiling looks,
   And know how well we 've sung.

However strong this rogue may be,
   Kind friends, if you 'll unite,
Should he peep in, oh, never fear,
   We 'll banish him to-night.

Difference of Color

God gave to Afric's sons
   A brow of sable dye,—
And spread the country of their birth
   Beneath a burning sky,—
And with a cheek of olive, made
   The little Hindoo child,
And darkly stained the forest tribes
   That roam our Western wild.

To me he gave a form
   Of fairer, whiter clay,—
But am I, therefore, in his sight,
   Respected more than they?—
No.—'Tis the hue of deeds and thoughts
   He traces in his Book,—
'Tis the *complexion of the heart*,
   On which he deigns to look.

Not by the tinted cheek,
That fades away so fast,
But by the *color of the soul*,
We shall be judged at last.
And God, the Judge, will look at me
With anger in His eyes,
If I my brother's darker brow
Should ever dare despise.

The Tree of Slavery

The
sin of
slavery
hardens the
heart, distempers
the mind, brutalizes
the holder, corrupts the
moral sense, inflames the
evil passions, turns men into
cruel monsters; it is "a witch
to the senses, a devil to the soul,
a thief to the pocket," a mildew to
the soil, and a curse to the nation; it
produces woe to man, woman, and child,
and draws from them sighs, tears, and
groans, that reach to the ear of the great God;
it reduces man to a beast—a thing—de-
faces the image of God on the mind,
takes away the key of knowledge,
robs man of the bible and his
soul!
The
root of this evil is
SLAVERY !!!!!!

Kate Barclay, 'Minnie May', 'Sambo's Toast', in *Minnie May with Other Rhymes and Stories* (1854)

Barclay's volume is composed of a mixture of short stories and poems on slavery and temperance themes. It is copiously illustrated with plates which have been lifted from the publisher John P. Jewett's edition of *Uncle Tom's Cabin* and then retitled to fit the new contexts. It might appear an utterly prosaic piece of publishing opportunism, aimed at the large children's market for abolition work, yet the poems are cleverly adapted to the child's perspective. The first poem, 'Minnie May', plays on the affection which the privileged child feels for the nurse. The poem as it reaches its conclusion has a Blakean economy. It deals with the passage of the child from innocence to experience; only here the experience is a stark warning that if you fall in love with your slave nurse you may well be horribly hurt because she can be sold away from you at any point. Minnie's visit to the slave market to try and talk to 'aunt Ruth', before she disappears for ever, only succeeds in having the old slave woman punished by her new master. The final three lines have a dark compression that tempts comparison with Blake's 'Nurses Song' from *Songs of Experience*.

Barclay's children's poems frequently manage this shift from childish happiness to utter despair with great skill. 'Sambo's Toast' is even more resonant, and is a brilliantly structured piece. It opens with a pseudo-Dickensian view of Christmas, all dancing children, rocking horses, joyful girls, and glad boys. Even the move to the slave quarters seems reassuring: the blacks are utterly stereotyped happy plantation 'darkies', with the generic titles of Chloe (courtesy of *Uncle Tom's Cabin*), Cato, Sambo, and 'Jack Woolly Head'. In their abject poverty and powerlessness they seem willing to give thanks for the fact that they are at least together for the moment. There is not a hint of rebellion in them. Nothing prepares the reader for the shocking conclusion with its emphatic repetition which cuts through the grammar, the *faux* black dialect, and the metrics, to tear the heart out of the matter: '"Old massa," he cried, "he hab a white face, | But a bery black heart, black heart."' The alliteration of the *b*s in that final line is stunning: 'white face . . . black heart, black heart' again has the lyric simplicity of the Wordsworth of the 'Lucy' poems, or the Blake of the *Songs of Experience*.

Minnie May

The flower of Savannah was sweet Minnie May,
With soft eyes of blue and brow open as day,
With lips ever ready to wreathe in a smile,
And wee merry dimples to dance round the while.

A sunbeam of summer was sweet Minnie May;
Her heart was so light and her spirit so gay,
Her friends were so true, so loving and fond,
She seemed to possess some bright fairy's kind wand.

But the sceptre of love in sweet Minnie May
Was the sceptre that ruled where'er it held sway;
And fairies might poise on invisible wing
To catch the joy notes as from her they would spring.

No cloud had e'er darkened o'er sweet Minnie May,
And life seemed to her but a bright summer day;
'Twas good just to live; and she lived but to love
And rejoice in the gifts of the Father above.

But trouble at length came to sweet Minnie May—
A shadow fell darkly across her smooth way.
"Aunt Ruth" was her nurse, and she loved her full well;
But now she was missing—where, no one would tell.

All over the premises searched Minnie May,
High and low, in and out, and every way;
She inquired of all, but not any would tell;
Though where "aunt Ruth" was they knew perfectly well.

Suspicion at last rose in sweet Minnie May;
She had heard there were slaves to be sold that day;
Could it be that this was the fate of "aunt Ruth"?
She ran to her mother and learned the sad truth.

Then fast fell the teardrops of sweet Minnie May;
The cloud was a dark one that shadowed her way;
She sought her lone room, and there fervently prayed
On Jesus the heart of "aunt Ruth" might be stayed.

Down she took then her Bible, and sweet Minnie May
Ran bounding along, stopping not by the way,
Till her hand tightly clasped "aunt Ruth's" dear old hand;
She heeded not then any master's command.

She leaned on her bosom there, sweet Minnie May,
For there those soft curls in her infancy lay;
She gave her the Bible with many a tear,
And bade her look upward in each trying fear.

There she sits on that slave block, sweet Minnie May,
And tries to shed light on "aunt Ruth's" darkened way;
She pleads with that master so stern and severe
To be kind to old nurse, to her ever dear.

Alas for your pleading now, sweet Minnie May;
His heart is of stone, and he lists not your lay;
Already he's angry, and threatens, e'en now,
To cause her to know at *his will* she must bow.

Sambo's Toast

'Tis a time of good cheer, a time of good cheer;
    Santa Claus is abroad in the land;
And "A happy New Year!" "A happy New Year!"
    Echoes gayly in every band.

Now the north and the south, the east and the west,
    Are in sympathy full and free;
For in each loved home St. Nick is a guest,
    And scatters his gifts merrily.

Some are costly and fine, some simple and poor,
    Some only a wish or a prayer;
But all are made welcome—all open the door
    To take with good will each a share.

The little girl dances and sings in her joy
    O'er her beautiful doll, all dressed:
"O, look at my rocking horse!" shouts the glad boy;
    "My gift is the best—is the best."

Some other a top has received or a cup;
    Another a drum or a fife;
A new set of china makes Lucy look up
    With smiles and a tear in glad strife.

New skates, or a sled, or a chair, or a book,
    Or a dress, or a coat, or a hat,
Or rabbit, or squirrel, or fish on a hook,
    Or a dear little dog, or a cat.

Fine, nice things, so many, some little ones get,
    Their hearts are quite full of delight;
While others, less favored of good things, have yet
    Been content with even their mite.

It is no matter what; when love's warm and true,
    And the spirit all free from guile,
You remember how happy such gifts make you,
    How they gladden your life a while.

On this happy New Year St. Nick made a call
    Where he never had called before—
'Twas in a slave's cabin, with low, smoky wall,
    And only the earth for a floor.

The negroes were sitting quite sullenly there,
    Heart and soul bound down as with chains;
He left them the gift of a warm, fervent prayer,
    Which filled them with love's purest flames.

They began to rejoice: one good thing was still
    Granted them, though hard was their lot—
Stern, selfish "old massa," with strong iron will,
    Had their family band parted not.

They hoped he ne'er would; and this brightened their eyes
    And made them look up with good cheer:
One blessing was left; this they would not despise;
    So their spirits from gloom rose clear.

Now Chloe prepared them their simple repast;
    On the table she placed just one dish;
It was all that she had, their first course and last;
    But gayly came with it the New Year's wish.

Then Sambo sat down in his rough, wooden chair;
    One hand he hung over the back;
In the other he held, steaming up in the air,
    A potato, taken from Jack.

He stuck up his foot as he laughingly said,
    "Here, Chloe; me just gib a toast;
Cum, Cato, and Susey, and Jack Woolly Head,
    Let tree cheers ring round all de coast."

> They eagerly listened: then with a good grace
> Each one with a will did his part:
> "Old massa," he cried, "he hab a white face,
> But a bery black heart, black heart."

Minstrelsy and the 'Ethiopian' and 'Nigger' songsters

'De New York Nigger', 'Black Sam', in *Christy's Panorama* (1846–56); 'The Old Brown Dog', 'Long Time Ago', in *The Negro Forget Me Not* (*c*.1850); 'South Carolina Gentleman', in *John Brown's Songster* (1863)

Black-face minstrelsy as a cultural phenomenon was ultimately demeaning to blacks, slave and free, and, when it is noticed at all, is now rightly maligned as a cultural phenomenon. Yet while the reductions and stereotyping of blacks, and of black dialect, must now be subjected to scrutiny, it is a fact that a huge popular audience was exposed to the issues of race and slavery through the literatures of minstrelsy. It is also a fact that poetry and song were very much at the heart of minstrel performance. This popular audience was a transatlantic one, and by the mid-nineteenth century the stars of North American minstrelsy, no less than the big stars of abolition, toured Britain. Using low comedy, buffoonery, and playing to the crudest and most sentimental fictions of nascent white racism, the troops of 'Ethiopian' singers performed for, and appealed to, a far wider and more eclectic audience than the abolition lecturers ever reached. One testimony to the huge cultural valency of this form of entertainment in England lies in the survival of black-face minstrelsy as a mainstream form into the 1960s and the age of television. *The Black and White Minstrel Show* was still attracting huge Saturday evening peak-time audiences in the late 1960s.

The songs reprinted below demonstrate that in its nineteenth-century heyday minstrelsy was an eclectic and transformative creative environment. Many of the songs come at issues of race and slavery from unexpected angles, or are capable of dealing with sorrow and trauma in pungent ways, which are all the more disturbing because of their comic and mimetic settings. Minstrelsy songs could be wolves in sheep's clothing, dealing with Northern prejudice against free blacks in the North and against whites in the South. It is consequently fitting that this anthology should conclude with some examples of minstrel verse selected from the songsters over their long chronological range.

Slavery saturates minstrel song and poetry in variegated ways. It did not escape the notice of the minstrel troupes that in some areas of the North abolition had a broad-based popularity which could be exploited. So in 1845 George Clark produced the song book *The Liberty Minstrel* full of unabashedly sentimental ballads telling of the tragic sale of 'The Quadroon Maid', or the horrific parting of 'The Blind Slave Boy' from his mother. 'The Slave Boy's Wish' (see pp. 525–6) was by the prominent woman abolitionist Eliza Lee Follen. This well-constructed little ballad shows how abolition sentimentality could translate directly into the minstrel marketplace. Yet not all the songs are as anodyne as those in *The Liberty Minstrel*. The plight of free blacks and ex-slaves in the North is dealt with in many songs. This can take direct forms, as in the strange 'De New York Nigger' where a white black-face actor sings of the prejudice blacks encounter in Manhattan, and sets the minstrelsy songs triumphantly off against abolition. Yet there are also more enigmatic and deeply disturbing songs which come at black loneliness and the cultural estrangement of the ex-slave. 'The Old Brown Dog' is a fine example: on the surface it is a poem about a stray whose master has died. On another level, however, it is a song about the plight of the masterless slave, who was only able to function socially within the structures of the slave system. There is a starkness about the language; the North's obliviousness to, and confusion about, the black ex-slave presence could hardly be more succinctly expressed than in the stanza: 'His name—his race—his business here, | Are hidden in a fog; | There seems to be a mystery | About that old brown dog.' Other songs go deeply into the horror of slave experience: for example the song 'Long Time Ago' is a plain narrative of a first-generation slave. He 'marries' another slave, and the couple are systematically used as 'breeders'; the master sells the children on. When the woman stops producing children the husband is sold down the river. In the enigmatic final lines it is impossible to say whether the black-face slave narrator tells us he has escaped as a runaway, or escaped to the afterlife, having been whipped to death. Some songs achieve remarkable power through having lulled the audience into a false sense of security. The extraordinary 'Black Sam' looks throughout its first three stanzas to be a typical example of the plantation darkie song, of the 'Ise a Happy Darkie' variety, where a comic and rotund figure sings of the contentment and high jinks on the old plantation. But the final stanza springs a trap: suddenly 'de fattest nigger dat you eber did see' goes to his master and asks if he can buy his freedom. When the master refuses, on the grounds that the slave is irreplaceable, his reaction is described with a sinister ambiguity. One reading of the last couplet is that he dances and grins with delight to know he is so valued by his master, yet that last line 'And I stretched my red mouf across from ear to ear' simultaneously suggests that he has cut his own throat in despair at his endless captivity. Ever adaptable, the songsters were a form which thrived in the Civil War and this anthology ends with a piece from *John Brown's Songster* of 1863. Here slavery is dealt with purely through an assault on the depravity and viciousness of the 'South Carolina Gentleman'. The verses are formally cleverly constructed: the third line is ingeniously pulled out into an ever-expanding inventory of criticism, leaving the reader hanging on the edge for the closure of the rhyme. It is noticeable, however, that one of the chief criticisms of the 'Gentlemen' of the South is their taint of miscegenation. They all have kinky hair which 'betrays an admixture with a race not particularly popular now'. It seems that in the music-hall ballads of 1863 blacks are no more popular in the North than the South.

De New York Nigger

When de Nigger's done at night washing up de china,
Den he sally out to go and see Miss Dinah.
Wid his Sunday go-to-meetings segar in his mouth
He care for no white folk, neder should he ought to,
His missy say to him, I tell you what, Jim,
Tink you gwan now to cut and come agin.

He walk to de Park, an'he hear such mity music,
A white man he did say enuff to make a dog sick,
He turn round to see who make de observation
An de sassy whites laugh like de very nation,
Jim was in de fashion, so he got into a passion.
'Cause de damn white trach was at hin a laffin.

Jim cut ahead an tink he never mind'em,
White folks got de manners—he tink de couldn't find 'em
He walk a little furder an tink he die a laffin,
To see his Dinah walkin'wid Massa Arfy Tappan,[1]
Ole Bobolition Glory, he live an'die in story.
De black man's friend, wid de black man's hour.

He gawn to de Bowery to see Rice[2] actin,
He tink he act de brack man much better dan de white 'un,
Only listen now, a nigga in a opera,
Rice wid a ball an'brush tink much properer,
He cut de pigeon wing, an' bring he do de handsome ting,
Wheel about and turn about, an' bring de money in.

De little house now, what is called de Olympic,
Wha massa Geo, Holland[3] makes de people grin,
Ching a ring, Pompey Smash, an, ride upon a rail, sir,
De little house coin de cash, while de big one ali fail
But I don,t like de house; I wish it was bigger,
'Cause dey neber, hab room to let in de nigga.

I wind it up now, I tink you say 'tis time, sir,
You got no reason, but you got plenty ob rhyme, sir,

[1] Arthur Tappan, leading abolitionist leader and financier.
[2] Rice was a leading 'Nigger Minstrel'.
[3] George Holland, another renowned minstrel performer with his own company.

I'se gwan to go away, but first I leave behind me,
What ebery brack man wish, in dis happy land ob liberty;
Here's success to Rice, to Dixon, and to Lester,
May dey neber want a friend, nor a hoe-cake to bake, sir.

SPOKEN.—Rice, Dixon, an' Lester, de proud supporters
ob be brack drama. may dey neber, want de encouragement de greatness ob de subject demands

Black Sam

TUNE—"Jim Brown."

I lib down in de holler whar de black snake go,
And I hab a wife dat's blacker dan de crow,
And we roast de hoe cake whan de sun's goin' down
'Case I am de fattest nigga in de town
I go ketch de possum, an my wife fry de fat,
And I chase de rackoon all round my hat.
   'Case I am de fattest nigga dat eber you did see,
   And all the gals of colour turn dar eye up at me.

When I go to de city, whar de niggars jump,
Den I take de banjo an I gib a thump,
And de niggas gin to hop, wid a haw! haw! haw!
'Case I am de gemman wot lays down de law;
And de gals of colour comes to the ball,
Phillis, Dinan, Susannah, and all.
   'Case I am de fattest nigga, &c.

I go to church a Sunday, an my wife look round
As de oder ladies squatted on de gound,
And she turn'd her lip up, case dey neber dress,
Haff so well as Dinah in her Sunday best;
She hab a Yellow apron hanging down before,
And her bustle stick out half a yard or more.
   'Case I am de fattest nigga, &c.

Once I say to massa, whar de cane brake grow,
I pay you for my freedom if you let me go,
And he tell dis nigga dat it neber can be,
'Case dat no sum ob money worth so much as me

Den I jump up an holler, even dis ting I hear,
And I stretch my red mouf across from ear to ear.
　　'Case I am de fattest nigga, &c.

The Old Brown Dog

There is an old brown dog,
　　That roams about our streets
But no one knows from whence he came,
　　Or where he sleeps or eats.
His name—his race—his business here,
　　Are hidden in a fog;
There seems to be a mystery
　　About that old brown dog.

Chorus.　Oh, that old brown dog—
　　　　　　That very old brown dog!
　　　　　There surely is a mystery
　　　　　　About that old brown dog!

He dogs his master round
　　Like most of them you see;
But through the longest winter day,
　　In one lone spot is he;
And there, with head between his paws,
　　He lies in the snow and rain,
As if some great misfortune
　　Perplexed his troubled brain.

Chorus.　Oh, that old brown dog, &c.

And oftentimes I stop
　　And gaze, and try to trace
The mournful thoughts, that seem to flit
　　Across his wrinkled face.
Perhaps he dreams of days
　　When filled with pleasure's cup;
Of days of sunshine, mirth and joy,
　　When he was but a pup.

Chorus.　Oh, that old brown dog, &c.

The voice he once obeyed,
    May long have died away;
But still he waits to hear its call,
    From weary day to day.
He dreams of days gone by,
    And he cannot help but weep,
To think his master's dead and gone,
    And left him in the street.

Chorus. Oh, that old brown dog, &c.

Enough! I do not wish
    To pry in his affairs;
But on his breast he seems to bear
    A weight of heavy cares.
His name—his voice—his business here,
    Are hidden in a fog;
There seems to be a mystery
    About that old brown dog.

Chorus. Oh, that old brown dog, &c.

Long Time Ago

In a little log cabin on old Virginny,
    Cousin John, hussa;
There lived ever since I come from Guinea,
    Long time ago.
Old massa bought me of a nigger driver,
    Oh oh oh oh oh oh;
Put me me in cornfield to hoe the potatoes
    Long time ago.

I staid with old massa good many summers,
    Cousin John, hussa;
All the time we have good dinners,
    Long time ago.
Oh every morn if we desire,
    Oh oh oh oh oh oh oh;
We used to bake the hoe cake before the fire,
    Long time ago.

Old Dina was cook and none of the worsest,
    Cousin John, hussa;
She use to bake the dodge without any crustes,
    Long time ago.
De way dey bake de hoe cake in Virginia neber tire,
    Oh oh oh oh oh oh oh;
De put it on de foot and hold it to de fire,
    Long time ago.

Den I thought I have old Dina for a wife,
    Cousin John, hussa;
So at old massa for to save de strifey,
    Long time ago;
Old Dina consented to have old Cæsar,
    Oh oh oh oh oh oh oh;
Soon popped the questions and did no more teaser,
    Long time ago.

We always have to ax before we get married,
    Cousin John, hussa;
So de ting was fixed I did no longer tarry,
    Long time ago.
Now I loves her to extraction,
    Oh oh oh oh oh oh oh:
And she loves me and bears de confexion,
    Long time ago.

Massa soon found we was good property,
    Cousin John, hussa;
He sold de little niggers and de money he did pocket,
    Long time ago.
But when old Dina didn't have no more,
    Oh oh oh oh oh oh oh oh;
So he sell old Ceaser and send him down de river,
    Long time ago.

But I dident stay long in de wild goose nation,
    Cousin John, hussa!
There de make de niggers work de plantation,
    Long time ago.
Oh ebery morn massa look sower,
    Oh oh oh oh oh oh oh;
Give de niggars thirty-nine ebery half hour,
    Long time ago.

South Carolina Gentleman

AIR—*The Fine Old English Gentleman*

Down in a small Palmetto State, the curious one may find
A ripping, tearing gentleman, of an uncommon kind;
A staggering, swaggering sort of chap, who takes his whisky straight,
And frequently condemns his eyes to that ultimate vengeance which
    a clergyman of high standing has assured us must be a sinner's fate;
This South Carolina gentleman, one of the present time.

You trace his genealogy, and not far back you'll see
A most undoubted octoroon, or, mayhap, a mustee;[1]
And if you note the shaggy locks that cluster on his brow,
You'll find that every other hair is varied with a kink that seldom
    denotes pure Caucasian[2] blood, but, on the contrary, betrays an
    admixture with a race not particularly popular now;
This South Carolina gentleman, one of the present time.

He always wears a full dress coat, pre-Adamite[3] in cut,
With waistcoat of the longest style, through which his ruffles jut;
Six breastpins deck his horrid front, and on his fingers shine
Whole invoices of diamond rings, which would hardly pass muster
    with the "Original Jacobs," in Chatham Street, for jewels gen-u-ine;
This South Carolina gentleman, one of the present time.

He chews tobacco by the pound, and spits upon the floor,
If there is not a box of sand behind the nearest door;
And when he takes his weekly spree, he clears a mighty track,
Of every thing that bears the shape of whisky-skin, gin and sugar,
    brandy sour, peach and honey, irrepressible cock-tail, rum and gum,
    and luscious apple-jack;
This South Carolina gentleman, one of the present time.

He takes to euchre[4] kindly, too, and plays an awful hand,
Especially when those he tricks, his style don't understand;
And if he wins, why then, he stoops to pocket all the stakes,

---

[1] Or 'mestee', racist term coming out of slave cultures denoting the offspring of a white person and a quadroon.

[2] A member of the white race; as used by the race theorist Blumenbach it denoted a person belonging to the ethnological division of humankind native to Europe and western and central Asia.

[3] Very old, literally existing before the first man, Adam.

[4] An American card game: if a player fails to make three tricks she or he is described as *euchred*.

But if he loses, then he says to the unfortunate stranger who had
    chanced to win, "It's my opinion that you are a cursed abolitionist,
    and if you don't leave South Carolina in one hour, you will be hung
    like a dog!"—but no offer to pay he makes;
This South Carolina gentleman, one of the present time.

Of course he's all the time in debt to those who credit give,
Yet manages upon the best the market yields to live;
But if a Northern creditor asks him his bill to heed,
This honorable gentleman instantly draws two bowie knives and
    a pistol, dons a blue cockade, and declares, that in consequence
    of the repeated aggressions of the North, and its gross violations
    of the Constitution, he feels that it would utterly degrade him to
    pay any debt whatever, and that in fact he has at last determined
    to SECEDE;
This S. Carolina gentleman, one of the present time.

Select Bibliography

General works on the history of slavery, memory, and the Diaspora

Anderson, S. E., *The Black Holocaust for Beginners* (Writers and Readers Publishing, 1995).

Andrews, William L., *To Tell a Free Story: The First Century of Afro American Auto-biography, 1760–1865* (University of Illinois Press, 1988).

Blackburn, Robin, *The Overthrow of Colonial Slavery 1776–1848* (Verso, 1990).

—— *The Making of New World Slavery from the Baroque to the Modern 1492–1800* (Verso, 1997).

Blackett, Richard J. M., *Building an Anti-Slavery Wall: Black Americans in the Atlantic Abolitionist Movement 1830–1860* (Cornell University Press, 1983).

Blanchot, Maurice, *The Writing of the Disaster* (University of Nebraska, New Bison Paperback edn., 1995).

Cunliffe, Marcus, *Chattel Slavery and Wage Slavery: The Anglo American Context 1830–1860* (University of Georgia Press, 1979).

Dash, J. Michael, *The Other America: Caribbean Literature in a New World Context* (University of Virginia Press, 1998).

Davis, David Brion, *The Problem of Slavery in the Age of Revolution* (1976; Oxford University Press, 1999).

—— *The Problem of Slavery in Western Culture* (Oxford University Press, 1988).

—— *The Emancipation Moment* (Fortenbaugh Memorial Lecture, 1983).

Diddleton, David, and Edwards, Derek (eds.), *Collective Remembering* (Sage, 1990).

Gates, Henry Louis (ed.), *Race, Writing and Difference* (University of Chicago Press, 1986).

—— *The Signifying Monkey* (Oxford University Press, 1988).

Gilroy, Paul, *The Black Atlantic: Modernity and Double Consciousness* (Verso, 1993).

—— *Small Acts* (Serpent's Tail, 1994).

Goldberg, David Theo, *Racist Culture: Philosophy and the Politics of Meaning* (Blackwell, 1993).

—— *Anatomy of Racism* (University of Minnesota Press, 1990).

Honour, Hugh, *The Image of the Black in Western Art*, part iv, 2 vols. (Harvard University Press, 1988).

Linebaugh, Peter, and Rediker, Marcus, *The Many-Headed Hydra: Sailors, Slaves, Commoners, and the Hidden History of the Revolutionary Atlantic* (Beacon Press, 2000).

Morgan, Philip D., 'The Black Experience in the British Empire', in P. J. Marshall and Alaine Low (eds.), *The Eighteenth Century*, Vol. 2 of *The Oxford History of the British Empire* (Oxford University Press, 1998).

Price, Richard (ed.), *Maroon Societies: Rebel Slave Communities in the Americas* (Anchor Doubleday, 1973).

Ricœur, Paul, *History and Truth*, trans. Charles Kelbley (Northwestern University Press, 1965).

Said, Edward, *Culture and Imperialism* (Vintage, 1993).

Tal, Kali, *Worlds of Hurt: Reading the Literatures of Trauma* (Cambridge University Press, 1996).

Tibbles, Anthony (ed.), *Transatlantic Anti-Slavery*, exhibition catalogue (Her Majesty's Stationery Office, 1994).

Wood, Marcus, *Blind Memory: Visual Representations of Slavery in England and America 1780–1865* (Manchester University Press, 2000).

—— *Slavery, Empathy, and Pornography* (Oxford University Press, 2002).

Young, James E., *The Texture of Memory: Holocaust Memorials and Meaning* (Yale University Press, 1993).

Young, Robert J. C., *Colonial Desire: Hybridity in Theory, Culture and Race* (Routledge, 1995).

English Poetry, Abolition, and Slavery

Anstey, Roger, *The Atlantic Slave Trade and British Abolition, 1760–1810* (Macmillan, 1975).

Ashfield, Andrew (ed.), *Romantic Women Poets 1788–1848*, vol. ii (Manchester University Press, 1998).

Barker, Anthony J., *The African Link: British Attitudes to the Negro in the Era of the African Slave Trade 1550–1807* (Frank Cass, 1978).

Basker, James G., *Amazing Grace: An Anthology of Poems about Slavery, 1660–1810* (Yale University Press, 2002).

Baum, Joan, *Mind-Forg'd Manacles: Slavery and the Romantic Poets* (Archon Books, 1994).

Billington, Louis, and Billington, Rosamund, '"Burning Zeal for Righteousness": Women in the British Anti-Slavery Society, 1820–1860', in Jane Rendall (ed.), *Equal or Different: Women's Politics 1800–1914* (Basil Blackwell, 1987).

Brantlinger, Patrick, *Rule of Darkness: British Literature and Imperialism, 1830–1914* (Cornell University Press, 1988).

Brooks, Chris, and Faulkner, Peter (eds.), *The White Man's Burdens: An Anthology of British Poetry of the Empire* (University of Exeter Press, 1996).

Brophy, Sarah, 'Elizabeth Barrett Browning's "The Runaway Slave at Pilgrim's Point" and the Politics of Interpretation', *Victorian Poetry*, 36/3 (1998), 273–88.

Carretta, Vincent, *Unchained Voices: An Anthology of Black Authors in the English Speaking World of the Eighteenth Century* (University Press of Kentucky, 1998).

Clarkson, Thomas, *The History of the Rise, Progress, and Accomplishment of the Abolition of the African Slave-Trade by the British Parliament*, 2 vols. (London, 1808).

Cowper, William, *The Letters and Prose Writings of William Cowper*, ed. James King, 5 vols. (Oxford University Press, 1988).

—— *The Poems of William Cowper*, ed. J. D. Baird and Charles Ryskamp, 3 vols. (Oxford University Press, 1990).

Dabydeen, David, *Hogarth's Blacks* (Manchester University Press, 1989).

Drescher, Seymour, 'Whose Abolition? Popular Pressure and the Ending of the British Slave Trade', *Past and Present*, 142 (1994), 136–66.

Dykes, Eva Beatrice, *The Negro in English Romantic Thought; or, A Study in Sympathy for the Oppressed* (Harcourt Brace, 1942).

Edwards, Bryan, *History, Civil and Commercial, of the British Colonies in the West Indies*, 3 vols. (J. Stockdale, 1793).

Equiano, Olaudah, *The Interesting Narrative and Other Writings* (1789; Penguin, 1995).

Erdman, D. V., 'Blake's Vision of Slavery', *Journal of the Warburg and Courtauld Institutes*, 15 (1952), 242–52.

Feldman, Paula R. (ed.), *British Woman Poets of the Romantic Era* (Johns Hopkins University Press, 1997).

Felsenstein, Frank, *English Trader, Indian Maid: Representing Gender, Race, and Slavery in the New World: An Inkle and Yarico Reader* (Johns Hopkins University Press, 1999).

Ferguson, Moira, *Subject to Others: British Women Writers and Colonial Slavery* (Routledge, 1992).

Fryer, Peter, *Staying Power: The History of Black People in Britain* (Pluto Press, 1984).

Gerzina, Gretchen, *Black London Life before Emancipation* (Rutgers University Press, 1995).

Hall, Catherine, *White, Male and Middle-Class: Explorations in Feminism and History* (Polity Press, 1992).

Hyam, Ronald, *Empire and Sexuality: The British Experience* (Manchester University Press, 1990).

Kitson, J. Peter, and Lee, Debbie (eds.), *Slavery, Abolition and Emancipation Writings in the British Romantic Period*, 8 vols. (Pickering & Chatto, 1999).

Lorimer, Douglas A., *Colour, Class and the Victorians: English Attitudes to the Negro in the Mid-Nineteenth Century* (Leicester University Press, 1978).

Midgley, Clare, *Women against Slavery: The British Campaigners, 1780–1870* (Routledge, 1992).

Morrison, Anthea, 'Coleridge's Greek Prize Ode on the Slave Trade', in J. R. Watson (ed.), *An Infinite Complexity: Essays in Romanticism* (Edinburgh University Press, 1983).

Newton, John, *An Authentic Narrative of Some Remarkable and Interesting Particulars in the Life of* ******, *in Fourteen Letters* (J. Johnson, 1762).

—— *Thoughts upon the African Slave Trade* (T. Buckland, J. Johnson, & J. Phillips, 1788).

—— *The Journal of a Slave Trader* (1750–2), ed. Bernard Martin and Mark Spurrell (Epworth Press, 1962).

Oldfield, J. R., *Popular Politics and British Anti-Slavery* (Manchester University Press, 1995).

Perera, S., *Reaches of Empire: The English Novel from Edgeworth to Dickens* (Columbia University Press, 1991).

Plasa, Carl, and Ring, Betty J. (eds.), *The Discourse of Slavery: Aphra Behn to Toni Morrison* (Routledge, 1994).

Sandiford, Keith, *Measuring the Moment: Strategies of Protest in Eighteenth-Century Afro-English Writing* (Associated Universities Press, 1988).

Sypher, Wylie, *Guinea's Captive Kings: British Anti-Slavery Literature of the Xviii'th Century* (University of North Carolina Press, 1942).

Thomas, Helen, *Romanticism and Slave Narratives* (Oxford University Press, 2000).

Tucker, Herbert F., 'Columbus in Chains: Tennyson and the Conquests of Monologue', *Harvard Library Bulletin* (1993), 43–64.

Walvin, James, *Black Ivory: A History of British Slavery* (Harper Collins, 1992).

—— (ed.), *Slavery and British Society 1776–1846* (Macmillan, 1982).

Wedderburn, Robert, *The Horrors of Slavery and Other Writings by Robert Wedderburn*, ed. Iain McCalman (Edinburgh University Press, 1991).

Wheeler, Roxann, *The Complexion of Race: Categories of Difference in Eighteenth-Century British Culture* (University of Pennsylvania Press, 2000).

American Poetry, Abolition, and Slavery

African American Poetry Full Text Data Base, Chadwyck Healey Inc., CD Rom (Virginia, 1994).

Appiah, Kwame Anthony, and Gates, Henry Louis, Jnr., *Africana: The Encyclopedia of the African and African American Experience* (Basic Civitas Books, 1999).

Beach, Christopher, *The Politics of Distinction: Whitman and the Discourses of Nineteenth Century America* (University of Georgia Press, 1996).

Bloom, Harold (ed.), *Toni Morrison* (Chelsea House, 1990).

Brown, William Wells, *The Anti-Slavery Harp: A Collection of Songs for Anti-Slavery Meetings* (Bela Marsh, 1848).

—— *The Black Man: His Antecedents, his Genius, and his Achievements* (T. Hamilton, 1863).

Cassuto, Leonard, *The Inhuman Race: The Racial Grotesque in American Literature and Culture* (Columbia University Press, 1997).

Dalton, Karen C. Chambers, '"The Alphabet is an Abolitionist": Literacy and African Americans in the Emancipation Era', *Massachusetts Review*, 32/4 (1992), 545–73.

Erkkila, Betsy, *Whitman the Political Poet* (Oxford University Press, 1989).

Farrison, William Edward, *William Wells Brown, Author and Reformer* (University of Chicago Press, 1969).

Finkelman, Paul, *Slavery in the Courtroom* (Library of Congress, 1985).

Fisher, Miles Mark, *Negro Slave Songs in the United States* (Citadel, 1990).

Foster, Frances Smith, *Written by Herself: Literary Production by African American Women, 1746–1892* (Indiana University Press, 1993).

Genovese, Elizabeth Foxe, *Within the Plantation Household* (University of North Carolina Press, 1990).

Jordan, Winthrop D., *White over Black: American Attitudes towards the Negro, 1550–1812* (W. W. Norton, 1977).

Klammer, Martin, *Whitman, Slavery and the Emergence of Leaves of Grass* (Pennsylvania State University Press, 1995).

Kolchin, Peter, *American Slavery* (Penguin, 1993).

Kraditor, Aileen, *Means and Ends in American Abolitionism* (Pantheon, 1969).

Lincoln, Jairus, *Anti-Slavery Melodies* (1843).

Lowell, James Russell, *Complete Poetical Works* (Houghton Mifflin & Co., 1896).

—— *The Biglow Papers [First Series]: A Critical Edition*, ed. Thomas Wortham (Northern Illinois University Press, 1977).

Ripley, C. Peter (ed.), *The Black Abolitionist Papers*, 5 vols. (University of North Carolina Press, 1985–92).

Ruchames, Louis, *The Abolitionists* (Capricorn, 1964).

Schwarz, Philip J., *The Roots of American Slavery: A Bibliographical Essay*, available at http://www.stratfordhall.org/schwarz.html.

Stewart, James Brewer, *Holy Warriors: The Abolitionists and American Slavery* (Farrar Straus & Giroux, 1993).

Stowe, Harriet Beecher, *Dred* (1992).

—— *Uncle Tom's Cabin* (1852; Norton, 1994).

Uncle Tom's Cabin, Web site, University of Virginia, http://jefferson.village.virginia.edu/utc/

Wolf, Hazel Catherine, *On Freedom's Altar: The Martyr Complex in the Abolition Movement* (University of Wisconsin Press, 1952).

Yellin, Jean Fagan, *Women and Sisters: The Antislavery Feminists in American Culture* (Yale University Press, 1991).

Index of Titles and First Lines